Crossword Solver

This book is intended to be a comprehensive reference guide for all crossword enthusiasts.

The book is divided up into sections under headings associated with the list of words. Each of these headings is listed in the contents page

As crosswords give clues and then the character length of the answer, we have categorised even further by dividing the words under their headings into their character length, i.e. apple being listed under 5.

Popular phrases have also been included under the headings and in these cases the space in between the words have been included as a character number, such as 'sticky wicket', which is calculated as 13 characters. Where names appear the space has been taken out and these are calculated without spaces, such as 'billclinton', calculated as 11 characters.

On the right hand side of each spread is a reference box, which lists the first heading entry on the page spread.

We hope that you find this crossword solver useful.

Oxford 2006

Contents

Crossword Solver

igloo

This edition published by Igloo Books Ltd 2006
Text © Igloo Books Limited 2006

ISBN: 1845613279

Writing, Project Management, Design & Typesetting
by HL Studios, Long Hanborough, Oxfordshire

Printed and bound in China

A copy of the British Library Cataloguing-in-Publication Data
is available from the British Library

Introduction

Crosswords are not just a fun hobby, if attempted regularly they will aid memory and overall mental ability. They can be frustrating however, and this book has been compiled to help in situations when a particular crossword proves difficult to complete.

Certain points are useful to bear in mind when attempting all crosswords. For example, start with an answer that you're sure of and build from there. A fill-in-the-blank clue, like "___ es Salaam", is a good place to begin, because the blank is easy to spot and there's no ambiguity about the answer.

If you have time to worry about where you are in the puzzle, it's best to work from the beginning of the word rather than the end. This is because English words have their greatest variation in spelling at the beginning. The letters WO- beginning a word, for instance, are much more helpful than -ED at the end.

Don't be afraid to take guesses, but also don't get too attached to answers that don't seem to be working out. Pencil in answers you remain unsure about.

Be wary of unlikely letter combinations that show up in a grid. An answer beginning PTB-, for example, indicates that something is probably wrong. PTB- just might start P.T. BARNUM, however, so you have to be alert.

Think of all the different meanings the clue words could have, because the constructor is probably not using the most obvious meanings. For example: the clue "Fast thinker" may lead to the answer DIETER, and "One with lots of bills" to a TELLER.

Learning words frequently used in crosswords can be a big help. ESTE is the name of an Italian Renaissance family for example, and an ANOA Celebes ox.

Modern crosswords have fewer esoteric words than older ones. Now, though, there is a large vocabulary of new words based on popular culture, from ANI DiFRANCO, EDA LESHAN and BRIAN ENO, to Nickelodeon's REN and STIMPY.

If you're ever asked for the name of a rock band in three letters, you can be almost certain the answer is either R.E.M. or E.L.O.

If you get stuck on a single square in a crossword, it helps to go through the alphabet testing each letter in turn.

For sections where you have some but not all the letters, try to guess the vowel-consonant pattern of the missing words. The second letter of an answer that also starts another answer is often an R, L, H or vowel. Getting a feel for what the answers look like may be enough to break the logjam. For plural answers or third-person singular verbs, try S at the end. Past-tense verbs may end in -ED.

Comparative and superlative answers almost always end in -ER and -EST.

If you're still stuck, you can check a dictionary or crossword solver (it's not cheating unless you consider it cheating) or do an online search.

Use pencil! You must be able to erase.

Read every clue, across and down. It is easy to miswrite a word, and reading the crossing clue is a useful check.

There is also a "zone approach" to solving.

The best way to solve a puzzle quickly is never to look at any clue more than once. Try to work one section of a puzzle at a time, and only that section. If your eye glances at a clue for another area that you know the answer to, don't fill it in immediately, because that would break the solving rhythm, you can simply put it on the back burner to answer later.

Read the clues in blocks. That is, read 1- through 4-Down, then write in the answers all at once. This saves looking-back-and-forth time.

Begin to read the next clue while you're filling in the previous answer. Ideally, your pencil should never stop writing.

The best advice, though, for any crossword contestant – superseding all the tips and techniques above – is to relax and solve at your own pace. Don't do anything different from your usual, and you'll probably work faster and make fewer mistakes.

The basics of a good Crossword

1 **Theme**: A theme makes a crossword more enjoyable by providing an additional challenge, hint and thrill of discovery to the solver. It is here that the creativity of the author stands out.

2 **Word Fill**: Good authors use words that are "lively" not obscure. Short words must be accessible to anyone with a reasonable knowledge and have a mix of current cultural and classical knowledge encompassing sports, literature, TV, film, etc. Diseases and other medical problems, cursing, ethnic and racial epithets, religious or other insults, sexual and some other bodily-function references are generally considered taboo words in crosswords. Obscure words, especially when they intersect, abbreviations no one uses, awkward excerpts from quotations and contrived words, are evidence of an unskilled author or a computer generated puzzle.

3 **Clues**: Must be factually accurate. They must match their answer in number and part of speech. They must not duplicate part of the answer. Ideally, no clue in a puzzle should duplicate an answer word anywhere in the grid. They must, at bare minimum, hint that an answer is an abbreviation or foreign word, or slang.

4 **Grid blacks**: Good authors tend to use as few black squares as possible. For a 15x15 puzzle size, about 37 black squares are considered the absolute limit. Crosswords with a higher count of black squares indicate an unskilled author or the use of a computer program.

5 **Word count**: For a 15x15 puzzle of average difficulty, 72-78 total words (counting both Across and Down words) is considered an acceptable range. If it is lower, it tends to make the puzzle very difficult for average solvers and if it is higher, will contain too many small words (4 letters or fewer) that tends to make a puzzle very bland and boring. Computer generated crosswords will suffer due to the latter.

Airlines

12
Scandinavian

11
Air jamaica
Continental

10
Aeromexico

Air jamaica
Icelandair

9
Aerlingus
Aircanada
Airfrance
Lotpolish
Lufthansa
Northwest
USairways

8
Aeroflot
Alitalia
American
Austrian
Canadian
Egyptair
Japanair
Mexicana
Swissair

7
Finnair
Olympic

6
Asiana
Iberia
Qantas
Sabena
Tapair

United

5
Varig

4
Elal
Thai

Algebra

19
Incomplete equation
Reversion of series
Root of an equation

18
Identical equation

17
Partial fractions

Positive quantity
Rational quantity
Residual quantity

16
Irreducible case
Radical quantity

13
Quadrinominal
Residual root

12
Quadrinomial

11
Rationalize

10
Parabolism
Polynomial
Quadratics

9
Imaginary
Quadratic
Transpose

7
Quadric
Quartic
Quintic

5
Radix

4
Real

Anatomy

19
Anticlinal vertebra
Columnar epithelium
Intercentral nerves
Pneumogastric
Nerve
Proximate principle
Reissner's mem-
brane
Rosenm.ller's organ
Semicircular canals
Sesamoid cartilages
Sudoriferous glands

Supraoccipital bone
Suprarenal capsules

18
Conjunctive tissue
Intercartilaginous
Maxillo-mandibular
Pepsinhydrochloric
Pit of the stomach
Poupart's ligament
Quadratojugal bone
Sensori-volitional
Splanchno-skeleton

Supraorbital point
Sympathetic system
Vermiform appendix

17
Connection tissue
Inhibitory nerves
Intertrochanteric
Lobule of the ear
Medulla oblongata
Obturator foramen
Omphalomesenteric
Peptohydrochloric

Perennibranchiate
Pharyngobranchial
Pleuropericardial
Pterygoid process
Sacculo-utricular
Sheath of Schwann
Sphenethmoid bone
Splanchnapophysis
Sympathetic nerve
Temperature sense
Temporo-auricular
Tympanic membrane
Umbilical vesicle
Virginal membrane

16
Achilles' tendon
Cardioinhibitory
Condylar foramen
Crystalline lens
Glossoepiglottic
Ichthyopterygium
Inhibitory-motor
Interventricular
Isodynamic foods
Leucocytogenesis
Lieno-intestinal
Maxillo-palatine

Medullary groove
Medullary sheath
Mucous membranes
Müllerian fibers
Musculocutaneous
Orbitosphenoidal
Pleuroperitoneal
Pleuroperitoneum
Polycotyledonary
Postzygapophysis
Praezygapophysis
Presphenoid bone
Primitive groove
Primitive sheath
Pterygomaxillary
Purkinje's cells
Sacculo-cochlear
Schwann's sheath
Sebaceous glands
Segmental organs
Subcartilaginous
Succus entericus
Superfecundation
Supplemental air
Supra-oesophagal
Temporomaxillary
Tenonian capsule
Thalamencephalon
Umbilical region
Vesicular column
White blood cell
White of the eye

15

Arterialization
Gastropneumatic
Infraclavicular
Interdigitation
Interfascicular
Interfollicular
Interganglionic
Intermandibular
Intermembranous
Intermesenteric
Intermetacarpal
Intermetatarsal
Interpedencular
Interphalangeal
Intussusception
Laryngotracheal
Malassimilation
Mandibular arch
Maxilloturbinal
Mesaticephalous
Mucous membrane
Mullerian ducts
Neck of a tooth

Neuro-epidermal
Occipital point
Olfactory organ
Omphalomesaraic
Palatopterygoid
Pathetic muscle
Pectoral girdle
Perilymphangial
Pituitary fossa
Prezygapophysis
Pterygopalatine
Pterygoquadrate
Radical vessels
Root of a tooth
Sagittal suture
Scalene muscles
Segmental tubes
Serous membrane
Shoulder girdle
Sigmoid flexure
Spermatogenetic
Spermatophorous
Sphenoethmoidal
Splanchnopleure
Squamozygomatic
Styloid process
Subconjunctival
Subpodophyllous
Superconception
Supersphenoidal
Supraclavicular
Suprascalpulary
Suprasphenoidal
Tarsometatarsal
Tarsometatarsus
Thermosystaltic
Tricuspid valve
Vasoconstrictor
Vaso-inhibitory
Ventro-inguinal
Vertebrarterial
Vesicoprostatic
Visceral arches
Visceral clefts
Visceroskeletal
Vital functions
White corpuscle

14

Abarticulation
Abdominal ring
Accrementitial
Accrementition
Adipose tissue
Amphiarthrosis
Anelectrotonus
Anthropotomist

Antitrochanter
Archipterygium
Auditory canal
Coarticulation
Coeliac artery
Coronal suture
Galactophorous
Gastroduodenal
Gastroepiploic
Hygrophthalmic
Hyperapophysis
Imparidigitate
Infrastapedial
Infratrochlear
Interarticular
Interauricular
Intercavernous
Intercondyloid
Intermaxillary
Interoperculum
Interstapedial
Intervertebral
Ischiocapsular
Mandibulohyoid
Medicommissure
Mediostapedial
Mentomeckelian
Mesaticephalic
Microcephalous
Muscular sense
Musculophrenic
Myelencephalic
Myelencephalon
Myodynamometer
Nasopharyngeal
Navicular bone
Nervous system
Neurapophysial
Oblique muscle
Occipital bone
Ophthalmometer
Ophthalmoscope
Opisthocoelous
Orbitosphenoid
Organ of Gorti
Palatine bones
Pathetic nerve
Pentadactyloid
Periganglionic
Plagiocephalic
Platycephalous
Pleurapophysis
Plowshare bone
Postcommissure
Postencephalon
Praecommissure
Prosencephalic
Prosencephalon
Protovertebral

Pseudobranchia
Pseudoturbinal
Pterygoid bone
Pulmocutaneous
Punctum caecum
Rennet stomach
Rhinencephalic
Rhinencephalon
Rods and cones
Sacrovertebral
Sanguification
Scaphocephalic
Scleroskeleton
Secreto-motory
Segmental duct
Semilunar bone
Sense organule
Septomaxillary
Serum globulin
Shoulder blade
Sigmoid valves
Spermatic cord
Spermatogenous
Spermatogonium
Sphenethmoidal
Sphenotic bone
Stationary air
Sternocoracoid
Stratification
Stylomaxillary
Subarachnoidal
Subendocardial
Subnotochordal
Subpericardial
Supermaxillary
Supra-acromial
Suprachoroidal
Supracondyloid
Supramaxillary
Supraoccipital
Suprastapedial
Supratrochlear
Text blindness
Thyroarytenoid
Transformation
Umbilical cord
Vertebro-iliac
Vital capacity
Vitreous humor
Wandering cell
Word blindness

13

Agglutination
Alisphenoidal
Anfractuosity
Aqueous humor

Axis cylinder
Cardiographic
Centrostaltic
Cylinder axis
Gastrocnemius
Gastrophrenic
Gastrosplenic
Genitourinary
Hepatogastric
Herpetotomist
Heteropelmous
Hyomandibular
Hypobranchial
Hypochondrium
Incapsulation
Incito-motory
Infrascapular
Infratemporal
Interalveolar
Interclavicle
Interglobular
Intermuscular
Interparietal
Interscapular
Intersesamoid
Interungulate
Mesencephalic
Mesencephalon
Mesobronchium
Mesocephalous
Mesopterygium
Metadiscoidal
Metamorphosis
Metanephritic
Metapterygium
Metencephalon
Mucous tissue
Musculospiral
Nasolachrymal
Nervomuscular
Neurapophysis
Neuro-central
Neuromuscular
Neuroskeleton
Occipitoaxial
Odontoid bone
Orbital index
Orthognathism
Orthognathous
Parabronchium
Parepididymis
Parotid gland
pelvic girdle
Peribranchial
Perichondrial
Perichondrium
Perilymphatic
Perivertebral
Petrosal bone

Plagiocephaly
Pleurocentrum
Pneumogastric
Polydactylism
Polyperythrin
Postoblongata
Post-temporal
Post-tympanic
Praeoperculum
Presphenoidal
Proteinaceous
Protovertebra
Proventriulus
Pterygopodium
Quadrate bone
Quadratojugal
Quadricipital
Recto-uterine
Recto-vesical
Scaphocephaly
Scapular arch
Semipenniform
Sense capsule
Serum albumin
Serum of milk
Shackle joint
Sinus venosus
Somatopleuric
Somatotropism
Spermatogemma
Spermatophore
Sphenoid bone
Splanchnology
Splanchnotomy
Splenial bone
Sternomastoid
Sternothyroid
Subepiglottic
Subepithelial
Subintestinal
Subpeduncular
Subperiosteal
Subperitoneal
Subsphenoidal
Superfetation
Supra-angular
Supraclavicle
Supra-ethmoid
Supratemporal
Sustentacular
Synchondrosis
Taste of buds
Temporofacial
Tendon reflex
Thoracic duct
Thyroid gland
Transpalatine
Transpiration
Trisplanchnic

Tympanic bone
Unciform bone
Vasoformative
Vesicouterine
Vesicovaginal
Vision purple
Visual purple
Visual yellow
Vitreous body
Vulvo-uterine
Word deafness
Word dumbness
Xiphiplastron

12

Aliethmoidal
Amphopeptone
Anaerobiotic
Anthropotomy
Antialbumose
Antibrachial
Antibrachium
Articulation
assimilation
Cephalostyle
Conjunctival
Cricothyroid
Fenestration
Genitocrural
Haematoblast
Haematoplast
Hemapophysis
Hemicerebrum
Hemorrhoidal
Hepatocystic
Heterocercal
Homoeomerous
Hypapophysis
Hypocleidium
Hypogastrium
Hypoplastron
Hyposkeletal
Idiomuscular
Incito-motor
Infraorbital
Infraspinous
Infrasternal
Infundibulum
Insalivation
Intercarotid
Intercentrum
Interdigital
Interlaminar
Interlobular
Intermaxilla
Intermembral
Internuncial

Interorbital
Interosseous
Interspinous
Intralobular
Irritability
Ischiorectal
Kinaesthesis
Macrobiotics
malnutrition
Median plane
Mesial plane
Mesocephalic
Mesocephalon
Mesocoracoid
Mesocuniform
Mesogastrium
Mesognathous
Mesoscapular
Metapophysis
Monophyodont
Muscle curve
Nasopalatine
Nasoturbinal
Nondeciduate
Olivary body
Organoleptic
Ossification
Osteocranium
Osteodentine
Osteogenetic
Osteoplastic
Paraglobulin
Parapophysis
Parasphenoid
Paridigitate
Paroccipital
Parumbilical
Pentadactyle
Pericellular
Perivisceral
Petromastoid
pineal gland
Placentation
Platycnemism
Platycoelian
Plicidentine
Podophyllous
Postclavicle
Postpalatine
Postscapular
Postsphenoid
Praecoracoid
Prebronchial
Premaxillary
Preoblongata
Preopercular
Preoperculum
Prevertebral
Propterygium

Proventricle
Pseudobranch
Pseudocoelia
Receptaculum
Rectovaginal
Renal-portal
Sacrosciatic
Sanguiferous
Schindylesis
Schizorhinal
Schneiderian
Sclerogenous
Solar plexus
Somatopleure
Spermatocyte
Spermococcus
Spermoplasma
Spermosphere
Sphenethmoid
Sphygmograph
Sphygmometer
Sphygmophone
Sphygmoscope
Spiritualism
Sternocostal
Stirrup bone
Stomatodaeum
Styloglossal
Stylomastoid
Subarytenoid
Subbronchial
Subcuticular
Submaxillary
Suboccipital
Subopercular
Suboperculum
Subpulmonary
Subscapulary
Subvertebral
Subzygomatic
Sudoriferous
Sudoriparous
Supermaxilla
Superspinous
Supraciliary
Supracranial
Suprahepatic
Supramaxilla
Supraorbitar
Supraspinous
Suprasternal
Supravaginal
Suspensorium
Sustentation
Sweat glands
Synarthrodia
Synarthrosis
Syndesmology
Synosteology

Syringocoele
Temporomalar
Tetanization
Thalamocoele
Thermogenous
Thoracometer
Trochanteric
Turacoverdin
Urinogenital
Vas deferens
Venous pulse
Verumontanum
Visual white
Vital tripod
Vivification
Vulvovaginal
Warm-blooded
Xiphisternum
Zygapophysis

11

Adenography
Admaxillary
Aesthesodic
Aganglionic
Agglutinate
Air bladder
Alisphenoid
Allantoidal
Amphistylic
Anallantoic
Anapophysis
Angiography
Animal heat
Anteorbital
Aponeurosis
Aponeurotic
Arachnoidal
Arbor vitae
Arteriology
Arteriotomy
Articularly
Astragaloid
Canaliculus
Collagenous
Collar bone
Comparative
Conjunctiva
Constrictor
Convolution
Costiferous
Cremasteric
Crotaphitic
Ganglionary
Gastrocolic
Haemapodous
Helicotrema

Hepatorenal
Herpetotomy
Heterocercy
Huckleberry
Hyparterial
Hypoglossal
Hyposternum
Ichthyotomy
Ideo-motion
Iliofemoral
Incapsulate
Indeciduate
Innervation
Inscription
Intercarpal
Intercrural
Interhaemal
Intermedium
Interneural
Intertarsal
Kymographic
Laniariform
Lumbosacral
Lymphangial
Lymphogenic
Masseterine
Median line
Mediastinal
Mediastinum
Mesogastric
Mesometrium
Mesonephric
Mesonephros
Mesopodiale
Mesoscapula
Mesosternal
Mesosternum
Metacromion
Metanephros
Metapodiale
Metasternum
Monocrotism
Musculation
Musculature
Myodynamics
Myohaematin
Nasal bones
Nasal index
Nasofrontal
Nerve fibre
Nervimotion
Neural arch
Neurenteric
Neurography
Nonvascular
Notochordal
Nummulation
Odontoblast
Odontoplast

Oestruation
Orbitonasal
Ornithotomy
Palatonares
Pampiniform
Parachordal
Paramastoid
Paraxanthin
Paroophoron
Pentacrinin
Peptogenous
Peptotoxine
Pericardial
Pericardium
Pericranial
Pericranium
Perienteron
Perineurial
Perineurium
Periodontal
Peritonaeum
Platycnemin
Pleurosteon
Polygastric
Polymastism
Polythelism
Postfrontal
Postglenoid
Postscapula
Post-tragus
Praecordial
Precoracoid
Prescapular
Presphenoid
Pretemporal
Procerebrum
Proctodaeum
Prognathism
Prognathous
Prosocoelia
Proteolysis
Pseudostoma
Sarcolactic
Scalpriform
Scapholunar
Schizocoele
Sclerotical
Sense organ
Sensibility
Skeletology
Spermoblast
Spermospore
Sphygmogram
Splint bone
Spontaneity
Stercobilin
Sternohyoid
Stethograph
Stethometer

Stimulation
Subacromial
Subaxillary
Subcoracoid
Subcorneous
Subthalamic
Suburethral
Supercarpal
Supersacral
Supracostal
Supraglotic
Supra-ilium
Supraspinal
Sympathetic
Syndesmosis
Synneorosis
Synosteosis
Syssarcosis
Teleorganic
Tetanomotor
Thermogenic
Thermotaxic
Throat pipe
Tibiotarsal
Tibiotarsus
Tongue bone
Trypsinogen
Twixt-brain
Tympanohyal
Uriniparous
Vasodentine
Vasodilator
Vena portae
Ventrimeson
Vertebrally
Vertebrated
Vis vitalis
Whitleather
Xanthophane

10

Aberration
Absorption
Acetabulum
Alum shale
Amylolytic
Anacrotism
Anamniotic
anatomical
Antagonist
Antitragus
Antorbital
Arthrology
Articulary
Asteriscus
Astragalar
Astragalus

Autogenous
Autostylic
Cancellous
Carnassial
Ceruminous
Compressor
Corniculum
Corrugator
Crotaphite
Cul-de-sac
Cytogenous
Gangliated
Ganglionic
Geniohyoid
glomerulus
Glossohyal
Haematosac
Hemicardia
Heterodont
Holorhinal
Hyosternum
Hypotarsus
Hypothenar
Ideo-motor
Ileocaecal
Iliolumbar
Infrahyoid
Inhibition
Innominate
Interbrain
Interlobar
Internasal
Interpubic
Interramal
Interrenal
Intracolic
Irritation
Katabolism
Kinaesodic
Leptorhine
Malpighian
Masseteric
Medullated
Megalocyte
Mesenteric
Mesenteron
Mesethmoid
Mesocaecum
Mesocoelia
Mesogaster
Mesophryon
Mesopodial
Mesorchium
Mesorectum
Mesovarium
Metabolism
Metabolize
Metacarpal
Metacarpus

Metapodial
Metastasis
Metatarsal
Metatarsus
Milk molar
Milk tooth
Monocrotic
Mucigenous
Muciparous
Myelocoele
Myelogenic
Myocardium
Nasobuccal
Nasoseptal
Nerve cell
Nervimotor
Neurilemma
Neurocoele
Oculomotor
Oculonasal
Odontogeny
Oligomyoid
Ornosternal
Omosternum
Ophthalmic
Opisthotic
Optocoelia
Optography
Osteoblast
Osteoclast
Osteocomma
Osteogenic
Osteoplast
Otocranial
Pancreatic
Pancreatin
Paralactic
Paralbumin
Parethmoid
Parovarium
Pepsinogen
Perimysial
Perimysium
Periosteal
Periosteum
Peripheral
Peritoneal
Peritoneum
Petrohyoid
Phalangian
Pharyngeal
Phlebology
Platetrope
Platyrhine
Pleurodont
Pneumology
Podarthrum
Praecordia
Precordial

4

Premaxilla
Preorbital
Prepollent
Prescapula
Presternum
Prochordal
Prognathic
Promontory
Pronephric
Pronephron
Propeptone
Propodiale
Prosocoele
Protractor
Protureter
Proximally
Psalterium
Quadriceps
Salivation
Sarcolemma
Sebiferous
Sebiparous
Secernment
Semiglutin
Seralbumen
Sesamoidal
Sincipital
Somatology
Sperm cell
Spermatism
Spermatoid
Spermatoon
Spirograph
Spiroscope
Splanchnic
Splenculus
Splenotomy
Stammering
Staphyline
Stephanion
Stomodaeum
Stylohyoid
Subclavian
Subcranial
Subglossal
Subglottic
Subhepatic
Subhyaloid
Sublingual
Sublobular
Suborbitar
Subpleural
Subspinous
Subvaginal
Supination
Suprahyoid
Suprapubic
Suprarenal

Surangular
Suspensory
Sweetbread
Symphyseal
Symplectic
Tachometer
Tentaculum
Testicular
Thigh bone
Thyrohyoid
Thyroideal
Tonsilitic
Trabecular
Tricipital
Tricrotism
Tricrotous
Trigastric
Trigeminal
Triquetrum
Trochanter
Trochleary
Turbinated
Urogenital
Via Lactea
Vocal tube
White cell
Xiphoidian
Zoˆtrophic
Zygosphene

9

Abduction
Absorbent
Adduction
Adenotomy
Aesthesia
Agennesis
Aggregate
Agminated
Aliseptal
Allantoid
Anabolism
Anacrotic
Anatomism
Anatomist
Angiology
Angiotomy
Antihelix
Apophysis
Apparatus
Arachnoid
Arthrodia
Arthrosis
Arytenoid
Associate
Auricular
Bronchial

Calcaneal
Calcaneum
Calcarine
Capitular
Cartilage
Caruncula
Coccygeal
Columella
Condyloid
Cornified
Corpuscle
Corrugent
Cotyledon
Cremaster
Cysticule
Funicular
Ginglymus
Gladiolus
Glomerule
Gomphosis
Hamstring
Harderian
Hindbrain
Hippotomy
Hyomental
Hyostylic
Hypoarion
Ileocolic
Iliopsoas
Ingestion
Ingluvies
Innervate
Insertion
Interhyal
Internode
Intestine
Intrinsic
Irritable
Ischiadic
Ischiatic
Katabolic
Kinesodic
Knee jerk
Kymograph
Labyrinth
Leucocyte
Lobulette
Lumbrical
Lymphatic
Malleolar
Malleolus
Manubrial
Manubrium
Manyplies
Maxillary
Meckelian
Medicornu
Medullary

Meibomian
Meningeal
Mesentery
Mesoarium
Mesocolon
Mesohepar
Mesonasal
Mesorhine
Mesostate
Metabolic
Metatarse
Metosteon
Microcyte
Microdont
Microseme
Morphotic
Mucinogen
M.llerian
Myeloplax
Mylohyoid
Myochrome
Navicular
Neurility
Neurocity
Neuroglia
Neuromere
Neuropore
Neurotome
Neurotomy
Notochord
Nutrition
Oblongata
Obturator
Occipital
Olecranal
Olecranon
Olfaction
Olfactory
Oncograph
Oncometer
Oogenesis
Opercular
Operculum
Opisthion
Optometer
Ossifying
Osteogeny
Osteomere
Osteotomy
Otoconite
Oviparous
Parorchis
Pectineal
Peptonoid
Perilymph
Periopic
Phrenosin
Phytotomy

Pia mater
Pituitary
Planiform
Popliteal
Postaxial
Postcornu
Posterior
Postnares
Praecornu
Praenares
Praenasal
Preaortic
Precrural
Predorsal
Prehallux
Prelumbar
Prepenial
Preputial
Prespinal
Pretibial
Procoelia
Propepsin
Propodial
Prorhinal
Prostatic
Pterygoid
Pupillary
Putrescin
Pygostyle
Pylangium
Pyramidal
Rabdoidal
Recurrent
Restiform
Reticular
Saphenous
Sarcology
Sartorial
Sartorius
Satellite
Scarfskin
Sciatical
Sclerotal
Sclerotic
Sebaceous
Secernent
Secretion
Secretory
Sectorial
Semilunar
Sensation
Sensorium
Sharebone
Shin bone
Short rib
Signature
Siphonium
Sonometer

Spermatic
Spermatin
Sphenotic
Sphincter
Squamosal
Stapedial
Stercolin
Stercorin
Sternebra
Stimulant
Stimulate
Stylohyal
Subcaudal
Subcostal
Sublingua
Sublumbar
Submental
Submucous
Subocular
Subsacral
Subserous
Supinator
Symphysis
Synangium
Syringeal
Systaltic
Tablature
Tectorial
Tegmentum
Tentorium
Thecodont
Thyrohyal
Tidal air
Tonometer
Trabecula
Transpire
Trapezium
Trapezoid
Tricrotic
Tricuspid
Trifacial
Trochlear
Umbilical
Umbilicus
Uncinatum
Uropygial
Uropygium
Urosacral
Utriculus
Vallecula
Vasomotor
Vena cava
Ventricle
Vertebral
Villosity
Voluntary
Whirlbone
Zygantrum

Zygomatic

8

Abductor
Abomasus
Achylous
Achymous
Acromial
Acromion
Actinost
Adducent
Adductor
Aeration
Afferent
Agastric
Agenesic
Agenesis
Air cell
Alinasal
Alveolus
Amniotic
Anabolic
Anastate
Anconeal
Anconeus
Anthelix
Arcturus
Asterion
Asternal
Asystole
Atlantal
Axillary
Callosan
Callosum
Calvaria
Cathodic
Centrale
Cephalic
Cerebral
Cerebrum
Clitoris
Cochlear
Conarium
Condylar
Coronary
Coronoid
Cotyloid
Cuboidal
Cuniform
Cutgrass
Euphuism
Fibulare
Ganglial
Gigerium
Glabella
Glutaeus
Hallucal

Hemisect
Homodont
Hydatoid
Hypaxial
Hypohyal
Illusion
Incisive
Irritate
Lymphoid
Mammilla
Mandible
Masseter
Megaseme
Membrane
Meninges
Meniscus
Mesaraic
Meseraic
Mesially
Mesodont
Mesoseme
Midbrain
Modiolus
Motility
Muciform
Myelonal
Myocomma
Myograph
Myolemma
Myotomic
Neuraxis
Odontoid
Oestrual
Omohyoid
Omoplate
Omphalic
Omphalos
Optogram
Organule
Osteogen
Otocrane
Otolitic
Otosteal
Oviducal
Pacinian
Palatial
Palatine
Palmitic
Palmitin
Pancreas
Paraxial
Parietal
Parietes
Parotoid
Parvolin
Patagium
Patellar
Paxywaxy

Perineal
Perineum
Periople
Periotic
Peroneal
Pessulus
Petrosal
Pisiform
Placenta
Plastron
Poplitic
Postanal
Postcava
Postoral
Praecava
Preaxial
Premolar
Prenasal
Prepubic
Prepubis
Proatlas
Procoelo
Pronator
Prorenal
Prostate
Protagon
Protamin
Proximad
Plerotic
Ptomaine
Pudendal
Pudendum
Pulvinar
Pyridine
Quadrate
Sacculus
Sagittal
Salivary
Sarcosin
Scaphoid
Sclerous
Semiring
Septulum
Serosity
Sesamoid
Shoulder
Sinciput
Skeleton
Sneezing
Sniffing
Spermary
Spermule
Sphenoid
Sphygmic
Spiracle
Splenial
Splenium
Splenius

Splenoid
Spondyle
Squamous
Striatum
Subdural
Subnasal
Subpubic
Subzonal
Sympathy
Synovial
Syntonin
Temporal
Tenonian
Teretial
Testicle
Tetanize
Thalamic
Thalamus
Thoracic
Tonicity
Tonsilar
Trochlea
Trochoid
Turbinal
Tympanic
Tympanum
Unciform
Unipolar
Urosteon
Urostyle
Vertebra
Vertebre
Vibrissa
Vinculum
Visceral
Windpipe
Wolffian
Ypsiloid

7

Abdomen
Acantha
Acrania
Adrenal
Air sac
Apohyal
Auricle
Canthus
Capsule
Carotid
Carpale
Centrum
Clinoid
Cnemial
Cochlea
Conchal
Condyle

6

Corneal
Cranial
Cricoid
Cryptal
Fascial
Frontal
Gizzard
Glenoid
Glottis
Gluteal
Gluteus
Gnathic
Hamatum
Hamulus
Hindgut
Humeral
Hyaloid
Hypural
Incisor
Ingesta
Ischiac
Ischial
Ischium
Jejunum
Jugular
Kneecap
Kneepan
Lacteal
Laniary
Larmier
Laterad
Laxator
Levator
Limbous
Malleal
Malleus
Mammary
Mastoid
Maxilla
Medulla
Melanin
Membral
Metopic
Midriff
Minimus
Mucific
Mucigen
Myogram
Myology
Myotome
Myotomy
Nostril
Obelion
Occiput
Olivary
Omental
Omentum
Opercle

Ophryon
Osteoid
Ostosis
Otolite
Oviduct
Oxyntic
Packwax
Palatic
Palmary
Parotic
Parotid
Patella
Pedicel
Peptone
Petrous
Phalanx
Phallus
Pharynx
Phrenic
Plantar
Plasmin
Pleural
Pleuric
Pontile
Preoral
Prepuce
Prootic
Proteid
protein
Ptyalin
Pudenda
Pudical
Pyloric
Pylorus
Pyridic
Pyrogen
Radiale
Retinal
Rhachis
Rotular
Sagitta
Sarcous
Scalene
Scapula
Sciatic
Scrotal
Scrotum
Secrete
Sensory
Serolin
Snoring
Splenic
Spongin
Stearic
Stearin
Sternal
Sternum
Stomach

Styloid
Synovia
Systole
Tactual
Tapetum
Tarsale
Tearpit
Tetanic
Tetanus
Thyroid
Tibiale
Trachea
Triceps
Trigone
Trophic
Trypsin
Tryptic
Turacin
Umbilic
Ungular
Urachus
Urethra
Urocyst
Urohyal
Utricle
Vaginal
Valvula
Ventrad
Ventral
Vesical
Vesicle
Villous
Wormian
Xiphias
Xiphoid
Zoˆtomy

6

Acinus
Adduct
Adnate
Aerate
Amnion
Antral
Artery
Atrium
Auriga
Axilla
Biceps
Caecum
Calcar
Canine
Cardia
Carpal
Carpus
Cloaca
Coccyx

Coelia
Collum
Concha
Corium
Cornea
Corona
Cortex
Costal
Cotyle
Crural
Cuboid
Cupola
Cuspid
Cystic
Fascia
Frenum
Genian
Gullet
Haemad
Hallux
Income
Inguen
Inject
Inogen
Kidney
Labium
Lanugo
Larynx
Lienal
Ligule
Limbus
Lumbal
Lunule
Magnum
Marrow
Matrix
Meatus
Medius
Member
Mental
Mesiad
Mesial
Midgut
Muscle
Myelon
Myolin
Nasion
Neurad
neuron
Nipple
Nuchal
Nympha
Ocular
Oecoid
Omasum
Orgasm
Origin
Ossify

Ostium
Output
Palate
Palmar
Papain
Paunch
Paxwax
Pecten
Pelvis
Pepsin
Peptic
Pleura
Plexus
Pollex
Portal
Pteron
Rachis
Radius
Ranine
Rectal
Rectum
Rectus
Retina
Rhinal
Rotula
Sacral
Sacrum
Sarkin
Secern
Sepsin
Serous
Skatol
Smegma
Spinal
Spleen
Splint
Stapes
Stasis
Stigma
Stroma
Suture
Syrinx
Taenia
Tarsal
Tarsus
Temple
Tendon
Tensor
Testis
Thenar
Thorax
Throat
Thymic
Thymus
Tibial
Tongue
Tonsil
Tragus

Tubule	Groin	Pubic	Tuber	Lung
Ulnare	Gyral	Pubis	Tunic	Milk
Ureter	Heart	Pudic	Udder	Milt
Uterus	Hymen	Pupil	Ulnar	Nail
Uvular	Hyoid	Pygal	Urine	Nose
Vagina	Ileac	Pyxis	Uvula	Palm
Venous	Ileum	Raphe	Vagal	Pial
Venter	Iliac	Renal	Vagus	Pith
Vertex	Ilial	Rumen	Velum	Pons
Vessel	Ilium	Scala	Venus	Pulp
Villus	Incus	Scull	Volar	Pyla
Viscus	Inial	Semen	Vomer	Rete
Vision	Inion	Sense	Vulva	Rima
Zygoma	Jugal	Serum	Wrist	Skin
	Liver	Sinew		Soly

5

	Malar	Skull		Tear
	Mamma	Slime	**4**	Tube
	Manus	Smell		Ulna
Ancon	Meros	Sperm	Anal	Uvea
Aorta	Meson	Spine	Anus	Vein
Atlas	Molar	Stoma	Axis	Womb
Axial	Mucus	Sural	Bulb	
Caput	Nares	Sweat	Caul	
Cutio	Nasal	Talus	Cord	**3**
Colon	Nates	Tarse	Crus	
Costa	Navel	Taste	Cusp	Ham
Crura	Nerve	Tease	Fang	Haw
Crypt	Orbit	Terma	Foot	Pap
Cubit	Penis	Thigh	Gill	Poo
Cutis	Pinna	Tibia	Iris	Pyx
Glans	Porta	Tonus	Iter	Rib
Glome	Psoas	Tooth	Knee	Toe
Ggonad	Pubes	Touch	Lobe	Vas

ANIMALS

6	5	Whale	Fish	3
			Frog	
Rabbit	Goose	**4**	Goat	Bat
Walrus	Mouse		Orca	Cat
	Sheep	Bear	Seal	Cow
	Snail	Deer	Toad	Dog
	Snake	Duck		Pig

Archaeology

19	16	15	14	13
Haunches of an arch	Heel of a rafter	Grouped columns	Heading course	Gutter member
Header			Hypotrachelium	Half-timbered
				Hanging stile

8

12
Gambrel roof
Ground plate
Ground table
Guttae band
Hanging rail
Hecatompedon
Hollow newel
Hyperthyrion

11
Ground plan
Hard finish
Hip molding
Hipped roof

10
Floor plan
foundation
Gorgoneion
Half round
Hip rafter

9
Foliation
Gradatory
Guilloche
Hexastyle
Hypethral
Hypostyle

8
Gargoyle
Gorgerin
Halfpace
Headroom
Hip knob
Hoarding

7
Frontal
Frustum
Galilee
Gargyle
Godroon
Gradine
Gradino
Groined

Halpace
Headway
Hogback
Housing

6
Facing
Fascia
Gablet
Gargle
Gather
Gothic

5
Facet
Flank
Flier

Flyer
Gable
Glyph
Groin
Gutta
Halve
Hanch
Hanse
Helix

4
Gain

3
Fur
Hip

Art

42
American Society for Testing and Materials

35
Art of the United States of America

32
Republican period of Chinese art

27
Degree of Colour Permanence

23
Free-standing Sculpture
Groupe du Bateau-lavoir

22
Abstract expressionism

Subliminal advertising

21
Royal Academy of Arts

20
Asymmetrical
Balance
Conversation
Galante
Corrugated
Cardboard

Asteroids

16
Beatrice Tinsley
Beatrice-Tinsley
Hartbeespoortdam
Kliment Ohridski
Kliment-Ohridski
Kosmodemyanskaya
Payne-Gaposchkin

15
BeatriceTinsley
Jonathan Murray

Jonathan-Murray
KlimentOhridski
Toatenmongakkai
Weidenschilling

14
Bellingshausen
Chernyshevskij
Czechoslovakia
Franklin Adams
Franklin-Adams
Franz Schubert
Franz-Schubert
Harimaya-Bashi

JonathanMurray
Louispharailda
Moore-Sitterly
Pasacentennium
Ruperto-Carola
Schwarzschilda
Skalnate Pleso
Skalnate-Pleso
Van Biesbroeck
van den Heuvel
Van-Biesbroeck
van-den-Heuvel
Vibert-Douglas
Vinterhansenia
Vsekhsvyatskij

13
Banachiewicza
Broederstroom
Ching Sung Yu
Ching-Sung-Yu
Christy Carol
Christy-Carol
Coonabarabran
Franceswright
FranklinAdams
FranzSchubert
Guo Shou Jing
Guo-Shou-Jing
Horn-d'Arturo

James Bradley
James-Bradley
Junepatterson
Klytaemnestra
Konstitutsiya
Pasasymphonia
Perseverantia
Pervictoralex
Petropolitana
Photographica
Pino Torinese
Pino-Torinese
Rockwell Kent
Rockwell-Kent
Saint-Exupery

Schwambraniya
Schwassmannia
Siding Spring
Siding-Spring
SkalnatePleso
Susanvictoria
Tripaxeptalis
Tsiolkovskaja
VanBiesbroeck
Vladvysotskij

12

Adzhimushkaj
Ambartsumian
Andrea Doria
Andrea-Doria
Andres Bello
Andres-Bello
Aristophanes
Armandhammer
Azerbajdzhan
Bakhchisaraj
Bobrovnikoff
Carlospotter
ChristyCarol
Chrysothemis
Daphne Plane
Daphne-Plane
David Bender
David-Bender
Gerasimovich
Heilongjiang
Horn-dArturo
Iso-Heikkila
JamesBradley
Jean-Jacques
Julian Loewe
Julian-Loewe
Kachuevskaya
Kazakhstania
Kiril-Metodi
Konoshenkova
Koussevitzky
Kovalevskaya
Kustaanheimo
Lappeenranta
Lobachevskij
Michelangelo
Milankovitch
Nordenmarkia
Nordenskiold
Novorossijsk
Olaus Magnus
Olaus-Magnus
Otto Schmidt
Otto-Schmidt
Patrick Gene

Patrick-Gene
PinoTorinese
Pittsburghia
Pyotr Pervyj
Pyotr-Pervyj
Quetzalcoatl
RockwellKent
Rutherfordia
Scheherezade
Shaposhnikov
Shostakovich
SidingSpring
Soyuz-Apollo
Stereoskopia
Tezcatlipoca
Transylvania
Uzbekistania
van de Hulst
van der Laan
van-de-Hulst
van-der-Laan
vandenHouvel
Vanderlinden
Wallenbergia
Washingtonia
Williams Bay
Williams-Bay
Zhongolovich
Zu Chong Zhi
Zu-Chong-Zhi

11

Aleksandrov
Amalasuntha
AndreaDoria
AndresBello
Annapavlova
Aposhanskij
Auravictrix
Baboquivari
Barnardiana
Bauersfelda
Bellerophon
Belopolskya
Bonsdorffia
Bruce Helin
Bruce-Helin
Byelorussia
Caiurlionis
Champollion
ChingSungYu
Chivilikhin
Chizhevskij
Coppernicus
DaphnePlane
DavidBender
Davidweilla

Demiddelaer
Desagneauxa
Descamisada
Dobronravin
Dobrovoleva
Dobrovolsky
Dostojevsky
Dzhanibekov
Eichsfeldia
El Leoncito
Fraternitas
Fredegundis
Fulchignoni
Geowilliams
Glasenappia
Goethe Link
Goethe-Link
Goldschmidt
Gondolatsch
Gudiachvili
GuoShouJing
Hameenlinna
Hannu Olavi
Hannu-Olavi
Harlansmith
Heidelberga
Hermentaria
Hertzsprung
Hoffmeister
Hohensteina
Hoshi-no-ie
Interkosmos
Ioannisiani
Jack London
Jack-London
JulianLoewe
Karl-Ontjes
Katsurahama
Kempchinsky
Kittisvaara
Kobuchizawa
Koskenniemi
Kressmannia
Kulikovskij
Leuschneria
Lev Tolstoj
Lev-Tolstoj
Linda Susan
Linda-Susan
Lindemannia
Lubos Perek
Lubos-Perek
Lunacharsky
Mason-Dixon
Maximiliana
Mehltretter
Mendelssohn
Michkovitch
Mitake-mura

Mussorgskia
Napolitania
Nei Monggol
Nei-Monggol
Neoptolemus
Oberndorfer
OlausMagnus
Omarkhayyam
Otto Struve
Otto-Struve
OttoSchmidt
Paavo Nurmi
Paavo-Nurmi
Parchomenko
PatrickGene
Penthesilea
Philoctetes
Philosophia
Pickeringia
Princetonia
Protesilaos
Prologencia
Pyatigoriya
PyotrPervyj
Rockefellia
Rumpelstilz
Rupertwildt
Rusthawelia
Sawyer Hogg
Sawyer-Hogg
Schlesinger
Schweikarda
Shakespeare
Stavropolis
Steveedberg
Stromgrenia
Stroobantia
Strugatskia
Tadjikistan
Taurinensis
Tchaikovsky
Terpsichore
Thrasymedes
Transvaalia
Trubetskaya
Tvardovskij
Tycho Brahe
Tycho-Brahe
Ultrajectum
Universitas
Vainu Bappu
Vainu-Bappu
Van De Kamp
Van Den Bos
Van-De-Kamp
Van-Den-Bos
Vasilevskis
Verbaandert
Victor Jara

Victor-Jara
Victorplatt
Violaumayer
Volkonskaya
Voronveliya
Vysheslavia
Wallenquist
WilliamsBay
Wratislavia
Yakhontovia
Yatsugatake
Yoshkar-Ola

10

Abanderada
Abastumani
Abundantia
Aesculapia
Aeternitas
Alleghenia
Alphonsina
Amphitrite
Amundsenia
Andromache
Angerhofer
Annagerman
Anne-Marie
Antarctica
Antilochus
Appenzella
Argelander
Armisticia
Astapovich
Astronomia
Athamantis
Baptistina
Barabashov
Barbarossa
Beljawskya
Beltrovata
Berbericia
Bernardina
Boksenberg
Bredichina
Bronislawa
BruceHelin
Bruchsalia
Budovicium
California
Carlvesely
Castafiore
Caupolican
Centenaria
Chebotarev
Christabel
Christophe
Chukokkala

Cincinnati
Clementina
Climenhaga
Coelestina
Comas Sola
Comas-Sola
Constantia
Crescentia
Cruikshank
Cunningham
De Sanctis
De-Sanctis
Dennispalm
Derevskaya
Desiderata
Di Martino
Di-Martino
El Djezair
El-Djezair
Eleutheria
Elisabetha
ElLeoncito
Epimetheus
Esclangona
Etheridgea
Euphrosyne
Florentina
Floris-Jan
Fracastoro
Friederike
Geertruida
Geographos
GoetheLink
Goldberger
Gothlandia
Groeneveld
Gutemberga
Hamiltonia
HannuOlavi
Harrington
Hatshepsut
Hekatostos
Helwerthia
Hephaistos
Hippodamia
Hyperborea
Imperatrix
Imprinetta
Incidentia
Interamnia
Irmintraud
JackLondon
Jacqueline
Jubilatrix
Kenrussell
Komsomolia
Kondratyuk
Kotelnikov
Krisbarons

Kristensen
Kvistaberg
Lagerkvist
Lappajarvi
Leopoldina
LevTolstoj
Liberatrix
Lilliputia
LindaSusan
Lindbladia
Lomonosowa
LubosPerek
Lysistrata
Makharadze
Malmquista
Mandeville
Marjaleena
Mark Twain
Mark-Twain
Massevitch
Matterania
Mayakovsky
McLaughlin
Mitlincoln
Montefiore
Nehalennia
NeiMonggol
Neugebauer
Nevanlinna
Nihondaira
Noviomagum
Oosterhoff
Ostrovskij
OttoStruve
PaavoNurmi
Pakhmutova
Paracelsus
Parthenope
Parvulesco
Perovskaya
Persephone
Pettengill
Philagoria
Philippina
Pieksamaki
Pokryshkin
Polonskaya
Polyhymnia
Polypoites
Portlandia
Prometheus
Proserpina
Punkaharju
Pyatiletka
Radishchev
Rantaseppa
Reinmuthia
Ristenpart
Robelmonte

Roberbauxa
Ruth Wolfe
Ruth-Wolfe
Samitchell
Savonlinna
SawyerHogg
Schaumasse
Sebastiana
Seeligeria
Sevastopol
Shklovskij
Silbermann
Simferopol
Sisigambis
Smilevskia
Sniadeckia
Sonneberga
Sophrosyne
Spiridonia
Stalingrad
Stellafane
Sternberga
Strattonia
Swedenborg
Talthybius
Tarkovskij
Tautenburg
Timresovia
Tovarishch
Trimberger
TychoBrahe
VainuBappu
van Altena
Van Houten
van-Altena
Van-Houten
vandeHulst
vanderLaan
Vehrenberg
Vernadskij
Veteraniya
VictorJara
Vincentina
Vladisvyat
von Sprang
von-Sprang
Waterfield
Westerlund
Westphalia
Whittemora
Wilhelmina
Winchester
Yugoslavia
Zerbinetta
Zhang Heng
Zhang-Heng
Zimmerwald
ZuChongZhi

9

Aavasaksa
Aconcagua
Adalberta
Adelgunde
Aeschylus
Agamemnon
Agrippina
Aiguillon
Akhmatova
Albertine
Albitskij
Alemannia
Alexandra
Alfaterna
Alschmitt
Amaryllis
Amherstia
Anacostia
Anastasia
Anatoliya
Anneliese
Antikleia
Antwerpia
Aphrodite
Apollonia
Aquilegia
Aquitania
Argentina
Aristaeus
Atanasoff
Athanasia
Austrasia
Automedon
Backlunda
Bagration
Baillauda
Balduinus
Bancilhon
Barcelona
Barringer
Bashkiria
Beethoven
Belinskij
Ben Mayer
Ben-Mayer
Benguella
Benjamina
Berendeya
Bernoulli
Bertholda
Boliviana
Bonestell
Botolphia
Bourgeois
Bouzareah
Boyarchuk

Brabantia
Bradfield
Brambilla
Brendelia
Brorfelde
Bruxelles
Burdigala
Burgundia
Burnhamia
Bussolini
Calpurnia
Cambridge
Campanula
Carpenter
Cebriones
Centesima
Chacornac
Charlotte
Charybdis
Chebyshev
Cheruskia
Chlosinde
Christine
Churyumov
Chuvashia
Colchagua
ComasSola
Concordia
Coubertin
Crommelin
Daghestan
Dangrania
De Sitter
De-Sitter
Debehogne
Decabrina
Deiphobus
Delportia
Dembowska
Demoulina
DeSanctis
Desdemona
Dieckvoss
DiMartino
Dionysius
Eddington
Edmondson
Efremiana
ElDjezair
Erbisbuhl
Ernestina
Esperanto
Espinette
Eugenisis
Eupraksia
Euripides
Euryanthe
Eurykleia
Farinella

Fedchenko
Fedynskij
Felicitas
Fernandus
Filipenko
Flagstaff
Flammario
Francette
Franklina
Franziska
Fringilla
Fukushima
Gabriella
Gajdariya
Galanthus
Gallagher
Galvarino
Gellivara
Genevieve
Genichesk
Geometria
Geraldina
Geramtina
Gershberg
Giacobini
Gilgamesh
Gingerich
Gonnessia
Goodricke
Greenberg
Greenwich
Griboedov
Griseldis
Guangdong
Guinevere
Hallstrom
Heinemann
Heiskanen
Helewalda
Helionape
Henderson
Henrietta
Herculina
Herodotus
Heyerdahl
Hilaritas
Hildegard
Hiroshima
Hollandia
Honkasalo
Hormuthia
Hypsipyle
Idelsonia
Idomeneus
Iku-Turso
Ilfpetrov
Industria
Iphigenia
Itzigsohn

Jarnefelt
Jaroslawa
Jekhovsky
Jim Young
Jim-Young
Jimarnold
Johnadams
Josephina
Jyvaskyla
Kacivelia
Kahrstedt
Kallavesi
Kandinsky
Kapteynia
Karbyshev
Karl Marx
Karl-Marx
Karolinum
Karttunen
Kartvelia
Kashirina
Kassandra
Katharina
Kaverznev
Kilmartin
Kirghizia
Kitt Peak
Kitt-Peak
Kleopatra
Knezevic'
Kobayashi
Kollontai
Kornensky
Kostinsky
Kriemhild
Kronstadt
Kukkamaki
Kunigunde
Kurchatov
Kurchenko
Kuznetsov
Lacadiera
Lacrimosa
Lagrangea
Lambrecht
Laurentia
Lencarter
Leningrad
Lermontov
Leukothea
Leverrier
Likhachev
Limburgia
Lipschutz
Lundmarka
Magdalena
Magnusson
Makarenko
Malaparte

Manuilova
Marbachia
Marceline
Margarita
Marghanna
MarkTwain
Mayrhofer
McAuliffe
McDonalda
McGetchin
Mechthild
Melpomene
Mendeleev
Messalina
Metcalfia
Metsahovi
Meyermann
Mikhailov
Mitchella
Mnemosyne
Moisseiev
Monterosa
Morosovia
Mr. Spock
Mr.-Spock
Mrinalini
Mundleria
Musashino
Nefertiti
Nepryadva
Newcombia
Nicholson
Nofretete
Normannia
Northcott
Nostalgia
Numerowia
O'Higgins
Okudzhava
Ole Romer
Ole-Romer
Olshaniya
Olympiada
Orelskaya
Ornamenta
Outeniqua
Palamedes
Paolicchi
Parysatis
Pasternak
Patientia
Patroclus
Patterson
Per Brahe
Per-Brahe
Phereclos
Philomela
Pierretta
Ponomarev

Pordenone
Predappia
Principia
Priscilla
Prokofjev
Proskurin
Prudentia
Queteleta
Quintilla
Radcliffe
Ra-Shalom
Ratisbona
Reginhild
Rollandia
Ron Helin
Ron-Helin
Rontaylor
Rosalinde
Rosamunde
Rosseland
Rovaniemi
RuthWolfe
Sakuntala
San Diego
San-Diego
Sapientla
Sarmiento
Scaltriti
Schaifers
Schmakova
Schneller
Seidelman
Seinajoki
Semiramis
Seraphina
Serkowski
Shcheglov
Shimoyama
Shiretoko
Shoemaker
Sholokhov
Sigelinde
Sillanpaa
Silvretta
Skovoroda
Skvortsov
Sodankyla
Soderblom
Sophocles
Soromundi
Spartacus
Spellmann
Steinmetz
Stephania
Steshenko
Sthenelos
Struveana
Subbotina
Sulamitis

Sundmania
Szmytowna
Tauntonia
Teneriffa
Tengstrom
Tercidina
Theobalda
Thersites
Thessalia
Thuringia
Thusnelda
Tisiphone
Tisserand
Tomeileen
Tsesevich
Tsvetaeva
Turkmenia
Underhill
Urhixidur
Valentine
vanAltena
VanDeKamp
VanDenBos
VanHouten
Villigera
Vindobona
Volgo-Don
Voloshina
vonSprang
Vyssotsky
Walinskia
Wasserman
Wendeline
Wesselink
Wetherill
Wingolfia
Wladilena
Xanthippe
Zahringia
Zeelandia
ZhangHeng
Zimmerman

8

Aaronson
Abalakin
Abkhazia
Academia
Achilles
Adelaide
Adelheid
Adelinda
Adolfine
Adrastea
Agematsu
Aguntina
Aidamina

Alagasta
Aletheia
Alhambra
Alikoski
Amalthea
Ambrosia
Amicitia
Amnestia
Anchises
Andersen
Andriana
Angelica
Angelina
Antigone
Antinous
Arabella
Arequipa
Arethusa
Ashbrook
Asmodeus
Asplinda
Asporina
Asterope
Astyanax
Atalante
Atkinson
Atlantis
Auricula
Autonoma
Avicenna
Baikonur
Bamberga
Bandusia
Bardwell
Bathilde
Bathseba
Bechuana
Belisana
Benkoela
BenMayer
Berenike
Bergholz
Berkeley
Bernheim
Berolina
Birgitta
Biryukov
Bohlinia
Bohrmann
Bornmann
Borrelly
Boweller
Brangane
Brasilia
Bressole
Brigitta
Bruckner
Brunhild
Brunonia

Buchwald
Bulgakov
Bulgaria
Buryatia
Caecilia
Caldeira
Calvinia
Campania
Campbell
Cannonia
Cantabia
Carnegia
Carolina
Catriona
Celestia
Ceplecha
Ceraskia
Cerberus
Cevenola
Chaldaea
Chalonge
Chapleya
Charlois
Chernykh
Chimaera
Chryseis
Chukotka
Cimmeria
Cindijon
Clarissa
Clematis
Clemence
Clorinde
Coconino
Cogshall
Colocolo
Columbia
Comacina
Coppelia
Cordelia
Cornelia
Cosicosi
Cottrell
Coventry
Daedalus
Daguerre
Dangreen
Deflotte
Dejanira
Dejopeja
Delphine
Delporte
Delsemme
DeSitter
Dikan'ka
Dimitrov
Diomedes
Dornburg
Dorothea

Drakonia
Duboshin
Dulcinea
Duncombe
Dynamene
Dzhangar
Educatio
Einstein
Eleonora
Elfriede
Ellicott
Emanuela
Endymion
Erfordia
Eriphyla
Ethiopia
Eucharis
Euphemia
Eurydike
Eurynome
Evdokiya
Everhart
Fanatica
Fantasia
Fatyanov
Feodosia
Ferguson
Fesenkov
Figneria
Filipoff
Forsytia
Fragaria
Freuchen
Friedman
Geldonia
Genoveva
Gentelec
Geranium
Gerlinde
Germania
Gersuind
Gismonda
Gordonia
Gorshkov
Grinevia
Guacolda
Guernica
Guyhurst
Gyldenia
Hadwiger
Hagihara
Halleria
Halliday
Hamburga
Hammonia
Hannibal
Happelia
Haremari
Harmonia

Hartmann
Hasegawa
Heckmann
Helsinki
Herberta
Hercynia
Hergiani
Hermione
Herodias
Herschel
Hersilia
Herzberg
Hesburgh
Hesperia
Hildburg
Hirayama
Hispania
Hoffmann
Hokkaido
Holmberg
Hooveria
Horemheb
Horrocks
Hungaria
Hurakawa
Ibarruri
Iduberga
Ilsebill
Ingeborg
Ingwelde
Irpedina
Isabella
Isergina
Jablunka
Janequeo
Jeffbell
Jessonda
JimYoung
Jugurtha
Julietta
Justitia
Kakhovka
Kalahari
Kalbaugh
Kalevala
Kalliope
Kallisto
Kalmykia
Kamenyar
Karamzin
KarlMarx
Kastalia
Katyusha
Kemerovo
Kemstach
Kharadze
Kirkwood
KittPeak
Klotilde

Klumpkea
Knezevic
Kniertje
Kobresia
Kohoutek
Konkolya
Korsunia
Kressida
Kukarkin
Kutaissi
La Plata
La Silla
La-Plata
La-Plata
La-Silla
Lachesis
Lacroute
Laetitia
Lamberta
Lampetia
Lampland
Lancelot
Landgraf
Laodamia
Lausanna
Lebofsky
Lemaitre
Leocadia
Leonardo
Leonisis
Leonteus
Leontina
Liaoning
Lictoria
Lilliana
Lindelof
Lindgren
Lipperta
Lorraine
Lubarsky
Lucienne
Lucretia
Ludmilla
Ludovica
Lupishko
Luscinia
Madeline
Magnitka
Magnolia
Maksutov
Malautra
Malzovia
Mancunia
Mannucci
Marcelle
Marconia
Maresjew
Margolin
Marianna

Marietta	Newtonia	Reginita	Stateira	Walraven
Maritima	Nicolaia	Repsolda	Stebbins	Waltraut
Marmulla	Nininger	Reunerta	Storeria	Waterman
Martelli	Nipponia	Rhodesia	Strackea	Watsonia
Martinez	Nocturna	Richilde	Subamara	Weissman
Martynov	Notburga	Ristiina	Svanetia	Werdandi
Massalia	Obruchev	RonHelin	Swetlana	Weringia
Massinga	Odysseus	Rosemary	Swissair	Whitford
Masursky	O'gyalla	Rosselia	Sylvania	Williams
Mathesis	OHiggins	Roswitha	Tamariwa	Winifred
Mathilde	Okavango	Roucarie	Tantalus	Wisibada
Mattiaca	Olbersia	Rutllant	Taratuta	Wolfiana
Mauderli	OleRomer	Safronov	Tavastia	Xinjiang
Mauritia	Oppolzer	Sakharov	Tekmessa	Yamamoto
McCauley	Ostanina	Saldanha	Tellervo	Zambesia
McCrosky	Ottegebe	Samantha	Tenojoki	Zamenhof
McCuskey	Paganini	San Juan	Terentia	Zaragoza
McFadden	Paijanne	San-Juan	Tergeste	Zelinsky
McNaught	Painleva	SanDiego	Terradas	Zhejiang
McVittie	Palisana	Sandrine	Teutonia	Zhongguo
Meliboea	Pandarus	Sarabhai	Texereau	Zichichi
Melnikov	Pannonia	Sarahill	The NORC	Zverdara
Melusina	Panopaea	Sarpedon	The-NORC	
Menelaus	Papagena	Scabiosa	Theodora	7
Mercedes	Paradise	Schiller	Theresia	
Meriones	Parenago	Schilowa	Timandra	Adriana
Mezzarco	Parsifal	Schlutia	Titicaca	Aehlita
Michelle	Pasadena	Schmadel	Tombaugh	Aemilia
Mielikki	Patricia	Schorria	Tombecka	Aethusa
Milbourn	Patsayev	Schubart	Torrence	Aetolia
Minnaert	Pawlowia	Schulhof	Triberga	Agassiz
Mireille	Pedersen	Schumann	Trusanda	Aguilar
Mitidika	Penelope	Schuster	Tubingia	A'Hearn
Modestia	PerBrahe	Schuyler	Turandot	Ahrensa
Moguntia	Perrotin	Seillier	Tuulikki	Aisleen
Moldavia	Phaethon	Sekanina	Tyumenia	Akiyama
Monachia	Phaetusa	Seleucus	Valdivia	Alamosa
Montague	Philippa	Semphyra	Vampilov	Alekhin
Morabito	Pielinen	Setouchi	Van Gent	Alfreda
Morrison	Piironen	Shandong	Van Herk	Algeria
Moskvina	Pikelner	Shanghai	Van-Gent	Algunde
Moultona	Planckia	Sharonov	Van-Herk	Alisary
Mozartia	Plaskett	Shavarsh	Varsavia	Alkeste
Mr.Spock	Platonov	Shen Guo	Vaticana	Alkmene
Mtskheta	Platzeck	Shen-Guo	Verbiest	Alsatia
Murakami	Pochaina	Sheragul	Veronika	Alstede
Murayama	Poincare	Shimanto	Victoria	Althaea
Murmansk	Polyxena	Shukshin	Vilyujsk	Alvarez
Naantali	Polzunov	Sibelius	Vinifera	Amazone
Nadezhda	Porphyro	Siebohme	Violetta	America
Nansenia	Posnania	Sijthoff	Virginia	Amneris
Nassovia	Postrema	Simonida	Virtanen	Ampella
Natascha	Poutanen	Sisyphus	Vladimir	Anahita
Nauheima	Praxedis	Sitarski	Von Lude	Annette
Nausikaa	Pretoria	Slovakia	Von-Lude	Antenor
Nekrasov	Preziosa	Smolensk	Wachmann	Anteros
Nephthys	Probitas	Sofievka	Walhalla	Antiope
Nesterov	Raimonda	Somville	Wallonia	Antonia
Neujmina	Raphaela	Standish	Walpurga	

Appella	Brunsia	Donnera	Gezelle	Isberga
Arachne	Budrosa	Dorffel	Gilmore	Jacchia
Arcadia	Burdett	Douglas	Ginevra	Jackson
Arctica	Caltech	Dresden	Glarona	Janacek
Arduina	Camelia	Druzhba	Glaukos	Jarmila
Ariadne	Camilla	Dubiago	Goberta	Jeffers
Aribeda	Camillo	Ducrosa	Gondola	Jiangxi
Arizona	Campins	Duponta	Granada	Jihlava
Armenia	Caprera	Durrell	Granule	Joensuu
Arnolda	Carelia	Dwornik	Grechko	Johanna
Arsinoe	Carlova	Dzhalil	Gregory	Jokaste
Artemis	Carrera	Edburga	Grietje	Jucunda
Aschera	Caubeta	Edisona	Grissom	Juliana
Askania	Cellino	Eduarda	Gryphia	Juvisia
Aspasia	Cetacea	Ehrsson	Guangxi	Kaarina
Astarte	Chagall	Elektra	Gubarev	Kajaani
Asteria	Chandra	Eltigen	Guizhou	Kalinin
Athalia	Chantal	Epstein	Gunhild	Kalypso
Atropos	Chaplin	Ercilla	Haffner	Kampala
Augusta	Chapman	Erigone	Hakoila	Kapitsa
Aurelia	Chaucer	Erminia	Handahl	Katanga
Ausonia	Chekhov	Estonia	Hanskya	Kathryn
Austria	Cherson	Eugenia	Harding	Kaverin
Bacchus	Chicago	Eukrate	Harriet	Kazbegi
Badenia	Chilton	Eulalia	Hartmut	Keldysh
Baetsle	Chkalov	Eunomia	Harvard	Kerstin
Barbara	Chloris	Euterpe	Harvill	Khanina
Barucci	Christa	Evenkia	Haworth	Kiangsu
Basilea	Cimbria	Fabiola	Helenos	Kieffer
Bateson	Claudia	Feldman	Henrika	Klemola
Baumann	Cloelia	Felicia	Herluga	Klymene
Baumeia	Colchis	Feronia	Herrick	Knopfia
Bavaria	Conrada	Ferreri	Hidalgo	Kobolda
Beadell	Corbett	Fidelio	Hildrun	Kochera
Beatrix	Corduba	Fiducia	Hirundo	Kokkola
Beckman	Cortusa	Floirac	Hodgson	Komarov
Begonia	Corvina	Fogelin	Holbaek	Koranna
Behrens	Cosette	Fortuna	Honoria	Korczak
Belgica	Cremona	Francis	Hopmann	Kordula
Bellona	Crisser	Franzia	Hoshino	Korolev
Belnika	Croatia	Frieden	Houssay	Koronis
Belyaev	Cunitza	Frostia	Houston	Kovacia
Bennett	Cydonia	Gabrova	Houzeau	Kozyrev
Beograd	Danmark	Gadolin	Huberta	Kulikov
Bethgea	Danubia	Gagarin	Huggins	Kunikov
Bettina	Davydov	Galahad	Humason	Kutuzov
Betulia	Deborah	Galatea	Hypatia	Kuzbass
Bezovec	Delmary	Galilea	Iguassu	Kythera
Biarmia	Delores	Ganymed	Iisalmi	Lagrula
Blazhko	Delvaux	Gardner	Ilinsky	Laocoon
Bohemia	Demeter	Garlena	Illyria	Laodica
Bologna	Dermott	Garumna	Ilmatar	LaPlata
Bolzano	d'Hotel	Gaussia	Imhilde	Larissa
Bononia	Dikanka	Gaviola	Imhotep	LaSilla
Borngen	Diotima	Gedania	Indiana	Lassell
Bradley	Dirikis	Gehrels	Iolanda	Laugier
Brandia	Dollfus	Georgia	Irenaea	Lautaro
Briseis	Dolores	Gerarda	Irkutsk	Lavonne
Brouwer	Domeyko	Gertrud	Irmgard	Lazarev

Lebedev	Millman	Pelagia	Sapporo	Tampere
Lederle	Minerva	Peltier	Satpaev	Tamriko
Leonora	Mineura	Petrina	Saucier	Tataria
Liberia	Mirnaya	Petunia	Schaber	Tatjana
Libussa	Mironov	Phaedra	Schalen	Tedesco
Liguria	Moeller	Phocaea	Scheila	Telamon
Lilofee	Moliere	Phyllis	Schmidt	TheNORC
Limpopo	Mombasa	Piazzia	Schober	Thernoe
Liriope	Montana	Piccolo	Schwall	Thomana
Livadia	Moravia	Pieters	Scythia	Thomsen
Lobelia	Muazzez	Pilcher	Segovia	Tianjin
Locarno	Namaqua	Pirogov	Selinur	Tinchen
Lohmann	Namibia	Planman	Semenov	Tinette
Lonnrot	Nanking	Plovdiv	Semirot	Titania
Lorbach	Natalie	Polonia	Seppina	Tjilaki
Loreley	Nealley	Poltava	Sequoia	Tjossem
Loretta	Nemausa	Pompeja	Severny	Tolkien
Loviisa	Nemesis	Pongola	Shaanxi	Tomyris
Lucerna	Nenetta	Porthan	Shapiro	Toronto
Lucidor	Nephele	Potomac	ShenGuo	Iristan
Lucifer	Nerthus	Preston	Shimizu	Troilus
Lugduna	Newburn	Priamus	Siberia	Tselina
Lumiere	Nezarka	Prieska	Sibylla	Tucapel
Lunaria	Nikonov	Primula	Sichuan	Turnera
Lutetia	Ningxia	Pulcova	Sicilia	Ueferji
Luthera	Nongorna	Pushkin	Sidonia	Ukraina
Luznice	Novikov	Qingbai	Siegena	Ulugbek
Maartje	Numidia	Rachele	Silesia	Ulyanov
Mabella	Nummela	Ragazza	Simeisa	Uppsala
Machado	Nurmela	Rebekka	Simonov	Ushakov
Magoeba	Octavia	Reddish	Slipher	Vaisala
Makhaon	Odishaw	Renauxa	Slipher	Valborg
Makover	Ogyalla	Requiem	Smetana	Valeria
Malabar	Okayama	Retsina	Smither	Valeska
Malaren	Oleshko	Rhodope	Sobolev	Vanadis
Manning	Olympia	Ricarda	Solvejg	VanGent
Margret	Onizuka	Richter	Somalia	VanHerk
Marilyn	Ophelia	Rickman	Soomana	Vavilov
Marlene	Oppavia	Ricouxa	Sootiyo	Velimir
Marmara	Orangia	Riviera	Spiraea	Vellamo
Marsden	Orlenok	Roberta	Spitzer	Velleda
Marshak	Orpheus	Robeson	Staehle	Venetia
Martebo	Ortutay	Roemera	Stearns	Venusia
Martina	O'Steen	Rogeria	Stentor	Veritas
Masaryk	Ostenia	Rokoske	Sterpin	Verveer
Mashona	Otthild	Romilda	Strenua	Veverka
Mathieu	Ottilia	Rosalia	Strobel	Vibilia
McElroy	Owensby	Rotraut	Suleika	Viipuri
Megaira	Paeonia	Rublyov	Sumiana	Vilnius
Melanie	Palatia	Rudneva	Surikov	Vittore
Melitta	Palomaa	Ruppina	Susanna	Volodia
Mellena	Paloque	Rusheva	Susilva	VonLude
Memoria	Panacea	Russell	Suvanto	Vundtia
Menippe	Pandora	Sabauda	Suvorov	Walbeck
Mertona	Papanov	Sabrina	Svetlov	Walkure
Messina	Pariana	Salazar	Syringa	Weisell
Michela	Patrice	Salonta	Tacitus	Whipple
Mikkeli	Paulina	Sanders	Taiyuan	Wilkens
Mildred	Peiroos	SanJuan	Tamblyn	Woltjer

Yabuuti
Yakutia
Yatskiv
Yeomans
Yesenin
Yi Xing
Yi-Xing
Zappala
Zeissia
Zelinda
Zellner
Zenobia
Zerlina
Zubaida
Zwetana

6

Aaltje
Aarhus
Abante
Abetti
Abnoba
Achaia
Adeona
Admete
Adonis
Adorea
Aegina
Aeolia
Aethra
Africa
Agathe
Agenor
Aglaja
AHearn
Ahnert
Aitken
Aksnes
Alauda
Albert
Albina
Alcock
Alekto
Aletta
Alfven
Alinda
Altona
Alupka
Alwine
Amalia
Amanda
Amelia
Amosov
Andree
Angara
Angola
Anitra

Ankara
Annika
Anubis
Aoluta
Apollo
Arabia
Arabis
Aralia
Arenda
Ariane
Arieso
Armida
Arnica
Arpola
Arthur
Astrea
Astrid
Athene
Atossa
Attica
Attila
Aurora
Azalea
Bahner
Baikal
Batten
Baucis
Beagle
Beatty
Bernes
Bertha
Bessel
Bianca
Bilkis
Binomi
Binzel
Birgit
Bishop
Bistro
Blaauw
Blixen
Bobone
Bohmia
Bojeva
Bokhan
Bolyai
Bondia
Boreas
Bowell
Bowell
Brahic
Brahms
Brauna
Brenda
Britta
Brixia
Brucia
Bruwer
Byblis

Carina
Carmen
Celuta
Chaika
Charis
Chimay
Chiron
Chopin
Clivia
Cohnia
Cosima
Cowell
Crimea
Crocus
Cucula
Cuffey
Cupido
Cybele
Cyrene
Dagmar
Dalera
Daliya
Daniel
Danjon
Danzig
Daphne
Darwin
Datura
Davida
Dawson
Delila
Denise
Derice
Devine
Devosa
Devota
dHotel
Dodona
Dorrit
Dorsey
Dresda
Drukar
Dudley
Dufour
Dunant
Dunbar
Duncan
Dunham
Dunlap
Dvorak
Dysona
Ebella
Eckert
Efimov
Egeria
Ehrdni
Eliane
Elinor
Elliot

Elvira
Epeios
Epyaxa
Eriepa
Erynia
Esther
Euboea
Eudora
Eunike
Europa
Evelyn
Fagnes
Fanale
Fayeta
Fennia
Finsen
Flavia
Florya
Fowler
Franke
French
Fricke
Frieda
Frigga
Frisia
Fujian
Fulvia
Gaffey
Galene
Gallia
Garber
Gaspra
Gawain
Gefion
Geisei
Geisha
Gelria
Gibson
Giclas
Giomus
Gisela
Glauke
Gliese
Glinka
Godiva
Goethe
Goffin
Golson
Gostin
Gotard
Gradie
Gramme
Gratia
Gretia
Gretry
Griqua
Grubba
Gudrun
Gudula

Guisan
Gunila
Gunlod
Gunnie
Gunter
Gyptis
Haidea
Hakone
Halawe
Halley
Haltia
Hamina
Handel
Harris
Hathor
Havnia
Hecuba
Hedera
Hedwig
Hekate
Hektor
Helena
Helina
Hencke
Henyey
Herald
Herero
Herget
Hermia
Hertha
Herzen
Hestia
Higson
Hirons
Hirose
Hissao
Holden
Holmia
Hubble
Huenna
Hughes
Hunnia
Hurban
Hybris
Hygiea
Ianthe
Icarus
Ilmari
Ilsewa
Imatra
Impala
Inanda
Ingrid
Inkeri
Irakli
Irmela
Ismene
Isolda
Istria

Italia	Lavrov	Mitaka	Pearce	Sahade
Ithaka	Lehigh	Mizuho	Pecker	Sahlia
Jakoba	Leloir	Modena	Peitho	Saimaa
Janice	Leonce	Mohler	Peking	Salome
Janina	Lepage	Monica	Pepita	Salvia
Jansky	Letaba	Monnig	Peraga	Sandra
Jarvis	Lexell	Moreau	Perkin	Sappho
Jeanne	Libera	Morris	Philia	Sarema
Jensch	Lieske	Moskva	Phryne	Sarita
Jerome	Lilaea	Mourao	Phthia	Saskia
Jo-Ann	Lilith	Muonio	Pierre	Sather
Joella	Lilium	Muriel	Pirola	Sazava
Josefa	Liller	Murray	Plavsk	Scanla
Jovita	Linzia	Muschi	Pobeda	Schilt
Judith	Lorcia	Mustel	Poesia	Scholl
Juhani	Losaka	Myrrha	Pogson	Scobee
Jurgen	Lottie	Nadeev	Polana	Scotti
Justus	Louise	Naerum	Polyxo	Scylla
Kaiser	Lowell	Nakano	Pomona	Selene
Kansas	Luanda	Naniwa	Porter	Scmele
Kaplan	Lucina	Navajo	Porvoo	Sendai
Kariba	Lugano	Neckar	Porzia	Seneca
Kataev	Lundia	Nerina	Priska	Sersic
Kayala	Luyten	Nestor	Prisma	Shajna
Keeler	Lyalya	Netzel	Prokne	Shipka
Kepler	Lydina	Newell	Prymno	Sigrid
Kevola	Lyubov	Nicole	Psyche	Sigune
Kienle	Magion	Niepce	Putnam	Simona
Kilopi	Magnya	Ninina	Pyrrha	Sirene
Kippes	Majuba	Nissen	Pythia	Sirona
Kitami	Maklaj	Nojiri	Quadea	Slavia
Klotho	Margot	Nyanza	Quaide	Smiley
Klytia	Marina	Nymphe	Rafita	Sofala
Knysna	Marion	Oceana	Raissa	Sophia
Kobzar	Martha	Odessa	Raksha	Sphinx
Kohsai	Martir	Oenone	Rarahu	Spicer
Kollaa	Matson	Ohsaki	Reaves	Srbija
Komaki	Mayall	Ohtaki	Reblin	Steina
Komppa	McCord	Oliver	Regina	Steins
Koyama	McMath	Olivia	Renate	Stobbe
Kresak	McNair	Oljato	Renzia	Strand
Kreusa	Medusa	Ontake	Reseda	Stuart
Krinov	Megumi	Oongaq	Resnik	Suevia
Kuiper	Melete	Orchis	Rhodia	Sumava
Kundry	Memnon	Oriola	Riceia	Sumida
Kuopio	Mentha	Orthos	Rimito	Sutton
Kypria	Menzel	Ortrud	Rodari	Suzuki
La Paz	Merapi	Osiris	Roehla	Swasey
La-Paz	Merlin	Ostara	Rosina	Swings
Ladoga	Merope	OSteen	Rostia	Sylvia
Lalage	Merxia	Oterma	Roxane	Tabora
Lameia	Michel	Pafuri	Ruanda	Taiwan
Landau	Mikawa	Palala	Rudaux	Talbot
Lanzia	Mikula	Pallas	Russia	Tamara
Laputa	Miller	Pamela	Ruvuma	Tanete
Larink	Millis	Pamina	Ruzena	Tanina
Larson	Mimosa	Parana	Sabine	Tauris
Latona	Miriam	Patria	Sadeya	Taylor
Latvia	Misuzu	Pawona	Safara	Tempel

Teucer	Weimar	Aster	Dante	Hanko
Thalia	Wesson	Atala	Dasha	Hanna
Thekla	Widorn	Atami	Davis	Hansa
Themis	Wisdom	Athor	Deira	Hapag
Thetis	Wright	Aunus	Dejan	Hapke
Thiele	Wrubel	Azabu	Delia	Hasek
Thisbe	Xanthe	Baade	Detre	Haupt
Tholen	Xizang	Bacon	Diana	Hawke
Thomas	Yan'an	Baily	Dibaj	Haydn
Tiflis	Yangel	Baize	Dione	Heard
Tikhov	Yarilo	Baker	Donar	Hebei
Tirela	Yeates	Balam	Doris	Hedda
Titius	Yerkes	Barks	Dugan	Heike
Tololo	YiXing	Barry	Durer	Helga
Tolosa	Yunnan	Barto	Edith	Helio
Tomita	Yvette	Beals	Edmee	Hella
Tornio	Yvonne	Beate	Edwin	Helma
Toyota	Zachia	Beira	Ekard	Henan
Tracie	Zelima	Bella	Elisa	Henry
Tuckia	Zhukov	Benda	Ellen	Herba
Tucson	Zimmer	Bengt	Elmer	Herge
Tugela	Zverev	Berna	Elpis	Hibbs
Tulipa	Zwicky	Beryl	Elyna	Hicks
Tunica	Zyskin	Beyer	Emita	Hilda
Tuorla		Birch	Ensor	Hippo
Ucclia	**5**	Bodea	Erato	Hirst
Uganda		Bodil	Erida	Holda
Ulrike	Aaryn	Botha	Erika	Holst
Umtata	Abell	Boury	Ethel	Honda
Undina	Adams	Boyce	Euler	Hoppe
Unitas	Adele	Boyer	Evans	Horta
Unsold	Adria	Brest	Evita	Horus
Upgren	Aegle	Brian	Fabre	Hubei
Urania	Aenna	Brita	Faina	Hunan
Ursina	Aeria	Brown	Fanny	Hveen
Ursula	Agnes	Bruna	Fatme	Hynek
Utopia	Agnia	Brunk	Felix	Iclea
Valdaj	Alain	Bryan	Fides	Iduna
Vassar	Alden	Bunke	Field	Iliya
Veeder	Algoa	Burns	Flora	Ilona
Vesale	Alice	Byron	Freda	Inari
Veseli	Aline	Candy	Freia	Innes
Vibeke	Alois	Carla	Fucik	Irene
Vieira	Altaj	Carol	Gaika	Isara
Vienna	Amata	Ceres	Galya	Isora
Vigdis	Amber	CERGA	Gansu	Izsak
Vihuri	Amici	Cesco	Genua	James
Viljev	Aneas	Chaka	Gerda	Jeans
Virton	Anhui	Chang	Gerti	Jenny
Virtus	Arago	Chant	Gibbs	Jetta
Visbor	Arete	China	Gogol	Jilin
Vivian	Arina	Chiny	Golia	Jones
Vltava	Arlon	Chloe	Gorgo	Juewa
Vogtia	Armor	Circe	Gorky	Jugta
Volkov	Arosa	Clara	Gotha	Julia
Vondel	Artek	Cline	Gotho	Jutta
Wagner	Asaph	Cyane	Grano	Kacha
Wallia	ASCII	Danae	Hagar	Kafka
Weaver	Aslog	Danby	Hajek	Kalle

Kanda	Mayre	Phaeo	Thyra	Asia
Karel	Medea	Picka	Tilia	Asta
Karen	Meeus	Pippa	Tirza	Aten
Karin	Metis	Pisek	Tokai	Aura
Kasan	Mette	Plzen	Tokio	Bach
Katja	Meyer	Polit	Troja	Bali
Kenya	Midas	Popov	Tsvet	Beer
Kerch	Mieke	Praha	Turku	Blok
Khama	Mikko	Prast	Tyche	Boda
Khufu	Milet	Pryor	Tynka	Brel
Kiang	Minsk	Puijo	Ulula	Buda
Kiess	Miune	Pumma	Union	Caia
Kilia	Mocia	Raahe	Vaasa	Carr
Kirik	Moira	Rauma	Vaino	Cava
Klare	Moore	Recha	Valda	Cook
Kochi	Mrkos	Regge	Verdi	Cora
Kolga	Munoz	Reiss	Vesta	CrAO
Konig	Naema	Remek	Vicia	Cuyo
Kopal	Namba	Rezia	Vilas	Dali
Kopff	Nancy	Rhoda	Vilho	Dato
Kotka	Nanna	Riema	Viola	Davy
Kozai	Nanon	Roman	Vilja	Dawn
Kullk	Ndola	Ryoma	Volga	Dido
Kumin	Neith	Sagan	Wanda	Dike
Kursk	Netto	Saito	Warck	Disa
Lahti	Niels	Salli	Watts	Dora
Landi	Nikko	Sampo	Wawel	Dudu
LaPaz	Niobe	Santa	Welch	Dzus
Lapko	Noemi	Sasha	Wells	Echo
Lauer	Nolli	Scott	Wempe	Edda
Laura	Nonie	Sedov	Werra	Edna
Legia	Norma	Seili	Wodan	Elba
Leona	Ocllo	Senta	Wotho	Ella
Lesya	OISCA	Shane	Xenia	Elly
Levin	Oishi	Sheba	Yalta	Elsa
Libya	Ojima	Shura	Yanan	Emma
Lilio	Onnie	Signe	Yazhi	Erda
Lioba	Orlov	Sigyn	Ylppo	Erin
Litva	Osita	Silke	Yorii	Erna
Ljuba	Oskar	Sinon	Young	Eros
Lohja	Ostro	Skiff	Zelia	Fama
Lomia	Otero	Skuld	Zeuxo	Fini
Lotis	Otila	Smith	Zomba	Fuji
Lucla	Ounas	Smuts		Gaby
Luisa	Padua	Sonja	4	Gaea
Lumen	Pales	Sorga		Gase
Lumme	Palma	Summa	Aase	Goto
Lydia	Paola	Suomi	Afra	Gudy
Lyyli	Paris	Swope	Ahti	Haas
Mally	Paton	Tammy	Aida	Hahn
Malva	Patry	Tanga	Ajax	Hale
Manto	Patsy	Tanya	Alex	Hall
Margo	Paula	Tapio	Alma	Hebe
Maria	Pauly	Tarka	Amor	Hela
Marlu	Peale	Tatry	Amun	Hera
Mateo	Pemba	Tatum	Anga	Hess
Matra	Penza	Tesla	Anna	Hill
Matti	Perec	Thais	Anza	Hind
Maury	Perth	Thora	Arne	Hoag
Mavis	Peter	Thule		Hopi

20

Hugo	Lois	Pele	Tone	Ate
Ilse	Lola	Pels	Toni	BAM
INAG	Lova	Pien	Toro	Bok
Inge	Luce	Pire	Tosa	Bus
Inna	Luda	Pori	Tsai	Cox
Iris	Lunn	Rabe	Tuva	Eos
Irma	Lyka	Reni	Ueta	Eri
Isis	Lyot	Resi	Ukko	Eva
Isko	Maja	Rhea	Ulla	Glo
Itha	Mary	Riga	Urda	Hay
Ivar	Mera	Rita	Ursa	Hel
Jena	Meta	Roka	Utra	Hus
Jens	Mila	Roma	Vala	Ida
Jole	Mimi	Rosa	Vera	Ino
Jose	Misa	Ruby	Webb	Isa
Juno	Mora	Ruth	West	ITA
Kalm	Musa	Saga	Wild	Iva
Kama	Naef	Sara	Wirt	May
Kate	Nasi	Savo	Witt	Oda
Kemi	Nata	Seki	Wood	Ops
Kevo	Nele	Shao	Wren	Owa
Kibi	Nemo	Siri	Wurm	Pax
Kiev	Neva	Sita	Xosa	Pia
King	Nike	Siva	Yrjo	Sax
Kira	Nina	Siwa	Yrsa	Tea
Kiso	Noel	Skip	Zita	Una
Klet	Nora	Soma	Zoya	Ute
Klio	Nuki	Stur	Zulu	Viv
Krat	Nuwa	Susi		Wil
Kron	Nysa	Svea		
Lada	Ohio	Taga	**3**	**2**
Leda	Olga	Tama		
Lena	Oort	Tana	Ada	Io
Leto	Opik	Tata	Aho	Li
Levy	Oulu	Thia	Amy	Sy
Lick	Pala	Tina	Ani	Wu
Lina	Paul	Tito	Ara	
			ASP	

Astrology

15
Sinister aspect

6
Trigon

5
Solar

Astronomy

26
Apex of the earth's motion

24
Rectification of a globe

22
Ascensional difference
Resolution of a nebula

21
Conservation of areas
Ground of the heavens

Variation of the moon

20
Lunisolar precession

Universal instrument

19

Crown of aberration
Magnitude of a star
Meridian instrument
Newtonian telescope

18

Ascending latitude
Inductive sciences
Limiting parallels
Physical astronomy
Pythagorean system
Transit instrument

17

Absolute equation
Magellenic clouds

16

Medicean planets
Nadir of the sun
Rational horizon
Secondary planet
Secular equation
Spots on the sun
Subconstellation
Telespectroscope

15

Annular eclipse
Galactic circle
Meridian circle
Ring micrometer
Tail of a comet
Vertical circle
Winter solstice
Zenith distance

14

Coma Berenices
Georgium Sidus
Heliocentrical
Neptunicentric
Saturnicentric
Southern Cross
Temporary star
Transit circle

Unformed stars
Variable stars
Vernal equinox

13

Anomalistical
Austral signs
Kepler's laws
Mean distance
Medusa's head
Multiple star
Radiant point
Radius vector
Selenocentric
Shooting star
Southern Fish
Ultrazodiacal
Upper transit
Zenith sector

12

astronomical
Comet-finder
Geocentrical
Meteoroscope
Mural circle
Normal place
Serpentarius
Solar system
Vernal signs
Water-bearer

11

Acronyctous
Antecedence
Astronomize
Conjunction
Globe valve
Hour circle
Nonagesimal
Occultation
Sagittarius
Seven stars
Spherograph
Triple star

10

Aberration
Acronychal
Almacantar
Almucantar
Altazimuth

Apparition
Astronomer
Cassiopeia
Collimator
Cometarium
Cometology
Great bear
Heliometer
Helioscope
Hour angle
Nebulosity
Opposition
Quadrivium
Refraction
Retrograde
Revolution
Selenology
Septentrio
Siderostat
Stargasing
Terminator
Uranometry

9

Aldebaran
Amplitude
Andromeda
Astrolabe
Astrology
Astronomy
Capricorn
Curtation
Hour line
Melpomene
Meteoroid
Midheaven
Milky Way
Monoceros
Ophiuchus
Satellite
Saturnian
Secondary
Star-read
Sun spots
Swordfish
Synodical
True time

8

Altitude
Apastron
Aphelion
Aquarius
Asterism
Canicula

Cosmical
Gelation
Heliacal
Heremite
Herschel
meridian
Nebulous
Northing
Nubecula
Nutation
Occulted
Quadrant
Sidereal
Solstice
Southing
Sporades
The Wain
Victoria
Zodiacal

7

Anomaly
Apogeal
Appulse
Apsidal
Canopus
Centaur
Cepheus
Combust
Curtate
Flexure
Horizon
Neptune
Nucleus
Radiant
Sagitta
Science
Scorpio
Serpens
Sextans
Sextant
Spheric
Transit
Uranian
Wagoner

6

Alioth
Apogee
Aquila
ARATUS
Atazir
Crater
Cygnus
Galaxy

Gemini
Gnomon
Hydrus
Lyraid
Nebula
Saturn
Sickle
Sirius
Sphere
Syzygy
Taurus
Tropic
Uranus
Virgin
Zodiac

5

Algol
Apsis
Aries
Comet
Hyads
Orbit
Orion
Phase
Regel
Rigel
Rille
South
Spica
Umbra
Vesta
Virgo

4

Ansa
Argo
Coma
Cusp
Harp
Lyra
Mars
Mira
Node
Rill
Twin
Ursa
Vega

3

Ara
RAM

Automobile Names

10
Ambassador
Mitsubishi
Volkswagen

9
Alfaromeo
Chevrolet

8
Cadillac
Chrysler
Mercedes
Plymouth
Vauxhall

7
Citroen
Citrone
Ferrari

Hyundai
Mercury
Peugeot
Pontiac
Porsche
Renault
Trabant

6
Datsun
Hyndai
Jaguar
Toyota

Toyoto

5
Buick
Dodge
Honda
Maxda
Skoda
Volga
Volvo

4
Fiat
Ford
Jeep
Jugo
Lada
Saab
Saub

3
BMW

Biology

19
Germinative vesicle
Saltatory evolution
Segmentation cavity
Segmentation
sphere
Virginal generation

18
Zymogenic organism

17
Anthropomorphitic
Electro-biologist
Germinal membrane
Sexual dimorphism

16
Archaeostomatous
General homology
Germinal vesicle
Hermaphroditical
Parthenogenitive
Promorphological
Sexual selection
Special homology

15
Amphibiological
Autofecundation
Electro-biology
Germinal layers
Hermaphroditism
Parthenogenesis
Parthenogenetic
Promorphologist
Saccharomycetes
Serial homology
Serial symmetry
Spermatogenesis
Streptobacteria

14
Centrolecithal
Coccobacterium
Cormophylogeny
Heteromorphous
Parent nucleus
Pro thyalosoma
Pseudobacteria
Specialization
Spherobacteria
Transformation
Variety hybrid
Viviparousness
Zona pellucida
Zonal symmetry

13
Archiblastula
Fertilization
Gemmification
Germinal spot
Glomuliferous
Hermaphrodism
hermaphrodite
Heterocarpism
Heterogenesis
Heterogenetic
Heteromorphic
Heteroplastic
Heterotactous
Homocategoric
Interosculant
Interosculate
Intracellular
Karyostenosis
Karyostenotic
Perivitelline
Polynucleolar
Proliferation
Promorphology
Prothyalosome
Protoorganism
Purpuriparous
Purpurogenous
Saccharomyces
Schizogenesis
Schizomycetes
Spermatozooid
Spirobacteria

Sporification
Sporuliferous
Sterilization
Streptococcus
Teratological
Tetraschistic
Transmutation
Triploblastic
Uniflagellate
Unity of type
Unsymmetrical
Vegeto-animal
Verticillated

12
Adosculation
Agamogenesis
Agamogenetic
Amphiblastic
Amphigenesis
Anamorphosis
Anaphroditic
Animalculism
Cytoblastema
Evolutionist
Gamomorphism
Gastrulation
Geneagenesis
Heterochrony
Heterogenist
Heterogenous
Heteromorphy
Histogenesis

Histogenetic
Histological
Homomorphism
Homosystemic
Hyperplastic
Impregnation
Inembryonate
Inequilobate
Intranuclear
Invagination
Karyokinesis
Karyokinetic
Parthenogeny
Pedunculated
Pleomorphism
Pneumaticity
Pneumococcus
Poison gland
Polymorphism
Polymorphous
Polyphyletic
Preformation
Protomorphic
Protoplasmic
Sarcina form
Scissiparity
Semeniferous
Seminiferous
Sperm morula
Spermatozoid
Spermatozoon
Sporogenesis
Streptothrix
Teleological
Transformism

Tridactylous
Uninucleated
Viviparously
Zona radiata
Zygomorphous

11

Abiogenesis
Abiogenetic
Amylobacter
Anamorphism
Archenteric
Archenteron
Auriculated
Autogenesis
Autogenetic
Coccosphere
Cytogenesis
Cytogenetic
Gamogenesis
Gamogenetic
Gastromyces
Gemmiferous
Gemmiparity
Gemmiparous
Gemmulation
Germ theory
Germiparity
Gymnocytode
Henogenesis
Hexapterous
Holoblastic
Homodromous
Homogenesis
Homogenetic
Homotypical
Hypoblastic
Hypospadias
Impregnable
Incremental
Inheritance
Interseptal
Karyoplasma
Kenogenesis
Kenogenetic
Palingenesy
Panspermist
Parablastic
Paranucleus
Parent cell
Penicillate
Pentamerous
Pericambium
Perigenesis
Perigenetic
Perinuclear
Photobiotic
Physiophyly

Plasmatical
Pneumatical
Polygenetic
Polynuclear
Polyplastic
Proliferate
Respiration
Sacciferous
Schizophyte
Seminifical
Spirochaete
Spontaneity
Sporiferous
Sporulation
Stereoplasm
Symmetrical
Teleologist
Tessellated
Trimorphism
Univalvular
Vacuolation
Variability
Vascularity
Vital force
Xenogenesis
Xenogenetic

10

Abbreviate
Abiogenist
Abiogenous
Ablastemic
Achromatic
Achromatin
Aerobiotic
Amphiaster
Anaerobies
Anthracoid
Ascococcus
Autogenous
Autonomous
Biologists
centrosome
Cyatholith
Cystoplast
Cytococcus
Gastrodisc
Geotropism
Gymnoplast
Heterogeny
Heterology
Heterotaxy
Histolysis
Histolytic
Histophyly
Homaxonial
Homodermic
Homogenous

Homologize
Homomorphy
Homonomous
Homophylic
Homoplasmy
Homoplasty
Hygroplasm
Hypodermis
Idioplasma
Impregnate
Intercross
Karyomiton
Morphology
Organology
Pangenesis
Pangenetic
Panspermic
Paramitome
Parenchyma
Persistent
Physiogeny
Plasmodial
Plasmodium
Plastidule
Polygenism
Polygenist
Polyspermy
Prepotency
Primordial
Pronucleus
Protoplasm
Protoplast
Resistance
Serotinous
Specialize
Spermalist
Structural
Structured
Syngenesis
Systemless
Testaceous
Torulaform
Transition
Tridactyle
Unicentral
Unilateral
Unilocular
Vacuolated
Vegetality
Vegetative
Vitalistic
Viviparity
Viviparous
Ypsiliform

9

Aeroscope
Alecithal

Anaerobic
Anhistous
Appendage
Archegony
Archetype
Bacterium
Biologist
Coccolith
Conjugate
Connivent
Cormogeny
Coronated
Cytoblast
Cytoplasm
Dichotomy
Duplicate
Fecundate
Gemmation
Generical
Geotropic
Germ cell
Germicide
Gymnocyte
Histogeny
Holoblast
Homestall
Homodemic
Homodermy
Homophyly
Homoplast
Homoplasy
Homopolic
Homotaxic
Homotaxis
Homotypal
Hypnocyst
Hypoblast
Idioplasm
Imitation
Panspermy
Parablast
Paragenic
Pathogene
Periblast
Periplast
Physicist
Plasmogen
Polygenic
Prepotent
Pseudopod
Sacciform
Saltation
Spirillum
Sterility
Sterilize
Structure
Subfamily
Symmetric
Syncytium

Tectology
Tegmental
Teleology
Tomentose
Two-sided
Unicelled
Unigenous
Uniramous
Unisexual
Unit deme
Univalved
Vegetable
Vitellary
Vitelline
Zoˆgamous
Zymogenic

8

Aberrant
Abiogeny
Abortive
Aerobies
Amoeboid
Ancestor
Antimere
Bacillus
Cytogeny
Galeated
Gastraea
Gastrula
Germogen
Heredity
Homogeny
Homology
Homonomy
Homotype
Homotypy
Hypoderm
Panzoism
Papulose
Phrenism
Plastide
Polygeny
Proximal
Sarcodic
Seminist
Spermist
Strobile
Subgenus
Subgroup
Symmetry
Taxology
Unformed
Vascular
Vasiform
Vitalism
Vitalist
Vitellus

Zoˆgenic
Zoˆgloea
Zoˆsperm
Zymogene

7

Aborted
Aerobic
Agamous
Ampulla
Anthrax
Asexual
Atavism
Germule
Globule
Halones
Idorgan

Imitate
Pasteur
Persona
planula
Plasson
Plastin
Promise
Saccate
Sarcina
Sarcode
Sarcoid
Segment
Sporule
Sterile
Toothed
Treadle
Vacuole
Variety
Vegetal

Zoˆcyst
Zoˆgamy
Zoˆlogy
Zygosis

6

Agamic
Apolar
Coccus
Cormus
Cytode
Cytula
Hybrid
Mantle
Phylon
Plasma
Saccus
Series

Tissue
Torula
Vibrio

5

Abort
Cells
Fusco
Gamic
Gemma
Genus
Group
Plasm
Whirl
Zoide
Zoism
Zooid

4

Cell
Corm
Disk
Germ
Node
Sack
Seta
That
Type

3

Ala
Sac

Botany

18

Connate-perfoliate
Hartshorn plantain
Illegitimate union
Lily of the valley
Love-lies-bleeding
Mock bishop's weed
Northern muscadine
Poor man's treacle
Primordial utricle
Resurrection plant
Saint James's-wort
Saint John's bread
Saint Peter's-wort
Saracens' consound
Self-fertilization
Squirting cucumber
Tergiferous plants
Thorny rest-harrow
Triplicate-ternate
Water feather-foil

17

Angiomonospermous
Gall of the earth
Glastonbury thorn
Guinea-hen flower
Hare's-tail grass
Horse-radish tree
Hottentot's bread
India-rubber tree

Jack-by-the-hedge
Jack-in-the-bush
Love-in-idleness
Marsh five-finger
Mountain licorice
Mountain mahogany
Neapolitan medlar
Proper receptacle
Quinque foliolate
Rat-tailed radish
Rattlesnake grass
Reed canary grass
Saint John's-wort
Scrophulariaceous
Separated flowers
Shepherd's needle
Siberian pea tree
Sidesaddle flower
Snake's-head iris
Squarrose-slashed
Squarroso-dentate
Star-of-Bethlehem
Star-of-the-earth
Stock gillyflower
Strawberry tomato
Swamp honeysuckle
Three-nerved leaf
Three-parted leaf
Unequally pinnate
Vegetable leather
Venus's navelwort
Wild balsam apple
Wild sarsaparilla

16

Abruptly pinnate
Caryophyllaceous
Cocculus Indicus
Collective fruit
Cribriform cells
Gingerbread tree
Gold of pleasure
Golden saxifrage
Ground liverwort
Hare's-foot fern
Hedgehog thistle
Herb Christopher
High-water shrub
Holly-leaved oak
Hottentot cherry
Imperfect flower
Included stamens
Jerusalem cherry
Ladies' eardrops
Life everlasting
Linnaea borealis
Lords and Ladies
Luxuriant flower
Man-of-the-earth
Marsh cinquefoil
Meadow saxifrage
Mesembryanthemum
Michaelmas daisy
Monocotyledonous
Mountain spinach
Mountain tobacco

New Zealand flax
Obdiplostemonous
Oppositipetalous
Oppositisepalous
Pea-flower tribe
Prince's feather
Quintuple-ribbed
Rattlesnake fern
Rattlesnake root
Rattlesnake weed
Robin's plantain
Scorpion's thorn
Seneca snakeroot
Serpent cucumber
Seven-year apple
Shepherd's purse
Shepherd's staff
Silk-cotton tree
Silver-bell tree
Strawberry blite
Three-lobed leaf
Trailing arbutus
Trembling poplar
Vegetable butter
Vegetable marrow
Vegetable oyster
Vertical anthers
Virginia cowslip
Virginia creeper
Water chinquapin
Water star grass

15

Alligator apple
Angiospermatous
Asclepiadaceous
Campylospermous
Compound flower
Conferruminated
Contortuplicate
Convolvulaceous
Forbidden fruit
Golden samphire
Golden-rod tree
Guatemala grass
Harefoot clover
Heterocephalous
Hypocrateriform
Indian cucumber
Indian plantain
Infundibuliform
Interfoliaceous
Intrafoliaceous
Intussusception
Jerusalem thorn
Joseph's flower
Jupiter's beard
Jupiter's staff
Ladies' tresses
Lady's bedstraw
Lamb's-quarters
Lavender cotton
Linnaean system
Lombardy poplar

Macrosporangium
Marsh pennywort
Menispermaceous
Microsporangium
Midsummer daisy
Moccasin flower
Monochlamydeous
Mother-of-thyme
Mountain damson
Mountain fringe
Mountain laurel
Mountain sorrel
Multiple fruits
Mushroom-headed
New Zealand tea
Noli-me-tangere
Old man's beard
Oppositifolious
Orbiculate leaf
Parthenogenesis
Partridge berry
Pepperidge bush
Peppermint tree
Pestilence weed
Phyllomorphosis
Pinkster flower
Porcupine grass
Protein crystal
Queen's delight
Quinquefoliated
Quinquevalvular
Rheumatism root
Rocket larkspur
Rogation flower
Rose of Jericho
Scorpion's tail
Self-fertilized
Semiamplexicaul
Sensitive plant
Seven-year vine
Shepherd's club
Sleep of plants
Spanish bayonet
Spanish buckeye
Spanish daggers
Spanish needles
Spattling-poppy
Spurred corolla
Stag-horn sumac
Starch hyacinth
Strawberry bush
Strawberry pear
Strawberry tree
Strawberry vine
Supertuberation
Supradecompound
Suprafoliaceous
Swamp sassafras
Sweet coltsfoot

Syncotyledonous
Telegraph plant
Toothache grass
Traveler's tree
Treacle mustard
Trumpet creeper
Turpentine tree
Umbraculiferous
Universal umbel
Vascular plants
Vascular system
Vascular tissue
Vasiform tissue
Vegetable sheep
Venus's flytrap
Venus's slipper
Vertical leaves
Viper's bugloss
Water chickweed
Water germander
Water horehound
Water pennywort
Water pimpernel
Water speedwell
White hellebore
White of a seed
Wind-fertilized
Winter lodgment
Witches' besoms
Witches' butter
Wood nightshade
Wood reed grass

14

Acanthocarpous
Acanthopodious
Adam's flannel
Adder's-tongue
Adversifolious
Alligator pear
Anacardiaceous
Angoumois moth
Anisostemonous
Anomaloflorous
Aspergilliform
Campanulaceous
Campylotropous
Compass flower
Corolliflorous
Cotton thistle
Cow's lungwort
Crown imperial
Crown-imperial
Cucurbitaceous
Galvanotropism
Gasteromycetes
Giant puffball

Globe amaranth
Graminifolious
Grape hyacinth
Grossification
Ground cypress
Ground hemlock
Haplostemonous
Hare's lettuce
Hedge bindweed
Hedgehog grass
Hercules' club
Heterochromous
Heterophyllous
Hippocrepiform
Horse purslain
Horse-chestnut
Hound's-tongue
Huntsman's cup
Hydrophytology
Hygroscopicity
Indian currant
Indian tobacco
Infra-axillary
Jack- in-a-box
Jacobaean lily
Jacob's ladder
Jamestown weed
Japan allspice
Jerusalem sage
Kangaroo apple
Kangaroo grass
Lady's cushion
Lady's garters
Lady's slipper
Lady's thimble
Lamb's lettuce
Leather flower
Leopard's bane
Lignum rhodium
Love-in-a-mist
Lycopodiaceous
Macrocephalous
Malpighiaceous
Marmalade tree
Marsh asphodel
Marsh marigold
Marsh rosemary
Marsh samphire
Marvel of Peru
Meadow foxtail
Meadow parsnip
Meadow saffron
Medullary rays
Melastomaceous
Monk's rhubarb
Monocarpellary
Mountain ebony
Mountain holly

Mourning bride
Multisiliquous
Mushroom spawn
None-so-pretty
Nucamentaceous
Nucumentaceous
Obdiplostemony
Old man's head
Paleophytology
Palisade cells
Paper mulberry
Papilionaceous
Passion flower
Pelican flower
Pheasant's eye
Photo-epinasty
Phytolithology
Pistilliferous
Plurifoliolate
Poison dogwood
Poison hemlock
Polemoniaceous
Polycarpellary
Polyembryonate
Porcupine wood
Portulacaceous
Prairie clover
Prairie turnip
Pride of China
Proper nectary
Protophytology
Quadricapsular
Quadriphyllous
Quaker buttons
Queensland nut
Quinquefarious
Quinquepartite
Radiate-veined
Ranal alliance
Ranunculaceous
Rejuvenescence
Rose of Sharon
Rotundifolious
Sapodilla plum
Savanna flower
Savanna wattle
Saxifragaceous
Scarlet runner
Scorpion grass
Scorpion senna
Scotch thistle
Semiflosculous
Sensitive fern
Sheep scabious
Slipper flower
Snake's-tongue
Soapberry tree
Soldier orchis
Solomon's seal

Spanish potato
Spindle-shaped
Sporangiophore
Sporting plant
Squirrel grass
Stag-horn fern
Sterculiaceous
Stinking cedar
Summer cypress
Supra-axillary
Swedish turnip
Sweet calabash
Sweet marjoram
Tartarian lamb
Tern peduncles
Tetrachotomous
Thalamiflorous
Three-cornered
Three-flowered
Toothache tree
Tortoise plant
Trachyspermous
Traveler's joy
Tree of heaven
Tripe-de-roche
Trumpet flower
Umbilical cord
United flowers
Valerianaceous
Venetian sumac
Verticillaster
Vervain mallow
Virginia stock
Virgin's bower
Wall pellitory
Wall pennywort
Water agrimony
Water chestnut
Water crowfoot
Water dropwort
Water hyacinth
Water plantain
Water purslane
Wayfaring tree
Weeping willow
West India tea
Wood germander
Xanthic colors
Xanthospermous
Zingiberaceous
Zinziberaceous

13

Acetabuliform
Adam's needle
Adenophyllous
Almond willow

Amarantaceous
Amaryllideous
Amygdalaceous
Andropetalous
Anemorphilous
Angiospermous
Anisopetalous
Anisophyllous
Anomophyllous
Antheriferous
Antherogenous
Asperifolious
Avignon berry
Calabash tree
Cleistogamous
Cochineal fig
Coelospermous
Compound leaf
Consolidation
Corn marigold
Cornu Ammonis
Corymbiferous
Costal-nerved
Custard apple
Cyanic colors
Geminiflorous
Gentianaceous
German millet
Globe thistle
Grapple plant
Ground cherry
Guernsey lily
Guinea grains
Guinea pepper
Gymnospermous
Gynodioecious
Hariali grass
Hart's clover
Hart's-tongue
Hedge mustard
Heptaphyllous
Heptaspermous
Herb Margaret
Herb of grace
Heterocarpism
Heterocarpous
Heterodromous
Heterosporous
Heterostylism
Heterotropous
Horse gentian
Horse parsley
Hyacinth bean
Hymenomycetes
Hypocarpogean
Hysteranthous
Imparipinnate
Indian mallow
Indian millet

Indian physic
Indian turnip
Induplicative
Inflorescence
Interaxillary
Interpetalary
Interpetiolar
Intraaxillary
Intrapetiolar
Involucellate
Jerusalem oak
Johnson grass
Labiatifloral
Lady's mantle
Laterifolious
Lattice plant
Leather plant
Leucophyllous
Licorice fern
Licorice weed
Lignification
Liguliflorous
Lily daffodil
Lily hyacinth
Lizard's tail
Loblolly pine
Loblolly tree
London rocket
Macropetalous
Macrophyllous
Macrozoospore
Magnoliaceous
Mangel-wurzel
Mangoldwurzel
Mariposa lily
Marrow squash
Marsh trefoil
Meadow beauty
Meiostemonous
Melon thistle
Membranaceous
Mexican poppy
Microphyllous
Microzoospore
Monkey flower
Monocephalous
Monocotyledon
Morning-glory
Mountain mint
Mountain rice
Mountain rose
Multicapsular
Musquash root
Mustard grape
Myriophyllous
Natural order
Nectariferous
Nutmeg flower
Oligopetalous

Oligosepalous
Oligospermous
Orchard grass
Orthospermous
Paddock stool
Paleobotanist
Palma Christi
Palmatisected
Papaveraceous
Pappoose root
Parrot's-bill
Parsley piert
Partridge pea
Pasque flower
Pencil flower
Penicilliform
Pentacapsular
Pentadelphous
Pentapetalous
Pentaphyllous
Pentaspermous
Pentastichous
Phanerogamian
Pheasant wood
Phyllocladium
Phyllodineous
Phyllophorous
Phylloxanthin
Physiological
Pichurim bean
Pickerel weed
Piney thistle
Pinnatilobate
Pistillaceous
Planipetalous
Plantain tree
Pleiophyllous
Pleurisy root
Pleurocarpous
Plumbagineous
Podocephalous
Polleniferous
Polliniferous
Polyadelphous
Polycotyledon
Polyembryonic
Polygonaceous
Poly-mountain
Poverty grass
Prickly poppy
Prickly withe
Primary pinna
Prince's pine
Prolification
Proterandrous
Proteranthous
Proterogynous
Pudding grass
Quadrifoliate

Quaker ladies
Quaking aspen
Quaking grass
Quillaia bark
Quinquenerved
Rabbits' ears
Radiciflorous
Ragged sailor
Randall grass
Reflorescence
Reindeer moss
Resting spore
Rose of China
Saddle-shaped
Salver-shaped
Sand-box tree
Sarmentaceous
Scarlet maple
Scimiter pods
Scouring rush
Scratch grass
Scrobiculated
Scythian lamb
Sea chickweed
Serpent withe
Service berry
Sexual method
Sheep's beard
Shooting star
Siberian crab
Simpler's joy
Single flower
Skunk cabbage
Sleep-at-noon
Snail trefoil
Snowball tree
Solar flowers
Sorediiferous
South-Sea tea
Spanish broom
Spanish cress
Spanish grass
Spanish juice
Spear thistle
Sphaerenchyma
Sphagnicolous
Spider orchis
Sporidiiferous
Spring beauty
Squirrel corn
Squitch grass
Star cucumber
Star hyacinth
Stem-clasping
Stenophyllous
Stone bramble
Stone parsley
Striped maple
Strobilaceous

Strombuliform
Strophiolated
Succade gourd
Sultan flower
Swamp cabbage
Sweet alyssum
Sweet maudlin
Sweet William
Swine thistle
Swine's cress
Sychnocarpous
Tansy mustard
Tartary wheat
Tassel flower
Tetradynamian
Tetradynamous
Tetrapetalous
Tetraphyllous
Tetrasepalous
Tetraspermous
Thermotropism
Three-pointed
Timothy grass
Torch thistle
Tower mustard
Trachycarpous
Transpiration
Tree wormwood
Tripinnatifid
Triplicostate
Tristigmatose
Turk's turban
Tussock grass
Umbelliferous
Umbrella leaf
Umbrella tree
Upland sumach
Vaginant leaf
Velvet flower
Venus's basin
Venus's pride
Victoria lily
Vine of Sodom
Viper's grass
Vital vessels
Wandering Jew
Water caltrop
Water flannel
Water lettuce
Water milfoil
Water parsnip
Water pitcher
Water soldier
Water trefoil
White campion
White currant
White lettuce
Whitlow grass
Wild allspice

Wild bergamot
Wild camomile
Wild hyacinth
Wild Irishman
Wild licorice
Wild marjoram
Wild pieplant
Wild plantain
Wild rosemary
Wild Spaniard
Wild tamarind
Winter cherry
Winter's bark
Xanthocarpous
Xiphophyllous
Zo˜sporangium

12

Acanthaceous
Achlamydeous
Acutifoliate
Adenophorous
Adventitious
Aetheogamous
Agglomerated
Agnus castus
Amentiferous
Amphicarpous
Anamorphosis
Anchovy pear
Angiosporous
Antherozooid
Anthocarpous
Antipetalous
Antisepalous
Apogeotropic
Cabbage rose
Calycifloral
Catapetalous
Caulocarpous
Conduplicate
Conglomerate
Consolidated
Coquilla nut
Corn parsley
Cotton grass
Cotton plant
Crane's-bill
Crape myrtle
Crucian carp
Cryptogamist
Cuckooflower
Curvicostate
Cutinization
Cynarrhodium
Cypress vine
Gamopetalous

Gamophyllous
Gamosepalous
Garnet berry
Gemmiflorate
Geraniaceous
Glandulation
Goat's beard
Goat's thorn
Goat's wheat
Golden chain
Goose tongue
Grape fungus
Green dragon
Ground furze
Ground swell
Guelderrose'
Guinea grass
Gymnocarpous
Gynantherous
Haematoxylon
Heart's-ease
Heather bell
Hedge garlic
Hedge hyssop
Hedge nettle
Heliotropism
Hemerocallis
Herd's grass
Heron's bill
Heterauxesis
Heterogonous
Heteromerous
Heterostyled
Hexacapsular
Hexapetalous
Hexaphyllous
Hibernaculum
Hog's fennel
Holy thistle
Homochromous
Honey flower
Honey locust
Hop hornbeam
Horned poppy
Horse cassia
Horse nettle
Horse-radish
Humble plant
Hydrotropism
Hyphomycetes
Hypophyllous
Hysterophyte
Iceland moss
Indehiscence
Indian berry
Indian bread
Indian cress
Indian grass
Indigo berry

Indigo plant
Involucrated
Isodiametric
Isostemonous
Jamaica rose
Japan quince
Japanese ivy
Jew's mallow
Joe-Pye weed
Jungermannia
Kidney vetch
King's spear
Labrador tea
Lady's bower
Lady's laces
Lady's smock
Lady's thumb
Lambert pine
Laticiferous
Leather leaf
Lenticellate
Leucadendron
Leucoplastid
Lignum-vitae
Linearensate
Liriodendron
Live-forever
Lobeliaceous
Loblolly bay
Lomentaceous
London pride
Malacca cane
Marginicidal
Marsh mallow
Meadow grass
Melanorrhoea
Mermaid weed
Metrosideros
Milk parsley
Milk thistle
Monadelphous
Monkey-bread
Monopetalous
Monophyllous
Monopyrenous
Monosepalous
Monospermous
Monostichous
Moon trefoil
Moss campion
Moth mullein
Mountain ash
Moving plant
Multicipital
Multifarious
Multiflorous
Multiseptate
Musk thistle
Native bread

Needle furze
Nomenclature
Northern spy
Nutmeg melon
Oblique leaf
Octopetalous
Octospermous
Octostichous
Oosporangium
Orange grass
Orchidaceous
Orthotropous
Oscillatoria
Ostrich fern
Oyster plant
Oyster-green
Pachycarpous
Paddock pipe
Palmatilobed
Pampas grass
Paradise nut
Parapetalous
Parsley fern
Pentachenium
Pentacoccous
Pepper dulse
Pepper elder
Perichaetial
Perichaetium
Peripetalous
Petaloideous
Phaenogamous
Phanerogamia
Phyllotactic
Pigeon berry
Pigeon grass
Pistillidium
Placentation
Placentiform
Plagiotropic
Planifolious
Pleurenchyma
Plume nutmeg
Pluripartite
Poison sumac
Pollen grain
Polyadelphia
Polyembryony
Polypetalous
Polyphyllous
Polysepalous
Polyspermous
Prairie dock
Prefloration
Prefoliation
Prickly pear
Prickly pole
Primary axis
Primulaceous

Pseudo-china
Pteridophyta
Pudding pipe
Pulveraceous
Purging flax
Pussy willow
Quadrijugous
Quicken tree
Quitch grass
Racemiferous
Ragged robin
Ramentaceous
Receptacular
Red gum-tree
Red mulberry
Rescue grass
Retrofracted
Rhizocarpous
Rhizophorous
Rhododendron
Ribbon grass
Ripple grass
Rose campion
Saffron wood
Salad burnet
Sallow thorn
Salmon berry
Santalaceous
Sapindaceous
Sapucaia nut
Sarsaparilla
Satin flower
Scitamineous
Sclerenchyma
Scorpionwort
Scotch broom
Scrophularia
Scurvy grass
Scutch grass
Scutelliform
Sea colander
Sea colewort
Sea daffodil
Sea lavender
Sea milkwort
Sea sandwort
Sea withwind
Sea wormwood
Semifloscule
Seminal leaf
Seneca grass
Septifarious
Septifolious
Sesame grass
Sheep laurel
Sheep sorrel
Shell flower
Silver grain
Slippery elm

Slough grass
Smoking bean
Snail clover
Snail flower
Snake's-head
Soboliferous
Sops in wine
Sops of wine
Southernwood
Spanish bean
Spanish moss
Spatter-dock
Spermogonium
Spermophytic
Sphaerospore
Spindle tree
Spinulescent
Spotted tree
Spring grass
Squirrel cup
Standergrass
Star thistle
Steeple bush
Stork's bill
Strangulated
Stringy bark
Strophanthus
Styptic weed
Suffruticose
Swamp laurel
Swamp willow
Sweet cicely
Sweet Cistus
Sweet clover
Sweet potato
Sweet sultan
Sweet willow
Switch grass
Sword-shaped
Synantherous
Syngenesious
Taphrenchyma
Teleutospore
Tenuifolious
Tetracoccous
Tetradynamia
Tetter berry
Thecasporous
Thermotropic
Thimbleberry
Three-leaved
Tick trefoil
Tiger flower
Tiger's-foot
Tobacco pipe
Touch-me-not
Trachenchyma
Tradescantia
Tread-softly

Tree of life
Triadelphous
Tribracteate
Trifoliolate
Troll flower
Trumpet leaf
Trumpet tree
Turkey beard
Turkey berry
Turkey wheat
Turtle grass
Twitch grass
Two-capsuled
Undershrieve
Unguiculated
Unicorn root
Unifollilate
Varnish tree
Velvet grass
Venus's comb
Venus's hair
Verbenaceous
Vernal grass
Vinegar tree
Voluble stem
Walking fern
Walking leaf
Water celery
Water locust
Water pepper
Water radish
Water rocket
Water shield
Water tupelo
Water violet
Water willow
Wedge-shaped
Wellingtonia
Wheel-shaped
White clover
White poplar
White spruce
Whitlow-wort
Whitten tree
Whortleberry
Wild bugloss
Wild comfrey
Wild service
Willow-thorn
Windsor bean
Winter berry
Winter bloom
Winter cress
Wolf's peach
Wood anemone
Yellow-golds

11

Acalysinous
Acarpellous
Acaulescent
Acinaciform
Acrocarpous
Acutilobate
Aestivation
Agrostology
Almond tree
Amentaceous
Amphigamous
Amphigenous
Amphitropal
Amplexicaul
Anantherous
Androtomous
Angienchyma
Anisomerous
Antheridium
Antidromous
Antitropous
Arbor vitae
Archegonium
Arrow grass
Artocarpous
Aspermatous
Autocarpian
Calceolaria
Calvessnout
Campanulate
Capillament
Catadromous
Cauliflower
Clinanthium
Collenchyma
Comb-shaped
Compositous
Conceptacle
Constricted
Contrayerva
Convolvulus
Corn cockle
Corn violet
Corniculate
Cotton rose
Crateriform
Cream-fruit
Cruciferous
Cryptogamia
Crystalloid
Curvinerved
Curviserial
Cycadaceous
Cyperaceous
Cypripedium
Fastigiated

Gang-flower
Gatling gun
Geitonogamy
Globe daisy
Globeflower
Glochidiate
Glycyrrhiza
Goat's bane
Goat's foot
Gold thread
Golden club
Golden hair
Golden seal
Goose grass
Grama grass
Grass vetch
Grass wrack
Grease bush
Grease wood
Green brier
Green heart
Green laver
Green-broom
Ground hele
Ground pine
Ground plum
Grugru palm
Guard cells
Guinea corn
Guinea plum
Guttiferous
Gymnocladus
Hare's-tail
Heath grass
Helichrysum
Heliotropic
Hemitropous
Heptagynous
Heptamerous
Heptandrous
Herb bennet
Herb Gerard
Herb Robert
Hercogamous
Hesperidium
Hex-androus
Hog's bread
Hollow root
Homomallous
Homotropous
Honeysuckle
Hormogonium
Horse sugar
Horse vetch
Huckleberry
Hydrotropic
Hymenophore
Hypocarpium
Icosandrous

Imbricative
Immarginate
Inantherate
Incrassated
Indehiscent
Indian bean
Indian corn
Indian pipe
Indian poke
Indian rice
Indian shot
Induplicate
Interrupted
Ipecacuanha
Jeffersonia
Jelly plant
Job's tears
Jupati palm
Kaffir corn
Kidney bean
Kneejointed
Knife grass
Laciniolate
Lady's comb
Lady's hair
Lady's seal
Lark's-heel
Latent buds
Latifolious
Leatherwood
Lemon grass
Lentiginose
Leopardwood
Lilly-pilly
Lion's foot
Lion's leaf
Lion's tail
Liquidambar
Lirelliform
Loculicidal
Locust bean
Locust tree
Loggerheads
Long purple
Loosestrife
Lung flower
Lung lichen
Lycotropous
Macrocystis
Macrosporic
Madeira nut
Maiden pink
Maiden plum
Maid's hair
Malabar nut
Malay apple
Manna grass
Mare's-tail
Marking nut

Marsh elder
Marsh grass
Maudlinwort
Meadow pink
Meadow sage
Melanosperm
Merithallus
Mesophloeum
Mesophyllum
Mexican tea
Microphytal
Microsporic
Milk vessel
Mist flower
Mock orange
Monadelphia
Monembryony
Monocarpous
Monoclinous
Monothalmic
Multijugous
Multiserial
Mummy wheat
Musk mallow
Musk orchis
Nemathecium
Nereocystis
Nimble Will
Noon-flower
Nutmeg wood
Nyctitropic
Oak leather
Obimbricate
Octolocular
Oligandrous
Oliganthous
Oligomerous
Oophoridium
Operculated
Orchidology
Ordeal bean
Ordeal root
Ordeal tree
Orthostichy
Orthotropic
Painted cup
Palissander
Panic grass
Paper birch
Paracorolla
Paripinnate
Parrot weed
Pear blight
Pear family
Peepul tree
Pelargonium
Penny cress
Penny grass
Pentagynous

Pentandrous
Pepper tree
Pepperbrand
Peppergrass
Perianthium
Periclinium
Peristerion
Perithecium
Petiolulate
Phaenogamia
Phototropic
Phycochrome
Phyllomania
Phyllotaxis
Phytelephas
Pigeon plum
Pigeon wood
Pine needle
Piperaceous
Planer tree
Pleurosigma
Podophyllum
Polyandrian
Polyandrous
Polycarpous
Polyrhizous
Polysporous
Pomegranate
Prickly ash
Proliferous
Prosenchyma
Protandrous
Proteaceous
Proterandry
Prothallium
Protococcus
Protogynous
Pseudo-bulb
Pseudospore
Pteridology
Purpleheart
Quadrivalve
Quick grass
Quince tree
Quincuncial
Radiatiform
Ragged lady
Raisin tree
Ramiflorous
Razor grass
Rectinerved
Rectiserial
Red currant
Red sanders
Reduplicate
Rest-harrow
Retinaculum
Rhamnaceous
Rhizanthous

Rhizomatous
Rose acacia
Rose family
Rose mallow
Rupturewort
Sacred bean
Sage willow
Salal-berry
Saloop bush
salsuginous
Sand spurry
Sandaliform
Sanguinaria
Sapotaceous
Sauce-alone
Scarlet oak
Scotch pine
Scratchweed
Scuppernong
Sea cabbage
Sea girdles
Sea purslan
Sea trumpet
Seed vessel
Selaginella
Sempervivum
Septiferous
Septifragal
Shave grass
Sheep's bit
Shield fern
Shingle oak
Sideroxylon
Sieve cells
Siliquiform
Silk flower
Silver bush
Silver tree
Silverberry
Slipperwort
Snake gourd
Snow flower
Solanaceous
Soldierwood
Sorrel tree
Sow thistle
Spanish elm
Spanish nut
Sparrowwort
Spathaceous
Spear grass
Spermaphore
Spermophyte
Spike grass
Sponge tree
Sporophoric
Spur pepper
Spurt grass
Squarrulose

Staggerbush
Staggerwort
Staminodium
Star flower
Stephanotis
Stick-tight
Stipitiform
Stipulation
Stone fruit
Stone-break
Stove plant
Strangulate
Strigillose
Styliferous
Stylopodium
Subaxillary
Subpetiolar
Sugar berry
Sugar maple
Sulphurwort
Supervolute
Supple-jack
Swallowtail
Swallowwort
Swamp maple
Sweet apple
Sweet grass
Swine grass
Sword grass
Symmetrical
Sympetalous
Synanthesis
Synsepalous
Tallow tree
Ten-o'clock
Tergeminate
Tern leaves
Testiculate
Tetracarpel
Tetragynous
Tetramerous
Tetrandrous
Tetrathecal
Thallophyte
Thimbleweed
Thorn apple
Thorn broom
Thoroughwax
Thyine wood
Tiger grass
Tilley seed
Towel gourd
Trabeculate
Tree clover
Tree sorrel
Trichomanes
Trichophore
Trifoliated
Tripetaloid

Tripetalous
Triphyllous
Triseralous
Trispermous
Tristichous
Trophosperm
Trumpet ash
Trumpetweed
Trumpetwood
Turk's head
Twin flower
Umbilicated
Unicapsular
Unifoliate
Urticaceous
Utricularia
Vaginervose
Velvet dock
Venous leaf
Vertebrated
Verticillus
Vine mildew
Vine sorrel
Virgouleuse
Wall barley
Wall pepper
Wart spurge
Water beech
Water cress
Water elder
Water lemon
Water nymph
Water thyme
Water torch
Water-withe
Welsh onion
Welwitschia
Wheat grass
Wheat thief
Whippletree
Whistlewood
White alder
White cedar
White daisy
White grass
White poppy
White-heart
Wild celery
Wild cherry
Wild mammee
Willow-herb
Willow-weed
Willow-wort
Wing-leaved
Wintergreen
Witch grass
Witch-hazel
Wolf's-claw
Wolf's-foot

30

Wolf's-milk
Wood betony
Wood laurel
Wood nettle
Wood sorrel
Wood- waxen
Woody fiber
Woolly butt
Xanthophyll
Xanthorhiza
Xanthorhoea
Xanthoxylum
Xerophilous
Xylocarpous
Xyridaceous
Zauschneria

10

Absinthium
Accrescent
Acephalous
Acinaceous
Acotyledon
Acrogenous
Aculeolate
Alabastrum
Allogamous
Ambigenous
Ambiparous
Amentiform
Amplectant
Anacardium
Anadromous
Anatropous
Ancipitous
Androecium
Androgynal
Androphore
Androspore
Angiosperm
Angola pea
Annotinous
Anthophore
Apiculated
Apocarpous
Apocyneous
Apothecium
Aristulate
Asarabacca
Ascigerous
Aspalathus
Astragalus
Athalamous
Autogamous
Cactaceous
Calceiform
Calliopsis

Calyciform
Calyculate
Cancellate
Carpellary
Carpogenic
Carpophore
Carpophyll
Carpophyte
Carpospore
Cascarilla
Cassideous
Cat's-foot
Caulescent
Cloudberry
Clove pink
Commissure
Complicate
Compositae
Compressed
Connective
Continuous
Coquelicot
Coral root
Coral tree
Coriaceous
Cormophyta
Corn poppy
Corn salad
Cornflower
Cottonweed
Cottonwood
Crab grass
Crakeberry
Crenulated
Crotalaria
Crowflower
Cuckoopint
Cucullated
Cyanophyll
Fornicated
Frontignan
Gama grass
Gaultheria
Glory tree
Glue plant
Gnaphalium
Goat's rue
Golden cup
Golden-rod
Goldylocks
Gooseberry
Gourd tree
Gramineous
Granadilla
Grass tree
Green gage
Ground ash
Ground ivy
Gymnosperm

Gynandrous
Hackmatack
Hair grass
Hand plant
Hard grass
Hare's-ear
Hart's-ear
Haustorium
Heliotrope
Hemigamous
Hen's-foot
Heptagynia
Heptandria
Herb Paris
Heterocyst
Heterogamy
Hexagynous
Hexamerous
Hobblebush
Hog peanut
Hog's bean
Holly rose
Holy grass
Homogamous
Homogonous
Hop clover
Horn poppy
Horse balm
Horse bean
Hydropiper
Hyoscyamus
Hypanthium
Hypogynous
Hyponastic
Icosandria
Immortelle
Inadherent
Incomplete
Indefinite
Indian bay
Indigofera
Indusiated
Innovation
Involucred
Involucret
Involucrum
Isostemony
Ivory palm
Jagua palm
Judas tree
Juncaceous
June grass
Kidneywort
Knapbottle
Knop sedge
Kyanophyll
Ladle wood
Lad's love
Lageniform

Lappaceous
Lauraceous
Laurestine
Lead plant
Leaf green
Leaf trace
Lenticelle
Letterwood
Leukoplast
Lignireose
Liliaceous
Lion's ear
Lithy tree
Live grass
Loculament
Love apple
Love grass
Lycoperdon
Lycopodium
Lyme grass
Macaw bush
Macaw tree
Macrospore
Madderwort
Mahwa tree
Maidenhair
Malacotoon
Male berry
Mallowwort
Malvaceous
Manchineel
Mandragora
Mango tree
Map lichen
Marcescent
Marguerite
May flower
Meadow rue
Meadowwort
Meliaceous
Melicotoon
Melocotoon
Membranous
Merenchyma
Microphyte
Microspore
Mignonette
Mocker nut
Monandrian
Monandrous
Monanthous
Monkey-cup
Monkflower
Monocotyle
Monogamous
Monogynian
Monogynous
Monomerous
Monopodial

Monopodium
Monothecal
Monotocous
Moonflower
Moor grass
Moss berry
Motherwort
Musk plant
Myrtaceous
Myrtle wax
Naked wood
Nannyberry
Nasturtion
Nasturtium
Nightshade
Nipplewort
Niter bush
Notorhizal
Octagynous
Octandrous
Octogynous
Oily grain
Opera girl
Orangeroot
Orchideous
Oscillaria
Paddlewood
Padow pipe
Paleaceous
Palmaceous
Palmatifid
Pancratium
Paper reed
Para grass
Paraphysis
Parastichy
Parkleaves
Passiflora
Pennyroyal
Pentagynia
Pentandria
Pepperidge
Peppermint
Pepperwort
Perfoliate
Perichaeth
Perigynium
Perigynous
Peristeria
Periwinkle
Persicaria
Petaliform
Phaeospore
Phelloderm
Phenogamia
Phototonus
Phycomater
Phyllodium
Physic nut

Phytolacca
Phytomeron
Pigeon pea
Pigeonfoot
Pileorhiza
Pinenchyma
Pinguicula
Pinnatifid
Pipsissewa
Pistillate
Pistillody
Pitch pine
Pixy stool
Plane tree
Pleurocarp
Podogynium
Poinsettia
Pointletcd
Poison ash
Poison ivy
Poison nut
Poison oak
Polemonium
Polyandria
Polyanthus
Polygamian
Polygamous
Polygynous
Polymerous
Polypodium
Polylocous
Polytomous
Pomiferous
Pompelmous
Pond spice
Prickmadam
Primordian
Princewood
Procambium
Procumbent
Propagulum
Prothallus
Protophyte
Prune tree
Pseudocarp
Puberulent
Pulsatilla
Quincewort
Quinquefid
Racemulose
Radication
Radiciform
Radiculose
Ramigerous
Ramiparous
Ranunculus
Rattleweed
Rattlewort
Ray floret

Receptacle
Reed grass
Resin bush
Retinerved
Rheinberry
Rhizophora
Rhizotaxis
Rhodosperm
Ribbonwood
Rigidulous
Rock cress
Rock tripe
Rondeletia
Rose apple
Rose elder
Rowan tree
Royal fern
Royal palm
Rubiaceous
Rubiginous
Salisburia
Sand grass
Sand myrtl
Sandalwood
Sanguinary
Sapan wood
Sappodilla
Saprophyte
Sarcobasis
Sarcoderma
Sarmentose
Sarmentous
Sarracenia
Sassy bark
Saxicolous
Scale moss
Schizocarp
Sclerotium
Screw bean
Screw pine
Screw tree
Scurfiness
Scyphiform
Sea fennel
Sea hulver
Sea lettuc
Sea rocket
Sea thongs
Sebiferous
Seed grain
Seed stalk
Seirospore
Semidouble
Semifloret
Semination
Sempervive
Septicidal
Setterwort
Sexlocular

Sheep pest
Sheepberry
Shepherdia
Sickle pod
Sicklewort
Siliculose
Silk grass
Silver fir
Silverboom
Silverweed
Slash pine
Smoke tree
Snake moss
Snapdragon
Sneezeweed
Sneezewood
Sneezewort
Snow plant
Soap plant
Soft grass
Solubility
Souari nut
Sour gourd
Spadiceous
Spermatium
Spermidium
Spermoderm
Sphrigosis
Spiderwort
Spike rush
Spinaceous
Spinescent
Spleenwort
Sporangium
Sporophore
Spurgewort
Squawberry
Staff tree
Stamineous
Star anise
Star apple
Star grass
Star jelly
Starchwort
Stavesacre
Stellulate
Stichidium
Stick-seed
Stigmatose
Stipellate
Stitchwort
Stone fern
Stone pine
Stramonium
Strawberry
Strelitzia
Strophiole
Subkingdom
Sugar beet

Sugar cane
Sugar pine
Sugar tree
Swarmspore
Sweet cane
Sweet corn
Sweet fern
Sweet flag
Sweet gale
Sweet John
Sweet leaf
Sweet rush
Sweetbrier
Sweetwater
Swinebread
Sword lily
Synanthous
Syncarpium
Syncarpous
Syngenesia
Synoecious
Tacamahaca
Tape grass
Tartareous
Tear-thumb
Tendrilled
Tetragonal
Tetragynia
Tetrandria
Tetraspore
Totterwort
Thecaphore
Throatwort
Thrum-eyed
Tiger lily
Tiger-foot
Tiliaceous
Tillandsia
Tonca bean
Tonka bean
Town cress
Tree onion
Triandrous
Triangular
Trichogyne
Tricoccous
Tricostate
Trifarious
Triflorous
Trinervate
Trioecious
Tripennate
Tripinnate
Triseriate
Triternate
Tumbleweed
Tupelo gum
Turban-top
Turbinated

Turkey oak
Turk's cap
Turtlehead
Two-lipped
Two-parted
Two-ranked
Umbellated
Umbellifer
Umbra tree
Unicostate
Uniflorous
Unilabiate
Uniovulate
Uniseptate
Uredospore
Urn mosses
Volutinous
Velvetleaf
Vespertine
Vine apple
Violaceous
Virescence
Viticulose
Wake-robin
Wall cress
Wallflower
Wart cress
Water aloe
Water arum
Water dock
Water flag
Water hemp
Water lily
Water pore
Water tree
Water vine
watermelon
Wax myrtle
Wheel tree
White pine
White sage
Whitethorn
Widow-wail
Wild basil
Wild brier
Wild cumin
Wild elder
Windflower
Wind-plant
Wine apple
Winter fat
Winterweed
Wire grass
Witch meal
Witch-tree
Woad-waxen
Wood fiber
Wood grass
Wood-layer

32

Woodwardia
Woody pear
Wool grass
Worm grass
Wych-hazel
Xanthidium
Xanthopous
Yellowroot
Yellowseed
Yellowwood
Yellowwort

Acapsular
Accumbent
Acropetal
Acrospire
Acrospore
Adansonia
Adderwort
Adelaster
Adelphous
Adventive
Aerophyte
Aggregate
Air plant
Alaternus
Aleuronic
Alfilaria
Alkekengi
Alternate
Alum root
Alveolate
Amaryllis
Anacharis
Anandrous
Ananthous
Androgyne
Andromeda
Anthodium
Anthotaxy
Apetalous
Aphyllous
Apiaceous
Apophysis
Arachnoid
Araucaria
Archangel
Argentate
Aroideous
Arrhizous
Arrowhead
Arrowroot
Artemisia
Artichoke
Asclepias
Ascospore

Asparagus
Aspermous
Assurgent
Azedarach
Botanical
Buckthorn
buttercup
Calcarate
Calendula
Calycinal
Calycular
Campanula
Candytuft
Carambola
Cardamine
Carnation
Carpellum
Carpology
Caryopsis
Cassidony
Casuarina
Caudicula
Cauliform
Celandine
Centaurea
Centinody
Claytonia
Club moss
Club root
Club-rush
Coadunate
Cocklebur
Cockscomb
Cockshead
Cocobolas
Colchicum
Coltsfoot
Columbine
Columella
Composite
Confluent
Congested
Conjugate
Contorted
Convolute
Coralline
Coralwort
Corchorus
Coreopsis
Coriander
Cork tree
Corn flag
Coronilla
Corymbose
Cotyledon
Cranberry
Crataegus
Cremocarp
Crenation

Crenature
Crenelled
Crosswort
Crowberry
Crow-silk
Cryptogam
Cuckoobud
Curvative
Cystocarp
Excurrent
Flagellum
Galingale
Gelsemium
Gemmation
Germander
Gladiolus
Glasswort
Glomerule
Glory pea
Glutinous
Goat weed
Gonophore
Goosefoot
Gossypium
Grapevine
Greengage
Greenweed
Groundnut
Groundsel
Gulf weed
Gynandria
Gynobasic
Gynoecium
Gynophore
Gypsywort
Hackberry
Hag-taper
Halophyte
Hamamelis
Hand tree
Hazelwort
Heartseed
Heath pea
Hellebore
Hexagynia
Hexandria
Hig-taper
Histogeny
Hollyhock
Homoptera
Honeyware
Honeywort
Hoop tree
Horehound
Horsefoot
Horseknop
Horsemint
Horsetail
Horseweed

Horsewood
Houseleek
Hydrangea
Hypericum
Hypoderma
Hypogeous
Hyponasty
Ice plant
Idioblast
Impatiens
Inclining
Incumbent
Induviate
Ink plant
Internode
Intextine
Intorsion
Involucel
Involucre
Involuted
Ironheads
Isonandra
Isosporic
Ivory nut
Jaborandi
Jacaranda
Jack tree
Jambolana
Japan pea
Jessamine
Jewelweed
Jew's-ear
Joint-fir
Jointweed
Jonquille
Julaceous
Juneberry
Kippernut
Knee holm
Knotberry
Knotgrass
Kohl-rabi
Lace-bark
Lady fern
Laminaria
Lanceolar
Lancewood
Laserwort
Lazarwort
Lead tree
Leaf scar
Leafstalk
Lent lily
Lenticula
Lepidoted
Leverwood
Libriform
Ligulated
Lima bean

Lima wood
Liverleaf
Locellate
Lousewort
Mad-apple
Male fern
Malpighia
Mangostan
Manzanita
Marrubium
Marsdenia
Mat grass
Maudeline
May apple
Mayflower
Medullary
Melastoma
Mesosperm
Milk tree
Mirabilis
Mistletoe
Miterwort
Monandria
Monecious
Moneywort
Monkshood
Monocotyl
Monoecian
Monogamia
Monogamic
Monogynia
Monoicous
Monosperm
Monotropa
Moosewood
Moschatel
Moss pink
Moss rose
Moss rush
Mouse-ear
Mousetail
Muscadine
Musciform
Musk pear
Musk root
Musk rose
Musk seed
Muskmelon
Myroxylon
Narcissus
Naseberry
Navelwort
Nectareal
Nectarine
Nepenthes
Nicotiana
Nine-bark
Nit grass
Nosebleed

Nosesmart	Pollinate	Sabadilla	Soap tree	Swine oat
Notchweed	Pollinium	Saccharum	Sorediate	Symmetric
Nullipore	Polygamia	Sack tree	Sour dock	Sympodial
Nut grass	Polygonum	Safflower	Sour plum	Sympodium
Oat grass	Polygynia	Sago palm	Sow bread	Tangerine
Obvoluted	Polyphore	Salt tree	Spadicose	Tanghinia
Ochreated	Polyporus	Sapodilla	Spearmint	Taqua-nut
Octandria	Pomaceous	Sarcocarp	Spearwood	Tartarian
Octogynia	Pompoleon	Sassafras	Spearwort	Tea plant
Oil gland	Pond lily	Satinwood	Speedwell	Tephrosia
Oleaceous	Porcelain	Saw grass	Sphagnous	Terebinth
Olivewood	Portulaca	Saxifraga	Spicewood	Thallogen
Olusatrum	Posterior	Saxifrage	Spiciform	Theobroma
Omphalode	Posticous	Scapeless	Spiculate	Thrumwort
One-sided	Pot plant	Scapiform	Spikenard	Toad pipe
Operculum	Prickwood	Scattered	Spiranthy	Toad rush
Orchidean	Primerole	Sclerogen	Spongiole	Toadstool
Orthogamy	Proembryo	Sclerosis	Spoonwood	Tolu tree
Oso-berry	Prostrate	Scrub oak	Spoonwort	Toothwort
Palsywort	Protonema	Scutellum	Sporidium	Torchwood
Pappiform	Pulmonary	Sea blite	Sporocarp	Torchwort
Parietary	Purcelane	Sea cocoa	Sporozoid	Tormentil
Parnassia	Puttyroot	Sea grape	Squamella	Transpire
Patchouly	Pycnidium	Sea grass	Squarrose	Trap tree
Paulownia	Pyracanth	Sea heath	Squawroot	Tree fern
Pearlwort	Quamoclit	Sea holly	Squawweed	Tree moss
Peat moss	Quebracho	Sea laces	Squinancy	Tree wool
Pellitory	Quillwort	Sea onion	Staminate	Treebeard
Pendulous	Radicated	Sea wrack	Staminode	Triandria
Pennywort	Rafflesia	Secundine	Stavewood	Trifolium
Perdifoil	Raspberry	Seed coat	Stellated	Trigamous
Perennial	Rattlebox	Seed down	Stem leaf	Trigynous
Perisperm	Reclinate	Seed leaf	Stichwort	Trijugate
Perispore	Reclining	Seed lobe	Stinkhorn	Trijugous
Peristome	Recurvate	Segregate	Stinkweed	Trimerous
Persimmon	Red birch	Self-heal	Stinkwood	Trinerved
Personate	Red cedar	Septenate	Stipitate	Triparted
Pertusate	Red ebony	Septulate	Stipulary	Tripmadam
Peterwort	Red maple	Sericeous	Stipulate	Trisected
Petiolary	Reed-mace	Sexualist	Stonecrop	Tunicated
Petiolule	Regmacarp	Shad bush	Stoneroot	Twayblade
Pettywhin	Renneting	Sharewort	Stoneweed	Twig rush
Phaenogam	Reservoir	Shea tree	Stonewort	Two-cleft
Phaseolus	Rhachilla	Shellbark	Strangury	Ulmaceous
Phellogen	Rhaphides	Shin leaf	Strychnos	Umbellule
Phillyrea	Rib grass	Siliquosa	Succubous	Umbilicus
Phytology	Rie grass	Siliquous	Succulent	Undivided
Pimpernel	Roan tree	Silk tree	Suffrance	Undulated
Pin grass	Rocambole	Silky oak	Surculose	Unijugate
Pine tree	Root hair	Skunkweed	Suspensor	Uniparous
pineapple	Root leaf	Smartweed	Swamp oak	Urbaniste
Pinedrops	Rootstock	Snake nut	Sweet bay	Vaccinium
Pinnulate	Rosaceous	Snakehead	Sweet gum	Vallecula
Pipe tree	Rosinweed	Snakeroot	Sweet pea	Vasculose
Piperidge	Royal bay	Snakeweed	Sweetroot	Vernation
Pistachio	Ruminated	Snakewood	Sweet-sop	Vernicose
Podosperm	Runcinate	Snowberry	Sweetweed	Vetchling
Poinciana	Ruta-baga	Snowflake	Sweetwood	Villosity
Pole bean	Rutaceous	Soap bark	Swietenia	Vimineous

Virgalieu
Vivacious
Vulviform
Wagenboom
Wall moss
Water can
Water poa
Waterleaf
Waterweed
Waterwort
Wax plant
Weech-elm
Whinberry
White elm
White fir
White oak
White rot
Whitebeam
Whiteblow
Whiteweed
Whitewort
Wild bean
Wild pink
Wild plum
Wild rice
Wild sage
Wild woad
Wildering
Wincopipe
Wineberry
Witch-elm
Withe-rod
Wolfberry
Wolfsbane
Wood cell
Wood fern
Wood lily
Wood rush
Wood sage
Wood vine
Wood-sare
Woundwort
Xiphidium
Yellowtop
Zapotilla
Zygophyte
Zygosperm

8

Abelmosk
Abutilon
Acanthus
Acarpous
Acauline
Achenium
Achilous
Aculeate

Adelphia
Adherent
Adiantum
Adnation
Aecidium
Aegilops
Aerocyst
Ageratum
Agrarian
Agrimony
Aigrette
Ailantus
Air cell
Alburnum
Gleurone
Algaroba
Algology
Allogamy
Amaranth
Angelica
Anophyte
Ant rice
Anthemis
Anthesis
Anticous
Antrorse
Apricots
Apterous
Araceous
Aristate
Ascidium
Asphodel
Atropous
Autogamy
Avenious
Axillary
Ayegreen
Bartlett
Biennial
Bindweed
Boxthorn
Calambac
Calamint
Calycled
Calyptra
Camellia
Cannabis
Capsicum
Carnauba
Castanea
Catapuce
Catchfly
Cat-tail
Caulicle
Celeriac
Cenanthy
Centaury
Cernuous
Cleavers

Clematis
Clypeate
Cockspur
Cockweed
Compound
Conferva
Conidium
Consound
Cornbind
Corollet
Coronule
Corymbed
Costmary
Coloured
Cowberry
Cowquake
Cowwheat
Crenated
Crowfoot
Crucifer
Cucumber
Culerage
Cuneated
Cup-moss
Cutgrass
Cyclamen
Cyclosis
Garcinia
Gardenia
Geminate
Geranium
Gill ale
Glabrate
Gladiate
Gladiole
Glaucous
Gloriosa
Gloxinia
Glumelle
Goat fig
Goldseed
Gonidial
Gonidium
Gonimous
Goutwort
Gromwell
Guaiacum
Guttifer
Gymnogen
Gynander
Gynobase
Hagberry
Hairbell
Hardbeam
Hardfern
Hardhack
Harebell
Harefoot
Hartwort

Hawkweed
Hawthorn
Heartpea
Hebetate
Hedgehog
Hemicarp
Hepatica
Hibiscus
Hip tree
Hireling
Hockherb
Hog plum
Holdfast
Homogamy
Homogony
Honewort
Hop tree
Hop vine
Hornbeam
Hornwort
Humifuse
Hyacinth
Hymenium
Hypogean
Illicium
Immersed
Incanous
Inclined
Incubous
Incurved
Indusium
Indutive
Induviae
Inermous
Inferior
Inflated
Inflexed
Inserted
Introrse
Ionidium
Irideous
Ironweed
Ironwood
Ironwort
Ivy bush
Japonica
Jeniquen
Juliform
Knapweed
Knitback
Knotweed
Knotwort
Krameria
Labdanum
Labiated
Laburnum
Lagopous
Lakeweed
Larkspur

lavender
Lawsonia
Leadwort
Leaf bud
Lecythis
Lenticel
Lichwale
Lichwort
Licorice
Lilywort
Live oak
Loculate
Loculous
Lodicule
Lungwort
Lustwort
Lygodium
Magnolia
Mahogany
Mandarin
Mandioca
Mandrake
Mangrove
Manicate
Marigold
Marjoram
Martagon
Mary-bud
Mat rush
Matfelon
May lily
Maybloom
Mericarp
Meristem
Mesocarp
Mezereon
Milk pea
Milkweed
Milkwort
Monander
Monocarp
Monoecia
Monogyny
Monopode
Moonseed
Moonwort
Moorball
Mulberry
Mulewort
Multifid
Muriform
Muscales
Mushroom
Muskwood
Mycelium
Myceloid
Myosotis
Napiform
Natchnee

Neckweed
Necrosis
Neishout
Nenuphar
Nidulant
Noisette
Nucament
Nucellus
Nuciform
Nudicaul
Nut pine
Nut rush
Nutation
Nymphaea
Oarsweed
Oil palm
Oil tree
Old maid
Oleander
Oleaster
Oncidium
Oneberry
Oogonium
Oophoric
Oophytic
Oosphere
Oosporic
Opposite
Orchanet
Origanum
Oxtongue
Pachonta
Padelion
Palmated
Palmetto
Pandanus
Panicled
Para nut
Parasite
Parietal
Parietes
Patience
Pea tree
Pea vine
Pearmain
Peduncle
Pennated
Pentafid
Perianth
Periblem
Pericarp
Periderm
Peridium
Perigone
Peronate
Petaline
Petalody
Petaloid
Pezizoid

Phormium
Phyllode
Phyllody
Phyllome
Phyllous
Picketee
Picotine
Pieplant
Pilewort
Piliform
Pillwort
Pimpillo
Pimpinel
Pinaster
Pineweed
Pin-eyed
Pinkroot
Pinnated
Pipevine
Pipewort
Pissabed
Pistacia
Pitahaya
Plantain
Plantule
Plastide
Platanus
Plumbago
Plumular
Pockwood
Podetium
Podocarp
Pokeweed
Polygamy
Polygony
Polypode
Polypody
Pondweed
Porkwood
Primrose
Prolific
Puffball
Purslane
Putchuck
Pyxidium
Quandong
Quartine
Queening
Quickens
Quincunx
Quintine
Racemule
Rachilla
Rachitis
Radicant
Radicule
Rambutan
Ramiform
Raphides

Ravenala
Reclined
Red pine
Redwithe
Reinette
ReliquiÊ
Rhizogan
Rhizogen
Richweed
Riga fir
Rockrose
Rockweed
Roseroot
Rosewort
Rosulate
Rotiform
Sabulose
Sainfoin
Saltbush
Saltwort
Samaroid
Sambucus
Samphire
Sandwort
Santalum
Sap ball
Sap tube
Sapindus
Sapucaia
Sargasso
Satyrion
Saw-wort
Scabious
Scabwort
Scallion
Scammony
Scarious
Sciuroid
Scleroid
Scullion
Sea appl
Sea bean
Sea holm
Sea kale
Sea pink
Sea pool
Sea reed
Seabeard
Sebesten
Seed bud
Seedling
Sepaline
Sepalody
Sepaloid
Sepalous
Septfoil
Serpolet
Serrated
Shagbark

Shamrock
Sheathed
Sicamore
Siderite
Silicula
Silicule
Silkweed
Siphonia
Skullcap
Smallage
Snapweed
Snowball
Snowdrop
Soaproot
Soapwort
Soldanel
Solidago
Soredium
Sour gum
Sourwood
Spathose
Spathous
Spekboom
Sphagnum
Spicated
Spicknel
Spikelet
Spiricle
Squamula
Squamule
Stapelia
Starwort
Stipular
Stipuled
Stomatic
Straight
Stramony
Strigose
Strigous
Strobile
Strumose
Suberous
Submerse
Suwarrow
Sycamore
Synedral
Tamarack
Tamarind
Tamarisk
Tarragon
Tea rose
Tea tree
Teaberry
Tentwort
Teosinte
Terminal
Thalamus
Thalline
Thalloid

Tickseed
Tidytips
Til tree
Tithymal
Toadflax
Tomentum
Toonwood
Torulose
Tracheid
Treasury
Tremella
Triander
Trichome
Trigynia
Trillium
Trinodal
Trioecia
Triticum
Truelove
Trumpets
Tuberose
Tuberous
Tuckahoe
Turmeric
Turnsole
Twinleaf
Umbellar
Umbellet
Urceolus
Uva-ursi
Vaginula
Vaginule
Valerian
Vascular
Vasculum
Veratrum
Vergaloo
Veronica
Verticil
Vexillum
Viburnum
Victoria
Vitellus
Wall pie
Wall rue
Wallwort
Wartweed
Wartwort
Wax palm
Wax tree
Waxberry
Waybread
Weigelia
Whanghee
Whitetop
Whitsour
Wig tree
Wild oat
Wistaria

36

Withvine
Withwind
Withwine
Wood nut
Wood oil
Woodbine
Woodroof
Wormseed
Wormwood
Wych-elm
Xanthium
Xenogamy
Yaw-weed
Yoncopin
Zoˆspore

7

Abaxial
Acantha
Accrete
Acerose
Aconite
Acrogen
Aculeus
Agynous
Albumen
Alcanna
Alecost
Alfalfa
Alkanet
Alyssum
Amorpha
Androus
Anemone
Apogamy
Apprest
Apricot
Arillus
Awlwort
Azarole
Baldwin
Bertram
Bivalve
Bristle
Cabbage
Calamus
Callose
Caltrop
Calycle
Calypso
Cambium
Cammock
Campion
Candock
Canella
Capsule
Caraway

Cardoon
Cassava
Catalpa
Catmint
Cauline
Cerrial
Climber
Comfrey
Conifer
Connate
Coontie
Corcule
Cordate
Corolla
Couhage
Cowbane
Cowhage
Cowitch
Cowslip
Coxcomb
Crampon
Creeper
Crinite
Crowtoe
Cucumis
Cudbear
Cudweed
Culrage
Cumfrey
Curcuma
Currant
Cyperus
Cypress
Cypsela
Fanlike
Fertile
Floccus
Folious
Fuchsia
Fulcrum
Gemmate
Gemmule
Genipap
Genista
Gentian
Gherkin
Ginseng
Girasol
Gladwyn
Goldcup
Golding
Gonakie
Gonimia
Gromill
Grumose
Grumous
Gutwort
Halesia
Hastile

Hautboy
Hawkbit
Healall
Hemlock
Henbane
Henware
Hepatic
Hickory
Hog gum
Hogweed
Honesty
Hypogyn
Incised
Inermis
Inverse
Ipomoea
Ivy tod
Jasmine
Jeterus
Jewbush
Jugated
Juglans
Juniper
Juwansa
Karatas
Kedlock
Kingcup
Kumquat
Labiate
Labiose
Lacinia
Lactuca
Leafcup
Lentisk
Lettuce
Lignify
Lignone
Lignose
Linseed
Lirella
Lituate
Lobated
Lobelet
Lobelia
Locular
Locusta
Lopseed
Lucerne
Lunular
Lychnis
Lycopod
Lyrated
MadroÒa
Madwort
Mahaled
Mahonia
Maithes
Mallows
Mammose

Mannite
Maranta
Margosa
Matweed
Mawseed
Maybush
Mayweed
Mealies
Medulla
Melilot
Melissa
Melluco
Mesquit
Milfoil
Monogam
Monogyn
Morelle
Morello
Morinda
Moringa
Mudwort
Mugweed
Mugwort
Mullein
Murlins
Muscoid
mustard
Narthex
Nectary
Nelumbo
Nervate
Nervose
Nervure
Nucleus
Oatmeal
Obovate
Octofid
Oilseed
Oophore
Oophyte
Oospore
Opuntia
Ostiole
Paleola
Palmite
Palmyra
Panacea
Panicle
Panicum
Pannose
Papaver
Pappose
Pappous
Papyrus
Parelle
Parsley
Parsnip
Partial
Partite

Patella
Pedicel
Peloria
Peloric
Perfect
Perilla
Petaled
Petiole
Petunia
Phalanx
Phallus
Phoenix
Pigweed
Pimenta
Pimento
Pinesap
Pinnule
Pinweed
Pitcher
Plerome
Plumula
Plumule
Pointal
Polygyn
Prangos
Primine
Primula
Puberty
Puccoon
Pumpion
Pumpkin
Pungent
Putamen
Quamash
Quercus
Quinate
Racemed
Radiant
Radiate
Radical
Radicel
Radicle
Ragweed
Ragwort
Ramenta
Rameous
Rampion
Ramsted
Red ash
Red bay
Red fir
Redhead
Redroot
Redweed
Redwood
Reptant
Restant
Rhachis
Rhamnus

Rhizine
Rhizoid
Rhizoma
Rhizome
Rhubarb
Ribwort
Ricinus
Ringent
Robinia
Rootcap
Rosebay
Roselle
Safflow
Saffron
Saligot
Salsafy
Salsify
Salsola
Sanicle
Sapwood
Sarment
Scyphus
Seawand
Seaware
Seaweed
Seedbox
Senecio
Sepaled
Sequoia
Service
Sessile
Setwall
Sexifid
Shallon
Shallot
Silicle
Siliqua
Silique
Sinapis
Skirret
Slashed
Sloakan
Soboles
Solanum
Sophora
Sorghum
Sorosis
Souring
Sowbane
Spathal
Spathed
Spicose
Spicous
Spicula
Spicule
Spignel
Spignet
Spinage
Spiraea

Spurrey
Stipula
Stipule
Stomate
Stopper
Stupose
Suberin
Succise
Succory
Supreme
Sutural
Syconus
Sympode
Synacmy
Syncarp
Syringa
Talipot
Tannier
Taproot
Tarweed
Tendril
Tercine
Thallus
Thistle
Thitsee
Thyrsus
Tigella
Tigelle
Tobacco
Trachea
Trefoil
Trifoly
Tumeric
Tunhoof
Turpeth
Tussock
Tylosis
Undated
Unequal
Upstart
Utricle
Valonia
Valvate
Vanilla
Vaulted
Ventral
Verbena
Vervain
Vesicle
Vetiver
Villose
Virgate
Vittate
Wallaba
Wanghee
Wanhorn
Wapatoo
Wappato
Warence

Watches
Waxwork
Whitish
Whortle
Wilding
Xylogen
Yellows
Zizania
Zostera

6

Abrupt
Acajou
Acinus
Adesmy
Adnate
Adonis
Agaric
Allium
Althea
Amomum
Ananas
Angio-
Anther
Arista
Arnica
Attire
Axilla
Azalea
Cactus
Calcar
Camass
Carina
Carrot
Cashew
Cassia
Catkin
Caudex
Caulis
Cedrat
Celery
Cereus
Cerris
Clover
Coccus
Cockle
Cohort
Cohosh
Coleus
Collar
Collum
Comose
Conium
Cormus
Cornel
Corymb
Cowage

Cowdie
Cowish
Cowrie
Crenel
Crinum
Crocus
Croton
Cupule
Cymoid
Cymous
Cymule
Double
Farina
Fauces
Female
Fiddle
Fleshy
Fringe
Fungus
Garget
Garlic
Ginger
Ginkgo
Gladen
Glumal
Goolde
Gunjah
Gyrose
Hamous
Harmel
Henbit
Hognut
Humiri
Hyphae
Hypnum
Imphee
Innate
Intine
Isatis
Jarnut
Kalmia
Kamala
Kawaka
Kecksy
Keeled
Kermes
Ketmie
Knawel
Kousso
Lablab
Lamina
Laurel
Laurus
Leafet
Legume
Lentil
Lichen
Lignin
Ligule

Lilial
Linden
Litchi
Locken
Loment
Longan
Loquat
Lorate
Lovage
Lucern
Lucuma
Lunary
Lupine
Lychee
Mabolo
Madder
Madnep
Maghet
Maquey
Mammee
Manioc
Mariet
Marram
Masked
Mastic
Mathes
Matico
Maypop
Mazard
Mentha
Midrib
Mildew
Millet
Mimosa
Moutan
Mullen
Muscat
Myrcia
Myrica
Myrtle
Naphew
Nardoo
Natant
Nectar
Nepeta
Nerved
Nettle
Nostoc
Notate
Nucule
Nuphar
Nutlet
Nutmeg
Ochrea
Offset
OÔdium
Oilnut
Orache
Orchid

Orchis
Organy
Orpine
Osmund
Oxalis
Oxbane
Oxheal
Pacane
Pachak
Paeony
Pagina
Paigle
Pappus
Parted
Pastel
Patent
Paunce
Pawpaw
Peanut
Pedate
Peplis
Perula
Peziza
Phleum
Phloem
Phyton
Pignut
Pileus
Pilose
Pindar
Pippin
Pistil
Pitted
Pollen
Poplar
Potato
Privet
Prunus
Ptyxis
Pusley
Pyrena
Pyrene
Quince
Quitch
Raceme
Radish
Raffia
Rament
Ramoon
Ramson
Ratany
Rattan
Redbud
Redtop
Rennet
Repent
Replum
Reseda
Rhaphe

Robert
Rocket
Rotund
Rubigo
Sabine
Sallow
Salvia
Sapota
Savine
Savory
Scypha
Secale
Seckel
Secund
Septum
Serial
Sesban
Sheath
Shield
Shumac
Silene
Sissoo
Smilax
Social
Solute
Sorema
Sorrel
Spadix
Sparse
Spatha
Spathe
Sporid
Spruce
Spurge
Spurry
Squash
Squill
Stamen
Stigma
Stipel
Stirps
Stolon
Stroma
Struma
Styrax
Sumach
Sundew
Suture
System
Tampoe
tangle
Tanier
Teasel
Tegmen
Thatch
Thrift
Tiller
Tomato
Trigyn

Tucuma
Tupelo
Turion
Turnep
Turnip
Tutsan
Twiner
Ulluco
Unguis
Ungula
Urtica
Vagina
Vanglo
Veined
Velate
vessel
Villus
Violet
Volvox
Waahoo
Walnut
Wampee
Warted
Weapon
Whahoo
Wicopy
Willow
Winged
Woolly
Yarnut
Yarrow
Yaupon
Youpon
Zachun
Zamang
Zinnia
Zonate

5

Abies
Agave
Akene
Alder
Algal
Ament
Anise
Anona
Arbor
Areca
Ascus
Aspen
Aster
Avena
Avens
Awned
Basil
Cacao

Calla
Calyx
Canna
Caper
Carex
Carob
Climb
Clove
Colza
Corol
Costa
Cress
Cumin
Cutin
Cycad
Cycas
Fruit
Fucus
Galea
Gemma
Glans
Glume
Gorse
Gourd
Grape
Grass
Guaco
Hazel
Heath
Henna
Hilar
Hilum
Holly
Hyrse
Ixtli
Jugum
Julus
Juvia
Kafal
Kauri
Kemps
Khaya
Kneed
larch
Latex
lemon
Lepal
Liana
Liber
Lichi
Lilac
Linum
Lotos
Lotus
Madia
Mahoe
Maize
Manna
Maple

Maqui
Maule
Medic
Melon
Merry
Moong
Morel
Moril
Morus
Mould
Mucor
Mucus
Mudar
Musci
Naiad
Napus
Navew
Nonda
Nondo
Nopal
Olive
Onion
Orpin
Orris
Orval
Oryza
Osier
Ovary
Ovate
Oxeye
Oxlip
Paddy
Palea
Palet
Panic
Pansy
Papaw
Paris
Peach
Pecan
Pelta
Peony
Petal
Phlox
Picea
Pinna
Pióon
Pinus
Piony
Pirie
Pixie
Plane
Plica
Plume
Pocan
Poley
Poppy
Pubes
Pulas

Pyrus	Sylva	Axis	Node	Veil
Pyxie	Tansy	Beet	Ocra	Vein
Pyxis	Tazel	Bulb	Okra	Vine
Quick	Tecum	Bunt	Olea	Ware
Radix	Tepal	Cane	Oval	Wavy
Ramee	Thorn	Cole	Palm	Weld
Ramie	Thrum	Coma	Pear	Whin
Rampe	Thuja	Cone	Pepo	Woad
Ranal	Thuya	Corm	Pine	Wood
Raphe	Thyme	Culm	Pink	Wort
Regma	Tokay	Cyma	Pita	Yamp
Rheum	Torus	Cyme	Pith	
Ribes	Tribe	Cyst	Plum	**3**
Rubus	Trica	Gale	Poke	
Runch	Tuber	Gean	Poly	Ash
Sabal	Tulip	Gill	Pome	Asp
Sagus	Turio	Gist	Prie	Awn
Salix	Ulmus	Gram	Pulp	Gem
Sappy	Umbel	Halm	Rape	Gum
Savoy	Uredo	Hemp	Rata	Hip
Scaly	Usnea	Holm	Reed	Hop
Scape	Velum	Horn	Rhea	Ivy
Scion	Vetch	Ilex	Rhus	Jag
Scoke	Vimen	Ixia	Rice	Jak
Scurf	Viola	Jack	Root	Kat
Seche	Vitis	Juba	Rush	Kex
Sedge	Vitta	Kail	Rust	Lid
Sedum	Volva	Kale	Sadr	Lip
Semen	Wheat	Kali	Sage	May
Senge	Whorl	Kava	Seat	Nep
Senna	Whort	Keel	Seed	Nut
Sepal	Whurt	Kelp	Sego	Oak
Serye	Withy	Leaf	Sida	Oat
Shola	Wrack	Leek	Sloe	Oca
Shrub	Xylem	Lily	Smut	Pea
Sieva	Xyris	Lime	Soja	Pip
Silva	Yacca	Limu	Sola	Poa
Situs	Yapon	Ling	Sorb	Pod
Sloke	Yeara	Loco	Stem	Pay
Sorgo	Yerba	Loof	Sunn	Rot
Sorus	Yucca	Lote	Tang	Rue
Sours	Yulan	Mace	Tare	Rye
Spawn	Yupon	Male	Taro	Sal
Spelt	Zamia	Milk	Teak	Sam
Spike	Zante	Mint	Teek	Seg
Spine	Zilla	Moha	Teil	Sex
Split	Zoned	Moly	Thea	Soy
Spore		Mora	Toon	Sun
Stalk	**4**	Moss	Tree	Ule
Sting		Moxa	Tube	Urn
Stipe	Alar	Mung	Tule	Uva
Stole	Alga	Musa	Tuna	Yam
Stoma	Aloe	Musk	Twin	Yew
Style	Anil	Nabk	Ulva	Zea
Swede	Axil	Nard	Upas	

Chemistry

19

Amylic fermentation
Compounds of carbon
Corrosive sublimate
Inorganic Chemistry
Spirit of hartshorn
Tartarized antimony
Tellureted hydrogen
Vegetation of salts
Volumetric analysis

18

Magnesium sulphate
Mercurous chloride
Naphthalene yellow
Proximate analysis
Saint Gobain glass
Semiphlogisticated
Silicofluoric acid
Structural formula

17

Applied chemistry
Aromatic compound
Coal-tar creosote
Hydrofluosilicate
Mineral chameleon
Nitrohydrochloric
Organic chemistry
Organic compounds
Patchouly camphor
Persulphocyanogen
Polytungstic acid
Sal microcosmicum
Salt of colcothar
Salt of hartshorn
Secondary alcohol
Separating funnel
Spirit of vitriol
Standard solution
Stannous chloride
Sulphophosphorous
Ultimate analysis

16

Actino-chemistry
Aethiops mineral
Aldehyde ammonia

Combining weight
Electro-chemical
Hemoglobinometer
Hydrargochloride
Hydrocarbostyril
Hydrosulphureted
Hyperoxymuriatic
Isosulphocyanate
Metasilicic acid
Microcosmic salt
Molecular weight
Nitro-chloroform
Octahedral borax
Organic analysis
Persulphocyanate
Phenyl hydrazine
Phenylic alcohol
Plaster of Paris
Polysilicic acid
Stereo-chemistry
Sulphantimonious
Sulphur trioxide
Supersulphureted
Vegetable alkali
Weldon's process

15

Cream of tartar
Hydrosulphurous
Hypercarbureted
Hyperoxygenized
Hyperoxymuriate
Hypophosphorous
Isosulphocyanic
Macro-chemistry
Mandarin yellow
Mercurification
Metric analysis
Naphthalene red
Naphthol yellow
Osmic tetroxide
Paranaphthalene
Permanent white
Persulphocyanic
Perthiocyanogen
Phenol aldehyde
Phosphoric acid
Physicochemical
Platinochloride
Platinum metals
Platinum sponge
Prismatic borax
Pyrophoric iron
Pyrotritartaric

Ruby of sulphur
Sal acetosellae
Sal catharticus
Stereo-chemical
Sulphantimonate
Sulphantimonite
Sulphocarbonate
Sulphonic group
Sulphophosphate
Sulphophosphite
Sulphotungstate
Sulphur alcohol
Sulphur auratum
Sulphur dioxide
Supercarbureted
Supersulphurize
Sympathetic ink
Tobacco camphor
Turnbull's blue
Violaquercitrin
Volatile alkali

14

Allantoic acid
Amylic alcohol
Antimoniureted
Antiphlogistic
Gelatification
Glycyrrhizimic
Haemochromogen
Hydrobilirubin
Hydrosulphuret
Hydrosulphuric
Hydrotellurate
Hypophosphoric
Hyposulphurous
Iatrochemistry
Licorice sugar
Mercurammonium
Metaphosphoric
Methaemoglobin
Methane series
Methyl alcohol
Methylene blue
Micro-chemical
Naphthoquinone
Neroli camphor
Neutralization
Nitrocellulose
Nitromagnesite
Nitrosaccharin
Nitrosalicylic
Oenanthylidene
Oil of vitriol

Organometallic
Oxyhaemocyanin
Paraphosphoric
Pentamethylene
Phenanthridine
Phenanthroline
Phenol alcohol
Phenyl hydrate
Photochemistry
Phytochemistry
Platinichloric
Platinochloric
Platinocyanide
Platinum black
Polymerization
Protocatechuic
Protosulphuret
Prussian green
Pure chemistry
Pyroantimonate
Pyrophosphoric
Red phosphorus
Redintegration
Sal culinarius
Sal Cyrenaicus
Sal diureticus
Sal duplicatum
Salt of lemons
Salt of Saturn
Salt of sorrel
Salt of tartar
Saltpeter acid
Sesquisulphide
Silicification
Silicofluoride
Silicotungstic
Spirit of salt
Stannofluoride
Sulphantimonic
Sulpharsenious
Sulphindigotic
Sulphocarbonic
Sulphocyanogen
Sulphostannate
Sulphotungstic
Supercarbonate
Superphosphate
Tetramethylene
Thermochemical
Tricarballylic
Tridimensional
Trimethylamine
Trinitrophenol
Turmeric paper
Unitary theory

Victoria green
Vitriolic acid
Vitriolization
Washing bottle

13

Achro o dextrin
Amniotic acid
Anthraquinone
Atomic theory
Atomic weight
Carburization
Cobalt yellow
Columbic acid
Configuration
Convallamarin
Coumaric acid
Cresylic acid
Croconic acid
Crotonic acid
Curcuma paper
Cyanuric acid
Hematinometer
Hydrocarburet
Hydrogenation
Hydrophlorone
Hydrotelluric
Hydroxylamine
Hyposulphuric
Iatrochemical
Luteocobaltic
Mannitic acid
Margaric acid
Mauve aniline
Mellitic acid
Melting point
Mesityl oxide
Metalammonium
Metantimonate
Metaphosphate
Metatungstate
Methyl orange
Methyl violet
Mineral acids
Monosulphuret
Mother liquor
Naphthalidine
Naphthylamine
Nascent state
Nitrification
Nitroglycerin
Nitromuriatic
Octonaphthene
Orthocarbonic

Oxyhemoglobin
Ozonification
Paranthracene
Pentachloride
Pentadecatoic
Percarbureted
Phaseomannite
Photochemical
Phthalic acid
Physostigmine
Phytochemical
Platinocyanic
Polysulphuret
Precipitation
Primary amine
Protosilicate
Protosulphide
Prussian blue
Pseudo-cumene
Pyroantimonic
Pyrophosphate
Pyrosulphuric
Quadrivalence
Quantivalence
Reconvertible
Rochelle salt
Ruberythrinic
Saccholactate
Sal absinthii
Sal alembroth
Sal sedativus
Sal Seignette
Salt of amber
Salt of Venus
Salt sedative
Scorification
Sedative salt
Silicofluoric
Soluble glass
Subcarbureted
Subtilization
Sulpharsenate
Sulpharsenite
Sulphoarsenic
Sulphocyanate
Sulphocyanide
Sulphostannic
Sulphur ether
Superchemical
Supersulphate
Tartar emetic
Terephthalate
Tetrathionate
Thiocarbonate
Thionaphthene
Thiosulphuric
Tridecatylene
Triethylamine
Umbellic acid

Umbelliferone
Unsymmetrical
Vapor density
Veratric acid
Volatile oils
White arsenic
White vitriol
Woulfe bottle
Xanthoproteic
Xanthoprotein
Xanthopuccine
Xanthorhamnin
Zircofluoride

12

Albuminoidal
Alcoholmeter
Arbor Dianae
Arseniureted
Atmolyzation
Aurochloride
Carbohydrate
Carbohydride
Caryophyllin
Coerulignone
Condensation
Cuminic acid
Gentiopikrin
Glycocholate
Glycyrrhizin
Hemialbumose
Hemimellitic
Hepatization
Homocerebrin
Hydrofluoric
Hydroquinone
Hydroxanthic
Hypochlorous
Incompatible
Inoxidizable
Lactoprotein
Laughing gas
Litmus paper
Manganesious
Menispermine
Mephitic air
Mesitylenate
Mesotartaric
Metalorganic
Metantimonic
Metasilicate
Metastannate
Metatungstic
Metavanadate
Methyl amine
Methyl ether
Methyl green

Milk of lime
Mineral salt
Mint camphor
Monocarbonic
Monosulphide
Multivalence
Mytilotoxine
Naphthalenic
Naphthazarin
Neurokeratin
Neutral salt
Nitrobenzene
Nitromethane
Nitroprussic
Nitrous acid
Noble metals
Nonoxygenous
Oenanthylate
Oenanthylous
Orthosilicic
Oxamethylane
Oxygenizable
Oxymethylene
Oxyquinoline
Oxysulphuret
Paracyanogen
Parrot green
Passive iron
Pentadecylic
Pentathionic
Periodic law
Permanganate
Persulphuret
Phenanthrene
Phloroglucin
Phosphureted
Phyllocyanin
Polychloride
Polychromate
Polysulphide
Polytungstic
Praseodymium
Primary salt
Proof spirit
proportional
Pyroarsenate
Pyrocatechin
Pyrosulphate
Pyrotartaric
Pyrotartrate
Pyrotungstic
Quadrivalent
Quantivalent
Quercitannic
Rectificator
Reduced iron
Rhabarbarine
Rhaponticine
Rhodammonium

Ricinelaidin
Ring formula
Rose aniline
Rose camphor
Saccharinate
Saccharonate
Saccholactic
Sal ammoniac
Sal prunella
Sal vitrioli
Salification
Salt of soda
Seleniureted
Semimetallic
Silicic acid
Spiritualize
Stearic acid
Sulpharsenic
Sulphocyanic
Sulphur acid
Sulphur base
Sulphur salt
Tellurhydric
Terebenthene
Terephthalic
Tersulphuret
Tetrathionic
Tetravalence
Thermifugine
Thiocarbonic
Thiosulphate
Titanic acid
Tricarbimide
Triglyceride
Trimethylene
Tripalmitate
Vanadic acid
Veratralbine
Vinegar lamp
Vitriolation
Vivification
Washing soda
Wood vinegar
Xanthic acid
Xanthogenate
Xanthoxylene
Zinc vitriol
Zo^chemistry

11

Alkalimetry
Amphichroic
Antialbumid
Antimonious
Antipeptone
Apomorphine
Aqua fortis

Athermanous
Aurocyanide
Backgrounds
Caffetannic
Calcigenous
Calcination
Cantharidin
Carbazotate
Cascarillin
Cementation
Colocynthin
combination
Convallarin
Convolvulin
Corrovaline
Crotonylene
Cryohydrate
Crystalloid
Cyanic acid
Gallotannic
Haemacyanin
Hemialbumin
Hemipeptone
Hemiprotein
Hendecatoic
Hennotannic
Herapathite
Hesperidene
Hexeikosane
Hydracrylic
Hydrargyrum
Hydrobromic
Hydrocarbon
Hydrogenate
Hydrogenium
Hydrogenize
Hydrosorbic
Hyoscyamine
Hyponitrous
Hypoxanthin
Indoaniline
Iodoquinine
Isocyanuric
Isonicotine
Lactic acid
Lactoabumin
Lauric acid
Leucaniline
Lithofellic
Malamethane
Manganesate
Manganesian
Manganesous
Marine acid
Mauvaniline
Melampyrite
Melissylene
Metachloral
Metacrolein

Metaldehyde
Metapeptone
Metasilicic
Metastannic
Metatitanic
Metavanadic
Methylamine
Methysticin
Molybdenous
Morintannic
Multivalent
Mustard oil
Naphthalate
Naphthalene
Naphthaline
Naphthalize
Nicotianine
Nigraniline
Nihil album
Nitraniline
Nitrocarbol
Nitrogenize
Nitrogenous
Nitroquinol
Nonmetallic
Oenanthylic
Oenothionic
Orthoxylene
Oxalic acid
Oxaluramide
Oxanilamide
Oxychloride
Oxygenation
Oxyhydrogen
Oxysulphide
Ozonization
Ozonometric
Ozonoscopic
Paraldehyde
Paris white
Pentadecane
Pentavalent
Percarburet
Perchlorate
Perchloride
Permanganic
Persulphate
Persulphide
Phenic acid
Phenol acid
Phenylamine
Phillygenin
Phosphonium
Phosphorate
Phosphorous
Phthalimide
Pilocarpine
Podophyllin
Polybromide

Polychroite
Polychromic
Polysilicic
Potassamide
Precipitant
Precipitate
Propylidene
Protoxidize
Pyoxanthose
Pyroarsenic
Pyrogallate
Pyrovanadic
Pyroxanthin
Quadribasic
Quartenylic
Quicksilver
Quindecylic
Quinhydrone
Replaceable
Respiration
Rhodeoretin
Ricinoleate
Saccharinic
Saccharonic
Sacchulmate
Safety tube
Sal Saturni
Sal volatil
Santoninate
Selenhydric
Sesqui salt
Sesquibasic
Sesquioxide
Spongy lead
Standardize
Stearoptene
Sublimation
Substituent
Substituted
Subsulphate
Subsulphide
Succinamate
Succinimide
Succinurate
Sulphanilic
Sulphaurate
Sulphionide
Sulpho salt
Sulphovinic
Sulphureted
Sulphydrate
Synanthrose
Synthetical
Tannic acid
Tartrovinic
Tautomerism
Terebilenic
Terebinthic
Terminology

Tersulphide
Tetradecane
Tetrakosane
Tetraphenol
Tetravalent
Theobromine
Thermolysis
Thiocyanate
Thiophthene
Trichloride
Tridecatoic
Triple salt
Trisnitrate
Trisulphide
Trithionate
Tropilidene
Ultramarine
Undecylenic
Unsaturated
Urechitoxin
Valerianate
Valeritrine
Violaniline
Vitriolated
Vortex atom
Wash bottle
Water glass
Wood spirit
Xanthogenic
Xyloquinone
Zinc methyl

10

Absinthate
Acidimeter
Acidimetry
Acolyctine
Adiactinic
Albuminate
Albuminoid
Albuminose
Alcoholate
Alkalamide
Allomerism
Allomerous
Alloxanate
Alloxantin
Ammoniated
Amygdalate
Anisomeric
Anthracene
Antimonate
Antimonite
Aqua regia
Arseniuret
Asparagine
Azobenzene

Azotometer
Cajuputene
Calabarine
Calendulin
Camphorate
Carbureted
Carburetor
Colchicine
Combustion
Conhydrine
Cryophorus
Cryptidine
Cryptopine
Gadolinium
Glutaconic
Glycoluric
Glycoluril
Haematosin
Helianthin
Helleborin
Hemicollin
Hesperidin
Hexavalent
Hydroguret
Hydrolytic
Ilixanthin
Indifulvin
Indifuscin
Indiglucin
Indigrubin
Indogenide
Indophenol
Invertible
Isethionic
Isodulcite
Lacturamic
Lantanuric
Lanthopine
Leucomaine
Leucophyll
Leucoturic
Lignoceric
Lithobilic
Logometric
Manganesic
Margaritic
Melaniline
Melezitose
Mercaptide
Mesaconate
Mesitylene
Mesoxalate
Metacetone
Metalbumin
Metaleptic
Metamerism
Metapectic
Metapectin
Metathesis

Metaxylene
Methionate
Methylated
Microcrith
Middle oil
Milk sugar
Mimotannic
Molybdenum
Monovalent
Monte-acid
Moroxylate
Naphthalic
Nesslerize
Neutrality
Neutralize
Nicotidine
Nitranilic
Nitrometer
Nitrophnol
Nitrosylic
Noropianic
Octavalent
Oenanthate
Oenanthone
Oleandrine
Open chain
Orange oil
Orsellinic
Osmic acid
Oxaldehyde
Oxamethane
Oxidulated
Oxyammonia
Oxybenzene
Oxybenzoic
Oxybutyric
Oxycaproic
Oxychloric
Oxyneurine
Ozonometry
Ozonoscope
Palladious
Palmitolic
Papaverine
Paraconine
Paracymene
Paramaleic
Parapectin
Paraxylene
Pelargonic
Pentabasic
Pentatomic
Perbromate
Perbromide
Percarbide
Perchloric
Perchromic
Peroxidize
Peucedanin

Philippium
Phloramine
Phosphatic
Phosphinic
Phosphonic
Phosphoric
Phosphorus
Phosphoryl
Phosphuret
Phytochimy
Picrotoxin
Piperidine
Piperylene
Polyatomic
Polychrome
Polyiodide
Polymerism
Polymerize
Polymerous
Polyvalent
Potassoxyl
Propionate
Pyrethrine
Pyroacetic
Pyroborate
Pyrocitric
Pyrogallic
Pyrogallol
Pyromalate
Pyromucate
Quadroxide
Quercitrin
Quinaldine
Quindecone
Quinizarin
Quinoidine
Resorcylic
Rhodizonic
Ricinoleic
Ricinolein
Roche alum
Roman alum
Rosaniline
Rufigallic
Ruthenious
Saccharate
Saccharine
Saccharone
Saccharose
Sacchulmic
Sacchulmin
Sal enixum
Sal Martis
Sal plumbi
Salicylate
Salicylide
Salicylite
Salicylous
Salifiable

Santoninic
Saponifier
Saturation
Seleniuret
Selenonium
Separatory
Sesquisalt
Silicified
Sinapoleic
Sinapoline
Solanicine
Solanidine
Spiroylous
Strychnine
Subsesqui-
Succinamic
Succinuric
Sulphamate
Sulphamide
Sulphauric
Sulphinate
Sulphinide
Sulphonate
Sulphonium
Sulphosalt
Sulphurate
Sulphurize
Sulphurous
Sulphydric
Superoxide
Suroxidate
Tartarated
Tartramate
Tartramide
Tartrazine
Tartronate
Tautomeric
Telerythin
Tellureted
Teracrylic
Terpenylic
Test paper
Tetrabasic
Tetraboric
Tetratomic
Theobromic
Thermolyze
Thiocyanic
Thionoline
Thiophenic
Thiophenol
Thiotolene
Trichromic
Trimesitic
Trithionic
Trivalence
Tropaeolin
Tubulation
Tubulature

Ustulation
Valeramide
Valerianic
Valeridine
Valerylene
Vapor bath
Vincetoxin
Vitriolate
Vivificate
Wolframate
Wolframium
Xanthamide
Xanthinine
Zinc amine
Zinc amyle
Zinc ethyl
Zinc oxide
Zo^melanin

9

Absinthic
Absinthin
Acetamide
Acetylene
Acidifier
Aconitine
Albuminin
Aldehydic
Allantoin
Allotropy
Alloxanic
Aluminate
Aluminium
Amic acid
Amygdalic
Amygdalin
Anhydride
Anthokyan
Antichlor
Antimonic
Arabinose
Argentous
Arsenious
Aspirator
Athermous
Atmolysis
Atmolyzer
Atomicity
Cacodylic
Camphoric
Cannabene
Caoutchin
Caprylate
Capsaicin
Capsicine
Carbamide
Carbamine

Carbimide
Carboxide
Carburize
Carthamin
Carvacrol
Casserole
Catalytic
Cathartin
Cobaltous
Colcothar
Collidine
Collodion
Colophene
Columbate
Columbium
Condenser
Conglutin
Coniferin
Conjugate
Cosmoline
Cotarnine
Cresorcin
Croconate
Crotonine
Cyamelide
Cyanurate
Gadolinia
Germanium
Glucoside
Glyceride
Glycerine
Glycolide
Granulose
Grossulin
Haematoin
Harmaline
Hecdecane
Hendecane
Hexabasic
Histozyme
Hydantoin
Hydramide
Hydramine
Hydrazine
Hydroxide
Hypogaeic
Ichthidin
Ichthulin
Igasurine
Indicator
Indigogen
Indigotic
Indigotin
Indihumin
Indiretin
Indirubin
Indoxylic
Inocarpin
Iodhydrin

Iridoline
Isatropic
Isocyanic
Isologous
Isomeride
Isomerism
Isopepsin
Jamaicine
Juglandin
Juniperin
Kairoline
Kreatinin
Kynurenic
Laburnine
Lactamide
Lactimide
Lactucone
Laevulose
Lanthanum
Lardacein
Larixinic
Laudanine
Lead tree
Lecanoric
Lecanorin
Leucoline
Levulinic
Levulosan
Light oil
Ligustrin
Linoleate
Lipochrin
Lupulinic
Magistery
Magnesium
Mandelate
Manganate
Manganese
Manganite
Manganous
Mannitate
Mannitose
Margarate
Margarone
Margarous
Marsh gas
Meconinic
Melanuric
Melilotic
Mellitate
Mercaptal
Mercaptan
Mercurous
Mesaconic
Mesitylol
Mesoxalic
Metalepsy
Metalline
Metalloid

44

Metameric
Methionic
Methylate
Methylene
Molybdate
Monatomic
Monobasic
Moroxylic
Munjistin
Mycomelic
Mydaleine
Mydatoxin
Myeloidin
Myristate
Myristone
Naphthene
Naphthide
Naphthoic
Narcotine
Neodymium
Nickeline
Nickelous
Nicotinic
Nigrosine
Nitrifier
Nitroform
Nitroleum
Nondecane
Nonylenic
Norwegium
Oenanthic
Oenanthol
Oenanthyl
Oleograph
Oleometer
Oleoptene
Oleoresin
Oreoselin
Organogen
Osmiamate
Ovalbumen
Oxalantin
Oxalurate
Oxamidine
Oxanilate
Oxanilide
Oxidation
Oxybromic
Oxycymene
Oxygenium
Oxygenize
Oxyphenic
Oxyphenol
Ozonation
Palladium
Palmitate
Palmitone
Parabanic
Paraconic

Paraffine
Paramalic
Paramylum
Parigenin
Parvoline
Passivity
Pentoxide
Perbromic
Periodate
Petroline
Phenicine
Phenolate
Phenylene
Phillyrin
Phloretic
Phloretin
Phlorizin
Phosphate
Phosphide
Phosphine
Phosphite
Phthalate
Phthalein
Phthalide
Pinacolin
Piperonal
Platinoid
Platinous
Plumbagin
Polybasic
Polygalic
Polymeric
Potassium
Practical
Prehnitic
Propargyl
Propidene
Propiolic
Propionic
Propionyl
Propylene
Protopine
Protosalt
Protoxide
Prussiate
Pure blue
Purpurate
Pyocyanin
Pyrethrin
Pyroboric
Pyromucic
Pyroxylin
Pyrroline
Quercitin
Quicklime
Quinidine
Quinizine
Raffinose
Retistene

Rhigolene
Rhodanate
Ricinolic
Roccellic
Rubiretin
Ruthenium
Saccharic
Saccharin
Safranine
Sal Jovis
Saleratus
Salicylal
Salicylic
Salicylol
Saligenin
Saliretin
Salt acid
Salt cake
Saltpetre
Sand bath
Santonate
Sapogenin
Saturated
Saturnine
Scheelium
Scillitin
Sclerotic
Scorifier
Secondary
Selenious
Semimetal
Seriation
Signature
Silicated
Sinapisin
Sincaline
Sinistrin
Sparteine
Stannoso-
Stearolic
Stentorin
Stibonium
Strontium
Strychnia
Strychnic
Stryphnic
Styphnate
Styrolene
Sublimate
Succinate
Sulphacid
Sulphamic
Sulphatic
Sulphato-
Sulphinic
Sulphonic
Sulphuret
Sulphuric
Sulphuryl

Supersalt
Sycoceric
Sycoceryl
Sylvanium
Symbolism
Synaptase
Synthesis
Tantalate
Tartarine
Tartarize
Tartralic
Tartramic
Tartrated
Tartrelic
Tartronic
Tartronyl
Tellurate
Telluride
Tellurite
Tellurium
Tellurize
Tellurous
Teraconic
Terpentic
Terpilene
Test tube
Tetrazone
Tetroxide
Tetrylene
Thallious
Thermogen
Thialdine
Thiophene
Titration
Toluidine
Toluylene
Trehalose
Triatomic
Tridecane
Trikosane
Trimellic
Tritylene
Trivalent
Tropidine
Tungstate
Undecolic
Undecylic
Univalent
Urechitin
Uroxanate
Vanadious
Vanillate
Vaporific
Veratrate
Veratrina
Veratrine
Verdigris
Vermilion
Violantin

Vitriolic
Water gas
Wine acid
Wolframic
Wrightine
Xanthogen
Xylindein
Xylostein
Ytterbium
Zirconate
Zirconium
Zymolysis
Zymophyte
Zymoscope

8

Abietine
Abietite
Aconitia
Acrolein
Actinium
Aethogen
Affinity
Albumose
Aldehyde
Alizarin
Alkaline
Alkaloid
Alkargen
Alkarsin
Allylene
Altheine
Ambreate
Amidogen
Ammonium
Amphigen
Analemma
Analysis
Anchusin
Anemonic
Anemonin
Antiarin
Antimony
Antozone
Apocynin
Argentic
Arnicine
Arsenate
Arsenide
Arsenite
Aspartic
Atmolyze
Atropine
Caffeine
Calumbin
Camphene
Cannabin

Capnomor	Hyoscine	Melamine	Oxygenic	Rubidine
Caproate	Igasuric	Melassic	Ozonizer	Rubidium
Capsicin	Ilmenium	Melissic	Paeonine	Rufiopin
Carbamic	Imesatin	Melissyl	Palladic	Ruthenic
Carbanil	Inactose	Melitose	Parietic	Rutylene
Carbazol	Inosinic	Mellitic	Parillin	Safranin
Carbinol	Invertin	Menthene	Pearlash	Samarium
Carbonic	Iodoform	Mercuric	Pectosic	Santalic
Carbonyl	Ipomoeic	Metallic	Pellicle	Santalin
Carboxyl	Iridious	Methenyl	Pelopium	Santonic
Carburet	Isatinic	Methoxyl	Pentacid	Santonin
Castorin	Isatogen	Methylal	Periodic	Saturant
Catechin	Isolable	Methylic	Perissad	Saturate
Cerealin	Isomeric	Molecule	Peroxide	Scandium
Cerebrin	Isoprene	Molybdic	Phenetol	Scheelin
Cerotene	Itaconic	Monamide	Phenylic	Scillain
Cobaltic	Jaborine	Monaminc	Phlorone	Scoparin
Columbic	Kapnomar	monoxide	Phocenic	Scyllite
Columbin	Kephalin	Monureid	Phocenin	Selenate
Compound	Keratose	Morindin	Phospham	Selenide
Condense	Krameric	Moringic	Photogen	Selenio-
Conyrine	Lactamic	Morphine	Phthalic	Selenite
Corallin	Lactonic	Mucamide	Phthalin	Selenium
Coumarin	Lactucic	Muconate	Phthalyl	Seminose
Creosote	Lactucin	Murexide	Picollne	Silicate
Cresylic	Lantanum	Murexoôn	Pinacone	Silicide
Crocetin	Laurinol	Muriated	Piperine	Silicify
Cucurbit	Lavúsium	Muriatic	Pittacal	Sinalbin
Cumidine	Lecithin	Murrayin	Platinic	Sinamine
Curarine	Lepidine	Muscarin	Platinum	Sinapate
Curcumin	Leucinic	Musculln	Plumbous	Sinapine
Cyanogen	Leuconic	Myristic	Pollenin	Sinigrin
Cyanuret	Levulose	Myristin	Polyacid	Sodamide
Cyanuric	Lichenin	Naphthol	Potashes	Solanine
Cymidine	Litharge	Naphthyl	Potassic	Spiraeic
Cymogene	Lobeline	Narceine	Propenyl	Stannate
Garancin	Locustic	Nataloin	Propinyl	Stannous
Gelatine	Lupinine	Negative	Propione	Stearate
Geranine	Lupuline	Neuridin	Propylic	Stearone
Glowlamp	Luteolin	Nickelic	Pulvinic	Stibious
Glucinum	Lutidine	Nicotine	Purpuric	Stilbene
Glutamic	Maclurin	Nitrated	Purpurin	Strontia
Glutaric	Magnesia	Nitrogen	Pyroacid	Strontic
Glyceryl	Magnesic	Nitrolic	Pyrocoll	Stycerin
Glycocin	Malamate	Nitrosyl	Quartane	Styphnic
Glycolyl	Malamide	Nitroxyl	Quartene	Styracin
Glyoxime	Malonate	Nonmetal	Quercite	Suberate
Gommelin	Maltonic	Nonylene	Quinazol	Suberone
Granatin	Mandelic	Octylene	Quininic	Sublimed
Hardness	Manganic	Oenocyan	Quinogen	Suboxide
Hematein	Mannitan	Olefiant	Racemate	Succinic
Hexdecyl	Mannitic	Onocerin	Rational	Succinyl
Hexylene	Mannitol	Opianine	Reaction	Sulphate
Hippuric	Margarin	Orpiment	Resinate	Sulphide
Homotype	Massicot	Orsellic	Resorcin	Sulphine
Hydracid	Masticin	Osmiamic	Rhodanic	Sulphion
Hydroxy-	Masticot	Oxaluric	Ricinine	Sulphite
Hydroxyl	Mauvene	Oxanilic	Rose oil	Sulphone
Hydruret	Meconate	Oxidizer	Rubianic	Suroxide

46

Syringin
Tantalic
Tantalum
Tartaric
Tartarum
Tartrate
Taurylic
Telluret
Telluric
Terebene
Terpinol
Tertiary
Tetra- A
Tetracid
Tetradic
Tetrazo-
Tetrinic
Tetrolic
Thallate
Thallene
Thalline
Thallium
Thallous
Thebaine
Thienone
Thionine
Thioxene
Titanate
Titanium
Titrated
Toluenyl
Toluole
Tolylene
Triamide
Triamine
Tribasic
Trigenic
Trioxide
Triticin
Tropeine
Tubulure
tungsten
Tungstic
Turmeric
Turmerol
Turnsole
Umbellic
Undecane
Uranitic
Uranoso-
Urethane
Uroxanic
Uvitonic
Valerate
Valerone
Valylene
Vanadate
Vanadite
Vanadium

Vanadous
Vanillic
Vanillin
Vanlllyl
Veratria
Veratric
Veratrol
Verditer
Vernonin
Violuric
Viridine
Vodanium
Vomicine
Vulpinic
Xanthate
Xanthide
Xanthose
Xeronate
Xylamide
Xylidine
Xylitone
Xyloidin
Xylorcin
Xylylene
Ytterbic
Yttrious
Zirconia
Zirconic
Zôchemy

7

Acerate
Acetate
Acetone
Acrylic
Adapter
Adopter
Alanine
Alantin
Albumen
Albumin
Alchemy
Alkanet
Alloxan
Alumina
Amarine
Ambreic
Ambrein
Ammonia
Amylate
Amylene
Amylose
Anethol
Angelic
Anilide
Aniline
Aricine

Arnicin
Arsenic
Asarone
Asbolin
Assamar
Aurated
Azoleic
Azotite
Cacaine
Cacodyl
Cadmium
Caesium
Caffeic
Calcium
Calomel
Caramel
Carbide
Carmine
Carotin
Catechu
Cedrene
Cerasin
Ceresin
Cerosin
Cerotic
Cerotin
Cetylic
Cocaine
Codeine
Creosol
Crocein
Crocose
Cuprous
Cyanate
Cyanide
Cyanine
Cydonin
Cymenol
Element
Formula
Gallate
GalleÔn
Gallium
Glacial
Glaucic
Gliadin
Glucina
Glucose
Glycide
Glyoxal
Gradate
Guiacol
Halogen
Harmine
Helenin
Helicin
Hematin
Heptane
Heptene

Heptine
Heptone
Hexacid
Holmium
Hordeic
Hordein
Hyacine
Hyaline
Hydride
Hydrous
Hygrine
Ichthin
Indazol
Indican
Indogen
Indolin
Indoxyl
Inosite
Inuloid
Ioduret
Iridium
Isatide
isolate
Isorcin
Isouric
Jalapin
Jervine
Juglone
Kairine
Kerasin
Keratin
Ketonic
Komenic
Kreatin
Lactate
Lactide
Lactone
Lactose
Lampate
Lanolin
Laurate
Laurone
Legumin
Levulin
Lilacin
Limonin
Linoxin
Lipinic
Lithium
Lophine
Lupinin
Lupulin
Magenta
Malamic
Malonic
Malonyl
Maltine
Maltose
Mannide

Mannite
Matrass
Meconin
Meletin
Mellate
Mellone
Menthol
Menthyl
Mercury
Mesityl
Metamer
Methane
Methene
Methide
Monacid
Morphia
Muconic
Mucusin
Mudarin
Murexan
Muriate
Myricin
Myricyl
Myronic
Myrosin
Naphtha
Nascent
Natrium
Neology
Neurine
Neutral
Nicotic
Niobate
Niobium
Nitrate
Nitride
Nitrify
Nitrile
Nitrite
Nitrose
Nitrous
Nonacid
Nonylic
Nuclein
Occlude
Octoate
Octylic
Odorine
Olefine
Olibene
Olivite
Ophelic
Opianic
Opianyl
Osmious
Ouretic
Oxalate
Oxaline
Oxamate

Oxamide
Oxidate
Oxidize
Oxindol
Oxiodic
Oxonate
Oxyacid
Oxysalt
Ozonize
Palmate
Parting
Passive
Paytine
Pectate
Pectose
Pectous
Pentane
Pentene
Pentine
Pentoic
Pentone
Persalt
Phenose
Phlorol
Phorone
Phycite
Picamar
Picrate
Pimaric
Pimelic
Piperic
Platina
Plumbic
Plumbum
Polymer
Populin
Potassa
Primary
Propane
Propene
Propine
Pyridyl
Pyruvic
Pyruvil
Quassin
Quinate
Quinine
Racemic
Reagent
Rectify
Residue
Resinic
Retinol
Rhodium
Ricinic
Rosolic
Rubidic
Rumicin
Salicin

Salicyl
Salmiac
Salogen
Saponin
Saponul
Scandia
Scandic
Scorify
Sebacic
Selenic
Septane
Septoic
Sericin
Sesqui-
Silicic
Silico-
Silicon
Silvate
Sinapic
Solania
Solvent
Sorbate
Sorbite
Stannic
Stanno-
Stannum
Stearyl
Stereo-
Stethal
Stibine
Stibium
Styrone
Subatom
Suberic
Sublime
Subsalt
Sucrate
Sucrose
Sulpho-
Sulphur
Sylvate
Tannate
Terbium
Terebic
Ternary
Terpene
Thallic
Thetine
Thialol
Thienyl
Thionic
Thionol
Thionyl
Thorium
Thulium
Thymate
Thymene
Tin cry
Titanic

Titano-
Titrate
Toluate
Toluene
Toluric
Trehala
Triacid
Triadic
Tropine
Turpeth
Undecyl
Uranate
Uranium
Uranous
Valence
Valency
Valeric
Valerin
Valero-
Valeryl
Vanadic
Vanadyl
Verdine
Vernine
Vesbium
Vinasse
Violine
Vitriol
Xanthic
Xanthin
Xenylic
Xeronic
Xylenol
Xyletic
Xylidic
Yttrium
Zincane
Zincous
Zircona
Zymogen

6

Acetal
Acetic
Acetin
Acetyl
Adipic
Alkali
Aludel
Alumen
Amidin
Amphid
Amylic
Anilic
Arabin
Arsine
Artiad

Aurate
Aurous
Azotic
Cadmic
Calcic
Carbon
Cardol
Carnin
Carvol
Casein
Cation
Cerium
Cetene
Cobalt
Conine
Cornin
Cresol
Crocin
Crocus
Cumene
Cupric
Cuprum
Cutose
Cyanin
Cymene
Gaduin
Gaidic
Gallic
Gallin
Gelose
Glucic
Gluten
Glycin
Helium
Heptad
Heptyl
Hexane
Hexene
Hexine
Hexone
Hircic
Hircin
Humate
Hydra
Hydric
Ignite
Ilicin
Indigo
Indium
Indoin
Inulin
Invert
Iodate
Iodide
Iodine
Iodous
Iridic
Isatin
Isomer

Isuret
Kalium
Ketine
Ketone
Kinate
Kinone
Kyanol
Laccic
Laccin
Lactam
Lactic
Lactirn
Lactin
Lactyl
Lampic
Laurin
Lethal
Leucin
Lithia
Lithic
Litmus
Luteic
Lutein
Luteo-
Luting
Lycine
Malate
Maleic
Maleyl
Melene
Mellic
Methal
Methol
Methyl
Minium
Morate
Mucate
Mycose
Myelin
Myosin
Neogen
Neroli
Nickel
Niobic
Nitric
Nitro-
Nitrol
Nitryl
Nonane
Nonoic
Nonone
Norium
Normal
Octane
Octene
Octoic
Octoyl
Oleate
Oleone

Oliban
Olivil
Olivin
Orcein
Ortho-
Osmate
Osmite
Osmium
Ossein
Oxacid
Oxalan
Oxalic
Oxalyl
Oxamic
Oxides
Oxonic
Oxygen
Ozonic
Palmic
Palmin
Paviin
Pectic
Pectin
Penta-
Pentad
Pentyl
Period
Peucil
Phenic
Phenol
Phenyl
Phyto-
Picene
Picric
Picryl
Pinite
Potash
Propyl
Proto-
Purree
Pyrene
Pyrrol
Quinia
Quinic
Retene
Revert
Rhodic
Roseo-
Rubian
Rutate

Salify
Saline
Santal
Sebate
Serine
Sienna
Silica
Silvan
Silver
Siphon
Smight
Sodio-
Sodium
Sorbic
Sorbin
Starch
Stibic
Strass
Styrol
Styryl
Super-
Sylvan
Sylvic
Tannin
Tartar
Taxine
Terbic
Terpin
Tetrad
Tetrol
Tetryl
Theine
Thoria
Thoric
Thulia
Thuyin
Thymic
Thymol
Tiglic
Tincal
Tolane
Toluic
Toluid
Toluyl
Trityl
Tropic
Ulmate
Uramil
Uranic
Uranin

Uranyl
Ureide
Uvitic
Verine
Vicine
Viscin
Vulpic
Wasium
Xylate
Xylene
Xylite
Yttria
Yttric
Zincic
Zinco-
Zirco-
Zymase
Zymose

5

Acids
Alban
Allyl
Aloin
Amide
Amido
Amine
Anion
Argon
Auric
Aurin
Cerin
Ceryl
Cetin
Cetyl
Crith
Cumic
Hemi-
Hemin
Hexad
Hexyl
Humic
Humin
Imide
Imido
Indin
Indol
Iodal

Iodic
Ketol
Kinic
Lipic
Lipyl
Malic
Melam
Metal
Morin
Mucic
Mucin
Nitre
Nitry
Nonyl
Nucin
Octad
Octyl
Odmyl
Olein
Opium
Orcin
Orgal
Osmic
Oxide
Oxime
Ozone
Para-
Param
Phase
Phene
Pinic
Rheic
Rhein
rouge
Rufol
Rutic
Rutin
Salol
Sodic
Split
Suint
Tared
Thio-
Tolyl
Triad
Trial
Tutty
Ulmic
Ulmin
Usnic

Vinic
Vinyl
Xenyl
Xylic
Xylol
Xylyl

4

Acid
Alum
Amic
Amyl
Aqua
Azo-
Calx
Cech
Geic
Gein
Gold
Hexa
Iron
Lead
Lute
Neo-
-ose
-ous
Oxid
Per-
Puri
Pyin
Rust
Soda
Sub-
Test
Tiza
Tri-
Uvic
Zein
Zinc
Zink

3

Al-
ñic
Tin
Wet

Climbing

25	23	Tahquitz Decimal System Yosemite Decimal System	20
Sewing-machine leg or arm	Double Fisherman's Knot		Traditional Climbing

Computer

19

Analytical graphics
Closed architecture
Compressed printing
Cursor-control keys
Cylinder addressing
Dependent variables
Explicit formatting
Fixed-length record
Full-screen display
Imbedded formatting
Overstrike printing

18

Character-oriented
Compacted printing
Daisywheel printer
Data transcription
Dedicated computer
Desktop publishing
Dot-matrix printer
Exploded pie chart
Hierarchical model
IEEE parallel port
Integrated circuit
Local area network
Logical operations
Macro instructions
Mainframe computer
Partitioned memory
Search and replace
Soft-sectored disk
Speech recognition
Supervisor program
Telecommunications

17

Assembly language
Backup procedures
Broadband channel
Computer hardware
Computer software
Context switching
Data input screen
Data transmission
Destructive write
Digitizing tablet
Graphics terminal
Network data base
Nonimpact printer

Numerical key pad
On-screen editing
Open architecture
Secondary storage
Serial processing
Thesaurus program

16

Absolute address
Acoustic coupler
Address register
Batch processing
Bold declaration
Boolean operator
Cathode ray tube
Cell referencing
Computer console
Computer program
Conditioned line
Dial-back system
Digital computer
Downloading data
Gallium arsenide
Graphics printer
Hard hyphenation
Hard-copy output
Hard-sector disk
Instruction time
Logic operations
Machine language
Operating system
Optical bar code
Read-only memory
Record structure
Relational model
Relative address
Report generator
Speech synthesis
Storage register
Teleconferencing
Utility programs

15

Analog computer
Background mode
Bar code reader
Blocked records
Command program
Copy protection
Data encryption
Data redundancy
Dvorak keyboard

Electronic mail
Flatbed plotter
Foreground mode
Formula Display
Graphics system
Ink Jet printer
Page formatting
Parity checking
QWERTY keyboard
Read/write head
Read-only media
Right-justified
Screen-oriented
Software piracy
Source document
Variable length
Word processing

14

Device address
Execution time
Expansion card
Expansion slot
Impact printer
Internal modem
Logic function
Logical record
Microprocessor
Output devices
Smart terminal
Sort key field
Tree structure
Turnkey system
Uploading data
Video graphics

13

Bubble memory
Buffer memory
Chain address
Chain printer
Coaxial cable
Cut and paste
Documentation
Dumb terminal
Function keys
Help facility
Laser printer
Machine cycle
Magnetic disk
Microcomputer
Object module

Reverse video
Sector method
Semiconductor
Supercomputer
Syntax errors
Table look-up
User friendly
Write-protect

12

Band printer
Binary digit
Carrier wave
Command menu
Control unit
Copy command
Demodulation
Drum plotter
Electron gun
Laser memory
Line printer
Logical file
Mailing list
Minicomputer
Mother board
Multitasking
Site license
Split screen
Tab settings
Touch screen
Tractor feed

11

Attenuation
Audio input
Auto-answer
Backup copy
Binary code
Bit-mapping
Boilerplate
Coprocessor
Dot command
Floppy disk
Form letter
Gantt chart
Index files
Information
Interpreter
Menu-driven
Microsecond
Multiplexer
Object code

Raster-scan
RGB monitor
Spreadsheet
Vacuum tube

10

Band width
CDROM drive
Data field
Disk drive
Encryption
Field mask
Fixed disk
Grid chart
Hard disks
Head crash
Initialize
Mail merge
Microphone
Modulation
Monochrome
Parameters
Parity bit
Picosecond
Psuedocode
Resolution
Subroutine
Transistor
Translator

9

Amplitude
Assembler
Attribute
Bar graph
Bold face
Branching
Character
Check bit
Clipboard
Data base
Digitizer
Directory
Disk drive
Emulation
Flat file
Flowchart
Frequency
Interrupt
Joy stick
Light pen
Megahertz

Microwave
Processor
Refreshed
Retrieval
Scan rate
Scrolling
Seek time
Subwoofer
Touch pad
Word wrap

8

Compiler
Computer
Cylinder
DVDdrive
End user
Firmware
First-in
Gigabyte
Hardcard
Hardware
Help key
Joystick
Keyboard
Kilobyte
Megabyte
Protocol

RAM disk
Register
Software
Speakers
Spooling
Template
Terminal
Volatile
Zipdrive

7

Address
Booting
Channel
Footers
Formula
FORTRAN
Headers
Looping
Monitor
Network
On-line
Printer
Program
Scanner

6

Buffer
Camera
Coding
Cursor
encode
I-time
Labels
Memory
MS-DOS
Nibble
Output
Prompt
Queues
Record
Screen
Update
Window

5

ASCII
Basic
Clock
Clone
Field
Forth

Index
Modem
Mouse
Phase
Pixel
Shell
Track
Virus

4

Baud
Byte
Cell
CP/M
Data
File
Font
Icon
Logo
Menu
MIPS
Node
Read
Sort
Word
Zoom

3

ADA
APL
Bit
CAD
CAM
CPU
Key
LAN
OCR
OEM
PBX

Cooking

19

Caciocavallo cheese
Danziger
Goldwasser
Lady Baltimore cake
Oysters Rockefeller

18

Cabernet Sauvignon
Danish blue cheese
Explorateur cheese
Jamaican hot chile

17

Back of the house
Caerphilly cheese
Immersion blender

Lancashire cheese
Oil of peppermint
Scalloped oysters
Trans fatty acids

16

Dagwood sandwich
Dandelion greens
Ice-cream makers
O'Brien potatoes
Oeufs la neige
Oil of spearmint
Puttanesca sauce
Scotched collops
Szechuan cuisine
Upside-down cake
Vacherin cheeses
Veal cordon bleu
Yankee pot roast

15

Alla puttanesca
Cabinet pudding
Chinese cabbage
Expiration date
Farmer's cheese
Fat substitutes
Hamburger press
Iceberg lettuce
Ice-cream scoop
Italian parsley
Italian sausage
Jambon persillé
Littleneck clam
Lyonnaise sauce
Madagascar bean
Napoleon cherry
Oakleaf lettuce
Pacific pompano
Palm-kernel oil
Pyramide cheese

Szechuan pepper
Taleggio cheese
unsalted butter
Valencia orange
Veal parmigiana
Watermelon tuna
Yellow-eyed pea

14

Cabbage turnip
Cabernet Franc
Danablu cheese
Danish lobster
Eastern oyster
Gum tragacanth
Habanero chile
JalapeÒo chile
Jamaica pepper
Kabocha squash
Kalamata olive
Kasseri cheese

Lambert cherry
Lamb's lettuce
Mackinaw trout
Nutmeg grinder
Oceanic bonito
Pacific oyster
Ragu Bolognese
Rainbow runner
Ramos gin fizz
Tabasco pepper
Water chestnut
Yard-long bean
Yellowfin tuna

13

Baba gannoujh
Baba ghanoush
Cactus leaves
Cutting board
Danish pastry
Earl Grey tea

Earth almonds
Farmer cheese
Fats and oils
Garbanzo bean
Garlic butter
Half-and-half
Hamburger bun
Icebox cookie
Le flottante
Jagging wheel
Juniper berry
Lady's finger
Macadamia nut
Mysost cheese
Nutmeg grater
Oaxaca cheese
Quatre épices
Queso fundido
Quinine water
Rainbow trout
Sabra liqueur
Safflower oil
Saint-Germain
Savoy cabbage
Tabasco Sauce
Vanilla sugar
Varietal wine
Variety meats
Veal Parmesan
Waldorf salad
Walleyed pike
Water biscuit
Yeast starter
Zapote blanco

12

Baguette pan
Bahmi goreng
Butyric acid
Caesar salad
Cafè au lait
Chili pepper
Curry powder
Danbo cheese
Dancy orange
Fuzzy squash
Galanga root
Game animals
Garam masala
Garde manger
Garlic bread
Gouda cheese
Haman's hats
Hamantaschen
Idaho potato
Jagermeister
Kaffeekuchen

Leaf lettuce
Macoun apple
Madeira cake
Nantua sauce
Napa cabbage
Navel orange
Palak paneer
Purple laver
Queso blanco
Queso fresco
Rack of lamb
Sacher torte
Saint-Honoré
Soupe-maigre
Spitchcocked
Table d'húte
Tamago somen
Tandoor oven
Tutti-frutti
Valpolicella
Veal Marengo
Yellow berry

11

Aji-no-moto
Bagna cauda
Benedictine
Bénédictine
Bloody Mary
Cactus pear
Cafè brélot
Cafè filtrè
Damson plum
Earthenware
Eccles cake
Edam cheese
Fuzzy melon
Fuzzy navel
Gallimaufry
Hairy melon
Half & half
Hydroponics
Icing sugar
Jack cheese
Kaffir lime
Label terms
Lactic acid
Nasi goreng
Ocean perch
Palak panir
Quadrettini
Quick bread
Rye whiskey
Sachertorte
Saint Andrè
Stabilizers
Tagliatelle

Tybo cheese
Veal Orloff
Vol-au-vent
Waffle iron
Xanthan gum
Yankee bean
Yeast bread
Zante grape
Zungenwurst

10

Azuki bean
Back bacon
Cacciatore
Corn syrup
Cuttlefish
Dutch oven
Eau de vie
Emulsifier
Fahrenheit
Farfallini
Farfallone
Game birds
Garden pea
Gingerroot
Gum arabic
Hot pepper
Jackrabbit
Lady apple
Ladyfinger
Lake trout
Maccheroni
Muttonfish
Nasturtium
Pain perdu
Palacsinta
Palm heart
Palm sugar
Pasteboard
Quesadilla
Ramos fizz
Semifreddo
Shortening
Spitchcock
Tagliarini
Tagliolini
Tamale pie
Ugli fruit
Unleavened
V.V.S.O.P.
Veal Oscar
Veal Oskar
Walnut oil
Water bath
Watercress
Watermelon
Yellowtail

Zabaglione

9

Amberjack
Asparagus
Baby corn
Chantilly
Cole slaw
Creamcake
Croquette
Croustade
Dacquoise
Earth nut
Earthnuts
Edelfaule
Egg cream
Entremets
Faba bean
Fastnacht
Fava bean
Galantine
Galingale
Gastropod
Hamburger
Ice cream
Jackfruit
Jambalaya
Kuro goma
Lagniappe
Lambrusco
Lyonnaise
Macédoine
Madeleine
Madrilène
Navy bean
Oat flour
Oenophile
Pack date
Radiatore
Radicchio
Rye flour
Sablefish
Saccharin
Saga blue
Sai-hashi
Scalloped
Shellfish
Tabbouleh
Tamarillo
Zinfandel

8

Allspice
Baguette
Bergamot
Consommé

Daiquiri
Dextrose
Duxelles
Extracts
Farfalle
Fasnacht
Flatfish
Flounder
Fructose
Galangal
Galliano
Guar gum
Hallacas
Ice milk
Ice wine
Imperial
Jalousie
Jamberry
Kaasdoop
Kamaboko
Kara age
Lagnappe
Macaroni
Macaroon
Macerate
Mackerel
Marinade
Meringue
Nabemono
Nam prik
Napoleon
Nut mill
Oat bran
Oenology
Pad thai
Paillard
Palm oil
Quenelle
Raclette
Rutabaga
Saganaki
Sautéing
Stuffing
Szechwan
Tandoori
Umeboshi
Univalve
V.S.O.P.
Vacherin
Vanillin
Wormseed
Wormwood
Yakimono
Yakinori
Yakitori
Yule log
Zucchini
Zuccotto

52

7

blanc
abalone
avocado
bacalao
baccal
bagoong
cabbage
Crouton
dariole
edamame
fagioli
fajitas
falafel
fat mop
fatback
felafel
galette
ganache
garbure
Garnish
ginseng
glucose
gweduck
haddock
hakusai
halibut
jaggery
kumquat
lactose
lahvosh
lamprey
Madeira
mafalda
maltose
Marsala
mollusk
nam pla
oatmeal
octopus
o-hashi
palmier
pompano
quetsch
ramekin
sabayon

saffron
sautéed
Scallop
Shirred
sirniki
sucrose
syrniki
tzimmes
vanilla
Vouvray
wassail
yaki fu
zakuska

6

babco
brandy
byssus
cactus
cutlet
daikon
éclair
Entrée
fagara
farfel
farina
fennel
fondue
garlic
ginger
haggis
hallah
halvah
hyssop
ichimi
Izarra
jambon
junket
Kahla
kampyo
kanten
lavosh
lychee
mutton
nameko
paella

pakora
plaice
quahog
quiche
quince
quinoa
rabbit
radish
ragot
raisin
rakkyo
saddle
Salmis
tagine
tahini
tajine
tamale
tamari
unmold
waffle
wakame
walnut
wasabe
wasabi
yarrow
zahtar
zester
zitoni
zombie
Zoutch

5

awabi
B & B
babka
bacon
bagel
Byrrh
cacao
chile
Crimp
crust
Curry
daizu
farce
farci

farle
glaze
gyoza
halva
icing
kabob
kamut
kasha
kashi
m,che
nacho
natto
offal
ozoni
pasta
quail
Quark
queso
raita
rakyo
ramen
sablè
Salmi
satay
sauté
spoom
Stuff
taffy
varak
varaq
wahoo
wurst
yeast
yucca
zuppa

4

baba
cafe
café
dust
EDTA
farl
fish
Gamy
gari

gyro
hake
hare
jack
kale
kuzu
lait
lamb
mace
naan
nuts
oats
oeuf
pain
ragu
sage
sago
saté
taco
udon
V.S.
vark
veal
yuca
yuzu
zest
ziti
zoni

3

dab
dal
eel
egg
ham
ice
jam
jus
nan
nap
tea
Udo
yam

Cricket

19	17	16	15	
It is not cricket	Bat-and-pad catch	Win by x wickets	Sticky Wicket	Batting Average Bowling average Innings victory Opening batsman

14

double century
night watchman
ton or century
triple century

13

spin (bowler)
wicket keeper
wicket maiden
win by x runs

12

Spectacles
economy rate
half century
lofted drive

11

cover drive
declaration
maiden over
strike rate

10

tail-ender
Test Match

9

hat trick
off drive
stonewall
wicket(s)

8

chinaman

leg side
on drive
run rate

7

country
innings
leg bye

6

run(s)
seamer

5

break

4

draw
duck
over

3

ODI

Crime

19

biological theories
brain lesion theory
clinical psychology
collection or stash
corporal punishment
correctional milieu
correctional nurses
correctional system
criminal harassment
crisis intervention
delinquency offense
diminished capacity
ethics professional
evidence collection
expressive violence
fast force injuries
fatal inquiries act
forensic psychiatry
forensic psychology
health care officer
HIV Nominal testing
homicide expressive
hospital provincial
hostile environment
injuries fast force
intrapsychic theory
life without parole
mandatory sen-
tences
Medium Secure
Units
murder first degree
offence delinquency

opportunities Model
performed frequency
philosophy human-
ism
physical aggression
professional ethics
psychological abuse
rape date rape drug
rates of occurrence
relative risk ratio
research case study
research evaluation
scientific approach
sentences mandato-
ry
triumvirate nursing
verbal abuse threat
violence expressive

18

bite mark injuries
capital punishment
child prostitution
child sexual abuse
computer forensics
convicted prisoner
corrections system
criminal profiling
criminogenic needs
digital technology
diversion programs
euthanasia passive
evidence invisible
evidence transient

false imprisonment
forensic dentistry
forensic interview
forensics computer
indictable offence
injuries bite mark
long term offender
mechanism of death
mental retardation
offence indictable
passive euthanasia
population at risk
prisoner convicted
probation Officers
restraint chemical
stalker erotomania
stockholm syndrome
suicide compulsory
temporary absences
therapeutic milieu
total institutions
victimology theory

17

attachment theory
clandestine abuse
consultant expert
covert aggression
crime Profits Law
criminally insane
cut incised wound
cycle of violence
dehospitalization
domestic homicide

domestic violence
emergency nursing
euthanasia active
evidence physical
evidence transfer
ex post fact laws
expert consultant
eyeball chemistry
forensic chaplain
forensic medicine
forensic services
forensic settings
habeas corpus act
hesitation wounds
homicide criminal
homicide domestic
injuries pattered
killer and slayer
les murdrorum law
medical Examiners
medicolegal death
nondiscrimination
organic disorders
parole assessment
pattered injuries
physical assaults
primum non nocere
research clinical
research forensic
restraining order
rethinking method
security hospital
security officers
sexual harassment
slashing(cutting)

structural models
total Institution
undomicile people
verbal aggression
warrant of remand
wounds hesitation

16

body temperature
caring & empathy
chain of custody
civil commitment
conceptual model
decentralization
domiciled people
driving injuries
evidence pattern
exigent evidence
expert testimony
federal statutes
female offenders
forensic nursing
forensic science
histology tissue
informed consent
injuries driving
insane criminals
insanity defence
insanity defense
legal psychology
lethal injection
living forensics
medical Examiner
overt aggression

self harm
uxoricide
war crime

8

bailiffs
cannabis
criminal
diabetes
drifters
drug use
epilepsy
evidence
exigency
facility
filicide
forensic
guardian
homeless
homicide
humanism
imbecile
injuries
insanity
juvenile
lividity

mens rea
misandry
misogamy
misogyny
neurosis
offender
outreach
penology
popcorns
prisoner
research
restrain
Rohypnol
security
slashing
spanking
stalking
time-out
violence

7

accused
autopsy
carving
collude
coroner

culture
custody
cutting
defence
endemic
hanging
hashish
neglect
prisons
purloin
stalker
suicide
summary

6

ageism
allege
bedlam
duress
family
guilty
heroin
indict
inmate
intent
lawyer

modosu
murder
native
parole
prison
rapist
remand
stigma
theory
trauma
victim

5

adult
agent
bogus
chlld
court
crime
haras
idiot
jails
judge
macks
trick
youth

4

care
clan
goal
hemp
host
jail
john
jury
pimp
race
rape
RCMP
risk

3

cut
DNA
EMT
HIV

Deserts

10

Australian
Chihuahuan
Patagonian
Taklamakan

8

Colorado
Kalahari

7

Arabian
Atacama

Iranian
Painted
Simpson
Sonoran

6

Gibson
Mojave

Saharan
Somali
Syrian
Turfan

5

Namib
Negev

Nubia
Ordos
Sinai
Sturt

4

Gobi
Thar

Ecclesiastical

19

Augustan confession

18

Ecclesiastical law

Unbloody sacrifice

17

Primitive Fathers
Sustentation fund
Transelementation
Trisacramentarian

16

Ecclesiastically
To take the veil
Tradition Sunday
Way of the cross

15

Antilogous pole
Antisabbatarian
Ecclesiasticism
Excommunication
Mixolydian mode
Pectorial cross

Spiritual court
Superordination
Transfiguratien
United Brethren
Vicar apostolic
Vice chancellor

14

Absolution day
Ecclesiastical
Infralapsarian
Passion Sunday
Pastoral staff
Sacramentarian
Standing order
Supralapsarian
To take orders

13

Administrator
Advent Sunday
Antinomianism
Apocrisiarius
Autocephalous
Establishment
Excommunicate
High festival
Holy Saturday
Impropriation
Incorruptible
Preconization
Rogation days
Rural deanery
Semi-Pelagian
Spy Wednesday
Stated supply
Stercorianism
Subdeaconship
Surplice fees
United Greeks
Vicar-general

12

Adessenarian
Annunciation
Antilegomena
Apollinarian
Conciliabule
Consociation
Denunciation
Dispensation
Ecclesiastic
Incameration
Metamorphist
Metropolitan
Minor orders
Misericordia
Pan-Anglican
Presbyterian
Presentation
Presentative

Processional
Quadragesima
Qualificator
Sabellianism
Septuagesima
Serpentinian
Southcottian
Spirituality
Stercoranism
Stercoranist
Sublapsarian
Superfrontal
Un-Romanized
Vicar forane
Voluntaryism

11

Adiaphorist
Adoptionism
Adoptionist
Aliturgical
Anniversary
Antependium
Antiburgher
Archdeacons
Augustinian
Calefactory
Catabaptist
Celestinian
Censureship
Conciliable
Free church
Grand vicar
Hieronymite
High priest
Iconodulist
Impropriate
Independent
Occidentals
Palm Sunday
Procuration
Proprietary
Sandemanian
Socinianism
Spiritualty
Superioress
Third order
Thunderbolt
Wesleyanism
White canon
White friar
Whittuesday

10

Absolution

Antinomian
Apotactite
Archdeacon
Artotyrite
Capitulary
Catechumen
Catholicos
Cerinthian
Commissary
Compounder
Conference
Consociate
Covenanter
Ecumenical
Illuminati
Jeronymite
Low-church
Metropolis
Monsignore
Octaemeron
Ordination
Parathesis
Pluralizer
Portionist
Procession
Provincial
Responsory
Rural dean
Semi-Arian
Semidouble
Sexagesima
Solifidian
Statocracy
Subchanter
Syncretist
Tersanctus
Trespasser
Vincentian
Whitmonday
Whitsunday

9

Abbeacute
Abelonian
Abstinent
Agnus Dei
Albigeois
Anathemas
Apostates
Apostolic
Appellant
Capitular
Colleague
Concordat
Cordelier
Crown tax
Ecclesial

hierarchy
Holy Week
Induction
Invisible
Jansenism
Jansenist
Martinmas
Methodism
Obedience
Officiant
Ostension
Parsonage
Patronage
Philatory
Pluralism
Pluralist
Plurality
Pluralize
Portioner
Preconize
Prothesis
Raskolnik
Recollect
Sabellian
Sarabaite
Spiritual
Subdeacon
Succentor
Suffragan
Surcingle
Surrogate
Synodical
Translate
Trigintal
Trisagion

8

Ablegate
Ablution
Accensor
Acephali
Anathema
Apostate
Aquarian
Armenian
Arminian
Asperges
Cardinal
Cellarer
Censured
Censures
Covenant
Libelant
Ministry
Mortuary
Mozzetta
Official

Oriental
Pastoral
Pectoral
Polemics
Primitia
Propound
Province
Recollet
Response
Rogation
Sacellum
Sinecure
Subprior
Sudarium
Suffrage
Superior
Surplice
Temporal
Terminal
Tertiary
Theatine
Thurible
Trappist
Ursuline
Vartabed
Vestment
Vexillum
Viaticum
Voidance
Wesleyan

7

Acolyte
Adamite
Advents
Alogian
Ampulla
Angelus
Apparel
Azymite
Censure
Cluniac
Deprive
Dignity
Formula
Frontal
Jacobin
Karaite
Kneeler
Menaion
Officer
Penance
Prelacy
Primacy
Proctor
Respond
Retable

Sanctus
Scotist
Seceder
Secular
Stylite
Synodal
Tonsure
Trental
Tunicle
Unalist
Urceole
Vespers

6

Advent
Annual

Camail
Church
Decree
Exarch
Gloria
Induct
Living
Mormon
Mystic
Nonage
Notary
Novice
Ordain
Parson
Patena
Placet
Rochet

Rubric
Seeker
Seraph
Simony
Switch
Tammuz
Tebeth
Tunker
Uniate
Venite

5

Amess
Amice
Canon
Corps

Glebe
Nisan
Paten
Prior
Proxy
Saint
Sivan
Somne
Stole
Stoup
Synod
Tisri
Tunic
Vicar
Vigil
Vocal
Water

4

Abib
Adar
Cope
Fund
Rota
Veil

3

Pax
Zif

Education

37

Mixed Laterality or
Lateral Confusion

36

Educational
Consultant/Diagnosti
cian

35

Test of English as
Foreign Language

34

Graduate
Management
Admission Test

33

College Level
Examination
Program

31

Licensed Clinical

Social Worker
Licensed
Professional
Counselor

30

Cumulative Grade
Point Average
Licensed Clinical
Psychologist
Medical College
Admission Test

29

Individualized
Education Plan
International Student
Advisor

28

Figure-Ground
Discrimination
Specific Language
Disability

27

Adaptive Physical
Education

Attention Deficit
Disorders
Exchange Scholar or
Student
Graduate Record
Examination
Multiple-choice
examination

26

Advanced
Placement Program
Comprehensive
Examinations
Early Intervention
Program
Professional
Accreditation
Rehabilitation Act of
1973
Scholastic
Assessment Test
Visting Scholar or
Student

25

Criterion Referenced
Test
Law School
Admission Test
Minimal Brain

Dysfunction
Orton-Gillingham
Approach
Psychological
Examination
Self-Contained
Classroom
Specialized
Accreditation

24

Distribution
Requirement
Letter of
Recommendation
Neurological
Examination
Preliminary
Examinations

23

Auditory
Discrimination
Foreign Student
Advisor
Modified Self-
Contained
Proprietary
Institution
Soft Neurological
Signs

22

Auditory Figure-
Ground
Behaviour
Modification
Central Nervous
System
Educational
Evaluation
Land-Grant
Institution
Multidisciplinary
Team
Orton Dyslexia
Society
Qualifying
Examination
Regional
Accreditation
Test of Spoken
English

21

Catastrophic
Reaction
Challenge
Examination
Child Study
Committee
Cooperative
Education

Credit-by-Examination
Eligibility Committee
Experiential Learning
Eye-Hand Coordination
Learning Disabilities
Miller Analogies Test
Open-book examination
Residence

Requirement
Spatial Relationships
Take-home examination
Visual Discrimination

20

All but dissertation
Application Deadline
Continuing

Education
Doctor of Philosophy
Electroencephalogram
Language Requirement
Liberal Arts College
Mid-term examination
Perceptual Abilities
Visual Figure-Ground

19

Assistant Professor
Associate Professor
Conceptual Disorder
Expressive Language
Grade-point average
Linguistic Approach
Make-up examination

Perceptual Handicap
Postdoctoral Fellow
Private Institution
Professional School
School Psychologist
Sight Word Approach
Spatial Orientation
Structural Analysis

Electronic terms

16

audiofrequencies
autotransformers
radiofrequencies

15

autotransformer
multiconductors
servomechanisms

14

audiofrequency
discriminators
multiconductor
permeabilities
radiofrequency
rectifications
semiconductors
servomechanism
thermoplastics
traceabilities

13

discriminator
ferromagnetic
galvanometers
interferences
localizations
milliammeters
piezoelectric
polarizations
preamplifiers
radioactivity
rectification

semiconductor
synchroscopes
thermoplastic
undershooting

12

candlepowers
coefficients
commutations
degradations
demodulating
demodulators
electrolytic
enhancements
galvanometer
hexadecimals
incandescent
interference
localization
megohmmeters
microamperes
milliammeter
milliamperes
milliseconds
permeability
polarization
preamplifier
rechargeable
redundancies
servomasters
servosystems
synchroscope
traceability

11

attenuators
backlighted

candlepower
coefficient
commutation
commutators
degradation
demodulated
demodulates
demodulator
diametrical
elongations
enhancement
fluorescent
hexadecimal
hypotenuses
integrators
megohmmeter
microampere
microfarads
microsecond
milliampere
millifarads
millisecond
multiplexer
nanoamperes
nanoseconds
patchboards
photodiodes
picoamperes
picoseconds
precessions
radarscopes
servomaster
servomotors
servosystem
switchboxes
telemetries
thermistors
thermostats
transducers
transistors

undershoots
wavelengths

10

amplidynes
asymmetric
attenuator
bandpasses
bolometers
bootstraps
burnishing
commutator
cotangents
darlington
degaussing
demodulate
dielectric
elongation
fidelities
hypotenuse
hystereses
hysteresis
inductions
integrator
laminating
lamination
microfarad
microfiche
microvolts
microwatts
microwaves
millifarad
millivolts
milliwatts
monopulses
nanoampere
nanofarads
nanometers

nanosecond
narrowband
partitions
patchboard
patchcords
penetrants
permalloys
photodiode
picoampere
picofarads
picosecond
precession
presetting
radarscope
recharging
reciprocal
rectifiers
redundancy
repulsions
resonances
resonators
servomotor
sinusoidal
solderless
thermistor
thermostat
transducer
transistor
transiting
undershoot
varnishing
voltmeters
wattmeters
waveguides
wavelength

9

amplidyne

antiseize
arresters
backlight
bolometer
bootstrap
broadband
burnished
burnishes
cotangent
crossbars
crossover
crosstalk
degaussed
degausses
degrading
duplexers
enameling
exponents
ferruling
filaments
induction
inductive
inductors
inversely
inverters
isometric
kinematic
klystrons
laminated
laminates
latencies
linearity
metrology
microvolt
microwatt
microwave
midranges
millivolt
milliwatt
monopulse
multiplex
nanofarad
nanometer
nanovolts
nanowatts
nonlinear
ohmmeters
overshoot
partition
patchcord
penetrant
permalloy
picofarad
picovolts
picowatts
pneumatic
polyphase

prognosis
radiating
recharged
recharges
recorders
rectifier
repelling
repulsion
resolvers
resonance
resonator
sheathing
shuttling
spectrums
sprockets
switchbox
telemetry
templates
threshold
transient
transited
undershot
unseating
varnished
varnishes
voltmeter
wattmeter
waveforms
waveguide

8

ammeters
anmeters
arrester
asbestos
avionics
bandpass
brackish
breakers
conduits
couplers
crossbar
dampings
degraded
degrades
discrete
dopplers
duplexer
emitters
emitting
enameled
erosions
exciters
exponent
ferrites

ferruled
ferrules
fidelity
filament
fixtures
inductor
inertial
inverses
inverter
isogonic
klystron
laminate
limiters
luminous
midrange
nanovolt
nanowatt
ohmmeter
orbiting
pentodes
pickoffs
picovolt
picowatt
plotters
polymers
radiated
radiates
readouts
recharge
recorder
repelled
resolver
resonant
rigidity
sawtooth
scanners
shunting
shuttled
shuttles
spanners
spectrum
sprocket
stimulus
tangents
template
tertiary
tetrodes
transits
unseated
wattages
waveform

7

ammeter
anmeter

bleeder
breaker
burnish
cations
chasses
chassis
coaxial
conduit
coronas
cosines
coupler
cutoffs
dampers
degauss
degrade
domains
doppler
ductile
emitted
emitter
enamels
erosion
exciter
ferrite
ferrule
fibrous
gimbals
hybrids
inphase
inverse
latency
limiter
lobings
lugging
megohms
nucleus
orbited
outputs
pentode
photons
pickoff
plasmas
plotter
polymer
presets
protons
radiate
readout
scanner
shunted
shuttle
slewing
spanner
stimuli
tangent
tensile
tetrode

tinning
transit
triodes
unseats
varnish
vernier
wattage

6

agonic
anodes
cation
corona
cosine
cutoff
damper
domain
enamel
gimbal
hybrid
lobing
lugged
lumens
megohm
nuclei
orbits
photon
plasma
preset
proton
repels
rotary
teflon
toggle
triode
unseat

5

anode
emits
inert
lumen
ohmic
orbit
repel
zener

4

emit

Engineering & Computer

40
Childseat Presence
Orientation
Detection
Proportioning
Control plus
Derivative Fu
Threshold Limit
Value Time-
Weighted Aver

39
Superconducting
Magnetic Energy
Storage

38
Underwriters
Laboratories
Incorporated

36
Combined Available
Residual Chlorine
Floating-Point
Operations Per
Second
Four-Terminal
Resistance
Measurement
International
Standards
Organization

35
Integrated Services
Digital Network
Proportioning
Control plus Integral
Unswept Volume/
Haskel gas boosters

34
Newtons 1st and
2nd laws of motion
Photondetector or

Quantum Detector

33
Optical Time Domain
Reflectometer
Thermal Coefficient
of Resistance

32
General
Communications
Interface
Negative
Temperature
Coefficient
Positive Temperature
Coefficient
Pressure Limit or
Proof Pressure
Reduced Instruction
Set Computer
Singel Ended Gas
Booster haskel
Skidmore Bolt
Tension Calibrator
Spontaneous Ignition
Temperature

31
Thermal Sensitivity
Coefficient

30
Basic Transportation
Reference
Canadian Standards
Association
Coloured Body or
Non Gray Body
Combined Residual
Chlorination
Gravitational
Potential Energy
Mineral-insulated
Thermocouple
Optical or Infrared
Resolution
Single-Plane
Balancing Machine

29
Compensated
Temperature Range
Diatomaceous Earth
Filtration
DSL - Digital
Subscriber Loop
Electromagnetic
Compatibility
Maximum Operating
Temperature
Reflected Energy
Compensation
Sinusoidal
Frequency
Response

28
Absolute Pressure
Transducer
Calcium Carbonate
Equivalent
Glass Transition
Temperature
Internal Reference
Electrode
Silicon-Controlled
Rectifier
Standard Electrode
Potential
Two Stage Gas
Booster Haskel
Uninterruptible
Power Supply

27
Analog-to-Digital
Converter
Calender-Van Dusen
Equation
Common Mode
Rejection Ratio
Digital-to-Analog
Converter
Distance Piece
Haskel Pumps
Newtons third law of
motion
Normal-mode
Rejection Ratio
Piezoelectric

Accelerometer

26
Absorption of Water
Vapour
Asynchronous
Communication
Global Positioning
Systems
Mounted Resonant
Frequency
Outlet Check Valve/
Haskel
Proportioning
Control Mode
Temperature Effect
On Span
Temperature Effect
On Zero

25
Biochemical Oxygen
Demand
Electromagnetic
Radiation
Fresnel Reflection
Losses
Inlet Check Valve/
Haskel
Normal Hydrogen
Electrode
Piezoresistive
Transducer
Reciprocating
Compressors
Salt Gradient Solar
Ponds
Scleroscope
Hardness Test
Synchronous
Rectification
Thermal Sensitivity
Shift
Total Harmonic
Distortion

24
Breakdown Voltage
Rating
Chlorine-Contact
Chamber

Colorimetric
Measurement
Compressibility
Factor Z
Digital Light
Processing
Digital Signal
Processor
Dose-Response
Evaluation
Dual-Slope A/D
Converter
Floating-Point
Processor
Gage Pressure
Transducer
Interchangeability
Error
Piezoelectric
Transducer
Saturated Vapor
Pressure
Short-Circuit
Protection
Single Ended Pump
Haskel
Supplementary
Insulation
Temperature
Compensation
Thermal Zero
Coefficient

23
Acceptable daily
Intake
Aliphatic Hydroxy
Acids
Attenuation
Coefficient
Breakpoint
Chlorination
CAS Registration
Number
Coefficient of
Friction
Cyclic Redundancy
Check
Differential
Correction
Discharge Time
Constant
Focal Point or
Distance

Precipitation Hardening
Source Frequency Effect
Staebler-Wronski Effect
Thermophotovoltaic Cell
Transient Recovery Time
Transient Response Time
Undervoltage Protection
Widmanstatten Structure

22

Air Pressure
Amplifier
Amperometric Titration
Best Fit Straight Line
Centrifugal Compressor
Chemical Oxygen Demand
Compression Efficiency
Gravimetric Efficiency
Hydraulic Conductivity
Neutral Density Filter
Nondestructive Testing

Pulse Width Modulation
Static Transfer Switch
Switching Power Supply
Temperature Resolution
Threading and Knurling
Train Lighting Battery
Transverse Sensitivity
Two-Colour Thermometry
Volt Microsecond Clamp
Zero Voltage Switching

21

Adaptive Equalization
Brinell Hardness Test
Burst Pressure Rating
Calibration Procedure
Certificate Authority
Client-Server Network
Compression Adiabatic
Current

Proportioning
Differential Pressure
Dissociation Constant
Efficiency Isothermal
Efficiency Volumetric
Electromagnetic Force
Fixed-Point Processor
Hydrogen Ion Activity
Insulation Resistance
Integral Nonlinearity
Lower Explosive Limit
Mechanical Hysteresis
Modulus of Elasticity
Parallel Transmission
Pulse Code Modulation
Pyroelectric Detector
Short-Circuit Current
Size-of-Source Effect
Step-Down Transformer
Total Regulation Band
Vickers Hardness Test
Voltage Stabilization
Volumetric Efficiency
Zero Power Resistance

20

Adiabatic Efficiency
Ambient Compensation
Archimedes principle
Atmospheric Pressure
Background Radiation
Bernoullis Principle
Binary Coded Decimal
Chlorine Requirement
Chromatic Aberration
Closeness of Control
Comparison Pyrometry
Critical Temperature
Dissipation Constant
Dry Bulb Temperature
Environmental Rating
Fundamental Particle
Geodetic Coordinates
Ignition Temperature
Infrared Thermometer
Method of Correction
Phase

Transformation
Rhodium 10%
Rhodium
Rhodium 13%
Rhodium
Rhodium 30%
Radiance Temperature
Security Certificate
Semiregulated Output
Solar Trough Systems
Squirrel Cage Motors
Standby Power Supply
Sub-critical Reactor
Synchronous Inverter
Temperature Derating
Thermal Conductivity
Transducer Vibration
Varnish Impregnation
Vibration Error Band
Wet Bulb Temperature
Wet/Dry Differential
Wet/Wet Differential

Environmental

13

ablation area
ablation cone
aboral cavity
abscisic acid
absolute date
absolute time
absolute zero
abutment load
abyssal plain
abyssal realm
abyssobenthic
abyssopelagic

accelerograph
accelerometer
acceptor stem
accommodation
acetaminophen
acetylcholine
acid drainage
acid strength
acid-dip test
acoustic wave
adaptive peak
advection fog
age structure
agglomeration
agglutination

air pollution
Aitken nuclei
allopolyploid
alveolar duct
ambient air
amniocentesis
amplification
anchor charge
andesite line
angle of bite
angle of draw
angle of pull
angle of rest
angling dozer
anidiomorphic

aniline point
annual labour
anode furnace
anterior horn
anthophyllite
anthracometer
anthropogenic
antiasthmatic
anticoagulant
anti-oncogene
antisense RNA
appropriation
aquarium test
aqueous humor
arbitration

areal geology
areal pattern
argentiferous
argentopyrite
argillization
aridity index
armored apron
armored cable
arrow diagram
arsenic bloom
arsenobismite
arsenoclasite
arterial road
Artesian Well
asbestos yarn

asexual spore
aspartic acid
asphalt stone
asphaltic ore
assay balance
asthenosphere
astrophyllite
atoll texture
atomic charge
atomic energy
atomic number
atomic volume
atomic weight
attrital coal
austenitizing
autochthonous
autohydration
autoinjection
autointrusion
automatic dam
autopolyploid
autosomal set
axial element
axial priming
azurmalachite
B lymphocytes
back mutation
back pressure
back rippings
backarc basin
back-bye work
backing deals
backing winds
backsight hub
backwardation
balance plane
balance sheet
balbiani ring
ball and test
bally seating
band conveyor
bank of cells
bank of ovens
bar channeler
bar timbering
barrel copper
barrel of oil
barrel washer
barren ground
barring scrap
barytocalcite
basal ganglia
basal sliding
basaltic dome
base analogue
base exchange
base fracture
base sequence
basic process

basic solvent
basidiomycete
bastard shale
batch charger
batch testing
bathymetrical
bathysophical
batter boards
Baume gravity
bauxite brick
bauxitic clay
bauxitization
Bayer process
beach deposit
beam building
bearing plate
bearing stake
bedding fault
bedding glide
bedding joint
bedding plane
before breast
Beien machine
Belfast truss
Belgian press
Belgian silex
belt capacity
belt conveyor
belt dressing
belt friction
bench working
benching iron
Bendelari jig
beneficiation
benign tumour
berm interval
Bertrand lens
Bessemer blow
beta particle
biaxial stone
big-stone bit
Bilharz table
billow clouds
binary system
Bingham model
biocentrism
bioenergetics
biotechnology
biotic factor
black diamond
black granite
black pigment
blacklead ore
Blair process
Blake breaker
Blake furnace
blast furnace
blasting cord
blasting fuse

blood islands
boiling point
bottomset bed
boulder train
Boulder winds
brachydactyly
breeding line
brownfields
buffer system
bulbar region
carbon sink
carbon source
carcinogens
cardiac cycle
catalytic RNA
catastrophism
cell division
cell membrane
central dogma
Charlesís law
chemical bond
chemical rock
chimeraplasty
chlorophyll A
cis dominance
clay minerals
closed system
coding strand
coevolution
concentration
Connate water
consumption
contour lines
control group
cooperativity
coral reefs
cosegregation
covalent bond
cover crops
critical mass
cross bedding
crossing over
cuprozippeite
cyclosilicate
dauerblastula
decomposers
decomposition
deforestation
demyelination
determination
deterministic
detritivore
deuterostomes
diprotic acid
disconformity
discontinuity
doppler lidar
doppler radar
double digest

Down syndrome
dysmorphology
E (exit) site
Earth systems
earthquakes
easterly wave
ecofeminism
effector cell
elastic limit
elastic solid
encapsidation
engine tenter
enhancer trap
environment
eolian placer
epeirogenesis
epidotization
epiianthinite
eq.sexplosive
eruptive vent
estramadurite
eucrystalline
euphotic zone
excited state
exogenous DNA
expansion bit
explosive oil
extension ore
extrapolation
F+(plus) cell
Fabian system
face conveyor
face sampling
faced crystal
facies change
facies fossil
faecal pellet
fall velocity
false bedding
false diamond
false horizon
fan structure
Far East Rand
farewell rock
farringtonite
fatigue limit
fatigue ratio
fault breccia
fault complex
fault fissure
fault surface
fault terrace
feather metal
Federov stage
feed pressure
feeder trough
fence diagram
ferrifayalite
ferritization

ferroelectric
ferrous oxide
ferrovanadium
Fersman's law
fertilization
fetid calcite
fiducial mark
fiducial time
field geology
filled valley
fine grinding
finger lifter
finishing jig
fire breeding
fire refining
firing a mine
first arrival
First World
flanking hole
flaser gabbro
flashy stream
fleckschiefer
flexural slip
flipping turn
float mineral
floating cone
floating reef
flohmig amber
floodplains
floor station
flotation oil
flow cleavage
flow gradient
fluvioglacial
fluxed pellet
fluxing stone
flying cradle
foam drilling
foaming agent
foaming earth
fog quenching
fold mountain
follower rail
footage block
force majeure
force of blow
forearc basin
forellenstein
foresight hub
forest marble
forge welding
foshallassite
fossiliferous
fossilization
foul-air duct
founder cells
fourmarierite
fractionation
fracture dome

fragmentation
framing table
France screen
francevillite
Frasch sulfur
fringing reef
frontal lobes
frontogenesis
frost wedging
fruiting body
gene mutation
gene splicing
gene transfer
genetic drift
gene-trapping
geochronology
geomorphology
Ginkgo biloba
ginney tender
glacial drift
glacial epoch
glaciofluvial
glaucochroite
glaucoma test
gliding plane
glimmer plate
glutamic acid
glyptogenesis
gobbing slate
going headway
gold poachers
gold sapphire
goliath crane
good delivery
Goodman miner
Gordon's rule
grab sampling
graded stream
gradient wind
grain gliding
gram-molecule
granitic rock
granitization
gravel powder
gravity corer
gravity fault
gravity meter
gravity plane
gray antimony
gray crescent
gray hematite
greasy luster
greasy quartz
green plans
green vitriol
grinding mill
gripping hole
gripping shot
grizzly chute

groove sample
ground sluice
ground spears
groundwater
grout curtain
grout machine
growler board
growth factor
guest element
gynandromorph
gypsification
Haarmann plow
Haase furnace
hag principle
half bearings
half-reaction
Halimond tube
Hallett table
hand cleaning
hand drilling
hand sampling
hand specimen
hand spraying
hand tramming
hanging bolts
haplodiploidy
Hardinge mill
hardness gage
hardness test
Hastings beds
hatchet stake
hatchettolite
hauchecornite
haul distance
haulage brake
haulage chain
haulage curve
haulage plant
haulage stage
headache post
heading blast
heap leaching
heap roasting
heap sampling
heat capacity
heat transfer
heaving shale
heavy mineral
Hensen's node
heptaphyllite
hermaphrodite
heteroblastic
heterogeneous
heteromorphic
heteroplasmon
heterothallic
heterotroph
hewing double
high pressure

high velocity
highmoor peat
hoisting crab
hoisting drum
hoisting jack
hoisting plug
hoisting rope
holing shovel
Holman Airleg
homeostasis
hopper dredge
horsetail ore
hose coupling
hot shortness
hot-blast man
hot-laid type
hot-quenching
hsianghualite
Hummer screen
humonigritite
hundredweight
hunting tooth
hurdle screen
hutch product
Huwood loader
Huwood slicer
hyaluronidase
hybridization
hydatogenesis
hydrargillite
hydrated lime
hydraulic ram
hydraulic set
hydraulicking
hydrodynamics
hydrogen bond
hydrohematite
hydronium ion
hydrous salts
hyperglycemia
hypersthenite
hypogene rock
Iceland agate
Icelandic low
ideal gas law
ideal section
idiochromatic
igneous cycle
ignition arch
ignition tube
Ilgner system
immersion cup
immune system
impact factor
impact screen
imperial jade
improved dial
in situ liner
incline bogie

incline shaft
inclined fold
inclined gage
incombustible
incorporation
index contour
index horizon
index mineral
Indian summer
indicated ore
indigo copper
indoor stroke
induction log
inequilibrium
injected hole
in-line valve
insecticide
inside kicker
inside marker
inside reamer
insular shelf
insular slope
interior span
interpolation
Intertrappean
intracellular
intratelluric
introgression
inverted fold
ionic bonding
iron refining
iron sulfides
ironstone cap
isocarbon map
isochromosome
isodimorphous
isodrosotherm
isogenic line
isogonic line
isoporic line
isostructural
Istrian stone
jackhead pump
jackknife rig
jacupirangite
jagging board
jasperization
jerking table
jet hydraulic
jet streams
jetting drill
jig indicator
johachidolite
Jolly balance
Joy microdyne
jubilee wagon
Judson powder
Jupiter steel
kalistrontite

kaolinization
kappa carbide
Karlsbad twin
kerogen shale
keronigritite
kettle bottom
kickoff point
kidney sulfur
kilbrickenite
kilkenny coal
kilobase (kb)
kilowatt-hour
kin selection
kindly ground
Kiruna method
knobbing fire
knotted slate
knuckle joint
Kollen garnet
kratochvilite
Kroll process
Krupp process
kwashiorkor
kyanophyllite
Labrador rock
ladder sollar
ladle furnace
Lambert's Law
lamellar flow
lame-skirting
lamp repairer
landing shaft
lang lay rope
lanyon shield
Larsen's pile
lashing chain
lattice water
law of motion
layer-loading
lead feldspar
lead motorman
lead selenide
lead silicate
leading place
leading stone
lead-well man
lechosos opal
left lang lay
left long lay
lengenbachite
length of lay
lens grinding
Leopard stone
lepidoblastic
lepidocrocite
Lepidodendron
leucitohedron
leucochalcite
leucoperthite

leucophyllite
leucosphenite
level surface
levelling rod
lifter spring
lifting block
lifting guard
light mineral
light railway
lightning gap
lignitic coal
limbic system
lime feldspar
limit of draw
lindstroemite
line brattice
line drilling
line of creep
line of force
line of sight
lineal travel
linear tetrad
link conveyor
linkage group
linoleic acid
listric fault
lithification
lithiophilite
lithiophorite
lithofracteur
lithoglyptics
lithophosphor
littoral zone
liver pyrites
livingstonite
load transfer
loaded filter
loader runner
loading chute
loading point
loading ratio
local current
location plan
location work
locking bolts
lockup clutch
logging chain
logging tongs
loosening bar
low explosive
low-level jet
lucid attrite
Luhrig vanner
Lurgi process
Lurmann front
luthos lazuli
lynx sapphire
machine miner
machine mines

machine screw
mackintoshite
macrodiagonal
macromolecule
macroporosity
maculose rock
Madeira topaz
Magma chamber
magnesia alum
magnesia mica
magnetic bort
magnetic flux
magnetic plug
magnetic pole
magnetosphere
magnochromite
main conveyor
main crosscut
Maine sampler
makeup bunker
makeup medium
malleablizing
Manebach twin
manganepidote
manganese ore
manhole cover
manual takeup
marathon mill
margarosanite
marginal zone
marine mining
marlstone ore
marmarization
marmorization
mass movement
mass shooting
master hauler
mastershifter
Maxton screen
measures head
mechanization
medium solids
Megabase (Mb)
megalopolis
melanostibite
melting house
melting point
merchant iron
merosymmetric
mesh aperture
mesh fraction
mesh of grind
meta-alunogen
meta-autunite
metabentonite
metahewettite
metakahlerite
metalimestone
metallic bond

metallic iron
metalliferous
metallization
metallography
metaschoepite
metastrengite
metavariscite
metazeunerite
meteoric iron
meteorologist
Michigan slip
microchemical
microfelsitic
microgranular
microhardness
microperthite
microporosity
microzonation
midocean rift
migmatization
millgrit rock
mill-head ore
milliangstrom
millibar (mb)
milling grade
milling width
milling yield
mine conveyor
mine drainage
mine examiner
mine motorman
mine surveyor
mineral bruto
mineral claim
mineral entry
mineral fibre
mineral field
mineral group
mineral lease
mineral paint
mineral resin
mineral right
mineral water
minerogenesis
miner's right
miners' rules
miner's wedge
mine-run coal
mine-run mica
minor element
minus station
minute of arc
miogesyncline
Mississippian
mitochondrion
mixed cements
mixed crystal
mobile loader
mock-infected

modeling clay
modifier gene
Mohr envelope
Mohr's theory
molders' rule
molding frame
molengraafite
molybdomenite
monazite sand
monkey wrench
monochromatic
monomineralic
monoschematic
Montana agate
moorland peat
moose pasture
morphogenesis
mortification
mosaic silver
mother liquor
motion driver
motive column
mottled slate
mountain cork
mountain flax
mountain meal
mountain milk
mountain soap
mountain wood
mounting pipe
muck shifting
muckle hammer
mud viscosity
mud wall cake
mudcap method
mudstone trap
multiple dike
multiple shot
multiple sill
multiple twin
mummification
Munroe effect
Murex process
Muscovy glass
Musso process
mutant allele
mutation rate
nailhead spar
Nansen bottle
national grid
native copper
natrochalcite
natrojarosite
natural glass
natural paper
natural resin
natural scale
natural slope
nautical mile

negative rake
nematoblastic
neo-darwinism
nephelinitoid
nerve impulse
neurotoxins
neutral point
N-frame brace
nickel glance
nickel pyrite
nickeliferous
night emerald
nitrification
nitrogen base
nitroglycerin
nitrous oxide
no-cut rounds
nominal price
nonconformity
noncoring bit
nonspin cable
nonstructural
normal stress
normal theory
Northern blot
Norwegian cut
nucleoprotein
nugget effect
nuisance dust
oblique block
oblique fault
oblique joint
Oceanic crust
oceanic front
offshore wind
oil flotation
oligosiderite
Oliver filter
one-part line
one-piece set
opalized wood
open canopy
open system
open traverse
opencast mine
opening stock
optical glass
ore developed
ore expectant
ore separator
organogenesis
oriented core
orifice meter
original hole
original lead
orthochlorite
orthodolomite
orthomagmatic
orthopinacoid

orthopyroxene
outcrop water
outflow winds
output device
outside stone
outside upset
outwash plain
overdominance
overlap fault
overrun brake
oversize core
oversize hole
overspringing
oxide mineral
oxide of iron
oxidized zone
oxyhornblende
Pacific suite
packing gland
paddle loader
paddle washer
pahoehoe lava
palaeocurrent
palaeoecology
palaeontology
palaeoseismic
palaeozoology
Paleozoic Era
panel barrier
panel slicing
panel testing
panel working
parabutlerite
parallel drum
parallel flow
parallel fold
parallelogram
paramagnetism
paraschoepite
paratellurite
parcel of air
Parian marble
particle size
parting flask
parting glass
parting slate
parts of line
party foreman
party manager
passing point
passing track
passive fault
passive metal
paste pumping
pastoralist
patent survey
patented rope
patio process
pearlite iron

peat blasting
pebble gravel
pebble powder
pedestal rock
pediment pass
pedimentation
peg structure
pellet powder
pendulum mill
Pennsylvanian
peptidyl site
percent error
percent yield
perched water
perfect frame
permanent set
permanent way
Permotriassic
PEST sequence
Petersen grab
petrification
petrochemical
petrolo-shale
phase control
phase diagram
phase shifter
Phenylalanine
Phleger corer
phosphorylate
photoelectric
phreatic line
phreatic zone
phytoplankton
picking chute
picking table
picrochromite
pillar caving
pillar robber
pin timbering
pioneer bench
pipe coupling
pipe elevator
pipe friction
pipe sampling
pitch working
pitching seam
placer ground
placer mining
plagioclastic
planetary lap
planetesimals
plank tubbing
plaster stone
plastic limit
plastic solid
plastic state
plastic yield
plate cleaner
platinic gold

platiniridium
plumbocalcite
plumboferrite
plumbogummite
plunger press
plus distance
plutonic rock
pneumatic jig
pneumatic ram
pneumatogenic
pneumatolysis
pneumatolytic
pocket hunter
pocket of gas
podzolization
point kriging
point of frog
poky mutation
polarity gene
pole strength
polirschiefer
polychroilite
polycistronic
polynigritite
poorly sorted
pop a boulder
pop-off valve
pore pressure
porous ground
porphyroblast
porphyroclast
Portland beds
positive rake
potential ore
potter's clay
pound-calorie
pouring basin
powder barrel
powder factor
powder monkey
powdered coal
power grizzly
power station
power takeoff
prairie soils
precious opal
Precipitation
premature set
present value
pressed amber
pressed cameo
pressed copal
pressure arch
pressure bump
pressure dome
pressure drop
pressure gage
pressure head
pressure ring

pressure wave
pressure wire
pretensioning
primary blast
primary coast
primary creep
primary metal
primary phase
primary shaft
primer charge
priming valve
Prins process
process scrap
project plans
prokaryotic
propeller fan
proportioning
protodolomite
protomylonite
proximity log
Prussian blue
pseudoboleite
pseudobreccia
pseudoleucite
pseudovolcano
psilomelanite
pteropod ooze
public domain
puddled steel
pulp dilution
pulverization
pump pressure
pumping shaft
purple blende
pyrheliometer
pyrophysalite
pyrostilpnite
quadrilateral
quarry powder
quartering in
quartz latite
quartz sinter
quartziferous
quenching tub
quinquevalent
rabbling tool
rack railroad
racking table
radial strain
radial stress
radiation fog
radioactivity
radiophyllite
radon progeny
rain shadow
raise climber
Raleigh's law
random mating
random sample

Rankine scale
ratchet drill
rate of grade
raw feed coal
Rayleigh wave
reaction line
reaction pair
reaction rate
reading frame
real property
real-time PCR
reaming pilot
reaming shell
recarburizing
recharge area
recharge zone
reciprocating
recirculation
reclamation
recombination
rectification
red manganese
reduced level
redundant DNA
refining heat
reforestation
refractometer
refrigeration
regulations
reheater load
relative time
relay haulage
relieving cut
remediation
remolded soil
rensselaerite
repeat region
reporter gene
reserve fault
reserved coal
residual clay
resin rodlets
resin-in-pulp
resinite coal
resinous coal
restoration
Retger's salt
return period
return stroke
reverberation
reverse fault
rheid folding
rheostat rope
rhodochrosite
rhombarsenite
ribosomal RNA
rib-side gate
rib-side pack
Richter scale

66

ridge terrace
right running
right-lateral
rinsing water
rise and fall
rising column
RNA replicase
roadside pack
roadway cable
rock cleavage
rock cone bit
rock cuttings
rock fracture
rock hardness
rock pedestal
rock pressure
rock sediment
rock splitter
rockbridgeite
rock-dust man
rocker bottom
rocker shovel
rock-fill dam
rocking lever
rod clearance
roentgenogram
Roesing wires
roll operator
roller screen
rolling plant
roof pressure
roof stringer
room conveyor
rope diameter
rope plucking
rotary boring
rotary dumper
rotary screen
rough diamond
roughing hole
roughing mill
roughing tool
rounding tool
rubbing stone
runback water
runic texture
running block
rupture front
rutherfordine
safety factor
safety powder
safety switch
sag structure
salvage count
salvage value
sampler liner
sampling pipe
Samson loader
sand bearings

sand diamonds
sand leaching
sandy alumina
sapropel-clay
sapropsammite
satellite DNA
satellite RNA
saturated air
scale cleaner
scalenohedron
schafarzikite
schiefer spar
schiller spar
schiller-fels
schreibersite
schuchardtite
Schumann plot
scintillation
scissor fault
scorification
Scotch pebble
scraper hoist
screen sizing
screened coal
screw shackle
second mining
second outlet
second weight
second worker
secondary air
secondary ash
secondary fan
sediment tube
sediment vein
sedimentation
sedimentology
seismic drill
seismic event
seismic focus
seismic noise
seismic waves
selected fill
self-assembly
semiconductor
semiwater gas
sensible heat
sensitiveness
septechlorite
series firing
serum albumin
service shaft
set of timber
settling cone
settling pond
settling sand
settling tank
severance tax
severed lands
shaft raising

shaft section
shaft sinking
shaft station
shaker chutes
shaker screen
shaking table
Shanklin sand
shaped charge
shatter index
shear failure
shear modulus
sheet deposit
sheeting caps
sheeting pile
shield basalt
shindle stone
shipper shaft
shock loading
shooting boat
shore terrace
short section
shot blasting
shothole plug
shovel loader
shovel trough
shutdown time
shutoff valve
Siberian ruby
side shearing
side-hitching
sidelong reef
sideroferrite
sideronatrite
sidewall core
sieve shakers
sieve texture
signal system
siliceous ore
silicious ore
silicon steel
silver glance
single outlet
sinking plant
size analysis
size fraction
size selector
sizing screen
skimming gate
skin friction
skip operator
skull cracker
slope failure
sorosilicates
Southern blot
space lattice
specific heat
star activity
static moment
static switch

stay-bolt tap
steam thawing
steatite talc
steel erector
steel support
steenstrupine
step-face bit
stepped stope
stereoisomers
stewardship
stick loading
stilling well
stilpnomelane
stoichiometry
stone content
stone dusting
stone tubbing
stope driller
stope scraper
stoping drill
stoping width
stopper maker
straight work
stranded rope
stratigrapher
stratigraphic
Stratovolcano
stratum plain
stray current
stretch fault
strike a lead
strike valley
string survey
stringer lead
stringer lode
stringer sets
stringer zone
strip packing
strong motion
stub switches
stull stoping
stump pulling
subconchoidal
subindividual
subvital gene
subweathering
suction blast
sugary quartz
sulfidization
sulfoarsenite
sulfonic acid
sulfur mining
super section
superexchange
superposition
surface break
surface drift
surface lines
surface slope

surface speed
surface water
Svedberg unit
swedenborgite
sweepwashings
swing parting
swivel trough
symmetry axis
syndicate man
target theory
tectosilicate
temperature
tetratype (T)
thermal plume
thermocline
Third World
thorn shrub
thymine dimer
tidal current
topoisomerase
trace element
trailing edge
transcription
transcriptome
translocation
transpiration
transposition
trophic level
troposphere
type II error
unshared pair
Vapor (water)
visual cortex
volcanic bomb
volcanic cone
volcanic dome
volcanic dust
Volcanic Neck
volcanic rock
water cycle
water table
Wilm's tumour
wind abrasion
zona reaction

12

ABC proteins
abernathyite
absolute age
abyssal zone
acceleration
accelerogram
acceptor arm
acceptor end
accretionary
accumulation
acetyl group

acid process
acidic oxide
aclinic line
acoustic log
acreage rent
active agent
active entry
active fault
active layer
actual yield
air pressure
Aleutian low
alkali metal
alkali rocks
allozygosity
alluvial fan
ampangabeite
amphidiploid
anastomosing
anemoclastic
angle of dip
angle of nip
angle trough
animal model
annual layer
annual value
annular kiln
anode copper
anode effect
anode metals
anorthoclase
anthracology
anthraconite
anticipation
antiparallel
apparent dip
apron feeder
aqua ammonia
aquifer test
arc shooting
Arctic suite
arfvedsonite
argillaceous
argyropyrite
argyrythrose
Arizona ruby
arm conveyor
arsenopyrite
asparagolite
asphalt rock
assay office
assembly rod
assimilation
astatization
astrogeology
asymmetrical
asymptomatic
atomic plane
ATP synthase

augen gneiss
augen schist
auger boring
auger mining
aurichalcite
austempering
authigenesis
authigenetic
autoantibody
autoimmunity
autozygosity
axial figure
axial stream
azure quartz
Babel quartz
back balance
back brusher
back filling
back heading
back of lode
back-end man
backing sand
backset beds
bacteriocide
bacteriostat
baffle board
baffle plate
balance brow
balance rope
balance shot
ball bearing
ball grinder
ball milling
balling tool
banded agate
bank measure
banner cloud
bar diggings
barbertonite
barbiturates
barchan dune
barge loader
barrier gate
barrier reef
barring down
Barry mining
basal arkose
basaluminite
base bullion
base failure
base station
basic lining
basonomelane
bastard cauk
batch feeder
bathyal zone
bathypelagic
batter level
battered set

baumhauerite
baymouth bar
beach mining
beach placer
beam compass
bearing door
becquerelite
bedding down
bedrock test
beehive coke
beehive kiln
beetle stone
Beilby layer
Belgian oven
Bell process
bellingerite
bclt cleaner
belt tripper
helyankinite
bench gravel
bench height
bench placer
bend tangent
Benioff zone
benthic zone
Bermuda high
bernardinite
berzelianite
Bessemer ore
beta blocker
betekhtinite
bichromatics
binary alloy
binary cycle
binding bolt
biochemistry
biodiversity
biogeography
biomass fuel
black garnet
black liquor
black powder
black silver
black smoker
bladder pump
blanket feed
blanket sand
blanket vein
blast hearth
blasting cap
blasting log
blasting mat
blasting oil
bottle cells
boulder size
bronchoscopy
bulk element
cannabinoids
capacitation

carbohydrase
carbohydrate
carbon cycle
carbon ratio
carnivores
carotid rete
cDNA library
cell lineage
Cenozoic Era
chalcopyrite
Charles' Law
Charon phage
Chattermarks
chemiosmosis
chemotherapy
chlorenchyma
chromocenter
cis-dominant
cladogenesis
clastic rock
coactivators
coat protein
codon repeat
cohesive end
cold front
cold glacier
commensalism
common law
composting
condensation
conductivity
conglomerate
constitutive
contour line
coordination
crystal form
cytochrome C
cytogenetics
cytoskeleton
debris slide
delamination
demography
denaturation
desalination
dimerization
disaccharide
displacement
dissociation
distributary
distribution
domesticated
dot blotting
double helix
droogmansite
dry adiabats
ecotourism
Ekman spiral
electrolysis
emigration

endonuclease
energy level
engine plane
enthalpy (H)
entry driver
entry stumps
epidemiology
equigranular
eriochalcite
escape shaft
etch pattern
eugosyncline
excess spoil
excitotoxins
exploitation
expressivity
exsolutional
extensometer
extinction
extralateral
F generation
face haulage
face of hole
faceted spur
facies fauna
Fagersta cut
fairchildite
fairfieldite
fall streaks
falling slag
false bottom
false galena
false gossan
fan cleavage
fan shooting
fanglomerate
fast country
fast junking
fata morgana
fatty luster
fault casing
fault groove
fault growth
fault inlier
fault mosaic
fault striae
fault strike
fault system
fault trough
feather alum
feather edge
feather ends
fee engineer
feed control
feed spindle
feldspar jig
feldspathide
feldspathoid
fermentation

fernandinite
Ferrel's law
ferreto zone
ferrinatrite
ferroedenite
ferrosilicon
fibrillation
fibroblastic
fibroferrite
fibrous peat
fiery dragon
figure stone
filter cloth
filter press
filter stick
fine grinder
fine-grained
finger board
finger chute
finger raise
finish grade
fire setting
firing cable
firing point
first mining
first motion
fishtail bit
fissure vein
fix-bitumens
fixed allele
fixed carbon
fixed guides
fixed screen
flagstaffite
flake copper
flake sulfur
flame spinel
flange wheel
flaxseed ore
fleischerite
flinty slate
float copper
float sulfur
floatability
flocculating
flocculation
flood basalt
flour copper
flour gypsum
flow banding
flow breccia
flow folding
flow texture
flowage fold
fluid column
fluid volume
fluorapatite
fluoredenite
fluorescence

fluxing lime
flying veins
focal sphere
fold breccia
followup tag
food chain
footprinting
foraminifera
forcing lift
foreign coal
foreset beds
forge cinder
form contour
formula unit
fossil copal
fossil flour
fossil fuels
fossil paper
fossil resin
foundry sand
four-way dip
fractography
fragile site
free radical
frontal wave
frost action
fuel cells
Fujita scale
funnel cloud
gamma rays
gastrulation
GC-rich area
gene cloning
gene linkage
gene mapping
gene product
gene therapy
genetic code
genetic load
geotechnical
giant nuclei
Gibbs energy
Giemsa stain
glacial soil
glacial till
glaciomarine
glass schorl
Glauber salt
glaucopyrite
Gli proteins
global scale
glomerocryst
Glossopteris
glucose test
glushinskite
glyptography
gold amalgam
gold cupride
gold milling

golden beryl
golden ocher
golden stone
goldfieldite
Gondwanaland
got-on-knobs
gouging shot
grab dredger
grab sampler
grading test
Graham ratio
grain growth
grainer salt
granite wash
granoblastic
granodiorite
graphic gold
gravity feed
gravity road
grease stone
grease table
greasy blaes
green charge
green marble
greenlandite
grid azimuth
Griffin mill
grindability
grinding aid
grip the rib
grooved drum
ground cover
ground fault
ground noise
ground plate
ground state
ground water
ground waves
growth curve
growth phase
guard magnet
guard screen
guide fossil
guide pulley
guide runner
gum dynamite
gypsum plate
Haase system
haelleflinta
hair zeolite
half blinded
half headers
Hall process
halotrichite
hammer drill
hammochrysos
hand cobbing
hand filling
hand scraper

hanging coal
hanging deal
hanging sets
hanging wall
hard heading
hard sorting
harmful dust
hartschiefer
haueynophyre
haulage boss
haulage cars
haulage clip
haulage drum
haulage hand
haulage rope
head section
heading seam
heading side
heading wall
heap closure
heap rinsing
heat balance
heated stone
heating back
heavy ground
heavy metals
hedenbergite
hemimorphism
hendersonite
heritability
heteroduplex
heterogenite
heterokaryon
heteroplasmy
heterosphere
heterotomous
heterozygote
high furnace
high voltage
high-grading
hinged apron
hitch cutter
holding rope
hole through
hollow quoin
holmquistite
homeoblastic
homeo-domain
homeothermal
homocysteine
hopper table
host element
hot material
hugger drive
Humboldt jig
humite group
hunting coal
hurdle sheet
hurricanes

hutch mender
hydrobiotite
hydrocyclone
hydrogen ion
hydrostatics
hydrotalcite
hydrothermal
hydrozincite
hyperfusible
hypermelanic
hypertension
hypogene ore
hypoglycemia
hypothalamus
hypothesis
ice concrete
Iceland spar
igneous rock
ignitability
igniter cord
illegal mine
ilmenorutile
impact glass
incandescent
incline hole
inclinometer
incontinence
incrustation
index fossil
Indian title
inert primer
inferred ore
infiltration
inflammation
infusion gun
ingot header
inhaul cable
inherent ash
inholdings
initial face
inner mantle
inquartation
insect cells
inside slope
inside stone
inside upset
insolation
intercalated
intercooling
interference
interkinesis
intermediate
intermontane
intersection
interstitial
intumescence
invagination
invasiveness
invert level

invert strut
invertebrate
inwall brick
iodide metal
ion channels
ion exchange
ionic radius
ionosphere
iron furnace
iron monarch
iron olivine
iron sampler
iron vitriol
irrespirable
Isbell table
isochore map
isodiametric
Isontic line
isoschizomer
jackhead pit
jackhead set
jeffersonite
jet drilling
jet piercing
jetting pump
johannsenite
johnstrupite
joint system
Jones riffle
judge rapper
junction box
kaemmererite
kaliophilite
kame terrace
karnasurtite
karpinskyite
karyokinesis
Kast furnace
katamorphism
Kelly filter
Kelvin scale
kentsmithite
keratinocyte
kerned stone
ketoacidosis
kettle dross
keyhole slot
kicker stone
kidney stone
killed steel
kiln cleaner
kinetic head
Kirkup table
klockmannite
knife switch
knipovichite
knistersalze
knockoff bit
knockout man

koehler lamp
Koepe sheave
Koepe system
Koepe winder
korzhinskite
kuprojarosit
labeled atom
labuntsovite
ladle filler
lagergestein
lagged liner
lambda phage
lambda plate
lamella roof
laminar flow
lamp cleaner
lamp station
lamprobolite
lamprophyric
lamproschist
land compass
land plaster
landslides
lapis lazuli
lapis matrix
larderellite
large nuclei
lateral draw
latex cement
Laue diagram
lava breccia
law of sines
lazarevicite
leached zone
lead niobate
lead sulfide
lead vitriol
leading edge
leading wire
leakage halo
leaky mutant
leatherstone
lefkasbestos
left-lateral
leonhardtite
leopard rock
lepidomelane
leptothermal
letter stone
leucitophyre
leucophanite
level course
lichenometry
life of mine
life science
lifted index
lifter holes
light alloys
light burden

light figure
limit charge
limit switch
lindackerite
line timbers
linear model
lining sight
linked veins
lip of shaft
lipoxygenase
liquefaction
liquid glass
lithidionite
lithifaction
lithium mica
lithogenesis
lithogenetic
litmus paper
little giant
little winds
load dropper
loaded wheel
loading boom
loading boss
loading head
loading pick
loading pole
loading ramp
locked fault
Lohmannizing
lok batanite
lomonosovite
London force
long section
loop circuit
loop haulage
looping mill
loose ground
loss of vend
lost closure
low red-heat
low velocity
Lowden drier
luciferinase
Lueders line
lueneburgite
lumber scale
luminescence
lunar crater
luxullianite
Lydian stone
macfarlanite
macgovernite
machine boss
machine tool
machine wall
macroclimate
macromeritic
magnetic dip

magnetometer
magnoferrite
magnussonite
mahogany ore
mailly stone
main endings
main haulage
mains firing
makeup water
malinowskite
malleability
malnutrition
Manebach law
manganblende
manless face
mansfieldite
marginal sea
marine humus
maritime air
marker block
Marsaut lamp
Marsh funnel
mass balance
mass density
mass diagram
mass profile
mass spectra
massifs long
massive rock
mass-wasting
master alloy
master joint
matrix metal
mean calorie
meander belt
meander line
medical lock
mediosilicic
meeting post
meizoseismal
melanasphalt
melanocratic
melanotekite
mellow amber
melting hole
melting shop
melting zone
mephitic air
mephitic gas
Merrit plate
mesh texture
mesosphere
Mesozoic Era
metabitumite
metabolism
metabrushite
metacinnabar
metadolomite
metal mining

metal powder
metallic ore
metallograph
metallometry
metallurgist
metamorphism
metasapropel
metasediment
metasomatism
metasomatite
metavolcanic
metering pin
methanephone
methanometer
method study
metric carat
Mexican onyx
miarolithite
Michigan cut
microballoon
microbreccia
microclastic
microclimate
microelement
microfluidal
microgeology
micrographic
micromeritic
micrometrics
microsection
microtubules
microvitrain
middletonite
milky quartz
mill furnace
mill sampler
minasragrite
mine captain
mine foreman
mine opening
mine tractor
mine wireman
mined strata
mined volume
mineragraphy
mineral acre
mineral belt
mineral deed
mineral fuel
mineral land
mineral salt
mineral vein
mineral wool
mineralogist
miner's dial
miner's horn
miner's inch
miner's lamp
miner's lung

miner's pick
mining claim
mining ditch
mining title
mining under
mining width
minnesotaite
mirror plane
mirror stone
misfire hole
missed round
mitigation
mitochondria
mixing depth
mixing ratio
mix-in-place
mobile crane
mobile drill
mobile hoist
Mohr balance
moisture man
molded cameo
molding hole
Mond process
monkey board
monkey chock
monkey drift
monkey shaft
monkey winch
Monongahelan
monopyroxene
Montana ruby
montebrasite
monticellite
moorband pan
motion study
motive power
motor cortex
motor driver
motor neuron
motor nipper
mottled iron
mountain tar
MS connector
mud blasting
mule skinner
mushroom jib
mustard gold
mutagenicity
mylonization
name of lode
narrow place
narrow stall
native state
native water
natural coke
natural face
natural sand
NCB recorder

neomesselite
nephelometry
neritic zone
nesosilicate
nesquehonite
neurogenesis
neutral axis
neutral salt
neutral zone
New York rod
Newlyn datum
nickel bloom
nickel green
nickel ocher
nickel oxide
nickel steel
nimbostratus
nitrocalcite
nitrogelatin
nominal area
nominal size
noncoal mine
non-parental
nontectonite
nonvitrified
normal depth
normal fault
normal field
normal price
normal scale
normal shift
norstrandite
notch effect
nozzle brick
nuçe ardente
nucleic acid
Nuée ardente
nugget model
Oamaru stone
object glass
oblique slip
ocean mixing
ocean trench
oil reserves
oligist iron
oligotrophic
olivine rock
olivinophyre
on short awn
on the track
onshore wind
opaque-durit
open circuit
open lagging
open working
opencut mine
opening shot
openpit mine
optical flat

optical sign
optimization
ordinary ray
ore blending
ore district
ore dressing
ore in sight
ore province
ore sampling
organic soil
organic test
oriented bit
original dip
orthoclasite
orthoclastic
orthorhombic
oryctologist
osarizawaite
oscillograph
oscilloscope
Osteoporosis
output shaft
outside face
outside wall
outside work
overbreaking
overcharging
overcrossing
overdrilling
overgrinding
oversize rod
Owen process
oxidized ore
oxyacetylene
oxygen index
oxygen lance
oxygen sag
oxygen steel
Pachuca tank
Pacific high
pack builder
paddle mixer
palingenesis
palygorskite
pan conveyor
pantellerite
pan-type car
parallel cut
paramagnetic
paramorphism
parasitology
paratacamite
Parr formula
particulates
Pascal's law
passing boss
patchiness
path diagram
pay material

pea iron ore
peacock coal
peak loading
pearl sinter
peat machine
pebble armor
Pele's tears
Pelton wheel
pencil stone
pendletonite
penning gate
pentahydrite
peptide bond
peraluminous
periodic law
permafrost
permanganate
permeability
petering out
petrifaction
petrofabrics
petrogenesis
petrographer
petrographic
petrophysics
pH regulator
pharmacolite
phase system
phosphorogen
photogeology
phototropism
phreatic gas
physical map
pick breaker
pick carrier
pick machine
pickeringite
picking belt
piece weight
Piggot corer
Pike process
pile sinking
pileus cloud
pillar burst
pillar drive
pillar split
pillow block
pilot burner
pilot method
pilot reamer
pilot tunnel
Pilz furnace
pimple metal
pinching out
pioneer road
pioneer wave
pipe fitting
pipe sampler
piston corer

piston speed
pit sampling
pitch circle
pitch length
pitching bar
placer claim
plagiohedral
plane course
plane figure
plane strain
plane stress
plane tender
plaster mill
plastic clay
plastic flow
plastic soil
plastic zone
Plast-Sponge
plate feeder
plate former
plate girder
plenargyrite
pleomorphism
plugged crib
plumbiferous
plumose mica
plunger case
plunger lift
plunger pump
pluripotency
pluvial lake
point defect
point driver
point source
Polar Viking
polarization
poling board
polled stone
pollen grain
polyargyrite
polymorphism
polyribosome
polysomatism
poppet valve
pop-shooting
population
porcelaneous
porcellanite
portal crane
positive ore
positive ray
positivism
possible ore
post puncher
potato stone
pottery spar
pouring gate
powder chest
powder house

powder metal
powdered ore
power barrow
power factor
power rammer
power shovel
prairie soil
precipitator
preheat zone
preselective
preservative
presplitting
pressure fan
prestressing
pricking bar
primary cell
primary clay
primary coil
primary mill
primary wave
primary zone
priming coat
priming tube
processioner
processivity
product rule
productivity
profilograph
project data
proof stress
propel shaft
property man
protoclastic
proton donor
proving hole
proving ring
prussic acid
pseudoallele
pseudogalena
psychrometer
psychrometry
puddingstone
pulp balance
pulp climate
pulp density
pulsator jig
pump chamber
pump station
pumping head
punch mining
puppet valve
pure bending
pure culture
putrefaction
pyralmandite
pyricaustate
pyritiferous
pyritization
pyritohedron

pyrobelonite
pyroclastics
pyrognostics
pyromorphite
pyrophyllite
pyrosmaltite
pyrostibnite
pyroxmangite
quadrivalent
quantitation
quantitative
quaquaversal
quarry drill
quarry floor
quarry waste
quarry water
quarter line
quarter post
quartz claim
quartz glass
quartz index
quartz wedge
radial dikes
radial drill
radioelement
radioisotope
radius ratio
ragged rolls
rail riffles
rain chamber
rainforest
raised shaft
raking strut
RAM mutation
ram operator
random stone
rank variety
rating flume
rattle boxes
rattler test
raw dolomite
raw material
Raymond mill
reaction rim
reamer shell
reamer stone
reaming ring
recalescence
record table
red antimony
red hematite
red iron ore
red lead ore
red lime mud
red orpiment
red zinc ore
redingtonite
reduced iron
refined iron

reflectivity
refuse rotor
regeneration
regional dip
rejuvenation
relative age
release mesh
relief holes
relief valve
repose angle
reserve base
residual oil
resilience
resiliometer
retinasphalt
return water
revegetation
reverse bend
reverse feed
reverse gear
RFLP mapping
rheomorphism
rhodium gold
rhombic mica
rhombohedron
ribbon brake
ridge fillet
right-of-way
rimmed steel
ring complex
ring crusher
Ring of Fire
ring tension
Rinman scale
ripple board
ripple index
ripple marks
rise heading
rising shaft
rittingerite
river mining
river pebble
river quartz
river system
rivet heater
rivet tester
riving seams
road cleaner
roaster slag
robot loader
rock asphalt
rock bolting
rock crusher
rock crystal
rock cycle
rock driller
rock drivage
rock dusting
rock failure

rock filling
rock glacier
rock kindred
rock leather
rocker sieve
rocking beam
rod coupling
rod elevator
rod friction
roll crusher
roll orebody
rolled metal
rolled plate
roller chain
Roman cement
roof bolting
roof control
roof cutting
roof pendant
root station
roof testing
roofing hole
rooseveltite
root deposit
rope driving
rope haulage
Ropp furnace
rose diagram
rose vitriol
rosin blende
Rossby waves
rotary drier
rotary drill
rotary fault
rotary table
rough ground
rougher cell
row shooting
royal barren
rubinglimmer
ruby alumina
ruby arsenic
ruling grade
run-in table
runner stick
running kiln
running lift
running rope
running sand
run-to-waste
rupture line
rupture zone
saddle block
safety catch
safety chain
safety check
safety clamp
safety glass
safety joint

safety latch
safety light
safety tools
safety valve
sal ammoniac
salable coal
saliniferous
salinization
salt furnace
salt prairie
sampler head
sampler tube
sampling bag
sampling tip
sand calcite
sand crusher
sand crystal
sandblasting
sanmartinite
saphir d'eau
sargent tube
sarsen stone
scale copper
scatter pile
schapbachite
schaum earth
scheteligite
schmiederite
schrotterite
schuilingite
sclerotinite
scotch block
Scotch topaz
scout boring
scrap picker
scrap sorter
scraper plow
screen chute
screen cloth
screen plate
screw feeder
seam contour
section boss
seepage line
segmentation
seismic area
seismic belt
seismic wave
seismic zone
select round
selenjoseite
self-rescuer
self-shooter
seligmannite
semifusinite
semiprecious
semivitreous
senarmontite
sense strand

series shots
serpentinite
setting plug
setting ring
settling box
settling pit
settling vat
sex reversal
sexual spore
shaft bottom
shaft casing
shaft collar
shaft guides
shaft lining
shaft pillar
shaft pocket
shaft siding
shaft signal
shaft survey
shaft tackle
shaft tunnel
shaking down
shale screen
shale shaker
shaley blaes
shallow well
shape factor
shaped stone
sharp gravel
shatter belt
shear bursts
shear of ore
shear strain
shear stress
shearing jib
sheave block
sheave wheel
sheep silver
sheep's-foot
sheet ground
sheet piling
sheet quarry
sheeted vein
sheeted zone
shelf quarry
shelter hole
sherardizing
sherry topaz
shin plaster
shipping ore
shivery post
shock losses
shoepite-III
short column
short period
shot instant
shot samples
shothole log
shovel dozer

shovel front
sick mercury
side shelves
side slicing
side stoping
sidehill cut
sideromelane
siderosphere
sidetracking
Sierra Leone
sighting hub
sigma factor
silent chain
silica brick
silification
silky luster
simatic rock
similar fold
Simplex pump
single block
single entry
single sling
sinker drill
sinking fire
sinking head
sinking lift
sinking pump
sinter plant
sinuous flow
size consist
sizing punch
skid-mounted
skip haulage
skirt plates
skleropelite
sklodowskite
skutterudite
slabbing cut
slack hauler
slag blanket
slickensides
sociobiology
soil horizon
soil profile
solar system
solifluction
somatic cell
somatostatin
SOS response
spermatocyte
stathmograph
static level
staurotypous
steady point
steady state
steam hammer
steam shovel
steam winder
steel casing

steel guides
steel needle
steel puller
steinmannite
stemming rod
stereosphere
stereovision
sternbergite
stetefeldite
sticky limit
stillwellite
stinger ream
stoichimetry
stone butter
stone clunch
stone duster
stone fields
stone gobber
stone hammer
stone of ore
stone planer
stone sawyer
stone spavin
stone weight
stone yellow
stony clunch
stope pillar
stoperperson
stopper hole
straightaway
strain break
strain burst
strain sheet
strata gases
strata-bound
straticulate
stratigraphy
stratosphere
streak plate
stream order
streamlining
strike fault
strike shift
strip mining
strip sample
strip thrust
stromatolite
stromatolith
stromeyerite
strong force
strontianite
stuffing box
Styrian jade
subgraywacke
subsidence
subsoil plow
substitution
substructure
subtense bar

subterranean
sucked stone
sucking pump
suction head
suction lift
sulfate test
sulfide zone
sulfur group
sump cleaner
Sunday stone
supercharger
supercoiling
superdusting
superlattice
superpushing
supply cager
surface area
surface clay
surface lift
surface loss
surface plan
surface wave
surge bunker
surge hopper
surge pulley
survey meter
survivorship
suture joint
swallet hole
sweating out
Swedish iron
sweep plates
swing loader
swing radius
swing roller
switch plate
switch point
switch throw
sycee silver
syenodiorite
synadelphite
synchroneity
synclinorium
synkinematic
synteny test
T Lymphocyte
teleological
telolecithal
teratogens
testosterone
tetracycline
thermosphere
thin section
thrust fault
time history
trans-acting
transcytosis
transduction
transfection

transfer RNA
transformant
transversion
triple point
tropopause
trunk stream
tsunamigenic
type I error
unconformity
urban sprawl
urbanization
valley train
vaporization
ventral horn
volcanic arc
volcanic ash
Volvocaceans
warm front
warm glacier
weathering
wilderness
wind farms
withdrawal
X chromosome
Y chromosome

11

abandonment
Abbe theory
ablatograph
Abney level
abysmal sea
accelerator
access road
accumulator
acesulfames
acetic acid
acid lining
acid sludge
acidic lava
acidization
acrocentric
active site
adult-onset
aftershocks
aggradation
agriculture
air density
aldosterone
allergens
alpha decay
alpha helix
altocumulus
altostratus
amber codon
amino group
amniography

amphetamine
amphibolite
amphipathic
anamorphism
anaphase II
anchor bolt
anchor jack
anchor prop
andersonite
anencephaly
angelellite
angle brace
angle level
anisodesmic
anisometric
anisotropic
annabergite
anode scrap
anode slime
anodic zone
anorthosite
anthocyanin
anthracitic
anthracosis
anticyclone
antioxidant
aplogranite
apomagmatic
apophyllite
aporhyolite
application
Appolt oven
apron plate
aquaculture
arable land
Aragon spar
arborescent
arc furnace
arc welding
arch blocks
arch girder
archenteron
Arctic haze
argentation
argillation
arteriogram
asbestiform
ash drawers
ashcroftine
assay grade
assay split
assay value
assay walls
association
asthenolith
astrakanite
atomic mass
atomic size
atomization

attack rate
attapulgite
attenuation
auricupride
aurostibite
autochthony
autoclastic
automorphic
autotroph
axial angle
axial plane
axial ratio
axial trace
Aztec stone
azure stone
b direction
back casing
back coming
back of ore
back ripper
back stopes
backfolding
backing off
backscatter
backup gear
bacon stone
baddeleyite
baeumlerite
baffle tube
baffle wall
bag process
baikerinite
balance bob
balance car
balance pit
balata belt
ball jasper
ball sizing
ballast car
baltimorite
band wander
banded coal
banded peat
banded vein
bandy metal
bank engine
bank gravel
bank height
bank mining
Banka drill
bar grizzly
barbosalite
barrel work
barren hole
barsanovite
basal plane
base charge
base course
basic front

basic grade
basic oxide
basic price
basic steel
basin range
basis price
basket core
bastnaesite
bathymetric
bathyscaphe
bathysphere
bathysystem
bathyvessel
battery ore
Baum washer
bay barrier
beach drift
beach ridge
bead theory
beam action
beam engine
bearing bed
bearing set
bears' muck
beater mill
bedded rock
bell sheave
bell socket
belt feeder
belt loader
bench claim
bench flume
bench scrap
bench slope
bend pulley
bend radius
beneficiate
benjaminite
bergschrund
berkeleyite
Berlin blue
Berlin iron
berthierine
bertrandite
berylliosis
beryllonite
beryloscope
beta quartz
beta-glucan
betechtinit
bicarbonate
bindheimite
bioleaching
biosphere
black light
black metal
black ocher
black roast
black rouge

black shale
Blanton cam
blast draft
bond energy
bond length
bond radius
Boyleís law
Boyle's Law
Brocken bow
calorimeter
calorimetry
carotenoids
cassiterite
cell theory
cement rock
cementation
chaparral
chloroplast
chloroquine
cholesterol
chondrocyte
chromoplast
Cinder cone
civil law
classifying
cobble size
codominance
coefficient
cointegrate
col plasmid
colinearity
colonoscopy
compartment
competition
Complex III
compression
concordance
conjugation
convergence
copper fist
corepressor
correlation
cytokinesis
cytoplasmic
dart leader
datum plane
death phase
debris flow
deciduous
decussation
deformation
degradation
delorenzite
deoxyribose
derepressed
determinant
development
dew point
diffraction

directivity
discharge
dissolution
DNA cloning
double bond
downwelling
dry climate
duplication
earth waves
ecosystem
eicosanoids
ejaculation
electrolyte
end moraine
endocytosis
endomitosis
endothelium
endothermic
energy flow
engorgement
entrainment
entropy (S)
entry table
environment
epiasterism
epididymite
epimagmatic
epinephrine
epiplankton
epistilbite
equilibrium
eremeyevite
error curve
erythrocyte
eskebornite
espley rock
etch figure
etch method
euchromatin
eutrophic
evaporation
evolution
exconjugant
exfoliation
exhaust fan
exomorphism
exonuclease
exploration
extirpate
face hammer
face height
face on end
face signal
face-airing
failed hole
fairy stone
fall ridder
false lapis
false stull

false topaz
fan exhaust
fan fireman
fast ground
fast powder
fatty amber
fault basin
fault bench
fault block
fault creep
fault gouge
fault heave
fault plane
fault scarp
fault shift
fault stuff
fault trace
fault trend
fault wedge
feather ore
fecundity
feed travel
feeder vein
feldspathic
fergusonite
Ferrel cell
ferriferous
ferrochrome
ferrogabbro
ferrosalite
ferroselite
ferrosilite
ferrospinel
ferruginate
ferruginous
fertility
fibrous wax
fiery cloud
fifth wheel
figure cuts
fill factor
filter cake
filter loss
filter pump
fine silver
finger grip
fingerprint
finnemanite
fire bridge
fire feeder
fire marble
fire runner
fired stone
firing line
first break
fishing tap
fissionable
fitness (W)
flake white

flash flood
flash roast
flask cells
flatworking
fleet angle
fleet wheel
flight line
float valve
flood plain
floor break
floor burst
flour agate
flow gneiss
fluorescein
fluorescent
fluorimetry
fluorometer
fluoroscope
fluoroscopy
flush water
fluted core
flux fusion
fluxing ore
flying reef
foamy amber
focal depth
fold system
fool's gold
foraminifer
force lines
forcing fan
forcing set
forechamber
Forel scale
forest peat
forge train
fork-filled
form energy
fossil fuel
fossil salt
franklinite
fresh water
fritzcheite
frontal fog
frontolysis
frost point
fungicide
fusion gene
game theory
gametophyte
gene family
gene fusion
genetic map
genomic DNA
geochemical
geosyncline
gill arches
Glacial ice
glacier ice

glaucophane
glial cells
glide plane
gneissosity
gob heading
gold matrix
gold quartz
goldamalgam
gondola car
gopher hole
gouge angle
gow caisson
grab bucket
grab-camera
grade scale
grade stake
graded coal
graded sand
Grahm's Law
gram weight
granophyric
granularity
granulation
graphic ore
grass roots
grassland
gravel bank
gravel mine
gravel pump
gravitation
gravity bar
gray cobalt
gray copper
gray matter
greasy feel
greasy gold
green acids
green flash
greenockite
greenschist
greet stone
griffithite
grit number
grizzly man
ground boss
ground prop
ground roll
ground wire
groundwater
group level
growth rate
guide frame
guide idler
guinea gold
Gulf Stream
gunned shot
gypsiferous
gyrocompass
hachure map

hack hammer
Hadley cell
Hadsel mill
haemophilia
hair copper
hair pyrite
half-course
half-life
half-marrow
half-period
halokinesis
hand boring
hand hammer
hand loader
hand mining
handpicking
hard bottom
hard ground
hard solder
hard vector
harzburgite
hat rollers
hatchettine
hatchettite
haueynitite
hausmannite
hawser laid
head motion
head pulley
head sheave
heart joint
hearthplate
heat energy
heat engine
heat island
heavy joist
heavy water
heinrichite
hemafibrite
hemimorphic
hemipelagic
hemipyramid
hengleinite
Henryís law
heptavalent
herbicide
herbivore
hetaerolite
heterotroph
hexahydrite
high pillar
high quartz
highwoodite
hinge fault
hinge point
hippocampus
hisingerite
hoe scraper
hogger pipe

hogger pump
Hogness box
hole layout
hole system
holing pick
holohyaline
homogeneity
homogeneous
homothallic
hondurasite
honey stone
hook tender
Hooke's law
hopper salt
horn silver
horn socket
horsfordite
hortonolite
hot forming
hot rolling
hot working
humboldtine
humboldtite
humic coals
Hundís rule
hurdy-gurdy
H-Y antigen
hyalophitic
hydatogenic
hydrocarbon
hydrogarnet
hydrogenate
hydrogenous
hydrography
hydrophilic
hydrophobic
hydrosphere
hydrostatic
hygroscopic
hypersthene
hypnum peat
hypohyaline
hypothermia
ice pellets
idioblastic
idiomorphic
ilesmannite
illiquation
Imlay table
impact cast
impact loss
impact mill
impact slag
impermeable
impregnated
in situ vat
incendivity
inclination
incline man

incoalation
incompetent
inderborite
India steel
Indian jade
inert anode
ingot pitch
initial dip
inoculation
inosilicate
inside face
inside gage
inside work
insufflator
intake area
integration
interbedded
interburden
intercalate
intercooler
intergrowth
interleaved
interrupter
intersertal
iodargyrite
iodembolite
iodobromite
iridescence
iridic gold
iris quartz
iron glance
iron oxides
iron pyrite
iron runner
iron series
irradiation
ishikawaite
isochronous
isogeotherm
isolith map
isomorphism
isomorphous
isopach map
isostannite
isovelocity
itacolumite
jack engine
jack setter
jackknifing
Jacob staff
jam riveter
jamb cutter
James table
Jarno taper
jasper opal
jaw breaker
jaw crusher
jet maximum
jib holeman

jig bushing
jig haulage
jigger work
jiggling in
joint plane
Jominy test
josephinite
Joule's law
jouph holes
K selection
karelianite
karpinskite
karyomegaly
kataclastic
K-bentonite
kennel coal
kerargyrite
keratophyre
key horizon
keystoneite
kibble rope
kilchoanite
kiln burner
kiln placer
kinetochore
king screen
klaprothine
Klaprothite
knee timber
knell stone
knox system
knoxvillite
knuckle man
koechlinite
Koepe hoist
kohlenhobel
kornerupine
krebs cycle
kupletskite
kurnakovite
kutnohorite
labradorite
lactic acid
ladder lode
ladder vein
laded metal
lading hole
ladle liner
lag deposit
lagging bar
laitakarite
lake breeze
Lake copper
laminations
lamp keeper
lamprophyre
land breeze
land pebble
land weight

landing box
landsliding
langbeinite
lansfordite
lapilliform
large shake
large split
large waves
latent heat
Latex spray
launder man
laundry box
lay of rope
layer depth
lazy girder
lead button
lead glance
leadhillite
leeside low
leightonite
length fast
length slow
leonhardite
leptynolite
lethal dose
lethal gene
leucocratic
leucopyrite
leukotriene
level drive
life span
lift hammer
lifting set
light water
lime mortar
lime shells
lime slaker
lindgrenite
line defect
line of dip
lineal foot
lining mark
linkage map
liskeardite
lithia mica
lithic tuff
lithofacies
lithogenesy
lithophysae
lithosphere
litidionite
lit-par-lit
lixiviation
load binder
load factor
loaded hole
loader boss
loader gate
loading pan

loam beater
Lobbe Hobel
local winds
lock paddle
locked test
loellingite
long column
longevity
loose goods
loose rails
loose stone
loose yards
losing iron
lost corner
love arrows
low powders
low voltage
lower break
lower plate
lubrication
lucky stone
lugeon test
lying money
lymph nodes
lyosorption
machine cut
machine nog
machine set
macroscopic
made ground
mafic front
magnetorque
main airway
main bottom
main engine
main facets
main firing
main intake
main levels
main return
maintenance
maitlandite
makeup shed
makeup time
making hole
male thread
mammillated
man machine
manandonite
mandelstone
manganolite
manganosite
manila rope
manipulator
mantle rock
margarodite
maria glass
marsh buggy
maskelynite

mass burn
mass copper
mass defect
mass effect
mass number
master lode
mate-killer
mating type
Mayari iron
mcgovernite
meager feel
mean stress
measurement
mediation
medium band
melanellite
melanterite
meliphanite
melting pot
menaccanite
meneghinite
mercury ore
mesh number
mesoclimate
mesocyclone
mesothermal
mesotrophic
meta-arkose
metacrystal
metadiabase
metadiorite
metal drift
metal notch
metal stone
metaleucite
metallogeny
Metamorphic
metarossite
metasomasis
metasomatic
metasomosis
metavauxite
metavoltine
meteorology
methylation
mica powder
mica schist
michenerite
microampere
microfacies
micronuclei
microscopic
microsecond
midalkalite
middle prop
midge stone
midworkings
mill feeder
milliampere

millidegree
milling bit
milling ore
millisecond
mine expert
mine ground
mine refuse
mineral fat
mineral tar
mineral wax
mineralizer
miner's bar
miner's box
miners' oil
miner's pan
mining camp
mining case
mining dial
minus sieve
minus sight
missed hole
mix-crystal
mixed cloud
mixed layer
mobile belt
Mocha stone
mogensenite
Mohr circle
Mohr's salt
mole mining
molten slag
molybdenite
monchiquite
Monel metal
monkey face
monkey hair
monkey hole
monkey roll
monoculture
monogenetic
monomaceral
montbrayite
montroseite
montroydite
mooihoekite
morbidity
morpholinos
mortality
mother gate
mother lode
mother rock
motive zone
mountainite
mud balance
mud logging
mud snapper
mud volcano
mudding off
muffle kiln

mule's foot
multihybrid
mutant site
muthmannite
mutualism
Mycorrhizae
naphtha gas
napoleonite
narrow gage
narrow work
natural gas
natural ore
neat cement
neck cutoff
neddylation
neighborite
nephelinite
nephropathy
Nernst film
nero-antico
neural tube
neurologist
neurulation
neutron log
nevyanskite
nickel iron
Nicol prism
night shift
nitrocotton
noble metal
noise level
noncore bit
nonmetallic
nonsequence
nonvitreous
norm system
normal fold
normal haul
northeaster
notopleural
noxious gas
NPN process
nuclear log
nucleometer
nucleoplasm
null allele
ocean basin
ochre codon
oil shale
old working
on long awn
oncogenesis
oncosimeter
one-way ram
onyx marble
opalescence
open hearth
open system
opener hole

opening out
ophicalcite
optic angle
optic nerve
orange heat
orchiectomy
ore cluster
ore control
ore crusher
ore deposit
ore genesis
ore geology
ore mineral
ore reserve
oreing down
organic ash
organogenic
orientation
orphan drug
orthogneiss
orthomarble
orthophyric
orthoschist
orthotectic
orthotropic
oryctognosy
oscillation
oscillogram
out of gage
outbreeding
outcrop map
outcropping
outer stone
outside tap
oval socket
overcasting
overgrazing
overrunning
overshoot
overtopping
overvoltage
overwinding
oxialyphite
oxyhydrogen
ozone layer
pack drawer
paleobotany
palladinite
pallas iron
panclastite
paper shale
paracelsian
parachrosis
paradigms
paragenesis
paragenetic
parahopeite
pararealgar
paravauxite

Parkerizing
Parrish arm
part miner
particulate
parting boy
party chief
passivation
paving sand
peacock ore
pebble dike
pebble jack
pebble mill
pebble size
pebblestone
pedogenesis
pegmatolite
Pele's hair
pelletizing
pencil mark
pennyweight
pentavalent
pentlandite
peptization
peralkaline
percolation
periblinite
periclasite
permeameter
permissible
persistence
persorption
pesticide
petrography
pH modifier
Phanerozoic
phase angle
phenhydrous
phillipsite
phosphalite
phosphatase
phosphorate
phosphorite
phosphorize
photosphere
phylloretin
pick lacing
pickup test
picric acid
picromerite
piedmontite
pig handler
pile drawer
pile driver
pile helmet
pillar boss
pillar coal
pillar line
pillar road
Pillow lava

pilot drill
pilot plant
pilot shaft
pilot valve
pilot wedge
pilotaxitic
pinion gear
pintle hook
pipe cutter
pipe factor
pipe prover
pistol pipe
pit foreman
pitchblende
pittasphalt
pivot shaft
placer gold
placer mine
plagihedral
plagioclase
plain pilot
plane fault
plane group
plane shear
plane table
planetology
plant scrap
plaster pit
plasticizer
plate tongs
plattnerite
playa basin
pleiotrophy
Pleistocene
pleochroism
plombierite
plugged bit
pluripotent
pluviometer
point agate
point group
pointed box
polar curve
polar front
polariscope
pole figure
poling back
pollen peat
pollution
polychroism
polychroite
polycrystal
polydactyly
polygenetic
polymignite
polypeptide
polyphenism
polysomatic
polysyngony

poppet head
poppy stone
porosimeter
porphyritic
portlandite
post puller
pot setting
potash alum
potash mica
potash spar
pottern ore
powder mine
power tongs
power train
Pratt truss
preaeration
Precambrian
precedent
precipitant
precipitate
premium tin
preparation
press cloth
pressurized
Pribnow box
primary dip
primary ore
prime mover
probability
proceedings
process lag
proliferate
prop cutter
prop drawer
prop sawyer
prop setter
propagation
prospecting
proteolytic
proterozoic
protogenous
protostomes
pryany lode
pseudomorph
pseudophite
pseudotopaz
psilomelane
public land
puddle roll
pull shovel
pulverulent
pump kettle
pumpellyite
pyramid cut
pyramid-set
pyrargyrite
pyrgeometer
pyrobitumen
pyrochroite

Pyroclastic
pyrogenesis
pyrogenetic
pyrophanite
pyropissite
pyrostibite
quake sheet
quaking bog
qualitative
quarey lode
quarfeloids
quarry body
quarry face
quarry lode
quartz boil
quartz gold
quartz lead
quartz mill
quartz mine
quartz reef
quicksilver
Quigley gun
quill shaft
rack-a-rock
radial axis
radioactive
radiocarbon
radiography
radiometric
raggy stone
rain shadow
raise borer
ramp valley
rangeland
ranging rod
rare earths
rarefaction
ratchet man
rathole bit
ray craters
razor stone
Reading jig
readthrough
reaming bit
reannealing
recarburize
reclamation
recombinant
reconnoiter
record hole
recuperator
recycling
red arsenic
red mercury
red nucleus
red vitriol
redledgeite
referencing
refrigerant

refuge hole
refuse worm
regular lay
reiteration
reject gate
relief well
replacement
replication
rescue team
resistivity
respiration
resplendent
restoration
retardation
retentivity
reticulated
revdanskite
reverberate
rewdanskito
rhabdomancy
rhabdophane
rhizosphere
rhodochrome
rhodotilite
rhomboclase
ribbed roll
richmondite
riffle bars
Rift system
rift valley
rigging bar
rigid ducts
rigid frame
rig-up time
rim texture
rim walking
ring stress
rip current
rippability
ripping bed
ripping lip
ripple mark
rising main
river claim
river drift
river plain
river right
rivet forge
RNA editing
road roller
roast stall
robinsonite
rock butter
rock dredge
rock duster
rock fabric
rock factor
rock gypsum
rock kicker

rock loader
rock pillar
rock quartz
rock series
rock shovel
rock stress
rock tunnel
rock weight
rocketsonde
rod millman
roentgenite
roll feeder
roll screen
roll sulfur
roller gate
roller grip
Roman ocher
Roman pearl
romanechite
roof bolter
rope cutter
rope driver
rope socket
rose copper
rose quartz
Ross feeder
rosthornite
rotary dump
rotary pump
roto finish
rotor cloud
rotten reef
rottenstone
rough stone
roundabouts
rubberstone
rubbing bed
rubblestone
rubbly reef
rubinblende
ruby blende
ruby copper
ruby silver
ruby spinel
ruby sulfur
run of lode
running dry
running off
run-of-mill
run-of-mine
runout fire
Russia iron
saddle reef
saddle vein
safety belt
safety door
safety fuse
safety gate
safety hook

safety lamp
safety lock
safety post
safety stop
salicylates
salinometer
salt bottom
salt bridge
salt effect
salt garden
salt of tin
salting out
sand bottle
sand filter
sand holder
sand muller
sand washer
sanguinaria
sarmientite
satin stone
saw-toothed
scaling bar
scarf joint
schairerite
schallerite
scheererite
schefferite
schistosity
schorl rock
schorlomite
schuetteite
schultenite
sclerometer
scoriaceous
scram drift
scram drive
scrap baler
scratch pan
scree plate
screen deck
screen pipe
screen room
screen size
screw mixer
scythestone
sea current
sealed area
Seale's lay
search coil
second-foot
section man
sector gate
sedimentary
seed charge
seed gypsum
segregation
seidozerite
seismic gap
seismogenic

Seismograph
seismometer
seismoscope
self stones
self-feeder
selfish DNA
semigelatin
semitrailer
sensitivity
serendibite
setting out
setting rod
settlingite
sex linkage
shadow zone
shaft cable
shaft house
shaft inset
shaft mixer
shaft space
shale break
sharp stone
shatter cut
shattuckite
shear plane
shear rivet
shear slide
shear steel
sheet metal
sheet piles
Shelby tube
shelf angle
shell cameo
shepherding
sheridanite
sherwoodite
shift lever
shiver spar
shock-proof
shore drift
shot boring
shot copper
shot firing
shot moment
shot runner
shot tamper
shotty gold
shuttle car
sialic rock
side thrust
sidecasting
side-laning
siderophile
sideroscope
sidetracked
siding over
siegburgite
sieve scale
sieve sizes

signal code
silica rock
silica sand
silicatosis
sillimanite
silver lead
silver sand
simple beam
single bond
single jack
single shot
single vein
sinkholes
Sirocco fan
sjoegrenite
skerrystone
skin effect
skip bucket
skip system
slack water
slag hearth
solid state
solid waste
source rock
spider cell
spliceosome
stability
state point
static E.P.
static head
static load
static tube
stauroscope
steady mass
steam point
steam stamp
steel cable
steel press
steel scrap
steelmaking
step socket
stereograph
stereoscopy
sterrettite
stibiconite
stinkquartz
stoker coal
Stokes' law
stone count
stone drift
stone ocher
stonecutter
stope board
stope hoist
stope miner
stoved salt
strain gage
strain rate
strait work

Straits tin
stranskiite
strap brake
strata bolt
stratascope
stream gold
stream tube
streamworks
stress drop
strike slip
strike-slip
strong acid
strong base
strong lode
strut tenon
Stub's gage
stull piece
stylotypite
subdrilling
sublimation
submergence
subsilicate
subvitreous
subvolcanic
suction fan
sugar stone
sulfatizing
sulfide ore
sulfur ball
sulfur dome
sumping bar
sumping cut
superficial
superfund
superheater
superimpose
supernatant
superpanner
supply pump
surface rig
surturbrand
suture zone
svanbergite
svitalskite
swage block
swamp buggy
Swedish bit
sweet roast
sweet water
swing angle
swing loose
swing shift
Swiss lapis
swivel head
swivel neck
swivel plug
swivel vise
syenogabbro
symbiosis

symon fault
symplectite
synchromesh
synchronism
synchronous
synergism
synorogenic
syntectonic
talus slope
teleseismic
temperature
terracing
tetrahedron
thalidomide
thermocline
thoracotomy
tidal inlet
totipotency
trait ratio
transformer
translation
travel time
triple bond
trophoblast
troposphere
tumor virus
unicellular
variegation
V-J joining
warm spring
Water cycle
water table
watershed
welded tuff
yield point
zinc finger

10

aa channel
ABC system
aberration
aboral end
absorption
abyssolith
achavalite
achromatic
acid leach
acid shock
acid steel
acid water
acoelomate
acre-yield
actinolite
activation
actual age
adaptation
Adenovirus

adrenaline
adrenergic
adult form
aerosols
aftershock
air parcel
allogeneic
Alu family
amino acid
amoebocyte
amphimixis
amphoteric
anagenesis
anaphase I
Anbauhobel
andalusite
andesinite
andrewsite
androecium
anemograph
anemometer
aneuploidy
angel dust
angiosperm
angle beam
angle hole
angledozer
anisotropy
annerodite
annotation
antagonist
antheridia
anthoinite
anthonyite
anthracene
anthracite
anthrafilt
antibiotic
antigens
Apricotine
apron feed
apron rope
apron wall
aqua regia
aquifers
aramayoite
arc cutter
arch forms
archegonia
Archeozoic
arenaceous
Arents tap
argyrodite
arrojadite
arsenicite
arsenolite
articulite
asbestosis
ascomycete

Asparagine
asperolite
asphaltite
asphyxiate
aspirating
assay foot
assay inch
assay plan
assessment
asteriated
astringent
atelestite
Atlas spar
atmosphere
attenuator
auger bits
auger head
auger hole
auriferous
aurosmirid
authigenic
autochthon
autogenous
automolite
autostoper
autrometer
avanturine
aventurine
avicennite
axial flow
axial line
azure spar
B form DNA
back acter
back break
back entry
back holes
back leads
back slope
back stope
background
bag filter
bag of gas
bag powder
balas ruby
ball stamp
ballistite
band chain
band scale
banded ore
bank claim
bank right
bank slope
bank water
bank yards
banker off
bar mining
bar screen
bare motor

barotrauma
barrandite
barroisite
barysilite
barysphere
basal body
basal reef
basal slip
base level
base metal
base price
basic lava
basic slag
bastnasite
bathymeter
bathymetry
bayldonite
beach face
bead tests
bearer bar
bearing-in
Becke line
Becke test
beech coal
beidellite
bell holes
bell screw
belly pipe
Belomorite
belonesite
belt creep
belt press
belt table
bench coal
bench face
bench mark
bend shaft
bend wheel
benstonite
bent sieve
bergbutter
berthonite
beryllides
berzeliite
beta decay
beudantite
bevel gear
Big Coal D
billietite
billy coal
bilobalide
bimagmatic
bin feeder
bing place
bioclastic
bioreactor
bipedalism
black body
black flux

black gold
black iron
black lead
black mica
black muck
black opal
black sand
blade mill
blank hole
blank pipe
blanketing
Blasjo cut
blastocoel
blastocyst
blastoderm
blastomere
blastopore
bottleneck
brain stem
brannerite
breakpoint
breakwater
breed true
bronchiole
brown clay
calcitonin
carcinogen
case law
catabolism
cell cycle
centromere
centrosome
cephalized
cerebellum
chalcedony
chalcocite
chemotaxis
chemotroph
chondrules
chromomere
chromosome
chrysotile
CIB method
coenzyme Q
Collection
combustion
compaction
competence
competency
complement
Complex II
Complex IV
compound
concatemer
concretion
conduction
cone sheet
congenital
conifers

consumer
contig map
convection
conversion
coral reef
correction
corridor
covariance
creatinine
crossbreed
ctenophore
cytochrome
decomposer
deep focus
deep water
deficiency
demography
deposition
dewindtite
diagenesis
diakinesis
dictyotene
dike swarm
dimorphism
disability
dispersion
divergence
DNA gyrase
DNA ligase
DNA marker
downstream
Drosophila
dust whirl
earthquake
echinoderm
ecotourism
elasticity
electron
embryology
emissivity
endemism
endodermis
endogenote
endogenous
engine pit
englishite
enigmatite
enrichment
eosphorite
epeirogeny
epibenthos
epidiabase
epididymis
epidiorite
epigenesis
epigenetic
epiphyte
epistolite
epithelial

epithermal
epsom salt
equivalent
erubescite
escarpment
etch angle
ethanamide
etiolation
euchlorine
eucryptite
eudidymite
eudiometer
eusapropel
evaluation
excavation
excess air
excitation
excitatory
exemptions
exhalation
exhaustion
exocytosis
exothermic
experiment
explosible
exsolution
extinction
extractant
extraction
extradosal
fabricator
face cleat
face entry
face right
face stone
facies map
Fahrenheit
fall table
false form
false gate
false ruby
famatinite
fan rating
fathometer
fatty acid
fault line
fault trap
fault vein
fault zone
fault-fold
feed ratio
feed shaft
feed speed
felsenmeer
felsophyre
ferghanite
ferricrete
ferricrust
ferrierite

ferroalloy
ferroboron
ferroxdure
ferruccite
feverstein
fichtelite
field work
fiery heap
fiery mine
filter aid
filter bed
filtration
fine metal
finger bar
finger bit
fink truss
fire agate
fire assay
fire grate
fire stink
fire styth
fireblende
fire-heavy
firing key
fishplates
flake mica
flame kiln
flame opal
flame test
flameproof
flank hole
flap valve
flash opal
flash over
flashpoint
flat drill
flat idler
flat joint
flat sheet
flavonoids
flint clay
flint mill
float coal
float dust
float gold
floatstone
flocculate
flocculent
flood tide
Floodplain
floor lift
floor sill
florencite
flos ferri
floss hole
flour gold
flour salt
flow layer
fluid wash

fluoborite
fluocerite
fluviatile
flux spoon
Flygt pump
fold fault
food chain
food web
foot clamp
force pump
forcherite
fore drift
forehearth
forepoling
foreshocks
forfeiture
forge iron
forge pigs
forge roll
forsterite
fossil ice
fossil ore
fossil wax
fossilized
foundation
fragmental
framed dam
frameshift
franckeite
frozen dew
gene locus
geneticist
geophysics
germ plasm
ginkgolide
giobertite
gips plate
gismondine
Glacialite
glaciation
glaciology
glass opal
glass sand
glass wool
glauberite
glaucolite
glauconite
glimmerite
glimmerton
glistening
glockerite
glory hole
glycocalyx
glycolysis
goergeyite
going bord
going road
gold fever
gold glass

gold topaz
goldichite
goldmanite
goniometer
gonnardite
goodletite
gorceixite
gouge clay
gouge rake
Gouy layer
graded bed
gradienter
grain gold
grain size
Granby car
granitizer
granophyre
granulator
granulitic
graphitite
graphitoid
grass crop
Grassellis
grate coal
gravel pit
gravimeter
gravimetry
graywether
great salt
green hole
green roof
green salt
greenalite
greenovite
greenstone
groroilite
ground fog
ground log
groundmass
grout core
grout hole
guardplate
gublin bat
gudmundite
guide core
guide rope
guillotine
guinea bed
gunningite
gust front
guy anchor
gymnosperm
hackmanite
hailstones
hailstreak
half width
halloysite
hamburgite
hammermill

hammerpick
hand auger
hand cable
hand frame
hanging-on
hard water
hartleyite
HAT medium
haulageway
Hauy's law
hawk's-eye
head grain
head piles
head shaft
head value
headsticks
headstocks
heap matte
heat value
heatstroke
heavy crop
heavy gold
heavy soil
heavy spar
heavy tiff
hecatolite
heeling in
heep stead
heliotrope
hellyerite
hemihedral
hemisphere
hemitropic
hemizygous
hemophilia
hemorrhage
hereditary
Hertz (Hz)
Hessís law
heterogamy
heulandite
hexagonite
hexavalent
high doors
high-grade
hilgardite
Hilt's law
hinged bar
hinterland
hitcher-on
hoegbomite
hoernesite
hohmannite
holing nog
hollandite
hollow dam
holoenzyme
holohedral
homoplasmy

homosphere
homozygote
hook block
Hooper jig
hopper car
hopperings
horn coral
hornblende
horse gear
horse whim
host range
hot miller
hot spring
house coal
huanghoite
huascolite
huebnerite
humboltite
humic acid
humid heat
humidostat
humus coal
hureaulite
hurlbarrow
hutch road
hyalophane
hybrid DNA
hydraulics
hydrograph
hydrolysis
hydrometer
hydroscope
hydrosizer
hydrotator
hyetometer
hygrometer
hygrometry
hypabyssal
hypermorph
hyperploid
hypocenter
hypothesis
hypsometer
hypsometry
hysteresis
ianthinite
ice nuclei
ice period
iddingsite
idiogenite
idle wheel
idler disk
idler gear
ignimbrite
illinition
ilmenitite
imbibition
immiscible
immunology

impalpable
impervious
imprinting
inbreeding
incestuous
inch-pound
inclinator
inclusions
incoherent
incubation
Indian-cut
indicolite
induration
inert dust
inertinite
infrasizer
ingot iron
ingot mold
ingredient
ingression
inhibition
initiation
inner core
insert bit
insert set
inspirator
integrator
intercepts
intercross
interferon
interfluve
intergrown
interphase
interplate
interstice
intradosal
intraplate
inundation
involution
ionic bond
ionization
ionosphere
iridosmine
Irish coal
iron black
iron froth
iron oxide
iron piler
iron stain
iron steel
ironmaster
ironworker
island arc
isogam map
isoleucine
isopachous
isopachyte
isopiestic
isoseismal

isothermal
isotopes
jack catch
jacket set
jackhammer
jacking up
jamb stick
jamesonite
jar collar
jasper bar
jedding ax
jeffersite
jenkinsite
jet streak
jet stream
jibbing-in
jig washer
jinny road
joaquinite
John Odges
joint line
joint rose
Joplin jig
Joy loader
jump sheet
jumper bar
junckerite
kaersutite
kaliborite
kalicinite
kamarezite
karyolymph
karyolysis
karyoplasm
karyoplast
katoptrite
kearsutite
keel wedge
keldyshite
kelyphytic
kentrolite
kerf stone
kersantite
kettleback
ketlnerite
Keweenawan
key blocks
K-feldspar
Khari salt
khinganite
khlopinite
Kick's law
kidney ore
kieselguhr
kimberlite
king brick
kink bands
klinkstone
knee brace

knee piece
knife edge
knobellite
knock down
knockstone
known mine
known vein
koettigite
kolbeckite
kolovraite
koninckite
kotulskite
kremersite
krennerite
kroehnkite
Krupp-Renn
kryptomere
laboratory
lac operon
lacroixite
lacustrine
lag gravel
lamination
lamp cabin
lamp house
land chain
langbanite
lanthanide
lanthanite
lapse rate
lard stone
large coal
large knot
lath frame
laubannite
laurdalite
laurionite
laurvikite
Lauth mill
laxmannite
laying out
lazy bench
leach dump
leach hole
leach pile
lead azide
lead ocher
lead wires
lead works
ledge rock
left twist
legrandite
Lehigh jig
lehrnerite
lenticular
lentil ore
leonardite
leopardite
leopoldite

lepidolite
letovicite
lettsomite
leucophane
leucophyre
level-free
levigation
levitation
Lewis acid
Lewis base
lewis hole
life cycle
lift joint
lightening
lillianite
limeburner
limit line
line oiler
lined gold
linophyric
lip screen
lipocorun
liquid air
liroconite
lithargite
lithionite
lithoglyph
lithologic
lithomarge
lithophile
live steam
liveingite
liver opal
liver rock
liverstone
loader-off
lobbying
local cell
local vent
locomotive
lode claim
log washer
loose rock
loranskite
lorettoite
lost level
lost river
lost water
love stone
lovozerite
low quartz
lower leaf
lumachelle
luminosity
lying wall
lymphocyte
macedonite
machineman
macro-axis

macroburst
macrograph
macromeres
macrophage
macroscale
Magnafloat
magnetized
main break
main drive
main entry
main shaft
maintenage
Majac mill
major face
malacolite
malladrite
mallardite
malthacite
mammillary
man engine
manasseite
man-of-war
marasmus
marble saw
Marcy mill
marekanite
mariposite
marker bed
market pot
marl slate
marm stone
marmorosis
martensite
martinsite
martourite
mascagnite
mass fibre
master pin
matlockite
matte fall
maucherite
meadow ore
mean depth
mechanized
medfordite
medmontite
meerschaum
megacity
megascopic
melaconite
melanchyme
melilitite
melteigite
merohedral
merozygote
merrillite
mesa-butte
mesenchyme
mesocratic

mesokaites
mesosphere
mesostasis
metabasite
metabolism
metabolite
metaborite
metafemale
metal bath
metallites
metallurgy
metamarble
metaplasia
metastasis
methionine
miargyrite
miarolitic
mica house
mica plate
microarray
microburst
microcline
microfarad
micrograph
microlitic
micromeres
micrometer
Micronizer
microplate
microscale
microscope
microscopy
microseism
middle cut
middle man
midfeather
mikheevite
mild earth
mild steel
mill scale
mill value
millidarcy
millifarad
milligauss
millihenry
mimetesite
mine hoist
mine mason
mine water
mineralize
mineralogy
mineraloid
minguzzite
mirabilite
mischmetal
miter gear
mitridaite
mixed dust
mixed face

mixer cone
mixing pit
MM diamond
modulating
Mohs scale
moil point
moissanite
molar mass
molecule
moluranite
molybdenum
monheimite
monoclinal
monohybrid
monovalent
montan wax
morass ore
morbid map
morenosite
morphology
mortar bed
mortar box
moss agate
mossy zinc
motor body
motor boss
mottramite
mucky hole
mud barrel
mud bucket
mud column
mud socket
mudcapping
multiphase
murasakite
murdochite
mussel bed
mutabilite
mutability
mutagens
mutation
myocardium
myogenesis
naumannite
neat lines
necrotroph
needle ore
negligence
N-end rule
neokerogen
neomorphic
nerve cell
Neuregulin
neuroblast
Neuropathy
neurospora
neutrality
neutralize
newjersite

night pair
niter cake
nodulizing
nonferrous
nontronite
normal air
normal arc
normal dip
novaculite
nowcasting
nucleation
nucleoside
nucleosome
nucleotide
nullisomic
nurse cell
nutcracker
nylon belt
octet rule
oil-temper
old silver
oleic acid
oligoclase
omega high
omnivore
oncologist
one on two
onyx agate
opal codon
open fault
open front
open light
open split
open stope
optic axis
optic sign
orangepeel
ordonezite
Ordovician
ore bridge
ore grader
ore hearth
ore pocket
ore strand
ore washer
organolite
orichalcum
orogenesis
orographic
orthoclase
orthogonal
orthoprism
orthoscope
Orton cone
oryctology
Otto cycle
outer core
outer gage
outgassing

outstation
overburden
overfiring
overloader
overmining
overthrust
overtravel
overturned
overwinder
ovum (Egg)
oxacalcite
oxbow lake
oxymagnite
ozone hole
pachnolite
paddy lamp
paint gold
paint mill
paint rock
palagonite
pale brick
palimpsest
palindrome
palustrine
palynology
pan feeder
panabasite
pandermite
pantograph
paper clay
paper coal
paper spar
paradamite
paragneiss
paragonite
parameters
paramoudra
paraschist
parasite
parasitism
paratomous
parsonsite
passivator
paste fill
paternally
pathfinder
pathogen
paulingite
pay gravel
pay streak
pea gravel
peak stope
pearl mica
pearl opal
pearl spar
pearlstone
peat press
peat spade
pecopteris

pedosphere
pegmatitic
Penang tin
pencil ore
penetrance
penroseite
periclinal
peridotite
peritectic
permafrost
permit man
perofskite
perovskite
peroxidase
persilicic
persistent
perthorite
phacellite
phagocytes
phaneritic
phase rule
phasemeter
phenocryst
phillipite
phlogopite
pholidoide
phosgenite
phosphorus
phyllonite
pick miner
pick money
pick tongs
piemontite
piercement
piezometer
pig caster
pig tailer
pigeonhole
pigsticker
pile group
pilehammer
pillar man
pilot hole
pilot lamp
pin puller
pin thread
pintadoite
pin-to-box
pin-to-pin
pipe clamp
pirssonite
pit bottom
pit mining
pit quarry
pitch line
pitchstone
pitman arm
Pitot tube
pitotmeter

pivot tube
plaffeiite
plagionite
planimeter
planimetry
plankton
planktonic
plasma jet
plastering
plasticity
plate roll
playa lake
pleiotropy
pleochroic
plow steel
plug drill
plug valve
plumb post
plus sight
pneumatics
poaching
poecilitic
poicilitic
poldometer
poikilitic
point bars
Polar Ajax
polar body
pole cells
pole chain
pole piece
pollutants
polybasite
polydymite
polyhalite
polylinker
polymerize
polyspermy
polytypism
poor fumes
population
pore space
pore water
porphyrite
porphyroid
port crown
post brake
post drill
post stone
posthumous
postmortem
pot bottom
pound-foot
powder box
powder keg
power pack
power unit
praseolite
precocious

precutting
predator
prediction
preference
prehnitoid
preplaning
previtrain
priguinite
probertite
processing
producer
production
productive
projection
prokaryote
prominence
pronucleus
proplastid
proportion
propositus
prospector
prospectus
proteasome
proteins
Proteomics
protoclase
protoplast
prototroph
protractor
proved ore
provenance
pseudogene
pseudojade
pull wheel
pulp assay
pulpit man
pulsometer
pulverizer
pump slope
pump stock
pump surge
punch prop
pure oxide
pure shear
pure steel
purple ore
pycnocline
pycnometer
pyralspite
pyrimidine
pyroaurite
pyrochlore
pyrolusite
pyroxenite
pyroxenoid
pyrrhotine
pyrrhotite
quarry sap
quarry-rid

quartation
quartering
quartz ore
quartzitic
Quaternary
quenselite
quick clay
quick test
quickening
R.Kprocess
rabbit-eye
rabbittite
rack frame
radial arm
radio link
radiogenic
radiograph
Radiolaria
radiolitic
radiometer
radiophone
radiosonde
rain gauge
rake blade
ralstonite
ramdohrite
random set
range line
range pole
rapid plow
rated load
rathite-II
rat-holing
ratiometer
reactivity
reamer bit
reclaiming
red cobalt
red schorl
red silver
red tide
reddingite
redox pair
redruthite
reef drive
reef knoll
reflection
reformer
refraction
refractory
regal jade
regression
relaxation
relief map
reluctance
remolinite
repression
rescue-car
resettable

resilience
resin jack
resistance
resolution
resource
respirator
rest magma
resurgence
retgersite
reticulate
reticulite
retinallte
retinosite
retracting
retrovirus
return air
return man
reussinite
revolution
rewash box
rhinestone
rhomb spar
rhyacolite
rhyodacite
rib lining
rib pillar
rickardite
riebecklte
riemannite
riffle box
right bank
right line
rigid arch
rigid foam
rill stope
rim flying
rimrocking
ring fault
ring holes
ring stone
ringed out
rip plates
river flat
river sand
rivet snap
rivet test
road metal
rock burst
rock chute
rock cover
rock cycle
rock drift
rock drill
rock fault
rock flour
rock glass
rock hound
rock miner
rock navvy

rock sharp
rock slide
rock slope
rock waste
rocker arm
rod puller
rod string
roll cloud
roll scale
roller bit
rolley man
roof drill
roof layer
roof shale
roof stone
roof-framy
room entry
rope guide
rope rider
roscherite
roscoelite
rose beryl
rose steel
rose topaz
rosickyite
rosin jack
rosin zinc
rotary bit
rothoffite
roughbacks
round hook
round kiln
round trip
roundstone
rowlandite
rubblerock
ruin agate
run levels
runner box
runoff pit
russellite
rusty gold
sabugalite
saddleback
safety car
safety hat
safflorite
salamander
salamstone
saliferous
salinity
Salmonella
salmonsite
salt block
salt horse
salt marsh
salt stock
salt table
samarskite

sample log
sand floor
santafeite
saponifier
sapphirine
saprophyte
sardachate
saryarkite
satellites
sathrolith
satin spar
satpaevite
sausserite
saussurite
scabblings
scale door
scamy post
scarbroite
scarcement
scavenging
scheibeite
schizolite
schoderite
schwatzite
scorzalite
Scotch pig
scout hole
scovillite
scowl bowl
scrap mica
scree bars
screen box
screenings
screw bell
screw pile
scrubstone
Seale rope
searlesite
seat earth
seat stone
sebkainite
Seger cone
seismicity
Seismitron
seismogram
seismology
s-electron
selenolite
semifusain
senescence
sengierite
separation
sequencing
serpentine
serpierite
set casing
set copper
set weight
setting up

settlement
sex linked
sex switch
sexduction
sex-lethal
seybertite
shaft cave
shaft foot
shaft mine
shaft wall
shake wave
shale band
shale dust
sharp fire
sharp sand
shear fold
shear wave
shear zone
shear-cake
sheer legs
sheet flow
sheet iron
sheet mica
sheet pile
sheet sand
sheet wash
shell lime
shell marl
shell pump
sherardize
shift gear
shift work
ship auger
shock bump
shock wave
shonkinite
shop rivet
shore reef
short coal
short hole
short shot
shoshonite
shot break
shot datum
shot depth
shot drill
shot firer
shot metal
shot point
shunt back
sicklerite
side basse
side piles
side trees
siemensite
sieve bend
sieve mesh
sight line
sigma heat

silication
silicified
silicinate
siliconize
sill depth
silting up
simple ore
simplotite
simpsonite
sinker bar
sinter bit
sinter cap
sinter set
siphon tap
siserskite
sismondine
site rivet
size range
skelp iron
skew plate
skip hoist
skip miner
skip shaft
skull drop
slab entry
slag buggy
slip model
slip plane
smelting
solubility
SOS repair
spacer DNA
speciation
speleothem
sperm cell
sphalerite
sporophyte
stalactite
stalagmite
statistics
staurolite
staurotide
steam main
Steart fan
steel arch
steel belt
steel jack
steel mill
steel prop
steel ring
steel sets
steel shot
steigerite
stell prop
step fault
stephanite
stercorite
stereogram
stevensite

stewartite
stibianite
stick-slip
sticky end
stiff clay
still coke
stinkstein
stinkstone
stochastic
stomates
stone band
stone bind
stone coal
stone dust
stone flax
stone land
stone mill
stone mine
stone sill
stone wall
stop codon
stopblocks
stove coal
strain bar
stratified
stratiform
straw boss
stream tin
streamline
street ell
stretchers
striations
strike cut
strip mine
Stripkolex
stromatite
strongback
struck out
structural
stub entry
stump prop
subalkalic
subangular
subaqueous
subcloning
subcooling
subduction
suberinite
subincline
subophitic
suboutcrop
subsidence
subsilicic
subslicing
subsoiling
substation
substitute
substoping
subsurface

subterrain
subterrane
sugar sand
sugar spar
sulfophile
sulfur ore
sump shaft
sump winze
sumping-in
sundiusite
sunk shaft
sunken pit
superalloy
superprint
surfactant
surge pipe
surge tank
suspension
swinestone
switchback
switchgear
symplectic
symplesite
synantetic
synchisite
synchronal
synchronic
synchysite
syngenetic
syntectite
tablemount
tailings
telomerase
terminator
test-cross
tetraploid
Ti plasmid
tidal bore
tidal wave
topography
topoisomer
topset bed
totipotent
tourmaline
toxicology
transcribe
transducer
transgenic
transition
transposon
travertine
troposhere
Tryptophan
turbidites
ubiquinone
understory
unique DNA
ventricles
vertebrate

vitamins
viviparous
wastewater
water well
wave front
wavelength
weathering
wetlands
wilderness
woodland
y-junction
zwitterion

9

A horizon
acanthite
acaricide
accessory
accretion
acellular
acervulus
acetamide
acetylene
aciculite
acid clay
acid cure
acid flux
acid rain
acid slag
acid soil
acid test
acidizing
aciniform
acopolado
acoustics
acre-foot
acre-inch
activator
adenosine
adipocyte
advection
aggregate
aggresome
A-horizon
alkalosis
allantois
allometry
almandite
altimeter
Ames test
amorphous
amphibole
amplitude
anabolism
anatectic
anchaduar
anchorage

andradite
anemogram
anemolite
aneuploid
angle-cut
anglesite
anhydride
anhydrite
anhydrock
anhydrous
animikite
annealing
anode mud
anorthite
anticline
anticodon
antimorph
aphanitic
aphrodite
apophysis
apoptosis
appraisal
A-protein
Aquiclude
aragonite
arbitrage
ardennite
areal map
argentate
argentine
argentite
argillite
arizonite
arkansite
armangite
arochlors
aromatite
arquerite
Arrestins
arteriole
arthritis
arthropod
arthurite
asbestine
ascharite
aschisite
aschistic
ascospore
ash curve
ash error
ash yield
asphaltic
aspirator
assay ton
asteroids
astochite
astridite
astrocyte
atacamite

Atlas ore
atriopore
attrition
austenite
austinite
authigene
automixis
autosomal
autospray
autotroph
auxiliary
auxotroph
Avalanche
axotomous
azulinhas
B horizon
back arch
back coal
back mine
back prop
back shot
back skin
back slip
back vent
back work
backblast
backcross
backjoint
backshift
backshore
backsight
backstamp
backstone
backswamp
baff ends
baikalite
baikerite
balistite
balkstone
ball clay
ball head
ball mill
ball vein
ballstone
balmaiden
balnstone
banalsite
bandylite
bank coal
bank head
bank pump
banqueria
bar drill
barequear
barequero
barnesite
barograph
barometer
Barr body

barricade
barrowman
barrowway
basaltine
base flow
base line
base plug
base rock
baselevel
bassetite
bastonite
batholith
bathygram
bathylith
bathysmal
bayleyite
beach ore
bean rock
beaverite
beckerite
bed claim
bed joint
bell mold
bell work
bolt slip
bementite
bench cut
bend test
benitoite
benthonic
benthos
bentonite
beraunite
bergalite
bergalith
bergenite
berkelium
bermanite
bernstein
beryllite
beryllium
bevel cut
B-horizon
bieberite
bikitaite
Bilateria
bilirubin
bing hole
biolistic
biologics
biomass
bionomics
biopelite
biosphere
black mud
black ore
black tin
black wad
blackdamp

blackjack
blacklung
blank bit
blasthole
body wave
bryophyte
C horizon
Cachectin
capital
capsomere
carbonate
carcinoma
carnotite
cartilage
catabolic
catalysis
causality
celecoxib
cell body
cell fate
cell wall
centriole
chaparral
chaperone
character
chemistry
choralite
chromatid
chromatin
cirrhosis
clarkeite
clay size
cleft lip
climate
coffinite
cognition
community
competent
Complex I
conjugate
corrosion
cortisone
cot value
cytoplasm
deflation
denatured
dendrites
detergent
dew point
dichogamy
dieback
diffusion
dilatancy
discharge
disease
divergent
DNA clone
dolostone
downburst

downdraft
dripstone
dumontite
dust size
earthflow
ecology
economics
ecosystem
ecotone
El Niño
electrode
element
embryonic
emissions
end point
endophyte
endosperm
endostyle
enhydrite
enhydrous
enstatite
enstenite
enzymes
eolianite
epicenter
epidosite
epigenite
epiphysis
epistasis
equal lay
erythrine
erythrite
escapeway
eschynite
eskolaite
esplanade
essential
estuary
etch line
etch ring
etch time
etch tube
ethmolith
eubitumen
eucairite
euchroite
eudialyte
eukaryote
eutaxitic
eutectoid
eutrophic
evaporate
evaporite
Evolution
ex vessel
excavator
exception
exfoliate
exit site

exogenote
exogenous
exosphere
explosive
extension
extralite
extrusion
extrusive
exudation
eye agate
ezcurrite
F protein
fabianite
face area
face boss
face left
face slip
face wall
facellite
factorial
fahlunite
fall line
fall wind
fall zone
famines
fan drift
fan scarp
fan shaft
fang bolt
fast cord
fast feed
fast gear
fast line
fast side
fat stone
fathogram
fault gap
fault set
Faust jig
f-duction
feed gear
feed pump
feed rate
feedwater
feldspars
feldstone
felsitoid
ferberite
ferganite
fermorite
ferrolite
fervanite
fibrolite
film mica
fine gold
fine sand
fine silt
fire bank
fire boss

fire door
fire kiln
fire opal
fire sand
fire seal
firebreak
firebrick
firestone
first aid
first bye
fissility
fitchered
fizelyite
flagellae
flagstone
flammable
flash box
flat arch
flat ends
flat hole
flat lode
flat rods
flat rope
flitching
float ore
floe rock
floodgate
floor cut
flop gate
flotation
flow line
flow rate
flow roll
flow unit
flowmeter
flowsheet
flue dust
fluellite
fluid cut
fluid ton
fluobaryt
fluometry
fluormica
fluorspar
fluxstone
foam plug
foam spar
focus map
fold axis
foliation
foot hole
foot wall
foot-acre
foot-yard
forbesite
fore dune
forebrain
foreigner
forensics

foreshift
foreshock
foreshore
foresight
formanite
formation
fornacite
foshagite
fossicker
fossilize
fowlerite
frame dam
frame set
framesite
frequency
frostbite
fuel cell
fungicide
gamma ray
gasohol
gastunite
g-banding
gene dose
gene flow
gene pair
gene pool
genophore
geologist
geosphere
germ cell
germ line
germarium
gin wheel
glaciated
glaucodot
gley soil
globulite
glutamate
glutamine
gmelinite
gob entry
Gohi iron
going off
gold dust
gold mine
gold opal
goldstone
gonorrhea
gonyerite
goosecoid
gooseneck
gophering
gopherman
gordonite
goshenite
goslarite
goutwater
grab iron
grabhooks

gradation
gradeline
grain tin
gram-atom
granitoid
granofels
granolith
grantsite
granulite
grate bar
graticule
grave wax
gray iron
green mud
green top
greensand
grenatite
greywacke
gross cut
gross ton
grossular
grovesite
grubstake
grunching
grunerite
guanosine
guide rod
gum copal
gun drill
gurhofite
guttering
habitat
hair salt
hairstone
half-cell
half-life
halfspace
halocline
haloxylin
hand gear
hand lamp
hand lead
hand whip
haplotype
hard coal
hard kiln
hard mica
hard rock
hard seat
hard spar
hardebank
hardening
harmotome
harpolith
harrisite
haul road
haulabout
hawleyite
HD allele

head coal	horsetail	intensity	jetstream	krantzite
head side	host rock	intercept	jews' tin	labyrinth
head tank	hot blast	interlock	jib crane	laccolite
headblock	hot-drawn	intersect	jig chain	laccolith
headboard	Hull cell	intrusion	johannite	lack clay
headframe	hung fire	intrusive	joint box	ladderway
headhouse	hung shot	inversion	joint set	ladle lip
headsword	huntilite	iodimetry	jordanite	lag fault
heapstead	hurricane	ionophore	julienite	lag phase
heat flow	hurry gum	iriginite	junk mill	lag screw
heat pump	hutchwork	iron (Fe)	junkerite	laihunite
heat unit	huttonite	iron alum	K antigen	lamellate
hectorite	hybridize	iron clay	kahlerite	laminated
hedyphane	hybridoma	iron mica	kaliphite	lamp rack
heintzite	hydration	iron sand	kalsilite	lamp room
helicitic	hydraulic	iron spar	kanamycin	lampadite
helictite	hydrology	iron talc	kaolinite	lamproite
heliolite	hydrolyze	ironsmith	karpatite	Lanarkian
helizitic	hydromica	ironstone	karyocyte	lanarkite
helper-up	hydrostat	ironworks	karyogamy	land rock
hemiprism	hygrostat	irruption	karyology	landerite
homolyois	hypogenic	isallobar	karyosome	landesite
hepatitis	hypomorph	isinglass	karyotype	landslide
herbicide	hypoploid	isoclinal	katungite	Lane mill
hercynite	ibuprofen	isoclinic	kayserite	lardalite
herderite	ice front	isodesmic	keeleyite	lardstone
herrerite	ice sheet	isofacial	keen sand	larsenite
hessonite	ice shelf	isogamous	kellerite	larvikite
heteropic	Ice stone	isometric	kelly bar	lasher-on
hewettite	ideal gas	isopycnic	kelyphite	last lift
hexagonal	idioblast	isostatic	Kema plow	latrobite
hexaploid	idrialite	isotropic	kermesite	laubanite
hiddenite	ignescent	itabirite	kesterite	lausenite
hide salt	ikunolite	J curve	kettleman	lautarite
high feed	imandrite	J segment	kick back	lava dome
high reef	imitation	jack boom	kieserite	Lava Flow
high seas	impactite	jack hole	kilocusec	Lava tube
high side	impedance	jack post	kilocycle	lavendine
hill peat	implosion	jackknife	kilometer	lavialite
hillslope	impotence	jackscrew	kimzeyite	lavrovite
hindostan	inclusion	jackshaft	kinematic	lawsonite
hintzeite	increment	jacky pit	king plle	lazulitic
Histidine	index bed	jacobsite	king post	lazy balk
histogram	indialite	jacutinga	kinradite	lead bath
hodge jig	indicator	jadeitite	kinzigite	lead edge
hoist boy	induction	jadeolite	kladnoite	lead fume
hold out!	indurated	jamb wall	kliachite	lead rail
holdenite	inert gas	James jig	knebelite	lead spar
hololeims	infilling	jaspagate	knife dog	lead tree
holystone	inflation	jasperine	knock out	leaf clay
homeo-box	infusible	jasperite	knockbark	lean clay
homocline	ingot saw	jasperoid	knox hole	lecontite
homologue	inhibitor	jaspidean	kobellite	left bank
honeycomb	initiator	jaspilite	kochenite	leg piece
Hopcalite	injection	jerry man	komatiite	lennilite
horn coal	inorganic	jet corer	konimeter	lenticule
horn lead	inselberg	jet mixer	kornelite	lentiform
horn tiff	insoluble	jet shale	koutekite	lernilite
horseback	inspector	jetloader	kramerite	lesleyite

leucitite
leucoxene
leupeptin
liebigite
life zone
lifelines
lift gate
lift pump
lightning
lignite A
lignite B
lime boil
lime mica
lime rock
limestone
limewater
limonitic
line drop
lineament
lineation
linishing
linnaeite
liposomes
liptinite
liquation
list mill
listy bed
lithodeme
lithogene
lithogeny
lithoidal
lithology
lithopone
lithospar
lithotope
lithotype
live boom
live load
live lode
liver ore
livestock
lixiviant
lizardite
load cell
load fold
loadstone
loam cake
lock sill
lode plot
lodestone
lodestuff
log phase
long clay
long hole
longitude
loop drag
loose end
lorandite
lost core

lost hole
Love wave
low blast
low doors
low level
low-grade
LP delays
lublinite
lucianite
ludlamite
ludwigite
luminance
lump coal
lussatite
lutaceous
lyophilic
lyophobic
lysogenic
machinist
macrodome
macroetch
maghemite
magistral
magmatist
Magnedisc
magnesite
magnesium
magnetics
magnetism
magnetite
magnitude
main arch
main brow
main fans
main gate
main hole
main road
main roof
main rope
mainshock
malachite
maldonite
malignant
malignite
malleable
malmstone
maltesite
mammogram
manganese
manganite
manometer
manoscope
manoscopy
marcasite
mare ball
margarite
marialite
marlstone
marmatite

marmolite
marsh gas
marsh ore
marsh pan
martenite
marundite
mass aqua
mass unit
matildite
matrosite
Mauna Loa
mean size
mechanics
medjidite
meehanite
megacycle
megaspore
meiospore
mellilite
mellorite
mendipite
mendozite
merogones
meroleims
merwinite
mesopause
mesoscale
messelite
metaclase
metacryst
metadurit
metaglyph
metallify
metalloid
metaphase
metashale
meteorite
meymacite
miarolite
micaceous
micrinite
micrinoid
microglia
microlite
microlith
microspar
microvolt
microwatt
middlings
migmatite
migration
milk-opal
mill head
mill hole
mill roll
mill shoe
mill test
millerite
millivolt

millstock
millstone
mine bank
mine cage
mine dial
mine door
mine dust
mine fill
mine fire
mine head
mine iron
mine jeep
mine lamp
mine prop
mine road
mine rock
mine skip
mine tons
mineral
mineworks
minyulite
mispickel
mixed ore
mix-metal
mizzonite
mock lead
mold plug
moldavite
moldboard
moldering
molybdite
monadnock
moncheite
Mono pump
monobasic
monocable
monocline
monograin
monoploid
monosomic
monsoon
montanite
montasite
monticule
montiform
monzonite
moonstone
moor peat
mordenite
morganite
mosaicism
moss form
moss peat
motometer
mousetrap
muck boss
muck iron
muck soil
mud auger

mud crack
mud flows
mud mixer
mudcracks
mud-laden
mugearite
mule shoe
multiplow
muscovado
muscovite
mutualism
myoclonus
myrickite
myrmekite
myxamoeba
N rod bit
N segment
nagyagite
nahcolite
nanotesla
nantokite
naphthode
natrolite
navajoite
neap tide
near-mesh
nelsonite
neocortex
Neolithic
nepheline
neptunism
neptunite
neuroglia
neutron
new scrap
niccolite
nickeline
nickelite
nigritite
ningyoite
Ni-resist
nitratine
nitrolite
noble gas
nocturnal
nomograph
nonwetted
normality
normative
north end
nose pipe
notochord
novackite
nozzleman
nucleolus
nucleus
nystagmus
obduction
objective

occlusion	pargasite	pilot bit	posepnyte	Q banding
oikocryst	parkerite	pilot bob	post hole	quarrying
oil shale	pass pipe	pinch out	post jack	quarryman
old scrap	passivity	pineapple	potassium	quartzite
old waste	patent ax	pipe clay	potential	quartzoid
oldhamite	patronite	pipe coil	potty ore	quartzose
Oligocene	pay limit	pipe grab	powderman	quartzous
oligonite	pay shoot	pipe jack	powellite	quebracho
olivenite	peak load	piped air	power arm	quenching
olivinite	pearceite	pipestone	pozzolana	quickness
olivinoid	pearl ash	pistacite	precision	quicksand
omphacite	peat moss	pit frame	precursor	quiescent
on sights	Pecos ore	pit guide	predation	quitclaim
oogenesis	pectolite	pit limit	priderite	R factor
open area	pediplane	pit shale	Primacord	R plasmid
open fire	pedogenic	pit slope	primitive	rack back
open fold	pedometer	pit water	primosome	rack gear
open hole	peg point	pitch arm	principal	radiating
open rock	pegmatite	pitch off	prod cast	radiation
open shop	pegmatoid	pitch ore	prod mark	radiohalo
operation	penciling	pitchwork	proflavin	radiolite
ophiolite	penninite	pitticite	proofread	radiumite
orbicular	penthrite	pituitary	prop wall	raffinate
ore block	pentolite	placodine	propagate	rail gage
ore chute	pentrough	planation	prop-free	rain gage
ore delfe	periblain	plane man	propylite	rain wash
ore guide	periclase	planerite	prosopite	rake vein
ore magma	pericline	planisher	protamine	rankinite
ore shoot	perimorph	plant mix	protogene	ransomite
ore stamp	permalloy	platinize	protogine	razor saw
ore trend	permeable	platynite	proustite	razorback
oregonite	permitted	pleonaste	psatyrite	reactance
organelle	persuader	plication	ptilolite	ream back
orientite	pesticide	plot mark	ptygmatic	recession
ornansite	petralite	plug dome	pucherite	recessive
orthodome	petrogeny	plug shot	pull hole	rectifier
osteolite	petroleum	plumb bob	pull rope	rectorite
outrigger	petrology	plumbline	pulpstone	recycling
overaging	phacolith	plumosite	pulverize	red chalk
overbreak	phanerite	plus mesh	pumiceous	red earth
overdrive	phenacite	plutonism	pump fist	red heart
overfired	phenakite	pneumatic	pump lift	red metal
overprint	phenocopy	point bar	pump load	red roast
oxidation	phenology	poisoning	pump slip	redd bing
ozocerite	phenotype	poker man	pump sump	reddleman
P element	pheromone	polarizer	pump tree	reductant
pack hole	pholerite	polianite	pure coal	reduction
pack wall	phonolite	polishing	purpurite	reef wash
paddy bit	phosphate	poll pick	push hole	regulator
Paleozoic	phosphide	pollucite	push wave	reinerite
palladium	photicite	pollution	pyramidal	reliction
pallasite	phthanite	polycrase	pyreneite	remanence
palleting	phytolith	polygonal	pyroclast	remission
panmictic	pick mine	polymorph	pyrogenic	remolding
papagoite	picrolite	polyphase	pyrolysis	renardite
paramecin	piecework	polyploid	pyrometer	renierite
parameter	pig metal	polytropy	pyrophane	repairman
paramorph	pigeonite	pop valve	pyroretin	replisome
parbigite	pile head	porpezite	pyroxenes	repressor

repulsion	rod shaft	sand flag	seat clay	simonyite
resection	rod shell	sand jack	seat rock	sincosite
reservoir	rod slack	sand mold	secondary	sinhalite
reset bit	rod spear	sand pipe	secretion	sintering
resetting	rod stand	sand pump	sectility	siphonage
residuals	rod stock	sand reef	sedentary	skim gate
residuite	rodingite	sand roll	segregate	skin rock
resin tin	rollerman	sand seam	seif dune	slabstone
resoiling	romometer	sand size	selection	slack box
resonance	roof bolt	sand trap	semiloose	slag dump
reticular	roof jack	sand wall	semseyite	slag lead
retorting	roof rock	sandburrs	separator	slaggable
reversion	roof work	sanded in	sepiolite	slip face
revetment	room boss	sandstone	septarian	slip rate
rhodesite	room neck	saprolite	septarium	Sniceball
rhodolite	root clay	saprolith	sequester	Snirtball
rhodonite	root hook	sartorite	serandite	Snockball
rhythmite	rope core	sassoline	severance	snow line
rice coal	rope drum	sassolite	seyberite	snowfield
richetite	roquesite	satellite	shaft kip	soapstone
ride over	rose opal	saturated	shaft set	sole mark
rifle bar	rosin tin	sauconite	shag boss	species
rifle nut	rotameter	saukovite	shale oil	spermatid
rift zone	rubbleman	sawsetter	shale pit	spirillum
right lay	rubellite	scabbling	shear cut	star dune
ring arch	rubicelle	scacchite	shelf sea	statistic
ring coal	ruby mica	scantling	shinarump	steam gas
ring dike	ruby sand	scapolite	shingling	steam jet
ring main	ruby zinc	scarifier	shoreline	steel bit
ring wall	rudaceous	scavenger	short awn	steel boy
rise face	runaround	scheelite	short run	steel ore
rivelaine	Ruoss jig	schematic	shortwall	stem cell
river bar	rush gold	schistose	shot bort	stenonite
RNA phage	ruthenium	schlieren	shot fast	step reef
road dust	S curve	schoepite	shot feed	step vein
rock base	sag meter	scholzite	shot rock	stichtite
rock body	sag tower	schorlite	shot soil	stiff mud
rock bolt	sagenitic	schungite	shotcrete	stiffener
rock bump	sahlinite	sclaffery	shrinkage	stiffness
rock cork	salimeter	scolecite	Siam ruby	sting-out
rock dust	salnatron	scooptram	sickening	stinkdamp
rock flow	salt boot	scopulite	side adit	stockpile
rock hole	salt cake	scorifier	side shot	stockwork
rock meal	salt cote	scoriform	side spit	stockyard
rock melt	salt dome	scorodite	sideboard	stokehole
rock milk	salt flat	scotching	sideplate	stokesite
rock rake	salt mine	scrap bar	siderodot	stoltzite
rock roll	salt plug	screening	siderogel	stomodeum
rock ruby	salt vein	screw fan	siderosis	stone pit
rock salt	salt wall	screwfeed	sidewalls	stone saw
rock silk	salt well	screwjack	siegenite	stonehead
rock slip	saltation	screwplug	siliceous	stonework
rock soap	saltpeter	sea bloom	silicosis	stool end
rock spar	saltworks	sea level	sillenite	stovepipe
rock type	sampleite	sea slick	silt size	strahlite
rock wool	samsonite	sea stack	silt trap	streaking
rockshaft	sand boil	sea state	siltation	streaming
rockslide	sand dike	seamanite	siltstone	strengite
rod proof	sand fill	seasoning	silvering	striation

strip pit
stripping
strontium
structure
strunzite
stylolite
subaerial
subarkose
subhedral
subjacent
sublimate
subsample
subsoil
substrate
succinite
sudburite
sulfonite
sulfydril
sulvanite
sump fuse
sump shot
sun check
sun crack
supercoil
supergene
surcharge
surf zone
surficial
surge bin
surveying
susannite
sussexite
swamp ore
swartzite
swing cut
swivelase
sylvanite
sylvester
sylvinite
symbiosis
synclinal
syncytium
synergism
syngeneic
synneusis
syntectic
synthesis
Tay-Sachs
telophase
teratogen
testicles
tholeiite
Threonine
thymidine
titration
topsoil
transform
trap rock
tributary

trihybrid
twin spot
ubiquitin
unit cell
variation
ventifact
viability
virulence
viscocity
Viscosity
volcanism
volcano
water gap
watershed
WD repeat
weak acid
weak base
weather
wild-type
X linkage
X:A ratio
Xenograft
Y linkage
yolk plug
zoologist

8

Abbe jar
ablation
abortion
abortive
ab plane
abrasion
abutment
acceptor
accuracy
achirite
achroite
acicular
acid fog
acid ore
acidosis
acoustic
acrosome
actinide
actinote
activity
acyl-CoA
adhesion
aerovane
A-factor
affected
air glow
air mass
albedo
alkanoyl
allotype

allozyme
Alluvium
altitude
altruism
amniotic
amplexus
amplicon
ampullae
amygdala
anabolic
anaerobe
analyzer
anaphase
anatexis
anauxite
ancylite
andesine
Andesite
andorite
anemia
Angstrom
anhedral
Animalia
ankerite
annivite
anorthic
antibody
apomixis
appendix
aquifuge
Aquitard
arcanite
arch rib
arch set
Archaean
argillic
Arginine
argulite
argyrite
argyrose
arkosite
armenite
arnimite
arrastra
arrastre
arrester
arsenate
arsenite
artesian
artifact
artinite
asbestos
asbestus
asbolane
asbolite
aseismic
Ash flow
ashstone
asperity

assembly
asterism
at grade
Atkinson
atomizer
attitude
attritus
augelite
auralite
autogamy
autolith
autosome
autunite
awaruite
axiolite
azurlite
bacalite
bacillus
backfill
backfire
backhand
backhaul
backlash
backrush
backstay
backwash
bacteria
baculite
badlands
baghouse
bakerite
banakite
banksman
bankwork
baralyme
bararite
barefoot
barequeo
barranca
barrings
barylite
basaltic
basanite
base box
base map
base ore
basement
basining
Baum jig
baum pot
bauxitic
bavenite
bay salt
bayerite
bc-joint
bean ore
bearsite
bed load
bed vein

bell jar
bell tap
bell top
belonite
belovite
benching
benzenol
beryloid
Bessemer
beta ray
beta tin
beta-DNA
betafite
betatron
beyerite
bilinite
bin gate
bing ore
bioassay
biofilms
biogenic
biophile
biramous
bivalent
blakeite
blankoff
blastula
blizzard
blotting
cancer
capacity
catalyst
cataract
catheter
cellular
cerebrum
chelator
chemical
chi site
chloride
chlorite
chordate
chromite
cleavage
coenzyme
cofactor
compound
consumer
cortisol
coupling
creatine
crevasse
cysteine
cytidine
cytology
cytosine
davidite
deletion
dementia

92

denature
desert
Devonian
dew cell
diagnose
dialysis
dihybrid
dilution
dip pole
dip slip
diplopia
Di-polar
diuretic
doldrums
dolomite
dominant
dopamine
dormancy
dry haze
dynamics
ebb tide
ecdysone
ecliptic
ectoderm
efficacy
effusion
electron
emeralds
emulsion
endoderm
energy
enhancer
enhydros
enthalpy
entryman
envelope
epigenic
epiphyte
epsomite
equiform
ericaite
erratics
eruption
eruptive
essexite
essonite
estrogen
etindite
eucolite
eugenics
euhedral
eulytite
euosmite
euploidy
eustatic
eutectic
eutomous
euxamite
euxenite

evaluate
evansite
evenkite
exploder
exposure
extrados
eye wall
eyesight
F factor
face run
fact cut
faheyite
fahlband
fairlead
fan fold
fan laws
fassaite
fast end
fat clay
fate map
faulting
faustite
Fauvelle
fayalite
feedhead
feldspar
felsitic
felstone
ferritin
fersmite
ferutile
fettling
fieldite
filiform
filigree
filtrate
fimbriae
fineness
fire rib
fireback
fireclay
firedamp
fishtail
fissures
fittings
fiveling
fixation
flagging
flapping
flat cut
flatiron
flatting
flawless
flexible
floating
floccule
florspar
flow law
flummery

fluorene
fluoride
fluorine
fluorite
flushing
fly gate
flywheel
foliated
food web
foot rod
footeite
footmark
footwall
forecast
foreland
forelimb
forepole
foul gas
founding
fourfold
fourling
foxbench
fraction
fracture
fragment
freezing
Fumarole
furanose
ganglion
gene map
genetics
genotype
geodetic
gin race
gin ring
ginorite
glassies
glessite
globular
glucagon
glycerol
G-M tube
gob dump
gob fire
gob pile
gob road
gob room
gob wall
go-devil
goethite
going in
Golconda
gold pan
goldfoil
goldleaf
Gondwana
gone off
gorgulho
gradient

grainers
grandite
granitic
granular
graphite
grayband
greigite
grinding
gritting
grothite
grouting
groutite
grub saw
grubbing
gugiaite
guillies
gumbrine
gummings
guniting
guy line
guy ring
guy rope
gyratory
hackiron
haeggite
half end
half set
hand jig
handyman
hangfire
hard way
hardener
hardhead
hardness
harmonic
harriers
hartsalz
Harz jig
hatching
hatchure
haulaway
hauynite
hawaiite
head end
headgear
headings
headland
headline
headrace
headroom
headrope
headtree
headwall
headwork
health
heatings
helenite
helicase
heliodor

Hematine
hematite
hemetite
hemidome
hemiopal
hemloite
henryite
hepatite
heredity
highwall
hillside
hjelmite
hoisting
hoistman
holdback
holdfast
Holocene
homeosis
homology
horadiam
hornfels
hoshiite
hot cell
hot spot
humacite
humidity
humiture
humocoll
humosite
hutching
hyacinth
hydroxyl
hypogeal
hypogeic
hypogene
ice plug
ice spar
identity
idiogram
idocrase
igdloite
ignition
ilmenite
immunity
impinger
improper
impurity
in vitro
incubate
inderite
infrared
ingotism
injector
inkstone
instroke
insulate
intersex
interval
intrados

invasion
inverted
iodyrite
iron hat
iron man
iron ore
iron pan
ironshot
ischemia
isochore
isochron
isocline
isogenic
isograde
isolator
isomeric
isopical
isopleth
isopynic
isoseism
Isostasy
isotherm
isotonic
isotropy
isotypic
Ixiolite
jack pit
jackhead
jackpipe
jackroll
jag bolt
jalpaite
jar mill
jarosite
jasponyx
jet coal
jet hole
jet mill
jet pump
jet rock
jetstone
jig brow
jig dips
Jim Crow
jimboite
jointing
jugglers
junction
junk DNA
Jurassic
jury rig
juvenile
kalicine
kalinite
kamacite
Kanawhan
kaolinic
kasolite
katazone

kb (kbp)
Keewatin
kerolite
keystone
kiln-dry
kingbolt
kirovite
kirvings
kleinite
klintite
kneading
knee pad
knobbing
knocking
knogging
kraurite
krausite
kundaite
kurtosis
kyrosite
lability
lag time
lake ore
lamellar
lamp cup
landfill
landform
landslip
lapidary
lard oil
laterite
laterlog
lathlike
latitude
Laurasia
lavatory
lavenite
lay rope
layering
lazulite
lazurite
leachate
leaching
lead lap
leadings
lean ore
leg wire
lehr man
lenticle
lepolite
let into
lethargy
leukemia
leveling
levelman
leverman
lievrite
lifeline
lighting

lightman
lignitic
ligurite
likasite
lime pan
lime pit
lime set
limonite
limurite
linarite
line map
lines up
linesman
link bar
linneite
liparite
list pan
litharge
lithoxyl
littoral
liverite
livesite
lixivium
loadings
load-out
loadstar
lobbying
location
lode tin
loeweite
lofthead
long awn
long run
long tom
longwall
loparite
lopezite
lopolith
loseyite
low coal
low gear
lucinite
lueshite
lug down
luminous
lump ore
lusakite
lutecite
luzonite
lymphoma
lynx eye
lysosome
machined
maculose
madogram
mafelsic
magazine
magmatic
magnesia

magnetic
main rod
main tie
main way
make gas
malinite
malleate
malonate
manchado
manshift
mantle
marbella
marokite
marshite
massicot
masuyite
mat pack
matraite
matter
maturity
mayenite
mboziite
measures
meiocyte
meionite
melanite
melatope
melilite
melinite
melonite
membrane
Menevian
menilite
meniscus
mephitis
merchant
meroxene
mesogene
mesohigh
mesolite
mesomere
Mesozoic
mesozone
metalist
metallic
metaloid
metamale
metamere
metamict
metasome
metaxite
miascite
Micanite
microbar
microite
midbrain
miersite
milarite
mil-foot

mill bar
mill car
mill ore
mill run
millibar
milligal
milltons
mimetene
mimetite
mine car
mine fan
mine run
mine tin
minehead
miscible
misenite
mock ore
modeling
modifier
Moe gage
moganite
mohavite
moisture
mojavite
molarity
moldings
molecule
momentum
monazite
monetite
monogene
monolith
monorail
monosomy
monotron
monument
moorband
morals
mosesite
motioner
motorman
mountain
mounting
muck bar
muck saw
mud belt
mud cake
mud cast
mud pump
mud ring
mud rush
mud scow
mud sump
mudcrack
mudstone
mutation
mylonite
myotonia
nacreous

nadorite
napthoid
nauckite
nebulite
neomorph
neoplasm
nephrite
new sand
nichrome
nickings
nicolite
niperyth
nitrogen
nobleite
nolanite
Nolvadex
nomogram
nonmetal
nose out
noselite
notching
noumeite
nuclease
nucleoid
nut coal
nutation
obsidian
oil base
oil pump
oil sand
oilstone
old hole
ollenite
on plane
oncogene
one shot
onofrite
onsetter
Ontarian
open off
open pot
opencast
openings
operator
orcelite
ordinate
ore band
ore boat
ore boil
ore dike
ore face
ore pipe
ore plot
ore sill
ore vein
ore zone
organism
ori site
oriental

oriented
orocline
orogenic
orometer
orpiment
ostracod
outburst
out-over
outslope
overcast
overgate
overhang
overhaul
overload
override
overrope
overshot
overside
oversize
overtime
overwind
oxammite
oxidizer
oxyphile
ozarkite
ozonizer
packfong
packsand
pagodite
Pahoehoe
painting
palasome
paleosol
pallidum
panabase
pan-edge
parabola
parallax
parasite
parental
parhelia
parisite
particle
pascoite
pat coal
pathogen
pavement
pavilion
pavonite
pay load
pay rock
pea coal
pea grit
pearlite
peastone
peat bed
peat bog
peat gel
peat hag

pedalfer
pedestal
pedigree
pediment
pedology
Pelletol
pendulum
penstock
pentagon
penthrit
peridote
perlitic
perthite
pervious
petalite
petaloid
petuntze
phengite
phosphor
phreatic
phthisis
phyllite
phyteral
pick boy
pickling
pickwork
picotite
piedmont
pier cap
pier dam
piercing
pig foot
pig lead
pigotite
pilarite
pile dam
pimelite
pinacoid
pinchbar
pine tar
pinguite
pinnacle
pipe bit
pipettes
pisanite
pisolite
pisolith
pit bank
pit boss
pit brow
pit cage
pit hand
pit hill
pit lamp
pit pony
pit prop
pit room
pit rope
pit sand

pit wood
placenta
plaiting
plankton
planning
planosol
plasma
platelet
platform
platinum
platting
plattman
plessite
plow cut
plucking
plug bit
plug box
plugging
plughole
plumbago
plumbing
plumbous
plumites
plutonic
poaching
poikilit
polarity
Polaroid
policy
polygene
polykras
polynite
polysome
polytypy
polyxene
pony set
pop shot
porosity
porphyry
porthole
positive
positron
pot kiln
pot lead
potarite
potassic
potentia
potstone
pounceon
prasopal
preblast
precious
prehnite
pre-mRNA
pressure
priceite
prillion
princess
producer

promoter
property
prophage
prophase
proppant
propping
prospect
protease
Proteome
proton
prove up
provirus
proximal
psammite
psephite
puddling
pull pin
pulsator
pumicite
pump bob
pump rod
PVC belt
pyribole
pyrolite
pyroxene
pyrrhite
pyruvate
quagmire
quantity
quarrier
quartzic
quincite
rabatage
rabbling
radiated
radium G
ragstone
rainwash
ram pump
rapakivi
rashings
Rasorite
rate law
raw coal
raw fuel
raw mica
reactant
reactive
receptor
recharge
recorder
recovery
red beds
red cake
red clay
red lead
reddsman
red-hard
reduzate

reef cap
reel boy
refikite
refinery
refining
regional
reglette
regolith
reheater
relevé
rendrock
reniform
replicon
rerailer
research
reserves
residual
residuum
resinite
resinoid
resinous
resistor
resource
reticule
retiform
retinite
reversal
reversed
reworked
Rf value
rhabdite
rheidity
rheology
rheostat
rhizobia
rhizoids
rhoenite
rholites
rhomboid
Rhyolite
rib boss
rib dust
rib hole
rib line
rib mesh
ribosome
ribozyme
rib-side
riders
rigidity
rime ice
ring ore
ring pit
ring-cut
rinneite
rip tide
riparian
rives in
roadhead

roadster
roasting
Roburite
rock bit
rock cut
rockfall
rockhead
rockwood
rod damp
rod dope
rod drag
rod drop
rod mill
rod plug
rod pull
rod slap
rod snap
roentgen
roestone
romanite
roof cut
rope lay
rosasite
rose bit
roselite
rosolite
rough ER
roughing
roughway
rozenite
ruberite
rubidium
ruby tin
ruinform
rumanite
ruminant
runoff
Sabalite
safreiro
sag bolt
sag pipe
sagenite
sagponds
saleeite
salesite
salinity
salitral
salmoite
saltspar
samarium
sampling
sand bar
sand bed
sandarac
sandrock
sanidine
saponite
sapphire
saprocol

sapropel
sardonyx
satelite
saw gang
scabbler
scaffold
scale-up
scalping
scandium
scantite
scarfing
scarring
scavenge
scawtite
schiller
scoopman
scorious
scrablag
scrubber
sculping
sea arch
sea cave
sea coal
sea sand
sea-foam
seal off
seamount
seam-out
seasoned
seconite
Sediment
selector
selenite
selenium
self-act
sellaite
selvedge
semiarid
semiopal
septaria
sericite
Serology
serotype
serumite
set i.d.
set o.d.
shackler
shagreen
sharpite
shattery
Shearing
shearpin
shedline
sheeters
sheeting
shelling
shepherd
shingler
shoo-fly

shooting
shore up
shothole
shotting
shoulder
shungite
siallite
siberite
sideline
siderite
siderosa
siderose
sidertil
sigloite
silcrete
silexite
silicate
silt box
Silurian
simetite
sinkhole
sipylite
skewness
skiagite
skialith
skimming
skimping
skipping
skirting
slabbing
slacking
slag car
slag pot
slagging
sludge
smelting
snowball
snowline
solution
spectrum
splicing
stacking
stations
stavrite
stealite
steatite
stellate
stem bag
stemming
stenting
step cut
stiblite
stibnite
stibnium
sticking
stilbite
stimulus
stoneman
stoopway

stop end
stopping
stottite
straddle
straight
stranded
strebbau
strength
stress
striated
strike 1
striking
stringer
stripper
struvite
stunning
suberain
subgrade
sublevel
substage
sulfuret
sum rule
sun gear
sun opal
sun vein
sundtite
sunshine
sunstone
superdip
supports
surveyor
sway rod
sweaters
sweating
sweeping
symmetry
symptoms
synapsis
syncline
syndrome
syntexis
taconite
taking
TATA box
tectonic
telomere
template
terminus
thalamus
toxins
traction
trenches
triploid
trisomic
tundra
tyrosine
upstream
vaccinia
values

96

variable
variance
velocity
visceral
volatile
windpipe
Windward
X linked
xenolith
Y linked
yolk sac
zygotene

7

aa lava
abaxial
abdomen
abiotic
abraded
abraser
abysmal
abyssal
acidize
acids
aciform
acinose
acinote
acinous
aclinal
aclinic
adenine
aerosol
agonist
Alanine
albumen
altered
alveoli
ammonia
amniote
ampulla
amylase
amyloid
analyte
anatase
anatomy
angling
angular
anilite
annelid
anomaly
anthill
antigen
AP site
aphrite
aphyric
aplitic
apogamy

apyrous
aqueous
Aquifer
Archaea
Archean
arching
arenite
aridity
arkosic
arroyos
arsenic
asbolan
asphalt
aspirin
assayer
astatic
asteria
atopite
atrophy
aureole
axinite
axoneme
axstone
azimuth
azorite
azurite
B cells
bacilli
backarc
backhoe
backing
bad air
bad top
baffler
bailiff
bailing
balance
ballast
ballers
balling
banking
bantams
baotite
bar rig
bar tin
barchan
barilla
baroque
barrier
barring
barytes
bases
basidia
bastard
bastite
bathyal
battery
bauxite
bazzite

bearers
bearing
bedding
bedrock
beeches
belgite
belland
bellies
bellite
bellows
bellund
belting
beltman
benches
benthos
biaxial
bicable
bigging
binnite
bioherm
biolite
biolith
biomass
biome
biota
biotite
bitumen
bivalve
blanket
blaster
blowout
boiling
bornite
Breccia
brittle
bronchi
budding
C plant
calcite
Caldera
caliche
Calorie
carrier
caspase
cathode
caudate
chimera
chorion
chronic
cinders
cistron
clastic
climate
cloning
cocaine
coesite
colloid
compost
control

coquina
crust
crystal
culture
cytohet
cytosol
decibel
delta
density
diabase
diamond
diatoms
digoxin
diorite
diploid
diurnal
drizzle
drought
drumlin
ecology
-ectomy
El Nino
El Niño
element
entropy
epaulet
epiboly
epidote
epigene
episome
epitaxy
epizone
Erinide
erinoid
erosion
erratic
estuary
etching
ethanol
euclase
euploid
europia
euscope
eustasy
eutaxic
euxinic
exinite
exinoid
exploit
express
eyebolt
F scale
face-on
fahlerz
fallers
fan cut
fatigue
fauna
feloids

felsite
felspar
fenster
feral
ferrate
ferride
ferrite
ferrous
fibrous
filling
fiorite
fire up
firebox
fireman
fishing
fissile
fission
fissure
fitting
flagger
flamper
flapper
flaring
flashes
flavins
flexing
Flexlok
flexure
flitter
floater
floocan
flood
flookan
flora
floured
flowage
fluting
fluvial
fluxing
flyrock
folding
foliate
footing
footman
forearc
forebay
foreman
foreset
forstid
forward
fossick
fouling
foyaite
fungi
G stone
gas law
genetic
geodesy
geology

gin pit
ginging
giraffe
girasol
gizzard
glacial
glacier
gladite
gliding
glimmer
glinite
gliosis
glucine
glucose
glycine
glyptic
gobbing
gondola
gonidia
goosing
gouging
gradall
grading
grampus
granite
granule
graphic
grapple
grating
graupel
gravity
grayite
greaser
greisen
grisley
grizzly
groover
grouter
grow-on
grunter
guanine
gudgeon
gummite
gunboat
gunniss
gyprock
gypsite
habitat
hachure
hairpin
halitic
halogen
hammada
handset
hang-up
haplite
haploid
hardhat
hardpan

harrock
hartine
hartite
hassing
haulage
hauling
headbox
heading
headway
heaving
hectare
hedging
helvite
hepatin
hessite
hillock
hircite
histone
hitcher
hoedown
hoelite
hogback
hoister
holding
hole-in
holeman
holings
hollows
homolog
hook-on
hopeite
hoppers
horizon
hormone
hot top
hotspot
howlite
H-piece
hulsite
humidex
humopel
humus
hunting
huntite
hushing
hutcher
hyaline
hyalite
hydrate
hydrite
hydrous
hyperon
hypoxia
ice age
ice cap
ice run
iceberg
igneous
igniter

ihleite
ijolite
ilesite
ill air
ilvaite
impound
impulse
in fork
in situ
in vivo
incline
indraft
inducer
inertia
inesite
ingress
inosine
in-over
insulin
inyoite
iranite
iridium
irinite
iserine
isobase
isobath
isocals
isocarb
isograd
isogram
isohume
isohyet
isolate
isoline
isolith
isomers
isopach
isorads
isotach
isotope
isotypy
isozyme
jacinth
jackleg
jadeite
jagoite
jam out
jarlite
jetters
jetting
jib end
jig bed
jig pin
jigging
joseite
joule
journal
journey
jumbler

jumbles
junking
kalamin
kandite
kaoleen
kaoline
kasoite
keatite
kehoite
kempite
keratin
kernite
kerogen
kerrite
key bed
kidneys
killing
kilneye
kilnman
kiloton
kindred
kingdom
kirving
kneeler
knuckle
kobeite
kriging
kunzite
kyanite
La Niña
lactate
lactose
lagging
lamella
lamings
lamping
lampman
lanchut
landing
landsat
langite
Langley
lantern
Lapilli
lardite
larnite
lashing
lash-up
latches
lateral
latosol
lattice
laueite
launder
laurite
lautite
layered
leacher
leadage

leaders
leakage
learies
leaving
leelite
leering
Leeward
lehiite
lengths
lensing
leonite
Leucine
leucite
leveler
library
lifters
lifting
lignite
limnite
line up
lineage
linkage
lionite
liptite
listing
lithium
lithoid
L-joint
loading
loaming
located
lockage
locknut
lockpin
lofting
logbook
loodwin
looping
loopway
loosing
louvers
low bed
lozenge
luckite
LULUs
Lumnite
lyddite
lysogen
mçlange
macadam
maceral
made up
maenite
magma
makings
malacon
malpais
mandrel
mandril

manhole
manlock
mapping
marlite
marsh
martite
mascons
maskeeg
massive
matting
mattock
maxwell
McGinty
meander
medulla
meeting
megabar
megalo-
-megaly
Megator
meiosis
melanic
mellite
melting
men on
mercury
metamic
methane
micelle
micrite
microbe
microhm
middles
middoor
miemite
miesite
milling
millman
mimetic
mimicry
Mineral
Miocene
misfire
mitosis
mixture
moating
modeler
mofette
mohsite
molasse
molding
mongrel
monitor
monomer
monsoon
montana
Montian
moorlog

Moraine
mordant
mortice
mortise
mossing
mossite
mourite
mucking
mud bit
mud gun
mud hog
mud log
mud pot
mudding
mudflow
mudline
muffler
mulch
muleway
mulling
mullite
mullock
mutagen
myeloma
nablock
nacrite
naphtha
nascent
Na-spar
natrite
natrium
natrona
needled
needles
neolite
neoteny
neritic
net cut
neuroid
neurula
neutral
neutron
ngavite
nickase
nicking
NIMBY
niobite
niobium
nitrate
nodular
Norbide
nordite
nose in
notcher
nowcast
N-truss
nuclein
nucleon

nucleus
nuclide
oil pot
okenite
old age
oldland
oligist
olivine
omnibus
on line
onegite
oogonia
olites
oolitic
opacite
opacity
opaline
opalite
opencut
opening
openset
ophitic
opiates
orbital
ore bed
ore bin
ore car
orebody
orepass
organic
orifice
orogeny
oronite
orthite
orthose
osmosis
-ostomy
otavite
outcrop
outfall
outlier
outtake
outwash
ovaries
overcut
overlap
overlay
overrun
ovulite
oxalite
oxidate
oxonite
ozone
packing
Pahrump
paludal
pancake
Pangaea

panhead
panning
Paragon
paralic
parting
passage
pasting
pattern
pay ore
pay out
pea ore
peatman
pedocal
pelagic
pelitic
penalty
pendant
penning
pentice
peptide
peptize
peridot
perlite
Permian
perpend
petcock
petrous
petzite
-philia
physics
picacho
picking
picture
piebald
piercer
pig bed
pinched
piotine
pipeman
pit ash
pit bar
pit eye
pitcher
pithead
pitting
pitwork
placebo
plasmid
plastic
plastid
-plasty
plateau
platina
plugged
plugman
plumbic
plummet
plumose

plunger
poleman
polygon
polymer
pontoon
pophole
popping
portage
posting
pot ore
potable
pothole
potting
pounder
power
preheat
prepare
present
presser
primary
primase
priming
probing
problem
process
produce
product
profile
proline
prolong
protein
protest
protist
protore
prypole
puddler
pullway
pumping
puncher
purines
purlins
putamen
pycnite
pyrabol
pyramid
pyrites
pyritic
quality
quarman
quarpit
quarrel
quarter
quartzy
R group
rabbler
raceway
rack up
racking

Radiata
radical
rafting
ragging
rainbow
raising
ramming
rappage
rapping
raspite
ratchet
rathite
rathole
rattler
rauvite
raw ore
raydist
raywork
realgar
reaming
recover
red dog
red mud
red ore
redrill
redsear
reefing
reeving
refusal
regulus
reinite
remnant
rending
replica
reserve
residue
resuing
retigen
retract
retreat
returns
retzian
reussin
rhenium
-rhexis
rhodite
rhodium
rhombic
rhombus
ribbing
ridding
riffler
rifling
rifting
rigging
rimrock
ringing
rinkite

rinsing
ripping
riveter
roadbed
roadman
roadway
roaster
robbing
rocking
rockman
rod bit
rod sag
rodding
rodlike
rollman
romeite
roofing
roof-up
ropeway
rosette
roweite
royalty
rubasse
run dry
runaway
runback
runners
running
rupture
rustler
sahlite
salband
salines
salmlak
saltbox
saltern
salting
saltpan
saltpit
salvage
sampler
sandbag
sandbar
sandhog
sandman
saponin
sappare
sarcoma
sardine
sardius
savanna
scabble
scaling
scallop
scalper
scarfer
scarify
scatter
science

scouter
scraper
scratch
screens
scronge
sealant
sealing
seating
seawall
seconds
sectile
section
secular
seeding
seismic
seizure
selvage
senaite
seriate
serrate
serving
set bit
setting
settler
shackle
shading
shaking
shalene
shamble
shammel
shangie
shearer
shifter
shingle
shining
shooter
shoring
shotter
showing
shuttle
sieving
sifting
silicic
silicon
silklay
sillite
silting
siltite
similor
singing
sinking
sinople
S-joint
skimmer
slacken
solvent
sorting
SOS box
species

statics
station
stemmer
stenton
step up
stibium
stickup
stinger
stinker
stirian
stoking
stooled
stooper
stoping
stopoff
stowage
stowing
stratum
studdle
stuffed
stumper
subarid
subbase
sublime
suction
sulfate
sulfide
sulfite
sullage
sulphur
sumping
sumpman
sun bed
support
surface
surfeit
surging
suspent
svabite
swallow
swamp
swilley
swither
syenite
sylvane
sylvine
sylvite
synapse
synform
syngamy
syntaxy
synteny
tabular
taiga
Tamofen
tension
terrace
texture
thymine

thyroid
tillite
titrant
tombolo
tonsils
topsoil
trachea
triplet
trisomy
tritium
trypsin
tsunami
tubulin
uridine
vaccine
vacuole
variant
variate
vesicle
vitamin
volcano
voltage
weather
wetland
X ray

6

a axis
a-axis
abrade
abzyme
achene
acidic
acmite
albedo
albino
albite
alkane
alkene
alkyne
allele
amnion
amorph
analog
anemia
anlage
annite
anoxia
anther
anthra
aplite
Apocal
arched
arcose
arkose
arroyo
artery

arthro
ashlar
AS-PCR
aspect
asthma
ataxia
ataxic
atom
atrium
augite
aurora
aurous
b axis
baaken
bahada
bailer
bajada
baking
ballas
banded
banket
barges
baring
barite
barium
barley
barrel
barren
barrow
baryta
Basalt
basket
basset
bating
batten
batter
bearer
beater
bedded
belite
belith
bellan
belled
benchy
berdan
binder
biomes
biopsy
bladed
blaize
bolide
bracts
buffer
bursae
callus
canopy
capsid
carbon
cation

cavern	fibrin	gridaw	hyper-	kicker
cervix	filler	groove	-iasis	killas
cirque	filter	grouan	icecap	kinase
city	finger	ground	idaite	kindly
cleave	firing	growan	illite	kishly
coccus	fitter	growth	-illus	klippe
-coele	flaggy	grueso	impact	kmaite
colony	flange	grundy	incrop	K-spar
column	flight	guides	indite	kunkur
contig	floats	gummer	indium	kuroko
core	Flotol	gunite	inerts	labile
cortex	flucan	gunnie	iingate	lacing
cosmid	flukan	gurlet	inlier	ladder
crater	fluken	gusset	inmost	ladler
craton	flumed	gutter	insert	lamina
Cullin	flurry	gypsum	inside	lander
curite	flysch	H wave	intake	lanugo
cutoff	fodder	haboob	iinvert	lapped
cyclin	forble	hackly	inwall	lasher
dacite	forcer	haiarn	iodine	lasque
Dalton	format	halide	iolite	latent
desert	fossil	halite	ionite	latite
digest	fother	hammer	ions	latten
dipole	freeze	hanger	iozite	lay-by
divide	fungus	harrie	isobar	layout
d-loop	fusion	harrow	isogal	lazuli
domain	gabbro	hasson	isogam	leader
dynein	galaxy	hauyne	isogon	league
ejecta	galena	hawser	isomer	leaser
embryo	gamete	hazard	isopic	lectin
energy	gangue	header	isopor	legend
enzyme	garnet	hearth	isovol	legume
eolian	gene	heat	jacket	lentil
equant	genome	heater	jailer	lesion
escape	GeoMan	height	jargon	levels
ethine	geyser	helium	jasper	levyne
ethyne	ginney	hewing	jenkin	lichen
eulite	girdle	hiatal	jib in	lifter
exotic	glance	hiatus	jigger	ligand
F.L.P.	Gleeds	hoggan	jockey	ligase
f.o.b.	gneiss	hogger	joggle	ligate
fabric	goaves	hoggin	joints	likely
facies	gobber	holers	jointy	limnic
facing	goffan	holing	jumble	linear
family	goiter	hoodoo	jumper	lingot
famine	gopher	hopper	junket	lining
fanner	gossan	hoppet	jkanase	linker
faunal	gotten	hoppit	kankar	linsey
feeder	gozzan	hotbed	kaolin	lintel
feinig	Graben	howell	karang	lipase
felite	graded	hugger	karyon	liquid
felsic	grader	humins	keeper	lithic
felted	graith	humite	kellow	litmus
femmer	granat	humper	Kelvin	litter
fender	grater	hungry	kernel	loader
fenite	gravel	hurdle	kettle	locker
ferric	grease	hyalin	kevell	loipon
fettle	greasy	hybrid	kibbal	lonkey
fibril	greave	Hydrox	kibble	looper

looses
lumber
lunker
luster
luting
lutite
lutose
lydite
lysate
lysine
maacle
macled
mafite
makeup
mallan
maltha
mantle
manway
marble
marcus
marker
marrow
martic
massif
matrix
matter
mature
median
medium
megger
member
mestre
meteor
metore
micron
middle
milled
miners
mining
minion
minium
mirage
mixing
mixite
mohole
monkey
montre
Morcol
morgen
morlop
mortar
morula
mosaic
mother
mottle
mucker
muckle
mud up
mudcap

muffle
muller
mundic
murine
muskeg
mutant
naetig
narrow
native
natron
nattle
nebula
needle
nekton
neuron
newton
nickel
nipple
nodule
Norite
normal
nosean
nosite
NSAIDs
nubber
Nuflex
nugget
nullah
o.m.s.
on air
oocyte
oogamy
oolite
oolith
opaque
operon
ophite
optics
option
orient
origin
ormolu
orogen
osmite
osmium
outlay
outlet
output
oxygen
P site
P wave
pacite
packer
paddle
panman
pascal
passby
patchy
patent

-pathy
patina
paxite
pearly
peat
pebble
pedion
peeler
pegleg
peldon
pelite
pelter
pelyte
-penia
period
pest
petite
phenol
phloem
photon
picker
picket
pickle
pickup
picral
pigsty
piking
piling
pillar
pillow
pinion
pinite
pinnel
pintle
piping
piracy
piston
pitchy
pitman
pitmen
placer
planar
planer
planet
plaque
plasma
plenum
plexus
ploidy
plunge
Pluton
pocket
podsol
Podzol
polder
poling
polish
pollux
pontil

poppet
porous
portal
porter
potash
potlid
potter
powder
premix
primer
profit
proper
proton
puddle
pulpit
pumice
pumper
pusher
pyrene
pyrite
pyrope
Q wave
quarry
quartz
queane
queery
quench
R wave
rabble
radial
radian
radium
radius
rakers
rammel
rammer
rap-in
rating
ravine
reamer
recast
recent
reddle
reduce
refine
refuse
regime
reject
relict
relief
rescue
retina
retort
return
rewash
-rhage
ribbon
ribose
ricket

riddle
riding
riffle
rig up
rigged
rigger
rig-up
rilles
riming
rincon
ringer
ripper
ripple
riprap
rising
risk
rock
rocker
rodman
rodney
roller
rondle
rooter
rosing
rosite
rotary
rotche
rotors
roxite
rubber
rubble
rudite
run in
runner
runoff
runout
rutile
S- mix
S wave
sabkha
saddle
safety
sagger
salina
saline
salite
samite
sample
sawyer
scabby
scalar
scaler
scales
scares
schist
sconce
scones
scoria
scotch

scovan
scowle
screen
scribe
scroll
scrowl
scruff
sculls
seated
sebkha
sector
segger
seiche
selfed
sensor
septum
series
Serine
shaker
sheath
sheave
sheets
shield
shiver
shoran
shorts
shovel
sialma
sienna
sierra
sights
silica
silver
sinker
sinter
siphon
sizing
skares
skerry
skewed
skirts
skulls
smog
soil
solute
somite
source
spines
spring
stator
stench
steppe
sterny
sticky
stifle
stitch
stoker
stones
stoper

stowce
strain
strake
straps
strata
streak
stream
stress
striae
strike
string
stripe
stroke
strong
stythe
sulfur
sumper
survey
swaugh
sweeps
switch
symbol
T cell
T Test
tendon
Tephra
terrae
tester
testes
tetrad
theory
thrush
thymus
tremor
trench
tundra
uracil
valine
vector
virion
viroid
volume
vulcan
weight
wobble
work
zygote

5

abime
abyss
actin
acute
agate
algae
alloy
andre

anion
anode
aorta
apron
aràte
areng
aréte
argil
argon
arite
armor
arrow
ascus
assay
asset
aster
atoll
augen
auger
auxin
azure
backs
bacon
balas
balls
banos
barer
barro
basic
basin
batch
baulk
beach
beads
beans
belly
bench
bends
berms
beryl
biard
billy
biome
biota
blade
blaes
blank
blast
block
blood
bog
bolus
breed
calyx
cata-
-cele
chalk
chase
chert

chute
-cide
clade
class
clone
coast
codon
color
comet
creep
cross
crust
delta
DNA
drift
Earth
Ecoli
elbow
entry
epoch
esker
evase
facet
fancy
fauld
fault
fauna
favas
F-box
feigh
felty
femic
fen
fetch
fetid
fetus
fiber
field
filty
fines
fiord
fired
fjord
flail
flame
flank
flaps
flask
flats
fleck
fleet
flint
float
floor
flora
floss
fluid
fluke
flume

fluor
flush
flute
focus
foehn
folia
foram
force
forge
-form
fouls
found
frame
front
genus
geode
girth
glady
gland
glare
glass
glebe
gleet
glide
glist
gloom
glory
going
goods
gorse
gouge
grade
grail
grain
grant
grate
grenz
greve
grike
gripe
groin
group
grout
grove
grube
gruff
grush
guide
gulch
gumbo
gummy
gunis
gurmy
guyed
guyot
habit
hards
haunt
hazel

heads	laser	nacre	plume	salar
heave	latch	nadir	plump	salic
helks	laths	naked	point	salts
henry	layer	nappe	poise	sands
hepat	leach	niche	polar	sandy
hertz	leads	nicol	potch	scale
heugh	lease	nital	pound	scall
hewer	ledge	niter	pouty	scalp
hexad	legua	nitro	power	scaly
hinge	lenad	noble	prase	scamy
hitch	lense	-noid	pregs	scarf
hoist	levee	noise	prill	scarp
horse	level	nonel	prion	scobs
horst	lidar	nosin	probe	scone
house	liner	notch	prong	scoop
hovel	lines	nowel	prove	score
hudge	lipid	Nujol	punch	scour
humus	lllano	nylon	puppy	scout
hurry	lodge	oakum	puron	scram
hutch	Loess	octad	quarl	scrap
hypo-	loooo	octet	queen	scree
-llla	loran	-ogen	queer	screw
lmago	lorry	oiled	quene	scrin
ingot	loupe	oiler	quick	sculp
inset	lower	onlap	quoin	seamy
lnvar	lumpy	opens	radar	sehta
iojap	lurry	order	radon	seize
-itis	lysis	organ	rails	serra
ivory	lytic	-osis	raise	setup
jager	lyway	outby	range	shadd
jelly	macle	oxbow	reach	shade
jetty	mafic	oxide	rebar	shaft
jitty	magma	ozone	recon	shake
joint	manto	paddy	reeve	shale
joren	maria	paint	relay	shaly
josen	marly	panel	relic	shank
joule	marsh	paste	resin	shard
judge	maser	patch	rests	shear
jumbo	match	patio	resue	sheen
junks	matte	pearl	-rhea	sheet
jutty	melee	perch	rheid	shelf
kapel	melle	peter	rhomb	shell
karat	metal	-pexy	rhums	sherd
karst	meter	phage	rider	shift
kelly	metra	phase	ridge	shirt
kepel	micas	phyre	rifle	shoad
kerve	midge	pilot	riser	shode
kevil	migma	pinch	rivet	shoot
kirve	minal	piper	roast	short
kloof	miner	pitch	roche	shunt
knock	miser	pivot	rosin	shute
knots	mixed	place	rotap	shuts
kyack	mixer	plain	rotch	sides
labor	model	plane	rotor	siege
ladle	moler	plant	rough	sieve
lagre	monad	plate	round	sight
Lahar	mouth	playa	royer	silex
laper	moyle	ploat	rural	sills
large	muton	plumb	sagre	sinks

skarn
skelp
skews
skirt
skrin
slack
slate
slide
slump
solid
spore
stack
state
stave
stead
steel
steep
stein
stele
stell
stent
stick
still
stilt
stint
stock
stoke
stomp
stone
stook
stool
stope
stove
strap
strek
stria
strip
strut
stull
stulm
stump
sugar
suite
surge
swamp
swarf
swarm
sweal
sweat
sweep
sweet
swell
swing
symon
taiga
talus
Taxol
T-DNA
thio-

-tomy
trait
trans
tumor
urban
value
varve
virus
yield
Z DNA

4

acid
acne
acre
acyl
agar
anus
arch
asci
ASOS
atom
axes
axil
axis
axon
back
bail
bajo
bald
ball
band
bank
bare
bark
base
bass
bead
Beam
bear
bede
beds
beef
bell
belt
bent
berm
beta
bias
biat
bile
bind
bing
Bomb
bond
bone
cave

cell
coal
core
data
deep
deme
didN
diet
dike
Dome
dose
dune
dyad
eddy
exon
face
fall
feed
fell
fill
film
fine
fire
firn
Fish
flag
flap
flat
flaw
floc
flot
flow
flue
flux
foid
foig
fold
foot
fork
form
foul
gale
gene
glia
glow
goaf
gold
goth
grab
grid
grit
grus
guag
guhr
gull
gunk
guss
gust
hade

hail
halo
hand
hang
hard
haul
head
heap
heat
heel
hess
high
hill
hole
home
hook
horn
host
hove
huel
hulk
hush
inby
iron
jack
jade
jamb
jeso
jock
jubs
jump
junk
kale
kame
kauk
kell
kelp
kerf
kick
kies
kill
kiln
kind
kink
kish
kist
knot
kolm
kong
kulm
lace
lade
lags
lair
lamp
land
lash
lath
lava

lawn
LDLC
lead
leaf
leak
lean
leap
lear
leat
leer
legs
lehr
lens
lift
lill
limb
lime
Line
list
load
lobs
loch
loci
lode
loma
lool
loom
lose
loup
lype
make
mall
Manx
marl
mask
mass
mast
mean
meet
mend
mesa
mesh
meta
mica
mill
mine
mire
mist
misy
moat
mode
Moho
mold
mole
moon
moor
moss
moya
mRNA

mscp
muck
mule
muon
mutu
naif
nail
neat
neck
ness
nest
névé
norm
nose
onyx
ooze
opal
oued
oven
pack
page
pair
papa
part
pass
pawl
peat
pena
pick
piel
pier
pike
pile
pill
ping
pion
pipe
plan
plat
plow
plug
plum
pole
pons
pool
pore
port
post
pour
puff
pulp
pump
quad
race
rack
raft
rail
rain
rait

rake
ramp
rang
rank
rasp
rate
rays
ream
redd
reds
reed
reef
reel
ribs
rift
rill
ring
rise
risk
road
roca
rock
rods
roke
roll
roof
room
rRNA
ruby
ruin
rush
rust
rute
salt
sand
sard
scab
scad
scar
scow
scum
scun
seal
seam
seat
self
sett
shed
shoe
shot
show
sial
side
silk
sill
silo
silt
sima
sing

sink
size
skew
skid
skip
slab
slag
slip
smog
soap
soil
soma
spit
star
stay
stem
step
stey
stip
stop
stow
stud
sump
sunk
swab
swad
swag
sway
talc
tarn
tide
till
tufa
Tuff
unit
Vent
wadi
warp
wash
watt
wave
well

3

AMP
amu
arc
Arg
arm
Ash
Asn
Asp
ATP
bag
bal
bar
bay

bed
ben
bin
bud
CAM
cap
cis
col
Cys
dam
dew
dip
DNA
EMS
eon
EPA
era
erg
eye
FAD
fan
FDA
fea
fen
fey
fix
fog
gas
Glu
Gly
GMO
gob
gor
GPS
gug
gum
gun
gut
guy
hag
Hfr
HGH
hit
hod
hot
HPA
Hsp
hub
ice
ion
jad
jam
jar
jaw
jet
jib
jig
jud
jug

keg
kep
keq
key
kip
kir
kit
kua
lag
lap
law
lay
LCR
LDH
led
leg
leu
lip
log
low
lpb
lue
lug
lyc
lys
MAC
map
mat
Met
MHC
mor
MPF
MRE
MRI
mud
mun
mvb
NCB
net
NIH
nil
nip
NMR
NPD
NRM
NSF
OCD
oil
opx
ore
ORF
pad
pan
pBR
PCP
PCR
peg
PEL
Phe

PID	rib	URF	Fe	SG
pie	rid	UTR	HQ	UV
pig	rig	Val	HW	
pin	rim	vug	HX	**1**
pit	rip	YAC	Ig	
pKa	RNA	zoo	IR	C
PKU	row		IS	G
ply	run	**2**	Ka	H
PNS	sag		Kb	K
pod	sal	ab	LD	L
pop	sap	AQ	Ma	N
pot	sax	AW	Mg	P
ppm	sea	AX	MS	Q
Pro	Ser	BC	NO	S
pry	set	bp	NP	T
put	SNP	Bt	NQ	U
QTL	STP	EC	NW	V
rag	Thr	ED	NX	
ram	TMA	ER	PD	
rap	TNF	EW	pH	
raw	TRM	EX	pK	
rho	Try		RF	

Female First Names

15

helen-elizabeth

14

helenelizabeth

12

anne-corinne
barbara-anne
christabella
lorettalorna
marie-jeanne

11

alejandrina
alexandrina
annecorinne
barbaraanne
cairistiona
constantina
constantine
diane-marie
guillemette

jackqueline
jacquenetta
jacquenette
mariejeanne
martguerita
minnaminnie
ulrikaumeko

10

alessandra
anastassia
andromache
anestassia
anna-diana
anna-diane
anna-maria
anne-marie
anthiathia
antoinette
antonietta
bernadette
bernardina
bernardine
bonnibelle
carmencita
carol-jean
cassaundra
christabel

christalle
christiana
christiane
cinderella
clarabelle
clementina
clementine
concettina
constancia
constantia
cristionna
dianemarie
donnamarie
elisabetta
enrichetta
ermengarde
ermentrude
estrellita
evangelina
evangeline
ferdinanda
ferdinande
fernandina
fredericka
frederique
friederike
gabriellia
georgeanna
georgeanne

georgianna
georgianne
gerhardine
gilbertina
gilbertine
hildagarde
hildegaard
hildegarde
holly-anne
hyacinthia
hyacinthie
jackquelin
jacqueline
jacquelynn
jaquenetta
jaquenette
marcellina
marcelline
margaretha
margarethe
margaretta
margarette
marguerite
mariquilla
melisandra
michaelina
michaeline
petronella
petronilla

petronille
philippine
stephannie
vilhelmina
wilhelmina
wilhelmine
willabella

9

albertina
albertine
alejandra
alexandra
allianora
ammamaria
anastasia
anastasie
andriette
angelique
anjanette
annabella
annabelle
annadiana
annadiane
annaliese
annamaria
annamarie
anneliese

annemarie
ann-marie
antonella
antonetta
appolonia
aprilette
augustina
augustine
bathsheba
benedetta
benedicta
benedikta
bernadene
bernadina
bernadine
bette-ann
betteanne
blondelle
bobinette
bridgette
brittaney
brunhilda
brunhilde
carmelina
carmelita
caroljean
cassandra
cassandre
cassandry
cassondra
catharina
catharine
catherina
catherine
cathyleen
celestina
celestine
celestyna
chantalle
charlotta
charlotte
charmaine
cherianne
cherilynn
christean
christian
christina
christine
christyna
claudelle
claudetta
claudette
clementia
cleopatra
concordia
consolata
constance
constancy
constanta

corabella
corabelle
corrianne
courtenay
cristabel
delphinia
desdemona
doloritas
dominique
donnajean
doralynne
ekaterina
elbertina
elbertine
elisabeth
elizabeth
emmalynne
enriqueta
ernestine
esmeralda
evangelia
evangelin
ezmeralda
fanchette
fleurette
florencia
florentia
francesca
francisca
franciska
francoise
frederica
gabriella
gabrielle
gavrielle
genevieve
georgetta
georgette
georgiana
geraldine
gerladina
gertrudis
gilemette
giulietta
goldarina
guendolen
guenevere
guglielma
guinevere
gwendolen
gwendolin
gwendolyn
harrietta
harriette
henrietta
henriette
henryetta
hephzibah
hildagard

hollyanne
hortensia
hyacintha
hyacinthe
isabelita
jacquelin
jacquelyn
jacquetta
jacquette
jeannette
jessamine
josephina
josephine
kara-lynn
kassandra
katharina
katharine
katherina
katherine
kimberlee
kimberley
kimberlyn
konstance
konstanze
krystalle
laurianne
louisette
maddalena
madelaine
madeleine
magdalena
magdalene
maighdiln
marchelle
margareta
margarete
margarita
maribelle
marie-ann
mariellen
marsiella
marybelle
maryellen
marylinda
marylynne
mehetabel
melisande
melisenda
mellicent
mellisent
meredithe
merrielle
michaella
michelina
micheline
miguelita
milissent
millicent
millisent

miof mela
mirabella
mirabelle
mireielle
modestine
morganica
mufinella
natividad
nicolette
nikoletta
philomena
pierrette
pollyanna
priscella
priscilla
quintilla
rafaelita
robinetta
robinette
rosabella
rosabelle
rosalinda
rosalinde
rosemaria
rosemarie
rosemonde
sallyanne
selestina
shandeigh
shoshanna
simonette
sophronia
stephanie
stephenie
susanetta
tanitansy
theodosia
theresina
theresita
thomasina
thomasine
valentina
valentine
veronique
wendeline
willamina
winnifred

8

adelaida
adelaide
adelheid
adriaens
adrianna
adrianne
adrienne
amabelle

anabella
anabelle
analiese
anallese
anallise
andreana
andriana
angelica
angelika
angelina
angeline
angelita
annabela
annabell
annalise
annelise
annmaria
annmarie
antonina
arabella
arabelle
aridatha
ashleigh
atalanta
aubrette
babbette
barbabra
barbette
batsheva
beatrice
beatrisa
bellanca
berenice
bernelle
bernetta
bernette
bethanne
betteann
beverlee
beverley
beverlie
birgitta
blakelee
blakeley
blondell
bobbette
brandais
brandice
brandise
brigitta
brigitte
brittani
brittany
britteny
brittney
camellia
cariotta
carlotta
carlynne

carmelia	clemence	estrella	halimeda	kamillah
carmella	clerissa	ethelind	harmonia	karalynn
carmelle	clotilda	etheline	harmonie	karilynn
carolann	collette	euphemia	harriett	kariotta
carolina	conchita	eustacia	harriott	karlotta
caroline	consuela	fanechka	hendrika	karlotte
carolyne	consuelo	faustina	henrieta	karolina
carolynn	coraline	faustine	herminia	karoline
carrissa	cordelia	federica	hermione	katerina
casandra	cordelie	felicdad	hilliary	katerine
catarina	cornelia	felicity	hortense	katharyn
caterina	cornelle	fernanda	hyacinth	katheryn
catherin	corrinne	fernande	ingaberg	kathleen
cathleen	costanza	fidelity	ingaborg	kathrine
cathlene	courtnay	fionnula	ingeberg	kathryne
cathrine	courtney	fiorenze	ingeborg	katrinka
catlaina	cristina	florance	iolanthe	katuscha
catriona	cristine	florella	isabella	kellyann
celestia	daniella	florence	isabelle	kerianne
celestyn	danielle	florenza	isahella	kiersten
charissa	danyelle	florette	jacintha	kimberli
charisse	danyette	florinda	jacinthe	kimberly
charlean	darlleen	francene	jackelyn	kirsteni
charleen	darrelle	francine	janeczka	klarrisa
charlena	delphine	francyne	jannelle	kristien
charlene	demetria	fredelia	jaquelin	kristina
charline	demetris	fredrika	jaquelyn	kristine
charmain	devondra	gabriela	jeanelle	krystyna
charmane	dolorita	gabriell	jeanette	laurette
charmian	domeniga	garnette	jeannine	la verne
charmine	dominica	gennifer	jeniffer	laetitia
charmion	donielle	genovera	jennette	latashia
chastity	doralynn	genvieve	jennifer	lauraine
cherilyn	dorolice	georgena	jennilee	lauralee
cherrita	dorolisa	georgeta	jermaine	laurella
chiquita	doroteya	georgina	jerrilee	lauretta
chloette	dorothea	georgine	jerrilyn	laurette
chrissie	dorothee	gerianna	jerrylee	leonanie
christal	drusilla	gerianne	jessalin	leonelle
christan	dulciana	germaine	jessalyn	leontine
christel	dulcinea	gerrilee	jessamyn	leontyne
christen	eachelle	gertruda	jesselyn	lisabeth
christie	ealasaid	gertrude	jillayne	lizabeth
christin	eleanora	giacinta	joceline	lorianna
christye	eleanore	gilberta	jocelyne	lorianne
chrysler	eleonora	gilberte	johannah	lorraine
chrystal	eleonore	gilligan	johnette	lorrayne
chrystel	elfrieda	ginnifer	jordanna	loutitia
cindelyn	elianora	giovanna	joscelin	lucienne
cinnamon	elianore	giuditta	josefina	lucretia
claresta	elisabet	giustina	josselyn	ludovika
claretta	elizabet	gloriana	joycelin	lynnelle
clarette	elladine	gloriane	julianna	lynnette
claribel	elsinore	gratiana	julianne	madalena
clarinda	emmaline	gretchen	julienne	madelena
clarissa	emmalynn	griselda	julietta	madelene
clarisse	emmeline	guillema	juliette	madelina
claudina	engracia	gwenette	kaitlynn	madeline
claudine	ernaline	gwenneth	kakalina	magdalen

109

maitilde
malissia
mallissa
mallorie
marcelia
marcella
marcelle
marcille
margalit
margaret
margeaux
margette
marianna
marianne
maribeth
marieann
marielle
marietta
mariette
marigold
marillin
marjorie
marquita
marrilee
marrissa
martelle
marthena
martynne
maryanna
maryanne
marybeth
maryjane
maryrose
mathilda
mathilde
maureene
maurizia
maybelle
mechelle
melantha
melicent
melisent
melloney
mercedes
meredith
meridith
merralee
merridie
merrilee
michaela
michelle
mignonne
milicent
mireille
modestia
morganne
murielle
nannette
natalina

nataline
natassia
nathalia
nathalie
nicholle
nicolina
nicoline
nikaniki
ninnetta
ninnette
odelinda
olivette
ortensia
pamelina
papagena
patience
patricia
patrizia
pauletta
paulette
pearline
penelopa
penelope
petronia
philippa
philippe
phillida
phyllida
pierette
prudence
quintana
quintina
rachelle
rafaelia
raphaela
rayshell
rebbecca
rebekkah
robinett
rochella
rochelle
rochette
rosaleen
rosalind
rosaline
rosalynd
rosamond
rosamund
roseanna
roseanne
roseline
rosemary
roshelle
rosmunda
rozamond
ruthanne
sallyann
samantha
sapphira

sapphire
sara-ann
sarajane
sashenka
scarlett
sharleen
sharlene
sharline
shaylynn
sheelagh
sherilyn
sherline
shirleen
shirlene
shirline
shoshana
sidonnie
starlene
stefania
stefanie
steffane
stephana
stephani
stephine
stoddard
sunshine
susannah
tabbatha
tabbitha
tallulah
tatiania
teresina
teresita
terri-jo
theadora
theodora
theressa
thomasin
tiffanie
timothea
tiphanie
toinette
tomasina
tomasine
ursulina
ursuline
valencia
valentia
veronica
veronika
veronike
victoria
violante
violetta
violette
virginia
virginie
vittoria
vivianna

vivianne
vivienne
vivyanne
willetta
willette
wilmette
winifred
yolanthe
yovonnda

7

abagael
abagail
abigael
abigail
abigale
adaline
adelice
adelina
adelind
adeline
adriana
adriane
adriena
aeriela
aeriell
agnella
agnesse
agretha
aigneis
aindrea
ainslee
ainsley
ainslie
alameda
alberta
alethea
alexina
alexine
alfreda
allegra
allison
allissa
allyson
almeria
aloisia
aloysia
alverta
alvinia
amaleta
amalita
amandie
amberly
amelina
ameline
amelita
analise

anatola
anderea
angelia
angelle
annabal
annabel
annalee
annetta
annette
annissa
annnora
anselma
anstice
antonia
antonie
arabela
arabele
ardelia
ardelis
ardella
ardelle
ardenia
ariadne
ariella
arielle
arlette
arleyne
arliene
arlinda
arluene
atlanta
atlante
auberta
augusta
auguste
aundrea
aurelea
aurelia
aurelie
aurilia
auroora
austina
austine
aveline
babette
barbara
beatrix
beatriz
beitris
belicia
belinda
bellina
bendite
benetta
benoite
bernete
bernice
bernita
bertina

bertine	carolyn	corette	dolores	farrand
bethany	carroll	corilla	dominga	fayette
bethena	cathrin	corinna	donella	felecia
bethina	cathryn	corinne	donelle	felicia
bettina	catrina	corissa	donetta	felicle
bettine	cecelia	corliss	doralia	felisha
beverie	ceciley	cornela	doralin	fenelia
beverly	cecilia	correna	doralyn	feodora
blancha	cecilla	corrina	dorelia	fidelia
blanche	celesta	corrine	dorella	filippa
blinnie	celeste	cortney	dorelle	florida
blondie	celinda	cosetta	doretta	florina
bobette	celinka	cosette	dorette	florrie
brandea	celisse	crissie	dorotea	flossie
brandie	chandal	cristal	dorothy	frances
breanne	chandra	cristen	dorthea	frankie
brianna	chantal	cristie	drucill	frannie
brianne	charita	cristin	dulcine	freddie
bridget	charity	crystal	edeline	gabriel
brietta	charlot	crystie	elberta	gabrila
brigida	chelsae	cthrine	eleanor	garland
britney	chelsea	cynthea	electra	gayleen
brittan	chelsey	cynthia	elenore	gaylene
brittne	chelsie	cynthie	elfreda	genevra
brittni	cherice	dalenna	elfrida	georgia
cacilia	cherida	daloris	elinore	georgie
cacilie	cherise	damaris	ellette	geralda
caitlin	cherish	danella	ellissa	germain
caitrin	cherlyn	danette	elonore	germana
callida	cheslie	daniela	elsbeth	gertrud
calypso	chiarra	daniele	elspeth	gianina
camella	chickie	daphene	emelina	gillian
camilla	chiquia	darelle	emeline	ginelle
camille	chloris	darleen	emelita	ginevra
candace	chrissy	darlene	emelyne	giorgia
candice	christa	darline	emiline	giralda
candida	christi	deborah	emlynne	gisella
candide	christy	dee dee	emmalee	giselle
caprice	chryste	deeanne	emmalyn	glenine
caralie	cissiee	deerdre	emogene	glennie
caressa	clareta	deirdre	eolanda	glennis
caresse	clarice	delcina	eolande	glynnis
carilyn	clarine	delcine	erminia	goldina
carissa	clarita	delilah	erminie	grethel
caritta	claudia	delinda	ernesta	grissel
carleen	claudie	delores	esmaria	gunilla
carlene	clemmie	deloria	estella	gusella
carlina	coletta	deloris	estelle	gweneth
carline	colette	demeter	ethelda	gwennie
carlita	colleen	demetra	ethelin	gwenora
carlota	collete	desirae	ethelyn	gwenore
carlynn	colline	desiree	eugenia	gwyneth
carmela	corabel	devinne	eugenie	haleigh
carmina	coralie	devonna	eulalie	halette
carmine	coralyn	devonne	evaleen	harlene
carmita	cordula	diahann	eveleen	harmony
carolan	corella	diandra	evelina	harriet
carolee	corenda	diannne	eveline	harriot
carolin	coretta	dierdre	fanchon	heather

hedvige	jilleen	kissiah	loralie	marilin
hedwiga	jillene	klarika	loralyn	marilyn
helaina	jillian	koralle	lorelei	marinna
helaine	jo-anne	kordula	lorelle	mariska
helenka	joannes	korella	lorenza	marissa
heloise	jocelin	koressa	loretta	maritsa
hermina	jocelyn	krissie	lorette	marjory
hermine	joellen	kristal	lorilee	marketa
hesther	joellyn	kristan	lorilyn	marlane
hillary	joelynn	kristel	lorinda	marleah
honoria	johanna	kristen	louella	marleen
horatia	johnath	kristin	luciana	marlena
idalina	joletta	kristyn	lucilia	marlene
idaline	jordain	krystal	lucille	marline
imogene	jordana	krystle	lucinda	martica
imojean	josepha	kynthia	lurette	martina
inesita	jourdan	kyrstin	lurleen	martita
ingunna	jsandye	ladonna	lurlene	maryann
lolande	juanita	lanette	lurline	marylee
iormina	juditha	laraine	lyndell	marylin
isabeau	juliana	larissa	lyndsay	marylou
isadora	juliane	laryssa	lyndsey	matelda
iseabal	juliann	latisha	lyndsie	matilda
isidora	julieta	latrena	lynelle	matilde
jacenta	julissa	latrina	lynette	maureen
jacinda	junette	laureen	lynnell	maurene
jacinta	justina	laurena	lynnett	maurine
jacklin	justine	laurene	mabelle	maurise
jacklyn	justinn	laurice	madalyn	maurita
jacquie	kaitlin	laverna	madelin	meaghan
jacynth	kaitlyn	laverne	madella	meghann
janella	kaleena	lavinia	madelle	melamie
janelle	kalinda	lavinie	madelon	melania
janenna	kalindi	leandra	madelyn	melanie
janessa	kamilah	leanora	madonna	melessa
janetta	kandace	leeanne	magdaia	melinda
janette	karalee	lenette	mahalia	melinde
janifer	karissa	leodora	malanie	melissa
jaquith	karleen	leoline	malinda	melisse
jasmina	karlene	leonora	malinde	melitta
jasmine	karylin	leonore	malissa	mellisa
jaynell	katalin	leticia	mallory	melodee
jeanine	kathlin	letisha	malorie	melodie
jeannie	kathryn	letitia	malvina	melonie
jehanna	katinka	letizia	malynda	meridel
jemimah	katleen	liliane	marabel	merilee
jenelle	katrina	lillian	marcela	merilyn
jeniece	katrine	lilllie	marcile	merissa
jenifer	katusha	lindsay	maressa	merlina
jenilee	kellina	lindsey	margalo	merline
jennica	kellsie	linette	margaux	merrile
jennine	keriann	linnell	margery	merrili
jeralee	kerrill	lisbeth	margret	merrill
jerrine	kerstin	lisetta	mariana	merrily
jessica	kessiah	lisette	mariann	micaela
jessika	kikelia	lizbeth	maribel	michele
jewelle	kirsten	lizette	maridel	michell
jillana	kirstin	loraine	mariele	miguela
jillane	kirstyn	loralee	marilee	mikaela

mildred
mildrid
minerva
minetta
minette
minnnie
miquela
mirabel
miranda
mirella
mirelle
mirilla
modesta
modesty
monique
morgana
morissa
moselle
mozelle
myranda
myrilla
myrlene
myrtice
nananne
nanette
natalee
natalie
natalya
natasha
nerissa
nichole
nicolea
nicolle
nikolia
ninetta
ninette
noelani
noellyn
novelia
octavia
olimpia
olympia
olympie
opalina
opaline
ophelia
ophelie
othelia
othella
othilia
othilie
ottilie
pamella
pandora
paolina
patrica
patrice
paulina
pauline

paulita
perrine
petrina
petunia
phaedra
phaidra
philipa
phillie
phillis
phyllis
phyllys
prissie
queenie
quentin
querida
rachael
rachele
rafaela
ramonda
randene
ranique
raquela
raychel
raynell
rebecca
rebecka
rebekah
renelle
rhiamon
rhianna
rhianon
riannon
rivalee
robenia
roberta
robinet
robinia
rochell
romonda
ronalda
ronnica
roobbie
rosabel
rosalia
rosalie
rosalyn
rosanna
rosanne
roseann
roselia
roselin
rosella
roselle
rosetta
rosette
roxanna
roxanne
rozalie
rozalin

rozanna
rozanne
rozella
rozelle
rubetta
ruperta
ruthann
sabrina
sadella
salaidh
samaria
saraann
sarette
saundra
scarlet
selinda
sephira
shandee
shandie
shandra
shannah
shannen
shannon
shantee
sharity
sharona
sharron
shawnee
shaylah
shaylyn
sheelah
sheeree
sheilah
shelagh
shelley
shellie
sherill
sherrie
shirlee
shirley
sibella
sibelle
sibilla
sibylla
sibylle
sidoney
sidonia
silvana
simonne
siobhan
siouxie
sonnnie
sosanna
stafani
starlin
steffie
stephie
stevana
stevena

stormie
suellen
susanna
susanne
susette
suzanna
suzanne
suzette
sybilla
sybille
sydelle
tabatha
tabitha
tamarah
tamarra
tammara
tamqrah
tatiana
teirtza
teodora
teressa
teriann
terrijo
tersina
theresa
therese
therine
thomasa
tierney
tiertza
tiffani
tiffany
tiphani
tiphany
tootsie
trescha
tuesday
valaree
valaria
valenka
valeria
valerie
valerye
vanessa
veradis
vernice
virgina
vitoria
viviana
viviene
viviyan
wenonah
whitney
winonah
wrennie
xaviera
yalonda
yasmeen
yevette

yolanda
yolande
yoshiko
zabrina
zitella
zsa zsa

6

aarika
adella
adelle
adiana
adoree
adorne
adrian
aeriel
agatha
agathe
agnese
agneta
agnola
aileen
ailene
ailina
ailsun
alaine
alanah
alanna
alayne
albina
alecia
aleece
alexia
alexis
alicea
alicia
alidia
alikee
alisha
alison
alissa
alisun
alleen
allene
allina
allsun
allyce
almeda
almeta
almira
almire
aloise
althea
alvera
alvina
alvira
alysia

alyson	ashley	blanch	carmen	corine
alyssa	ashlie	blinni	carmon	coriss
amabel	astrid	blinny	carola	cornie
amalea	astrix	blisse	carole	correy
amalee	athena	blithe	carree	corrie
amalia	athene	blondy	carrie	crissy
amalie	aubine	blythe	cassey	crista
amalle	aubree	bobbee	cassie	cristi
amanda	aubrey	bobbie	cathee	cristy
amandi	aubrie	bobbye	cathie	crysta
amandy	audrey	bobina	catina	cybill
amargo	audrie	bobine	catlee	cymbre
amelia	audrye	bonita	catlin	cyndia
amelie	aurlie	bonnee	cecile	cyndie
amitie	aurora	bonnie	cecily	cynthy
anabal	aurore	brande	celene	daffie
anabel	austin	brandi	celina	dagmar
andeee	averil	brandy	celine	dahlia
andrea	averyl	breena	chanda	dalsey
andree	avivah	brenda	channa	daisie
androi	babara	brenna	charil	dalila
andria	babbie	briana	charin	dallas
anetta	babita	bridie	charis	damara
anette	bambie	brigid	charla	damita
angela	barbee	brigit	charyl	danell
angele	barbey	briney	chelsy	danica
anissa	barbie	brinna	cherey	danice
anitra	barbra	britni	cherie	danika
anjela	barrie	britta	cherin	danila
annice	beckie	britte	cherri	danita
annora	beilul	brooke	cherry	dannie
ansley	belita	brooks	cherye	dannye
anthea	belvia	bryana	cheryl	daphna
anthia	benita	brynna	chicky	daphne
arabel	bennie	brynne	chrysa	darbie
ardath	berget	bunnie	cicely	darcee
ardeen	bernie	calida	cicily	darcey
ardene	berrie	calley	cindee	darcie
ardine	bertha	callie	cindie	dareen
ardisj	berthe	camala	cindra	darell
ardith	bertie	camila	claire	darice
ardyce	beryle	camile	clarey	darryl
ardyth	bessie	cammie	clarie	darsey
aretha	betsey	candie	claude	darsie
ariana	bettye	candis	clemmy	daveen
ariela	beulah	candra	cloris	daveta
arlana	bianca	carena	clovis	davida
arleen	bianka	caresa	coleen	davina
arlena	bibbie	carina	colene	davine
arlene	bibbye	carine	collen	davita
arleta	biddie	carita	collie	deanna
arlina	bidget	carlee	connie	deanne
arline	billie	carlen	cookie	debbie
arlyne	billye	carley	cordey	debera
ashely	binnie	carlie	cordie	debora
ashien	birdie	carlin	coreen	deeann
ashlan	birgit	carlye	corena	deedee
ashlee	blaire	carlyn	corene	dehlia
ashlen	blanca	carmel	corina	deidre

114

delila	elinor	fianna	gretta	janaye
delora	elisha	fidela	guenna	janean
denice	elissa	fifine	guinna	janeen
denise	ellene	filide	gussie	janela
dennie	ellynn	fionna	gustie	janene
denyse	elmira	floria	gwenni	janeta
deonne	elnora	florie	gwenny	janeva
desiri	elnore	floris	gwynne	janice
devina	eloisa	florri	hadria	janina
devora	eloise	florry	hailee	janine
dianna	elvera	flossi	halley	janith
dianne	elvina	flossy	hallie	jannel
dinnie	elvira	franky	hannah	jasmin
dionis	elwira	franni	hannie	jaymee
dionne	elysee	franny	hannis	jazmin
dniren	elysha	frayda	harley	jeanie
dolley	elysia	freddi	harlie	jeanna
dollie	elyssa	freddy	harrie	jeanne
domini	emalee	fredia	hattie	jelene
donica	emalia	fredra	hayley	jemima
donnie	emelda	freida	heddie	jemmie
doreen	emelia	frieda	hedvig	jenica
dorena	emilee	fulvia	hedwig	jenine
dorene	emilia	gabbey	heidie	jennee
dorian	emilie	gabbie	helena	jennie
dorice	emlynn	galina	helene	jerrie
dorine	emylee	garnet	henrie	jessie
dorisa	enrica	gaynor	hermia	jewell
dorise	enrika	geneva	hertha	jillie
dorita	ericha	gennie	hester	jo ann
dorree	ericka	george	hestia	joanie
dorrie	erinna	gerrie	hettie	jo-ann
dorris	ermina	gertie	hilary	joanna
dorthy	estele	gianna	hollie	joanne
dottie	estell	gillan	ianthe	jobina
dreddy	esther	gillie	idalia	jobyna
drucie	eudora	ginger	idelle	joeann
drusie	eugine	ginnie	idette	joelie
dulcea	eunice	gisela	ileana	joella
dulcia	evania	gisele	ileane	joelle
dulcie	evanne	giulia	ilyssa	joelly
dulsea	evelyn	gizela	imelda	johnna
dyanna	evonne	gladys	imogen	joleen
dyanne	fallon	glenda	indira	jolene
eadith	fancie	glenna	inessa	joline
eartha	fannie	gloria	ingrid	jolynn
easter	farand	glynda	isabel	jonell
ebonee	farica	glynis	isobel	jordan
editha	farrah	godiva	ivette	jorrie
edithe	faunie	goldia	ivonne	josefa
edwina	fawnia	goldie	izabel	joyann
edythe	faydra	gracia	jackie	joyous
eileen	fayina	gracie	jaclin	judith
eimile	faythe	gratia	jaclyn	juieta
eirena	fedora	grayce	jacqui	juliet
elaina	felice	grazia	jaimie	julina
elaine	felipa	gretal	jamima	juline
elayne	felita	gretel	jammie	julita
elicia	feliza	gretna	janaya	junina

kailey	kissee	lindsy	marian	moreen
kalila	kissie	linell	marice	morena
kalina	kittie	linnea	mariel	morgan
kameko	kizzee	linnet	marijo	morgen
kamila	kizzie	linnie	marika	muffin
karena	korney	lissie	marina	mureil
karina	korrie	livvie	marion	murial
karine	krissy	livvyy	marisa	muriel
karisa	krista	lizzie	marita	myriam
karita	kriste	loella	mariya	myrtia
karlee	kristi	loleta	marjie	myrtie
karlen	kristy	lolita	marlee	myrtle
karlie	krysta	lonnie	marley	nadean
karlyn	kylila	lorain	marlie	nadeen
karmen	kylynn	loreen	marlyn	nadine
karola	lainey	lorena	marney	nadiya
karole	lanita	lorene	marnia	nalani
karoly	larina	lorine	marnie	nancee
karrah	larine	lorita	marris	nancey
karrie	larisa	lorrie	marsha	nancie
kassey	laural	lorrin	martha	nanete
kassia	lauree	lottie	marthe	nanice
kassie	laurel	louisa	martie	nanine
kathie	lauren	louise	maryjo	nannie
kathye	laurie	lucila	marysa	nariko
katina	lauryn	lucina	mattie	natala
katine	lavena	lucine	maudie	neilla
katlin	lavina	lucita	maxine	neille
kattie	layney	luella	meagan	nellie
kaycee	leanna	luelle	meggie	nerita
kaylee	leanor	lulita	meghan	nertie
kayley	lebbie	lyndel	melany	nessie
kaylil	leeann	lynett	melesa	nettie
kaylyn	leelah	lynnea	melina	nettle
keeley	leigha	lynnet	melisa	nichol
keelia	leilah	lynsey	melita	nickie
kelcey	leisha	maddie	mellie	nicola
kelcie	leland	madlen	melody	nicole
kelila	lenora	madlin	melony	nicoli
kellen	lenore	maegan	melosa	nikkie
kelley	leoine	maggee	mercie	nissle
kellia	leonie	maggie	meriel	noella
kellie	leshia	mahala	merola	noelle
kelsey	lesley	maible	merrie	noelyn
kendra	leslie	maisey	mersey	nolana
kendre	lethia	maisie	michal	nollie
kerrie	lettie	malena	michel	nonnah
kerrin	lexine	malina	mickie	norean
kesley	lezlie	malory	mignon	noreen
keslie	lianna	mandie	milena	norene
kessia	lianne	marcia	millie	norina
kettie	libbey	marcie	milzie	norine
kevina	libbie	mareah	minnie	norrie
kimbra	lilian	marena	miriam	odelia
kimmie	lilias	marget	missie	odella
kippie	lilith	margie	mollee	odelle
kirbee	lillis	margit	mollie	odessa
kirbie	lilyan	margot	monica	odetta
kirsti	lindie	mariam	monika	odette

odilia
odille
ofelia
ofella
ofilia
olenka
olivia
olivie
olympe
ondrea
oneida
oralee
oralia
oralie
oralla
oralle
orelee
orelia
orelie
orella
orelle
oriana
orsola
paloma
pamela
pammie
pansie
pattie
paulie
pearla
pearle
pegeen
peggie
pennie
pepita
persis
phedra
phelia
philis
philly
phoebe
phylis
phylys
pietra
portia
prisca
quinta
rachel
raeann
ralina
ramona
randee
randie
ranice
raquel
rebeca
rebeka
reggie
regina

regine
renata
renate
renell
rennie
revkah
rhetta
rhodia
rhodie
rhonda
rianon
rickie
rivkah
roanna
roanne
robbie
robbin
robbyn
robena
robina
rodina
romola
romona
ronica
ronnie
rosana
rosene
rosina
rosita
roslyn
rowena
roxana
roxane
roxine
rozele
rozina
rubina
ruthie
sabina
sabine
saidee
sallee
sallie
saloma
salome
salomi
samara
sandie
sandra
sandye
sarena
sarene
sarina
sarine
sarita
sascha
saudra
savina
selena

selene
selina
seline
serena
serene
shaina
shaine
shalna
shalne
shanda
shandy
shanie
shanna
shanon
shanta
sharai
sharia
sharla
sharon
sharyl
shauna
shawna
shayla
shayna
shayne
sheela
sheena
sheila
shelba
shelbi
shelby
shelia
shelli
shelly
sheree
sherie
sherri
sherry
sherye
sheryl
sianna
sibbie
sibeal
sibley
sigrid
sileas
silvia
silvie
simona
simone
sindee
sisely
sisile
sissie
siusan
sondra
sonnie
sophey
sophia

sophie
sorcha
stacee
stacey
stacia
stacie
starla
steffi
stella
stepha
stephi
stesha
stormi
stormy
susana
susann
suzann
sybila
sydney
sylvia
tabbie
tabina
tallia
tallie
tallou
talyah
tamara
tamera
tamiko
tammie
tandie
tanhya
tarrah
tawnya
tawsha
teddie
teresa
terese
terrie
terrye
tessie
thalia
thekla
thelma
tiffie
tildie
tillie
timmie
tommie
torrie
tracee
tracey
tracie
trenna
tressa
tricia
trisha
trista
trixie

trudey
trudie
ulrica
ulrika
ulrike
ursala
ursola
ursula
valeda
valene
valera
valery
valida
valina
vallie
vannie
velvet
venita
verena
verene
veriee
verile
verina
verine
vickie
vinita
vinnie
violet
virgie
vivian
vivien
vivyan
vonnie
wallie
wallis
walliw
wandie
wandis
waneta
wanids
wendie
wendye
wenona
wileen
willie
willow
willyt
wilona
wilone
winnah
winnie
winona
wynnie
xylina
yasmin
yelena
yettie
yolane
ysabel

yvette
yvonne
zahara
zandra
zaneta
zilvia
zondra
zonnya
zorana
zorina
zorine
zsazsa
zulema
zuzana

5

aaren
abbey
abbie
abbye
adara
addia
addie
adela
adele
adena
adina
adora
adore
adrea
adria
afton
agace
agata
aggie
agnes
aidan
ailee
ailey
ailis
ailyn
aimee
aimil
alana
alane
aleda
aleen
alena
alene
aleta
alexa
alexi
alfie
alica
alice
alida
alika

alina
aline
alisa
aliza
allie
allis
allix
allyn
allys
alyce
alyda
alysa
alyse
alyss
amara
amata
amber
ambur
amily
andee
andie
andra
anett
angel
angie
angil
anica
anita
annie
annis
anthe
april
arden
ardis
ardra
ardys
ariel
arlee
arlen
arlie
arlyn
ashia
ashil
ashla
ashli
ashly
astra
aubry
audie
audra
audre
audry
aurea
aurel
auria
aurie
aviva
avril
avrit

bambi
bamby
barbe
barbi
barby
barry
basia
becca
becka
becki
becky
bekki
belia
bella
belle
belva
benni
benny
beret
berna
berni
berny
berri
berry
berta
berte
berti
berty
beryl
bessy
betsy
betta
bette
betti
betty
bevvy
bibby
biddy
billi
billy
binni
binny
blair
blake
bliss
bobbe
bobbi
bobby
bonni
bonny
brana
brear
brena
brenn
brett
bride
brier
brina
brinn

briny
brita
britt
brook
bryna
brynn
buffy
bunni
bunny
cahra
calla
calli
cally
camel
cammi
cammy
candi
candy
caren
carey
caria
carie
caril
carin
carla
carly
carma
carol
caron
carri
carry
caryl
caryn
casey
casie
cassi
cassy
catha
cathe
cathi
cathy
catie
cayla
cecil
celia
celie
celka
celle
cesya
charo
chere
cheri
chery
chloe
chris
cilka
cinda
cindi
cindy

cissy
clair
clara
clare
clari
clary
codee
codie
colly
conni
conny
coral
cordi
cordy
corey
corie
corly
corny
corri
corry
cybil
cynde
cyndi
cyndy
dacey
dacia
dacle
daffi
daffy
daile
daisi
daisy
dalia
dania
danit
danna
danni
danny
danya
darby
darci
darcy
darda
daria
darla
daron
darya
daryl
daryn
dasha
dasie
dasya
datha
daune
dawna
dayle
dayna
ddene
deana

deane	ebony	fawne	gusti	jaine
debbi	eddie	fayre	gusty	jamie
debby	edita	fayth	gypsy	jandy
debee	edith	ferne	haily	janel
debor	ediva	fiann	haley	janet
debra	edyth	filia	halie	janey
dedie	effie	fiona	halli	jania
dedra	eilis	fleur	hally	janie
deena	elana	flora	hanna	janis
deeyn	elane	flore	hanni	janka
deina	eleen	flori	hanny	janna
delia	elena	flory	happy	janot
della	elene	frank	harli	jayme
delly	eleni	freda	harri	jayne
denna	elfie	fredi	hatti	jeana
denni	elisa	gabbi	hatty	jeane
denny	elise	gabey	hazel	jemie
denys	elita	gabie	heath	jemmy
devan	eliza	gale	hedda	jenda
devin	ellen	gates	heddi	jenna
devon	ellie	gavra	heida	jenni
diana	ellyn	gayel	heidi	jenny
diane	elora	gayla	helen	jerry
diann	elset	gayle	helga	jessa
diena	elsey	gelya	helge	jesse
dinah	elsie	genia	helli	jessi
dinny	elyse	genna	helsa	jessy
dione	emera	genni	helyn	jewel
dixie	emili	genny	henka	jilli
dodie	emily	gerda	herta	jilly
dolli	emlyn	gerri	hetti	jinny
dolly	emmey	gerry	hetty	joana
donia	emmie	gerta	hilda	joane
donna	emmye	gerti	hilde	joann
donni	emyle	gerty	hildy	jobey
donny	erena	giana	hinda	jobie
dorey	erica	gilda	holli	jobye
doria	erika	gilli	holly	jodee
dorie	erina	gilly	honey	jodie
doris	erinn	ginni	honor	joela
dorri	ertha	ginny	hulda	joell
dorry	essie	gipsy	hynda	joete
dotti	estel	gladi	ibbie	johna
dotty	ester	gleda	idell	joice
dredi	ethel	glenn	ilene	jolee
drona	ethyl	glori	ilise	jolie
druci	ettie	glory	ilysa	jolyn
drucy	evita	golda	ilyse	jonie
drusi	evvie	goldi	inger	jonis
drusy	eydie	goldy	irena	jorey
dulce	faina	grace	irene	jorie
dulci	faith	grata	irina	jorry
dulcy	fancy	greer	irita	josee
dusty	fania	greta	issie	josey
dyana	fanni	grete	ivett	josie
dyane	fanny	grier	ivory	joyan
dyann	fanya	gussi	jacki	joyce
dynah	farah	gussy	jacky	juana
eadie	farra	gusta	jaime	judie

119

judye	kiele	liane	mable	meggy
julee	kiley	libbi	maddi	melba
julia	kimmi	libby	maddy	mella
julie	kimmy	licha	madel	melli
junia	kinna	lidia	madge	melly
junie	kippy	liesa	magda	melva
jyoti	kirby	lilah	maggi	merci
kacey	kitti	lilas	maggy	mercy
kacie	kitty	lilia	maiga	meris
kaela	klara	lilla	maire	merla
kaila	koral	lilli	malia	merle
kaile	koren	lilly	malva	merna
kalie	korie	linda	mamie	merry
kalli	korry	lindi	manda	meryl
kally	kylen	lindy	mandi	micki
kandy	kylie	linea	mandy	micky
kania	lacee	linet	manon	midge
kanya	lacey	linzy	manya	milka
karee	lacie	lisha	marci	milli
karel	laina	lishe	marcy	milly
karen	lanae	lissa	maren	minda
karia	laney	lissi	marga	mindy
karie	lanie	lissy	marge	minna
karil	lanna	liuka	margi	minne
karin	lanni	livia	margo	minni
karla	lanny	livvy	margy	minny
karly	latia	lizzy	maria	minta
karna	laura	loise	marie	miran
karol	laure	lolly	marin	mirna
karon	lauri	lonce	maris	misha
karry	layla	lonna	marja	missy
karyl	layne	lonni	marje	misti
karyn	leann	loree	marji	misty
kasey	leela	loren	marjy	mitzi
kassi	leena	loria	marla	moina
katee	leesa	lorie	marlo	moira
katey	leese	lorna	marna	molli
katha	legra	lorne	marne	molly
kathe	leigh	lorri	marni	mommy
kathi	leila	lorry	marta	monah
kathy	lelah	lotta	marti	moria
katie	lelia	lotte	marty	morna
katti	lenee	lotti	marya	moyna
katya	lenka	lotty	maryl	moyra
kayla	lenna	lucia	marys	muire
kayle	leola	lucie	masha	myrah
keely	leona	lucky	matti	myrle
kelci	leone	luisa	matty	myrna
kelcy	leora	luise	maude	myrta
kelli	lesli	lydia	maura	nadia
kelly	lesly	lydie	maure	nadya
kelsi	lesya	lynda	mavis	nance
kelsy	letta	lynde	mavra	nanci
kenna	letti	lyndy	maxie	nancy
kerri	letty	lynea	meade	nanni
kerry	lexie	lynna	meara	nanny
ketti	lexis	lynne	megan	nanon
ketty	leyla	lyssa	megen	naoma
kevyn	liana	mabel	meggi	naomi

natka	patty	rhody	sheri	terra
natty	paula	rhona	shina	terri
neala	paule	riane	shirl	terry
nedda	pauli	ricca	siana	terza
neely	pauly	ricki	sibby	tessa
neila	pavia	ricky	sibel	tessi
neile	pavla	rikki	sibyl	tessy
nelia	pearl	roana	silva	theda
nelie	peggi	robbi	sioux	tiena
nelle	peggy	robby	sissy	tiffi
nelli	penni	robin	sofia	tiffy
nelly	penny	robyn	sofie	tilda
nerta	peria	rodie	sonia	tildi
nerte	perla	ronda	sonja	tildy
nerti	perle	ronna	sonni	tilly
nerty	perri	ronni	sonny	timmi
nessa	perry	ronny	sonya	timmy
nessi	petra	rorie	sophi	tisha
nessy	phebe	rosie	stace	tobey
nesta	piper	roxie	staci	tobye
netta	pippa	rubia	stacy	tommi
netti	pippy	rubie	starr	tommy
netty	polly	ruthe	stefa	tonia
nevsa	poppy	ruthi	storm	tonie
neysa	prudi	ruthy	sukey	tonya
nicki	prudy	ryann	sunny	tonye
nicky	quinn	rycca	susan	torey
nicol	rahal	sabra	susie	torie
nikki	rahel	sacha	suzie	traci
ninon	raina	sadie	sybil	tracy
nissa	raine	sadye	sybyl	tresa
nisse	rakel	salli	sydel	trina
nissy	randa	sally	tabbi	trish
nixie	randi	sammy	tabby	trixi
noami	randy	sande	taffy	trixy
noell	ranee	sandi	talia	truda
noemi	rania	sandy	tally	trude
nolie	ranna	sarah	talya	trudi
nonah	rasia	saree	tamar	trudy
nonie	rasla	sasha	tamma	trula
nonna	raven	sayre	tammi	twila
norah	rayna	seana	tammy	twyla
norma	reeba	selia	tamra	tybie
norri	reena	selie	tandi	umeko
norry	reeta	sella	tandy	valli
nydia	reeva	selle	tania	vally
nyssa	regan	selma	tansy	valma
odele	reggi	shana	tanya	valry
olive	reiko	shane	tarah	vanda
ollie	reina	shani	tarra	vania
olwen	reine	shara	taryn	vanna
onida	renae	shari	tasha	vanni
paige	renee	sharl	tasia	vanny
pammi	renie	shaun	tatum	vanya
pammy	retha	shawn	tedda	velma
pansy	reyna	sheba	teddi	venus
paola	rheba	shela	teddy	verla
patsy	rheta	shell	tedra	verna
patti	rhoda	shena	teena	vevay

vicki	adel	bili	dina	eula
vicky	adey	bill	dion	evey
vikki	aggi	bird	dita	evie
vikky	aggy	bree	dode	evvy
vilma	agna	bren	dodi	eyde
vinni	aida	bria	dody	fara
vinny	aila	brit	doll	faun
viola	aile	bryn	dona	fawn
viole	aili	cami	dora	faye
vitia	aime	cara	dore	fern
vivia	ajay	cari	dori	fifi
vivie	alex	caro	doro	fina
vonni	alfi	cary	dory	flor
vonny	alfy	casi	dosi	flss
wally	alia	cass	doti	fran
wanda	alie	cate	dyan	fred
wenda	alis	cati	dyna	gabi
wendi	alix	caty	ouda	gaby
wondy	alla	caye	ebba	gael
wilie	alli	ceil	eddi	gall
willa	alix	cele	eddy	gale
willi	ally	chad	edee	gaye
willy	alma	cher	eden	gena
wilma	alta	chlo	edie	gene
wilow	alys	ciel	edin	geri
windy	arnie	clea	edna	gert
winna	amii	clem	elga	glgl
winne	amll	cleo	elie	gill
winni	amye	clio	elka	gina
winny	andi	cloe	elke	glad
wylma	andy	codi	ella	glen
wynne	anet	cody	elle	glyn
wynny	ange	cora	elli	gnni
xenia	angy	cori	elly	gray
xylia	ania	cory	elna	gwen
yetta	anna	crin	elsa	gwyn
yetty	anne	cris	else	hali
yoshi	anni	dacy	elsi	hana
zarah	anny	dael	elsy	heda
zaria	anya	dale	elva	hedi
zarla	arda	dana	elyn	hedy
zelda	arly	dani	emma	hope
zelma	aryn	dara	emmi	ibby
zenia	asia	darb	emmy	ilka
zonda	audi	dari	enid	illa
zorah	audy	dasi	eran	ilsa
	aura	dawn	erda	ilse
4	avie	debi	erin	ines
	avis	dede	erma	inez
	babb	dela	erna	inga
abbe	babs	dell	eryn	inge
abbi	barb	dena	esma	inna
abby	bari	deni	esme	iona
abra	bebe	deny	essa	iris
adah	bell	deva	essy	irma
adan	bert	devi	esta	isis
adda	bess	dian	etta	issi
addi	beth	didi	etti	issy
addy	bibi	dido	etty	ivie

jada	kyla	maxy	raye	tami
jade	kyle	maye	reba	tana
jami	lacy	mead	rebe	tani
jana	lana	mela	remy	tara
jane	lane	merl	rena	tate
jany	lani	meta	rene	tedi
jean	lara	mimi	reta	tera
jena	lari	mina	rhea	teri
jeni	lark	mira	rica	tess
jenn	leah	moll	rici	thea
jere	leda	mona	riki	theo
jeri	leia	mora	rina	thia
jess	lela	mufi	risa	tiff
jill	lena	myra	rita	timi
joan	leta	nada	riva	tina
jobi	lexi	nady	rivi	tine
joby	lexy	nana	rivy	tish
jodi	lian	nani	roby	tobe
jody	lida	nara	roch	tobi
joey	lila	nari	roda	toby
jojo	lily	nata	rodi	toma
joli	lina	neda	rois	tomi
joly	lind	nedi	romy	toni
joni	linn	nell	rona	tony
jori	lira	nert	rora	tori
josi	lisa	nike	rori	tory
josy	lise	niki	rory	tova
joya	lita	nina	rosa	tove
joye	liva	nita	rose	trix
judi	livy	noel	rosy	tybi
judy	liza	nola	rowe	tyne
juli	lois	nomi	roxi	ulla
june	lola	nona	roxy	ursa
kacy	lona	noni	roze	vale
kaia	loni	nora	rubi	veda
kaja	lora	olga	ruby	vera
kala	lori	olia	ruth	vere
kali	lory	oliy	saba	vida
kara	luce	olly	sada	viki
kare	luci	olva	sara	vina
kari	lucy	oona	sari	vita
kary	lula	opal	sean	viva
kass	lulu	orel	seka	vivi
kata	lura	orly	sela	vyky
kate	lusa	orsa	sena	waly
kath	lyda	otha	shae	wini
kati	lynn	page	shay	wren
katy	mada	pepi	shea	wynn
kaye	mady	peri	shel	xena
keri	maia	perl	sher	ynes
kiah	mair	peta	shir	ynez
kial	mala	phil	sile	yoko
kipp	mame	pier	star	zara
kira	mara	pooh	suki	zena
kiri	mari	pris	sula	zita
kora	marj	prue	susi	zola
kore	mary	rafa	susy	zora
kori	maud	rana	suzi	
kris	maxi	rani	suzy	

3

ada
adi
ali
ame
ami
amy
ana
ann
ara
ava
ayn
bab
bea
bee
bel
bev
cal
cam
clo
con
cyb
deb
dee
del

dix
doe
dot
dre
dru
eba
eda
ede
edi
edy
ema
eva
eve
evy
fae
fan
fay
fey
flo
gae
gay
gui
gus
ida
ina
ira
isa

ivy
jan
jen
joy
kai
kat
kay
kim
kip
kit
koo
kym
lea
lee
lia
lib
lil
lin
liv
liz
lou
luz
lyn
mab
mae
mag
max

may
meg
mei
mel
mia
mil
min
nan
nat
ola
ora
pam
pat
peg
pen
pet
pia
pru
rae
raf
ray
rea
ree
rey
ros
row
roz

sal
sam
sib
sue
ted
tim
ula
una
uta
val
van
vin
viv
zea
zia
zoe

2

ag
de
di
em
jo
ki
lu
vi

Finance

17

A mortgage-backed
Absolute priority
Accruing interest
Adverse selection
Announcement date
Authorized shares
Average measures
Back-to-back loan
Bellwether issues
Best-efforts sale
Blue-chip company
Canadian agencies
Capital budgeting
Capital rationing
Capital structure
Collection policy
Collective wisdom
Commission broker
Commission houses
Compound interest
Convenience yield

Convertible bonds
Convertible price
Corporate charter
Corporate finance
Cost of its funds
Counterpart items
Counterparty risk
Country selection
Cross-border risk
Cumulative voting
Debt displacement
Debt/equity ratio
Debt equity ratio
Dedicated capital
Differential swap
Diffusion process
Discrete variable
Disintermediation
Dividend clawback
Economic earnings
Economic exposure
Edge corporations
Efficient markets

Either-way market
Enhanced indexing
Equity multiplier
Euroequity issues
Evaluation period
Events of default
Exchange controls
Exchange of stock
Exempt securities
Fair market price
Field warehousing
Figuring the tail
Financial control
Five Cs of credit
Fixed price basis
Flight to quality
Forced conversion
Forward Fed funds
Full-payout lease
Futures contracts
Guarantor program
Homemade dividend
Homemade leverage

Horizontal merger
Horizontal spread
Implied repo rate
Income statements
Information costs
Intangible assets
Intercompany loan
Interest coverage
Interest payments
Interest rate cap
Intermediate-term
Investment income
Investor's equity
Last-In-First-Out
Legal investments
Letter of comment
Level-coupon bond
Leveraged buy-out
Limited liability
Linear regression
Liquidation value
Liquidity premium
Macaulay duration

Management buyout
Marginal tax rate
Market-book ratio
Market-if-touched
Measurement error
Minimum purchases
Minority interest
Modified duration
Money market fund
Mortgage duration
mortgage pipeline
Multifamily loans
Natural logarithm
Negative covenant
Negative duration
Net present value
Net profit margin
Net salvage value
New-issues market
Nominal cash flow
Non-insured plans
Notification date
Official reserves

Collateral pool
Commercial risk
Completion risk
Compound option
Consumer credit
Core competency
Corner A Market
Corporate bonds
Cost of capital
Cost of funding
Coupon payments
Coverage ratios
Credible signal
Credit analysis
Currency basket
Currency future
Currency option
Current account
Date of payment
Dead cat bounce
Debt instrument
Debt limitation
Debt securities
Default premium
Deferred equity
Defined benefit
Delivery notice
Delivery points
Demand deposits
Dilutive effect
Discount factor
Discount period
Discount window
Diversification
Dividend policy
Dividend rights
Dollar duration
Domestic market
Doubling option
Dynamic hedging
Economic income
Embedded option
Endowment funds
Equivalent loan
European option
Excess reserves
Exchange-listed
Execution costs
Expected return
Expiration date
Extendable bond
External market
Factor analysis
Federal Reserve
Field warehouse
Financial lease
Financial press
Financial ratio
Fixed-annuities

Fixed-rate loan
Flat price risk
Floating supply
Form efficiency
Forward premium
Free cash flows
General partner
Geographic risk
Government bond
Hedging demands
High-yield bond
Holding company
Hybrid security
Index arbitrage
Indicated yield
Insider trading
Insolvency risk
Internal market
Intrinsic value
Inverted market
Investment bank
Invoice billing
Ladder strategy
Leverage ratios
Leveraged lease
Limited partner
Lines of credit
Lookback option
Majority voting
Making delivery
Market clearing
Market overhang
Marketed claims
Maturity spread
Monetary policy
Mortgage-backed
Municipal notes
National market
Nationalization
Negotiated sale
Net asset value
Omnibus account
One man picture
Operating cycle
Operating lease
Opportunity set
Original margin
Paid in surplus
Phone switching
Portfolio yield
Preferred stock
Primary dealers
Program trading
Progress review
Promissory note
Property rights
Public offering
Purchase method
Pure index fund

Random variable
Realized return
Registered bond
Reopen an issue
Reported factor
Required return
Reset frequency
Residual assets
Residual claims
Residual losses
Residual method
Retention ratio
Reversing trade
Rights offering
Risk free asset
Risk management
Risk-free asset
Riskless return
Scale enhancing
Seasoned issues
Secondary issue
Settlement date
Settlement rate
Settlement risk
Shark repellant
Simple interest
Simple prospect
Spot rate curve
Spread strategy
Stated maturity
Stock exchanges
Stock selection
Stop-loss order
Straight voting
Structured debt
Substitute sale
Swap assignment
Systematic risk
Take a position
Taking delivery
Tandem programs
Temporal method
Three-phase DDM
Tick-test rules
Trade on top of
Turnaround time
Upstairs market
Value-added tax
Venture capital
Vertical merger
Vertical spread
Volatility risk
Wanted for cash
Window contract
Winners's curse
Withdrawal plan
Withholding tax
Working capital

14

Acquiring firm
Agency problem
Aging schedule
Alpha equation
Annuity factor
Asset turnover
Attribute bias
Automatic stay
Autoregressive
Balance sheet.
Balance sheets
Basic IRR rule
Basket options
Bill of lading
Bond agreement
Bond indenture
Budget deficit
Bull-bear bond
Bulldog market
Business cycle
Business risks
Buy on opening
Call an option
Call provision
Capital budget
Capital flight
Capital market
Capitalization
Carrying value
Cash and carry
Cash budgeting
Cash commodity
Claim dilution
Collateralized
Commitment fee
Contract month
Convertibility
Cost of equity
Counterparties
Coupon payment
Credit quality
Credit scoring
Crediting rate
Cross holdings
Crossover rate
Current assets
Current coupon
Custodial fees
Date of record
Dealer options
Debenture bond
Deferred taxes
Delivery price
Dividend yield
Earnings yield
Economic rents

Economic union
Effective date
Effective rate
Equity options
European Union
Ex post return
Exact matching
Excess returns
Exchange offer
Exchange rates
Exercise price
Exercise value
Expected value
Ex-rights date
Extension date
Extension swap
Federal agency
Financial plan
Financial risk
Flip-flop note
Floor planning
Foreign market
Forward market
Friction costs
Futures market
Futures option
Futures prices
Geometric mean
Gestation repo
Gross interest
Group of seven
Growth manager
Holding period
Horizon return
Indirect quote
Inflation risk
Interest rates
Intermediation
Inventory loan
Leveraged beta
Liability swap
Life insurance
Line of credit
Liquidity risk
Long-term debt
Management fee
Margin account
Market sectors
Mark-to-market
Matador market
Maturity phase
Maturity value
MBS Depository
Moving average
Municipal bond
Municipalities
Negative carry
Net book value
Net investment

Neutral period
Noncash charge
Normal deviate
Note agreement
Odd lot dealer
One-factor APT
One-way market
Open contracts
Operating risk
Option premium
Overnight repo
Pension plans
Personal trust
Political risk
Positive carry
Positive float
Price momentum
price/earnings
Primary market
Principal only
Profit margins
Program trades
Pyramid scheme
Quality option
Quality spread
rate of return
Real cash flow
Reference rate
Relative value
Reorganization
Required yield
Reserve ratios
Residual claim
Residual value
Retention rate
Risk arbitrage
Risk-free rate
Safety cushion
Sales forecast
Samurai market
Seasoned issue
Securitization
Self-selection
Short interest
Short position
Short straddle
Shortfall risk
Signaling view
Sovereign risk
Standard error
Stock dividend
Stopping curve
Straight value
Tactical Asset
Tangible asset
Taxable income
Term Fed Funds
Term insurance

Term structure
Terminal value
Terms of trade
The firm being
Tick indicator
Tracking error
Transfer agent
Transfer price
Treasury bills
Treasury bonds
Treasury notes
Treasury stock
Uncovered call
Universal life
Unmatched book
Unsecured debt
Visible supply
Waiting period
Weekend effect
Workout period
Yield to worst

13

Acquired firm
Agency theory
Annual report
Asset classes
Backwardation
Balance sheet
Balanced fund
Basic balance
Basket trades
Beta equation
Blue-sky laws
Bond covenant
Bond indexing
Bootstrapping
Bretton Woods
Bubble theory
Business risk
Buy on margin
Call swaption
Capital gains
Capital lease
Capital stock
Carring costs
Cash delivery
Cash discount
Cash dividend
Clean opinion
Clearinghouse
Closed-end fu
Closing range
Common market
Common shares
Consolidation
Cost of carry

Cost of funds
Counter trade
Credit period
Credit rating
Credit spread
Cross default
Cross hedging
Currency risk
Currency swap
Current issue
Current ratio
Current yield
Cushion bonds
Customs union
Dealer market
Debt capacity
Debt leverage
Decision tree
Deed of trust
Deferred call
Delivery date
Delta neutral
Discount bond
Discount rate
Distributions
Diversifiable
Dividend rate
Dollar return
Dutch auction
Earning power
Economic risk
Efficient set
Equity collar
Equity kicker
Equity market
Equityholders
Euro straight
Euroyen bonds
Exante return
Excess return
Exchange rate
Exchange risk
Expense ratio
Expropriation
Federal funds
Eirm specific
Eirm-specific
Fiscal policy
Fisher effect
Floating lien
Formula basis
Forward cover
Eorward rates
Forward trade
Fourth market
Free on board
Free reserves
Funding ratio

Futures price
Globalization
Gold standard
Good delivery
Grantor trust
Group of five
Hard currency
Herstatt risk
Host security
Human capital
Index warrant
Institutional
Insured plans
Interest rate
Invoice price
Joint account
Legal capital
Lifting a leg
Listed stocks
Locked market
long position
Long straddle
Make a market
Managed float
Market prices
Market return
Market timing
Marketability
Maturity date
MBS servicing
Merchant bank
Mismatch bond
Monetary gold
Money manager
Money markets
Mortgage bond
Mortgage rate
Mutual offset
Net financing
Nominal price
Nonredeemable
Nonrefundable
Non-tradables
Offered price
Open interest
Open position
Open-end fund
Opening price
Opportunities
Option seller
Option writer
Other capital
Other sources
Outright rate
Parallel loan
Pass-throughs
Payment float
Payout ratios

Pension plans
Perfect hedge
Periodic rate
Pipeline risk
Pit committee
Plain vanilla
Plan sponsors
Plowback rate
Present value
Presold issue
Privatization
Probabilities
Product cycle
Profit margin
Project loans
Project notes
Protectionism
Proxy contest
Purchase fund
Put an option
Put provision
Range forward
Refunded bond
Regional fund
Residual risk
Retail credit
Riskless rate
Salvage value
Samurai bonds
Selling group
Selling short
Shareholders
Short selling
Short squeeze
Shortage cost
Soft currency
Specific risk
Spread income
Stock markets
Stockholder's
Stockholders'
Stripped bond
Supermajority
Support level
Surplus funds
Swap buy-back
Swap reversal
Sweep account
Systemic risk
Taking a view
Term premiums
Terms of sale
Thinly traded
Time deposits
Time value of
Time-weighted
Timing option
Total returns

Total revenue
Trading costs
Trading paper
Trading posts
Trading range
Treasury Bond
Treynor index
Trust receipt
U.S. Treasury
Uncovered put
Underwriter's
Underwriters'
Unfunded debt
Utility value
Value manager
Vanilla issue
Variable cost
Variable life
Variance rule
Voting rights
Wasting asset
With dividend
W-type bottom
Yankee market
Yield to call
Zero-sum game

12

48-hour rule
Accrual bond
Acquisitions
Agency basis
Agency costs
Amortization
Anticipation
Arbitrageurs
Asian option
At-the-money
Average life
Black market
Block trades
Block voting
Blow-off top
Bulldog bond
Buy on close
Call options
Call premium
Capital gain
Capital loss
Cash markets
Chinese wall
Closing sale
Common stock
Confirmation
Conglomerate
Correlations
Counterparty

Country beta
Country risk
Covered call
Crawling peg
Cum dividend
Debt service
Default risk
Demand shock
Depreciation
Direct lease
Direct paper
Direct quote
Diversifying
Dollar bonds
Equity claim
Equity floor
Eurocurrency
Factor model
Fallout risk
Fixed assets
Floor broker
Floor trader
Foreign bond
Forward rate
Forward sale
Funding risk
Future value
Global bonds
Gross spread
Growth phase
Growth rates
Growth stock
Immunization
Implied call
Income stock
Index option
Indexed bond
Insured bond
Interest fee
In-the-money
Invoice date
Jensen Index
lead manager
Letter stock
Liquid asset
Load-to-load
Long coupons
Market cycle
Market maker
Market model
Market order
Market price
Market timer
Market value
Matched book
Money market
Money supply
Moral hazard
mutual funds

No-load fund
Open account
Opening sale
Option price
Overshooting
Parity value
Pass-through
Payment date
Payout ratio
pension plan
Premium bond
Price takers
Product risk
Purchase and
Put swaption
Quick assets
Real capital
Registration
Regulation A
Regulation D
Regulation M
Regulation Q
Reinvestment
Remainderman
Rental lease
Reproducible
Revenue bond
Revenue fund
Reverse Repo
Rights issue
Risk classes
Risk indexes
Risk neutral
Risk premium
Sales charge
Samurai bond
Search costs
Secured debt
Securitizing
Serial bonds
Shareholders
Sharpe ratio
Side effects
Sinking fund
Soft dollars
Spot lending
Spot markets
Stakeholders
Steady state
Step-up bond
Stock market
Stock option
Stock rights
Stock ticker
Stockholders
Strike index
Strike price
Supply shock
Tax-deferred

Tender offer
The Exchange
Third market
Tight market
Time deposit
Time premium
Total return
Trade credit
Trading halt
Transactions
Underperform
Underpricing
Underwriters
Underwriting
Underwritten
Uptick trade
Value dating
Volatilition
White knight
Yankee bonds

11

Acquisition
Aggregation
All or none
All-in cost
Annuity due
Back office
Basis point
Basis price
Bear market
Bearer bond
Block house
Block trade
Boilerplate
Bond points
Bondholders
Book profit
Book runner
Bought deal
Brady bonds
Broker loan
Bull market
Bull spread
Bullet loan
Call option
Capitalized
Cash budget
Certificate
Circus swap
Clean price
Coefficient
Commissions
Commodities
Competition
Composition
Compounding

Convergence
Convertible
Corporation
Correlation
Coupon rate
Covariances
Covered Put
Credit risk
Cross rates
Crown jewel
Day trading
Dealer loan
Debt market
Debt relief
Debtholders
Decile rank
Delta hedge
Depreciates
Derivatives
Devaluation
Dirty float
Dirty price
Discounting
Distributed
Diversified
Dollar roll
Enhancement
Equity swap
Eurocredits
Eurodollars
Event study
Ex-dividend
Fixed asset
Fixed-dates
Flat trades
Flower bond
Freddie Mac
Fund family
Funded debt
Global fund
Gray market
Growth rate
Hedge ratio
Homogeneity
Homogeneous
Hurdle rate
Income bond
Income fund
Index model
Information
Instruments
Inventories
Investments
Junior debt
Ledger cash
Liabilities
Limit order
Limit price
Liquidating

Liquidation
Lock-up CDs
Maintenance
Margin call
Market risk
Merchandise
Multiperiod
Mutual fund
Netting out
Nonrecourse
NPV profile
Offer price
Open order
Open-outcry
Origination
Outsourcing
Overperform
Partnership
Passthrough
Performance
Perquisites
Poison pill
Pool factor
Prepayement
Prepayments
Probability
Put options
Quanto swap
Quick ratio
Random walk
Real assets
Real market
Rebalancing
Receivables
Reclamation
Record date
Red herring
Replacement
Requirement
Retracement
Revaluation
Risk averse
Risky asset
Section 482
Securitized
Securitizes
Senior debt
Series bond
Shareholder
Shogun bond
Short bonds
Short hedge
Sight draft
Specialists
Spreadsheet
Standby fee
Stock index
Stock split
Stockholder

Street name
Strike rate
Strong form
Swap option
Syndication
Take-up fee
Target firm
The foreign
Theoretical
Thin market
To maturity
Trade draft
Trade house
Traditional
Transaction
Translation
Underwriter
Undewriting
Unique risk
Unleveraged
Wall Street
Warehousing
Whole loans
With rights
Yankee bond
Yield curve
Yield ratio
Zero uptick
Zero-coupon

10

Acceptance
Acquiree's
Acquirer's
Ad valorem
Allocation
Amortizing
Arms index
Asset swap
Assignment
Baker Plan
Bank draft
Bank loans
Bankruptcy
Basis risk
Bond value
Book value
Call price
Cash cycle
Cash flows
Cash offer
Cash ratio
Collateral
Commission
Commitment
Competence
Compounded

Controller
Conversion
Correlated
Covariance
Covered or
Cum rights
Currencies
Debentures
Debt ratio
Debtholder
Defeasance
Depreciate
Derivative
Deviations
Divergence
EAFE index
Efficiency
Endogenous
Equity cap
Euro lines
Eurodollar
Evaluation
Evening up
Event risk
Expiration
Extinguish
Face value
Fair price
Fiat money
First-call
Fixed cost
Flat price
Free float
Free rider
Full price
Ginnie Mae
Hedge fund
High price
High yield
Historical
Horizontal
In the box
Index fund
Investment
Jumbo loan
Junk bonds
Last split
Lease Rate
Liquidator
Loan value
Long bonds
Long hedge
Mail float
Match fund
Maturities
Money base
Muni bonds
Net assets
Net change

Net income
Net period
Notice day
On the run
Open order
Operations
OTC market
P/E effect
P/E ratios
Paper gain
Par values
Perpetuity
Poison put
Portfolios
Post-audit
Prepayemts
Prepayment
Price risk
Priced out
Prime rate
Prospectus
Proxy vote
Put option
Receivable
Redeemable
Refundable
Regression
Reinvested
Repurchase
Risk lover
Risk prone
Roll dates
Round-trip
Round-turn
Securities
Sell hedge
Sell short
Semistrong
Settlement
Short book
Short sale
Simulation
Specialist
Speculator
Spot month
Spot price
Spot rates
Spot trade
Stop order
Subsidiary
Sunk costs
Sushi bond
Syndicated
Syndicates
Synthetics
Systematic
Tax shield
Technician
TED spread

Term bonds
Term repos
Term trust
Time decay
Time draft
Time value
Trade date
Trade debt
Treasuries
True lease
Trust deed
Turnaround
Unbundling
Underlying
Underwrite
Value date
Volatility
Wallflower
Watch list
Whole life
Wire house
World Bank
Write-down

9

Accretion
Actionist
Agreement
Arbitrage
Ask price
Asymmetry
Balancing
Bank line
Bank wire
Bear raid
Benchmark
Big Board
Book cash
Call date
Call risk
Cash flow
Chartists
Commodity
Contracts
Covenants
Creditors
Day order
Debt swap
Dependent
Deviation
Dividends
Downgrade
Drop lock
Eurobonds
Euroclear
Euro-note
Exchanges

Execution
Exercised
Ex-rights
Extension
Factoring
Fair game
Fed funds
Forfaiter
Free cash
Frictions
Front fee
Go-around
Greenmail
Hot money
Indenture
Inflation
Insolvent
Insurance
Intrinsic
Inventory
Investors
Junk bond
Level pay
Leveraged
Liability
LIBO rate
Liquidity
Load fund
Long-term
Look-thru
Low price
Markowitz
Mortgagee
Mortgager
Mortgages
Multiples
Muni bond
Municipal
Net float
Net lease
Net worth
New money
Objective
Offerings
Open book
Open repo
P/E ratio
Par value
Parameter
Placement
Portfolio
Positions
Preferred
Principal
Prospects
Put price
Quotation
Rate lock

Rate risk
Rate swap
Rationing
Real time
Refunding
Registrar
Residuals
Rights-on
Roll over
Round lot
Rule 144a
Seniority
Spot rate
Spreading
Statement
Subpart F
Swap rate
Swap sale
Switching
Syndicate
Tax books
Tax haven
Technical
Term loan
Term repo
The close
Tick-test
Tombstone
Treasurer
Two-state
Variables
Variances
Weak form
Yankee CD

8

Accretes
Acquired
Acquiree
Acquirer
Amortize
Analysts
Banker's
Big Bang
Binomial
Breakout
Bundling
Buy-back
Buydowns
Calendar
Callable
Cash cow
Churning
Claimant
Comanger
Compare
Compound

Conflict
Contango
Contract
Covenant
Cramdown
Creditor
Currency
De facto
Dealer's
Defaults
Delivery
Dilution
Discount
Dividend
Domestic
Downtick
Due bill
Duration
Earnings
Euro CDs
Eurobank
Eurobond
Exchange
Exercise
Expensed
Exposure
Floating
Goodwill
Indexing
Industry
Insiders
Interest
Investor
Invoices
Lessor's
Leverage
Lock-out
Long run
Marginal
Maturing
Maturity
MBS pool
Modeling
Mortgage
Novation
NPV rule
Payables
Payments
Pipeline
Position
Premiums
Purchase
Put bond
Reaction
Receiver
Recourse
Related
Reserves

Reverses
Rollover
Safekeep
Scale in
Security
Shirking
Shopping
Slippage
Spectail
Spin-off
Standard
Stockout
Straddle
Strategy
Swaption
Take-out
Takeover
Tax swap
Tom next
Top down
T-period
Trader's
Tranches
Treasury
Turnover
Variable
Variance
Warrants
Weighted
Yield to

7

Accrual
Actuals
Agent's
Alizari
Analyst
Annuity
Arsenic
Average
Back-up
Balance
Bidding
BONDPAR
Bracket
brokers
Capital
Cashout
Control
Current
Dealers
Default
Deficit
Deliver
Detrend
Erosion
Exhange

Expense
Expires
Fedwire
Finance
Floater
Forward
Futures
Gearing
Generic
Give up
GNMA-II
Haircut
Hedging
Holders
Holding
Initial
Invoice
J-curve
Kiretsu
Leakage
Lease's
Leasing
Lenders
Lockbox
Manager
Markets
Mergers
Monitor
Netting
Nominal
Odd lot
Offered
Options
Pairoff
Partner
Payback
Paydown
Picture
Pooling
Premium
Pricing
Program
Quantos
Quarter
Ratings
Reserve
Returns
Revenue
Signals
Spinoff
Spreads
Step-up
Straddl
Subject
Time to
Traders
Trading
Tranche

Utility
Warrant
Without
Workout
Z score

6

Accept
Active
Actual
Agency
Angels
Annual
Assets
Bidder
Boning
Borrow
Bourse
Branch
Broker
Budget
Buy in
Buyout
Called
Circle
Collar
Common
Consol
Convex
Coupon
Credit
Dealer
Demand
Equity
Ethics
Factor
Filter
Future
Growth
Handle
Harvey
Hedges
Hedgie
Hubris
Hybrid
Issuer
Issues
Lambda
Lease
Leases
Lender
Lessee
Lessor

Liquid
Margin
Market
Mature
Merger
NASDAQ
Nearby
Offers
Offset
Option
Pay-up
Period
Pickup
Prepay
Prices
Quoted
Rating
Ratios
Retail
Retire
Return
Rights
Sector
Series
Shares
Sheets
Signal
Sinker
Spread
Stocks
Street
Strong
Swissy
Target
Tender
Tenors
Trader
Trades
Trough
Uptick
Volume
Writer
Wields
Z bond

5

Agent
Alpha
Asked
Asset
Banks
Basis
Betas

Board
Bogey
Bonds
Break
Cable
Calls
Cards
Carry
Clear
Costs
Cover
Curve
Debts
Delta
Draft
Euros
Float
Floor
Forex
Funds
Gains
Gamma
Gilts
Gross
Hedge
Issue
Kappa
Lease
Liens
Loans
Means
Merge
Mimic
Model
Money
Munis
Nexus
Noise
Notes
Offer
Order
Paper
Phase
Pivot
Point
Price
Proxy
Rally
Range
Ratio
Repos
Right
Rings
Risks

Rules
Scale
Scalp
Short
Speed
Split
Stock
Sucre
Swaps
Tenor
Theta
Total
Trade
Trend
Value
Whole
Wi wi
Woody
World
Yield

4

Agio
Away
Bane
Bank
Bear
Beta
Bids
Bond
Book
Buck
Bull
Call
Cash
Cost
Date
Debt
Fail
Fees
Fill
Firm
Flow
Fund
Lead
Lend
Lien
Loan
Long
Mean
Note
Peak
Plan

Plug
Plus
Post
Puke
Puts
Rate
Repo
Risk
Sale
See:
Shop
Size
Span
Spot
Swap
Tail
Take
Tick
Time
Type
View
Wash
Yard
Zero

3

Ask
Bar
Bid
Buy
Cap
Car
CDs
Fed
Hit
IRR
Lag
Par
Pit
PSA
Put
Run
The

2

BA
CD
DM
NM
Wi

French Composers

10
Saintsaens

8
Couperin
Massenet
Monsigny

7
Berlioz
Debussy
Delibes
Legrand
Milhaud
Poulenc

6
Godard
Gounod
Rameau
Rampal
Rivier

5
Auric
Bizet
Dukas
Faure
Ravel
Satie

4
Lalo

French Writers

10
Baudelaire

9
Corneille

8
Beauvoir
Bergerac
Flaubert
Rousseau
Stendhal
Voltaire

7
Cocteau
Colette
Moliere
Rimbaud

6
Balzac
France

Musset
Pascal
Proust
Racine
Sartre

5
Camus
Dumas
Verne

4
Gide
Hugo
Sand
Zola

3
Nin

Fruit Names

12
Passionfruit

11
Pomegranate

10
Breadfruit
Grapefruit
Mangostine

9
Jackfruit
Tangerine

8
Mandarin
Rambutan
Tamarind

7
Apricot
Avocado
Kumquat

6
Banana
Lychee
Orange
Papaya
Pomelo
Tomato

5
Apple

Grape
Guava
Lemon
Mango
Peach

4
Pear
Plum

Furniture

10
chandelier
nightstand

9
footstool

8
armchair
bookcase
endtable

7
armoire

cabinet
dresser
drysink
ottoman

6
buffet
carpet
rocker

torche

5
chair
couch
setee
shelf
stool
table

4
desk
lamp

3
bar
bed

Gemstones

11
Lapislazuli

10
Aquamarine
Tourmaline

9
Moonstone
Turquoise

8
Amethyst
Feldspar
Sapphire
Sardonyx

7
Apatite
Citrine
Diamond
Emerald

6
Garnet
Jasper

Quartz
Spinal
Zircon

5
Agate
Amber
Beryl
Coral
Pearl

Topaz

4
Jade
Onyx
Opal
Ruby

Geology

19
Interstratification
Lacustrine deposits

18
Columnar structure
Cumu-cirro-stratus
Indusial limestone
Mountain limestone
Phanerocrystalline
Tetrakishexahedron

17
Calciferous epoch

Cretaceous period
Cryptocrystalline
Laurentian period
Old red sandstone
Sedimentary rocks
Uniformitarianism

16
Ichthyocoprolite
Infusorial earth
Micro-geological
Phanerite series
Saliferous rocks
Subcarboniferous
Transition rocks
Unconformability

15
Anticlinal axis
Cliff limestone
Cumbrian system
Hamilton period
Interstratified
Intrusive rocks
Llandeilo group
Natural history
Oriskany period
Plutonic action
Plutonic theory
Primitive rocks
Stratigraphical
Supercretaceous
Supracretaceous
Tertiary period

Tetrahexahedral
Tetrahexahedron

14
Alabama period
Colorado group
Conformability
Hastings sands
Longmynd rocks
Millstone girt
Panidiomorphic
Plutonic rocks
Schoharie grit
Tetartohedrism
Trenton period
Trisoctahedron
Uniformitarian

13
Acadian epoch
Anticlinorium
Aqueous rocks
Catastrophism
Catastrophist
Coal measures
Cross bedding
Cumulostratus
Genesee epoch
Globuliferous
Harlech group
Interstratify
Laramie group
Lingula flags
Micro-geology
Porcelainized

Portage group
Potsdam group
Primary rocks
Purbeck stone
Reverse fault
Saddle-shaped
Salina period
Stalactitical
Strombuliform
Terrace epoch
Tetartohedral
Unconformable
Uralitization
Wenlock group

12

Cone-in-cone
Conglomerate
Geanticlinal
Geosynclinal
Intercolline
Lithological
Ludlow group
Paleozoology
Plastic clay
Posttertiary
Purbeck beds
Quaquaversal
Quebec group
Secondary ag
Stratigraphy
Stromatology
Synclinorium
Tertiary age
Thrust plane
Unconformity
Unstratified
Vesiculation

11

Agglomerate
Catastrophe
Conformable
Corniferous
Granitiform
Helminthite
Line of dip
Muschelkalk

Paleolithic
Pleistocene
Pretertiary
Puerco beds
Schistosity
Segregation
Stalactical
Subapennine
Subcolumnar
Tetrahedral
Trimorphism

10

Accretions
Anticlinal
Clinometer
Clinometry
Coal field
Coal plant
Concretion
Cordillera
Coromandel
Geological
Greenstone
Jura-trias
Oryctology
Pitchstone
Poecilitic
Poikilitic
Preglacial
Primordial
Psychozoic
Quaternary
Slate clay
Stalactite
Stalagmite
Subaqueous
Tautozonal
Tetragonal
Uniformism
Variolitic
Weald clay
Weathering

9

Alternant
Azoic age
Cainozoic

Corallian
Coral-rag
Corrasion
Foliation
geologist
Geologize
Granulite
Graywacke
Greensand
Gritstone
Ichnology
Intrusion
Laccolith
Oligocene
Paleolith
Paleozoic
Paxillose
Pleiocene
Plutonian
Plutonism
Protozoic
Sand gall
Sand pipe
Schistous
Segregate
Septarium
Sheepback
Solfatara
Stockwork
Synclinal
Thalassic
Tilestone
Triclinic
Trimetric
Underclay
Uniclinal
Variolite
Vulcanian
Weathered

8

Ablation
Alluvium
Archaean
Cenozoic
Cleavage
Coal bed
Foliated
Geognosy
Glaciate

Huronian
Hypogene
Hypozoic
Intruded
Inverted
Jurassic
Laterite
Peperino
Phreatic
piedmont
Pliocene
Porphyry
Sediment
Senonian
Silurian
Syncline
Tectonic
Tephrite
Tertiary
Tesseral
Tessular
Trachyte
Triassic
Trilling
Trimorph
Turonian
Twinning
Uniaxial

7

Corrade
Cumulus
Cyclone
Geology
Granite
Hogback
Hornito
Ice age
Igneous
Intrude
Knotted
Liassic
Miocene
Permian
Pluvial
Primary
Seiches
Shingle
Stratum
Taconic

Terrace
Terrane
Twinned
Volcano
Wealden

6

Ammite
Basalt
Coulee
Gneiss
Keuper
Oolite
Period
quartz
Rhetic
Schist
Shiver
Strata
Uplift

5

Crust
Fault
Gault
Heave
Joint
Loess
Pitch
Shale
Talus
Trass
Trias
Utica
Wacky

4

Crag
Grit
Jura
Lias
Slag
Till
Trap
Twin

German Composers

11

Duerrenmatt
Grillparzer
Humperdinck
Mendelssohn
Morgenstern

9

Beethoven
Bouterwerk
Hauptmann

8

Brentano

Bruckner
Dohnanyi
Gryphius
Hoffmann
Schiller
Schubert
Schuman
Telemann

7

Berlioz
Joseffy
Moerike
Mosonyi
Nikisch
Novalis
Poldind
Reineke

Romberg
Strauss

6

Anhalt
Bartok
Brahms
Brecht
Dorati
Frisch
Goethe
Handel
Herder
Hollerr
Kalman
Kleist
Kodaly
Mozart

Polgar
Sandor
Schutz
Wagner

5

Boell
Grass
Grimm
Haydn
Heine
Hesse
Kafka
Lehar
Liszt
Riulke
Rozsa
Serly

Szell
Trakl
Weber
Zsolt

4

Bach
Mann
Paul
Weil

3

Orf

Greek

13

Anthropotokos

11

Amphictyony
Apokalupsis

9

Anthropos

8

Archaios
Basileia

Basileus
Paidiske

7

Angeion
Biblion
Paideia

6

Amoibe
Byblos
Eryops
Koilia

5

Nomos
Onoma

4

Ouai

Greek Writers

12

Aristophanes

11

Apollonius
Callimachus

10

Pythagorus
Theocritus
Thucydides

9

Aeschulus

Euripides
Herodotus
Lucretius
Sophocles

8

Menander
Plutarch
Theognis

Xenophon

7

Alcaeus

6

Alcman
Hesidod

Pindar
Sappho
Strabo

5

Aesop
Homer
Plato
Solon

Hebrew

7 Nephesh

6 Askara / Neqeba

5 Almah / Arets / Padah

4 Aviv / Olam

Islands

12 Greatbritain / Nowfoundland

11 Southampton

10 Hispaniola / Madagascar

9 Ellesmere / Greenland / Mellville / Newguinea

8 Hokkaiso / Mindanao / Srilanka / Sulawesi / Tasmania / Victoria

7 Britaln

Iceland / Ireland / Sumatra

6 Baffin / Borneo / Honshu / Kyushu

5 Banks / Devon / Luzon

4 Cuba / Java

Italian Composers

11 Leoncavallo

10 Boccherini

Pallestrina

9 Donizetti / Scarlatti

8 Albinoni / Ambrosio / Catalani / Gabrieli / Paganini / Respighi

7 Bellini / Corelli / Martini / Menotti / Puccini / Rossinsi

Salieri / Torelli / Vivaldi

5 Verdi

Italian Writers

10 Campanella / Pirandello

9 Boccaccio / Fogazzaro / Lampedusa / Lorenzini

8 Carducci / Leeopardi / Sciascia

7 Alfieri / Aquinas / Aretino

Calvino / Collodi / Darezzo / Dassisi / Deledda / Ferrari / Foscolo / Goldoni / Manzoni / Mazzini

6 Basile / Favero / Labini / Pavese

5 Dante / Monti

Porta / Verga

4 Levi

3 Eco

Jargon Speak

31

dichlorodiphenyl-trichloroethane

27

assemblerprogram-merfriendly
graphicaluserinter-facebased

26

nondeterminis-ticpolynomial

25

generalpurposepro-gramming
smallerthancharac-tersized
waybehindthestate-oftheart

24

altmodealtmode-cokebottle
quadruplebucky-cokebottle
terminateandstayres-ident

23

metaloxidesemicon-ductor
mithacker-turnednsaspook
offtheorganization-chart
preindustrialrevolu-tion
programminglan-guagelike

22

conditional-

21

architecturedepen-dent
backward-compatibility
controlmetacoke-bottle
institutionalsounding
instructionsper-second
knowledge-manipulation
neverwasstateoft-heart
transactionprocess-ing

20

bondageand-discipline
characterbycharacter
internationalization
megabytesofmain-store
microprocessor-driven
nonvirtualaddressing
operatingsystemstaff
phrasefrequency-based
returnfromsubroutine
securitycompromis-ing
trademarksuperscript

19

conformityenforcing
incomprehensibility
microprocessor-based
multiplehierarchies
nationallampoonnerd

---

compilation
dungeonsand-dragonslike
megabytesof-massstorage
niagarafalls-equivalent

18

abstractionsidered
backwardcompatible
berserkosurrealist
cardpunchemulating
collisiondetection
extrovertedsensate
guiltbyassociation
informationsharing
informationstorage
microcomputerbased
millionthofasecond
montypythoninspace
multibilliondollar
overgeneralization
pseudomathematical
resourceallocation
resourcemanage-ment
resynchronizations
reverseengineering
telecommunications

17

anarchosurrealist
antiauthoritarian
blacklettergothic
burnbeforereading
charactergraphics
commercialization
compilerdependent
countercommercial
depersonalization
deterministically
directorybrowsing
drillingequipment
electromechanical
emergencypoweroff
exceptionhandling
formversuscontent
furthercompressed
garbagecollection
hackersubversives
hardwaredesigning
higherdimensional
highestunitvolume
inappropriateness

---

paragraphplusoffset
quadruplebuckyclear
structuredassembler
technicalspecialist

18

informationhiding
macropreprocessor
manufacturability
misunderstandings
muchunderutilized
multipleprecision
newlineterminated
nineteenseventies
nonstandardlength
paleontologically
phaseofthemoonbug
philosophunculism
programmerhostile
projectprogrammer
selfadvertisement
selfreferentially
singletaskingonly
sourcedistributed
superconductivity
systemmaintenance
tabulatingmachine

16

alltheworldsavax
assumedreachable
autobogotiphobia
banananananananana
bicapitalization
businessoriented
cellularautomata
characterization
computerlanguage
computerrefereed
computersecurity
controlaltinsert
crossreferencing
eclsupercomputer
electroncarrying
enthusiastically
fabricationsetup
featureencrusted
gigainstructions
hardwarespecific
incomprehensibly
industrystandard
informationspace
interoperability
lossageresistant
machinedependent
memorymanage-ment
miscommunication
misconfiguration
nondeterministic

---

nonorthogonality
optionshiftclick
overgeneralizing
phototypesetting
powertransducing
programautomated
pseudoscientific
registercoloring
reimplementation
reinitialization
reversedeightbit
searchanddestroy
searchandreplace
securitybreaking
securitycracking
segmentaddressed
selfsatisfaction
shortsightedness
signalprocessing
stateoftheworldp
superprogrammers
teenageoryounger
thoughtprovoking
threedimensional
threetimeslonger
typewriterpaired

15

administrations
anarchoverbiage
anthropological
authoritatively
behindthescenes
berserkerwizard
bettermotivated
byteaddressable
characteristics
cheaprestaurant
computermachine
computerrelated
computerscience
congratulations
controlmetabang
correspondingly
crossreferenced
crossreferences
customercontrol
differentiating
earthshattering
ekswiezedzedwie
ekswiezeezeewie
embeddedsystems
englishlanguage
englishspeakers

englishspeaking
epidemiological
errorcorrecting
eventprocessing
exceptionfilled
extraordinarily
fandomconnected
foreignlanguage
fourcolorglossy
generalizations
graphicscontrol
hahaonlyserious
hewlettpackards
hightemperature
hyphenseparated
imageprocessing
implementations
improvisational
inappropriately
inarticulations
inconspicuously
individualistic
inputtokenizing
intensification
interchangeable
interchangeably
interruptdriven
jargonification
longestablished
machinelanguage
machinereadable
maintainability
memoryintensive
memoryshuffling
merchantability
metainformation
microcontroller
microfortnights
microprocessors
microtechnology
missioncritical
monkeywrenchers
nanofabrication
nonquantifiable
nonsequentially
numbercrunching
oftdemonstrated
operatingsystem
personification
platinumiridium
postscriptbased
programmability
pseudocharacter
pseudolanguages
psychedelicware
rationalization
reconfiguration
representations

roomtemperature
ruleboundedness
russianlanguage
segmentedmemory
selfcompetitive
selfreplicating
selfreplication
semiconsciously
semiimmediately
semiindependent
semiintelligen
semiobsolescent
semirespectable
semiunderground
servicebusiness
simplyconnected
singlecharacter
sixteenfingered
standardization
storeandforward
superprogrammer
surreptitiously
synchronization
tenniselbowlike
timingdependent
transformations
transistorlogic
unadventurously
undistinguished
unintentionally
vendorsupported
waystoreproduce
wellintentioned
writeonlymemory

14

accelerometers
administration
administrative
administrators
affectionately
ahrteeefaykyoo
algoldescended
allcapitalized
alltoofrequent
alphabetically
anticonformist
asciimonospace
assemblerlevel
backapostrophe
blinkenlichten
bogoncomputron
busindependent
capitalization
carnegiemellon
characterbased

characterizing
chromodynamics
clustergeeking
coconspirators
collegedegreed
colorblindness
commaseparated
commercialized
communications
compilerlinker
configurations
confrontations
considerations
constellations
conversational
copyprotection
correspondence
correspondents
counterculture
countermeasure
crosslicensing
crossreference
crosssectional
curvaceousness
databasetheory
datastructures
decommissioned
defenestration
discriminating
discrimination
distinguishing
doughnutshaped
eisacompatible
electronically
electronicmail
errordetecting
etymologically
exponentiation
expressiveness
featurectomies
featurefulness
filemanagement
fingerpointing
frenchspeaking
fundamentalist
garbagecollect
generalization
generalpurpose
hackeroriented
hackerstandard
identification
idiosyncracies
illconditioned
illegaladdress
inconvenienced
initialization
inputcharacter
insufficiently

intellectually
interjectively
ironoxidebased
kruhftsmanship
lastinfirstout
letterbyletter
littleendfirst
lookenspeepers
lowestpriority
lowreliability
lowsingledigit
macroexpansion
magneticbubble
malfunctioning
mathematically
mathematicians
merryprankster
metaphorically
microcomputers
microfortnight
microprocessor
millifortnight
mindbogglingly
misconceptions
multitendriled
nanotechnology
nativelanguage
nearsuperhuman
nineteensixtyx
nondestructive
nondeterminism
nonfunctioning
noninteractive
nonintuitively
nonoverlapping
nonprogrammers
nowobsolescent
objectionablec
objectoriented
onescomplement
orderofarrival
overengineered
oversimplified
overtheweekend
overwhelmingly
parallaxsecond
pathologically
persontoperson
piesliceshaped
preconceptions
preferritecore
preoccupations
printedcircuit
problemsolving
programoverlay
pronunciations
proofofconcept
psychosexually

purepositional
puzzleoriented
quadruplebucky
quantification
recapitulation
redistribution
referencecount
regexphandling
reorganization
representation
requestforhelp
responsibility
retrocomputing
samedayservice
satisfactorily
sciencefiction
screenhandling
screenoriented
selfabsorption
selfdescribing
selfexpressive
selfrespecting
selfsubverting
semihumorously
simultaneously
singlemolecule
singlestepping
smokeproducing
sophistication
soundrecording
sourceportable
specialpurpose
specifications
spitzensparken
spoonerization
springerverlag
subdirectories
submicronsized
supercomputers
superficiality
syncronization
systematically
thermalcycling
thousanddollar
timepromptwait
twopersonsized
twoscomplement
ultraheavyduty
uncontrollably
understandable
understatement
unmaintainable
unsurprisingly
userextensible
userobsequious
variablelength
vaxocentricity
versioncontrol

wakingsleeping
washingmachine
wellthoughtout
wellunderstood
wholepolyester
wringlewrangle
writeprotected
yabacompatible

13

abbreviations
accomplishing
acknowledging
addisonwesley
administrator
advthanksance
affordability
alternatively
ambimoustrous
americanstyle
analretentive
appropriately
approximately
approximation
archeological
architectures
asciistandard
assassinating
assassination
atdhvaannkcse
automagically
automatically
awkwardnesses
awtohmajiklee
baadermeinhof
backformation
blinkenlights
blockoriented
blockprinting
booleanvalued
braincomputer
braindamaging
bugcompatible
bulletinboard
bureaucracies
bureaucratese
buzzwordladen
caseblindness
casesensitive
characterized
characterizes
characteronly
circumscribed
circumstances
circumventing
classsubclass
codeintensive

combatability
commemoration
commoncarrier
communicating
communication
communicators
compatibility
complications
comprehending
computational
computeraided
concentrating
concentration
condescending
consciousness
conspicuously
constructions
contradiction
contributions
conversations
copyprotected
corresponding
craftsmanship
crossmounting
cruftsmanship
cryptographic
datadependent
defenestrated
deliberations
demonstrating
demonstration
dereferencing
deterministic
disadvantages
disappearance
disassembling
disconnection
discontinuity
discordianism
diskaccessing
diskcompactor
disseminating
dissemination
distinguished
distinguishes
distressingly
distributions
doubleohseven
emohteeessess
encapsulation
encouragement
enlightenment
ethnocentrism
exceptionally
exivyleaguers
exponentially
extendedascii
extensibility
exterminating

extinguishers
fieldoriented
floatingpoint
floorstanding
flowofcontrol
frobnosticate
frustratingly
functionality
fundamentally
gefingerpoken
granularities
graphicsmacro
hackerculture
hackerrelated
hackerwritten
hackification
halfseriously
handoptimized
healthfoodist
humanreadable
humpdayboinks
idiomatically
illstructured
impossibility
inadvertently
inconsistency
incorporating
incrementally
independently
inexperienced
informational
installations
instantiation
instructional
intellivision
intentionally
interactively
interestingly
interjections
international
internetstyle
interpolation
interrogative
interruptions
intrinsically
inventiveness
investigating
investigation
irrecoverably
jargonfriends
justification
kayjeebeevaks
knowledgeably
languagestyle
languageusing
letterquality
lozengeshaped
lunaticfringe
mailtonetnews

manufacturers
manufacturing
memorylimited
metasyntactic
methodologies
microcomputer
microfloppies
microhobbyist
middleinitial
millennialong
millilampsons
minicomputers
mittengrabben
modelrailroad
modifications
nanocomputers
nanofortnight
nonalphabetic
nonbytestream
noncommercial
nonconducting
nonconforming
noncontiguous
nonelectronic
nonexpendable
nonfunctional
nonoptimality
nonreversible
northandsouth
nowdemolished
obliviousness
opportunities
optimizations
organizations
orthogonality
orthogonalize
overestimated
packeddecimal
parenthesized
participation
peculiarities
personalities
personalmicro
philosophical
pointandclick
porkvegetable
postaladdress
practitioners
predominantly
preoccupation
preprocessors
presentations
prewinchester
professionals
proliferation
pronouncement
protechnology
psychological
qualification

quickanddirty
radionuclides
ramifications
recentlyslain
reconfiguring
reimplemented
reincarnation
relationships
repercussions
representable
restrictively
restructuring
rollercoaster
salescritters
sarcastically
selfconscious
selfcontained
selfevidently
selfmodifying
selfreference
semiapproving
semiautomatic
semiconductor
semilegendary
semiseriously
shrinkwrapped
shubniggurath
signaltonoise
significantly
signmagnitude
singleplatter
singletasking
sixletterisms
skipcharacter
smalltalklike
smartprograms
sophisticated
sparcstations
specification
spectacularly
speculatively
spontaneously
squeakyvoiced
statistically
statisticians
storedprogram
straightfaced
strangulation
streetaddress
stylistically
substitutions
superannuated
supercomputer
superficially
syntactically
technological
telecommuting
textformatter
theoretically

thermodynamic
thousandpound
threequarters
tickpersecond
timeconsuming
timeimmediate
topicoriented
traditionally
transferrable
transparently
transportable
typographical
unambiguously
uncapitalized
uncomfortable
unconditional
undeliverable
underestimate
undergraduate
understanding
unexplainable
unforgettable
unfortunately
unimaginative
uninteresting
unixlookalike
unixworkalike
unparenthisey
unprecedented
unpredictable
unpredictably
unreliability
unwindprotect
uppercaseonly
userinterface
userspecified
vacuumcleaner
veryhighlevel
virtualmemory
volleyballers
wellconnected
winniethepooh
worldbuilding
worldgirdling

12

abbreviation
abstractions
accelerating
acceleration
accidentally
accompanying
accomplished
accomplishes
accumulation
acknowledges
additionally

administered
adulterating
aggressively
alllowercase
alternatives
anglebracket
announcement
anthologized
anticipation
antiphysical
applications
appreciating
appreciation
appreciative
approximated
arrangements
articulation
artificially
astonishment
astoundingly
astronomical
asymmetrical
authenticity
availability
baseregister
befuddlement
birkenstocks
blackonblack
blackongreen
bodylanguage
bogodynamics
boobytrapped
bottlenecked
braindamaged
breathoflife
britishstyle
broadcasting
brotherinlaw
buddhanature
bullsessions
bullshitting
businesslike
caesarcypher
calculations
cancellation
canonicality
capabilities
centenarians
characterize
christianity
cluelessness
coefficients
coincidences
collectively
combinations
commandbased
commercially
communicates
comparatives

compellingly
complemented
compositions
comprehended
computations
computerized
concentrated
concentrates
conceptually
conclusively
condensation
conditioning
confettilike
congruential
connotations
consequences
consequently
considerable
considerably
consistently
conspiracies
constipation
constituency
constituents
construction
constructive
contiguously
continuously
contractions
contributors
conventional
coordinating
coordinators
corporations
costofliving
countenanced
crackingring
crashandburn
crockishness
crossposting
crossproduct
curaretipped
customizable
czechoslovak
daisychained
deadlocklike
declarations
declassified
defenestrate
deinhibiting
deliberately
demonstrably
demonstrated
denomination
descriptions
determinedly
developments
dictionaries
difficulties

disagreement
disappointed
disapproving
disastrously
disgustitude
disorganized
disseminated
distinctions
distributing
dividebyzero
doubleglitch
doublequotes
dynamicstore
eightycolumn
electrically
embarrassing
encapsulated
encapsulates
encompassing
encountering
enhancements
enshrinement
environments
epsilondelta
equivalently
esthetically
euphoniously
everchanging
exaggeration
exhortations
expectations
experiencing
experimental
explanations
extrasomatic
faithholding
featurectomy
featureladen
fieldsupport
firefighting
flamethrower
floatinghead
fontdiddling
forceallcaps
friendliness
functionally
futurologist
gameoriented
generational
geographical
getcharacter
gettogethers
goaldirected
godzillagram
gohdienamiks
gonkyoolaytr
gratuitously
greatersized
hackandslash

hackerbladet
hackernature
halfderisive
halfjokingly
handlettered
hardtodetect
hardweirilee
harmlessness
hierarchical
highlighting
highoverhead
historically
humanfactors
hypothetical
illuminating
immoderately
immortalized
implementing
implementors
implications
impressively
inadequacies
incantations
incautiously
incompetence
incompletely
incorporated
incorrectspa
increasingly
incrementing
indefinitely
independence
inflectional
infrequently
infringement
inscriptions
insecteating
institutions
instructions
instrumental
intelligence
interactions
interjection
interleaving
intermachine
interminably
interoperate
interpreting
interprocess
intersection
interspersed
interstellar
irresistibly
irreversibly
irritatingly
japanesefood
journalistic
laboratories
languageplay

littleendian
locksmithing
longdistance
longdrawnout
lowbandwidth
lowintensity
macroproblem
magneticdisk
maintainance
malfunctions
manipulation
manufactured
manufacturer
marginalized
marketdriven
mathematical
memorymapped
metalanguage
metalcutting
metaphorical
methodically
microcentury
microproblem
microsystems
middleendian
millennarian
millilampson
milliseconds
minifloppies
missedemfive
misspellings
modification
monomaniacal
monumentally
moonlighting
muchimproved
multicolored
multileveled
multitasking
musicplaying
mysteriosity
mysteriously
mythological
nanocomputer
nearadjacent
nearsynonyms
newlycreated
nonaddictive
nonintuitive
nonnewtonian
nonobservant
nonoperative
nonpermanent
nonsklarkish
nontechnical
notification
nowlegendary
obsolescence
occasionally

oldfashioned
oldtimerhood
optimization
organization
oscillations
outofcontrol
outperformed
outrageously
overfeatured
overpowering
overwhelming
oxyacetylene
parenthesize
participants
participated
participates
particularly
pathological
pccompatible
pejoratively
periodically
perpetration
perpetrators
perversities
philosophers
philosophies
phonetically
placeholders
pointtopoint
pomdependent
poppencorken
powercycling
precisionist
predictively
predominates
prenticehall
preprocessor
proboscatory
processspawn
proportional
prototypical
pseudogerman
pseudorandom
psychometric
publicaccess
publications
publicschool
punchcutting
purposefully
quadrathorpe
quantifiable
quasiacronym
questionable
radioactives
rationalized
reallocating
reciprocally
recognizable
recognizably

reconnecting
recreational
rectocranial
redesignated
reintroduced
relationship
relinquished
relinquishes
representing
reproduction
requirements
respectively
restrictions
resubmitting
ridiculously
rightcontrol
rockclimbing
romannumeral
rubbernecken
rulegoverned
russianstyle
salescritter
sardonically
scandinavian
schoolshaped
schrodingers
screenhiding
secondsystem
seeteeessess
selfeducated
selfeffacing
selfselected
semideponent
semihumorous
semiinfinite
semimythical
semisemistar
sextidecimal
sfconvention
shubinternet
significance
similarsized
singleengine
singleplayer
singlequotes
sixletterism
skillfocused
slipperiness
softweirilee
specifically
speculations
spellchecker
springenwerk
stillcurrent
stillunusual
stormtrooper
streetnumber
stuhbrooteen
stuhdleekaps

subconscious
subprocesses
subsequently
substituting
successfully
successively
sufficiently
supernatural
surprisingly
surroundings
swashbuckler
symbolobject
synonymously
tastefulness
technologies
technophobes
temporaryuse
theatrically
thermometers
thoughtfully
threepronged
tickticktick
timecritical
timeextended
touchscreens
touchtypists
trailblazers
transactions
transformers
transforming
transitively
translations
transporting
tremendously
trivialities
truthfulness
typechecking
typographers
unacceptable
unapostrophe
unassailably
unbelievable
undergrounds
underplumage
underpowered
undiscovered
undocumented
unexpectedly
unflattering
ungracefully
unimaginably
universities
unmanageable
unmodifiable
unpopularity
unproductive
unreasonable
unreasonably
unstructured

unsuspecting
updownupdown
userfriendly
usersupplied
vaxocentrism
veeblefester
veeblefetzer
vocabularies
welldesigned
wizardliness
wordoriented
workstations

11

abbreviated
abstraction
absurdities
accelerated
accompanied
accompanies
accordingly
accumulated
accumulates
accumulator
accusations
acronymized
addressable
addressbook
adolescence
affiliation
aficionados
aimlessness
alterations
alternation
alternative
analogizing
analogously
antecedents
anticipated
apostrophes
appointment
appreciated
apprehended
approaching
arbitrarily
armorplated
arrangement
articulated
asphyxiated
assimilates
association
associative
assumptions
astonishing
astronomers
attachments
authorities

automobiles
autorelated
autorouting
bangperbuck
barfulation
beleaguered
belllabsism
berkeleyism
berzerkeley
bigendfirst
blackpowder
bletcherous
blowenfusen
bottlenecks
bowdlerized
boxological
braindamage
brainwashed
buckminster
bulletproof
busywaiting
calculators
canonically
capitalized
catchphrase
celebration
challenging
charityware
checkpoints
chipandwire
chronicling
circulation
classically
clusterfuck
codewalkers
coevolution
cognoscenti
coincidence
coinventors
collections
comfortable
comfortably
commandline
commitments
communities
compactness
compatibles
compensates
competitors
complaining
complicated
compounding
compressing
compromised
compuserves
computeroid
conditioned
confessions
confusingly

conjectured
conjunction
connections
consciously
consequence
considering
constituted
constrained
constraints
constricted
constructed
contentfree
contestants
contextfree
contracting
contraction
contributed
contributes
controlflow
controllers
convenience
conventions
convergence
cooperating
cooperative
copyediting
copywronged
coroutining
corporation
correctable
corrections
correctness
correlation
corresponds
creamcheese
creationism
creaturitis
cretinosity
crippleware
dangerously
darkonlight
daydreaming
decompiling
defensively
definitions
degenerates
depeditated
derivatives
descendants
descriptors
destination
destructive
determining
devastating
development
differences
differently
difficultto
dimensioned

diminishing
directories
disappeared
disassemble
discussions
disquieting
dissipation
dissociated
distasteful
distinction
distinctive
distressing
distributed
documenting
doublesided
doublespace
drastically
dynamically
educational
effectively
efficiently
egotistical
ekswiezizee
electricity
electronics
embaressing
emefftecell
emergencies
emmailleure
emotionally
emphasizing
encompasses
encountered
endangering
endorsement
engineering
enhancement
enlightened
enthusiasts
environment
epochmaking
equivalents
essentially
established
etymologies
evaluations
evangelists
everpopular
exaggerated
exceedingly
excessively
exclusively
executables
executioner
exemplifies
expeditions
experienced
experiences
experiments

explication
expressions
expurgation
fabrication
facilitates
fallthrough
familystyle
fascinating
fascination
fashionable
feasibility
featurerich
ferritecore
fieldeffect
fieldtested
finelytuned
fissionable
flexibility
flexowriter
flourishing
forthcoming
fortranlike
fortunately
foundations
francophone
frantically
fritterware
frontshiftl
frustration
functioning
gameplaying
generalized
generalizes
generically
gestapolike
glareridden
goodnatured
governments
gradstudent
grammatical
greaterthan
greyandblue
habituating
hackandslay
hackerspeak
hackishness
hairiferous
handhacking
handholding
handshaking
handwriting
harvardyale
headhunters
heavyhanded
heisenbergs
helpfulness
hieperspays
hierarchies
higherlevel

highpowered
highquality
highranking
hightraffic
hitchhikers
hofstadters
hypothesize
identically
identifiers
identifying
illassorted
illuminates
illuminatus
illustrated
illustrates
imagination
imaginative
immediately
impartially
implemented
implication
importantly
improvement
incessantly
incoherence
incontinent
incorrectly
incremental
incremented
indications
indirection
individuals
ingredients
inhabitants
initialized
initializer
innovations
instability
instruction
instruments
intentional
interacting
interaction
interactive
interchange
intercourse
interesting
interfacing
interpreted
interpreter
interrupted
interviewed
introverted
intuitively
irritations
jargonjokes
judiciously
kellybootle
keybindings

keyboarding
kluhstergee
kompyootron
largeformat
laserwriter
leadingedge
learsiegler
leftcontrol
leisuretime
letterbased
letterforms
limitations
linguistics
loadaverage
lobotomized
ludicrously
machohflops
macintoshes
maintainers
maintaining
maldesigned
maliciously
maneuvering
manipulated
marvelously
massstorage
mathematics
meaningless
measurement
mechanistic
medievalism
mediumlevel
meritocracy
metamagical
microfloppy
microscopic
millimeters
millisecond
minimumsize
mirrorimage
misbehavior
misdesigned
misfeatures
misinformed
misspelling
multiplayer
multiplexed
multiregion
multivendor
mumblewango
mustachioed
myersbriggs
nanocentury
necessarily
necessities
neepneeping
negotiation
neopaganism
neuromancer

neverending
newscasters
newsposting
newsreaders
newsreading
noncomputer
nonemphatic
nonexistent
nonmaskable
nonnegative
nonphysical
nonportable
nonstandard
nontechical
nooperation
notoriously
notsohumble
nottinghams
nowdeceased
nowobsolete
nowstandard
obscenities
obsessively
obstruction
occupations
offlavender
opensystems
operational
opportunity
originality
originating
oscillation
overflowing
overlapping
overrunning
overstating
overwriting
overwritten
parallelism
paraphrased
parasitizes
parenthisey
patronizing
penetrating
penetration
perceptions
perceptrons
peripherals
permanently
perpetrated
perpetrates
perpetrator
perpetually
persistence
personality
personified
pesimiezing
pessimizing
placefiller

playfulness
pluggandisp
pointlessly
politicians
polyandrous
popularized
populations
portability
possibility
potentially
powerhungry
powersupply
practically
precautions
predictable
preexisting
prereleased
presupposes
prettyprint
prevaricate
prioritizer
priteeprint
probability
professions
programmers
prominently
promotional
promulgated
pronouncing
propagating
propagation
proportions
proselytize
protections
protohacker
pseudoprime
psychedelic
punchedcard
punctuation
punishments
purportedly
quantifiers
quantifying
questioners
questioning
railroading
rainbowhued
readability
readytoship
realization
recognition
recommended
reconfigure
recoverable
recursively
redirecting
redirection
redundantly
reflections

reflexively
regenerated
regionalism
registering
reimplement
reinstalled
reinventing
reliability
religiously
reluctantly
remembering
replacement
replicating
represented
reproducing
requirement
researchers
resemblance
respectable
respondents
restaurants
restricting
restriction
restrictive
revelations
revolutions
rightsideup
roleplaying
roomfilling
sacrificing
scatologism
scratchmark
screamingly
scrutinized
selfassumed
selfevident
selfinverse
selflocking
selftorture
semiserious
sensibility
sensitivity
seriousness
sexadecimal
showstopper
sichtseeren
sideeffects
sieberkruhd
sieberpuhnk
sieberspays
simulations
singlepoint
singlesided
singlespace
sohsentrizm
soundeffect
spacecombat
specialcase
specialized

specializes
specialties
speculative
spoonerisms
squashedbug
statistical
stereotypes
stimulating
stimulation
structuring
stubroutine
subcultures
submariners
submissions
subnetworks
subproblems
subroutines
substituted
suchandsuch
suitwearers
superiority
surrounding
symmetrical
synchronize
synesthetic
synthesizer
synthesizes
systemlevel
techinician
technically
teleporting
temporarily
terminating
termination
testbedding
thencurrent
theological
theoretical
thirdperson
threatening
threefinger
threeletter
threesickly
tieneekruhd
timekeeping
timesharing
topstwentee
traditional
trailblazer
trampolines
transaction
transformed
transformer
transitions
translating
translation
treekillers
trespassing
tricktheeye

truthvalues
twosyllable
typewriters
typographic
unambiguous
unanimously
unappealing
unavailable
unbreakable
uncertainty
unconscious
underground
underlining
underscores
understands
understated
underweight
undesirable
undoubtedly
unequivocal
unexplained
unfortunate
uninspiring
unintuitive
universally
universitys
unnecessary
unprotected
unpublished
unspeakable
unspeakably
unspecified
unsupported
unsurpassed
unswizzling
unusability
unvarnished
uselessness
uservisible
utilization
verbdoubled
voluntarily
washingtons
watercooled
wavelengths
wellbehaved
welldefined
wellsprings
wellthumbed
wellwritten
whitesmiths
wildcarding
willingness
wireservice
workarounds
worshippers
wraparounds
writtenonly
wroughtiron

zerocontent

10

absolutely
abstemious
abstracted
abundances
acceptable
acceptably
acceptance
accordance
accounting
accurately
accustomed
acquainted
activehigh
activities
addressing
adequately
adjectives
admittedly
advantages
adventures
aeligature
aesthetics
affections
afterwards
agreedupon
ahrteeefem
aicomplete
algorithms
allnighter
allocating
allocation
alternates
analogizes
analytical
andpersand
anglicized
anglosaxon
announcing
annoyingly
antinomies
antisocial
antithesis
apolitical
apparently
approaches
archeology
archetypal
archetypes
archhacker
architects
assemblers
assignment
assistance
associated

associates
astonishes
astounding
attempting
attoparsec
attractive
attributed
australian
awtobohgot
awtohmajik
aychseeeff
backplanes
backusnaur
barfucious
bartlemuds
beekyooess
beethovens
beginnings
benchmarks
berserking
betterread
biological
bitbashing
blahdeblah
bluntended
bogosities
bogotified
bookstores
boondoggle
bootstraps
bottomsten
boundaries
bracketing
braindeath
breathless
bresenhams
briefcases
brilliance
britishers
broadcasts
broadsword
brokenness
bruteforce
bugchasing
bullwinkle
burlesques
buttondown
buttonhook
bystanders
bytebybyte
bytesexual
calculator
calibrated
campuswide
candidates
capability
capitalist
cardreader
carelessly

categories
challenges
characters
choppedoff
christened
circleplus
circulated
clarifying
classified
clattering
clawfooted
claymation
cleverness
clobbering
cloverleaf
codesigned
codewalker
coherently
coinreturn
coinventor
cokebottle
collection
collective
collectors
combatable
comicstrip
commanders
commenting
commitment
comparable
competence
complained
complaints
completely
complexity
components
compressed
compuserve
computings
computrons
concealing
conditions
configured
conforming
confounded
confronted
connecting
connection
connectors
considered
consisting
consonants
constantly
constructs
consulting
containeth
containing
contigents
continuing

contrasted
conversely
converters
conviction
convincing
convoluted
cooperated
copylefted
copyrights
coresident
correcting
correlated
correlates
counterspy
creatively
creativity
creaturism
cretinisms
critically
criticisms
criticized
crockitude
crocknicle
crucifixes
ctrlaltdel
curmudgeon
cyberspace
datamation
deadpanned
decapitate
decompiler
decoration
defaulting
definitely
delicacies
delicately
delimiters
depeditate
depositing
deprecated
deprecates
derisively
derivation
derivative
descenders
descending
describing
designedin
determined
developers
developing
diabolical
difference
directions
disappears
discarding
disclaimer
discordian
discourage

discovered
discreetly
discussing
disgusting
dishonesty
disordered
dispatches
displaying
dissolving
distinctly
distracted
distribute
documented
dongledisk
downloaded
downsizers
droolproof
drummemory
dumbeddown
dumpkopfen
duplicated
duplicates
easywriter
economical
eemohticon
efficiency
elaborated
electrical
electrolux
eliminated
elsewehere
elucidated
emphasized
emphasizes
emulations
encounters
encouraged
encourages
engineered
enrollment
entrenched
eradicated
especially
essentials
evacuating
evaluation
evangelize
eventually
everybodys
exceptions
executable
exhibiting
exoticbeer
expansions
expecially
explaining
explicitly
exploiting
explosives

expressing
exstudents
extensions
extracting
extraction
eyeglazing
facetoface
facilities
fandangoes
fascinated
fastaccess
feathering
featureful
featuritis
fertilizer
fiendishly
filesystem
finetuning
firebottle
flatscreen
flattening
flattering
flowcharts
fluegelman
foamrubber
followupto
footprints
foredoomed
foreground
formalisms
formations
formatters
fortythird
fourletter
fractional
framemaker
freeloader
frequently
frobbotzim
frobnicate
frobnikayt
frobnitzem
frontpanel
fruitfully
frustrated
fullscreen
functional
functioned
generality
generalize
generating
generation
generative
generators
genericize
generously
gentlemans
girlfriend
gonkulator

goodfellow
gosperisms
government
gracefully
grovelling
grudgingly
guaranteed
guidelines
habitually
hackercorp
hackerdoms
hackerisms
hackerlike
hackerseye
hackertype
hackintosh
halfcooked
halflength
halfsmiley
halfuncial
hardwarily
headtotail
heckendorn
heisenbugs
hgentleman
hiezenbuhg
highschool
highvolume
historians
historical
hofstadter
homebrewed
hotandsour
humanlevel
humanscale
humorously
hyperspace
hyphenless
hysterical
icebreaker
identifier
identifies
ideologies
illadvised
illbehaved
illdefined
illuminati
imaginable
impatience
implements
implicitly
importance
improperly
improvised
inclusions
increasing
incredibly
indicating
indication

indictment
indirectly
inelegance
inevitably
infamously
inferences
inflection
influenced
informally
inherently
initialize
initiative
innovation
innovative
insertions
inspection
instructed
integrated
interested
interfaced
interfaces
interferes
internally
interrupts
intimately
intimating
intriguing
introduced
introduces
invariably
inventions
investment
invocation
ironically
ironmonger
irritating
irritation
iterations
itsrelated
jargonlike
keypunches
keystrokes
kiteflying
konstantin
largescale
latinbased
laundromat
lengthened
letterbomb
lightspeed
lightyears
linguistic
linkedlist
literalize
logicaland
lovecrafts
lowdensity
lowercased
lowquality

lubricants
lumberjack
macdinking
machinable
machoflops
macintrash
macrotapes
magnifying
mailformat
mainframes
maintained
maintainer
makintrash
makrohtayp
malformity
malodorous
management
maneuvered
manifested
manifestly
marginally
marketable
marketings
marketroid
marvelmans
mastercard
mcgrawhill
measurable
mechanical
mechanisms
meditation
mentioning
metalevels
microbased
microhertz
microlenat
micromotor
microphone
microtapes
microvaxen
microwaved
middlename
middlepart
milkshakes
mindlessly
minifloppy
minniboink
minorities
misaligned
misfeature
misleading
mismatches
misspelled
mistakenly
modechange
moderately
moderation
modifiable
modularity

modulation
mollyguard
monitoring
monomaniac
monospaced
moreorless
motivation
moustaches
multimedia
multiplier
mythically
nanohtekno
nauseating
navigation
nearfuture
needlessly
negatively
neglecting
neologisms
netiquette
networking
nevernever
newsgroups
newspapers
newsreader
nodebynode
noncompact
noncontact
nondisplay
nonhackers
nonhackish
nonnatural
nonobvious
nonoptimal
nonseriali
nontenured
nontrivial
nonuniform
nonworking
notesfiles
noticeably
notionally
nowdefunct
npannoying
npcomplete
obfuscated
objections
objectivec
obligation
observable
obtusosity
occasional
occurrence
octothorpe
oenophiles
officially
oftenheard
omnivorous
oneplusone

operations
optimizers
optimizing
ordinarily
originally
originated
originates
originator
ostensibly
outputting
outwaiting
overcoming
overflowed
overlapped
overlaying
overloaded
overpriced
overridden
overstrike
overweight
pagelayout
painlessly
paperbased
paralleled
parameters
parasitize
parkinsons
passworded
pastyfaced
patterning
perfection
perforated
performing
perroutine
personally
personkind
pertaining
perversely
perversity
phlogiston
physically
physicists
pianoforte
piledriver
pinpointed
pioneering
pizzasized
plaguelike
plainascii
plexiglass
politeness
popculture
popularity
population
positioned
positively
possessing
postfixing
potsticker

pournelles
poweroftwo
practicals
practicing
pranksters
precedence
predicated
prediction
prepending
prerelease
presentday
presenting
preserving
presidents
presumably
pretenders
prevalence
preventing
previously
primitives
principles
privileged
privileges
procedures
proceeding
processing
processors
production
productive
professors
profoundly
prominence
pronounced
pronounces
propagated
propagates
properties
protecting
protection
protective
prototyped
protracted
protruding
pseudodown
pseudosuit
psilocybin
publicized
pufferfish
punishment
putatively
qualifiers
quantifier
quantities
quasiquote
questioner
quotations
rabbitears
randomness
raytracing

reasonable
reasonably
recipients
recognized
recompiled
recovering
rectangles
recursions
referenced
references
reflecting
reflection
reflectors
refraining
regardless
registered
regularity
regulating
reinforced
reinvented
relational
relatively
relativity
reluctance
remarkable
remarkably
remembered
renderings
repeatable
repeatedly
replicated
replicator
reportedly
represents
requesting
researcher
resembling
resistance
respective
responding
restricted
retirement
rhealstone
rhetorical
rightbrain
rightfully
robustness
rocketsled
rotational
safeguards
salesdroid
salesthing
sandbender
saturation
sawtoothed
scheduling
schematics
schroeppel
scientists

scratchpad
scribbling
seeareleff
selections
selfparody
selftaught
semiclosed
semiliquid
semismiley
separation
serialized
serialline
serialport
settlement
shimmering
shitohgram
shortening
shortlived
shortrange
shotgunned
sideeffect
signifying
similarity
simplified
simulating
simulation
singlefont
singlestep
situations
skillfully
slopsucker
slowaccess
smallscale
snarfnbarf
sneakernet
socialized
softcopies
softwarily
solidstate
soundalike
sourceless
spaceborne
spacecadet
spaceships
specialist
specifying
speculated
spoonerism
squeamious
squirrelly
statements
statistics
stereotype
stimulated
strategies
streetjive
streetname
stresstest
stroustrup

structured
structures
studlycaps
stunningly
stylebooks
subclasses
subculture
subdomains
subjective
submission
suboptimal
subprogram
subroutine
subsequent
subtleties
subvariety
successors
succinctly
succumbing
suggesting
superseded
supervisor
supplanted
supporting
supposedly
suppresses
surprising
surrounded
suspicions
synecdoche
synthesize
tabulating
techniques
technonerd
terminally
terminated
terminates
terminator
textstream
thankfully
theatrical
thenraging
theorizing
thirdparty
thirtyfive
thoroughly
threestate
timeddelay
timetested
tolerances
toolanddie
toploading
trademarks
traditions
trampoline
transcends
translated
translates
travelling

traversing
tredecimal
treekiller
triviality
truehacker
trumpeting
twinengine
typewriter
ultimately
ultrasonic
unabridged
unaffected
unbelieved
uncommonly
uncreative
uncritical
undergoing
undergrads
underlined
underlying
underscore
understand
understood
undertaken
undertones
undigested
undirected
undisputed
unesthetic
unexpected
unfamiliar
unforeseen
unfreezing
unfriendly
ungrounded
uninformed
unintended
university
unixhaters
unixtounix
unkillable
unlamented
unnumbered
unofficial
unpleasant
unplugging
unprepared
unreadable
unreliable
unrelieved
unresolved
unsociable
unsolvable
unstressed
unverified
upsidedown
usenetters
utterances
validating

validation
variations
vectorized
veneration
victimized
viewpoints
wallbanger
wankometer
warranties
weaknesses
weirdcomix
wellchosen
westerners
whitespace
wholeearth
wildcarded
winningest
workaround
worshipped
wraparound
writenotch
yesterdays
zipperhead

9

absorbing
academics
accepting
accessing
according
accreting
acronymic
activelow
activists
adamantly
addictive
additions
addressed
addresses
adhackery
adherence
adherents
adhockery
adjusting
afflicted
aftersale
aggrieved
agreement
airplanes
aliveness
allegedly
allelbows
allocated
allocates
allocator
allusions
alphabets

amazingly
americans
amphigory
amplified
amusement
amusingly
analogies
ancestors
animation
annealing
annotated
announced
answering
antivirus
apartment
apologies
appearing
appending
appetizer
approvals
archivers
archiving
arguments
armpitnet
arrogance
ascending
asciionly
asianmade
assembled
assembler
assertion
assertive
asterisks
attacking
attaining
attempted
attending
attitudes
attracted
audiences
augmented
authority
automated
available
avoidable
awesomely
awfulness
aychpuhks
backarrow
backpacks
backprime
backquote
backslant
backslash
backspark
backwards
backwhack
bagbiting
baremetal

barfulous
bartlemud
bartlmuhd
basements
basically
basiclike
battlecry
beeessdee
behaviour
believing
belonging
berserker
bestknown
bicycling
bietseksu
bigendian
biologist
biosphere
birthyear
bisecting
bitfields
bitmapped
bitpaired
blatantly
blearyeye
bludgeons
bluegreen
bogometer
bohzohtik
bothering
boundless
braindead
branching
brandname
breathing
brightest
brotherly
brunvands
bsuffixed
bugforbug
bugginess
buildings
buzzwords
bypassing
byteorder
bythebook
calendars
callahans
canonical
capturing
cardpunch
carefully
cargocult
caseblind
castersup
certainly
chemicals
chernenko
chernobyl

childrens
chockfull
cintercal
civilized
clanguage
clarified
classical
cleverness
clobbered
clutching
coauthors
cocktails
codebooks
cofounder
coherence
coincided
coincides
collation
collected
combative
combining
comesfrom
commanded
commented
community
companies
comparing
competing
compilers
completed
composing
compounds
computers
computing
computron
concerned
concluded
condemned
conducted
confronts
confusing
connected
considers
consisted
constants
consuming
contained
container
continues
contracts
contrasts
contrived
converges
converted
convicted
convinced
copybroke
corrected
correctly

corrupted
countries
crawlways
creatures
crippling
criticism
criticize
crossfire
crosspost
crunching
curlicues
currently
customers
customize
cybercrud
cyberpunk
damoclean
databases
dataglove
deadlines
deathblow
debuggers
decidedly
decisions
declaring
decorated
decorator
decsystem
dedicated
deedeetee
defective
defenders
delighted
delikweir
delimiter
delivered
delusions
demanding
densities
depending
depicting
deposited
depressed
derezzing
descended
described
describes
deserving
designers
designing
desirable
destroyed
detailing
detection
developed
developer
devouring
dhrystone
diagonals

differing
dijkstras
dinosaurs
directing
direction
directive
disappear
disasters
disbanded
disbelief
discarded
discordia
discourse
discussed
discusses
disguised
dishonest
diskdrive
diskettes
dioponocd
dispersed
displaced
displayed
distances
distorted
disturbed
diverging
documents
domainist
dominance
dominated
dominates
donothing
doubtless
dreariest
droppings
dubiosity
dumplings
dutifully
dutybound
dwindling
ecologies
economics
education
effective
eksekseks
elemental
elephants
elevation
elevators
eloquence
emergence
emergency
emoticons
emphasize
employees
employers
emulating
emulation

emulators
enclosing
enclosure
encounter
encourage
encrusted
endlessly
endoffile
endpoints
enforcing
engineers
enhancers
enjoyable
enjoyment
envelopes
equations
equipment
escalator
escapades
esspeeull
esthetics
etherhose
ethnicity
europeans
everyones
evidenced
evidently
examining
excepting
exchanged
exchanges
exclaimed
excrement
executing
exhausted
exhibited
existence
expanding
expecting
expending
explained
exploding
exploring
expressed
expresses
extending
extremely
eyestrain
fascistic
fashioned
feanorian
featuring
featurism
feechrizm
ferrosity
fictional
fictively
fightonet
filenames

filtering
fingerers
finishing
firechild
fireworks
firstname
fivepound
fixedsize
flakiness
flatascii
flatlined
flavoured
floppynet
flutzpahs
folklores
following
followups
forestall
forgeries
formalism
formation
formative
formatter
foundered
foundries
fourcolor
fractions
fragments
frequency
frobnitzm
frontends
fruitless
fulfilled
fullsized
functions
funkiness
gathering
gayissues
generally
generated
generates
generator
gensymmed
genuinely
gibsonian
gigabytes
glitschen
goddesses
gosperism
gradually
graduates
granholme
graphical
greatwall
greetings
grovelled
guiltware
gullivers
hackerdom

hackerism
hackishly
hackitude
hackorama
halitosis
handsdown
handtuned
happening
happyface
hardcoded
hardshell
hardwired
headaches
headwords
heavyduty
heavyporn
heinleins
heisenbug
highlevel
highnoise
highspeed
highusage
histories
hobbyists
hockeypux
honorable
hopefully
hostility
hotrodder
humongous
humorless
humungous
hunchback
hurriedly
hypercard
hypercube
ignorance
illicitly
imitation
imitators
immensely
impressed
improving
incidence
including
incontext
increased
increases
indenting
indicated
indicates
induction
industrys
infecting
infection
inferiors
infobooks
informash
infringes

ingrained
inherited
Initially
initiated
innocence
inscribed
inserting
insertion
insisting
inspected
installed
instances
instantly
insulting
intending
intensely
intensity
interests
interface
interlisp
internals
intervals
interword
inventing
inventors
inversely
inverters
involving
isolation
isopropyl
iterating
iterative
judgement
justified
keyboards
keystroke
kilobytes
kilograms
kopeeleft
kruhdweir
kuhmpielr
lalaberry
languages
largesite
latenight
latinized
latterday
lectroids
leftarrow
leftbrain
leftright
legalisms
lempelziv
lexiphage
liability
liberally
libraries
lifetimes
linearity

linguists
listening
literally
localarea
localized
locations
logically
logicalor
longjohns
loserhood
lowercase
lowsignal
macerated
macrology
macrotape
magazines
maggotbox
magically
magicians
magnifier
mainframe
maintains
manifests
marketing
massively
materials
maximally
mccarthys
mechanics
megabytes
megaflops
megapenny
melvilles
memorizes
mentality
mentioned
messaging
messdross
metaphors
metathing
microcode
microreid
microsoft
microtape
microwave
miniboink
ministers
misfeechr
misparsed
misplaced
misquoted
misspells
mistyping
mixedcase
mnemonics
moderated
modifying
molecules
mongolian

morsecode
mortality
motivated
motorolas
movements
mpyooting
muhltishn
muhnchkin
multibyte
multician
multitask
multiuser
munchkins
musicians
mutilates
mysteries
namespace
nanoacres
nanoagent
nastygram
naturally
neartotal
neophiles
neophilia
neotenous
networked
newsadmin
newsfroup
newsgroup
nominated
nonebcdic
nonhacker
nonlinear
nonplayer
nonprofit
nonrandom
notequals
nourished
numbering
numerical
objection
objective
obligated
obscenely
obscurity
observers
observing
obstacles
obviosity
obviously
occasions
occupying
offending
officials
ohfileeuh
oldtimers
olivedrab
oneliners
onevolume

operating
operation
operators
opponents
optimized
orangered
organized
orientals
orphaning
outandout
outbreaks
outdoorsy
outlasted
outofband
outsiders
overblown
overflows
overheard
overloads
oversight
oversized
overtaken
overtones
overwrite
pachyderm
painfully
paradoxes
parallels
parodying
partially
particles
partisans
pascalish
passwords
pastiches
patiently
paychecks
penalties
pepperoil
perceived
perfectly
performed
persuaded
perturbed
perverted
pessimize
phonecard
photocopy
phreaking
piggishly
pinkshirt
pioneered
pipelined
pipelines
pipesinta
placement
plurality
pluralize
pointless

politesse
political
positions
possessed
posthippy
posturing
practiced
practices
preceding
precisely
predating
predicted
pregnancy
presented
presently
preserved
pretended
prevented
primarily
printable
printouts
prnounced
proceeded
processed
processes
producing
profiling
promising
promoteth
promoting
prospects
protected
protocols
pseudonym
publicity
published
publishes
punchline
purchased
purported
purposely
purveying
purveyors
qualifier
qualifies
quarterly
questions
quuxandum
radiation
rampantly
ratracing
reachable
readwrite
realworld
reasoning
rebooting
recognize
recollate
recommend

recording
recursive
redesigns
reference
reflected
registers
regularly
rejection
relegated
relevance
religions
remaining
remarking
remembers
removable
repeating
replacing
reporting
represent
reprinted
reproduce
requested
requester
requiring
reseating
resembles
reserving
residence
resistors
resources
respected
responded
responses
restoring
resturant
resulting
retaining
retconned
retreated
retrocult
returning
revealing
reverence
revisions
revolving
rewritten
rightmeta
riscbased
runlength
sanitized
satirical
satisfied
satisfies
scattered
scavenged
scavenger
scenarios
scheduled
scheduler

schedules
schnappen
scholarly
scrambled
scrambler
scratches
screaming
scribbled
scribbles
scrozzled
searching
seemingly
seepeeyoo
segmented
selecting
selection
semantics
semicolon
sendenary
sensation
sentences
separated
sequences
seriously
seventies
sevenyear
shareware
sharpener
shelfware
shitogram
shockwave
shoelaces
shortened
shortterm
shoulders
shrinking
signalled
signetics
signified
signifies
silliness
sillywalk
similarly
simulated
simulator
singlebit
sitenames
situation
skeptical
slashouts
smalltalk
smartdata
smuggling
snailmail
snowballs
softwares
somebodys
sometimes
sorcerers

spacedout
spaceship
specified
specifier
specifies
specimens
spellings
spellname
spiciness
spirogyra
splatters
splitting
spotspark
spreading
sprinkled
stability
stairstep
standards
stanfords
starscape
statecode
statement
statistic
stickslip
stirfried
strangoly
streaking
stripping
struggled
stupidity
subatomic
subdomain
subgenius
subgroups
subjargon
subjected
subscribe
substance
subverted
successes
succumbed
suffering
suggested
suggester
sullivans
sunstools
superiors
supermans
supermini
superuser
supported
supremely
surplused
surprised
surprises
surviving
suspected
suspended
sustained

swallowed
swissarmy
switching
swizzling
syllables
symbolics
sysadmins
takeovers
tanstaafl
targeting
taxpayers
technical
techspeak
tediously
teeteewic
teitelman
teletypes
tendollar
tenfinger
tennisnet
tenthyear
tenyeared
terminals
teteatete
texhacker
texmaster
texnician
textbooks
textronix
textually
theorists
thompsons
thousands
thrashing
threefoot
thunklike
tictactoe
tiedemann
timedelay
timeslice
timestamp
tmpostfix
tolerably
tolerance
tolerates
topsecret
torpedoes
touchmenu
touchtype
touristic
tradeoffs
transfers
trapdoors
travelers
travelled
traverses
triangles
triggered
truncated

tutorials
twiddling
twinkling
twoforone
twotothen
typefaces
typically
ultrafast
unadorned
unbounded
unbracket
undefined
underflow
undergone
underline
underpass
undertake
underwear
undesired
undivided
unhelpful
uniformly
unixbased
unmatched
unmerited
unobvious
unrelated
unshifted
untouched
untutored
unusually
unwilling
uppercase
usenetter
usernames
utilities
vachement
vacuumvax
vannevars
vaporware
variables
variation
varieties
variously
vaxectomy
verbosely
viceversa
videogame
violating
violation
violently
virtually
vyssotsky
waitresss
wakesleep
wandering
wankiness
wannabees
wargaming

wedgitude
wellknown
westcoast
whetstone
whistling
wildcards
willfully
windmills
windowing
winnitude
wireheads
wordbased
worshiped
worthless
wrestling
writeonce
writeonly
wuthering
yarmulkes
yoobeedee
yooessjee
yooshyang
zerobased
zigamorph

8

aborting
abridged
absurdly
accented
accepted
accessed
accounts
achieved
achieves
acquired
acronyms
actively
activity
actually
adagency
adhocity
adjusted
admirers
advanced
advances
affected
afflicts
ahrteeem
ahrteeie
aihacker
aliasing
allascii
allnight
allowing
alluding
altering

aluminum
amateurs
anagrams
analyzer
androids
annoying
anointed
anothers
answered
antinazi
antonyms
appeared
appended
applying
apprised
approved
archiver
archives
arranged
arriving
articles
ascribed
assembly
assigned
assorted
assuming
atlantas
attached
attacked
attained
attempts
attended
attested
atypical
aviation
avoiding
aychelel
baaaaaaz
babbages
backslat
bagbiter
balanced
balloons
bandykin
bangpath
barriers
basement
bathtubs
bearings
becoming
bedquilt
beefdead
beertema
behaving
believed
believes
bellcore
belonged
benefits

berkliks
betatest
billions
binaries
bitching
bitfield
bithorpe
bitlevel
bleached
bleating
bleepers
blinking
blithely
blocking
bogosity
bogosort
bogotify
boinkcon
bonehead
booklets
boottape
boottime
bothered
bottomup
bouncing
boxology
bozolike
brackets
breaking
breakout
breathed
breathes
bridging
bringing
brothers
browsing
brunners
buckling
buffered
building
burritos
busywait
buttocks
bypasses
cabinets
caffeine
callback
capitals
capitull
capslock
captures
careless
careware
carrolls
carrying
cartoons
cascaded
casually
catching

catfight
centered
chadless
chaining
chainsaw
changing
channels
cheatham
checking
chernohb
chiclets
chomping
choosing
chuckles
circling
circuits
cixelsyd
claiming
classics
cleaning
cleanser
clearing
clothing
clownish
clueless
clunkier
coinages
colleges
coloured
coltrane
combined
combines
commands
comments
commoner
commonly
communes
commuter
companys
compared
competes
compiled
compiler
compiles
composed
computed
computer
computes
concerns
confetti
confined
confirms
conforms
confused
confuses
connects
connotes
consists
consoles

consumed
consumer
consumes
contacts
contains
contents
contexts
controlb
controlc
controlo
controls
controlz
conveyed
copyleft
cornered
corrupts
counters
counting
countrys
couriers
covertly
crackers
cracking
cramming
cranking
crashing
crawling
creation
creative
credited
creeping
critical
crockish
crowther
crudware
crufties
crunched
crunches
crunchly
cuisines
cultures
currency
currents
customer
cuteness
dangling
darkness
datagram
daytoday
deadbeef
debacles
deceased
declared
declasse
decoding
decrepit
defanged
defining
degraded

delights
delimits
demigods
denizens
denoting
depended
deprived
deranged
derisory
deriving
deserves
designed
designer
detached
detailed
detected
dewdneys
diagrams
dialects
dickless
diddling
diehands
ulehards
dieresis
digraphs
directed
directly
disabled
disagree
disaster
discards
disclave
discount
discover
diskette
diskless
diskordi
disliked
dismount
dispatch
displays
disputes
disquiet
disrupts
dissolve
distance
distract
dividing
divisors
doggerel
dolphins
domainos
domestos
doorstop
doubling
doubters
dousings
download
draining

drawings
drawnout
drescher
dropouts
dropping
duhblyoo
dumpling
dungeons
dyslexic
earmarks
ebcdicvs
echomail
eclipsed
editions
educated
eerotiks
efaykyoo
effeepee
efteepee
eightbit
eighties
elegance
elements
elevator
emailing
emanates
embossed
emerging
emoticon
cmulated
emulator
enclosed
encoding
endeavor
endtoend
enforced
enjoying
ensuring
entering
entirely
entities
entitled
entrails
entrance
environs
equality
escaping
esseedee
essohess
esteemed
esthetic
ethernet
evidence
evolving
examples
excludes
execling
executed
executes

exhibits
existing
expanded
expander
expected
expended
explains
exploded
exploits
explored
extended
extremes
fabritek
facility
factoids
failures
families
famously
fanciers
fandango
fanzines
favorite
featured
features
feechrie
feelings
ferreted
feynmans
fidonews
fighting
figuring
filename
filtered
finality
fingered
fingerer
finished
firesign
fishkill
fixtures
flagship
flamewar
flashing
flatfile
flatline
flattens
flipping
floating
flooring
floppies
flurries
flushing
focusing
followed
follower
followup
fondness
forcibly
forearms

forehead
foreseen
foreword
formally
formerly
formulas
fortrans
fortrash
founding
fourleaf
fourpack
fourpass
fractals
freeware
freezing
friendly
frieohdz
frobbing
frobbozz
frobnits
frobnitz
frobnool
frobnule
frontend
fronting
fruhbotz
fuckware
fulfills
fullbore
funniest
fuzzball
gallaher
garments
gateways
gaylords
generals
genitals
geometry
gestured
gestures
gewerken
ghostjob
gillions
glassfet
glitched
glitches
glitshen
globally
globbing
glossies
gnashing
gnoomaks
golfball
goodness
grabbing
granting
graphics
greatest
greeting

grepping	infested	listings	minimize	nonascii
grimoire	inflated	litmaath	minority	nonlocal
grinding	informed	livelock	minutely	nonsense
grinning	ingerman	liveware	mirabile	nonunixy
grouping	initials	loadings	mismatch	nonvaxen
grumbled	insanely	loathing	misquote	nonwanks
gubblick	insanity	location	misspelt	normally
habitues	inserted	lockpick	mistakes	notation
hackerly	insisted	logfiles	miswarts	notional
hackerom	inspired	loggedin	mixtures	nthlevel
hackings	integers	logoized	modelled	numbered
hakspeek	intended	longgone	modemoid	numerals
haldeman	interact	longterm	modestly	nyetwork
halfanos	intercal	loopback	modified	objected
halfbyte	internet	loosened	modifier	observed
halfmesh	intruder	lossages	mongrels	observer
halfword	invented	louellas	monikers	observes
hamradio	inverted	lowlevel	monitors	obtained
handling	invoices	lsbfirst	monocase	occluded
handwave	involved	luckless	monsters	occupied
happened	involves	lunchbox	mornings	occupies
hardboot	iterated	lurching	mourning	octonary
hardcore	johnsons	machines	movement	oddities
hardened	jokingly	macintoy	msbfirst	offbyone
hardiest	journals	macnelly	mudheads	offended
hardwary	joyously	magicked	muhltiks	offering
harmless	judgment	majority	mumblage	officers
harvards	juggling	makintoy	mumbleco	offtaste
hassling	junkfood	managers	mumbling	oldstyle
headsets	kildalls	mangiare	munchies	oldtimer
heinlein	kilobaud	manmonth	munching	ondemand
highhalf	kilobyte	manually	munchkin	oneinten
highways	kilogram	marching	mutating	oneliner
hoarding	knitting	marketed	mutation	onesided
hobbyist	kohkbotl	massaged	muttered	onscreen
hoequist	kreeping	massages	mutually	onthefly
holidays	kremvaks	matching	mystical	openplan
homebrew	kruhftee	maturity	mythical	operated
hopcroft	labeling	meanings	nameless	operator
humidity	labelled	measured	namepart	opposing
hundreds	lamented	measures	nanoacre	optimize
hyperwin	lampoons	meatware	nanocode	optional
ieteeess	langston	mediates	nanohbot	ordering
ignoring	lastname	memetics	nastiest	organism
imaspzap	latterly	memories	national	oriented
imitated	laughing	memorize	neatness	outcomes
imitates	launched	mentally	needless	outdated
impaired	lawsuits	mentions	neepneep	outgoing
impinged	learning	menuitis	negation	outhouse
implying	lectures	messages	negative	outright
improved	leftmeta	messloss	neithout	outshore
improves	legalese	messydos	neopagan	outsider
included	lessthan	metaname	neteeket	overcoat
includes	limiting	metarule	networks	overflow
incoming	linearly	microvax	newgroup	overhead
indented	linkable	migrated	newlines	overkill
indexing	linkdead	mililamp	newswire	overlaps
inducing	listened	milliard	niceties	overload
infected	listener	mindless	nonaryan	override

oxbridge
packaged
packages
panfried
papernet
parodied
parodies
partners
passages
passions
patching
patented
patently
pathname
patients
patterns
peeohdee
poroonto
performs
personae
pestered
phrasing
physical
pictures
pivoting
planners
planning
pleasing
plingnet
plotters
plotting
pluggery
plumbing
plunging
pointerd
pointers
pointing
policies
polished
politely
politics
polygons
porsches
portable
portably
portions
possibly
postings
poweroff
preceded
predated
predates
prefaces
prefixed
prefixes
premises
prepaged
prepared
presents

pretzels
prevents
printers
printing
priority
probable
probably
problems
produced
produces
products
programs
projects
promised
promises
promoted
promptly
properly
proposed
provably
provided
provides
prowling
pseudoop
publicly
punching
purposes
pushdown
quarters
querying
rambling
randomly
rasputin
rational
reaction
readable
readonly
realized
realizes
realtime
rebooted
received
receiver
recently
recorded
recycled
redlined
reducing
reflects
regarded
register
regulars
reinvent
rejected
rejoiced
rektomee
relating
relative
relaying

released
releases
relegate
reliable
reliably
reliance
reloaded
remained
remarked
reminder
remotely
removing
renaming
rendered
replaced
replaces
replying
reported
reporter
reposted
requests
required
requires
research
reserved
resolved
resolver
resource
respects
responds
restless
restored
resulted
retained
retrying
returned
retyping
revealed
reversed
reviewed
revising
reviving
revolves
rewarded
riscchip
ritchies
rotating
rotation
routines
rudeness
rzerklee
saltines
sampling
satirist
saylskri
scanning
scarcity
scraping
scrawled

screwage
screwily
scrogged
scrozzle
searches
sections
security
seepeeem
segfault
segments
selected
sendmail
sequence
serviced
services
sessions
severely
severity
sflovers
shambles
sharkfin
shifting
shipment
shipping
shooting
shopping
shortest
shouting
sideways
silently
simplest
simpsons
sitename
skuhzzee
sleeping
slightly
slowness
smallest
snarfing
snatches
snausing
snooping
socalled
societys
softboot
softcopy
softwary
solvable
someones
sophonts
spacewar
spanning
spawning
speakers
speaking
specmark
spectace
speeches
speeding

spelling
spending
spinning
spitting
sponsors
spoofing
spoolers
spooling
spotting
spurning
squiggle
squiggly
stackers
stalling
stallman
stamping
starship
starting
startups
statuses
stealing
steaming
steepest
stellner
stickers
sticking
stopping
storable
storages
stranger
straying
stressed
strictly
striking
strongly
students
studying
stuffing
stumbled
stumbles
stunning
stupidly
subgenre
subjects
subshell
suddenly
suffered
suffixes
suggests
suitable
suitably
sunspots
suntools
supernal
superset
superzap
supplied
supports
supposed

survives	triggers	variance	ability	babbage
sussmans	tripping	variants	aborted	backing
swapping	troopers	verbally	accused	backups
swimmers	tropisms	versions	achtung	backuss
swimming	trubshaw	videotex	actions	bagbiet
swinging	trunnion	viewable	adapted	bananas
switched	trusting	villains	adapter	bandits
switches	tuesdays	violated	adaptor	banging
symptoms	tunafish	visicalc	adduced	banners
synonyms	turistic	visitors	adgered	barries
sysadmin	turistik	visually	adopted	bashing
sysmangr	tweaking	voicenet	adspeak	batches
szechuan	twiddled	vomiting	affairs	bbnlisp
talented	twodigit	walloper	aiighhh	bboards
tapedeck	twolevel	wannabee	aimless	beanies
targeted	twostate	wargames	aliased	bearing
teaching	typename	wascawwy	aliases	beating
techtalk	typified	watching	alleged	beavers
tempfile	ugliness	weakness	allowed	becomes
teraflop	uletters	websters	alltech	beebord
terminak	unbolted	weekends	alsoran	beeenef
terribly	uncalled	weeklong	altered	behaved
texnique	uncommon	weirdest	altmode	behaves
textonly	underbar	whatmark	amazing	beloved
theaters	underlie	whistles	amounts	beranek
thenhead	undertow	whitehot	amulets	berklix
theorems	unfairly	whiteout	amusing	besides
theories	unfreeze	widening	analyze	bierces
thermite	unipress	wildcard	android	biggest
therteen	uniquely	wildchar	animals	bigname
thingkoh	unixlike	winitood	annoyed	bignuhm
thinking	unlikely	wirehead	answers	bignums
thisyear	unneeded	wizardly	antfarm	bigoted
threeday	unpacked	wizardry	antonov	bigsite
throwing	unparsed	wizeewig	appalls	binders
ticklist	unsolved	wordfill	appears	binding
timezone	unsquare	wordlike	applies	bitblit
tinycrud	unstable	wordplay	apriori	bitwide
tinymuds	untapped	workable	arcades	blandly
toasters	untested	worldcon	arising	blankly
toeprint	untimely	wormhole	armando	blaring
tofflers	untoward	worrying	arpanet	blaster
toggling	unusable	worships	arrived	blender
tolkiens	unuseful	wrasslin	arrives	blinded
toplevel	unveiled	wreathed	artists	blitter
totality	unwanted	wretched	aspects	bloated
touching	updating	wringing	asserts	blocked
tourists	upstairs	writable	asshole	blowing
townname	upthread	xeroxifs	assumed	blurred
toyboxes	upthrust	yooietis	assured	bobbles
tracking	uptospec	yushiang	asuckin	boinkon
traction	username	zeerohth	atsized	bombing
trainees	uttering		attacks	bonking
training	uucponly		authors	booting
trapdoor	validity	7	aviator	borrows
traveled	valspeak		avoided	botches
trawling	valuable	abbrevs	awarded	bottles
treating	vannevar	abermud	aychpee	bounces
trendoid	variably	abiding	ayohess	bozoish

bozotic	clearly	dechead	drawers	evolved
bramage	clients	decided	drawing	evolves
breaker	closely	deckers	drecnet	exactly
brechen	closest	decoder	dreknet	exalted
breedle	closing	decreed	drexler	excised
briefly	clothes	dectape	drifted	excited
broadly	cockney	deduced	drivers	exerted
brohket	columns	defacto	dropins	exhorts
brookss	comical	defense	dropped	exiting
buffers	comicss	defined	drugged	exitser
bugbear	conveys	defines	ducking	expands
buglike	conways	degrees	dueling	expects
bullitt	cookies	deleted	duhmass	experts
bumming	cooling	demoing	dumbass	expired
bundled	copying	demoted	dummics	expires
burning	corners	denotes	earlier	exposes
buttons	corresp	density	echoing	extends
byeloho	counter	depends	edisons	exusers
cabeese	coupled	depicts	editing	fabbing
cabling	couples	derived	editors	factors
caboose	courses	derives	eeeevil	fahlman
calling	covered	designs	effects	failing
caltech	cowlike	desired	efforts	faintly
cameras	cracked	desires	eisabus	falling
capable	cracker	desktop	elapses	fandoms
carried	crafted	details	elderly	fannish
carrier	cramped	devices	emailed	fanzine
carries	crashed	devised	emerged	farming
casting	crashes	devnuhl	emesdos	fastest
catalog	crayola	devoted	employs	fatally
causing	crayons	diddled	enabled	favored
ceiling	created	differs	enables	feeding
cellars	creator	digraph	enclose	feeling
chances	credits	dimpled	encoded	feeping
changed	cringed	directs	encoder	fellows
changer	crossed	disable	encodes	feynman
changes	crowded	discard	endings	fidonet
charges	crufted	discord	endless	fighter
charter	cruftie	disease	enforce	figured
chasing	cruncha	disgust	engaged	figures
chatter	cryppie	dislike	engages	filling
cheaper	cubicle	dismiss	engines	finally
checked	cuckoos	display	enjoyed	finding
chewing	culling	ditched	ensuing	fingers
chiclet	cutouts	diverts	ensures	finggrs
choices	cutters	divided	entered	firisss
chomper	cutting	divides	entrees	fishnet
chopped	cynical	doctors	entries	fitting
circles	dadazen	dogwash	equally	fixable
circlex	daemons	dollars	equated	flamage
claimed	damaged	domains	equates	flamers
clapped	dancing	dongles	erotics	flaming
clarkes	dangers	doubled	escapes	flashed
classes	dawkins	doubles	eschers	flavors
cleaned	deadpan	doubted	eschews	fleshed
cleaner	dealing	dowhile	etching	flipped
cleanly	debated	downers	ethical	floated
cleared	deboned	dragged	evening	flowers
clearer	decades	dragons	evoking	flushed

flyback	greener	ibmness	largish	matched
flytrap	grinder	icecube	lasting	matcher
follows	gripper	iconify	latency	matches
fooling	grokked	ignored	lawyers	mathout
forcing	gronked	ignores	layered	mattels
forgets	grossly	ikzizee	layouts	matters
formats	grounds	illness	leaders	maurits
forming	grouped	impedes	leading	mauvais
forsale	grovels	implied	learned	mcilroy
fossils	growing	implies	leaving	meaning
founded	growled	inchers	lebling	meddler
founder	grunted	indents	leftism	medical
framing	guarded	indexed	legends	meeting
frednet	gubbish	induced	lengths	members
freerun	guhbish	induces	lensman	mergers
freshly	guhmbee	infects	letters	merging
friends	hackers	infocom	letting	messdog
frobbed	hacking	informs	license	messdos
frobozz	hackish	inhouse	lightly	methods
frobule	hairier	injokes	limited	mindset
frotzed	hakspek	insects	lingers	minutes
frowned	halting	inserts	linpack	misbuhg
frowney	handcut	insides	linting	missing
fruhboz	handing	intends	lispers	mistake
fucking	handled	invites	listing	misused
fudging	handler	invoked	loading	miswart
fuhglee	handles	invokes	located	miswort
funding	hanging	islands	locates	mitisms
funkier	hanlons	jackets	logbook	mmuless
funnier	hapless	jaggies	logical	mobiles
furrows	happens	jiffies	longago	mockups
gaining	happily	judging	longest	mohtahs
galileo	harried	jumping	longjmp	mohtohs
garbled	harriss	junkies	looking	molotov
garplee	hassles	keeping	loosely	moments
gathers	hatched	kernels	lossage	mondays
gawking	haywire	keyable	lowcost	morning
gaybree	headers	keyboid	lowrent	morriss
geekdom	heading	keycaps	lurkers	mortals
germans	hearers	kicking	lurking	moscone
getting	hearing	kidding	maarten	moskvax
gibsons	heavier	kildall	macdink	motions
giggles	heavily	killing	maclisp	motives
gillett	heights	killjob	magical	mounted
gillion	helping	kindest	magtape	mpyootr
glasfet	highbit	knights	mahnjed	mudders
glazeth	hipness	knowing	mailers	mudding
glorked	hitting	krasner	mailing	mudhead
glowing	hobbies	kremvax	makdink	multics
gnumacs	holders	kruhnch	managed	mumbled
gobbles	holding	kuhspee	manager	muppets
gonking	hookers	kuttner	mangled	murders
gosmacs	hopping	kwertee	mangler	murphys
gozinta	horrors	labeled	manuals	mushdos
gozmaks	housing	lacking	mapping	musical
granted	humanid	lampson	markers	mutated
grasped	hurried	landing	markets	nailing
grazing	hurting	largely	marking	nanobot
greatly	huskies	largest	massbus	nastier

natures
nauseam
naziism
needing
nerdoid
nesting
nethack
netiket
netnews
netrock
netters
netwide
nfslike
nightly
niklaus
nodding
nondata
nonlisp
nonunix
nonzero
notable
notably
noticed
notices
notions
notwork
novices
nthyear
nuances
numbers
objects
obliged
octaval
offense
offered
offices
offline
oldtime
onehalf
oneline
oneshot
oobleck
ooblick
opcodes
opening
opiates
opposed
optical
options
ordered
origins
outcome
outgrow
outputs
outrage
outside
overall
overlap
overlay

overrun
overtly
overuse
packets
packing
padding
padgett
parking
parsing
parties
partway
pascals
passing
pasting
patched
patches
patents
payment
payware
ncclass
peanuts
peeohem
pending
peoples
peppers
perfory
periods
perlisc
permits
persent
persons
peruser
petscii
petskee
phrases
phreaks
physics
pickier
picking
piglets
pinning
pirates
pkwares
placing
planned
players
playing
playpen
pleased
ploktuh
plugged
plurals
pockets
podtype
pointed
pointer
politer
polling
popping

portion
poseurs
posters
posting
pounded
powered
poweron
powerup
praying
predate
prefers
prepend
pressed
pretzel
pricing
princes
printed
printer
proglet
program
protons
proudly
proving
prowler
psytons
pulling
pumping
punched
punches
punning
pushing
pushjay
putting
puzzles
pythons
quarter
quickly
quietly
quoting
quuxare
quuxuum
rabidly
raisins
randoms
rapidly
ratings
ravioli
reached
reaches
readers
readily
reading
reality
realize
reasons
rebuild
rebuilt
recalls
recipes

reclaim
recover
recycle
reduced
reduces
reeling
refined
refused
refuses
refuted
regeksp
regexps
regreet
rehosed
rejects
related
relates
relaxed
relaxen
release
remains
remarks
removed
remover
removes
renamed
renders
repeats
replace
replied
replies
reports
reputed
resides
resists
restart
restore
results
retains
retired
retrohk
returns
reusing
reveals
revered
revised
revived
rewards
rewrite
rhyming
riddles
rituals
rmgroup
roached
rollers
rolling
rooting
rotated
roughly

routing
rubbage
rumored
running
runtime
russian
sadness
sailing
salamin
samples
samsara
sandbox
sayings
scanner
schemes
scraped
screens
screwed
scruffy
seconds
seduces
seeking
selects
sellars
selling
selvage
senders
sending
sensors
sequels
servers
servoid
servoyd
setting
settled
shadows
sharing
sharply
shatner
sheenyu
shelves
shifted
shocked
shorter
shortly
showbiz
showers
showing
shugart
shyster
sighted
signals
sigplan
silence
sillier
simpler
sisfrog
sitting
sixpack

158

sixties
sjoberg
skating
skilled
skipped
skulker
slammed
slashes
slaying
sleeves
sliding
slinger
slogans
slowest
slowing
smashed
smeared
smoking
sneaked
snivitz
soaking
soandso
sockets
solving
sorting
sounded
sources
spacing
sparest
sparked
spawned
speaker
spectre
speling
spelled
spewing
spicier
spilled
spooler
springs
sprouts
sqiggle
squared
squares
stacked
stacker
stances
started
station
staying
steamed
stemmed
sternly
stomped
stopped
stories
storing
stoutly
streaks

strikes
strings
strudel
studied
studies
stuffed
subside
subtler
subtype
sucking
surfers
surfing
surveys
sussman
swabbie
swamped
swapped
swapper
swaying
sweeter
symbols
sysfrog
sysiwyg
sysprog
systeme
systems
sysvile
tactics
takeout
talking
tangled
tarasco
teacher
teaches
techies
teching
techref
telebit
telecom
telerat
teleray
telling
tempted
tending
tenexen
tenexes
tengwar
tenices
tenured
terpree
tersely
testers
testing
texinfo
texpert
theatre
thinker
thinner
thlevel

threads
thrills
thyrsus
tickets
tiedyed
tighter
tightly
tilting
tinymud
toasted
toaster
toddler
toggled
tolkien
tooland
topdown
topsten
torches
tostada
totally
tourist
towards
tracing
tracked
trapped
trashed
trashes
travels
trawler
treated
trigger
trinary
tripped
tropism
trusted
tshirts
tunnels
turning
tweaked
tweneks
twenexs
twinkie
twitted
twonkie
twospot
typical
typists
uhplohd
ullmans
unaware
unbrace
uncanny
unclear
uncurly
unequal
unfixed
unhappy
unician
univacs

unixism
unixoid
unknown
untried
unusual
unwedge
uparrow
updates
usascii
usedcar
useless
usenets
ushaped
usually
utastro
utsally
uttered
utterly
uucpnet
vadding
vaguely
vaksekt
validly
varying
veegrep
veggies
vending
vendors
verbage
verging
victims
viewers
viewing
viruses
visibly
visited
voicing
volumes
vomited
vovodeo
waiting
walking
wanggoh
wanking
warning
warrens
washing
wasting
watched
watchen
watches
weapons
wearing
wedding
wedging
weenies
weights
westley
wetware

whatcha
whoopee
widgets
wiggles
willing
wilsons
windows
winnage
winners
winning
wishing
wizards
wonders
wongkee
working
woudlnt
wouldbe
wouldnt
wouldve
wrapped
wrapper
writeln
writers
writing
wwiiera
wysiwyg
yeatman
yesorno
yooniks
yoosnet
yooznet
younger
zealots
zenlike
zenning
zeroing
zipcode
zippart
zizzing
zorkmid

6

abbrev
abuses
acting
action
active
adamss
addams
adding
addons
admins
agency
agents
ageold
aideth
aiword

alices	bitmap	castrz	cubing	dubbed
allman	bitter	caused	cursed	duckie
allows	bjarne	causes	curses	dumbed
alonzo	blamed	cavers	curves	dumped
alters	blanks	caving	cycles	dvorak
alwasy	blasta	cblock	daemon	dynner
amazed	blazer	cbreak	dahnkn	earths
amdahl	bletch	cdroms	dammit	easier
amigas	blivet	ceased	dances	easily
amused	blobby	center	dating	easter
analog	blocks	chacha	deadly	eating
andres	blugle	chains	dealer	ebcdic
annoys	boards	chairs	deckle	edited
apples	bodily	checks	decnet	edsger
applin	bogged	cheers	deedee	eeksee
approx	bogons	childs	deemed	eemaks
argued	bogued	chives	deemon	eemayl
arises	bohgon	choked	deeped	eeohef
arrays	bohgos	chores	deeper	eeohel
arrows	bohgot	chunks	deeply	egging
artlst	boiled	cities	deerez	eksoff
asking	boksol	claims	deevoh	eksohr
ataris	bolted	clarus	defioc	eksref
atlatl	bombed	clocks	dehose	elbows
atsien	boojum	closed	dekhed	elders
avatar	booted	closer	delays	eleear
avidly	boring	clouds	delint	elites
awocum	bosses	clover	demons	elvish
badass	bother	clunky	denary	encode
baggie	bounds	cmuish	denies	ending
baking	bourne	cobols	depths	enjoys
balked	boutin	cocked	derezz	ensued
banged	braces	coding	devils	ensure
banned	brader	coiled	diablo	enters
banner	braino	coined	dialin	eproms
barbox	brains	colors	digits	equals
barfed	brayno	comers	dinged	erased
barked	breaks	comics	dingle	errors
barred	broket	coming	dining	escher
bartle	brooks	commas	dinner	essexs
basics	btests	condom	diodes	evenly
bboard	buffer	consts	dipped	events
beanie	bufsiz	cooked	dismay	exclam
beards	buglix	copied	disuse	execlp
beasts	buhkee	copier	dogcow	exists
begins	burble	copies	donggl	fabled
beings	burner	coping	dongle	fables
bethke	burnin	copper	donned	fading
better	bushog	corner	donuts	failed
bibles	butted	costly	doomed	fairly
bigger	butter	counts	doubly	fandom
bignum	buying	courts	doused	faster
bigots	buyout	covers	dozois	faults
bikers	buzzes	cranks	drafts	favors
biksee	cables	crimes	dreams	feanor
bitand	called	crocks	drivel	feeper
bitblt	camels	crocky	driver	feetch
bitchy	canned	crowds	drives	fepped
biting	carted	crufty	drones	fflush

filing	gensym	hiccup	junked	likely
finest	ghosts	hiding	junkie	liking
finkel	giants	higher	kahuna	limits
firing	giegoh	highly	kajiya	linked
firiss	giving	hikers	kaleid	linkee
firmly	gladly	hiking	karmic	linker
fixing	glyphs	hillis	kbline	lisper
flakey	gnarly	hinfix	keepen	listed
flamer	gonkar	hobbit	kellys	lister
flames	gonken	hogans	kemeny	livein
flavor	gonkst	hogged	keycap	living
flipee	goroot	hooked	keypad	loaded
flippy	gosper	hoonuh	keytop	loader
floats	gotcha	hoping	kgbvax	locked
floors	graced	hopper	khakis	logged
flower	grapes	hordes	killed	logout
fluids	grault	hosery	killer	longer
flying	grawlt	hosing	kisses	looked
folded	greens	hosted	klasik	loomed
foobar	greets	hotels	kludge	looser
foobaz	grinds	housed	kluged	losers
fooled	gritch	houses	kluges	losing
fooqux	groper	huhngg	klugey	loudly
foovax	groups	humans	knocks	louies
forced	gruhnj	hunger	knuths	lovely
forces	grunge	hungus	kohbol	lowend
forged	grungy	hurled	korean	lowest
forked	guests	ibmish	kreetn	lowres
formed	guides	ibmism	kretch	lparen
former	gungho	idioms	kripee	lurked
formvs	gunned	idiots	kruhft	lurker
fortee	guotie	images	kurtzs	lusers
forums	gurfle	imbued	kwontm	lusing
frames	habits	imnsho	kwuhks	luster
freaks	hacent	impcom	labels	lyrics
freela	hacked	inband	labors	macros
freely	hacker	inches	lading	mailed
friode	hactrn	incore	landin	mailer
froggy	hakish	injoke	landon	mainly
frontl	hakmem	inline	lapses	makers
frotzt	halves	inning	laptop	making
fruity	hammer	inputs	larger	makroh
frying	handed	inquir	lasers	makrol
ftping	hanged	interj	lately	malloc
fucked	harder	isabus	latest	manged
fucker	hardly	issued	laughs	manger
fuckin	hardsf	issues	layers	manggo
fudged	harper	jageez	laying	manner
fueled	having	jammed	lchaim	mapped
fuggly	hayman	japans	leader	marked
fuller	headed	jedgar	leaves	marker
fuzzed	header	jeesee	leftit	markup
fverbs	hearts	jiaozi	lesser	markus
gagged	heated	joined	letter	mascot
gained	heeded	joiner	lettrs	masked
galore	heksit	joking	levels	masons
gaming	hellop	joplin	lewiss	masses
garply	helped	judges	lexers	master
gatech	henson	jumped	lighto	maters

mating	noclue	pclone	pusher	rincon
matter	nogood	pctalk	quarks	ringer
mccune	noises	pcware	queued	rising
meeces	nonibm	pedals	queues	rivals
meegoh	nonits	peedee	quiche	robots
meenoh	nonmmu	peeves	quirks	robson
mender	noting	perlis	quoted	rolled
merely	nouned	pesiml	quotes	roller
merged	novels	phased	quuces	rooted
merger	nphard	phreak	quuxes	rounds
merges	nsfnet	picked	qwerty	routed
merits	nuking	pieces	racing	router
mesdos	nuksee	pineal	racist	routes
messed	number	pinged	raised	rparen
metiks	nuncio	pinned	raises	rubber
michal	nybble	pissed	ranged	rubiks
micros	occams	pixels	raping	rucker
milder	occurs	pizzas	rarely	rudely
mildly	octets	pkease	ratfor	rulers
minded	oddest	pkware	rating	rushed
misbug	oeuvre	placed	ratios	safely
misfee	ohgyre	places	ravers	sagans
missed	oifing	planes	raving	salvos
misuse	online	plants	rayahl	sanity
mitism	ooblik	plates	reader	saving
mobies	oolien	played	readme	saying
models	opcode	player	really	scuzzy
modems	opened	playte	realms	seadog
modula	operas	plokta	reaped	sealed
mohbee	optics	ploogh	reaper	seemed
months	orally	points	rebels	seggie
moores	orders	poking	rebonk	segvee
morals	organs	poorly	reboot	seismo
mosfet	others	popjay	recall	seksee
mostly	outlet	popped	recast	sender
mouses	output	ported	recode	senses
movies	overly	posing	record	served
moving	packed	posses	refers	server
mowsoh	pacman	posted	reflex	serves
muhmbl	padded	poster	refuse	setjmp
nailed	paging	pounds	regexp	seusss
namely	paints	poured	reined	sewing
nanoay	paired	pranks	relays	sexier
nanohk	panels	prices	relied	sexism
narnia	papers	primer	relies	shades
nather	parens	printf	reload	shaman
nearly	parity	prints	remain	shames
neatly	parked	prizes	remove	shamos
needed	parlor	problm	repair	shaped
neewis	parsec	prolog	reread	shapes
nerves	parsed	proofs	retcon	shared
nested	parser	proved	retkon	shares
nethak	partly	psyton	reuses	sharps
newbie	passed	pulled	review	sheets
nicely	passes	pulses	rewind	shells
niches	passwd	punchy	rhumba	shiang
nickle	paying	purely	rhymes	shiftl
nights	pcisms	purest	richer	shifts
nlietz	pcland	pushed	rights	shirts

sholes
showed
sigint
signed
siphon
sizeof
skiing
skills
skrozl
slangy
sleeps
sliced
slides
slowed
slower
slowly
slurps
smears
smells
smiley
smiths
smokey
smurfs
snares
solved
solver
solves
soodoh
soozee
sorted
sortof
sounds
spaced
spaces
sparks
speaks
speeds
spends
spices
spifee
spiffy
spikes
splitp
spooge
spooks
spoons
sports
spying
stacks
stages
stampe
stamps
stands
stared
starts
stated
statep
states
steals

sticks
stiffy
stints
stolls
stored
stores
stover
straws
strips
stunts
styles
subset
sucker
suited
summed
summer
supper
surely
surfer
swamps
sweeps
swifts
swiped
sysgen
sysops
tables
taboos
taking
talked
talker
taller
tanked
taoism
tartan
tasted
tastes
tayste
techie
teekoh
telnet
tended
termed
terpri
tested
tester
texhax
thanks
theirs
themas
themed
theres
theyve
things
thingz
thinko
thinks
thirds
thuhnk
thumbs

thunks
tiedye
tigger
timing
tinged
titled
titles
todays
toking
topics
traced
traces
tracks
trades
trains
traits
trends
tricks
trufan
trunks
truths
trying
tubing
tucked
tunefs
tuning
turist
turned
tvedit
twenex
twonky
twopin
twoway
typing
ultrix
unable
unduly
unfair
unibus
unices
unicos
unions
unisys
united
unixen
unixes
unless
unlike
unlink
unload
unpack
unreal
unsafe
unsung
untrue
unused
unwind
upload
upsets

usages
usenet
usenix
userid
usnail
usualy
vading
valued
values
varied
varies
vaxism
vaxmud
vaxuum
veedif
veiled
verbed
verges
vernor
versed
vetted
vgrind
viewed
vinges
visits
vogons
vowels
wabbit
waiter
waitss
walbeg
walend
walked
wanted
warner
washed
wasted
wastes
watusi
weakly
wedged
wedgie
wedjit
weeble
weekly
weemba
weenie
weenix
welded
whales
whatll
whilst
whited
whizzy
wibble
widely
wildly
winged
winked

winkey
winner
wiring
wirths
wishes
wokked
woldoh
wonked
wonton
worked
worlds
writer
writes
wubble
xeroxs
yanked
yearly
yields
zappas
zapped
zenned
zeroed

5

abend
acres
adger
adhoc
adhok
adhos
admin
aften
after
ailab
aimed
alles
amiga
amock
amper
ansee
aptly
areal
areas
arent
ascii
asked
askee
atari
atest
atoms
atpar
bachs
badly
badob
balls
bands
bangs

barfs	chips	ebsee	foodp	hangs
based	cited	egzek	fooey	harts
bases	clike	eksch	fools	hates
baums	clods	eksee	forks	heads
bbses	clued	ekskl	forms	heaps
beams	coats	elisp	freds	hears
beans	coded	elses	frobn	helps
bears	coder	emacs	frobs	heres
beats	codes	email	frodo	hexit
beeuh	color	ended	frotz	hides
bells	comes	endif	fseek	hired
belts	comix	eniac	ftell	hires
bheer	cones	enjoy	fubar	holds
biffs	contr	ensue	fudds	holes
biker	cores	enyay	funky	homes
bilbo	corge	epics	fused	honor
bills	costs	eprom	fuses	hooks
bilos	coups	erics	gains	hopes
binds	crays	essoh	galls	honod
bitee	cruft	euwww	games	hoser
bites	ctest	ewoks	gangs	hoses
bitty	cults	excmu	gated	hosts
bixie	curod	exits	gears	hours
blech	curly	faced	gecos	hpsux
bleep	cuspy	faces	geeks	humma
bogon	daily	facts	geoff	humor
bogue	dared	faded	gerfl	hunan
boing	dated	fails	gives	hunts
boink	dates	falls	glark	hyper
boksn	dazed	famed	glich	icons
bombs	dbase	farms	glims	ideas
bones	decks	fates	glohb	imper
books	defun	favor	glork	imply
boots	demoh	feeds	gnnnn	inode
bored	demos	feeld	gnoll	intel
bosss	derez	feels	goals	inuit
boxed	desks	feepr	godel	itchy
boxen	dials	femto	going	items
boxes	dictu	fewer	gomez	iuclc
boynk	diffs	fiber	gongs	iwant
brohk	dijit	filed	gonna	iwbni
brses	dikes	files	gonzo	iyfeg
btest	dinky	filks	gored	jacks
bucky	disks	filtr	gotos	jaffe
bumps	dodgy	finds	grich	jafkl
burns	doing	fired	grink	jeans
burps	dokoh	fires	grmbl	jedgr
bushs	dongl	fitip	grohk	jerst
bytes	doors	fives	groks	jifkl
calls	dougs	fixed	gronk	jilly
cards	dreck	fixer	grows	joked
cares	droid	fixes	gulps	joker
cases	drops	flags	gumby	jokes
casts	drugs	flarp	gunch	jumpa
ccitt	drums	flaym	gurus	jumps
cedes	dryly	flows	hacks	karla
cents	dumps	folds	hafta	kazar
chars	dwimc	folks	halon	kbaud
ching	early	fonts	hands	keane

keeps	lover	nouns	puhdl	sewer
kells	loves	nroff	pushj	shoes
kinds	lpmud	nuked	pyoob	shops
kings	lured	nyooz	quant	shows
klone	lurks	obsex	quuxo	sides
klooj	luser	oddly	quuxu	signs
kluge	lwall	olcuc	quuxy	sinks
kluhb	mains	older	races	sisee
kluhj	makes	omits	randm	sisop
knees	males	oobee	rarer	sissy
knits	mango	oogrp	rasta	sitee
knows	mangy	opcon	rates	sites
knuth	mates	opted	raver	sixes
koans	mazes	orama	react	sizes
kreet	mbogo	orbar	reads	skigl
kretn	mcbee	outer	reels	skipa
kudos	means	outta	regex	skits
kuhdr	megoh	owned	rehug	skrog
kuhlr	melts	owner	relay	skroo
kwess	memes	packs	reply	slots
kwoht	mensa	padme	reset	slows
labor	metaw	paged	reuse	snarf
lacks	milli	pages	rider	snide
lapin	minds	pairs	rigor	snooz
laser	mines	palms	rings	snuck
lcase	minis	param	rises	socks
leads	mitai	paren	risks	softy
leksr	mitdm	parts	rites	sohsh
lemme	mixed	pasta	roles	sorts
lenat	modes	paths	roofs	soups
lerps	moons	pauls	rooms	sovok
levys	moree	pcbus	roots	soxen
lexer	moria	pcism	rotfl	spake
libes	motas	peetz	rtfaq	sparc
liked	motos	penee	ruled	specs
likes	motss	peter	rules	spied
lined	mouso	phils	rumor	spiel
lines	moved	phrog	runes	spock
links	moves	picks	runix	spooj
lions	msdos	piles	rytit	spots
lipit	muggs	pkarc	sadly	stang
lisps	muhng	pkpak	safes	stapp
lispy	muhnj	pkzip	sagan	stdio
lists	munge	plans	sagas	stems
lived	mungs	plays	sales	steps
lives	myths	playt	saved	stoll
loads	named	pling	saver	stops
loeil	names	plonk	saves	stubs
login	needs	plugh	saygn	sucks
logon	newer	polls	scars	suits
loins	nicht	popup	schwa	sunos
looks	niebl	pored	scrog	suzie
looms	nifty	ports	seats	synch
loony	niven	posed	seems	sysop
loops	noddy	posix	segee	takes
loozr	nohop	posts	semee	tales
loser	nomex	pours	semie	talks
loses	noted	proms	sends	taped
loved	notes	pubic	sethi	tapes

tarrs
tasks
teams
tears
techs
tecos
teens
tells
tends
tenex
terms
tests
texts
thatd
thats
thred
thunk
licks
timed
timer
times
tired
tires
titee
tmerk
tmrcs
tools
toons
towns
traps
trays
trccs
tries
trits
troff
troyd
tubes
tuned
turbo
turns
twink
twins
typed
types
typos
uarts
uhhuh
units
unixs
unjam
users
using
uunet
vadim
vaksn
vaxen
vdiff
veins
verbs

vgrep
vhlls
views
vinge
vlsis
volts
wabit
wages
wagon
waits
wakes
walks
wangk
wango
wanks
wanky
wants
warts
waves
wears
weebl
weeds
whatd
whats
whips
whorl
wibni
wider
wigan
wilde
wimps
wimpy
wiped
wired
wires
wirth
wizzy
wohrz
woken
wonky
words
works
worms
worng
wraps
wugga
xists
xyzzy
yabuh
yards
years
yeech
youll
youre
youve
yoyos
yucky
zeros
zilog

zizee
zorch
zowie

4

abbr
acrz
adas
adds
adjr
agre
aids
aims
ants
aosa
aose
aosg
aosh
apls
apps
aree
args
argv
arms
arts
asks
atto
awlt
aych
aydz
ayos
azaz
baen
bakw
bamf
barf
bars
bayt
bcnu
bcpl
bfmi
biet
biff
bios
birk
bits
blit
blok
boas
bohg
boks
bonk
bork
bots
bozo
budy
bugs

buhg
caps
cars
cats
cdev
chas
chdr
chuq
cing
cisc
clos
comm
comp
cond
conj
cons
conv
cops
cows
cpio
cpus
cray
crlf
cron
ctrl
ctss
cues
cuss
cuts
dain
daym
days
ddts
decs
dekl
deni
dens
dept
devo
dies
diff
dike
dink
dinr
dirk
doch
doco
docs
does
dogs
dont
dood
dots
dper
dtrt
dwim
ears
eats
eggs

eine
ends
enkw
eras
eris
etla
ever
evry
exch
excl
exec
expo
eyes
fans
farl
fatt
feep
fees
fopt
fido
filk
fits
foaf
foby
foom
foop
foos
fora
freq
frob
ftpd
fuck
fuer
fugu
fuhd
gcos
geef
geek
gems
gets
ghod
giga
gigo
gips
glas
gnoo
gnus
gobs
gods
goin
gonk
gorp
gosp
goto
grep
grok
guns
guts
guys

hakr
hese
hexa
hhoj
hhok
hhos
hits
hlls
hoax
hohl
holy
hops
howd
hows
hpux
ibms
icmp
imao
imho
init
intj
intp
ipsc
isbn
isms
isnt
itis
itll
jams
jaws
jedr
jews
jfcl
jiga
jips
jobs
jonl
jour
jrst
keir
kerl
kids
kips
kitn
klug
koan
kohd
kons
konz
korj
korn
kray
kree
kret
krul
kudr
kuhl
kung
kyoo

kzor
labs
lalr
larn
laws
layz
leds
lerp
lets
lfes
lies
linc
ling
lite
loch
logs
losj
lots
luvs
macs
maps
mayt
mbat
mecc
meeb
meem
mega
mego
megs
mels
meme
meta
mftl
mgmt
mime
minn
mips
misc
mits
mkfs
moby
mods
mody
mohd
moof
morf
moro
morz
mrcs
msec
muds
mult
muss
nand
nano
nbit
neep
nerd
nets

news
nibl
ning
nism
nnnn
nntp
noop
nooz
nual
nuhs
nuke
nuxi
nyet
obtw
odds
odor
ohms
oktl
ones
oois
orig
oses
ours
owns
parc
parm
pays
pcjr
pcrt
peon
perf
perh
perl
peta
pico
pidl
piet
pigs
pins
pipn
plow
pmed
pnch
pnet
popj
pops
poss
pree
pref
pres
prex
prob
prov
pube
puns
puts
qual
ques
quoi

quux
ralf
ravs
ravz
rays
rehi
rely
reps
rfcs
rife
rios
risc
rizm
rkal
rmss
rods
roff
roms
rotf
rows
rsts
rtfm
runs
sais
sayl
says
sbrk
sccs
scsi
sctv
sees
segv
selv
sets
sevn
sexa
sfla
shes
shit
sidr
sigs
siks
slak
smop
sots
spam
sqrt
sued
suff
suhx
suns
suzy
svid
swob
sync
syns
tabs
tans
tarr

tata
tayt
teco
tekh
temp
tera
texi
thru
tiem
ties
tits
tlas
tmrc
tnxe
tons
topl
tops
toto
toys
tric
trit
tron
truc
tscb
tsrs
ttfn
ttys
ture
uart
ucsc
unto
used
user
uses
uucp
vahr
vaks
vbar
veeb
veir
vhll
viel
vlsi
vnet
wank
wars
ways
weve
whos
wimp
wins
worz
wuhg
wwii
wyse
xinu
xmen
xoff
xref

yaba
yacc
yaun
yhwh
yoyo
yyyy
zeet
zork
zotz
zwei

3

ack
adb
ade
adj
adm
ads
adv
afk
aha
aho
ahr
ais
aka
alt
anl
ans
aoj
aos
apl
app
aql
arg
arl
asr
avg
awk
aws
baz
bbc
bbl
bbn
bbs
bcd
bei
bfi
bif
bix
blt
bnf
boh
bok
bps
bqs
bra
brb

brk
brs
bsd
btw
bwq
cav
cbw
cdr
cfc
chr
cis
clm
cmd
cms
cmu
com
cpp
cpv
crc
csh
csl
cty
cul
cuz
cwd
dak
das
dbx
dce
ddt
der
dev
dik
dir
dma
dms
dmu
doc
dok
dos
dpb
dte
dup
dvi
ebk
ebs
edp
edu
eeg
eek
eep
eff
eir
eks
elf
enq
ent
eof
eol

eot
eou
esc
esp
esr
ess
elx
exa
exe
fab
faq
fax
fds
feh
fep
fet
fft
fie
fmh
fod
foh
foo
fpu
ftp
fud
fya
fyi
gak
gen
ges
gfr
glf
gls
goo
gov
gpl
gpv
gur
has
hbd
hcf
hec
hed
hes
hie
hll
ics
ids
ien
iff
ilk
ing
int
ipm
iri
irp
irq
isa
isi

ism
iso
ist
its
ive
jcl
jee
jen
jfk
jkg
joh
jpl
jrl
jrn
jun
kar
kbt
kby
ked
ket
kom
ldb
ler
les
lex
lgp
lof
lol
lpt
lsd
lsh
mca
med
mee
mem
mhz
mil
mip
mir
mll
mmm
mmu
mod
mrc
msb
mts
mwm
nak
nfs
nls
nmi
nom
noo
nop
nsa
nth
nul
obs
oed

oic
oid
oif
ood
ook
ool
oop
ooz
ops
ord
org
orl
osc
osf
oui
owt
oyf
pak
pao
pbd
poo
pdl
pib
pio
pom
ppn
pre
qcd
quu
qux
qvq
rav
rec
ree
ref
rez
rfc
rfe
rms
rom
rpc
rpg
rpi
rsh
rsn
rsx
rti
rtm
rus
sdb
sed
sep
sfs
sie
sig
sio
sna
snr
sok

sos	vcc	ci	ip	rn
spl	vdd	ck	je	rs
syn	vff	cm	ji	rt
sys	vga	cn	jn	rx
tac	vic	cp	jp	sf
tak	vms	cr	kb	sh
tbs	vol	cs	kc	si
tcb	vom	cu	kh	sn
tcp	wie	dd	kl	sp
tdm	wpi	dg	kr	sq
ter	wrt	dh	lf	su
tex	wtf	dp	ln	te
thx	wth	dz	ls	th
tia	xct	ee	mb	tk
tla	xed	ef	mc	tl
tnx	xen	er	ml	tm
toi	xmp	es	mm	tr
trs	xor	fd	np	ts
tsp	xxx	ff	nt	uc
tsr	yes	fp	ob	uh
txt	yoo	fr	oo	ul
ubd	yup	fs	os	vg
uhp		fx	oy	vm
und	**2**	gb	oz	vr
uok		gc	pc	vs
upi	af	gd	pd	ws
urg	ai	gi	ph	xl
usg	ap	gr	pn	xs
usr	aw	gs	pp	xt
uzi	ay	hh	ps	xx
vac	bc	hp	pw	ya
vad	bl	hq	qa	yo
vak	cc	ic	rf	yu
var	ch	ie	rl	
vax		im	rm	

King James Bible Words

18

mahershalalhashbaz
overinterpretation

17

chushanrishathaim

16

bashanhavothjair
chepharhaammonai
covenantbreakers

evilfavouredness
kibrothhattaavah
lovingkindnesses
selahammahlekoth
unprofitableness

15

abelbethmaachah
acknowledgement
administrations
almondiblathaim
apharsathchites
berodachbaladan
bloodguiltiness
confectionaries

fellowdisciples
fellowlabourers
helkathhazzurim
inconsistencies
interpretations
kneadingtroughs
merodachbaladan
notwithstanding
prognosticators
ramathaimzophim
righteousnesses
stumblingblocks
threshingfloors
tilgathpilneser
unrighteousness
zaphnathpaaneah

14

accomplishment
administration
affectionately
bethdiblathaim
bethlehemjudah
communications
constellations
contemptuously
contradictions
deceivableness
dwellingplaces
fellowcitizens
fellowlabourer

fellowprisoner
fellowservants
grapegatherers
grapegleanings
interpretation
jegarsahadutha
kedeshnaphtali
lasciviousness
lookingglasses
lovingkindness
maalehacrabbim
misrephothmaim
nebuchadnezzar
nebuchadrezzar
nergalsharezer
presumptuously

principalities
reconciliation
representative
sanctification
shamefacedness
shoulderpieces
strengthenedst
stumblingblock
stumblingstone
superscription
threshingfloor
threshingplace
tiglathpileser
transgressions
uncircumcision
unsatisfactory

13

accomplishing
acknowledgeth
acknowledging
apharsachites
ashdothpisgah
bethjeshimoth
bethmarcaboth
blasphemously
bountifulness
brokenhearted
calebephratah
chislothtabor
circumspectly
communication
concupiscence
congregations
consecrations
contradicting
contradiction
contradictory
controversies
deceitfulness
demonstration
determination
disappointeth
discrepancies
dissimulation
doubletongued
dwellingplace
eleloheisrael
elonbethhanan
establishment
fellowhelpers
fellowservant
fellowsoldier
fellowworkers
firstbegotten
foreknowledge

forgetfulness
forgivenesses
grapegatherer
handkerchiefs
hazarhatticon
imperfections
imprisonments
inappropriate
inconsistency
incorruptible
intentionally
intercessions
intermeddleth
interpolation
interrogating
interrogation
jehovahshalom
jerahmeelites
justification
kirjathhuzoth
kirjathjearim
kirjathsannah
kirjathsepher
longsuffering
magormissabib
maliciousness
manifestation
masterbuilder
meribahkadesh
moneychangers
moreshethgath
netophathites
overspreading
pharaohhophra
pharaohnechoh
plenteousness
predestinated
purifications
remmonmethoar
reproachfully
righteousness
sheepshearers
shetharboznai
shihorlibnath
signification
snorkelwacker
stonesquarers
strengtheneth
strengthening
succothbenoth
superstitious
supplications
swaddlingband
sweetsmelling
syriadamascus
syrophenician
taanathshiloh

tenderhearted
thanksgivings
thessalonians
transgressest
transgresseth
transgressing
transgression
transgressors
treacherously
trucebreakers
uncircumcised
uncleannesses
uncorruptible
uncorruptness
understandest
understandeth
understanding
unreproveable
unrighteously
whereinsoever
whithersoever
womenservants

12

abominations
accompanying
accomplished
acknowledged
acquaintance
administered
adulteresses
alexandrians
allonbachuth
apothecaries
appertaineth
armourbearer
ashterathite
astonishment
atarothaddar
baalshalisha
backslidings
beerlahairoi
belteshazzar
bethazmaveth
bethbaalmeon
bethhaccerem
bethjesimoth
bethlehemite
bloodthirsty
breastplates
bridechamber
brokenfooted
brokenhanded
buryingplace
candlesticks
caterpillers

chamberlains
chastisement
chedorlaomer
cheerfulness
childbearing
chrysoprasus
circumcising
circumcision
clovenfooted
commandments
commendation
commonwealth
communicated
comprehended
condemnation
confirmation
confiscation
congratulate
congregation
consecration
considerably
consolations
conspirators
constraineth
consultation
consummation
contemptible
contrariwise
contribution
conveniently
conversation
convocations
countenances
courageously
covetousness
delicateness
deliverances
descriptions
despitefully
destructions
disannulleth
disannulling
disappointed
discomfiture
discontented
dishonourest
dishonoureth
disobedience
dispensation
dispossessed
disputations
disquietness
distributeth
distributing
distribution
ecclesiastes
encapsulated

enchantments
endeavouring
enlightening
epaphroditus
eshkalonites
establisheth
evilmerodach
extortioners
eyewitnesses
fainthearted
faithfulness
feebleminded
feedingplace
fellowhelper
foreordained
fornications
frankincense
gittahhepher
grasshoppers
graveclothes
grievousness
guestchamber
hazazontamar
hazezontamar
henceforward
hungerbitten
hypocritical
hypothetical
imaginations
immutability
impoverished
imprisonment
incompatible
inconsistent
incontinency
incorruption
inflammation
inheritances
inscriptions
insufficient
insurrection
intelligence
intercession
intermission
interpreting
jabeshgilead
jashubilehem
jehoshabeath
jehovahjireh
jehovahnissi
jerubbesheth
jezreelitess
joshbekashah
jurisdiction
kadeshbarnea
kerenhappuch
lamentations

maachathites
magnificence
maidservants
malchielites
manahethites
marketplaces
marvellously
mecherathite
mephibosheth
merryhearted
meshillemith
meshillemoth
meshullemeth
ministration
moneylenders
multipliedst
nathanmelech
netophathite
nevertheless
nicolaitanes
organization
outstretched
overshadowed
overthroweth
parshandatha
particularly
peradventure
persecutions
perseverance
perspectives
perverseness
pharaohnecho
philadelphia
philosophers
phylacteries
pleasantness
pomegranates
predestinate
preparations
presumptuous
principality
proclamation
prophesyings
propitiation
prosperously
provocations
pruninghooks
purification
ramathmizpeh
ramothgilead
recompensest
recompensing
regeneration
remembrances
restingplace
resurrection
sacrificedst
satisfaction
satisfactory

schoolmaster
shimeathites
shimronmeron
shuthalhites
slanderously
slothfulness
specifically
stedfastness
stiffhearted
stouthearted
strengthened
stubbornness
sufficiently
superstition
supplication
suspiciously
syriamaachah
tahtimhodshi
terribleness
thankfulness
thanksgiving
thessalonica
threatenings
thunderbolts
timnathheres
timnathserah
tranquillity
transfigured
transforming
transgressed
transgressor
tribulations
unaccustomed
unchangeable
uncompressed
undergirding
undersetters
unfaithfully
unprofitable
unquenchable
unreasonable
unscientific
unsearchable
variableness
vinedressers
watersprings
wellfavoured
wellpleasing
whoremongers
withersoever
wretchedness
zarethshahar

11

abelmeholah
abelmizraim
abelshittim

abomination
acceptation
accompanied
accordingly
acknowledge
acquainting
admonishing
adrammelech
adramyttium
advantageth
adversaries
adversities
affectioned
afflictions
ambassadors
ambushments
ammishaddai
anethothite
antichrists
apostleship
appearances
appertained
appointment
apprehended
approacheth
approaching
aristarchus
aristobulus
ashdothites
astrologers
atarothadar
attentively
authorities
aznothtabor
baalathbeer
baalperazim
babylonians
backbitings
backsliding
banquetings
bartholomew
battlements
beerothites
benefactors
benevolence
bethlebaoth
bethmaachah
bethshemesh
bethshemite
bethshittah
bethtappuah
blasphemers
blasphemest
blasphemeth
blasphemies
blaspheming
blasphemous
blessedness
blindfolded

bondservant
bondservice
bountifully
breastplate
brigandines
brotherhood
canaanitess
canaanitish
candlestick
carefulness
carmelitess
caterpiller
chalkstones
challengeth
challenging
chamberlain
charchemish
cherethites
circumcised
circumspect
cockatrices
cockcrowing
cogitations
comfortable
comfortably
comfortedst
comfortless
commandedst
commandment
commissions
communicate
compassions
complainers
complaining
complicates
composition
compoundeth
confederacy
confederate
confidences
confidently
conflicting
conformable
consciences
consecrated
consentedst
consequence
considerest
considereth
considering
consistency
consolation
constrained
consumption
contentions
contentious
contentment
continually
continuance

controversy
convocation
coppersmith
corinthians
corruptible
counsellors
countenance
counterpart
countervail
courteously
deceitfully
declaration
deliciously
delightsome
deliverance
deliveredst
description
desolations
desperately
destruction
determinate
deuteronomy
differences
diminishing
disannulled
disbelieved
discomfited
discontinue
discouraged
discovereth
discovering
discussions
disobedient
dispersions
displeasure
disposition
disputation
dissemblers
dissembleth
distinction
distraction
distributed
diversities
divinations
divorcement
documentary
doorkeepers
downsitting
dromedaries
drunkenness
earthquakes
edification
effectually
emboldeneth
embroiderer
enchantment
encountered
endeavoured
enlargement

enlightened
entertained
ephesdammim
ephraimites
ephrathites
eshtaulites
established
estimations
evangelists
eveningtide
everlasting
examination
exceedingly
executioner
exhortation
expectation
explanation
explanatory
extortioner
tearfulness
fellowheirs
firstfruits
flourisheth
flourishing
foolishness
forbearance
torefathers
forgiveness
fornication
fornicators
forwardness
foundations
frowardness
frustrateth
furtherance
furthermore
gazingstock
gederathite
gederothaim
genealogies
generations
gershonites
girgashites
governments
grandmother
grasshopper
haahashtari
habitations
hadadrimmon
hamathzobah
hammoleketh
handbreadth
handmaidens
handwriting
hardhearted
haughtiness
hazargaddah
hazarmaveth
hazelelponi

hearkenedst
horhagidgad
hospitality
householder
humiliation
hundredfold
hypocrisies
illuminated
imagination
immediately
immortality
implication
importunity
incontinent
indignation
industrious
inexcusable
infirmities
ingathering
inhabitants
inheritance
innumerable
inquisition
inscription
inspiration
instructers
instructing
instruction
instruments
intercessor
interesting
intermeddle
interpreted
interpreter
irrefutable
ishmaelites
ishmeelites
israelitish
jaareoregim
jahleelites
jahzeelites
jeberechiah
jehoshaphat
journeyings
jushabhesed
kirharaseth
kirhareseth
kirjatharba
kirjatharim
kirjathbaal
lamentation
languisheth
languishing
leanfleshed
lengthening
lieutenants
maachathite
machnadebai
magistrates

maidservant
maintainest
maintenance
malefactors
manservants
marketplace
marvelously
meholathite
melchisedec
melchizedek
menchildren
menpleasers
menservants
menstealers
merchandise
merchantmen
meronothite
meshelemiah
meshezabeel
mesopotamia
methegammah
midianitish
ministereth
ministering
miscarrying
mischievous
multiplieth
multiplying
naughtiness
nebushasban
nebuzaradan
necessities
necromancer
nephishesim
neverthless
nourishment
observation
occurrences
offscouring
onesiphorus
opportunity
oppositions
oppressions
overcharged
overfloweth
overflowing
overrunning
overturneth
overwhelmed
painfulness
peacemakers
perfectness
performance
perpetually
persecutest
persecuting
persecution
persecutors
pestilences

philippians
philistines
pirathonite
plentifully
pomegranate
possessions
preeminence
premeditate
preparation
prescribing
probability
problematic
proclaimeth
proclaiming
profaneness
progenitors
pronouncing
prophesieth
prophesying
provocation
punishments
quaternions
questioning
recommended
recompences
recompensed
reconciling
reformation
regemmelech
rememberest
remembereth
remembering
remembrance
repetitions
replenished
reproachest
reproacheth
resemblance
restitution
restrainest
revelations
righteously
rimmonparez
ringstraked
romamtiezer
sabachthani
sackclothes
sacrificeth
sacrificing
salutations
samothracia
sanctifieth
sanctuaries
secondarily
sennacherib
sepharvites
seventeenth
shaalbonite
shallecheth

shalmaneser
shamelessly
shearjashub
shechemites
sheepmaster
shemidaites
shemiramoth
shephathiah
sheshbazzar
shillemites
shimronites
shoelatchet
shumathites
shuphamites
silverlings
silversmith
similitudes
skilfulness
slingstones
slumberings
snuffdishes
solemnities
soothsayers
soothsaying
spiritually
stablisheth
stewardship
stiffnecked
storehouses
straightway
straiteneth
stretchedst
suchathites
sufficiency
sumptuously
superfluity
superfluous
susanchites
tabernacles
taskmasters
tehaphnehes
tempestuous
temptations
terrestrial
testifiedst
testimonies
thankworthy
thenceforth
theophanies
thitherward
threatening
thunderings
tobadonijah
trachonitis
traffickers
transferred
transformed
translation
transparent

treacherous
trespassing
tribulation
tributaries
turtledoves
unadvisedly
unbelievers
unbelieving
unblameable
unblameably
uncertainly
uncleanness
uncondemned
ungodliness
unmanagable
unrebukable
unrighteous
unspeakable
unspecified
unwittingly
uprightness
uzzensherah
voluntarily
watercourse
waterspouts
wellbeloved
wheresoever
wherewithal
whisperings
whoremonger
winebibbers
winepresses
winterhouse
witchcrafts
withdrawest
withdraweth
withheldest
withholdeth
wonderfully
wonderously
workmanship
worshippers
worshippeth
worshipping
yesternight
zareathites
zebulunites
zurishaddai

10

abiezrites
abominable
abominably
abstinence
abundantly
acceptable
acceptably

acceptance
accomplish
accounting
accusation
accustomed
acquainted
admiration
admonished
admonition
adonibezek
adonizedec
adullamite
adulterers
adulteress
adulteries
adulterous
advantaged
adventured
advisement
affections
afflictest
affliction
affrighted
afterwards
ahiramites
ahithophel
aholibamah
alammelech
alexandria
altogether
amalekites
ambassador
ambushment
ammonitess
amphipolis
anammelech
andronicus
anetothite
anointedst
answerable
answeredst
antichrist
antipatris
antothijah
apharsites
apothecary
apparelled
apparently
appearance
appointeth
appreciate
approached
archevites
areopagite
arimathaea
armageddon
artaxerxes
artificers
ashbelites

ashdodites
asrielites
assemblies
assembling
assumption
astonished
astrologer
asyncritus
atonements
attendance
baalberith
baalhermon
baalzephon
babylonish
backbiters
backbiteth
backbiting
backslider
baharumite
balancings
bamothbaal
banishment
banqueting
barbarians
barrenness
bartimaeus
bathrabbim
battlement
bedchamber
beerothite
beeshterah
beforehand
beforetime
beginnings
believable
belshazzar
benejaakan
benjamites
beseeching
betharabah
bethhoglah
bethnimrah
bethpazzez
bethphelet
birthright
bishoprick
bitterness
bizjothjah
blasphemed
blasphemer
boisterous
bottomless
bridegroom
brigandine
brightness
broughtest
burdensome
busybodies
butlership

calamities
canaanites
cankerworm
caphthorim
caphtorims
cappadocia
carbuncles
carchemish
carelessly
carpenters
centurions
ceremonies
chalcedony
chaldaeans
chambering
chancellor
changeable
chargeable
charitably
chastenest
chasteneth
chastening
chastiseth
cheerfully
cherethims
cherisheth
chesulloth
chinnereth
chinneroth
christians
chronicles
chrysolyte
circumcise
cockatrice
collection
colossians
comeliness
comforters
comforteth
commandest
commandeth
commanding
commendeth
commending
commission
committest
committeth
committing
commodious
commotions
companions
comparable
comparison
compassest
compasseth
compassing
compassion
compellest
complained

complaints
completely
comprehend
compressed
concealeth
conceiving
conception
concerneth
concerning
concluding
conclusion
conclusive
concubines
condemnest
condemneth
condemning
condescend
conditions
confection
conference
confesseth
confessing
confession
confidence
confirmeth
confirming
confounded
connection
conquering
conquerors
conscience
consecrate
consenting
considered
consistent
consisteth
conspiracy
constantly
constraint
constructs
consulteth
containeth
containing
contemneth
contendest
contendeth
contending
contention
continueth
continuing
convenient
conversant
conversion
converteth
converting
convinceth
convincing
copulation
correcteth

correction
corrupters
corrupteth
corrupting
corruption
costliness
counselled
counsellor
countrymen
courageous
covenanted
craftiness
crookbackt
cumulative
cupbearers
dabbasheth
dalmanutha
damascenes
deceivings
dedicating
dedication
degenerate
delectable
delicacies
delicately
delightest
delighteth
deliverest
delivereth
delivering
department
descendeth
descending
describeth
desolation
despiteful
destroyers
destroyest
destroyeth
destroying
determined
detestable
difference
diligently
diminished
diotrephes
disallowed
disappoint
discerneth
discerning
discharged
discipline
discourage
discovered
discreetly
discretion
discussion
disguiseth
dishonesty

disinherit
disorderly
displeased
dispossess
disputings
disquieted
dissembled
dissension
dissolvest
dissolving
distinctly
distracted
distressed
distresses
distribute
divination
doorkeeper
drowsiness
earthquake
ebedmelech
effeminate
eighteenth
elishaphat
emboldened
employment
emulations
enchanters
encouraged
endangered
endeavours
engravings
entangleth
enterprise
entreateth
ephraimite
ephrathite
epicureans
esarhaddon
especially
estimation
ethiopians
euroclydon
evangelist
everything
excellency
exchangers
execration
executedst
exerciseth
exhaustive
experience
experiment
eyeservice
eziongaber
eziongeber
faithfully
fallowdeer
falsifying
fashioneth

fashioning
fatfleshed
fatherless
favourable
feebleness
fellowship
fierceness
filthiness
firebrands
firstfruit
firstlings
flattereth
flatteries
flattering
fleshhooks
flourished
fluttereth
followedst
forbeareth
forbearing
forbiddeth
forbidding
foreigners
forerunner
foreseeing
forewarned
forgettest
forgetteth
forgetting
fornicator
forsookest
fortresses
fortunatus
foundation
fourfooted
foursquare
fourteenth
friendship
fulfilling
gainsayers
gainsaying
galilaeans
gatherings
gathhepher
gathrimmon
gazathites
generation
gennesaret
gentleness
gergesenes
gershonite
geshurites
gethsemane
gibeathite
gibeonites
gileadites
girgashite
glistering
glittering

gloominess
glorifieth
glorifying
gloriously
gluttonous
goldsmiths
goodliness
gorgeously
government
graciously
grayheaded
greediness
greyheaded
grievously
grudgingly
guiltiness
habaziniah
habergeons
habitation
hachmonite
hailstones
hammedatha
hammothdor
handmaiden
handstaves
hanochites
harvestman
hashabniah
hashbadana
havothjair
hazaraddar
hazarshual
hazarsusah
hazarsusim
hearkeneth
hearkening
hebronites
henceforth
hepherites
heretofore
hermogenes
hermonites
hezronites
hierapolis
highminded
hindermost
historical
honourable
horsehoofs
horseleach
households
humbleness
huphamites
husbandman
husbandmen
hushathite
hypocrites
hypothesis
idolatries

idolatrous
ignorantly
illustrate
impediment
impenitent
implacable
impossible
impoverish
imprisoned
inclosings
increasest
increaseth
increasing
incredible
indication
individual
infallible
influences
inhabitant
inhabiters
inhabitest
inhabiteth
Inhabiting
inheriteth
iniquities
Inordinate
instructed
instructer
instructor
instrument
intreaties
inventions
ishbibenob
ishbosheth
ishmaelite
ishmeelite
israelites
ittahkazin
izeharites
jachinites
jashubites
jealousies
jeezerites
jehaleleel
jehoiachin
jehonathan
jesharelah
jeshohaiah
jezreelite
jiphthahel
journeying
joyfulness
justifieth
justifying
kadmonites
kehelathah
kenizzites
kiriathaim
kirjathaim

kohathites
korathites
laboratory
lamentable
languished
laodiceans
lefthanded
lengthened
liberality
libertines
lighteneth
lightnings
likeminded
lillywhite
longwinged
macedonian
machirites
magistrate
magnifical
mahalaleel
mahanehdan
maintained
malchishua
malefactor
manassites
manifested
manifestly
manservant
manslayers
marvellous
mattathias
mattithiah
meditation
mehetabeel
melchishua
menstruous
messengers
methuselah
michmethah
middlemost
midianites
millstones
ministered
mishmannah
mishraites
mithredath
moderately
moderation
morasthite
mournfully
multiplied
multitudes
murmurings
naamathite
needlework
neglecting
nehelamite
neighbours
nemuelites

nephthalim
nethermost
netophathi
newsgroups
nineteenth
noteworthy
nourisheth
nourishing
occasioned
occupation
oftentimes
oliveyards
omnipotent
operations
oppresseth
oppressing
oppression
oppressors
ordinances
originally
outlandish
outrageous
overcharge
overcometh
overflowed
overlaying
overlooked
overshadow
overspread
overtaketh
overthrown
overturned
pahathmoab
palmerworm
parchments
partiality
particular
passengers
patriarchs
pelethites
pennyworth
pentateuch
perceivest
perceiveth
perceiving
perezuzzah
perfecting
perfection
performeth
performing
perizzites
permission
pernicious
perplexity
persecuted
persecutor
persuadest
persuadeth
persuading

persuasion
pertaineth
pertaining
perversely
perverteth
perverting
pestilence
philipians
philistine
philologus
philosophy
physicians
pihahiroth
pilgrimage
plaistered
plantation
plowshares
pollutions
possessest
possesseth
possessing
possession
possessors
postscript
potipherah
pourtrayed
praetorium
preferring
preparedst
presbytery
prescribed
presenting
preservest
preserveth
presidents
presumably
prevailest
prevaileth
preventest
previously
priesthood
princesses
principles
proceedeth
proceeding
proclaimed
professing
profession
profitable
prolongeth
promisedst
pronounced
prophecies
prophesied
prophetess
proportion
proselytes
prospereth
prosperity

prosperous
prostitute
protection
protesting
providence
provokedst
psalteries
publisheth
punishment
purloining
purtenance
putrifying
questioned
quickeneth
quickening
quicksands
ramathlehi
rearranged
reasonable
reasonably
rebellious
receivedst
rechabites
recompence
recompense
reconciled
recovering
redeemedst
redemption
refraineth
refresheth
refreshing
remembered
repentance
repentings
reproached
reproaches
reprobates
reputation
resolution
respecteth
restrained
reubenites
revelation
revellings
reverenced
ringleader
rottenness
sacrificed
sacrifices
salutation
samaritans
samgarnebo
sanctified
satisfiest
satisfieth
satisfying
scarceness
scattereth

scattering
scourgings
scriptures
searchings
selfwilled
separateth
separating
separation
sepharvaim
sepulchres
shaalabbin
shabbethai
shahazimah
shamefully
shamsherai
sharpeneth
shechaniah
sheepcotes
sheepfolds
sheepskins
shelanites
shephatiah
shephuphan
shibboleth
shigionoth
shilonites
shipmaster
shuhamites
shunammite
sicknesses
signifieth
signifying
simeonites
similitude
simplicity
singleness
slanderers
slanderest
slandereth
slumbereth
sojourners
sojourneth
sojourning
solitarily
soothsayer
speechless
spitefully
spreadings
sprinkleth
sprinkling
stablished
staggereth
stammerers
stammering
stargazers
stedfastly
storehouse
straitened
straitness

strangling
strengthen
stretchest
stretcheth
stretching
subjection
submitting
subscribed
subsequent
subverting
succeedest
sufferings
sufficient
supplanted
suppliants
suretiship
surfeiting
surmisings
sustenance
swalloweth
synagogues
tabernacle
tachmonite
talebearer
tarpelites
telharesha
temperance
temptation
tenderness
tentmakers
terrifiest
testifieth
testifying
themselves
theophilus
thereabout
thimnathah
thirteenth
thirtyfold
thoroughly
thoughtest
threatened
threescore
thresholds
throughout
thundereth
tirathites
tormentors
traditions
transgress
translated
travailest
travaileth
travailing
travellers
travelleth
travelling
traversing
treasurers

treasurest
treasuries
trespassed
trespasses
triumphant
triumphing
trogyllium
troubledst
trumpeters
tumultuous
turtledove
uncovereth
underneath
understand
understood
unfaithful
unfruitful
university
unleavened
unmerciful
unmoveable
unobserved
unoccupied
unprepared
unpunished
unsatiable
untempered
unthankful
unworthily
upbraideth
uzzielites
valiantest
vehemently
virtuously
visitation
wanderings
wantonness
watchtower
waterflood
wellspring
whatsoever
whensoever
whereabout
whirlwinds
whisperers
whomsoever
wickedness
wilderness
winebibber
witchcraft
withholden
witnesseth
witnessing
wondrously
workfellow
worshipped
worshipper
wrestlings
wrongfully

wroughtest
yokefellow
yourselves
zamzummims
zebulonite
zelophehad
zephonites
zeredathah
zerubbabel
zorathites

9

aaronites
abhorrest
abhorreth
abhorring
abiezrite
abimelech
abishalom
abolished
aboundeth
abounding
abundance
acceptest
accepteth
accepting
acclaimed
accompany
according
accounted
additions
admitedly
adulterer
adultress
advantage
adventure
adversary
adversity
advertise
affecteth
affection
afflicted
affording
aforehand
aforetime
afternoon
afterward
agreement
ahasuerus
ahimelech
ahisamach
ahishahar
alabaster
alexander
alienated
allowance
almsdeeds

amalekite
amazement
ambassage
amminadab
amminadib
ammizabad
ammonites
amounting
amramites
anaharath
ancestors
anointest
anointing
answerest
answereth
answering
antiquity
antothite
apollonia
appeareth
appearing
appeaseth
appertain
appointed
apprehend
approvest
approveth
approving
aramitess
arbathite
archangel
archelaus
archippus
areopagus
arguments
arrogancy
artificer
artillery
ascendeth
ascending
ashchenaz
asherites
ashtaroth
ashteroth
ashtoreth
ashurites
assaulted
assembled
associate
assurance
assuredly
assyrians
athenians
atonement
attending
attentive
authority
available
axletrees

baalhamon
baalhanan
baalhazor
baaltamar
baalzebub
babblings
bachrites
bakbakkar
bakbukiah
bakemeats
baptizest
baptizeth
baptizing
barachias
barbarian
barbarous
barhumite
barnfloor
barzillai
bashemath
bathsheba
battering
beautiful
bechorath
beckoning
beelzebub
beersheba
befalleth
begettest
begetteth
beginnest
beginning
beguiling
behaviour
beholdest
beholdeth
beholding
believers
believest
believeth
believing
belongest
belongeth
belonging
bemoaning
beneberak
benjamite
benzoheth
berachiah
bereaveth
berechiah
berothite
besodeiah
bethabara
bethanath
bethanoth
betharbel
bethbarah
bethbirei

bethdagon	carriages	concubine	damnation	discerned
bethelite	causeless	condemned	dangerous	discerner
bethgader	celebrate	condition	darkeneth	discharge
bethgamul	celestial	conducted	daughters	disciples
bethharan	centurion	conferred	dayspring	disdained
bethhogla	certainly	confessed	decapolis	disfigure
bethhoron	certainty	confident	deceitful	disguised
bethlehem	certified	confirmed	deceivers	dishonest
bethpalet	chaldeans	conformed	deceiveth	dishonour
bethphage	challenge	confusing	deceiving	dismaying
bethrapha	chameleon	confusion	declareth	dismissed
bethrehob	champaign	congealed	declaring	disobeyed
bethsaida	chapiters	connected	declineth	dispersed
bethshean	charashim	consented	decreased	displayed
betrayers	chargedst	consorted	dedicated	displease
betrayest	chastened	conspired	defendest	disposing
betrayeth	chastised	constrain	defending	disputing
betrothed	chemarims	consulted	deferreth	dissolved
bewaileth	chenaanah	consulter	defiledst	divisions
bewitched	chenaniah	consumeth	defrauded	doctrines
bewrayeth	chephirah	consuming	dehavites	dominions
biography	cherished	contained	delicates	doubtless
birzavith	cherubims	contemned	delighted	dromedary
blackness	childhood	contended	delivered	drunkards
blameless	childless	continual	deliverer	dunghills
blaspheme	chorashan	continued	delusions	dwellings
blasphemy	christian	continues	demetrius	earnestly
bleatings	cinneroth	converted	departeth	effectual
blemishes	citations	convicted	departing	egyptians
blessings	clamorous	convinced	departure	eightieth
blindness	cleanness	coriander	descended	ekronites
blossomed	cleanseth	cormorant	described	elihoenai
boanerges	cleansing	cornelius	describes	elihoreph
boastings	clearness	cornfloor	deserveth	elimelech
bondmaids	combining	corrected	deserving	eliphalet
bondwoman	comforted	corrupted	desirable	elipheleh
bondwomen	comforter	corruptly	desiredst	eliphelet
borroweth	commanded	countries	despaired	elisabeth
bountiful	commander	couplings	desperate	elizaphan
bracelets	commended	courteous	despisers	elkoshite
breakings	commented	covenants	despisest	embracing
breatheth	committed	coveredst	despiseth	embroider
breathing	commotion	coverings	despising	emptiness
brickkiln	communing	crackling	destitute	emulation
brimstone	communion	cracknels	destroyed	encampeth
broidered	community	craftsman	destroyer	encamping
brotherly	compacted	craftsmen	determine	enchanter
buildedst	companied	creatures	devotions	encourage
buildings	companies	creditors	devourest	endeavour
bulrushes	companion	croucheth	devoureth	enflaming
burnished	comparing	crownedst	devouring	engrafted
canaanite	compassed	crucified	different	enhakkore
capernaum	compelled	cucumbers	differeth	enlargeth
caphtorim	complaint	cumbereth	differing	enlarging
captivity	concealed	cumbrance	dignities	enlighten
carbuncle	conceived	cunningly	diligence	enmishpat
carefully	concision	cupbearer	dionysius	enquirest
carmelite	concluded	curiously	directeth	enrichest
carpenter	concourse	cyrenians	direction	ensamples

enshemesh	fervently	galleries	headstone	inventors
entangled	fictional	gammadims	hearkened	invisible
entappuah	fifteenth	garnished	heaviness	iphedeiah
entertain	fightings	garrisons	heberites	irshemesh
entrances	firebrand	gatherest	hebrewess	ismachiah
entreated	firmament	gathereth	helekites	israelite
epaenetus	firstborn	gathering	hephzibah	izharites
ephesians	firstling	gendereth	hereafter	jaazaniah
ephphatha	firstripe	genealogy	heritages	jaminites
escheweth	fisherman	generally	herodians	jashobeam
espousals	fishermen	gibbethon	hindereth	jebusites
establish	fishhooks	gibeonite	hoarfrost	jecholiah
esteemeth	fishpools	gileadite	honeycomb	jechonias
esteeming	fleshhook	ginnethon	honourest	jehalelel
estranged	followers	girgasite	honoureth	jehezekel
ethiopian	followeth	gleanings	horseback	jehizkiah
euphrates	following	glorified	hoshaphat	jehoaddan
evidences	foolishly	goatskins	household	jehohanan
evidently	footnotes	godliness	housetops	jehoiakim
evildoers	footsteps	goldsmith	howsoever	jehoiarib
exactions	footstool	goodliest	humbledst	jehonadab
examining	forasmuch	governors	hundredth	jehosheba
exceedest	forbidden	greatness	husbandry	jehoshuah
exceedeth	forefront	greenness	hymenaeus	jehozabad
exceeding	foreheads	greetings	hypocrisy	jehozadak
excellent	foreigner	greyhound	hypocrite	jehudijah
excellest	foreseeth	grievance	identical	jekabzeel
excelleth	foreskins	groanings	idolaters	jekuthiel
executest	forfeited	guiltless	ignorance	jeoparded
executeth	forgavest	habergeon	ijeabarim	jephunneh
executing	forgetful	habitable	illyricum	jerahmeel
execution	forgiveth	hachallah	imagineth	jerubbaal
exercised	forgiving	hadadezer	immutable	jerusalem
exhorteth	forgotten	hadarezer	imperious	jeshebeab
exhorting	forsaketh	hagarenes	important	jeshishai
exorcists	forsaking	hagarites	inability	jezerites
expecting	forsomuch	hallohesh	incidents	jezrahiah
expedient	forthwith	hamathite	inclineth	joshaphat
expounded	fortified	hammelech	including	joshaviah
expressed	forwarded	hamulites	increased	josiphiah
expressly	fountains	handmaids	incurable	jotbathah
extendeth	fourscore	handywork	infirmity	journeyed
extensive	fragments	hannathon	inflicted	judgments
extortion	freewoman	happeneth	infolding	justified
extremely	frontiers	hardeneth	inhabited	justifier
extremity	frontlets	harmonies	inherited	kerchiefs
faintness	frowardly	harnepher	inheritor	kinsfolks
faithless	frustrate	harnessed	injurious	kinswoman
falsehood	fryingpan	harosheth	injustice	kinswomen
familiars	fugitives	haruphite	innermost	kirharesh
farthings	fulfilled	hashabiah	innocency	knowledge
fashioned	furbished	hashabnah	innocents	korahites
fastening	furiously	hashmonah	instantly	labourers
faultless	furnished	hassenaah	integrity	laboureth
favourest	furniture	hasteneth	intendest	labouring
favoureth	furthered	hatefully	intending	landmarks
fearfully	gadarenes	haughtily	interpret	languages
feathered	galatians	hazarenan	intreated	largeness
feignedly	galilaean	headbands	intruding	leaveneth

leviathan
levitical
leviticus
liberally
lightened
lightness
lightning
lingereth
lionesses
loathsome
loftiness
lookforin
loruhamah
lowliness
maachathi
macedonia
machbanai
machbenah
machpelah
madmannah
magdalene
magicians
magnified
mahazioth
makheloth
malchijah
malchiram
malicious
malignity
mandrakes
manslayer
maranatha
marchedst
marriages
marvelled
masteries
mathusala
mattaniah
mattathah
mazzaroth
measuring
medicines
mehetabel
mentioned
meonothai
merarites
merathaim
merchants
mercurius
mercyseat
meribbaal
meshullam
mesobaite
messenger
methusael
midianite
migdalgad
mightiest
millstone

ministers
minstrels
mischiefs
miserable
miserably
mispereth
moabitess
moabitish
moderator
moistened
mollified
momentous
monuments
mortality
mortgaged
motheaten
mountains
multitude
munitions
murderers
murmurers
murmuring
musicians
mustereth
mysteries
nakedness
naphtuhim
narcissus
narrative
nathanael
naturally
nazarenes
nazarites
necessary
necessity
neglected
negligent
nehushtan
neighbour
neighings
nethaneel
nethaniah
nethinims
newsgroup
nicodemus
nicopolis
ninevites
northward
nourished
nourisher
numberest
numbering
obedience
obeisance
oblations
obscurity
observers
observest
observeth

obstinate
obtaineth
obtaining
obviously
occasions
occupiers
occupieth
occurrent
offenders
offerings
offspring
ointments
oliveyard
operation
oppressed
oppressor
ordaineth
orderings
ordinance
ornaments
ossifrage
ostriches
otherwise
ourselves
outgoings
outwardly
overdrive
overflown
overlived
overseers
oversight
overtaken
overthrew
overthrow
overwhelm
pacifieth
padanaram
paintedst
palestina
palestine
palluites
pamphylia
paradoxes
paramours
pardoneth
parmashta
partakers
partakest
parthians
partition
partridge
pasdammim
passovers
pathrusim
patiently
patriarch
patrimony
pavilions
peaceable

peaceably
pedigrees
pentecost
perceived
perdition
perezuzza
perfected
perfectly
performed
perisheth
perishing
perizzite
permitted
perpetual
perplexed
persecute
persuaded
pertained
perverted
pestilent
pethahiah
petitions
pharisees
pharzites
philistia
philistim
phygellus
physician
piercings
plainness
plantedst
plantings
plausible
pleadings
pleasures
plenteous
plentiful
plumbline
pochereth
polishing
polluting
pollution
pondereth
possessed
possessor
posterity
potentate
potsherds
practices
practised
pransings
preachest
preacheth
preaching
preferred
preparest
prepareth
preparing
presented

presently
preserved
preserver
prevailed
prevented
principal
priscilla
prisoners
privately
proceeded
prochorus
procureth
profaneth
profaning
professed
profiteth
profiting
prolonged
promising
promoting
promotion
pronounce
proselyte
prospered
protested
provender
provideth
providing
provinces
provision
provoketh
provoking
prudently
ptolemais
publicans
publickly
published
purchased
purifieth
purifying
purposeth
purposing
questions
quickened
quietness
rabshakeh
ramathite
readiness
reasoning
rebellest
rebellion
receiveth
receiving
reckoneth
reckoning
reconcile
recovered
redeemeth
redeeming

referring	rudiments	sheminith	springing	therefore
refrained	sabtechah	shepherds	sprinkled	therefrom
refreshed	sackcloth	sherebiah	stability	thereinto
refusedst	sacrifice	shewbread	staggered	thereunto
regardest	sacrilege	shilonite	standards	thereupon
regardeth	sadducees	shiphmite	stephanas	therewith
regarding	safeguard	shipwreck	stiffened	thickness
rehearsed	salathiel	shortened	stomacher	thirsteth
rejecteth	salvation	shoulders	stoutness	thirtieth
rejoicest	samaritan	shouldest	straitest	thousands
rejoiceth	sanballat	shoutings	strangely	threefold
rejoicing	sanctuary	shulamite	strangers	thresheth
relieveth	sansannah	shuthelah	strangled	threshing
religious	sapphires	sibbechai	stretched	threshold
remainder	sarsechim	sibbolcth	stripling	thronging
remainest	satisfied	sidonians	strivings	throughly
remaineth	savourest	signified	strongest	thrusteth
remaining	scapegoat	sincerely	struggled	thundered
remission	scattered	sincerity	stumbleth	timotheus
renderest	scholarly	situation	stumbling	tirshatha
rendereth	scorpions	sixteenth	subduedst	tolerable
rendering	scourgeth	sixtyfold	subjected	tormented
renounced	scourging	skilfully	submitted	tottering
repairing	scrabbled	skippedst	subscribe	townclerk
repeateth	scripture	slackness	substance	tradition
repentest	seafaring	slandered	subverted	translate
repenteth	searchest	slaughter	succeeded	travailed
repenting	searcheth	slimepits	succoured	travelled
replenish	searching	slumbered	succourer	traveller
reprobate	seditions	smootheth	sucklings	treachery
reproveth	semachiah	soberness	sufferest	treasured
requested	sentences	sodomites	suffereth	treasurer
requirest	separated	sojourned	suffering	treasures
requireth	sepulchre	sojourner	sufficeth	trembleth
requiring	seraphims	solemnity	sunrising	trembling
requiting	serjeants	something	supplieth	tributary
resembled	servitude	sometimes	supposing	trickleth
reserveth	sevenfold	sophereth	surprised	triumphed
resisteth	seventeen	sorcerers	sustained	trophimus
respected	severally	sorceress	swaddling	troublest
respecter	shaashgaz	sorceries	swallowed	troubleth
responses	shadowing	sorroweth	sweetness	troubling
restoreth	shaharaim	sorrowful	swellings	troublous
restraint	shamariah	sorrowing	sycomores	trustedst
retaineth	sharonite	sosipater	synagogue	tubalcain
returneth	sharpened	sosthenes	tacklings	twentieth
returning	sharpness	soundness	tahanites	twinkling
reubenite	shaulites	southward	tahapanes	uncertain
revealeth	shealtiel	sparingly	tahpanhes	unclothed
revengers	shebaniah	speakings	tanhumeth	uncovered
revengeth	shecaniah	specially	temanites	undefiled
revenging	sheepcote	spectacle	temperate	undertake
reverence	sheepfold	spikenard	terrified	undertook
revilings	shehariah	spiritual	tertullus	undressed
revolters	shelemiah	spokesman	testament	unequally
revolting	shelomith	spreadest	testified	unfeigned
rewardeth	shelomoth	spreadeth	testimony	unlearned
righteous	shelumiel	spreading	thaddaeus	unmarried
robertson	shemariah	springeth	tharshish	unmindful

unperfect
unsavoury
unskilful
unspotted
unstopped
unweighed
upbraided
upholdest
upholdeth
upholding
uppermost
uprightly
utterance
uttermost
vagabonds
vainglory
vajezatha
valiantly
vanisheth
vengeance
vermilion
vestments
vexations
vineyards
violently
virginity
voluntary
wallowing
wanderers
wanderest
wandereth
wandering
wasteness
watchings
wateredst
waterpots
wayfaring
weakeneth
weariness
wearisome
weightier
wherefore
whereinto
whereunto
whereupon
wherewith
whirlwind
whispered
whisperer
wholesome
whoredoms
whosoever
widowhood
willingly
winepress
winnoweth
withdrawn
withereth

withstand
withstood
witnessed
witnesses
wittingly
womankind
wonderful
wondering
woundedst
yesterday
zaanannim
zacchaeus
zachariah
zacharias
zarephath
zealously
zechariah
zephaniah
zephathah
zidonians
zorobabel

8

abednego
abelmaim
abhorred
abialbon
abiasaph
abiathar
abinadab
abounded
absolute
abundant
accepted
accounts
accurate
accursed
accusers
accuseth
accusing
aceldama
achaicus
achmetha
achshaph
acquaint
activity
actually
addicted
addition
adithaim
admonish
adonijah
adonikam
adoniram
adoption
adorneth

adorning
adultery
advanced
advocate
affected
affinity
affirmed
affright
ahinadab
aholibah
ahuzzath
akrabbim
alienate
alleging
allegory
alleluia
alloweth
almighty
alphaeus
altereth
although
ambushes
american
amethyst
aminadab
ammonite
amorites
amraphel
analysis
anathema
anathoth
ancients
anointed
answered
anything
anywhere
apollyon
apostles
appealed
appeared
appeased
appetite
approach
approved
arabians
arcturus
arelites
argument
aridatha
armholes
arodites
aroerite
arphaxad
arrested
arriving
articles
arvadite
asarelah

ascended
ascribed
ashkelon
ashkenaz
ashpenaz
asnapper
assaying
assemble
assembly
assented
asshurim
assigned
asswaged
assyrian
astaroth
astonied
athaliah
attained
attempts
attended
audience
augustus
availeth
avengeth
avenging
avoiding
avouched
azmaveth
baalmeon
baalpeor
baaseiah
babbling
backbone
backside
backward
balances
baldness
banished
baptisms
baptized
barabbas
barachel
barefoot
barjesus
barnabas
barsabas
bastards
bathshua
battered
bdellium
beauties
beautify
becamest
beckoned
becometh
bedstead
beeliada
beerelim

befallen
beggarly
begotten
beguiled
behaveth
beheaded
behemoth
belaites
believed
believer
believes
belonged
bemoaned
benefits
benhadad
benhanan
benjamin
berachah
bereaved
beriites
berothah
berothai
besieged
besought
bestowed
betharam
bethaven
bethemek
bethesda
bethezel
bethmeon
bethpeor
bethshan
betrayed
bettered
bewailed
bezaleel
biblical
bigthana
birthday
bithynia
bitterly
blackish
blasting
bleating
blessest
blesseth
blessing
blindeth
blossoms
blotteth
blotting
blueness
boasters
boastest
boasteth
boasting
boldness

bondmaid	casiphia	clothest	crescens	desolate
borrowed	casluhim	clothing	cretians	despised
borrower	castaway	clusters	crisping	detailed
bracelet	castedst	colhozeh	crossway	detained
brambles	catcheth	coloured	crownest	devilish
branches	causeway	combined	crowneth	deviseth
brandish	cemetery	combines	crowning	devoured
brawlers	cenchrea	comforts	cumbered	devourer
brawling	chaldean	comments	cursedst	dibongad
breaches	chaldees	commonly	cursings	diggedst
breakest	chambers	communed	curtains	diligent
breaketh	champion	compared	cuttings	diminish
breaking	chanceth	complain	cyrenian	dinaites
breathed	changers	complete	cyrenius	dinhabah
breeches	changest	compound	daberath	directed
breeding	changeth	computer	dainties	directly
brethren	changing	conaniah	dalmatia	disallow
bridleth	channels	conceits	damascus	disannul
bringers	chapiter	conceive	damnable	disciple
bringest	chargers	conclude	darkened	disclose
bringeth	chargest	conflict	darkness	discover
bringing	charging	confound	daughers	discreet
brothers	chariots	confused	daughter	diseased
bruising	charmers	cononiah	deadness	diseases
bucklers	charming	consider	dealings	disgrace
buffeted	chastise	constant	decayeth	disguise
builders	cheating	consumed	deceased	dismayed
buildest	checking	contempt	deceived	dispatch
buildeth	cheereth	continue	deceiver	disperse
building	cheerful	contrary	decently	disposed
bullocks	chelubai	contrite	decision	disprove
bulwarks	chesalon	converts	deckedst	disputed
burdened	chestnut	conveyed	declared	disputer
burnings	chickens	convince	declined	disquiet
bursting	chiefest	cottages	decrease	dissolve
business	childish	coucheth	dedicate	distress
busybody	children	couching	deepness	divideth
buttocks	choicest	couldest	defaming	dividing
caesarea	choosest	coulters	defenced	diviners
caiaphas	chooseth	councils	defended	divineth
calamity	choosing	counsels	deferred	divining
caldrons	chorazin	counteth	defilers	division
calledst	churches	counting	defileth	divorced
camphire	churlish	coupleth	delayeth	doctrine
cankered	churning	coupling	delicate	document
captains	cinnamon	covenant	delights	dominion
captives	circuits	coverest	delivery	doubteth
carcases	cisterns	covereth	delusion	doubtful
careless	citizens	covering	demanded	doubting
carmites	claiming	coveteth	denounce	downward
carnally	clappeth	covetous	departed	dragging
carriage	claudius	crashing	deprived	dreadful
carriest	cleansed	createth	deputies	dreamers
carrieth	cleanses	creation	derision	dreameth
carrying	clearing	creature	describe	dressers
carshena	cleaveth	credible	desirest	dresseth
carvingg	clemency	creditor	desireth	drinkers
carvings	cleophas	creepeth	desiring	drinketh
casement	climbeth	creeping	desirous	drinking

182

droppeth
dropping
drunkard
drusilla
dulcimer
dunghill
dwellers
dwellest
dwelleth
dwelling
earrings
eastward
ebenezer
ebiasaph
edifieth
edifying
edomites
effected
egyptian
eighteen
elamites
elbethel
election
elements
eleventh
eliasaph
eliashib
eliathah
elioenai
elishama
elisheba
elnathan
elonites
eloquent
elzaphan
embalmed
embraced
emeralds
emmanuel
employed
emptiers
encamped
endamage
endanger
endureth
enduring
eneglaim
engannim
engraven
engraver
enhaddah
enjoined
enlarged
enquired
enriched
enrimmon
ensample
ensnared
entangle

entereth
entering
enticeth
enticing
entirely
entities
entrance
envyings
epaphras
ephesian
ephratah
episodes
epistles
equality
eranites
escapeth
escaping
eschewed
eshtemoa
eshtemoh
espoused
esteemed
estimate
eternity
ethiopia
eutychus
evenings
eventide
evermore
evidence
evildoer
exacteth
exaction
exactors
exaltest
exalteth
examined
examples
exceeded
excelled
excepted
exchange
excluded
excusing
executed
exempted
exercise
exhorted
expected
expelled
expenses
explains
exploits
extended
extolled
eyebrows
eyesalve
eyesight
ezrahite

faintest
fainteth
faithful
familiar
families
famished
farewell
farthing
fashions
fastened
fastings
fatlings
favoured
feasting
feathers
feignest
festival
fetcheth
fidelity
fiftieth
fighteth
fighting
filledst
filleted
finished
finisher
firepans
flattery
fleddest
flourish
followed
forcible
forecast
forehead
foreknew
foreknow
foremost
forepart
foreship
foreskin
foretell
foretold
forewarn
forgiven
forsaken
forswear
fortieth
fortress
fouledst
foundest
fountain
fourfold
fourteen
freckled
freewill
frequent
fretteth
fretting
friendly

fruitful
fugitive
furlongs
furnaces
gabbatha
galbanum
gamaliel
gardener
garlands
garments
garrison
gathered
gatherer
gedaliah
gederite
gederoth
geliloth
gemariah
gendered
generate
gentiles
genubath
gezrites
giblites
giddalti
gilonite
ginnetho
gittites
gizonite
gladness
gleaning
gloriest
glorieth
glorious
glorying
gnasheth
gnashing
golgotha
gomorrah
gomorrha
goodlier
goodness
gorgeous
governor
gracious
gravings
greatest
grecians
greedily
greenish
greeteth
greeting
grieveth
grieving
grievous
grinders
grinding
groaneth
groaning

grounded
grudging
gudgodah
habakkuk
hachilah
hachmoni
hadashah
hadassah
hadattah
hagerite
haggites
hakkatan
hallowed
halohesh
hamongog
hanameel
hananeel
hananiah
handfuls
handleth
handling
handmaid
hangings
haphraim
happened
hararite
harbonah
hardened
hardness
harhaiah
harmless
harodite
harorite
harumaph
hasadiah
hasenuah
hashubah
hashupha
hastened
hatcheth
hazarded
hazeroth
headlong
healings
heardest
heartily
heavenly
heresies
heretick
hereunto
herewith
heritage
herodias
herodion
herschel
hezekiah
hiddekel
higgaion
highness

highways	internet	josaphat	lionlike	mejarkon
hindered	intreaty	josedech	loatheth	melatiah
hindmost	invasion	josibiah	lodgings	melchiah
hireling	invented	journeys	longedst	memorial
hitherto	inwardly	joyfully	lordship	mentions
hittites	irnahash	jozachar	lowering	meonenim
hizkijah	iscariot	judgment	lukewarm	mephaath
hodaviah	ishmaiah	kedemoth	lunatick	meraioth
holiness	ishmerai	kenezite	lycaonia	merchant
homeborn	issachar	killedst	lysanias	merciful
honestly	ithrites	kindleth	maaseiah	meremoth
honoured	izrahiah	kindness	madmenah	merodach
horonaim	izrahite	kindreds	magician	meshobab
horonite	jaakobah	kingdoms	magpiash	meteyard
horrible	jahaziah	kinsfolk	mahalath	michaiah
horribly	jahaziel	kirheres	mahanaim	michmash
horseman	jahzerah	kithlish	mahavite	midnight
horsemen	jangling	kneeling	mahlites	midwives
hoshaiah	japhleti	knocketh	mainsail	migdalol
hostages	jaresiah	knocking	maintain	mightest
housetop	jathniel	korahite	majority	mightier
howlings	jealousy	korhites	makkedah	mighties
humbleth	jealeral	kushaiah	malchiah	mightily
humility	jebusite	laboured	malchiel	mikneiah
hundreds	jecamiah	labourer	maleleel	millions
hungered	jecoliah	lahairoi	mallothi	miniamin
husbands	jeconiah	lamented	manahath	minished
idleness	jedidiah	landmark	manasseh	minister
idolater	jeduthun	language	manasses	ministry
idolatry	jehdeiah	languish	manifest	minstrel
igdaliah	jehoadah	lanterns	manifold	miracles
ignominy	jehoahaz	laodicea	mansions	mischief
ignorant	jehoiada	lapidoth	maonites	miseries
imagined	jehoshua	lasharon	mareshah	mistress
immanuel	jehubbah	laugheth	mariners	mithnite
immortal	jekameam	laughing	marishes	mitylene
imparted	jekamiah	laughter	marriage	moabites
impotent	jeopardy	launched	marrieth	mockings
impudent	jephthae	lawfully	marrying	moisture
imputeth	jephthah	lawgiver	masrekah	monogram
imputing	jeremiah	leanness	material	monsters
inasmuch	jeremias	learning	mattanah	mordecai
incensed	jeremoth	leathern	mattatha	moreover
incident	jerimoth	leavened	mattenai	mortally
inclined	jeroboam	lebbaeus	matthias	moseroth
inclosed	jerushah	lengthen	mattocks	mountain
increase	jeshaiah	lentiles	mealtime	mounting
indebted	jeshanah	leopards	measured	mourners
inditing	jeshimon	letushim	measures	mourneth
infamous	jeshurun	lewdness	mebunnai	mourning
inferior	jesimiel	libnites	meddleth	moveable
infinite	jesuites	lifetime	meddling	mufflers
informed	jezaniah	lightest	mediator	mulberry
iniquity	jimnites	lighteth	medicine	multiple
innocent	jochebed	lighting	meditate	multiply
insomuch	jogbehah	likeness	meekness	munition
instance	joinings	likewise	megiddon	murderer
instruct	joktheel	limiteth	mehujael	murmured
intended	jonathan	lingered	mehunims	mushites

mustered	ordereth	phaltiel	pricking	reckoned
muttered	ordinary	pharisee	princess	recorded
naamites	ornament	phenicia	prisoner	recorder
nahaliel	oughtest	philemon	problems	redeemed
nahallal	outcasts	philetus	proclaim	redeemer
nahamani	outlived	philippi	procured	reelaiah
naphtali	overcame	phinehas	profaned	reformed
narrowed	overcome	pibeseth	profited	refuseth
narrower	overflow	pictures	profound	regarded
narrowly	overlaid	pierceth	promised	register
nativity	overmuch	piercing	promises	rehabiah
nazarene	overpass	pilgrims	promoted	rehearse
nazareth	overpast	pinnacle	prophecy	rehoboam
nazarite	overplus	pirathon	prophesy	rehoboth
neapolis	overseer	pitchers	prophets	reignest
nebaioth	overtake	plaister	proposed	reigneth
nebajoth	overtook	plaiting	prospect	reigning
neballat	overturn	planters	proverbs	rejected
nedabiah	pacified	planteth	provided	rejoiced
neesings	painting	planting	provides	released
nehemiah	paleness	playedst	province	relieved
nehushta	parables	pleadeth	provoked	religion
neighing	paradise	pleasant	prudence	remained
nephtoah	pardoned	pleaseth	psalmist	remaliah
nephusim	parlours	pleasing	psaltery	remember
netophah	parmenas	pleasure	publican	remitted
networks	partaker	pleiades	punished	remotely
nineteen	partners	plotteth	purchase	removeth
nobleman	passages	plucketh	pureness	removing
noontide	passedst	pointing	purified	rendered
northern	passions	polished	purifier	renewest
nostrils	passover	polluted	purposed	renewing
numbered	pastures	pondered	purposes	renowned
numerous	patience	populous	pursuers	repaired
obededom	patrobas	portions	pursueth	repairer
obedient	patterns	positive	pursuing	repayeth
obeyedst	pavement	possible	quantity	repented
oblation	pavilion	postings	quarries	rephaiah
observed	peacocks	potiphar	quarters	rephaims
observer	peculiar	potsherd	quenched	rephidim
obtained	pedahzur	pouredst	question	replaced
occasion	pekahiah	pourtray	quieteth	repliest
occupied	pelaliah	powerful	quivered	replying
offences	pelatiah	practise	rabsaris	reported
offended	pelonite	praiseth	railings	reproach
offender	peninnah	praising	ransomed	reproofs
offereth	penknife	pransing	rattleth	reproved
offering	perceive	preached	rattling	reprover
officers	perfumed	preacher	ravening	requests
ofttimes	perfumes	precepts	ravenous	required
ointment	pergamos	precious	ravished	requited
onesimus	perilous	prepared	reacheth	rereward
openings	perished	presence	reaching	rescueth
opinions	perjured	presents	reasoned	research
opposest	persians	preserve	rebelled	resemble
opposeth	persuade	presseth	rebuketh	reserved
opposite	perverse	pressfat	rebuking	resisted
orchards	petition	presumed	received	resolved
ordained	peulthai	pretence	receiver	resorted

response	security	shipping	speedily	suggests
restored	sedition	shooters	spendest	sukkiims
restorer	seducers	shooteth	spendeth	sundered
restrain	seduceth	shooting	spitting	supplant
retained	seducing	shophach	spoilers	supplied
returned	seedtime	shoulder	spoilest	supposed
revealed	seething	shouteth	spoileth	sureties
revealer	selected	shouting	spoiling	surnamed
revenged	seleucia	shunites	sporting	swaddled
revenger	selfsame	shutteth	sprinkle	swearers
revenges	selfwill	shutting	stablish	sweareth
revenues	selvedge	sibbecai	stamping	swearing
reverend	senators	sickness	stanched	sweeping
revilers	sentence	silvanus	standard	swelling
revilest	separate	singular	standest	swimmest
reviving	sepharad	siphmoth	standeth	swimmeth
revolted	sequence	sixscore	standing	sycamine
rewarded	serpents	skipping	statutes	sycomore
rewarder	servants	slanders	stoaloth	syntyche
riddance	servedst	sleepest	stealing	syracuse
ripening	servitor	sleepeth	stedfast	tabbaoth
roarings	settings	sleeping	steppeth	tabering
roasteth	selllest	slightly	stewards	tabrimon
roebucks	settling	slingers	sticketh	tackling
rumbling	severity	slippery	stillest	tahpenes
sabbaths	shaalbim	slippeth	stilleth	tapestry
sabtecha	shaaraim	slothful	stingeth	tarriest
saltness	shadrach	sluggard	stinketh	tarrieth
saltpits	shalisha	smallest	stinking	tarrying
saluteth	shambles	smelleth	stirreth	tarshish
sanctify	shameful	smelling	stirring	tattlers
sapphira	shamhuth	smoother	stoodest	taunting
sapphire	shammoth	snorting	stoopeth	taxation
sardites	shammuah	snuffers	stooping	teachers
sardonyx	sharezer	snuffeth	stoppeth	teachest
satiated	sharuhen	sobriety	straight	teacheth
saturday	shearers	sodering	straiten	teaching
saviours	sheariah	sodomite	straitly	tebaliah
scabbard	shearing	sofsongs	stranger	tehinnah
scaffold	shebarim	soldiers	strength	tekoites
scarcely	sheddeth	solemnly	stricken	telassar
sceptres	shedding	solitary	striketh	telharsa
scoffers	shemaiah	solution	stringed	telmelah
scorched	shemeber	somebody	stripped	temanite
scorners	shemidah	sometime	striveth	tempered
scornest	shenazar	somewhat	striving	temporal
scorneth	shepherd	sorcerer	stronger	tempteth
scornful	sherezer	sorrowed	strongly	tempting
scorning	sheriffs	soundeth	stubborn	teraphim
scorpion	sheshach	sounding	studieth	terraces
scourged	shewedst	sparkled	stumbled	terrible
scourges	shilshah	sparrows	subdueth	terribly
scythian	shimeath	speakest	suborned	testator
searched	shimites	speaketh	subtilly	tetrarch
seasoned	shimrath	speaking	subtilty	thankful
seatward	shimrith	spearmen	suckling	thanking
secretly	shimshai	specific	suddenly	thelasar
secundus	shiphrah	speckled	suffered	thereout
securely	shiphtan	speeches	sufficed	thickets

thinkest
thinketh
thinking
thirsted
thirteen
thistles
thorough
thoughts
thousand
threaten
threshed
threwest
thronged
throwing
thunders
thyatira
tiberias
tiberius
timbrels
tinkling
tirhakah
tirhanah
tishbite
togarmah
together
tolaites
tomorrow
torments
tortoise
tortured
tossings
toucheth
touching
traffick
traitors
treaders
treadeth
treading
treasure
treasury
treatise
trembled
trespass
trimmest
troubled
troubler
troubles
trumpets
trustest
trusteth
trusting
tryphena
tryphosa
twilight
twoedged
tychicus
tyrannus
uchicago
unawares

unbelief
unbiased
uncomely
ungirded
unicorns
unjustly
unlawful
unlikely
unseemly
unstable
unstated
untarred
untimely
untoward
unwalled
unwashen
unworthy
upharsin
upholden
uprising
uttereth
uttering
vagabond
vanished
vanities
variance
vaunteth
vehement
venomous
veracity
verbatim
verified
versions
vestures
vexation
victuals
vigilant
vigorous
villages
vineyard
violated
violence
virtuous
visitest
visiteth
visiting
vocation
vomiteth
vultures
wakeneth
walkedst
wallowed
wandered
wardrobe
warriors
washings
watchers
watcheth
watchful

watching
watchman
watchmen
waterest
watereth
watering
waterloo
waterpot
wavereth
wavering
waymarks
weakened
weakness
wearieth
weigheth
weighing
westward
whirleth
whoredom
wickedly
wideness
wilfully
winnowed
wintered
withdraw
withdrew
withered
withheld
withhold
wondered
wondrous
wormwood
worthies
worthily
wouldest
woundeth
wounding
wrathful
wreathed
wreathen
wrestled
wretched
wringing
wrinkles
writings
wrongeth
yieldeth
yielding
youngest
youthful
zalmonah
zalmunna
zarhites
zartanah
zebadiah
zebedees
zedekiah
zemaraim
zemarite

zerahiah
zererath
zidkijah
ziphites
zipporah
zoheleth

7

abaddon
abagtha
abasing
abideth
abiding
abiezer
abigail
abihail
abilene
ability
abimael
abinoam
abishag
abishai
abishua
abishur
abjects
abodest
abolish
abraham
absalom
absence
abstain
abusers
abusing
account
accused
accuser
actions
adamant
adjured
admatha
admired
adoraim
adorned
adullam
adummim
advised
affairs
afflict
agagite
against
agreeth
agrippa
aground
aharhel
ahasbai
ahaziah
ahiezer

ahimaaz
ahimoth
ahinoam
ahishar
ahohite
aholiab
aijalon
alameth
alamoth
alemeth
allowed
almodad
almonds
already
altered
amariah
amashai
amasiah
amaziah
amiable
amittai
ammihud
amongst
amorite
amplias
anakims
ananiah
ananias
anchors
ancient
angered
anguish
another
answers
antioch
antipas
apelles
aphekah
apollos
apostle
apparel
appears
appease
applied
appoint
approve
arabian
araunah
archers
archite
ardites
arguing
ariseth
arising
armenia
armoury
arrayed
arrival
arrived

artemas	barrels	bilshan	bulrush	chatter
article	baskets	bindeth	bunches	checked
aruboth	basmath	binding	bundles	checker
asahiah	bastard	bishlam	burdens	cheeses
asareel	battles	bishops	buriers	chelluh
ascends	bazlith	bithiah	burneth	chemosh
ascribe	bazluth	bithron	burning	chenani
asenath	bealiah	bittern	burying	cherish
ashamed	bealoth	blacker	butlers	cherith
ashriel	bearers	blasted	calamus	chesnut
ashvath	bearest	blastus	caldron	cheweth
askelon	beareth	blemish	calkers	chiding
aspatha	bearing	blessed	callest	chiefly
assault	beatest	blinded	calleth	chileab
assayed	beateth	bloomed	calling	chilion
assumed	beating	blossom	calvary	chilmad
assumes	because	blotted	calveth	chimham
assured	bedeiah	bloweth	candace	chimney
asswage	beeroth	blowing	candles	chisleu
assyria	begging	boasted	caphtor	chislon
asunder	beguile	bocheru	captain	chittim
asuppim	behaved	boiling	captive	chozeba
ataroth	behoved	bolster	carcase	christs
athaiah	beliefs	bondage	careful	cilicia
athirst	believe	bondman	carried	circuit
attalia	bellies	bondmen	castest	cistern
attempt	bellows	bonnets	casteth	citizen
attired	beloved	booties	casting	claimed
augment	benaiah	borders	castles	clamour
austere	benammi	boscath	causest	clapped
authors	benches	bottles	causeth	claudia
avenged	bendeth	bottoms	causing	cleanse
avenger	bending	bozkath	ceaseth	clearer
avoided	beneath	brakest	ceasing	clearly
awakest	benefit	bramble	ceiling	cleaved
awaketh	benhail	bravery	cellars	clement
awaking	beraiah	brawler	censers	cleopas
azaliah	bereave	breadth	certain	climbed
azaniah	berites	breaker	certify	clipped
azarael	bernice	breasts	chalcol	closest
azareel	berries	breathe	chaldea	closets
azariah	beseech	bribery	chamber	clothed
azaziah	besides	bridles	chamois	clothes
azrikam	besiege	briefly	chanaan	clouted
baalath	bestead	broader	changed	cluster
baalgad	bethany	broadus	changes	collars
babbler	bethcar	broided	channel	college
babylon	bethink	broiled	chapmen	collops
badgers	bethuel	brother	charged	colosse
badness	bethzur	brought	charger	colours
bahurim	betimes	bruised	charges	combine
baladan	betonim	bruises	chariot	comfort
balance	betroth	brutish	charity	comings
banners	between	buckets	charmed	command
banquet	betwixt	buckler	charmer	commend
baptism	biddeth	builded	charran	comment
baptist	bidding	builder	chaseth	commune
baptize	bigthan	bukkiah	chasing	compact
barjona	billows	bullock	chasten	company

compare	current	denieth	driedst	enhazor
compass	cursest	denying	driveth	enjoyed
conceal	curseth	deposed	driving	enlarge
conceit	cursing	deputed	dropped	enquire
concern	curtain	derided	drought	enquiry
concord	custody	descend	drowned	enrogel
condemn	customs	descent	drunken	ensigns
conduct	cuttest	deserts	dryshod	entered
conduit	cutteth	deserve	dumping	enticed
confess	cutting	desired	dungeon	entreat
confirm	cymbals	desires	durable	entries
conquer	cypress	despair	dwelled	enviest
consent	dabareh	despise	earnest	envieth
consist	dalaiah	despite	earneth	envious
consult	dalphon	destroy	earring	environ
consume	damaris	details	earthen	envying
contain	damsels	devices	earthly	ephesus
contemn	dancing	devised	ebronah	ephraim
contend	dandled	devoted	edified	ephrath
content	danites	diamond	edition	epistle
convert	danjaan	diblaim	editors	equally
corinth	darkish	diblath	edomite	erastus
corners	darling	diddest	elealeh	erected
cornets	dasheth	didymus	eleasah	escaped
corpses	daubing	diggeth	eleazar	eshbaal
correct	dawning	dignity	elected	eshtaol
corrupt	daysman	dimness	elegant	estates
cottage	daytime	dimonah	elhanan	eternal
couched	deacons	dippeth	eliadah	ethanim
couches	dealers	discern	eliahba	ethbaal
coulter	dealest	discord	eliakim	eubulus
council	dealeth	discuss	elienai	eunuchs
counsel	dealing	disease	eliezer	euodias
counted	debates	dispute	eliphal	evening
country	deborah	distaff	eliphaz	evident
coupled	debtors	distant	eliseus	exacted
courage	decayed	ditches	elishah	exactly
courses	decease	diverse	elishua	exalted
cousins	deceits	divided	elkanah	examine
covered	deceive	divider	ellasar	example
coveted	decided	divorce	elmodam	exclude
craveth	deckest	dizahab	elpalet	excused
created	decketh	doctors	elparan	execute
creates	declare	dodanim	eltekeh	expired
creator	decline	dodavah	eltekon	explain
crimson	decreed	doleful	eltolad	expound
cripple	decrees	dophkah	elzabad	express
crispus	dedanim	doubled	embrace	extenso
crooked	defamed	doubted	emerald	extinct
cropped	defence	dragons	emerods	extreme
crowned	defiled	draught	eminent	eyelids
crucify	defraud	drawers	emptied	ezekias
cruelly	degrees	draweth	enabled	ezekiel
cruelty	delaiah	drawing	endless	faileth
crushed	delayed	dreamed	endured	failing
crystal	delight	dreamer	enemies	fainted
cunning	delilah	dressed	engaged	fairest
curdled	deliver	dresser	engines	fallest
curious	denials	drewest	engrave	falleth

189

falling	foameth	gederah	hammath	herdmen
falsely	foaming	gemalli	hammers	herself
famines	foldeth	general	hamonah	heshbon
fanners	folding	genesis	hamutal	heshmon
farther	follows	gentile	handful	hethlon
fashion	foolish	gerizim	handled	highest
fastest	footmen	gershom	handles	highway
fasting	forbare	gershon	hangeth	hilkiah
fathers	forbear	geshuri	hanging	himself
fathoms	forborn	getteth	hanniel	hissing
fatling	forcing	getting	happens	history
fatness	foresaw	gibeath	happier	hittite
fattest	forests	gideoni	haradah	hivites
fearest	forgave	gilalai	harbona	hizkiah
feareth	forgers	girdest	harlots	hodaiah
fearful	forgive	girdeth	harmony	hodevah
fearing	formeth	girding	harness	hodijah
feasted	forsake	girdles	harpers	holdest
feebler	forsook	gittaim	harping	holdeth
feedest	fortify	gittite	harrows	holding
feedeth	forward	glasses	harvest	holiest
feeding	founded	gleaned	hasshub	holyday
feeling	founder	glitter	hasteth	honesty
feigned	fowlers	glorify	hastily	honours
fellest	frameth	glutton	hasting	hopkins
felling	frankly	gnashed	hasupha	horites
felloes	freedom	goddess	hateful	hornets
fellows	freeman	godhead	hathath	hosanna
fervent	fresher	goliath	hatipha	hoshama
fetched	fretted	goodman	hattush	hottest
fetters	friends	gospels	haughty	houghed
fewness	fringes	graffed	havilah	howbeit
fiercer	froward	granted	hazaiah	however
fifteen	fulfill	graveth	hazerim	howling
fifties	fullers	graving	healeth	humbled
figures	fulness	gravity	healing	hundred
fillest	furbish	greater	heapeth	hungred
filleth	furious	greatly	hearers	hunters
fillets	furnace	greaves	hearest	huntest
filling	furnish	grieved	heareth	hunteth
finally	furrows	grisled	hearing	hunting
findest	further	groaned	hearken	hurleth
findeth	gabriel	gropeth	hearted	hurling
finding	gaddest	groweth	heathen	hurtful
fingers	gaddiel	guiding	heavens	hurting
finland	gadites	gunites	heavier	husband
firkins	gainsay	gurbaal	heavily	ibneiah
fishers	galatia	gutters	hebrews	ibnijah
fishing	galilee	habaiah	hedrick	ichabod
fitches	gallant	habakuk	heights	iconium
fitteth	gallery	hadoram	heinous	idumaea
flagons	gallows	hadrach	helkath	imagery
flaming	gardens	hagabah	helmets	imagine
flatter	garlick	haggeri	helpers	implead
fleeing	garment	haggiah	helpeth	imposed
fleshly	garmite	haggith	helping	imputed
flowers	garners	hakupha	hemlock	incense
floweth	garnish	halteth	henadad	incline
flowing	gazites	halting	herdman	inclose

infants	jeroham	kinsman	levites	maktesh
infidel	jerusha	kinsmen	liberal	malachi
inflame	jesaiah	kirioth	liberty	malcham
inhabit	jeshuah	kirjath	libyans	malchus
inherit	jesting	kishion	licence	mallows
injured	jesurun	kneaded	licketh	malluch
inkhorn	jetheth	kneeled	liftest	mankind
instant	jethlah	knewest	lifteth	manners
instead	jezebel	knocked	lifting	mantles
intents	jezliah	knowest	lighted	maralah
intreat	jezreel	knoweth	lighten	marched
invaded	jidlaph	knowing	lighter	markest
invited	jiphtah	kolaiah	lightly	marketh
involve	joatham	labours	likened	markets
inwards	johanan	lachish	limited	married
ishijah	joiakim	lackest	lineage	marsena
ishmael	joiarib	lacketh	lintels	martyrs
islands	joining	lacking	lioness	marvels
ismaiah	jokdeam	lancets	liquors	masters
isshiah	jokmeam	landing	listeth	mastery
italian	jokneam	lappeth	literal	matches
itching	jokshan	lapwing	litters	matters
ithamar	jonadab	lasting	loadeth	matthan
ithream	jorkoam	latchet	locusts	matthat
ithrite	josabad	lattice	lodebar	matthew
ituraea	jotbath	laughed	lodgest	mattock
jaasiel	journey	lawless	lodgeth	meadows
jaaziah	jozabad	lawyers	lodging	meanest
jaaziel	jozadak	layedst	loftily	meaneth
jabneel	judgest	lazarus	longest	meaning
jacinth	judgeth	leaders	longeth	measure
jahazah	judging	leadest	longing	meddled
jahdiel	jumping	leadeth	lookest	meetest
jahleel	juniper	leaneth	looketh	meeteth
jahzeel	jupiter	leaning	looking	meeting
jahziel	justice	leaping	looseth	megiddo
jairite	justify	learned	loosing	mehuman
jambres	kabzeel	leasing	lotheth	mehunim
jamlech	kadmiel	leather	lothing	mekonah
janohah	karnaim	leaveth	lovedst	melteth
japheth	kattath	leaving	lucifer	melting
japhlet	kedemah	lebanah	lurking	members
jarmuth	keepers	lebanon	lusteth	memphis
javelin	keepest	lebaoth	lusting	memucan
jawbone	keepeth	lebonah	lydians	menahem
jealous	keeping	leddest	maachah	mending
jedaiah	kelaiah	leftest	maadiah	mention
jediael	kenites	legions	maarath	meraiah
jedidah	kerioth	lehabim	maasiai	mercies
jehieli	kernels	leisure	maaziah	merging
jehoash	keturah	lendeth	madness	meribah
jehoram	kibzaim	leopard	magbish	merrily
jehovah	kidneys	leprosy	magdala	meshach
jehucal	killest	leprous	magdiel	meshech
jeremai	killeth	letters	magnify	message
jeribai	killing	lettest	mahalah	messiah
jericho	kindled	letteth	maharai	messias
jerijah	kindred	letting	maidens	mezahab
jerioth	kingdom	leummim	majesty	micaiah

michael	needest	outwent	phrases	praying
michmas	needeth	overlay	phrygia	precept
midwife	needful	overran	physics	prepare
mijamin	neglect	oversee	pierced	present
mikloth	neighed	oznites	pigeons	pressed
milalai	neither	painful	pildash	presses
miletum	nephews	painted	pillars	presume
miletus	nephish	palaces	pillows	prevail
mincing	nettles	palsies	pisidia	prevent
mindful	network	paltiel	pisseth	pricked
minding	newborn	paltite	pitched	priests
mingled	newness	panteth	pitcher	princes
minnith	nibshan	parable	pitieth	printed
miphkad	nicanor	parched	pitiful	prisons
miracle	nicolas	parents	plagued	private
mishael	nineveh	parlour	plagues	privily
misheal	nisroch	parnach	plainly	problem
missing	noadiah	parteth	planets	proceed
misused	noisome	partial	planted	process
mithcah	noonday	parties	platted	procure
mixture	notable	parting	platter	produce
mizraim	nothing	partner	players	profane
moabite	nourish	parvaim	playeth	profess
moadiah	numbers	passage	playing	prolong
mockers	nursing	passest	pleaded	promise
mockest	nurture	passeth	pleased	promote
mocketh	nymphas	passing	pledges	prophet
mocking	obadiah	passion	plowers	prosper
moladah	obeyeth	pastors	ploweth	protest
monthly	obeying	pasture	plowing	proudly
morever	obscure	pathros	plowman	proverb
morning	observe	pathway	plowmen	proveth
morsels	offence	patient	plucked	provide
mortify	offered	pattern	plummet	proving
mothers	officer	payment	pointed	provoke
motions	offices	pedahel	pollute	prudent
mounted	oftener	pedaiah	pommels	pruning
mourned	oldness	pelaiah	pontius	publick
mourner	olympas	pelican	poorest	publish
movedst	omitted	peoples	poplars	publius
mowings	openest	perazim	poratha	puffeth
murders	openeth	perfect	porches	puhites
murrain	opening	perform	porcius	pulling
musical	opinion	perfume	porters	punites
mustard	opposed	perhaps	portion	purgeth
mystery	oppress	persian	possess	purging
naarath	oracles	persons	posting	purpose
naashon	oration	persude	pottage	pursued
naasson	orchard	pertain	potters	pursuer
nahalal	ordered	pervert	poureth	pushing
nahalol	orderly	pethuel	pouring	puteoli
naharai	orphans	phanuel	poverty	puttest
nahshon	ostrich	pharaoh	powders	putteth
nailing	othniel	pharosh	praised	putting
naphish	outcast	pharpar	praises	quaking
nations	outline	phaseah	prating	quarrel
natural	outmost	phenice	prayers	quarter
naughty	outside	phichol	prayest	quartus
neariah	outward	phlegon	prayeth	quicken

quickly	rentest	sabaoth	sentest	sheshan
quieted	repayed	sabbath	seraiah	shethar
quietly	rephael	sabeans	sergius	shewest
raamiah	rephaim	sackbut	serpent	sheweth
raamses	replies	saddled	servant	shewing
rabbath	reproof	sadness	servest	shibmah
rabbith	reprove	saffron	serveth	shicron
rabboni	reputed	sailing	service	shields
rafters	request	sailors	servile	shilhim
railing	require	salamis	serving	shillem
raiment	requite	salchah	settest	shiloah
rainbow	rescued	salmone	setteth	shiloni
raiseth	reserve	saluted	setting	shimeah
raising	resheph	samaria	settled	shimeam
raisins	residue	samsung	seventh	shimeon
rakkath	resolve	sandals	seventy	shimrom
rameses	respect	sardine	several	shimron
rampart	respite	sardius	severed	shineth
ranging	restest	sarepta	shachia	shining
reached	resteth	satiate	shadows	shipmen
reaches	resting	satisfy	shaketh	shishak
readest	restore	saviour	shaking	shitrai
readeth	retired	savours	shallum	shittah
reading	returns	savoury	shallun	shittim
reality	revenge	sayings	shalmai	shivers
realize	revenue	scabbed	shalman	shobach
reapers	reverse	scaleth	shameth	shochoh
reapest	reviled	scarest	shamgar	shophan
reapeth	revised	scarlet	shammah	shorter
reaping	revived	scatter	shammai	shortly
reasons	rewards	sceptre	shammua	shouted
rebecca	rhegium	scholar	shapham	shovels
rebekah	ribband	science	shaphan	showers
rebuked	rightly	scorner	shaphat	shrines
rebuker	rioting	scoured	shapher	shubael
rebukes	riotous	scourge	sharaim	shuhite
receipt	riphath	scraped	sharpen	shunned
receive	rithmah	screech	sharper	shupham
records	roareth	scribes	sharply	shuppim
recount	roaring	sealest	shashai	shushan
recover	roasted	sealeth	shashak	shuttle
reddish	robbers	sealing	shavsha	sibraim
redness	robbery	seasons	shearer	sighest
redound	robbeth	secacah	sheaves	sigheth
refined	roebuck	secrets	shebuel	sighing
refiner	rogelim	section	shechem	signets
refrain	rolleth	seduced	shedder	signify
refresh	rolling	seekest	shedeur	silence
refused	roughly	seeketh	shekels	sincere
regions	rubbing	seeking	sheleph	singers
reigned	rubbish	seemeth	shelesh	singeth
rejoice	ruhamah	seirath	shelomi	singing
release	ruinous	sellers	shelter	sinners
relieve	rumours	sellest	shemaah	sinnest
remnant	runnest	selleth	shemida	sinneth
removed	runneth	sendest	shemuel	sinning
remphan	running	sendeth	shepham	sisamai
rending	rusheth	sending	sheresh	sisters
renewed	rushing	sensual	sheshai	sittest

sitteth	spotted	susanna	theudas	twelfth
sitting	spouses	sustain	thicker	twofold
situate	springs	swallow	thicket	unclean
sixteen	squared	swarest	thieves	uncover
skilful	squares	sweeter	thirdly	unction
skipped	stachys	sweetly	thirsty	unequal
slacked	stagger	swelled	thistle	ungodly
slander	stalled	swerved	thither	unicorn
slayeth	stamped	swifter	thought	unknown
slaying	stately	swiftly	thrones	unloose
sleeper	station	swollen	through	untaken
sleight	stature	swooned	thummim	upbraid
slewest	statute	syriack	thunder	upright
slidden	stayeth	syrians	thyself	uttered
slideth	stealth	taanach	tibhath	utterly
slipped	stephen	tabbath	tidings	valiant
sluices	stepped	taberah	tikvath	valleys
slumber	steward	tabitha	tillage	valuest
smelled	stilled	tablets	tillest	vapours
smiters	stirred	tabrets	tilleth	variety
smitest	stoicks	talents	timaeus	various
smiteth	stomach	talitha	timbrel	venison
smiting	stonest	talkers	timnath	venture
smitten	stoning	talkest	timnite	version
smoking	stooped	talketh	timothy	vessels
smotest	stopped	talking	tiphsah	vesture
sneezed	stories	taphath	tithing	victory
snuffed	straits	tappuah	tobijah	victual
soberly	strakes	taralah	toiling	village
society	strange	targets	tongues	villany
sockets	strawed	tarried	tookest	vinegar
sojourn	streams	tasteth	topheth	vintage
soldier	streets	taverns	torches	violent
solomon	stretch	teacher	torment	virgins
somehow	strifes	teareth	toronto	visible
someone	striker	tedious	totally	visions
sopater	strings	tekoite	touched	visited
sorcery	stripes	telabib	trading	vomited
sorrows	strived	tellest	trained	vowedst
sottish	striven	telleth	traitor	vulture
sounded	strokes	telling	trample	wagging
sources	strowed	tempest	travail	wailing
sowedst	stubble	temples	treader	waiteth
spakest	stumble	tempted	treason	waiting
spanned	subdued	tempter	tremble	wakened
spareth	subject	tendeth	tribute	walkest
sparing	suburbs	terrify	trimmed	walketh
sparrow	subvert	terrors	triumph	walking
speaker	succeed	tertius	trodden	wanteth
special	success	testify	trouble	wanting
spewing	succoth	thahash	troughs	warfare
spicery	succour	thanked	trumpet	warmeth
spilled	sucking	theatre	trusted	warming
spindle	suffice	thereat	tumbled	warning
spirits	support	thereby	tumults	warreth
spitted	suppose	therein	turnest	warring
spittle	supreme	thereof	turneth	warrior
spoiled	surface	thereon	turning	washest
spoiler	surname	thereto	turtles	washing

washpot
wasteth
wasting
watched
watcher
watches
watered
watmath
wayside
wealthy
weapons
weareth
wearied
wearing
weather
weavest
wedding
wedlock
weepest
weepeth
weeping
weighed
weights
weighty
welcome
welfare
wentest
western
wheaten
whereas
whereby
wherein
whereof
whereon
whereto
whether
whisper
whither
whoever
whoring
whorish
willeth
willing
willows
wimples
winding
windows
winefat
winketh
winneth
wishing
without
witness
wizards
wonders
woollen
workers
worketh
working

workman
workmen
worldly
worship
wotteth
wounded
wrapped
wreaths
wrestle
wringed
wrinkle
writest
writeth
writing
written
wronged
wrought
yearned
yielded
younger
zaanaim
zabdiel
zabulon
zacchur
zaretan
zarthan
zealous
zebedee
zeboiim
zebudah
zebulun
zelotes
zephath
zeruiah
zilthai
ziphion
ziphron
zobebah
zorites

6

abarim
abased
abated
abdeel
abdiel
abidah
abidan
abihud
abijah
abijam
abiram
abital
abitub
aboard
abound
abroad

absent
abused
accept
access
accord
accuse
achaia
achbor
achish
achsah
achzib
acquit
action
adadah
adaiah
adalia
adamah
adbeel
adders
addeth
adjure
adoram
adriel
advice
advise
aeneas
affect
affirm
afraid
afresh
agabus
agates
agreed
agrees
aharah
ahasai
ahihud
ahijah
ahikam
ahilud
ahiman
ahiram
ahitub
aholah
ahumai
ahuzam
aileth
ajalon
albeit
aliens
allied
allure
almond
almost
altars
always
amalek
amasai
amazed

ambush
amends
amerce
ammiel
anaiah
anamim
anchor
andrew
angels
ankles
anoint
answer
anyone
aphiah
aphrah
aphses
apiece
aplcen
aplvax
appaim
appeal
appear
apphia
apples
aprons
aquila
arabah
arabia
aramis
ararat
arbite
archer
arches
aretas
aridai
aright
arioch
arisai
arkite
armies
armoni
armour
around
arphad
arrest
arrive
arrows
arumah
asahel
asaiah
ascend
ascent
ashbea
ashbel
ashdod
ashima
ashnah
askest
asketh

asking
asleep
asriel
assent
asshur
assist
assume
assure
astray
atarah
athach
athens
athlai
atroth
attain
attend
attent
attire
author
avenge
averse
avites
awaked
azekah
azotus
azriel
azubah
baalah
baalim
baalis
baanah
baasha
backed
badest
bajith
bakbuk
bakers
baketh
balaam
bamoth
banded
banner
barbed
barber
barest
bariah
barked
barkos
barley
barrel
barren
baruch
basest
bashan
basket
basons
bathed
battle
beacon

195

beards	biteth	busied	chelal	cornet
bearer	bitnet	butler	chelub	corpse
beasts	bitten	butter	cheran	costly
beaten	bitter	buyest	cherub	couple
beauty	biztha	buyeth	chesed	course
became	blains	buzite	chesil	courts
becher	blamed	byways	chests	cousin
become	blocks	byword	chewed	covers
beerah	bloody	cabbon	chezib	covert
beetle	boards	cabins	chidon	crafty
beeves	bochim	caesar	choice	craved
befall	bodies	cainan	choked	create
befell	bodily	calcol	choler	cretes
before	boiled	called	choose	criest
beggar	boldly	calneh	chosen	crieth
begged	bolled	calved	christ	crimes
behalf	bolted	calves	church	crouch
behave	booths	calvin	cieled	crowns
beheld	border	camels	circle	crumbs
behind	borrow	camest	cities	crying
behold	bosses	camped	claims	cubits
belial	bottle	canaan	clauda	cuckow
belied	bottom	candle	cleave	cummin
belief	boughs	canker	clefts	cursed
bellow	bought	canneh	cliffs	curses
belong	bounds	cannot	clifts	cursor
bemoan	bounty	carcas	closed	cushan
beninu	bowels	careah	closer	custom
benoni	boweth	career	closet	cuthah
beriah	bowing	carest	clothe	cymbal
berith	bowmen	careth	cloths	cyprus
beside	bozrah	caring	clouds	cyrene
bestir	branch	carmel	cloudy	dagger
bestow	brands	carnal	clouts	dainty
bethel	brasen	carpus	cloven	damage
bether	brayed	carved	cnidus	damned
bethul	breach	cassia	coasts	damsel
betray	breaks	castle	cockle	danced
better	breast	castor	coffer	dances
beulah	breath	cattle	coffin	danger
bewail	bribes	caught	collar	daniel
beware	bricks	caused	colony	dannah
bewray	bridle	causes	colour	darius
beyond	briers	ceased	comely	darken
bichri	bright	cedars	comers	darkly
bidden	brings	cedron	comest	darkon
bidkar	broken	censer	cometh	dashed
bigtha	brooks	cephas	coming	dathan
bigvai	bruise	chafed	commit	daubed
bildad	bucket	chains	common	deacon
bileam	budded	chance	compel	deadly
bilgah	buffet	change	coniah	dealer
bilgai	bundle	chapel	conies	dearly
bilhah	burden	charge	convey	dearth
bilhan	burial	chased	copied	deaths
bimhal	buried	chaste	coping	debase
binnui	burned	chebar	copper	debate
birsha	bushel	cheeks	corban	debtor
bishop	bushes	cheese	corner	deceit

decide	driven	equals	festus	fuller
decked	driver	equity	fetcht	furrow
decree	dropsy	erites	fewest	gabbai
deemed	droves	errand	fields	gadite
deeper	dureth	erreth	fierce	gained
deeply	during	errors	figure	galeed
defeat	duties	esaias	filled	galley
defend	eagles	escape	fillet	gallim
defied	earing	eschew	filthy	gallio
defile	earthy	eshban	finest	garden
degree	easier	eshcol	finger	garner
demand	easily	eshean	fining	gashmu
denial	easter	eshton	finish	gather
denied	eaters	espied	fisher	gavest
depart	eatest	estate	fishes	gazing
depths	eateth	esteem	fitted	gazzam
deputy	eating	esther	flagon	gedeon
deride	edmund	ethnan	flakes	gehazi
descry	effect	eunice	flames	gender
desert	eglaim	eunuch	flanks	geneva
desire	eighth	exceed	flayed	genius
detail	eighty	except	fleece	gentle
detain	either	excess	fleeth	gently
detest	eladah	excuse	fleshy	gerahs
device	elasah	exhort	flieth	gesham
devils	eldaah	exodus	flight	geshem
devise	elders	expect	flinty	geshur
devote	eldest	expert	floats	gether
devour	eleven	extend	flocks	giants
devout	eliada	eznite	floods	gibbar
diadem	elidad	fables	floors	gibeah
differ	elijah	fadeth	flowed	gibeon
digest	elisha	fading	flower	giddel
digged	elizur	failed	flying	gideon
diklah	elnaam	fairer	fodder	gilboa
dilean	elpaal	fairly	folden	gilead
dimnah	eluzai	fallen	follow	gilgal
dinner	elymas	fallow	forbad	ginath
dipped	embalm	family	forbid	girded
direct	emmaus	famine	forced	girdle
dishan	empire	famish	forces	givest
dishes	employ	famous	forest	giveth
dishon	encamp	fasted	forgat	giving
distil	endeth	fasten	forged	gladly
divers	ending	father	forget	gnawed
divide	endued	fatted	forgot	goblet
divine	endure	fatter	formed	goings
doctor	engedi	faults	former	golden
doings	enjoin	faulty	fought	goodly
dorcas	enmity	favour	fouled	gopher
dothan	enough	feared	fourth	goshen
doting	enrich	feasts	fowler	gospel
double	ensign	feeble	framed	gotten
doubts	entice	felled	freely	gourds
dragon	entire	feller	friend	govern
drawer	envied	fellow	fringe	grapes
dreams	envies	female	frozen	graved
drieth	ephlal	fenced	fruits	gravel
drinks	ephron	ferret	fulfil	graven

graves	haters	hidest	idbash	japhia
grease	hatest	hideth	idiots	jaroah
grecia	hateth	hiding	idumea	jarvis
greece	hating	higher	ikkesh	jashen
greedy	hatita	highly	images	jasher
greeks	hatred	hillel	impart	jashub
griefs	hattil	hinder	impose	jasiel
grieve	hauran	hinges	impute	jasper
ground	havens	hinnom	indeed	jattir
groves	having	hirest	infamy	jearim
growth	havock	hither	infant	jebusi
grudge	hazael	hivite	inform	jeezer
guests	haziel	hodesh	inside	jehiah
guided	healed	hodiah	intend	jehiel
guides	healer	hoglah	intent	jehudi
guilty	health	hoised	invade	jehush
gushed	heaped	holden	invent	jemima
gutter	hearer	holier	inward	jemuel
hadlai	hearth	holily	irijah	jeremy
hagaba	hearts	hollow	irpeel	jeriah
hagaii	hearty	holpen	isaiah	jeriel
haggai	healed	homers	ishbah	jeruel
hakkoz	heaved	honest	ishbak	jesher
halhul	heaven	honour	ishiah	jeshua
haling	hebrew	hopeth	ishpan	jesiah
hallow	hebron	hophni	ishtob	jether
halted	hedged	hoping	ishuah	jethro
hamath	hedges	horims	ishuai	jewels
hammer	heifer	horite	island	jewess
hammon	height	hormah	israel	jewish
hamuel	helbah	hornet	issued	jeziah
hanani	helbon	horror	issues	jeziel
handed	heldai	horses	ithiel	jezoar
handle	heleph	hoshea	ithmah	jhuapl
hanged	helkai	hotham	ithnan	jibsam
haniel	helmet	hothan	ithran	jimnah
hannah	helped	hothir	itself	joahaz
hanoch	helper	houses	izehar	joanna
happen	hemath	howled	jaakan	joelah
harden	hemdan	hukkok	jaalah	joezer
harder	henoch	huldah	jaalam	joiada
hardly	hepher	humble	jaanai	joined
hareph	herald	humbly	jaasau	joints
hareth	hereby	humtah	jaazer	joktan
harhas	herein	hunger	jabbok	jordan
harhur	hereof	hungry	jabesh	joseph
hariph	heresh	hunted	jabneh	joshah
harlot	heresy	hunter	jachan	joshua
haroeh	hermas	hupham	jachin	josiah
harped	hermes	huppah	jaddua	josias
harrow	hermon	huppim	jahath	jotbah
harsha	hewers	hushah	jahaza	jotham
hashem	heweth	hushai	jahdai	joyful
hashub	hezeki	husham	jahmai	joying
hashum	hezion	hushim	jahzah	joyous
hasrah	hezrai	huzzab	jailor	jubile
hasted	hezron	hyssop	jairus	judaea
hasten	hiddai	ibleam	jannes	judged
hatach	hidden	idalah	janoah	judges

judith	leader	lowest	melicu	months
julius	league	loweth	melita	moriah
justle	leaned	lowing	melody	morrow
justly	leaped	lubims	melons	morsel
justus	leaved	lucius	melted	mortal
juttah	leaven	luhith	melzar	mortar
kadesh	leaves	lusted	member	morter
kallai	lebana	lysias	memory	mosera
kareah	ledges	lystra	merari	mother
karkaa	legion	maacah	merely	mouldy
karkor	lemuel	maadai	merged	mounts
kartah	lender	machir	merges	mouths
kartan	length	madest	meritt	moveth
kedesh	lepers	madian	mesech	moving
keeper	leshem	madmen	meshes	muppim
keilah	lesser	mahali	messes	murder
kelita	letter	mahath	meunim	murmur
kemuel	levite	mahlah	miamin	musick
kenath	lewdly	mahlon	mibhar	musing
kenite	libnah	maiden	mibsam	mutter
kettle	licked	maimed	mibzar	mutual
kicked	lifted	makers	michah	muzzle
kidron	lifter	makest	michal	myrtle
killed	lights	maketh	michri	myself
kindle	ligure	making	midday	naamah
kindly	liketh	malice	middin	naaman
kingly	liking	mammon	middle	naarah
kishon	lilies	manaen	midian	naarai
kissed	lintel	manger	mielke	naaran
kisses	liquor	manner	migdol	naboth
kitron	listed	manoah	mighty	nachon
kittim	listen	mantle	migron	nachor
knives	little	marble	milcah	nahari
kohath	lively	marcus	milcom	nahash
laadah	livest	marked	mildew	nahath
laadan	liveth	market	millet	naioth
labour	living	maroth	minded	namely
lacked	lizard	marred	mingle	nameth
ladder	loaden	marrow	minish	napkin
ladeth	loammi	martha	miriam	narrow
ladies	loathe	martyr	misery	nathan
lading	loaves	marvel	misgab	nation
lahmam	locked	mashal	mishal	native
laidst	locust	masons	misham	nature
lamech	lodged	massah	mishma	naught
lament	london	master	missed	nearer
landed	longed	matred	mizpah	needed
lapped	longer	matrix	mizpar	needle
lasted	looked	mattan	mizpeh	nekoda
lately	loosed	matter	mizzah	nemuel
latter	lordly	mayest	mnason	nepheg
launch	loseth	meadow	mocked	nephew
lavers	lothed	mearah	mocker	nereus
lavish	louder	meddle	modern	nergal
lawful	lovely	medeba	modest	neriah
lawyer	lovers	median	molech	nether
layest	lovest	mehida	moloch	neziah
layeth	loveth	melchi	molten	nibhaz
laying	loving	melech	moment	nights

nimrah	pasach	plague	purple	relied
nimrim	paseah	plains	purses	relief
nimrod	pashur	planes	pursue	remain
nimshi	passed	planks	pushed	remark
ninety	pastor	plants	putiel	remedy
nineve	patara	plates	pygarg	remeth
nobles	patmos	played	quails	remmon
nobody	paulus	player	quaked	remove
noised	paweth	please	queens	render
nophah	payeth	pledge	quench	renown
notice	pearls	plenty	quiver	repair
nought	peeled	plough	quotes	repent
novice	peeped	plowed	raamah	rephah
number	peleth	pluckt	rabbah	report
nursed	peniel	plunge	rabmag	rescue
obcyod	penuel	points	rachab	resent
object	penury	poison	rachal	resist
obtain	people	policy	rachel	resort
occupy	peresh	polled	raddai	rested
occurs	perida	pollux	rageth	result
odious	perils	ponder	ragged	retain
odours	perish	pontus	raging	retire
offend	permit	poorer	raguel	return
office	persia	poplar	railed	reuben
olives	persis	porter	railer	reumah
olivet	person	posted	rained	reveal
onions	peruda	potter	raised	revile
onward	pestle	pounds	raiser	revive
onycha	pethor	poured	rakkon	revolt
opened	phalec	powder	ramath	reward
openly	phallu	powers	ramiah	rezeph
ophrah	phalti	praise	ramoth	rhodes
oppose	pharah	prayed	ranges	riblah
oracle	phares	prayer	ransom	richer
orator	pharez	preach	rashly	riches
ordain	philip	prefer	rather	richly
organs	phrase	pretty	ravens	ridden
ospray	phurah	prices	reader	riddle
others	phuvah	pricks	reaiah	riders
ouches	pieces	priest	really	rideth
outrun	pierce	prince	reaped	ridges
owners	pigeon	prisca	reaper	riding
owneth	pilate	prised	reared	rifled
paarai	pileha	prison	reason	rigour
pacify	pillar	profit	rebels	rimmon
paddle	pilled	proofs	rebuke	rinnah
pagiel	pillow	proper	recall	rinsed
pained	pilots	proved	rechab	ripped
palace	piltai	pruned	rechah	risest
pannag	pineth	psalms	reckon	riseth
panted	pining	pudens	record	rising
paphos	pipers	puffed	redeem	rissah
parbar	pisgah	pulled	refers	rivers
parcel	pispah	pulpit	refine	rizpah
pardon	pithom	punish	refuge	roared
parosh	pithon	purely	refuse	robbed
parted	pitied	purged	regard	robber
partly	placed	purify	region	roboam
paruah	places	purity	reject	rohgah

200

rolled	search	sherah	sinner	stacks
roller	seared	sherds	sippai	stacte
romans	season	shewed	sirion	stairs
rooted	seated	shield	sisera	stakes
rotten	second	shihon	sister	stalks
rovers	secret	shihor	sitnah	stalls
rowers	secure	shilhi	skirts	starts
rowing	seduce	shiloh	slaves	states
rubies	seeing	shimea	slayer	status
rudder	seemed	shimei	slings	staves
ruined	seemly	shimhi	slowly	stayed
rulers	seethe	shimma	smiths	steads
rulest	seized	shimon	smooth	steady
ruleth	seller	shimri	smyrna	sticks
ruling	selves	shinab	snared	stings
rumour	senaah	shinar	snares	stocks
rushed	senate	shined	snatch	stolen
rushes	sender	shiphi	soaked	stoned
sabtah	senses	shisha	sochoh	stones
saddle	senuah	shobab	socket	stools
safely	seorim	shobai	sodden	stormy
safety	sephar	shobal	sodoma	strain
saidst	served	shobek	soever	strait
sailed	sethur	shocho	softer	strake
saints	setter	shocks	softly	stream
salcah	settle	shoham	solace	street
sallai	sevens	shomer	solemn	strife
salmon	sewest	should	sooner	strike
salome	seweth	shovel	sorely	string
salted	shaaph	shower	sorrow	stripe
salute	shadow	shrank	sought	stript
samlah	shaked	shroud	sounds	strive
sample	shaken	shrubs	source	stroke
samson	shalem	shuham	sowest	strong
samuel	shalim	shunem	soweth	strove
saphir	shamed	sibmah	sowing	struck
saraph	shamer	sichem	spared	subdue
sardis	shamir	sickle	sparks	submit
sargon	shamma	sickly	spears	subtil
saruch	shapen	siddim	speech	sucked
satest	shapes	sifted	speedy	sudden
satyrs	sharai	sighed	spiced	suffer
savest	sharar	sights	spices	summer
saveth	sharon	signed	spider	sunday
saving	shaved	signet	spirit	sunder
savour	shaveh	silent	spoils	sundry
sawest	shaven	siloah	spoken	supped
sayest	sheath	siloam	spokes	supper
saying	shebah	silver	spoons	supple
scales	shebam	simeon	spouse	supply
scarce	sheber	simple	sprang	surely
schism	shebna	simply	spread	surety
school	sheets	sinews	sprigs	swarms
scorch	shekel	sinful	spring	swords
scrape	shelah	singed	sprout	sychar
scribe	shemer	singer	sprung	sychem
scroll	shenir	single	spunge	syrian
scurvy	shephi	sinite	square	tabeal
sealed	shepho	sinned	stable	tabeel

tables	thrice	upheld	wastes	zabbud
tabret	throat	uphold	waters	zaccai
taches	throne	uproar	waxeth	zaccur
tacked	throng	upside	waxing	zacher
tadmor	thrown	upward	weaken	zalaph
tahath	thrust	urbane	weaker	zalmon
tahrea	thumbs	urgent	wealth	zanoah
takest	thyine	urijah	weaned	zaphon
taketh	tikvah	useful	weapon	zareah
taking	tiling	usurer	weasel	zatthu
talent	tilled	utmost	weaver	zebaim
talked	tiller	uzziah	weight	zebina
taller	timber	uzziel	whales	zeboim
talmai	timnah	vainly	wheels	zelzah
talmon	tingle	valley	whelps	zemira
tammuz	tirzah	valour	whence	zephon
tanach	tithes	valued	whiles	zereda
tanner	titles	vaniah	whilst	zeresh
target	tittle	vanish	whited	zereth
tarsus	tizite	vanity	whiter	zeruah
tartak	tobiah	vapour	wholly	zetham
tartan	tochen	vashni	whores	zethan
tasted	tolled	vashti	wicked	zethar
tatnai	tokens	verily	widows	zibeon
taught	tongue	verity	wilily	zibiah
taxing	tophel	vessel	willow	zichri
tebeth	tophet	vestry	window	ziddim
tekoah	tossed	viewed	winged	ziklag
telaim	toward	vilely	winked	zillah
temani	towers	vilest	winter	zilpah
temeni	traded	vipers	wipeth	zimmah
temper	trance	virgin	wiping	zimran
temple	travel	virtue	wisdom	ziphah
tender	trench	visage	wisely	zippor
tenons	tribes	vision	wished	zithri
teresh	triest	voices	withal	zoheth
termed	trieth	volume	wither	zophah
terror	troops	vophsi	within	zophai
thamah	trough	vowest	wizard	zophar
thamar	trusty	voweth	woeful	zophim
thanks	trying	voyage	wolves	zoreah
thebez	tumult	wafers	wonder	zuriel
thefts	turned	wagons	worker	zuzims
theirs	turtle	wailed	worlds	
thence	tutors	waited	worthy	5
theory	twelve	waketh	wounds	
therin	twenty	waking	wraths	aaron
therof	twined	walked	wreath	abana
thighs	undone	walled	writer	abase
things	unholy	wallow	writes	abdon
thirst	united	wander	yahweh	abhor
thirty	unjust	wanted	yearly	abiah
thomas	unlade	wanton	yelled	abida
thongs	unless	warmed	yellow	abide
thorns	unlike	warned	yonder	abiel
though	unripe	warred	youths	abihu
thread	unruly	washed	zaanan	abiud
threat	unshod	wasted	zaavan	abner
thresh	unwise	waster	zabbai	

202

abode	allon	aroer	basis	boils
about	allow	arose	bason	bonds
above	almon	arpad	bathe	bones
abram	almug	array	baths	books
abuse	aloes	arrow	bavai	booth
accad	alone	arvad	beams	booty
accho	along	asaph	beans	bored
achan	aloof	ascii	beard	borne
achar	aloth	ashan	bears	bosom
achaz	aloud	asher	beast	bosor
achim	alpha	ashes	bebai	botch
achor	altar	ashur	bedad	bough
achsa	alter	aside	bedan	bound
acres	alush	asiel	beera	bowed
adami	alvah	asked	beeri	bowls
addan	alvan	asnah	began	bozez
addar	alway	assay	begat	brake
added	amana	asses	beget	brand
adder	amasa	assir	begin	brass
addon	amber	assos	begun	bread
adiel	amend	assur	being	break
adina	amiss	athos	bekah	breed
adino	ammah	attai	belah	bribe
adlai	ammon	avims	belch	brick
admah	amnon	avith	bells	bride
admit	among	avoid	belly	brier
adnah	amram	await	berea	bring
adorn	anani	awake	bered	brink
adria	anath	aware	beryl	broad
aenon	angel	awoke	besai	brood
afoot	anger	azbuk	beset	brook
afore	angle	azgad	besom	broth
after	angry	aziel	besor	brown
again	aniam	aziza	betah	bruit
agate	anise	azmon	beten	brute
agone	ankle	azzah	bezai	build
agony	annas	azzan	bezek	built
agree	anvil	azzur	bezer	bukki
ahava	apace	baale	bible	bulls
ahban	apart	baali	binea	bunah
ahead	aphek	baana	birds	bunch
ahiah	aphik	baara	birth	bunni
ahiam	aplvm	babel	black	burnt
ahian	appii	babes	blade	burst
ahira	apple	backs	blame	bushy
ahlab	apply	baked	blast	buyer
ahlai	arbah	baken	blaze	cabul
ahoah	archi	baker	bless	cakes
aiath	ardon	balac	blind	calah
aided	areli	balah	block	caleb
ailed	argob	balak	blood	calno
akkub	argue	bamah	blown	calve
alarm	arieh	bands	blunt	camel
algum	ariel	banks	blush	camon
aliah	arise	barak	bmers	camps
alian	armed	barns	board	canst
alien	arnan	based	boast	cared
alike	arnon	baser	boats	cares
alive	arodi	bases	bohan	carmi

carry	cover	dodai	eliah	feels
cases	covet	doers	eliam	feign
catch	cozbi	doesn	elias	felix
cauls	craft	doest	eliel	fence
cause	crane	doeth	elihu	ferry
caves	creek	doing	elika	fetch
cease	creep	doors	eliud	fever
cedar	crept	doted	eloth	fewer
chaff	crete	doubt	emims	fgrep
chain	cried	dough	emins	field
chant	cries	doves	emmor	fiery
chapt	crime	dowry	empty	fifth
chase	cross	drams	ended	fifty
cheap	crown	drank	endif	fight
check	crude	drave	endor	files
cheek	cruel	drawn	endow	filth
cheer	cruse	dread	enemy	final
chest	crush	dream	enjoy	finer
chide	cubit	dregs	enoch	fires
chief	cured	dress	enosh	first
child	cures	dried	ensue	firth
chios	curse	drink	enter	fists
chiun	cushi	drive	entry	fitly
chloe	cycle	drops	ephah	fixed
chode	cyrus	dross	ephai	flags
choke	dagon	drove	epher	flame
chose	daily	drown	ephod	flash
churl	dance	drunk	equal	flesh
chuza	darda	dukes	erech	flies
claim	darts	dumah	erred	flint
clave	davem	durst	error	flock
claws	david	dwarf	eshek	flood
clean	deals	dwell	esrom	floor
clear	dealt	dwelt	etham	flour
cleft	death	dying	ethan	flute
cliff	debir	eagle	ether	foals
clift	debts	eared	ethni	folds
climb	decay	early	event	folks
cloak	dedan	earth	every	folly
clods	deeds	eased	evils	fools
cloke	deeps	eaten	exact	force
close	defer	eater	exalt	fords
cloth	dekar	ebony	excel	forks
cloud	delay	edged	exile	forms
coals	demas	edges	expel	forth
coast	depth	edify	extol	forts
coats	derbe	edrei	ezbai	forty
colts	deuel	eglah	ezbon	forum
comes	devil	eglon	faces	found
coney	diana	egypt	facts	fowls
cooks	dibon	eight	faint	foxes
coral	dibri	ekron	fairs	frail
cords	didst	elath	faith	frame
cosam	diest	eldad	falls	fraud
cotes	dieth	elder	false	freed
couch	dimon	elead	fared	fresh
could	dinah	elect	fault	fried
count	dined	eleph	fears	frogs
court	ditch	eliab	feast	front

frost	grain	hazor	horam	jalon
fruit	grant	heads	horeb	james
fully	grape	heady	horem	jamin
gaash	grass	heaps	horns	janna
gaddi	grate	heard	horse	janum
gaham	grave	heart	hosah	japho
gahar	great	heath	hosea	jarah
gains	greek	heave	hosen	jareb
gaius	green	heavy	hosts	jared
galal	greet	heber	hotly	jarha
gamul	grief	hedge	hough	jarib
gaped	grind	heels	hours	jason
gareb	groan	hegai	house	javan
gatam	grope	heirs	hukok	jazer
gates	gross	helah	hurai	jaziz
gazer	group	helam	huram	jebus
gazez	grove	heleb	husks	jehud
gebal	grown	heled	hymns	jeiel
geber	guard	helek	ibhar	jerah
gebim	guest	helem	ibzan	jered
geder	guide	helez	idols	jesse
gedor	guile	helon	igeal	jesui
gerar	guilt	helps	image	jesus
geuel	habor	helve	imlah	jetur
gezer	hadad	hemam	immer	jeuel
ghost	hadar	heman	imnah	jeush
giant	hadid	hence	imrah	jewel
gibea	hadst	herbs	india	jewry
gidom	hagab	herds	inner	jezer
gifts	hagar	heres	irons	jimna
gihon	haggi	herod	isaac	jireh
giloh	hairs	heron	iscah	joash
gimzo	hairy	hesed	ishma	jobab
girdd	halah	hewed	ishod	jogli
girls	halak	hewer	ishui	johns
gispa	haman	hezir	isles	joint
given	hamor	hezro	ispah	jokim
giver	hamul	hilen	issue	jonah
gives	hanan	hills	isuah	jonan
glass	hands	hinds	italy	jonas
glean	hanes	hirah	items	joppa
glede	hangs	hiram	ithai	jorah
glory	hanun	hired	ithra	jorai
gnash	haply	hires	ittai	joram
goads	happy	hoary	ivory	jorim
goath	haran	hobab	izhar	joses
goats	harim	hobah	jaala	joyed
godly	harod	hoham	jabal	jubal
goest	harps	holds	jabez	jucal
goeth	harts	holes	jabin	judah
going	harum	holon	jacob	judas
golan	haruz	homam	jadau	judea
gomer	haste	homer	jadon	judge
goods	hasty	honey	jagur	juice
gored	hatch	honor	jahaz	julia
gourd	hated	hoods	jahdo	junia
gozan	haunt	hoofs	jakan	kanah
grace	haven	hooks	jakeh	kedar
graff	hazel	hoped	jakim	kenan

kenaz	liver	media	nahum	other
keros	lives	meets	nails	othni
kezia	locks	mehir	naked	ought
keziz	lodge	melea	named	outer
kinah	lofty	menan	names	ovens
kinds	loins	merab	naomi	owest
kings	looks	mercy	navel	oweth
kishi	loops	mered	naves	owner
kison	loose	meres	nebai	ozias
knead	lords	merom	nebat	paces
kneel	lotan	meroz	necho	padan
knees	lothe	merry	necks	padon
knife	loved	mesha	needs	pains
knock	lover	meted	needy	palal
knops	loves	micah	nehum	pallu
known	lower	micha	neiel	palms
knows	lowly	midst	nekeb	palsy
korah	lubim	might	nests	palti
laban	lucas	milch	nevor	pangs
laded	lucre	millo	newly	paper
laden	ludim	mills	nezib	paran
lahad	lusts	minds	niger	parts
lahmi	lusty	minni	night	paths
laish	lycia	minus	ninth	paved
lakum	lydda	mirma	nisan	payed
lambs	lydia	mirth	nitre	peace
lamps	lying	mites	nobah	pearl
lance	maath	mitre	noble	pekah
lands	machi	mixed	nodab	pekod
lanes	madai	mizar	nogah	peleg
large	madon	moist	nohah	pelet
lasea	magog	moles	noise	pence
lasha	mahli	molid	north	penny
later	mahol	money	noses	peres
latin	maids	month	noted	perez
laugh	major	moons	notes	perga
laver	makaz	moreh	nunes	peril
learn	maker	moses	nurse	peter
least	makes	mount	oaths	phebe
leave	males	mourn	oboth	plece
lecah	mamre	mouse	occur	piety
leeks	maneh	mouth	ocran	pinon
leper	manna	moved	odour	piped
liars	maoch	mover	offer	pipes
libni	marah	moves	often	piram
libya	march	mower	oiled	pison
liers	marks	mozah	olive	pitch
liest	marry	mules	omega	place
lieth	marys	multi	omers	plain
light	massa	mused	opens	plant
liked	masts	mushi	ophel	plate
liken	mates	myrrh	ophir	plead
likhi	matri	mysia	ophni	pluck
limit	means	nabal	order	poets
linen	meant	nadab	organ	point
lines	meats	nagge	orion	polls
linus	medad	naham	ornan	ponds
lions	medan	nahbi	orpah	pools
lived	medes	nahor	oshea	porch

posts	reply	scalp	shock	smote
pound	resen	scant	shoco	snail
pours	rests	scent	shoes	snare
power	reuel	sceva	shone	snout
press	rezia	scoff	shook	snowy
price	rezin	scorn	shoot	sober
pride	rezon	scrip	shore	socho
print	rhesa	seals	shorn	socoh
privy	rhoda	seats	short	sodom
prize	ribai	sebat	shout	soles
proof	rider	sechu	shows	solve
proud	right	seeds	shred	songs
prove	rings	seers	shuah	sorek
prune	risen	seest	shual	sorer
psalm	rites	seeth	shuni	sores
pulse	river	segub	siaha	sorry
punon	roast	seize	sides	sorts
purer	robes	selah	sidon	sotai
purge	rocks	seled	siege	souls
purim	rolls	semei	sieve	sound
purse	roman	seneh	sighs	south
quake	roofs	senir	sight	sowed
queen	rooms	sense	signs	sower
quick	roots	serah	sihon	space
quiet	ropes	sered	sihor	spain
quite	rough	serug	silas	spake
rabbi	round	serve	silla	spare
ragau	rouse	seven	silly	spark
raged	rowed	sever	simon	speak
rahab	royal	sewed	simri	spear
raham	ruddy	shade	sinai	speed
rahel	rufus	shady	since	spend
rainy	ruins	shaft	sinew	spent
raise	ruled	shage	sinim	spice
rakem	ruler	shake	sirah	spied
ramah	rumah	shall	sivan	spies
range	sabta	shalt	sixth	spilt
ranks	sacar	shama	sixty	spite
rapha	sacks	shame	skies	spoil
raphu	sadly	shape	skill	spoke
raven	sadoc	share	skins	spoon
ravin	saint	sharp	skirt	sport
razor	saith	shaul	skull	spots
reach	sakes	shave	slack	spued
ready	salah	sheaf	slain	staff
reaia	salem	sheal	slang	stain
realm	salim	shear	slave	stalk
rebel	sallu	sheba	sleep	stall
reeds	salma	sheep	slept	stamp
refer	samos	sheet	slide	stand
regem	sarah	shema	slime	stank
rehob	sarai	sherd	sling	stare
rehum	sarid	sheth	slips	stars
reign	saron	sheva	small	state
reins	satan	shimi	smart	stays
rekem	satyr	shine	smell	stead
remit	saved	ships	smite	steal
renew	sawed	shiza	smith	steel
repay	scall	shobi	smoke	steep

steps	tarry	tooth	vines	woods
stern	tasks	topaz	viols	words
stick	taste	topic	viper	works
stiff	taunt	torch	visit	world
still	taxed	touch	voice	worms
sting	taxes	towel	vomit	worse
stink	teach	tower	vowed	worst
stirs	tears	towns	wafer	worth
stock	teats	trade	wages	would
stole	tebah	train	wagon	wound
stone	teeth	traps	waked	woven
stony	tekel	tread	walls	wrath
stood	tekoa	trees	wants	wrest
stool	telah	trial	wards	wring
stoop	telem	tribe	wares	write
store	tells	tried	waste	wrong
stork	teman	troas	watch	wrote
storm	tempt	trode	water	wroth
story	tenor	troop	waved	wrung
stout	tenth	truly	waves	yearn
straw	tents	trump	waxed	years
strip	terah	trust	waxen	yield
stuck	thank	truth	weary	yoked
studs	thara	tubal	weave	yokes
study	theft	turns	wedge	young
stuff	their	twain	weeds	yours
stump	there	twice	weeks	youth
suits	these	twigs	weigh	zabad
super	thick	twins	wells	zabdi
sware	thief	tyrus	wench	zabud
swarm	thigh	ummah	whale	zadok
swear	thine	uncle	wheat	zaham
sweat	thing	under	wheel	zarah
sweep	think	unite	whelp	zared
sweet	third	unity	where	zattu
swell	thorn	until	which	zavan
swept	those	uphaz	while	zebah
swift	three	upper	whips	zebul
swine	threw	urged	white	zedad
swoon	throw	uriah	whole	zelah
sword	thumb	urias	whore	zelek
sworn	tibni	uriel	whose	zenan
syene	tidal	usest	whoso	zenas
syria	tilon	useth	widow	zephi
table	times	using	wiles	zepho
tabor	timna	usual	winds	zerah
tahan	timon	usurp	windy	zered
tails	tiras	usury	wines	zeror
taken	tired	uthai	wings	zibia
taker	tires	utter	wiped	zidon
takes	tiria	uzzah	wires	zimri
tales	tithe	uzzia	wiser	zizah
talks	title	vails	witch	zobah
tamah	titus	value	withs	zohar
tamar	today	vaunt	witty	zorah
tamed	token	venom	wives	
tarah	tolad	vexed	woman	4
tarea	tombs	vials	wombs	
tares	tongs	viler	women	

abba	arad	beon	cave	diet
abda	arah	beor	chew	dine
abdi	aram	bera	chop	dirt
abel	aran	beri	chub	dish
abez	arba	best	chun	dodo
abia	arms	bier	city	doeg
abib	army	bill	clad	doer
able	arod	bind	clap	does
acre	arts	bird	clay	dogs
acts	arza	bite	coal	done
adah	aser	bits	coat	door
adam	asia	blew	cock	dost
adar	asps	blot	cold	dote
addi	atad	blow	colt	doth
ader	ater	blue	come	dove
adin	aunt	boar	cook	down
adna	aven	boat	cool	drag
afar	avim	boaz	coos	draw
agag	away	body	copy	drew
agar	axes	boil	cord	drop
aged	azal	bold	core	dues
agee	azaz	bolt	corn	duke
ages	azel	bond	cost	dull
ague	azem	bone	crag	dumb
agur	azor	book	crew	dung
ahab	azur	booz	crib	dura
ahaz	baal	bore	crop	dust
aher	babe	born	crow	duty
ahio	baca	both	cumi	dyed
aiah	back	bowl	cups	each
aija	bade	bows	cure	ears
ajah	bags	boys	cush	ease
akan	bake	bray	cuth	east
alas	bald	bred	dale	easy
alms	ball	brim	dara	ebal
also	balm	brow	dare	ebed
amad	band	buds	dark	eber
amal	bani	bull	dart	echo
amam	bank	burn	dash	edar
amen	bare	bury	date	eden
ammi	bark	bush	daub	eder
amok	barn	busy	dave	edge
amon	barr	buys	dawn	edom
amos	bars	buzi	days	eggs
amoz	base	cage	dead	ehud
amzi	bath	cain	deaf	eker
anab	bats	cake	deal	elah
anah	beam	calf	dear	elam
anak	bear	call	debt	elim
anan	beat	calm	deck	elms
anem	beds	came	deed	eloi
aner	been	camp	deep	elon
anim	beer	cana	deer	else
anna	bees	cane	defy	elul
anon	bela	care	dens	enam
ants	bell	cart	deny	enan
anub	bend	case	dial	ends
apes	beno	cast	died	enos
arab	bent	caul	dies	envy

eran	foam	hail	hori	kine
esau	foes	hair	horn	king
esek	fold	hale	host	kish
esli	folk	half	hour	kiss
espy	food	hali	howl	kite
etam	fool	hall	huge	knee
even	fool	halt	hunt	knew
ever	ford	hand	huri	knit
evil	form	hang	hurl	knop
ewes	fort	hara	hurt	know
eyed	foul	hard	husk	kore
eyes	four	hare	hymn	kwan
ezar	fowl	harm	ibri	lace
ezel	fray	harp	iddo	lack
ezem	free	hart	idle	lade
ezer	fret	hast	idol	lads
ezra	from	hate	igal	lady
ezrl	fuel	hath	ijon	lael
face	full	hats	iloi	lald
fact	fury	have	imla	lain
fade	gaal	hawk	imna	lake
fail	gaba	hazo	imri	lama
fain	gadi	head	into	lamb
fair	gain	heal	irad	lame
fall	gall	heap	iram	lamp
fame	gaps	hear	iron	land
fare	gate	heat	ishi	last
farm	gath	heed	isle	late
fast	gave	heel	isui	laud
fats	gaza	hege	itch	laws
fear	gaze	heir	ivah	lead
feed	geba	held	izri	leaf
feel	gera	heli	jada	leah
feet	giah	hell	jael	lean
fell	gier	helm	jair	leap
felt	gift	help	jaws	lees
fens	gins	hems	jehu	left
figs	girl	hena	jeuz	legs
file	girt	herb	jews	lehi
fill	give	herd	joab	lend
find	glad	here	joah	lent
fine	gnat	hers	joed	less
fins	gnaw	heth	joel	lest
fire	goad	hewn	joha	leth
firm	goat	hide	john	levi
fish	gods	hiel	join	levy
fist	goes	high	jona	lewd
five	gold	hill	jose	liar
flag	gone	hind	juda	lice
flat	good	hire	jude	lick
flax	gore	hiss	just	lied
flay	gray	hoar	keep	lien
flea	grew	hold	kept	lies
fled	grey	hole	keys	life
flee	grow	holy	kick	lift
flew	gulf	home	kids	lign
flow	guni	hoof	kill	like
flux	gush	hook	kiln	lily
foal	haft	hope	kind	lime

line	mine	ohad	pomp	rosh
lion	mint	ohel	pool	rows
lips	mire	ohio	poor	rude
list	miry	omar	port	ruin
live	misc	omer	post	rule
loaf	miss	omit	pots	rump
loan	mist	omri	pour	runs
lock	mite	onam	pray	rush
loft	mixt	onan	prey	rust
lois	moab	once	puah	ruth
long	mock	ones	pull	sack
look	mole	only	pure	safe
lord	moon	onyx	push	said
lose	more	open	quit	sail
loss	most	oreb	raca	sake
lost	mote	oren	race	sala
lots	moth	osee	rage	sale
loud	move	ours	rags	salt
love	mown	oven	rail	salu
luke	moza	over	rain	same
lump	much	owed	rama	sand
lurk	mule	owls	rams	sang
lust	muse	oxen	rang	sank
maai	must	ozem	rank	saph
maaz	myra	ozni	rare	sara
made	naam	paid	rase	saul
maid	nail	pain	rash	save
mail	nain	pair	rate	sawn
make	name	pale	read	saws
male	naum	palm	reap	says
many	navy	pans	rear	scab
maon	neah	pant	reba	scan
mara	near	paps	reed	scum
mark	nebo	pare	reel	seal
mars	neck	part	rely	seam
mart	need	pass	rend	seas
mary	neri	past	rent	seat
mash	nest	pate	rest	seba
mast	nets	path	ribs	sect
mate	news	paul	rich	seed
maul	next	paws	ride	seek
meah	nigh	peep	ring	seem
meal	nine	peor	riot	seen
mean	noah	phut	ripe	seer
meat	none	pick	rise	sees
mede	noon	pile	road	seir
meek	noph	pine	roar	sela
meet	nose	pins	robe	self
melt	note	pipe	rock	sell
mend	nows	piss	rode	send
mene	nuts	pits	rods	sent
mesh	oaks	pity	roes	seth
mess	oars	plat	roll	shed
mete	oath	play	rome	shem
mice	obal	plea	roof	shen
mile	obed	plow	room	shew
milk	obey	plus	root	ship
mill	obil	pole	rope	shoa
mind	oded	poll	rose	shod

shoe	suah	trow	weep	zoan
shot	such	true	well	zoar
show	suck	turn	went	zoba
shua	suit	tyre	wept	zuar
shun	sung	ucal	were	zuph
shur	sunk	ucla	wert	
shut	sure	ulai	west	**3**
sick	susi	ulam	what	
side	swan	ulla	when	abi
sift	swim	undo	whet	act
sigh	tail	unni	whip	add
sign	take	unto	whit	ado
silk	tale	upon	whom	age
sina	talk	urge	wide	ago
sing	tall	urim	wife	aha
sink	tame	used	wild	ahi
sins	tank	uses	will	ain
sion	tare	uucp	wilt	air
sirs	task	uzai	wind	all
sith	tear	uzal	wine	ami
sits	teil	uzza	wing	and
size	tell	uzzi	wink	ans
skin	tema	vail	wipe	ant
skip	tend	vain	wise	any
slay	tens	vale	wish	apl
slew	tent	vats	wist	apt
slip	text	veil	with	ara
slow	than	vein	woes	ard
snow	that	vent	wolf	are
soap	thee	very	womb	ark
sodi	them	vial	wont	arm
soft	then	vice	wood	art
soil	they	view	woof	asa
sold	thin	vile	wool	ash
sole	this	vine	word	ask
some	thou	viol	work	asp
song	thus	void	worm	ass
sons	tied	vows	wove	ate
soon	tile	wail	wrap	aul
sore	till	wait	xxii	ava
sort	time	wake	yarn	awe
soul	tire	walk	year	axe
sour	toah	wall	yell	bad
sown	toes	want	yoke	bag
span	tohu	ward	york	bar
spat	toil	ware	your	bat
sped	tola	warm	zair	bay
spin	told	warn	zara	bed
spit	toll	warp	zaza	bee
spot	tomb	wars	zeal	beg
spue	took	wash	zeeb	bel
spun	tool	wasn	zeri	ben
star	tops	wast	ziba	bid
stay	torn	wave	ziha	bin
stdc	toss	ways	zina	bit
stem	town	weak	zlon	bnr
step	trap	wear	zior	bow
stir	tree	webs	ziph	box
stop	trip	week	ziza	

212

boy	for	jhu	old	sop
bud	fos	jim	one	sow
bul	fox	job	ono	spy
but	fro	joe	our	sue
buy	ftp	jot	out	sum
buz	fun	joy	owe	sun
cab	gad	jwm	owl	sup
can	gap	key	own	sur
cis	gat	kid	pai	tar
clh	gay	kin	pan	tek
cmu	gem	kir	pau	ten
com	gen	koa	paw	the
cor	get	koz	pay	thy
cow	gin	lad	pen	tie
coz	gmt	lap	pin	tin
cry	gob	law	pit	tip
cud	god	lay	pot	tob
cup	gog	led	pua	toe
cut	got	leg	pul	toi
dam	gur	let	pur	too
dan	guy	lid	put	top
day	had	lie	ram	tou
dec	hai	lip	ran	tow
den	hal	lod	raw	try
dew	ham	log	red	tut
did	hap	lop	rei	two
die	has	lot	reu	uel
dig	hay	low	rib	uri
dim	hem	lud	rid	use
dip	hen	luz	rie	usr
dog	her	mad	rip	vex
don	hew	man	rob	vow
dor	hid	mar	rod	wag
dry	him	mat	roe	war
due	hin	maw	rot	was
ear	hip	may	row	wax
eat	his	men	rue	way
egg	hit	met	run	web
ehi	hod	mon	sad	wen
eli	hor	mps	sap	wet
end	hot	nay	sat	who
ere	how	ner	saw	why
eri	hul	net	say	win
err	hur	new	sea	wit
est	huz	nob	see	woe
etc	ice	nod	sei	won
eve	ico	noe	sem	wot
evi	iim	non	set	yea
ewe	ill	nor	sew	yes
eye	ink	not	she	yet
fan	inn	nov	sia	you
far	ira	now	sin	zer
fat	iri	nun	sir	zia
fed	iru	oak	sit	zif
few	isn	oar	six	zin
fig	its	odd	sky	ziz
fir	jah	off	soc	zur
fit	jaw	oft	sod	
fly	jew	oil	son	

213

2

ah	do	is	og	to
ai	ed	it	oh	up
am	er	je	ok	ur
an	ex	ll	on	us
ar	go	lo	or	uz
as	ha	me	ot	ve
at	he	my	ox	vi
be	ho	nb	pt	we
by	id	nd	rd	ye
	if	no	re	yn
	in	nt	ro	
	ir	of	so	

Kings & Queens

19
Bonnieprincecharlie
Carolineofbrunswick
Catherineofbraganza

18
Eleanorofaquitane
Elizabethbowesleyon
Elizabethwoodville
Nicholasbreakspear
Provisionsofoxford

17
Carolineofansbach
Catherineofaragon
Catherineofvalois
Philipmountbatten
Philippapfhainaut
Theyoungpretender

16
Dukeofcumberland
Hammerofthescots
Ladyoftheenglish
Mariafitzherbert
Maryqueenofscots
Pontefractcastle
Queenannesbounty
Routofwinchester
Westminsterabbey

15
Actofsettlement
Catherinehoward
Charlottesophia
Dukeofaquitaine
Elizabethofyork
Georgeofdenmark
Guildforddudley
Hundredyearswar
Margaretofanjou
Seconbaronswar
Simondemontfort
Themerrymonarch
Theoldpretender
Williamoforange
Williamwalworth

14
Dorotheajordan
Empressofindia
Henriettamaria
Olivercromwell
Peasantsrevolt
Robertdevereux
Robertthebruce
Sarahchurchill
Sophiadorothea
Stephenlangton
Stirlingbridge
Theblackprince
Thevirginqueen
Thomascromwell
Treatyoftroyes
Warsoftheroses
Williammarshal
Williamwallace

13
Anneofbohemia
Anneofdenmark
Bosworthfield
Catherineparr
Dukeofwindsor
Edwardseymour
Goodqueenbess
Gunpowderplot
Hubertdeburgh
Lambertsimnel
Robertcatesby
Rogermortimer
Thesailorking
Thomasfairfax
Wallissimpson

12
Albertedward
Anneofcleves
Domesdaybook
Farmergeorge
Hubertwalter
Ladyjanegrey
Maryofmodena
Newmodelarmy
Ninedayqueen
Robertdudley
Stoneofscone
Thebaronswar
Theconqueror
Thomasbecket
Thomaswolsey
Tuberculosis
Williamcecil

11
Bannockburn
Bolingbroke
Couerdelion
ElizabethII
Empressmaud
InnocentIII
Janeseymour
Johnofgaunt
Marydebohun
Plantagenet
Waltertirel

10
Adulterine
Anneboleyn
Annenevill
Berengaria
Bloodymary
Buckingham
Curtmantle
EdwardIII
ElizabethI
Johndudley
Longshanks
Lucywalter
Magnacarta
Maryofteck
Popishplot
RichardIII
Roundheads
Shrewsbury
Tewkesbury
Thebuilder
Thomasmore
Tinchebrai

Titusoates
Walsingham
WilliamIII

9
Agincourt
Alexandra
Babington
Beauclerc
Brandynan
CharlesII
EdwardIII
EdwardVII
GeorgeIII
Guyfawkes
HenryVIII
Influenza
Jacobites
Lancaster
Lionheart
RichardII
Runnymede
Sevenoaks
Whiteship
WilliamII
WilliamIV

8
Adelaide
AdrianIV
Annehyde
CharlesI
Culloden
Edgehill
EdwardII
EdwardIV

EdwardVI
GeorgeII
GeorgeIV
GeorgeVI
HenryIII
HenryVII
Isabella
Johncade
Lackland
PhilipII
Poitiers
RichardI
Ryehouse
Stalbans
Theboyne

Victoria
Wattyler
WilliamI

7

EdwardI
EdwardV
Falkirk
GeorgeI
GeorgeV
Hanover
HenryII
HenryIV

HenryYVI
Hotspur
JamesII
Lollard
Matilda
Polltax
Ridolphi
Saladin
Stephen

6

Addled
Albert

HenryI
HenryV
JamesI
MaryII
Stuart
Towton

5

Adela
Breda
Crecy
MaryI
Rufus

Stoke
Tudor

4

Anne
Joan
John

Lakes

10

Tanganyika

9

Athabaska
Greatbear
Nicaragua

8

Balkash
Issykkul
Manitoba
Michigan
Reindeer
Superior
Titicaca
Victoria
Winnipeg

7

Caspian
Kokonor
Ontario
Torrens

6

Baikal

Ladoga
Rudolf
Vanern

5

Huron
Nyasa
Onega
Urmia

4

Aral
Chad
Erie
Salt

Law

19

Comparison of hands
Conclusive evidence
Consensual contract
Constructive crimes
Consultary response
Corruption of blood
Couchant and levant
Marriage settlement
Presumption of fact
Principal challenge
Special plea in bar
Symbolical delivery
Threatening letters
Unilateral contract
View of frankpledge

Violent presumption
Warrant of attorney
Yielding and paying

18

Adverse possession
Arrest of judgment
Collation of seals
Confusion of goods
Malicious mischief
Presumption of law
Qualified property
Quantity of estate
Scandalum magnatum
Tenure by fee alms
Vindictive damages

Writing obligatory

17

A writ of account
Abstract of title
Abuse of distress
Act of bankruptcy
Cross-examination
Guardian ad litem
Joint and several
Material evidence
Negative pregnant
Oyer and terminer
Petition of right
Procuration money
Residuary legatee
Special injuction

Superstitious use
To wage one's law
Transitory action
Unlawful assembly
Vacant succession

16

A mensa et thoro
Act of attainder
Attorney-general
Collateral issue
Custos rotulorum
General demurrer
Hearsay evidence
Judgment summons
Multifariousness
Novel assignment

Privileged debts
Residuary clause
Residuary devise
Special demurrer
Special pleading
Special property
Vested remainder
View of premises
Voluntary escape
Writ of tresayle

15

Amicable action
Common barrator
Common lewdness
Common nuisance
Criminal action

General verdict
General warrant
Gross adventure
Particular lien
Personal action
Police offenses
Posse comitatus
Precatory words
Promissory note
Public nuisance
Quantum valebat
Separate estate
Simple contract
Special pleader
Special verdict
Specific legacy
Stale affidavit
Tender of issue
Things personal
Trustee process
Undue influence
Utter barrister
Vice chancellor
Voluntary waste
Wager of battle

14

Administration
Ancient lights
Audita querela
Common carrier
Corpus delicti
Extinguishment
Heriot service
High constable
Inferior court
Innocent party
Instance Court
Irreplevisable
Mala prohibita
Miscontinuance
Natural person
Orphans' court
Ouster le main
Parol contract
Penal statutes
Popular action
Post-obit bond
Probable cause
Probatory term
Quantum meruit
Representative
Search warrant
Simple larceny
Special damage
Spiriting away

Subinfeudation
To assure upon
To lay a venue
To wage battle
Vexatious suit
Watch and ward
Welsh mortgage

13

Acceptilation
administrator
Admortization
Ambidexterity
appropriation
Consolidation
Co-respondent
Cross-examine
Gaol delivery
General agent
General issue
Grand larceny
Gross average
Habeas corpus
Incorporation
Interlocution
Interlocutory
Interrogatory
Issuable plea
Joint tenancy
Judgment debt
justification
Maiden assize
Major offense
Mortgage deed
Obiter dictum
Office- found
Paraphernalia
Prevarication
Prison breach
Qualified fee
Rehypothecate
Remainder-man
Resulting use
Special issue
Synallagmatic
Third-borough
Toll and team
Traverse jury
Tyburn ticket
Vested legacy
Wife's equity

12

Accumulation
Acquiescence

Amortization
Appropriator
Cohabitation
Common scold
Compensation
Compurgation
Confirmation
Contribution
Contumacious
Conveyancing
Cooling time
Counter bond
Counter plea
Counterclaim
Cross action
General lien
Great cattle
Hereditament
Hypothecator
Incapability
Incapacitate
Incompetency
Incumbrancer
interference
Interlocutor
Interpleader
Joint tenant
Jurisconsult
jurisdiction
Mainpernable
Manslaughter
Miscognizant
Misdirection
Mixed action
Non obstante
Non-feasance
Parol arrest
Patent right
Peace of God
Penal action
Pourpresture
prescription
Prescriptive
Pro confesso
Protestation
Quo warranto
Recognizance
Renunciation
Res judicata
Reversionary
Scire facias
Sequestrator
Special jury
Stale demand
Substraction
Surrejoinder
Survivorship
Terre-tenant

Transmission
Trinity term
Unincumbered
Usufructuary
Vadium vivum
Verification
Wager of law
Water course

11

Advancement
Affiliation
Affirmation
Alien enemy
Appointment
Arraignment
Asportation
Collegatary
Commandment
Commutation
Complainant
Concealment
Concionator
Condonation
Confederacy
Conservator
Constituent
Contenement
Contentious
Contingency
Continuance
Conveyancer
Counterpart
Court lands
Court-baron
Disturbance
Encumbrance
Hue and cry
Hypothecate
Incompetent
Incorporeal
Incumbrance
Indifferent
Infeodation
Infeoffment
Infeudation
information
Inhabitancy
Inofficious
inquisition
Interferant
Jactitation
Malfeasance
Misdemeanor
Misfeasance
Mispleading

Next friend
Nihil debet
Nihil dicit
Office copy
Partnership
Permutation
Personality
Precontract
Presentment
Preterition
Pro re nata
Prosecution
Provocation
Purpresture
Ransom bill
Real action
Real assets
Reassurance
Re-demption
Redisseizin
Redisseizor
Rent charge
Repleviable
Requisition
Reservation
Reversioner
Safe-pledge
Single bill
Stipulation
Struck jury
Subornation
Subrogation
Subtraction
Suit custom
Supersedeas
Surrenderee
Surrenderor
Title deeds
Tort feasor
Traversable
Trusteeship
Unavoidable
Water gavel

10

Abalienate
Absolution
Absque hoc
Accomplice
Acquitting
Act of God
Adjustment
Administer
Aid prayer
Alienation
Allegation

Ambidexter
Ambulatory
Ampliation
Annexation
Assignment
Attornment
Away-going
Betterment
Clear days
Cognizance
Commorancy
Competency
Confession
Connivance
Connusance
Consensual
Conspiracy
Contingent
Conversion
Conveyance
Conviction
Coparcener
Copyholder
Court-leet
Covenantee
Covenantor
Cumulative
Disorderly
Extendible
Grand jury
Imparlance
Imprimatur
Incapacity
Indictment
Inducement
Infectious
Inhabitant
Inhibition
injunction
Inquisitor
Insolvency
Instrument
Intendment
Interplead
Intervener
Intestable
Invocation
Limitation
Mainpernor
Mala in se
Memorandum
Misjoinder
Misprision
Mutiny act
Negligence
Nisi prius
Nonability
Nonjoinder

Obligation
Part owner
Particular
Party wall
Penal code
Peremption
Perquisite
Personable
Personalty
Possession
Procedendo
Proceeding
Procession
Procurator
Prosecutor
Punishment
Rank modus
Recognitor
Recognizee
Recognizor
Redisseize
Redundancy
Rehibition
Rehibitory
Remittitur
Reputation
Respondent
Return day
Returnable
Schism act
Settlement
Speciality
Spoliation
Submission
Suggestion
Surplusage
Surrebuter
Table rent
Test paper
Tithingman
Tortiously
Trespasser
Trust deed
Unattached
Underlease
Vicontiels
Ward penny

9

Abandonee
Abatement
Abduction
Accession
Accessory
Accretion
Acquittal

Ademption
Admeasure
Adminicle
Admission
Adversary
Affidavit
Affirmant
Agistment
Agreement
Allocatur
Allotment
Amendment
Anatocism
Apparitor
Appellant
Appendant
Appointee
Appointor
Assumpsit
Attendant
Authentic
Averpenny
Cautioner
Cautionry
Certainty
Cognation
Collusion
Committee
Commodate
Commorant
Complaint
Condition
Confirmee
Conjugium
Connusant
Contumacy
Coparceny
Coshering
Coverture
Curtilage
Customary
Ejectment
Equitable
Executory
Extortion
Forthwith
Franchise
Garnishee
Good will
Guarantor
High seas
Homestead
Hospitium
Housebote
Hundreder
Ignoramus
Impleader
Incapable

Indenture
Infection
Insolvent
Intestate
Intrusion
Jointress
Mainprise
Malicious
Mandatary
Messenger
Mortgagee
Mortgager
Mutuality
Necessary
Nontenure
Nuisancer
Onomastic
Parcenary
Plaintiff
Pleadings
Port toll
Pourparty
Precedent
Prejudice
Premunire
Prescribe
Principal
Proponent
Prosecute
Protester
Pulsation
Purchaser
Purgation
Quitclaim
Recaption
Receiptor
Recognize
Recoveree
Recoveror
Reddendum
Refresher
Rejoinder
Reliction
Remainder
Rent seck
Repleader
Res geste
Retortion
Reversion
Routously
Sequester
Servitude
Severance
Similiter
Solicitor
Specialty
Suability
Subreader

Subtenant
Surcharge
Surrejoin
Surrender
Testament
Testatrix
Testimony
Theftbote
Tolsester
Traverser
Utter bar
Viability
Vicontiel
Voir dire
Volunteer
Ward-corn
Warrantee
Warranter
Warrantor
Withernam
Wrongdoer

8

Abeyance
Accepter
Addition
Agnation
Aleatory
Allodial
Allodium
Alluvion
Amortize
Ancestor
Appellee
Appellor
Assignee
Assignor
Assistor
Attentat
Attorney
Averment
Avulsion
Burglary
Cadaster
Caducary
Capacity
Cartbote
Carucage
Coercion
Cognatus
Cognizee
Cognizor
Cognomen
Cognovit
Commonty
Conjuror

Connusor
Contango
Contempt
contract
Conusant
Copyhold
Cosinage
Cottager
Covenant
Covinous
Cursitor
Disclaim
Distrain
Distress
Easement
Gravamen
Guardian
Habendum
Incident
Indictee
Indictor
Infamous
Informer
Innuendo
Insanity
John Doe
Jointure
Laudator
Location
Mandamus
Manovery
Marksman
Messuage
Mistrial
Mittimus
Mortgage
Mortmain
Mulierty
Muniment
Novation
Ordinary
Overrule
Parcener
Pernancy
Personal
Petition
Placitum
Plainant
Poundage
Praecipe
Promisee
Promisor
Property
Proposal
Purchase
Purparty
Quitrent
Rebuttal

Rebutter
Receiver
Recovery
Redemise
redirect
Relatrix
Relicted
Remitter
Remittor
Renounce
Replevin
Reprizes
Retainer
Reversed
Reverter
Scienter
Seashore
Sentence
Singular
Spinster
Stultify
Subagent
Sublease
Subpoena
Surrebut
Survivor
Suspense
Syngraph
Talesman
Talliage
Taxation
Teinland
Tenement
Terminer
Testator
Tortious
Transfer
Trespass
Usufruct
Vacation
Vadimony
Validity
Variance
Viscount
Voidable
Wainbote
Wehrgelt
Weregild
Wodegeld

7

Abandum
Accrete
Accruer
Acquest
Actuary

Affiant
Agistor
Alienee
Alimony
Aliunde
Arraign
Assault
Attaint
Average
Avowant
Caption
Codicil
Cognate
Cognati
Comfort
Compass
Compear
Concord
Concuss
Condone
Consent
Constat
Contest
Conusor
Cornage
Country
Curtesy
Defence
Earnest
Enfeoff
Escheat
Estreat
Execute
Exhibit
Falsify
Fiction
Fishery
Fixture
Freight
Grantee
Grantor
Holiday
Housage
Impeach
Implead
Indicia
Infancy
Infeoff
Inherit
Injuria
Inquest
Invalid
Jeofail
Joinder
Justify
Mistake
Misuser
Mutuary

Nonsuit
Nonterm
Nonuser
Nullity
Partner
Paviage
Payable
Perempt
Perjury
Piscary
Pleader
Pledgor
Plenary
Pluries
Pooling
Precept
Precipe
Premise
Prondor
Present
Privity
Probate
Process
Profert
Promise
Protest
Pursuit
Purview
Reality
Recital
Recoupe
Recover
Reentry
Relator
Release
Replevy
Reprise
Rescous
Reseize
Residue
Respite
Robbery
Set-off
Slander
Suicide
Summons
Tacking
Tailage
Taxable
Tenancy
Testacy
Testate
Testify
Tithing
Triable
Trustee
Verdict
Vesture

Vouchee
Voucher
Vouchor
Wainage
Warrant
Waveson
Witness

6

Abator
Accord
Accuse
Affirm
Affray
Agnate
Answer
Appeal
Arrest
Assets
Assign
Assize
Assume
Assure
Avoids
Bigamy
Caveat
Client
Cocket
Common
Corody
Cosher
Covert
Custom
Cypres
Damage
Defend
Eloign
Enjoin
Entail
Equity
Expert
Factum
Heresy
Hydage
Ignore
Imparl
Indict
Infamy
Infant
Infect
Malice
Marque
Mayhem
Merger
Mulier
Orator

Owelty
Parcel
Pardon
Parole
Pawnee
Pawnor
Pernor
Person
Plaint
Pledge
Postea
Puisne
Pursue
Realty
Recite
Recuse
Redeem
Rejoin
Remedy
Remise
Rescue
Revert
Reward
Rioter
Ruling
Salvor
Script
Seizin
Seizor
Semble
Specie
Stirps
Suable
Suborn
Suitor
Surety
Syndic
Tenant

Tender
Termer
Termor
Terrar
Trover
Twaite
Umpire
Vacant
Vadium
Vested
Viable
Viewer
Waiver
Walker

5

Actor
Adeem
Agist
Alias
Alibi
Array
Arson
Avoid
Cause
Close
Copal
Count
Covin
Culpa
Curia
Eject
Estop
Evict
Force
Fraud
Gavel

Grace
Grant
Howdy
Judge
Jural
Jurat
Juror
Legal
Major
Maker
Manor
Mesne
Modus
Novel
Overt
Panel
Parol
Payor
Plead
Prest
Privy
Prize
Quash
Rebut
Recto
Reply
Seize
Sever
Spado
Swear
Tenor
Teste
Theft
Third
Trial
Trier
Trior
Trust

Usury
Valid
Venue
Visne
Vouch
Wager
Waive
Waste
Wreck

4

Abet
Able
Arms
Aver
Avow
Case
Cost
File
Jury
Levy
Mise
Nude
Oath
Owel
Oyer
Pais
Plea
Rape
real
Rent
Riot
Rout
Rule
Said
Same
Sole

Stay
Suit
Tail
Tale
Tend
Term
Text
Toft
Toll
Tolt
Tort
Ulna
User
Utas
Wend
Will
Writ

3

Nul
Rob
Sue
Tac
Tax
Tol
Try
Use
Vis

2

In

1

M

Male First Names

13

christophorus
shellysheldon

12

bartholomeus
massimiliano
maximilianus

11

archaimbaud
archambault
bartolomeo
bartholomew
christoffer
christoforo
christopher
clerkclaude
constantine
constantino
konstantine

worthington

10

alessandro
alexandros
archibaldo
bartholemy
bartolomeo
batholomew
beauregard
christiano
christoper

christophe
cirstoforo
claudianus
claybourne
clementius
constantin
eziechiele
fitzgerald
franciskus
hieronymus
huntington
konstantin
kristoffer
kristoforo

kristopher
maximilian
maximilien
montgomery
rutherford
saunderson
sebastiano
sigismondo
sigismundo
stanislaus
sutherland
wainwright
washington
westbrooke

9

alejandro
aleksandr
alexander
alexandre
alexandro
alisander
ambrosius
archibald
archibold
aristotle
armstrong
augustine
bartolemo
benedetto
benedicto
beniamino
bertrando
broderick
chevalier
christian
christoph
claiborne
clayborne
cleavland
cleveland
cornelius
creighton
cristiano
cristobal
demetrius
dominique
ellswerth
ellsworth
engelbert
englebert
ethelbert
fairleigh
ferdinand
forrester
francesco
francisco
francklin
francklyn
fransisco
frasquito
frederich
frederick
frederico
frederigo
friedrich
friedrick
gabriello
gallagher
gaultiero

giselbert
gottfried
granville
gregorius
grenville
gualterio
guglielmo
guillaume
guillermo
heindrick
henderson
heriberto
ingelbert
inglebert
jefferson
johnathan
johnathon
justinian
kendricks
kristofer
kristofor
leicester
llewellyn
llywellyn
mackenzie
marcellus
marmaduke
matthaeus
nathanael
nathanial
nathaniel
nickolaus
patrizius
radcliffe
rafaellle
raffaello
reginauld
reinaldos
remington
richmound
rochester
roosevelt
salvatore
sanderson
sebastian
sebastien
sheffield
sherlocke
shurlocke
siegfried
sigismond
sigismund
silvester
standford
stanfield
stanislas
stanislaw

stanleigh
stephanus
stillmann
sutherlan
sylvester
templeton
teodorico
theodoric
thorndike
thorstein
timotheus
valentijn
valentine
valentino
wadsworth
wakefield
westbrook
westleigh
whittaker
winifield
zachariah
zacharias
zackariah
zechariah

8

adelbert
adolphus
aguistin
alasdair
alastair
alasteir
albrecht
aldridge
alexandr
algernon
alistair
allister
allistir
aloysius
alphonse
alphonso
ambrosio
anatollo
anderson
angelico
antonino
antonius
augustin
augustus
bancroft
barbabas
barnabas
barnebas
bartlett
basilius

bearnard
beaufort
bendicty
benedick
benedict
benedikt
benjamen
benjamin
benyamin
berkeley
bernardo
bernhard
bertrand
boniface
bradford
brantley
brewster
broderic
caldwell
carleton
cchaddie
cecilius
chadwick
chalmers
chandler
charlton
chauncey
chrissie
christie
christos
chrotoem
claiborn
clarance
clarence
claudell
claudian
claudius
clayborn
clemente
clifford
consalve
courtnay
courtney
crawford
crichton
cristian
cyrillus
davidson
delainey
demetris
dennison
dietrich
dionisio
dionysus
domenico
dominick
douglass

ebeneser
ebenezer
eberhard
eldredge
eldridge
elsworth
emanuele
emmanuel
emmerich
ephrayim
ernestus
ethelred
eugenius
ezechiel
ezequiel
farleigh
faulkner
federico
ferguson
fernando
fielding
filbarto
filberto
flemming
fletcher
forester
franchot
francois
franklin
franklyn
frederic
frederik
fredrick
freedman
freeland
gabriele
gamaliel
gardener
gardiner
garfield
gauthier
gayelord
geoffrey
gerhardt
germaine
germayne
gherardo
gilberto
giordano
giovanni
giuseppe
giustino
gonzales
gradeigh
grantham
granthem
grantley

greggory
gregoire
gregorio
griffith
griswold
guilbert
gustavus
hadleigh
hamilton
hansiain
harcourt
harrison
hartwell
harwilll
hastings
heinrick
hendrick
hercules
herculie
hernando
herschel
hilarius
hilliard
horatius
hugibert
humberto
humfried
humphrey
hunfredo
hurleigh
ignacius
ignatius
immanuel
jedediah
jedidiah
jefferey
jephthah
jeremiah
jeremias
jermaine
jermayne
johannes
jonathan
jonathon
jourdain
kahaleel
kendrick
kingsley
kingston
koenraad
krishnah
kristian
lancelot
langsdon
langston
laughton
laurence
lawrence
leighton

leonardo
leonhard
leonidas
lionello
lockwood
lodovico
lothaire
lothario
lowrance
ludovico
marcello
marchall
marietta
marshall
martainn
mattheus
matthias
matthieu
matthiew
mauricio
maurizio
meredeth
meredith
mitchael
mitchell
mohammed
mohandas
mohandis
montague
mordecai
mortimer
muhammad
napoleon
nataniel
nathanil
nehemiah
nicholas
nickolai
nickolas
nicolais
nikolaos
nikolaus
northrop
northrup
octavius
olenolin
oliviero
onofredo
orbadiah
osbourne
packston
panchito
papageno
parrnell
parsifal
pasquale
patricio
patrizio
pembroke

perceval
percival
philbert
phillipe
phillipp
prentice
prentiss
prescott
rafaello
raffarty
rafferty
raimondo
raimundo
randolph
reginald
reinaldo
reinhard
reinhold
reinwald
reynolds
riccardo
richardo
richmond
ricoriki
robinson
rockwell
roderich
roderick
roderigo
rodolphe
rodrique
rriocard
ruggiero
ruprecht
rutledge
salomone
salvador
salvidor
saunders
scarface
schuyler
sergeant
shepherd
sheppard
shepperd
sheridan
sherlock
sherwood
sherwynd
shurlock
shurwood
sigfried
silvanus
simmonds
sinclair
sinclare
somerset
staffard
stafford

stanford
stanwood
sterling
stillman
stirling
sullivan
taddeusz
tarrance
terencio
terrance
terrence
thaddeus
thatcher
thebault
thedrick
theobald
theodore
thornton
thorsten
thorvald
thurstan
thurston
timothee
torrance
torrence
townsend
tremaine
tremayne
trumaine
valdemar
valentin
vincents
vincenty
virgilio
vittorio
vladamir
vladimir
waldemar
wallache
waverley
whitaker
winfield
winthrop
wolfgang
zaccaria
zacharia
zacharie
zacherie
zebadiah
zedekiah

7

abelard
abraham
abrahan
addison
adolphe

adolpho
adriano
agustin
ailbert
alanson
alaster
alberik
alberto
aldrich
alfonse
alfonso
alfredo
alister
allayne
alphard
alyosha
ambrose
ambrosi
amerigo
anatole
andonis
andreas
anthony
antoine
antonin
antonio
armando
arnaldo
arnoldo
artemas
artemis
artemus
auberon
augusto
aurthur
averell
averill
avictor
avigdor
baillie
balduin
baldwin
barclay
barnabe
barnaby
barnard
barnett
barrett
barthel
bartlet
bartram
baryram
basilio
bastian
bastien
baudoin
beltran
bendick
bennett

bentlee	clemens	erasmus	georgie	hillier
bentley	clement	erastus	gerardo	hillyer
berkley	clemmie	ermanno	gerhard	hoebart
bernard	cointon	ernesto	germain	homerus
bernarr	coleman	erskine	gerrard	horacio
bertram	conrade	esteban	giacobo	horatio
bradley	conrado	estevan	giacomo	huberto
bradney	corbett	etienne	giacopo	humbert
branden	cordell	eugenio	giavani	humfrey
brander	cornall	eustace	giffard	humfrid
brandon	cornell	everard	gifford	huntlee
brandtr	craggie	everett	gilbert	huntley
brandyn	creight	ezekiel	gilburt	hussein
brannon	curtice	fabiano	giorgio	ibrahim
brendan	cyrille	fairfax	giraldo	ichabod
brenden	dalston	fairlie	glenden	ignacio
brendin	damiano	falkner	glendon	ignazio
brendis	darnall	farrell	goddard	ingamar
brendon	darnell	felicio	goddart	ingemar
brennan	darrell	felizio	godfree	isadore
brennen	darrick	ferrell	godfrey	isidore
brigham	davidde	fidelio	gonzalo	isidoro
brockie	de witt	filbert	gothart	jackson
broddie	delaney	filippo	graehme	jacques
bronnie	delbert	filmore	granger	jameson
bronson	delmore	findlay	grannie	jamison
bryanty	demetre	findley	gregoor	jarrett
burgess	demetri	fleming	gregory	jeffrey
burnaby	derrick	florian	griffie	jeramey
burnard	derward	forrest	griffin	jeramie
caddric	desmond	forster	gunther	jeremie
calhoun	desmund	francis	gustave	jermain
callean	devland	frankie	gustavo	jerrold
cameron	diarmid	frannie	guthrey	jerrome
carling	dimitri	franzen	guthrie	joachim
carlyle	dimitry	frasier	hadrian	joaquin
carmine	domenic	frazier	haleigh	johnnie
carolus	domingo	freddie	harbert	joseito
carroll	dominic	fredric	harland	joshuah
cassius	dominik	freeman	hartley	justino
cecilio	donaugh	freemon	harwell	karlens
chaddie	donavon	fremont	hasheem	kearney
chancey	donnell	gabriel	haskell	kendall
chariot	donovan	gallard	haslett	kendell
charles	douglas	gardner	hayward	kennedy
charley	dunstan	garrard	haywood	kenneth
charlie	durante	garreth	hazlett	kennett
chaunce	durward	garrett	heinrik	kennith
chester	eadmund	garrick	hendrik	kerwinn
cheston	edgardo	garrott	herbert	killian
chickie	edouard	garwood	hercule	kimball
chilton	eduardo	gaspard	hermann	kimbell
chrisse	ellerey	gasparo	herrick	kincaid
chrissy	elliott	gaylord	hershel	kingsly
christy	ellwood	gearalt	heywood	kinsley
cirillo	emanuel	gearard	hilario	klemens
claudio	emerson	geoffry	hillard	klement
clayson	enrique	geordie	hillary	kliment
clayton	ephraim	georges	hillery	krishna

222

krispin
kristos
lambert
lammond
laurens
laurent
lauritz
lazarus
leeland
lennard
leonard
leonerd
leopold
leupold
lincoln
lindsay
lindsey
lombard
lonnard
lorenzo
luciano
madison
mahmoud
malachi
malcolm
mallory
manfred
marcelo
marlowe
marshal
martino
massimo
mathian
mathias
matthew
matthus
mattias
maurice
maurise
maurits
maxwell
maynard
maynord
merrick
merrill
michael
michail
michale
micheal
micheil
michele
millard
mitchel
murdoch
murdock
nealson
neville
niccolo
nichole

nichols
nickola
nicolai
nicolas
nicolis
nikolai
nikolas
nikolos
norbert
normand
obadiah
obadias
obediah
obidiah
olivero
olivier
orlando
orville
osborne
osbourn
othello
pacorro
padgett
padraic
padraig
padriac
paquito
parnell
pascale
patrice
patrick
pebrook
pepillo
pernell
peterus
phillip
phineas
pierson
pietrek
pinchas
preston
purcell
quentin
quillan
quincey
quinlan
quintin
quinton
quintus
raimund
raleigh
rancell
randall
randell
randolf
ransell
raphael
raymond
raymund

raynard
reamonn
redford
reinald
reinold
renaldo
renault
reynard
reynold
ricardo
richard
richart
rickard
rickert
rinaldo
riobard
riordan
ritchie
robbert
roberto
robinet
roderic
rodolfo
rodolph
rodrick
rodrigo
rogerio
rolando
rolland
rollins
rowland
rudiger
rudolfo
rudolph
rudyard
ruperto
russell
ruttger
salomon
sampson
samuele
sanders
sanford
sansone
sargent
sauncho
saunder
saundra
sauveur
sawyere
scottie
sergent
seymour
shannan
shannon
shaughn
sheffie
shelden
shelley

shelton
shepard
sherman
shermie
sherwin
sigfrid
sigmund
sigvard
silvain
silvano
skipper
skippie
skipton
solomon
spencer
spenser
staford
stanley
stanton
stavros
stearne
stefano
steffen
stephan
stephen
steward
stewart
talbert
tedmund
teodoor
teodoro
terence
terrell
terrill
thacher
thaddus
thadeus
thaxter
thedric
theodor
thibaud
thibaut
thornie
tiebold
tiebout
timofei
timoteo
timothy
tirrell
toiboid
travers
tremain
trenton
tristam
tristan
trstram
trueman
trumann
tymothy

ulberto
ulysses
umberto
urbanus
vasilis
vassili
vassily
vaughan
victoir
vidovic
vidovik
vincent
vincenz
wallace
walther
waverly
wayland
webster
wendall
wendell
wernher
westley
wheeler
whitman
whitney
wilbert
wilburt
wilfred
wilfrid
wilhelm
willard
willdon
william
windham
winfred
winslow
winston
woodman
woodrow
wyndham
ximenes
ximenez
xymenes
yanaton
yardley
yehudit
zachary
zachery
zebedee
zebulen
zebulon

abbott
abramo
adolph
adrian

adrien	austen	brodie	corney	devlin
agosto	austin	bronny	cornie	dewain
aguste	averil	brooke	correy	dewitt
aharon	aylmar	brooks	corrie	dexter
alaric	aylmer	brucie	cortie	dickie
albert	bailey	bryant	cosimo	dieter
aldous	bailie	buckie	craggy	dillie
aldric	barney	buddie	creigh	dillon
aldwin	barnie	buiron	crosby	dmitri
alejoa	barret	burlie	cullan	donall
alexei	barrie	burtie	cullen	donalt
alexio	barris	burton	culley	donnie
alexis	barron	byrann	cullie	dorian
alfons	bartel	caesar	cullin	dougie
alford	bartie	calvin	culver	dudley
alfred	barton	carlie	curcio	duffie
allard	bacilo	carlin	curran	dugald
alleyn	baxter	carlos	currey	duncan
alonso	bayard	carney	currie	durand
alonzo	bealle	carrol	curtis	durant
aluino	bendix	carson	cyrill	dwayne
ambros	benito	carter	dallas	dwight
anatol	benjie	carver	dallis	earlie
ancell	bennie	caspar	dallon	earvin
anders	benoit	casper	dalton	eberto
andras	benson	cassle	damian	edgard
andrea	benton	cazzie	damien	edmund
andrej	berkie	cedric	daniel	eduard
andres	berkly	cesare	dannel	eduino
andrew	bernie	cesaro	dannie	edvard
andrey	bertie	chaddy	darbee	edward
andris	berton	chance	d'arcy	egbert
andros	billie	chicky	darill	elbert
andrus	blaine	chrisy	darius	elijah
angeli	blayne	chucho	darrel	elisha
angelo	bobbie	cirilo	darren	ellary
ansell	bogart	claire	darrin	ellery
anselm	boigie	clarke	darryl	elliot
antone	bondie	clemmy	darwin	elmore
antoni	bondon	cletis	daryle	elston
antons	boonie	cletus	davide	elwood
antony	boothe	clevey	delano	emelen
araldo	borden	clevie	delmar	emilio
archer	bordie	cobbie	delmer	emmery
archie	bourke	collin	delmor	emmett
armand	boycey	colman	demott	emmott
arnold	boycie	colver	dennet	enrico
arnuad	bradan	conant	denney	ephrem
artair	braden	conney	dennie	erhard
arther	bradly	connie	dennis	erhart
arthur	brandy	connor	denver	ernest
arturo	brewer	conrad	derick	errick
ashbey	briano	conroy	dermot	erroll
ashley	briant	conway	derrek	esdras
ashlin	briggs	cooper	derrik	ettore
ashton	brnaba	corbet	derril	eugene
aubert	brnaby	corbie	derron	evelin
aubrey	brocky	corbin	derwin	evelyn
august	broddy	cordie	devlen	evered

224

fabian	gasper	hamnet	ingmar	julius
fabien	gaston	hanson	ingram	justen
falito	gawain	harald	ingrim	justin
farlay	gayler	harlan	inness	justis
farlee	gaylor	harlen	iorgos	justus
farley	georas	harley	irvine	kahlil
farlie	george	harlin	irving	kaiser
farrel	georgi	harman	irwinn	kalvin
farris	georgy	harmon	isacco	kareem
felice	gerald	harold	isador	karlan
felike	gerard	haroun	isaiah	karlik
feliks	gerick	harper	isiahi	karlis
felipe	gerome	harris	isidor	karney
feodor	gerrie	harvey	isidro	karoly
ferdie	gianni	hashim	israel	kaspar
fergus	gibbie	haskel	issiah	kasper
ferrel	gideon	hastie	jackie	keefer
ferris	giffer	hayden	jacobo	keelby
fidole	giffie	haydon	jaimie	keenan
fields	gilles	hayyim	jamaal	kelbee
filmer	ginger	hebert	jamesy	kellby
finlay	giorgi	hector	jamill	kellen
finley	giraud	henrik	jammal	kelley
fletch	giulio	herbie	jarrad	kelsey
fonsie	giusto	herman	jarred	kelvin
fonzie	godard	hermie	jarret	kelwin
forbes	godart	hermon	jarrid	kendal
forest	godfry	herold	jarrod	kennan
foster	godwin	hersch	jarvis	kennie
fowler	goober	hervey	jasper	kenton
franky	goraud	hewett	javier	kenyon
franny	gordan	hewitt	jaymie	kermie
frants	gorden	hilary	jayson	kermit
frasco	gordie	hillel	jdavie	kerwin
fraser	gordon	hillie	jeffie	khalil
frazer	gradey	hilton	jeffry	kienan
freddy	graeme	hirsch	jerald	kilian
fredek	graham	hobard	jereme	killie
fulton	grange	hobart	jeremy	kimble
gabbie	granny	holden	jerome	kinnie
gaelan	gregor	hollis	jeromy	kippar
galvan	griffy	holmes	jerrie	kipper
galven	grover	homere	jervis	kippie
galvin	gunner	horace	jessee	konrad
gannie	guntar	horten	jessey	krisha
gannon	gunter	horton	jessie	kristo
garald	gustaf	howard	jethro	kurtis
gardie	gustav	hubert	jimmie	lamond
gareth	guthry	hughie	johann	lamont
garner	hadlee	hugues	johnny	lannie
garold	hadley	hunter	jordan	launce
garrek	hailey	hurlee	jordon	lauren
garret	hakeem	hurley	jorgan	laurie
garrik	hallsy	husain	joseph	lawton
garrot	halsey	husein	joshia	layton
garvey	hamish	ignace	joshua	lazare
garvin	hamlen	ilaire	josiah	lazaro
garwin	hamlin	ilario	josias	leland
gaspar	hammad	inglis	julian	lemmie

lemuel	mattie	nickie	porter	rowney
lenard	maurie	nicola	portie	royall
lennie	maximo	nikita	powell	ruddie
leonid	melvin	nikola	prince	rudolf
lesley	melvyn	nilson	putnam	rupert
leslie	menard	noland	putnem	rustie
lester	mendel	nollie	quincy	rustin
lewiss	mendie	norbie	raddie	rutger
lezley	merell	norman	rafael	rutter
lindon	merill	normie	ragnar	saleem
linoel	merrel	norrie	rainer	salmon
lionel	mervin	norris	ramsay	salomo
lonnie	merwin	norton	ramsey	sammie
lorant	merwyn	nowell	randal	samson
lorens	michal	oberon	randie	samuel
lorrie	michel	oliver	ransom	sancho
lovell	mickey	onfroi	rawley	sander
lowell	mickie	orazio	rayner	sandor
loydie	miguel	orland	raynor	sandro
lucais	mikael	osbert	reagan	sanson
lucian	mikkel	osborn	reagen	sascha
lucias	miller	osgood	reggie	sawyer
lucien	miltie	osmond	reggis	sayers
lucius	milton	osmund	reidar	sayres
ludvig	mischa	oswald	reider	scotti
ludwig	moises	oswell	reilly	scotty
lutero	moishe	paddie	renado	seamus
luther	monroe	padget	renard	sergei
maddie	morgan	palmer	renato	sergio
magnum	morgen	pancho	renaud	seumas
mahmud	morgun	parker	reuben	seward
maison	morltz	pascal	reuven	shadow
malchy	morlee	patric	ricard	shaine
malvin	morley	patten	richie	shalom
mandel	morrie	pattie	rickey	shamus
mannie	morris	pattin	rickie	shanan
manolo	morten	patton	ripley	shayne
manuel	mortie	paulie	roarke	sheffy
marcel	morton	pavlov	robbie	shelby
marcos	muffin	paxton	robers	shermy
marcus	munmro	payton	robert	sholom
marijn	munroe	peadar	rockey	sidnee
marion	murray	pearce	rockie	sidney
marius	murvyn	peirce	roddie	siffre
markos	mychal	pennie	rodger	silvan
markus	myrvyn	penrod	rodney	silvio
marlin	myrwyn	pepito	rogers	simeon
marlon	nappie	perice	roland	simone
marlow	natale	perkin	roldan	siward
marten	nathan	perren	rollie	skelly
martie	nealon	peyter	rollin	skippy
martin	neddie	peyton	romain	skylar
martyn	nelson	philip	ronald	skyler
marven	nester	pierce	ronnie	sloane
marvin	nestor	pierre	rooney	smitty
marwin	nevile	pieter	roscoe	sollie
mathew	nevins	pietro	rossie	sonnie
matias	newton	pincas	rourke	spence
matteo	nickey	pincus	rouvin	spense

stacee
stanly
stavro
stearn
stefan
sterne
steven
stevie
stinky
stuart
sumner
sutton
sydney
sylvan
tabbie
taddeo
tadeas
tailor
talbot
tallie
tammie
tanner
tanney
tannie
taylor
teador
teddie
tedman
temple
teodor
terrel
thaine
thatch
thayne
thomas
thorin
thorny
thorpe
tibold
timmie
tobiah
tobias
toddie
tomaso
tomkin
tomlin
tommie
tonnie
torrey
torrin
towney
townie
tracey
tracie
traver
travis
travus
trefor
trevar

trever
trevor
truman
tucker
tuckie
tulley
turner
tybalt
tyrone
ulises
ulrich
ulrick
urbain
urbano
vachel
vaclav
vasili
vasily
vaughn
vergil
vernen
verney
vernon
vernor
victor
vinnie
vinson
virgie
virgil
waiter
walden
waldon
walker
wallas
wallie
wallis
walton
warden
waring
warner
warren
waylan
waylen
waylin
waylon
weidar
weider
welbie
wendel
werner
wesley
weston
weylin
whitby
wilbur
wilden
wildon
willem
willey

willie
willis
wilmar
wilmer
wilton
winnie
wittie
wolfie
woodie
worden
worthy
wright
wyatan
xavier
xerxes
yancey
yankee
yehudi
yorgos
yorker
zollie

5

aaron
abbey
abbie
abbot
abdel
abdul
abner
abram
abran
adair
adamo
adams
addie
adham
adlai
adler
adolf
aguie
ahmad
ahmed
aksel
alain
alair
aland
alano
alard
albie
alden
aldin
aldis
aldon
aldus
alfie
alick

allan
allen
alley
allie
allin
allyn
aloin
alric
aluin
alvan
alvie
alvin
alvis
alwin
alwyn
amble
amery
amory
andie
andre
angel
angie
angus
ansel
anson
antin
anton
archy
ariel
arlan
arlen
arley
arlin
arman
armin
arney
arnie
arron
artie
artur
artus
arvie
arvin
ashby
asher
augie
avery
avram
avrom
aymer
baily
baird
banky
barde
barny
baron
barri
harry
barth

barty
basil
baxie
beale
bengt
benji
benjy
benny
berke
berky
berne
berny
berti
berty
bevan
bevin
bevon
billy
binky
birch
biron
bjorn
blair
blake
blane
bobby
bogey
bondy
boone
boony
boote
booth
bordy
boris
bowie
boyce
brade
brady
brand
brant
brent
brett
brian
brice
brien
brigg
brion
britt
brock
brody
brook
brose
bruce
bruis
bruno
bryan
bryce
bryon
bucky

buddy	corty	duffy	felix	halsy
burch	cosme	dukey	ferdy	hamel
burke	cosmo	dukie	fidel	hamid
burty	costa	dwain	field	hamil
butch	court	dylan	filip	hanan
byram	cozmo	eamon	flinn	hardy
byran	craig	earle	flint	harry
byrle	cross	early	flory	hasty
byrom	cully	eddie	floyd	haven
byron	curry	edgar	flynn	hayes
caleb	cyril	edlin	frank	hazel
camey	cyrus	edmon	frans	heall
cammy	dagny	edsel	franz	heath
carce	dalis	edwin	fraze	henri
carey	dalli	efrem	fritz	henry
carlo	damon	efren	gabby	herby
carly	danie	olden	gabie	hermy
carny	danny	eldin	gaile	hersh
caryl	dante	oldon	galen	herve
casar	danya	elias	ganny	hewet
casey	darby	elihu	gardy	hewie
cecil	darcy	eliot	garek	hilly
cello	daron	ellis	garey	hinze
cesar	darin	elmer	garik	hiram
chadd	dario	elnar	garry	hobey
chaim	daron	elroy	garth	hobie
chane	daryl	elton	garvy	hodge
chase	daven	elvin	gavan	hogan
chevy	davey	elvis	gaven	holly
chick	david	elvyn	gavin	homer
chico	davie	elwin	gawen	horst
chris	davin	elwyn	gayle	howey
chuck	davis	emery	geoff	howie
clair	davon	emile	georg	hubey
clare	deane	emlen	gerek	hubie
clark	decca	emlyn	gerik	hyatt
claus	denis	emmet	gerri	hyman
cleon	denny	emmit	gerry	hymie
clerc	denys	emory	gibby	iggie
cleve	derby	ennis	giffy	ignaz
cliff	derek	enoch	giles	ingar
clint	derry	erich	glenn	inger
clive	devin	erick	glynn	ingra
clyde	dewey	ermin	goran	inigo
clyve	dewie	ernie	gordy	innis
clywd	dicky	ernst	grace	iorgo
cobby	diego	errol	grady	iosep
codie	dilan	ervin	graig	irvin
colan	dilly	erwin	grant	irwin
colas	dolph	ethan	gregg	isaac
colby	donal	euell	griff	isaak
colet	donny	eugen	grove	izaak
colin	dorey	eward	guido	jabez
conan	dorie	ewart	gunar	jacky
conny	dougy	ewell	hagan	jacob
corby	doyle	faber	hagen	jaime
cordy	drake	fabio	haily	jakie
corey	drugi	farly	hakim	jakob
corny	duane	felic	haley	jamal

james	keven	marlo	nefen	pedro
jamey	kevin	marsh	neill	penny
jamie	kevon	marty	neils	percy
jamil	kiley	marve	neron	perry
janek	killy	mason	nevil	peter
janos	kinny	mateo	nevin	petey
jarad	kippy	mathe	niall	piggy
jareb	kirby	matty	nicko	piotr
jared	klaus	maury	nicky	pippo
jarib	kleon	maxie	nicol	porty
jarid	korey	maxim	niels	prent
jasen	kylie	mayer	nigel	price
jason	laird	mayne	nikki	prinz
jasun	lamar	mayor	nikos	pryce
jayme	lance	meade	niles	pyotr
jecho	laney	meier	niven	quent
jeddy	lanie	mendy	noach	quill
jeffy	lanny	merle	nobie	quinn
jeno	larry	merry	noble	quint
jerad	lawry	meryl	nolan	rabbi
jerri	lazar	meyer	nolly	raddy
jerry	lefty	micah	norby	ralph
jesse	leigh	micky	normy	ramon
jesus	lemar	mikel	norry	rance
jimmy	lemmy	mikey	north	randi
jocko	lenci	mikol	oates	randy
jodie	leroi	miles	odell	raoul
johan	leroy	milty	ogdan	ravid
johny	levey	miner	ogden	raviv
jonah	levin	minor	ogdon	reade
jonas	levon	mitch	ollie	reece
jorge	lewes	moise	olvan	reese
jozef	lewie	monro	omero	regan
judah	lindy	monte	onfre	regen
judas	linus	monti	orion	reggy
judon	lisle	monty	orlan	remus
jules	lloyd	moore	orran	reube
julie	locke	mordy	orren	rhett
julio	logan	morey	orrin	richy
kaine	lonny	morie	orson	ricki
kaleb	loren	morly	orton	ricky
kalil	lorin	morry	ossie	rikki
kalle	lorne	morse	ozzie	riley
karel	lorry	morty	pablo	ringo
karim	louie	moses	paddy	robby
kayne	louis	moshe	paige	robin
keane	lucas	mozes	paolo	rocky
keary	lucho	murry	parke	roddy
keefe	lucio	mycah	parry	rodge
keene	luigi	myles	paten	roger
keith	lukas	myron	patin	roley
kelby	lydon	nahum	paton	rolfe
kelly	lyell	nappy	patsy	rollo
kenny	lyman	natal	patty	rolph
kenon	maddy	natty	paulo	roman
kerby	major	neale	pauly	romeo
liormy	manny	neall	pavel	ronny
kerry	marco	nealy	paxton	rorke
kevan	mario	neddy	peder	rosco

rossy	taite	waldo	amos	bryn
rowan	tally	wally	andy	buck
rowen	tamas	walsh	ange	budd
royal	tammy	warde	arch	burg
royce	tanny	wayne	arel	burk
ruben	teddy	weber	arie	burl
rubin	tedie	welby	arin	burr
ruddy	terri	welch	ario	burt
rudie	terry	wells	arne	cale
rufus	thain	welsh	arni	calv
rurik	thane	wiatt	arny	care
rusty	thoma	wilek	aron	carl
ryley	thorn	wiley	arri	carr
salem	tiler	willi	arte	cart
salim	timmy	willy	arty	cary
sammy	titos	winny	arvy	case
sandy	titus	witty	aube	cash
sarge	tobie	wolfy	augy	cass
sasha	tobin	woody	axel	cece
saxon	tobit	worth	bail	chad
sayor	toddy	wyatt	bald	chan
sayre	tomas	wylie	balc	chas
scott	tommy	xenos	bank	chen
selby	torey	xever	bard	ches
selig	torin	yance	barn	chel
serge	torre	yancy	barr	chev
shane	torry	yorgo	bart	chic
shaun	towny	yorke	bary	chip
shawn	trace	yulma	base	ciro
sheff	tracy	yurik	baxy	clay
shell	trent	zared	bear	clem
sherm	tripp	zelig	beau	clim
sibyl	tucky	zolly	beck	cobb
silas	tudor		benn	codi
simon	tully	**4**	bent	cody
skell	tyler		berk	cole
skipp	tymon	abba	bern	conn
slade	tynan	abbe	bert	coop
sloan	tyrus	abby	bill	cord
smith	tyson	abel	bing	cori
solly	udale	abeu	bink	cort
sonny	udall	abey	birk	cory
spike	udell	abie	bond	cris
stacy	ulick	adam	bone	cull
stern	ulric	adan	boot	curr
steve	upton	addy	bord	curt
stevy	urban	akim	borg	dael
sully	uriah	alan	boyd	dale
sunny	uriel	aldo	brad	dall
svend	urson	alec	bram	dalt
sylas	valle	alex	bran	dame
syman	vance	alfy	bren	dana
symon	vanya	alic	bret	dane
tabby	verge	alix	brew	dani
taber	verne	alon	brig	darb
tabor	vince	alva	brit	dare
tadeo	vinny	alvy	brod	darn
tades	virge	amby	brok	dave
tadio	waite		bron	davy

dean	fitz	iago	knox	neel
deck	flem	iain	kort	neil
dell	flin	iggy	kory	nels
dene	fons	igor	kris	nero
derk	fonz	ikey	kurt	nial
desi	ford	isac	kyle	nick
devy	foss	isak	lalo	nico
dick	fran	itch	land	niel
dill	fred	ivan	lane	niki
dino	free	ivar	lars	niko
dion	gabe	iver	leif	nils
dirk	gabi	ives	leon	noah
dolf	gaby	ivor	levi	noak
donn	gael	izak	levy	noam
dore	gage	izzy	liam	nobe
dory	gail	jack	lief	noby
doug	gale	jake	linc	noel
drew	gard	jard	lind	noll
drud	gare	jase	link	obed
duff	garv	jaye	linn	obie
duke	gary	jean	lion	odey
duky	gene	jedd	lock	odie
dunc	geno	jeff	lowe	olag
dunn	geri	jehu	luca	olav
earl	gery	jens	luce	olin
eben	gian	jere	luis	olly
edan	gibb	jess	luke	omar
eddy	giff	jeth	lyle	oran
edik	gill	jock	lynn	oren
egan	gino	jodi	lyon	orin
egon	glen	jody	mace	otes
egor	glyn	joel	mack	otho
elia	gram	joey	maje	otis
elmo	gran	john	mano	otto
emmy	gray	jone	marc	owen
enos	greg	jory	mark	ozzy
erek	gris	jose	mart	pace
eric	griz	josh	marv	paco
erie	guss	juan	mata	page
erik	hale	judd	matt	pail
erin	hall	jude	maxy	pall
erny	hank	jule	mead	palm
esme	hans	kain	meir	park
esra	harp	kale	merv	pate
etan	hart	kane	mick	paul
ethe	harv	karl	mike	penn
evan	haze	kean	mile	pepe
even	herb	keen	mill	pete
evin	herc	keir	milo	petr
evyn	hewe	kele	milt	phil
ewan	hill	kenn	mord	phip
ewen	holt	kent	mort	pooh
ezra	hort	kerk	mose	port
ezri	hoyt	kerr	moss	poul
fabe	hube	kiel	myca	pren
fair	huey	kile	myer	puff
farr	hugh	king	mylo	rabi
ferd	hugo	kipp	nate	rafe
finn	hunt	kirk	neal	raff

rafi	tito	**3**	dun	lou
ralf	tobe		dur	loy
rand	toby	abe	eal	lyn
raul	todd	ade	edd	mac
ravi	tome	ado	eli	mal
read	tony	alf	ely	man
redd	tore	ali	erl	mar
reed	torr	any	erv	max
rees	town	ara	far	mel
reid	trev	ari	fax	mic
rene	trey	art	fee	moe
rhys	trip	arv	fin	nap
rice	tris	asa	gal	nat
rich	troy	ase	gan	ned
rick	tuck	ash	gar	nev
ring	tull	ave	gav	nil
robb	vail	axe	gay	noe
rock	vale	ban	gib	nye
rodd	vern	bar	gil	oby
rolf	vick	bat	gun	ode
roma	vite	bax	gus	odo
rory	vito	bay	guy	ody
ross	vlad	ben	had	ole
roth	wade	ber	hal	orv
rube	wain	bev	ham	pat
ruby	wait	bil	hew	pen
rudd	wake	bob	ian	pip
rudy	wald	boy	ike	rab
rufe	walt	bud	ira	rad
russ	wang	cad	irv	ram
ryan	ward	cal	isa	ray
ryon	ware	cam	ive	red
ryun	wash	car	jae	reg
saul	webb	caz	jan	rem
saxe	west	ced	jay	rex
scot	whit	che	jed	rey
sean	will	cly	jim	ric
seth	wilt	cob	job	rik
shae	winn	con	joe	rip
shaw	wolf	cos	jon	rob
shay	wood	dag	jud	rod
shea	wynn	dal	ken	rog
shem	yale	dan	ker	roi
shep	yank	dar	kev	ron
skip	yard	dav	kim	roy
skye	york	del	kin	ruy
stan	yule	den	kip	sal
sven	yuma	der	kit	sam
swen	yuri	des	law	saw
tabb	yves	dev	lay	sax
tadd	yvon	dew	lee	say
tait	yvor	dex	lek	see
tann	zach	dom	lem	sid
tate	zack	don	leo	sig
tedd	zane	dov	les	sim
temp	zeke	doy	lev	sky
theo	zerk	dru	lew	sly
thom		dud	lin	sol
thor			lon	son

stu	ugo	win	**2**	el
syd	uri	wit		em
tab	val	wye		ev
tad	van	wyn	ab	hi
tam	vic	yul	ad	hy
tan	vin	zak	al	jo
ted	von	zeb	ax	ky
tim	wat	zed	bo	ly
tod	way		cy	my
tom	web		eb	si
tye	wes		ed	ty

Mathematics

19

Congruency of lines
Impossible quantity
Increasing function
Mechanical solution
Reciprocal equation

18

Absolute curvature
Arbitrary function
Arbitrary quantity
Continued fraction
Intermediate terms
Nine points circle
Reciprocal figures
Regular polyhedron
Significant figure
Tabular difference
Triangular numbers
Unknown quantities
Vanishing fraction
Vertex of an angle

17

Aspect of a plane
Concurring figure
Congruent figures
Converging series
Implicit function
Inflected cycloid
Mean proportional
Nodated hyperbola
Orthotomic circle
Osculatory circle
Paracentric curve
Periodic function

Pyramidal numbers
Recurring decimal
Reverse operation
Tetrahedral angle
Theorem of Pappus
To vary uniformly
Universal theorem
Unlike quantities
Unlimited problem
Variable quantity
Vertex of a curve

16

Abstract numbers
Alternate angles
Amicable numbers
Applicate number
Ascending series
Axis of symmetry
Cubical parabola
Curve or surface
Imperfect number
Known quantities
Reciprocal ratio
Recurring series
Regression point
Triplicate ratio

15

Abundant number
Axis of a curve
Conical surface
Conjugate point
Curtate cycloid
Imperfect power
Inverse figures
Isoperimetrical
Ordinate figure

Regular polygon
Residual figure
Transverse axis
Twisted surface
Umbilical point

14

Hyperbolically
Interior angle
Internal angle
Interpretation
Inverse points
Isorropic line
multiplication
Orthographical
Quarter square
Theta function
Ultimate ratio
Unidimensional
Warped surface

13

Antilogarithm
Antiparallels
Approximation
Conic section
Curve tracing
Infinitesimal
Integrability
Interpolation
Interscendent
Mesologarithm
Positive sign
Quadruplicate
Rectification
Right pyramid
Row of points
Ruled surface

Tangent plane
Tautochronous
Transmutation
Twisted curve

12

Anallagmatic
Harmonically
Hyperbolical
Intersection
Isoperimetry
Manifoldness
Median point
Multiplicand
Oblique line
Orthomorphic
Proportional
Radical sign
Reciprocally
Round bodies
Triple ratio
Unlike signs
Wave surface
Whole number

11

Acute angle
Alternately
Alternation
Anchor ring
Contraction
Curvilinead
Icosahedral
Icosahedron
Inclination
Indivisible
Integration
Interfacial

Interpolate
Irreducible
Mass center
Median line
Occult line
Orthocenter
Permutation
Probability
Progression
Proposition
Quadrinodal
Rectifiable
Tautochrone
Tetrahedron
Transversal

10

A fortiori
Abbreviate
Anharmonic
Concurrent
Consequent
Conversion
Curvograph
Cyclometry
Cylindroid
Expression
Geodesical
Goniometry
Harmonical
Inequation
Integrable
Invariable
Invariance
Involution
Irrational
Major axis
Minus sign
Multiplier

Octahedron
Orthotomic
Osculation
Osculatory
Osculatrix
Proportion
Quadrature
Quaternion
Reciprocal
Supplement
Tangential
Tetragonal
Transverse
Trilateral
Trinominal
Trochoidal

9

Alternate
Asymmetry
Asymptote
Coinitial
Congruity
Conjugate
Cube root
Curvature
Glissando
Hodograph
Increment
Induction
Integrate
Intercept
Invariant
Inversion
Isosceles
Magnitude
Numerator
Operation
Orthotomy
Parameter
Plus sign
Potential
Quadrable
Ray point
Rectangle

Remainder
Resolvent
Resultant
Rheometry
Tangental
Transform
Transpose
Trapezium
Trapezoid
Trihedral
Trihedron
Trilinear
Trinomial
Undecagon
Unicursal

8

Absolute
Addition
Additive
Adjacent
Aliquant
Altitude
Amblygon
Analysis
Cardioid
Conchoid
Confocal
Conicoid
Constant
Coplanar
Crunodal
Cylinder
Equation
Function
Identity
Incenter
Inclined
Infinite
Infinity
Integral
Involute
Mantissa
Multiple
Multiply

Negative
Nonplane
Oblongum
Operator
Ordinate
Orthogon
Osculate
Repetend
Residual
Rhomboid
Roulette
Tetragon
Tractory
Tractrix
Triangle
Trinodal
Trochoid
Vertical
Vinculum

7

Algebra
Aliquot
Annulus
Apothem
Apotome
Contact
Content
Crunode
Cyclide
Cycloid
Develop
Fluxion
Formula
Geodesy
Inverse
Nonagon
Numeric
Oblatum
Oblique
Octagon
Operand
Problem
Product
Quadric

Quantic
Quantu
Radiant
Surface
Tangent
Theorem
Trapeze
Trident
Trisect
Umbilic

6

Acnode
Axioms
Divide
Factor
Isagon
Median
Medium
Member
Monome
Normal
Oblate
Octant
Oxygon
Plexus
Porime
Radian
Radius
Reason
Sector
Sphere
Symbol
Tensor
Ungula
Vector
Versed
Versor
Vertex

5

Angle
Apsis

Axiom
Conic
Cubic
Curve
Groin
Ideal
Minus
Nappe
Octicoddly
Prime
Radix
Ratio
Rhomb
Rider
Right
Scale
Torse
Torus
Wedge
Witch

4

Arch
Axis
Cone
Cube
Cusp
Even
Join
Mean
Node
Plus
Term
Tore
Unit

3

Arc
Net

Mechanics

#				
19	**18**	**17**	**16**	**15**
Conservative system	Accelerated motion	Rope transmission	Tangential force	Addendum circle
Neutral equilibrium	Moment of a couple	Tangential stress	To turn a flange	Neutral surface
	Skew bevel gearing		Virtual velocity	Shaping machine
	Universal coupling			Testing machine

Undershut valve
Universal chuck
Universal joint

14

Connecting rod
Reaction wheel
Reversing gear
Self-adjusting
Self-contained
Speed recorder
Spinning jenny
Sprocket wheel
Thermic weight
Traverse drill
Virtual moment
Wheel and axle

13

Marine engine
Ratchet brace
Ratchet wheel
Rocking shaft
Running block
Shrouded gear
Surface gauge
Surface plate
Tangent screw
Unit of power
Upright drill
Walking wheel
Working point

12

Countershaft
Moving force
Scroll chuck
Shroud plate
Spade handle

Spiral wheel
Tetraspaston
Virtual work
Vis impressa
Wing gudgeon

11

Accumulator
Cutter head
Regenerator
Safety cage
Socket bolt
Speed lathe
Stop motion
Swash plate
Tension rod
To turn off
Troll plate
Turn-buckle
Turret head
Union joint
Valve chest
Water snail

10

Angle iron
Crank axle
Cross axle
Cutter bar
Main brace
Male screw
Master tap
Oval chuck
Rock shaft
Rocker arm
Star wheel
Strap head
Suspension
Tool-stock
Topsoiling

Valve face
Valve seat
Valve stem
Valve yoke
Vis mortua
Wall frame
Web member
Web system

9

Air brake
Alligator
Angle bar
Crank pin
Crosshead
Crown-saw
Metergram
Regulator
Resultant
Set screw
Side tool
Slip link
Soleplate
Split pin
Spur gear
Sun wheel
Tentation
Tool-rest
Traveller
Way shaft
Wheelwork
Worm gear

8

Abutment
Conveyor
Coupling
Manifold
Momental
Momentum

Reaction
Shafting
Stub end
Telltale
Trochlea
Unclutch
Vis viva
Wall box
Wallower

7

Concave
Cropper
Cut-off
Rabbler
Segment
Shifter
Slabber
Slipper
Spindle
Succula
Tailpin
Take-up
Tension
Thimble
Torsion
Trigger
Trippet
Trundle
Whirtle
Whisket

6

Action
Centre
Matrix
Nipple
Rundle
Saddle
Shears

Sleeve
Taglia
Tappet
Tenter
Toggle
Torque
Travel
Trolly

5

Arbor
Brass
Crank
Crown
Cuddy
Molar
Slush
Strip
Swing
Wiper
Wrist

4

Cage
Muff
Neck
Rung
Shim
Snug
Stop
Stud
Teat
Vice
Whip

3

Cup
Tap
Toe

Metallurgy

16

Reducing furnace

15

Phosphor-bronze

14

German process

13

Queen's metal

12

German steel
Touch-needle

11

Hearth ends

Pistol pipe
Recarbonize
Tough-pitch
Tunnel head
White metal

10

Tap cinder

9

Greillade
Hot-short
Red-short
Tempering

8
Blooming
Lighting
Packfong
Puddling

7
Bulldog
Foxtail
Liquate
Looping
Testing
Torrefy

Tutenag
Zincify

6
Petong
Rondle
Rotatn

Tambac
Temper
Tombac

5
Torta

4
Lool
Pipe
Slag
Test
Tile

Meteorology

12
Aerosiderite

11
Anticyclone

9
Anthelion
Rain band

8
Aerolite

7
Thunder
Tornado
Typhoon

6
Trough

Military

19
Limber box or chest
Traversing platform

18
Practicable breach
Suspension of arms

17
General hospitals
Geneva convention
To take the field
Undercharged mine
Way of the rounds

16
Adjutant general
Counter approach
Countervallation
Court of Inquiry
Traversing plate

15
Concussion fuse
Contravallation
Countermovement
Floating bridge
General officer
Heavy artillery
Horizontal fire
Partisan ranger
Position finder
Provost marshal
Stand of colors
Stratarithmetry
Strategic point
Trench cavalier

14
Counter parole
Covering party
General guides
General orders
Guard of honor
Sergeant major
Special orders
Storming party
Strategic line

Undress parade

13
Accelerograph
Centesimation
Counter round
Coup d'oeil .
Honors of war
Place of arms
Quartermaster
Splinterproof
Stack of arms
Stand of arms
Tower bastion
Trumpet major
Vertical fire
Water battery
Watering call

12
Aide-de-camp
contribution
Corporalship
Counterguard
Countermarch
Counterscarf

Counterwheel
Coup de main
Geneva cross
Guard detail
Horse Guards
Light barrel
Line of fire
Picket guard
Solid square
Stone-mortar
Support arms
Tete-de-pont
Trou-de-loup
Under canvas

11
Aid-de-camp
Antestature
Counterfort
Countermine
Countersign
Coupe-gorge
Covered way
Crémaillére
Crow's-foot
Grand guard
Heavy metal

Heavy-armed
Light horse
Pass-parole
Pesent arms
Picket line
Point-blank
Sabretasche
Scale armor
Secure arms
Smart money
Stock purse
Swallowtail
Table money
Thumb stall

10
Angel shot
Contramure
Covert way
Cross fire
Crown side
Cul-de-sac
Guard duty
Guardhouse
Heavy fire
Light ball
Neutralize

Pack train
Pontvolant
Sally por
Sap roller
Skirmisher
Smoke ball
Substitute
Terreplein
Tirailleur
Tube pouch
Unattached
Under arms

9

Ambulance
Ambuscade
Artificer
Assistant
Camonflet
Caponiere
Carbineer
Cartridge
Field day
Formation
Furniture
Gabionage
Grapeshot
Grenadier
Guardroom
Half-pike
Petardier
Pommelion
Sap fagot
Sarrasine
Star fort
Tenaillon
Vauntmure
Voltigeur
Volunteer
Zumbooruk

8

Adjutant
Approach
Assembly
Bastions
Camisade
Canister
Cavalier
Consigne
Corporal
Corridor
Crotchet
Crowfoot
Galloper
Garrison
Gauntlet
Gendarme
Horseman
Partisan
Pass box
Pauldron
Pavilion
Pederero
Peterero
Ployment
Saucisse
Sergeant
Shabrack
Spontoon
Squadron
Stockade
Strategy
Surround
Tenaille
Traphole
Traverse
Trepeget
Turnpike
Unlimber
Vanguard
Zomboruk

7

Abattis
Bastion
Brigade
Carbine
Cavalry
Contour
Corbeil
Coupure
Crampet
Crampit
Cunette
Curtain
Cuvette
Frontal
General
Goudron
Grommet
Halberd
Palanka
Pannier
Pavisor
Perrier
Pioneer
Platoon
Plongee
Pontoon
Present
Private
Quarter
Salient
Scalado
Stacket
Station
Stative
Stifler
Summons
Surface
Trumpet
Tumbril
Vanfess

Vidette

6

Affair
Cartel
Cordon
Cornet
Crater
Harrow
Hussar
Pannel
Parade
Parole
Patrol
Pavise
Petard
Picket
Police
Pompon
Saikyr
Salute
Sapper
Sentry
Sillon
Sortie
Summon
Tattoo
Trefle
Trench
Turret
Uncase
Zareba
Zeriba
Zouave

5

Alert
Cavin
Crown

Flank
Grape
Hobit
Pivot
Sabot
Salvo
Scarp
Sight
Squad
Storm
Swive
Talus
Trace
Trail
Train
Tread
Troop
Truce
Uhlan
Yager

4

Foul
Halt
Park
Pike
Ploy
Port
Size
Tour

3

Arm
Gun
Sap
Spy
Tap

Mountains

11

Sierramadre

10

Adirondack
Macdonnell

8

Ccaucasus
Himalaya
Pyrenees
Tienshan

7

Adamawa

Khingan
Kjollen

6

Brooks
Pontic
Taurus

5

Altai
Andes
Atlas
Ozark
Pamir
Rocky

4

Alps
URral

Music

19

Unequal temperament

18

Consecutive chords
Thematic catalogue
Thirty-second note

17

Accidental chords
Corno di bassetto
Harmonic interval
Rhythmical accent
Sixty-fourth note

16

Auxiliary scales

15

Concerted piece
Contrary motion
Cornet à piston
Gregorian chant
Parallel motion
Perfect cadence
Pneumatic lever
Primitive chord
Programme music
Semidiatessaron
Wind instrument

14

Attendant keys
Concertmeister
Continued bass
Harmonic triad
Quadruple time
Quintuple time
Semidemiquaver
Sixteenth note
Sounding-board
Triple measure
Trumpet marine

13

Accompaniment
Adjunct notes
Close harmony
Compound time
Contrafagotto
Contrapuntist
Hand director
Kapellmeister
Partial tones
Passion music
Perfect chord
Phrygian mode
Sounding post
Superdominant
Thorough bass
Transcription
Transposition

12

Abbreviation
Acciaccatura
Aeolian mode
Anticipation
Appoggiatura
Augmentation
Common chord
Contrapuntal
Counterpoint
Half cadence
Holding note
Instrumental
Passing note
Passing tone
Quarter note
Registration
Repercussion
Semidiapason
Semidiapente
Sesquialtera
Tonic sol-fa
Volti subito

11

Accelerando
Arrangement
Capriccioso
Common time
Concertante

Consecutive
Contrabasso
Contratenor
Cracovienne
Grand piano
Great organ
Great scale
Harmoniphon
Harpsichord
Homophonous
Hydraulicon
Liedertafel
Passacaglio
Pedal organ
Plain chant
Poco a poco
Polyphonist
Prestissimo
Progression
Rallentando
Retardation
Rinforzando
Seventeenth
Solfeggiare
Solmization
String band
Subdominant
Subsemitone
Symphonious
Syncopation
Third sound
Triple time
Tuning fork
Violoncello

10

A cappella
accidental
Affettuoso
After-note
Allegretto
Cantatrice
Colorature
Concertino
Consonancy
Contrabass
Derivative
Grace note
Half shift
Hand organ
Harmonical
Improperia

Intermezzo
Kent bugle
Kettledrum
Lentamente
Pedal note
Pianissimo
Pianoforte
Pianograph
Polyphonic
Portamento
Recitative
Recitativo
Reed organ
repetition
Ritardando
Ritornello
Scherzando
Semichorus
Semiditone
Semiquaver
Sesquitone
Soavemente
Sotto voce
Sound post
Stringendo
Submediant
Supertonic
Tarantella
Thirteenth
Time-table
Tone color
Transcript
Transition
Tremolando
Undulation
Villanella
Vox humana
Whole note
Wind chest

9

Accompany
Accordion
Allemande
Altissimo
Alto clef
Andantino
Antiphone
Archilute
Authentic
Cacophony
Cantabile

Capriccio
Conductor
Consonant
Contralto
Crescendo
Fifteenth
Gems-horn
Generator
Half note
Half step
Harmonics
Harmonist
Harmonize
Hexachord
Homophony
Imitation
Impromptu
Interlude
Krakowiak
Lacrimoso
Languente
Larghetto
Leitmotif
Partition
Pastorale
Pizzicato
Polonaise
Polychord
Polyphony
Prolation
Quartette
Quickstep
Quintette
Quodlibet
Reed pipe
Reed stop
Ripienist
Roundelay
Saxophone
Semibreve
Semibrief
Septimole
Seraphine
Sightsman
Signature
Sixteenth
Solfeggio
Sopranist
Sostenuto
Spiritoso
Symphonic
Syncopate
Tablature
Tambourin

Theorbist
Transpose
Tripodian
Variation
Volkslied
Wind band
Wood wind
Woodblock

8

Accentor
Accolade
Addition
Al segno
Arpeggio
Canzonet
Carillon
Cavatina
Concerto
Continuo
Cromorna
Crotalum
Crotchet
Figurate
Fingered
Grazioso
Harmonic
Hornpipe
Infinite
Infinito
Interval
Intonate
Krumhorn
Legatura
Leggiero
Lentando
Parlante
Pastoral
Phrasing
Pianette
Quantity
Quinible
Quintole
Recorder
Reedwork
Relative
Rhapsody
Ritenuto
Sax-tuba
Semitone
Septette
Sequence
Serenade
Serenate
Sestetto
Sextetto
Sextolet

Sextuple
Sforzato
Smorsato
Sonatina
Spiccato
Staccato
Sticcado
Sub-bass
Subtonic
Symphony
Taborine
Telltale
Terzetto
Thematic
Tonality
Tremando
Trichord
Trombone
Vigoroso
Virginal
Virtuoso

7

Adjunct
Agitato
Allegro
Althorn
Amoroso
Andante
Ariette
Attacca
Cadenza
Calando
Cantata
Canzone
Capelle
Codetta
Concord
Conduct
Counter
Fagotto
Figural
Figured
Gambist
Gustoso
Hautboy
Kapelle
Keynote
Kussier
Natural
Partita
Pianino
Pibcorn
Piccolo
Piffara
Planxty
Polacca

Pomposo
Quatuor
Rackett
Recital
Related
Replica
Ripieno
Romance
Rosalia
Roulade
Roundel
Sackbut
Sambuke
Sanctus
Saxhorn
Scherzo
Secondo
Septuor
Seventh
Sistren
Slurred
Soloist
Soprano
Sordine
Sticker
Stretto
Syncope
Taboret
Tambour
Tampion
Tam-tam
Testudo
Theorbo
Timbrel
Timpano
Tipping
Toccata
Tompion
Tracker
Tremolo
Triplet
Tritone
Trumpet
Twelfth
Tympano
Violone

6

Adagio
Arioso
Ballet
Copula
Cornet
Figure
Finale
Finger
Florid

Giusto
Hopper
Invert
Kerana
Leader
Legato
Lesson
Phrase
Piatti
Plagal
Presto
Quaver
Repeat
Rhythm
Sempre
Sestet
Sonata
Sordet
Spinet
Strain
Subito
Syrinx
Taille
Temper
Tercet
Thesis
Tierce
Timbre
Timist
Tongue
Treble
Trigon
Trillo
Triole
Unison
upbeat
Violin
Vivace
Volume

5

Assai
Close
Comes
Comma
Croma
Croud
Cruth
Crwth
Drone
Fifth
Galop
Gamut
Gavot
Large
Largo
Lento

Piano
Pieno
Piper
Polka
Primo
Quill
Quint
Rebec
Regal
Rondo
Rotta
Scena
Score
Segno
Senza
Shake
Sharp
Shawm
Sixth
Soave
Sopra
Stave
Suite
Swell
Tabor
Tacet
Tardo
Tasto
Tempo
Tenor
Tenth
Theme
Third
Tonic
Tosto
Triad
Trill
Tutti
Viola
Volta
Volti

4

Alto
Aria
Clef
Coda
Cord
Glee
Leap
Lied
Loco
Long
Lute
Lyre
Poco
Reed

Rota
Rote
Skip
Slur
Solo
Stop
Tact

Tone
Trio
Tuba
Tune
Vary
Viol

3
Alt
Jig
Kin

Pi˜
Sol
Tie

2
La
Re
SI

Mythology

17
echidnehesperides

16
tuathadedananaan
unarmoredsoldier

15
ganapatihardiya
mountaincentaur
quantummechanic
templepriestess

14
baluchitherium
biasdnasrogaig
callicantzaros
carnivorousape
earthelemental
freezingsphere
gelatinouscube
glasgaibleanir
ichthyocentaur
metacollinarum
odontotyrannus
tuathadedanaan
waterelemental

13
brobdinagians
callicantzari
calygreyhound
chesterbelloc
draconcopedes
fireelemental
forestcentaur
gnomishwizard

hyman topodes
koplieutenant
mabonmamodron
mountainnymph
plainscentaur
questingbeast
quiveringhloh
ricabooracker
slidringtanni
watermoccasin

12
achiyalabopa
airelemental
archeologist
bandersnatch
blackpudding
blackunicorn
blatantbeast
brownpudding
burach-bhadi
cameloparbel
cynocephalus
draconcopede
energyvortex
erichthonius
glollinkambi
guardiannaga
gullinbursti
hippocentaur
koboldshaman
koboldzombie
leathergolem
leontophonus
lilliputians
madscientist
maricomorion
meshekenabec
miehtshozjin
mokelembembe
mythological
orangedragon
picktreebrag
prockgwinter

quetzalcoatl
smierragatto
spottedjelly
templepriest
violetfungus
waldmannlein
whiteunicorn
woodland-elf
yellowdragon

11
aesculapius
allocamelus
amphisbaena
anaskelades
barbeddevil
barrowwight
blackdragon
bloodybones
boabhansith
burachbhadi
cadwallader
carnivorous
cheng-hwang
chichevache
cinnamolgus
cynocephali
dadhikravan
daoinesidhe
electriceel
ettinzombie
flitterbick
floatingeye
formicoleon
gartersnake
ghulibeaban
giantbeetle
giantspider
giantzombie
gnomezombie
gollinkambi
grayunicorn
greendragon
heliodromos

hippocampus
horneddevll
humanzombie
ironpiercer
jormungandr
keystonekop
koboldmummy
kopsergeant
largekobold
lurkerabove
lyonpoisson
memecoleous
mirmecoleon
monicodiata
monoscelans
mooseweibel
muircartach
Mythologist
orc-captain
rockpiercer
rumptifusel
rustmonster
saggitarius
scolopendra
steamvortex
stymphalian
Terpsichore
thunderbird
titanothere
twrchtrywth
vampirelord
Water nymph
whitedragon
yellowlight
ysgithyrwyn
zoroastrian

10
aidohevedo
aigamuchas
amphiptere
archangels
argopelter
ashozushta

bhainsaura
bluedragon
bogeybeast
borogroves
brollachan
callirrhoe
callitrice
camelopard
cametennus
catoblepas
catoblepta
cavespider
charadrius
chenghwang
cockatrice
crookelegs
cynamolgus
demogorgon
dustvortex
ellerwoman
epidaurian
ereshkigal
erymanthos
ettinmummy
Euhemerism
Euhemerize
eymanthian
feng-hwang
fenriswolf
firevortex
fleshgolem
frostgiant
gaibleanir
gandharvas
gargouille
garudabird
gelatinous
giantmimic
giantmummy
gillygaloo
gioldaoram
girtablili
gnomemummy
goldennaga
graydragon

grœnteeth
gueniviere
guyascutus
gweniviere
gwynapnudd
hamadryads
heliopolis
hidebehind
hildirisin
hippocrene
hippodamia
hippogriff
hippogryph
hiyakudori
homunculus
hrodvitnir
humanmummy
iarnvithja
innungagap
jabberwock
jackalwere
jinshinuwo
kamaitachi
kirtimukha
koboldlord
kopkaptain
largemimic
leprechaun
lieutenant
lufferlang
maildaemon
mantichora
mantiserra
masterlich
maugmolach
nalfeshnee
nuckelavee
ochrejelly
onocentaur
polyphemus
Prometheus
purpleworm
saehrimnir
salamander
satyrefish
seaserpent
secundille
shopkeeper
shrovetide
smallmimic
soldierant
stonegiant
stonegolem
strawgolem
stymphalus
teakettler
tripoderoo
tsuchigumo

uilebheist
vampirebat
vourukasha
waterdemon
waternymph
watertroll
werejackal
werewolves
winterwolf
yatagarasu
yellowmold
yggdrasill
ysbaddaden
zolostraya

9

acipenser
aeschylus
ajaekapad
alcyoneus
Aphrodite
apocrypha
archangel
areopenop
atargatis
baalzebub
balthazar
barbarian
baryachre
belmarduk
bergelmir
blacknaga
bluejelly
bonedevil
brownmold
bundahish
cailleach
caladrius
cantharus
cantzaros
capricorn
catamount
cavewoman
centycore
chameleon
chamnaill
claygolem
conopenii
corocotta
cutercuss
cynamolgi
diocletan
dwarfking
dwarflord
easgsaint
elemental

elfzombie
elvenking
ephemerus
ephialtes
erymathus
feifrefiz
fenghwang
firedrake
firegiant
fomorians
gandareva
gandharva
giddyfish
gigelorum
gizdhubar
glawackus
gligamesh
gnomeking
gnomelord
green-elf
greenmold
guirivulu
guyanoosa
hamadryad
hatchling
hedleykow
hellhound
hildisvin
hillgiant
hippocerf
hobgoblin
hobthrush
hoopsnake
houyhnhnm
hraesvelg
hsingtien
huahutiao
hydrippus
icevortex
ihuaivulu
iphigenia
iphimedia
irongolem
jotunheim
keresaspa
khubilgan
killerbee
launcelot
leocrotta
leucrotta
leviathan
littledog
lykopolis
lyonsbane
manabozho
manticore
manticory
mantocore

mazainyan
Melpomene
merrymaid
monoceros
mordororc
mythology
narasinha
nunyenunc
oceanides
orcshaman
orczombie
palesmurt
papstesel
parandrus
partessus
pegpowler
pemphredo
pendragon
polyhymna
priestess
prirthous
pyragones
quivering
ratramnus
reddragon
rocktroll
ropegolem
Sagittary
sasbonsam
sciapodia
scientist
sea horse
semiramis
slamander
soonerdog
swamfisck
tarandrus
terrobuli
tisiphone
umberhulk
unarmored
vithafnir
vorysmort
vyantaras
Water god
wayzgoose
woodgolem
woodnymph
woodwives
yggdrasil

8

achelous
achilles
acidblob
adrastus

aeternae
ahuizotl
aitvaras
allerion
Ambrosia
analopos
aptaleon
arcadian
arimaspi
asmodeus
attracta
baphomet
bargvest
barometz
Basilisk
behemoth
bergfolk
bialozar
bogeyman
bonachus
bonnacon
borametz
borogove
briareus
bubastos
bwbachod
calliope
cantzari
centaurs
cerastes
Cerberus
chamrosh
chatloup
cherruve
cherubim
chrysaor
cockfish
corineus
crocotte
curupira
dadjikra
daedalus
daedelus
delphyne
demilich
dispater
ecidemon
electric
elf-lord
elfmummy
epimacus
erechire
erinnyes
eschylus
floating
fogcloud
fomorian
freezing

frumious
gacanagh
ganconer
ganeshra
gargoyle
giantant
giantbat
giantcel
giantrat
gleipner
glooscap
goatfete
gogmagog
grayooze
gremlins
grey-elf
griffeth
guardian
gumberoo
gwragedd
hairymeg
holzfrau
homocane
hornworm
housecat
hrimfaxi
hrothgar
Hyperion
icedevil
icetroll
ipopodes
keystone
khumbaba
kreutzet
kukulkan
lamassus
lancelot
largecat
largedog
lavellan
lofriska
lokapala
longworm
lucidius
lungwang
lurikeen
lybbarde
manabush
mandrake
marilith
mechanic
melusine
minocane
Minotaur
mixcoatl
moccasin
Morpheus
mountain

mushrush
mushussu
myrmadon
myrmedon
myrmidon
nagaloka
nependis
niflheim
oceanide
odysseus
ogreking
ogrelord
olog-hai
opinicus
orcmummy
oresteia
pantheon
panthera
papillon
nasiphae
Phalthon
phillylo
picktree
Pierides
pingfeng
pitfiend
pitviper
pleiades
portunes
poseidon
potharni
pyrallis
pyrausta
queenbee
rabidrat
ragnarok
raksasas
rameagle
ratatosk
ricabook
rockmole
roperite
sciapods
scitalis
scorpion
scythian
seraphim
sergeant
sevienda
sewerrat
shagamaw
shahapet
skinfaxi
skogsfru
sleipnir
spriggan
stellone
steropes

stringes
succubus
Tantalus
tarasque
Tartarus
Terminus
tichiang
tragopan
tulihand
unicorne
unycorne
uruk-hai
vaettrar
valhalla
valkyrie
varengan
werewolf
wudewose
wolfwere
woodwife
woolyhen
yeenoghu
ygdrasil
yllerion
ypotryll

7

Acheron
alborak
alburaq
alcyone
aloadai
Anteros
anthias
antlion
apsaras
arcades
Ariadne
artemis
artemus
astarte
astraea
attagen
aurochs
Bacchus
banshee
basadae
beowulf
biasdna
bicorne
billdad
bittern
blatant
blemyae
boabhan
boggart

bonasus
boobrie
brahmin
brillig
brontes
brownie
bugaboo
bugbear
bulchin
calopus
camelot
capacti
capalus
captain
catfish
caveman
cecrops
celphie
centaur
chapula
cheiron
chimera
chronos
circhos
cirsith
crocula
cualgne
culhwch
cyclops
dendain
derceto
direach
dwarves
empusae
enfield
erinyes
Erlking
eternae
euterpe
evilorc
faeries
fairies
fanesii
fanesus
fireant
gabriel
ganesha
gawaine
gerahav
glastig
gnomish
goofang
gremian
gremlin
grendel
griffin
gryphon
gudunna

gwinter
hafgygr
halcyon
haniver
hanuman
harpies
haugbui
havfine
heabani
hillorc
hobhole
huldras
humbaba
impaler
incubus
irizima
ivlthja
jinshin
juiblex
kakmora
kaptain
karfish
kinnara
kundrav
lampeia
lapiths
lernean
lindorm
lucifer
lumerpa
lympago
mahomet
margygr
martlet
matsaya
mermaid
merrows
microbe
midgard
monster
mordred
morgana
morholt
moruach
moruadh
mumakil
murrisk
musimon
musimus
muspill
narwhal
Nemesis
nereids
nidhogg
nimurta
ninevah
nisidia
oedipus

ogoncho
onniont
orcrist
orestes
owlbear
padfoot
Pandora
parande
pegasus
peredur
Perseus
phineus
Phoebus
phoenix
piercer
pontarf
Proteus
pudding
quantum
quechua
rabican
ratwere
rawhead
redmold
rednaga
rosualt
samurai
sarabha
satyral
scaipod
sekamet
senmurv
shriker
simurgh
sirrush
sisiutl
skoffin
soldier
spotted
srogaig
ssuling
stalker
stirges
stringe
sumargh
takujui
Talaria
tanagra
taotieh
Taranis
templar
thingut
tienkou
tityron
tityrus
topodes
tourist
trapper
tristan

ubastet
unicorn
unycorn
uranian
urukhai
vampire
wererat
xanthos
xiphius
ygraine
ypotain
ziphius

6

achlis
alecto
alicha
alphyn
alsvid
altion
alvand
amarok
ambize
angels
angulo
Anubis
apollo
arakho
arthur
asgard
assuit
astrea
athena
athene
auroch
aurora
Avatar
avesta
bagwyn
balios
balrog
barbed
barrow
bayard
beaban
belloc
bodach
boojum
brazen
buccas
bunyip
burach
caecus
cecith
cephus
charon
charus

cherub
chilin
cottus
daemon
danaan
daoine
daoram
djinni
djinns
dracus
dragon
drakes
dryads
dwarfs
eitidh
energy
enkidu
ercine
facahn
faerie
fafnir
fairie
fenris
fingal
forest
freyja
fungus
fylgja
garasu
garter
garuda
gawain
geryon
ghlinn
gimbal
goblin
golden
gorgon
gotama
graeae
grylio
guduna
guivre
gwaine
haokah
hathor
healer
hecate
hedley
henziz
hermes
hezrou
hobbit
hoenir
horned
hozjin
huginn
huldra
hunkus

icaros
icarus
iffrlt
ishtar
isolde
jackal
jaguar
jalpan
jeduah
jubjub
kargas
kaukas
kelpie
killer
kitten
knight
Kobold
kraken
kronos
kulili
lamiae
lapith
lemers
lemure
lilith
little
loyres
lurker
lycaon
magera
makara
manasa
marduk
master
mbembe
medusa
merlin
merrow
miehts
milamo
mimick
modron
mokele
mordor
muninn
muyans
myrmex
nacken
nagini
naiads
nazgul
Nereid
Nereis
nesnas
nessus
nymphs
oannes
ophois
oracle

orange
oreads
orthos
osiris
osquip
pegasi
pekhet
pelion
pelops
peluda
phooka
phykis
plains
Plutus
Pomona
priest
purple
python
qiqion
quasit
raiden
redcap
remora
rinjin
sargon
satyre
satyrs
schrat
scylla
semuru
seraph
shaman
shoney
sirens
slithy
sooner
sphere
Sphinx
spider
squonk
srvara
stirge
tanuki
tauris
taurus
temple
Thalia
Themis
tiamat
tlaloc
triton
trolls
trywth
tsuchi
tuatha
typhon
unnati
Urania
uranos

Uranus
valtar
vamana
varaha
varuna
violet
vishap
vishnu
vortex
vulcan
vuokho
winter
wizard
wraith
wumpus
wyvern
yahoos
Yaksha
yellow
yendor
yffrit
ygrain
zombie
zushta

5

abaia
abath
Aegis
aetna
afanc
agape
agapi
alfil
ammut
anaye
angel
angka
annwn
apres
areop
arges
Argus
arion
arrak
avanc
azael
bennu
biasd
bjara
bogey
bogle
borak
brash
bucca
buraq
busse

Ceres
cetus
cheng
chirn
circe
crumh
cuero
deino
devil
divis
djinn
dobie
draci
drake
dryad
dwarf
earth
eller
elves
erato
ettin
faery
fairy
falin
fauns
fetch
fiend
flesh
freki
frost
galon
ganga
ghost
ghoul
giant
giles
gizeh
gnome
golem
green
guard
gulon
gwain
Hades
harpy
hodag
horus
hound
houri
hsiao
hsing
huahu
human
humma
huppe
hwang
hydra
hyman

ifrit
ixion
jappa
jelly
jerff
jinni
jinns
jumar
Kalpa
karga
kilin
kirni
koori
kudan
kylin
lamia
lemer
light
mohon
magog
manes
medea
mimic
mimsy
Minos
mummy
nagas
naiad
nakki
nandi
nauru
niont
nisse
nixie
nurse
nykur
nymph
ochre
orcus
Oread
pajar
panku
peist
pheng
piasa
Pluto
pooka
prion
prock
pygmy
pyong
queen
rabid
rogue
rompo
rothe
safat
sahab

satyr
sedus
serra
sesha
sewer
shmoo
shuck
sidhe
siren
small
snake
snark
steam
stone
straw
talos
tatsu
taurt
tengu
Thoth
titan
toves
troll
twrch
tygre
umber
urisk
uther
vedic
Venus
viper
vorys
vrock
vrtra
water
white
wight
wivre
yahoo
yfrit
zruty

4

aido
aker
alan
apis
apop
apsu
Argo
baku
bucu
ccoa
ceyx
chac
clio

crom
dies
donn
eale
easg
enyo
eros
etna
faun
feng
fire
frek
gaia
garm
geri
ghul
giol
giza
glas
gwyn
gyes
gyre
haug
hell
hera
hill
hulk
jinn
juno
Kali
kiau
king
knei
krni
lich
loki
long
lord
mail
mara
mold
mole
mome
muse
naga
nakk
odin
ogre
ooze
ossa
otos
ovda
para
pwca
rahu
rath
reem
rigi

rock
rope
rukh
rust
seth
seti
tarn
tove
twas
uruk
urus
vlad
wabe
warg
wolf

wood
worm
xorn
yale
yali
Yama
yata
yeti
ylio
ymir
Yoni
zeus

3

aja
anu
bel
eel
elf
eye
fog
gog
hel
hob
hoo
ice

imp
isa
kop
mad
nix
nun
oni
orc
pan
pit
puk
pup
rat
red
roc

rok
Sop
tyr
xan
ziz

2

al
ea
hu
io
su
zu

Nations

10

Azerbaijan
Bangladesh
Elsalvador
Ivorycoast
Kazakhstan
Kyrgyzstan
Luxembourg
Madagascar
Mauritania
Mozambique
Newzealand
Northkorea
Seychelles
Southkorea
Tajikistan
Uzbekistan
Yugoslavia

9

Argentina
Australia
Capeverde
Costarica
Guatemala
Indonesia
Lithuania
Macedonia
Mauritius
Nicaragua
Sanmarino
Singapore
Swaziland
Venezuela

8

Barbados
Botswana
Bulgaria
Cambodia
Cameroon
Colombia
Djibouti
Dominica
Ethiopia
Honduras
Hongkong
Kiribati
Malaysia
Maldives
Mongolia
Pakistan
Paraguay
Portugal
Slovakia
Slovenia
Srilanka
Suriname
Tanzania
Thailand
Zimbabwe

7

Albania
Algeria
Andorra
Antigua
Armenia
Austria
Bahamas

Bahrain
Belarus
Belgium
Bolivia
Burundi
Comoros
Croatia
Denmark
Ecuador
Eritrea
Estonia
Finland
Georgia
Germany
Grenada
Hungary
Iceland
Ireland
Jamaica
Lebanon
Lesotho
Liberia
Moldova
Morocco
Nigeria
Romania
Senegal
Somalia
Stlucia
Tunisia
Ukraine
Uruguay
Vanuata
Vietnam

6

Angola
Belize
Bhutan
Bosnia
Brazil
Brunei
Canada
Cyprus
France
Gambia
Greece
Guinea
Guyana
Israel
Jordan
Kuwait
Latvia
Malawi
Mexico
Monaco
Norway
Panama
Poland
Russia
Rwanda
Sweden
Taiwan
Turkey
Tuvalu
Uganda
Zambia

5

Benin
Burma

Chile
China
Congo
Egypt
Gabon
Ghana
Haiti
India
Italy
Japan
Kenya
Libya
Malta
Nepal
Niger
Qatar
Spain
Sudan
Syria
Tonga
Yemen
Zaire

4

Chad
Cuba
Fiji
Iran
Iraq
Laos
Mali
Oman
Peru
Togo

Oceans

13 Mediterranean

10 Southchina

9 Caribbean
Eastchina

8 Adriatic
Atlantic

7 Andaman
Caspian
Okotsk
Pacific

6 Arctic

Baltic
Bering
Hudson
Indian

5 Black
Japan
North

4 Azov

3 Red

Palaeontology

17 Woolly rhinoceros

15
Ichthyopterygia
Labyrinthodonta
Paleontological
Paleornithology

14
Asterophyllite
Cyathophylloid
Ichthyosaurian
Labyrinthodont
Lepidodendroid
Paleontologist

13
Archaeopteryx
Ichthyosauria
Ichthyosaurus
Labyrinthodon
Lepidodendrid
Lepidodendron
Plesiosaurian
Proterosaurus
Pteranodontia

Pythonomorpha
Titanotherium

12
Anthropolite
Camarasaurus
Paleotherian
Paleotherium
Paleotheroid
Pelicosauria
Placodermata
Plesiosauria
Plesiosaurus
Pterodactyli
Pterosaurian
Tetracoralla
Theriodontia
Thunderstone
Uintatherium
Ventriculite

11
Anoplothere
Arenicolite
Asterolepis
Cephalaspis
Corallinite
Coryphodont
Ichthyolite
Ichthyornis

Ichthyosaur
Paleobotany
Paleosaurus
Paleozooogy
Paradoxides
Placodermal
Pleiosaurus
Protohippus
Pterichthys
Pterodactyl
Pterosauria
Teleosaurus
Tentaculite
Thecodontia
Theriodonta
Theromorpha
Thunderbolt
Tichorrhine
Tillodontia

10
Anaptychus
Archimedes
Coccosteus
Iguanodont
Inoceramus
Juniperite
Laminarite
Lycopodite
Oryctology
Palapteryx

Paleothere
Pecopteris
Pentamerus
Placodermi
Plesiosaur
Pliohippus
Pliosaurus
Pteranodon
Theriodont
Trinucleus
Tubiporite
Ulodendron

9
Amblypoda
Antholite
Clidastes
Coprolite
Iguanodon
Lithocarp
Palmacite
Placoderm
Productus
Psarolite
Pterosaur
Pycnodont
Taxeopoda
Teleosaur
Thecodont
Theropoda
Toxodonta

Trilobita
Trilobite
Turbinite
Turrilite

8
Ammonite
Calamite
Capstone
Conchite
Jewstone
Lunulite
Polypite
Trochite

7
Asaphus
Juncite
Laelaps
Lituite
Phacops
Toxodon
Turbite

6
Atrypa
Pinite

Philosophy

15
Antepredicament

14
Contraposition
Preîxistentism
Sensationalism
Transcendental

13
Contradictory

12
A posteriori
Continuative
Spiritualism

11
Affirmative
Amphibolous
Consequence
Crocodility
Voluntarism

10
Ampliative
Antecedent
Assumption
Conclusion
Consequent
Contraries
Conversion
Convertend
Phenomenal
Scepticism

9
Abduction
Absolutes
Aesthetic
Crocodile

8
A priori
Abstract
Analyses
Analysis
Concrete
Contrary

Converse
Psychism
Quotiety

7
Apagoge
Connote

5
Cynic

Physics

19
Adhesive attraction
Magneto- electrical
Magneto-electricity
Torricellian vacuum
Wheatstone's bridge

18
Corpuscular theory
Remanent magnet-
ism
Residual magnetism
Sympathetic sounds
Thermoelectrometer
Unipolar induction
Unit of resistance

17
Accidental colors
Magnetic elements
Microspectroscope
Thermoelectricity
Water thermometer
Wave of vibration

16
Galvanic battery
Graphite battery
Insulating stool
Sonorous figures
Specific gravity
Thermometrograph

15
Achromatic lens
Aplanatic focus
Catelectrotonic
Conjugate focus
Converging rays
Impenetrability
Radiomicrometer
Sensitive flame
Solar phosphori
Storage battery
Telepolariscope
Telestereoscope
Telethermometer
Thermobarometer
Vitre-o-electic
Water barometer
Wheel barometer

14
Absolute space
Catadioptrical
Gramme machine
Image Purkinje
Magnetic storm
Microtasimeter
Radiant energy
Stereoelectric
Tantalus's cup
Thermoelectric
Twelfth-second
Whirling table

13
Absolute zero
Galvanic pile
Geissler tube
Roric figures
Specific heat
Sprengel pump
Thermocurrent
Thermodynamic
Thermovoltaic
Transpiration
Virtual focus
Volumenometer
Water battery
Zeeman effect

12
Anorthoscope
Astatic pair
Cone of rays
Galvanometer
Galvanoscope
Idioelectric
Impenetrable
Imponderable
Inductometer
interference
Irrotational
Kaleidophone
Magnetograph
Magnetometer
Nonconductor
Spectrometer
Spectroscope
Thermal unit
Thermochrosy
Thermoscopic
Thermostatic
Transudation
Unit of heat
Unit of work
Visual angle
Water hammer
Wave surface
Zircon light

11
Aeolotropic
Agonic line
Amperometer
Anaclastics
Anisotropic
Calorimetry
Calorimotor
Gas battery
Gyrostatics
Ice machine
Incoercible
Inductorium
Inductrical
Interrupter
Isodiabatic
Nonelectric
Opeidoscope
Persistency
Restitution
Seismograph
Seismometer
Seismoscope
Spherometer
Stereometer
Temperature
Thaumatrope
Thermograph
Thermometer
Thermoscope

Ultraviolet
Volumescope
Wave length
Wave theory
White light
Zero method
Zinco-polar

10

Aberration
Achromatic
Aeolotropy
Anaclastic
Anelectric
Atmosphere
Attraction
Axial line
Conduction
Gyrostatic
Inducteous
Isentropic
Kinematics
Microphone
Milliweber
Multiplier
Otheoscope
Pachometer
Phonograph
Photometer
Piezometer
Radiometer
Radiophone
Radiophony

Regelation
Resistance
Teinoscope
Tenthmetre
Thermopile
Thermostat
Trichromic
Undulation
Void space
Voltameter
Wave front

9

Acoustics
Adiabatic
Aplanatic
Arcometer
Extension
Hydrogode
Incidence
Inductive
Influence
Intensity
Interfere
Isopycnic
Isotropic
Megameter
Osmometer
Osmometry
Passivity
Portative
Pyrometer
Reflector

Repulsion
Rheometer
Rheoscope
Telephone
Vibration
Viscosity
Voltmeter
Volumeter
Wattmeter
Y current

8

Adhesion
Adynamic
Air pump
Analyzer
Aperture
Armature
Atmology
Buoyancy
Gyrostat
Inductor
Insulite
Isotropy
Kinetics
Megadyne
Megalerg
Molecule
Particle
Regelate
Reotrope
Tenacity
Ultrared

Unipolar
Unit jar
Vergency
Voltaism

7

Ammeter
Astatic
Caloric
Gravity
Inertia
isolate
Kinetic
Photics
Quantum
Reostat
Tasimer
Telpher
Voltage
Zincode
Zincous

6

Liquid
Magnet
Megerg
Micron
Odylic
Period
Ripple
Smooth

Stable
Static
Vacuum
Virial

5

Force
Gauge
Odyle
Phase
Vapor
Weber

4

Atmo
Atom
Node
Volt
Watt
Wave

3

Ray

2

Od

Places

14

beltway bandit
czechoslovakia
jefferson city
north carolina
salt lake city

13

beltwaybandit
jeffersoncity
liechtenstein
massachusetts
new hampshire
north vietnam

northcarolina
oklahoma city
pennsylvanian
philadelphian
san francisco
santo domingo
south african
south dakotan
south vietnam
west virginia

12

buenos aires
east germany
indianapolis
kuala lampur

leopoldville
mountainview
newhampshire
north dakota
northvietnam
oklahomacity
pennsylvania
philadelphia
portauprince
rhode island
saltlakecity
san salvador
sanfrancisco
santodomingo
saudi arabia
sierra leone
south africa

south dakota
south korean
southafrican
southdakotan
southvietnam
soviet union
thessalonika
vatican city
westvirginia

11

afghanistan
albuquerque
archipegalo
archipelago
argentinian

brazzaville
buenosaires
carson city
connecticut
costa rican
daressalaam
east german
eastgermany
grandcayman
great falls
indian hill
ivory coast
kualalampur
little rock
los angeles
mauritanian
mexico city

minneapolis
mississippi
murray hill
netherlands
new orleans
new zealand
north korea
northdakota
ouagadougou
palestinian
philippines
portofspain
rhodeisland
salvadorian
sansalvador
saudiarabia
sierraleone
sioux falls
south korea
southafrica
southdakota
southkorean
sovietunion
springfield
switzerland
tallahassee
tegucigalpa
upper volta
vaticancity
yugoslavian

10

addisababa
australian
babylonian
batonrouge
berlinwall
birmingham
burlington
california
carolinian
carsoncity
charleston
concordian
copenhagen
costa rica
costarican
eastgerman
franciscan
greatfalls
guatemalan
harrisburg
indianhill
indonesian
irishwoman
ivorycoast

libreville
littlerock
losangeles
louisville
luxembourg
madagascar
manchester
mauritania
mexicocity
mogadiscio
montevideo
montpelier
murrayhill
new guinea
new jersey
new mexico
neworleans
newzealand
nicaraguan
northkorea
nouakchott
panamanian
philippino
piscataway
pittsburgh
providence
rawalpindi
sacramento
san marino
scotswoman
senegalese
siouxfalls
southkorea
tananarive
uppervolta
venezuelan
vietnamese
washington
wellington
welshwoman
wilmington
winchester
yugoslavia

9

amsterdam
anchorage
annapolis
argentina
ascension
australia
baltimore
bell core
bostonian
brazilian
bucharest

bulgarian
cambodian
ceylonese
charlotte
chicagoan
cleveland
columbian
costarica
desmoines
ecuadoran
elsavador
eluethera
ethiopian
floridian
frankfort
galapagos
guadelupe
guatemala
hampshire
icelandic
indonesia
jerusalem
jordanian
kalamazoo
las vegas
londinium
louisiana
malaysian
milwaukee
minnesota
mongolian
mongoloid
mongomery
muscovite
nashville
nebraskan
new delhi
newguinea
newjersey
newmexico
newyorker
nicaragua
oregonian
pakistani
palestine
palo alto
philipino
phnompenh
pittsburg
protonovo
pyongyang
reykjavik
salisbury
sanmarino
santiagan
santorini
singapore
stockholm

taiwanese
tennessee
ulanbator
venezuela
vientiane
wisconsin

8

alabaman
albanian
algerian
american
andorran
angelino
arizonan
asuncion
athenian
atlantan
austrian
bahamian
bathurst
bedouine
belgrade
bellcore
benghazi
berkeley
berliner
bismarck
bolivian
brasilia
brussels
budapest
bulgaria
cambodia
cameroon
canadian
canberra
carolina
cheyenne
colorado
columbia
columbus
damascus
delaware
djakarta
dubliner
eluethra
eluthera
endicott
ethiopia
filipino
fortlamy
freetown
georgian
hartford
helsinki

honduras
hongkong
honolulu
illinois
irishman
jamaican
japanese
katmandu
khartoum
kingston
lasvegas
lebanese
lentucky
liberian
londoner
malaysia
managuan
maryland
michigan
missouri
mongolia
monrovia
nebraska
nepalese
new york
newdelhi
nigerian
oklahoma
olympian
pakistan
paloalto
paraguay
parisian
parisien
pekinese
peruvian
portland
portugal
pretoria
richmond
rumanian
salvador
san jose
santa fe
santiago
saqqarat
scotsman
skiathos
somalian
spaniard
sudanese
tanzania
thailand
thessaly
tobagoan
trinidad
tunisian
usumbura

valletta
viennese
virginia
welchman
welshman

7

abidjan
alabama
alaskan
albania
algeria
algiers
america
andorra
ankaran
arabian
arizona
arkanas
atlanta
augusta
austria
babylon
baghdad
bahamas
bahrain
bangkok
bayarea
bedouln
beijing
belgian
belgium
beltway
bermuda
boisian
bolivia
boswash
burundi
caracas
chicago
chilean
chinese
conakry
concord
dahomey
dakotan
denmark
detroit
ecuador
eluthra
england
english
finland
florida
gambian
georgia
germany

ghanian
guinean
haitian
hanover
houston
hungary
icarian
iceland
indiana
ireland
israeli
jackson
jamaica
kampala
kinston
kuwaiti
lansing
laosian
lebanon
liberia
lincoln
madison
managua
memphis
mexican
montana
morocco
nairobi
newyork
nicosia
nigeria
norfolk
oakland
olympia
orlando
ottawan
phoenix
raleigh
rangoon
redbank
rumania
russian
rwandan
sanfran
sanjose
santafe
saqqara
saudian
seattle
senegal
somalia
spanish
stlouis
swedish
teheran
trenton
tripoli
tunisia

turkish
ugandan
uruguay
vatican
vermont
vietnam
wichita
wyoming
yangtze
yaounde
yucatan
zambian

6

abicos
aeqean
alaska
albany
ankara
arabia
arubas
athens
austln
bahama
bamako
bangui
berlin
berner
beruit
bhutan
bogota
boston
brazil
burman
canada
cayman
celtic
ceylon
cyprus
dakota
dallas
denver
dublin
france
french
gaelic
gambia
german
greece
guinea
guymas
havana
hawaii
helena
icaros
indian
israel

jordan
juneau
kenyan
kigali
korean
kuwait
lesbos
libian
libyan
lisbon
london
lusaka
madrid
malawi
manila
memnos
mexico
monaco
moscow
muscat
nevada
newark
niamey
norway
oregon
ottawa
panama
peking
peking
pierre
poland
polish
prague
riyadh
russia
rwanda
saigon
samnos
samoan
sofian
stpaul
sweden
syrian
taipei
taiwan
tehran
thimbu
tirana
tobago
togoan
topeka
turkey
uganda
vienna
warsaw
yemeni
zambia

5

abico
accra
agean
amman
aruba
boise
burma
cairo
chile
china
colom
congo
cuban
dakar
dover
fargo
gabon
ghana
greek
haiti
hanoi
hmong
hunan
idaho
india
iowan
irani
iraqi
irish
japan
kabul
kenya
korea
lagos
lanas
lapaz
libya
maine
malta
miami
nepal
niger
omaha
paris
quito
roman
salem
samoa
saudi
scots
seoul
sofia
spain
sudan
swede
swiss

syria
texan
texas
thera
tokyo
tunis
vaduz
wales
welch
welsh

yemen
zomba

4

apia
bern
bonn
celt

chad
cuba
iowa
iran
iraq
laos
lima
lome
mali
nyny

ohio
oman
oslo
peru
rome
sana
togo
troy
utah

3

usa

2

dc
uk

Politics

19

balance of payments
black consciousness
breach of the peace
checks and balances
Christian Democrats
classical economics
collective security
communist mani-
festo
cult of personality
cultural revolution
diminishing returns
diplomatic immunity
executive privilege
front organizations
independent counsel
massive retaliation
national liberation
public opinion poll
sphere of influence

18

affirmative action
ballistic missiles
civil disobedience
constitutional law
consumer activists
counter-revolution
division of labour
European
Community
limited government
Muslim Brotherhood
passive resistance
people's democracy
persona non gratis

private enterprise
self-determination
steering committee
storm in a tea cup
straddle the fence
territorial waters

17

balance of terror
conspiracy theory
constitutionalism
contempt of court
deficit financing
equal opportunity
greenhouse effect
guerrilla warfare
inalienable right
industrialization
international law
multiple warheads
national interest
non-proliferation
political capital
political realism
primary elections
satellite country
secondary boycott
shuttle diplomacy
supply and demand
unemployment rate

16

academic freedom
adversary system
aggregate demand
aggregate supply
anti-clericalism

Attorney General
balance of power
balance of trade
chain of command
church and state
collectivization
decentralization
direct democracy
displaced person
dyed-in-the-wool
economic warfare
internationalism
local government
Marxism-Leninism
non-intervention
philosopher king
political access
political asylum
political theory
public ownership
social Darwinism
summit diplomacy
Vatican Councils
women's movement
world government

15

anti-trust laws
balanced budget
Carter Doctrine
civil liberties
competitiveness
counter-culture
divide and rule
double jeopardy
economic growth
fellow traveler
free enterprise
interventionism

judicial review
kitchen cabinet
Monroe Doctrine
multilateralism
nationalization
petit bourgeois
planned economy
plenipotentiary
political party
prior restraint
public interest
pyrrhic victory
Reagan Doctrine
sit-down strike
social contract
Social Security
social services
standing orders
totalitarianism
Truman Doctrine

14

accountability
Achilles' heel
administration
anti-communism
bill of rights
business cycle
centralization
class struggle
discrimination
draconian laws
ecclesiastical
egalitarianism
eminent domain
featherbedding
foreign policy
fundamentalism
general strike

implied powers
incomes policy
incrementalism
indoctrination
infrastructure
interest group
invisible hand
labor movement
libertarianism
macroeconomics
microeconomics
millenarianism
modus operandi
Napoleonic law
natural rights
naturalization
nuclear family
party platform
point of order
politicization
pressure group
price controls
prime minister
private sector
public opinion
redistribution
rehabilitation
representation
secularization
silver-tongued
social justice
social welfare
states' rights
United Nations
utilitarianism
vicious circle
ways and means
westernization
white elephant

13

acculturation
anti-Semitism
appropriation
authoritarian
balkanization
carte blanche
civil service
collaboration
commercialism
common Market
confederation
court martial
desegregation
direct action
domino theory
eleventh hour
establishment
ethnocentrism
Eurocommunism
expropriation
fait accompli
fireside chat
fiscal policy
fourth estate
globalization
gold standard
grandstanding
habeas corpus
hard currency
head of state
incorporation
individualism
intellectuals
jurisprudence
laissez-faire
law and order
leisure class
Machiavellian
market forces
mass hysteria
mixed economy
modus vivendi
municipal law
national debt
nonconformist
normalization
privatization
protectionism
public morals
public sector
puppet regime
raison d'etat
raison d'etre
rank and file
raw materials
regimentation

revolutionary
right to work
rule of thumb
secret ballot
socialization
stare decisis
surplus value
welfare state
working class

12

act of state
adjudication
aide-de-camp
anthropology
arms control
belligerency
bilateralism
black market
block voting
brinkmanship
capitulation
carpetbagger
civil rights
codification
collectivism
collegialism
colonization
commonwealth
conciliation
conservatism
conservative
constitution
cosmopolitan
demographics
dictatorship
divine right
emancipation
embezzlement
entrepreneur
expansionism
exploitation
fifth column
gerontocracy
good offices
Gordian knot
human rights
humanitarian
iconoclastic
import quota
infiltration
insurrection
intervention
iron curtain
isolationism
jurisdiction
Keynesianism

labour union
legitimation
maritime law
mercantilism
minimum wage
mobilization
money supply
nation state
obsolescence
olive branch
omnibus bill
open society
paramilitary
parochialism
polarization
police power
police state
productivity
protectorate
public works
quid pro quo
ratification
rehabilitate
repatriation
rubber stamp
ruling class
toxic wastes
united front
universalism

11

adjournment
ahistorical
apologetics
appeasement
arbitration
aristocracy
arraignment
bureaucracy
by-election
casus belli
closed shop
coexistence
colonialism
common good
competition
consumption
containment
corporation
coup d'etat
credibility
criminology
destabilize
devaluation
dirty linen
disarmament
doctrinaire

due process
equilibrium
evangelical
extradition
figure-head
free market
geopolitics
gerrymander
immigration
impeachment
imperialism
integration
ivory tower
legislation
legislature
limited war
martial law
materialism
McCarthyism
meritocracy
methodology
mudslinging
nationalism
natural law
negotiation
Nobel Prize
nonpartisan
nonviolence
opportunism
ozone layer
pan-African
pan-Islamic
paternalism
pocket veto
pork-barrel
post mortem
prerogative
proletariat
prosecution
provocation
reactionary
Realpolitik
red herring
regionalism
reparations
retaliation
revisionism
segregation
show trials
sovereignty
speculation
stagflation
subsistence
syndicalism
third party
Third World
trade union
trusteeship

underground
ward heeler
Warsaw Pact

10

abdication
abrogation
absolutism
aggression
allegiance
ambassador
annexation
apolitical
automation
bipartisan
Bolshevism
brigandage
Capitalism
censorship
chauvinism
collective
common law
compromise
consortium
conspiracy
dark horse
delegation
depression
deterrence
devolution
ecumenical
electorate
emigration
euthanasia
evangelism
ex officio
expatriate
federalism
federation
filibuster
free trade
income tax
indexation
indictment
INF Treaty
injunction
insurgence
investment
Jacobinism
landlocked
leadership
legalistic
legislator
legitimacy
liberalism
liberation
magistrate

Malthusian
mass media
matriarchy
messianism
monetarism
muckraking
multipolar
neutrality
nomination
nonaligned
opposition
oppression
parliament
party line
patriarchy
patriotism
per capita
pigeonhole
plebiscite
plutocracy
politician
possession
pro choice
propaganda
providence
referendum
repression
revolution
right-wing
sacred cow
separatism
status quo
straw vote
subversive
succession
superpower
unilateral
usurpation
vox populi
World Bank
xenophobia

9

acid test
affidavit
affluence
agitation
amendment
anarchism
apologist
arbitrary
armistice
austerity
autocracy
bicameral
big stick
bilateral

blacklist
bourgeois
caliphate
canon law
civil war
coalition
Cominform
Comintern
commissar
Communism
consensus
criterion
dead heat
deflation
demagogue
democracy
despotism
dialectic
diplomacy
directive
dissident
dogmatism
earmarked
economics
ecumenism
equal pay
Fabianism
feudalism
franchise
guerrilla
hierarchy
holocaust
incentive
inflation
insurgent
judiciary
lame duck
landslide
left-wing
logistics
manifesto
mediation
mercenary
New Right
obscenity
oligarchy
oligopoly
ombudsman
orthodoxy
partition
patrician
patrimony
patronage
pluralism
political
pragmatic
precedent
prejudice

president
probation
rationing
rebellion
recession
reprisals
sanctions
sanctuary
secession
sectarian
servitude
skinheads
socialism
sovereign
Star Wars
statesman
symposium
syndicate
synthesis
terrorism
terrorist
theocracy
total war
vigilante
war crime
yardstick
Zeitgeist

8

activism
affluent
agitprop
agrarian
alliance
altruism
archives
autarchy
autonomy
blockade
centrism
charisma
civilian
clemency
coercion
Cold War
congress
consumer
contract
covenant
currency
de facto
deadlock
delegate
doctrine
domestic
drawback
election

emeritus
feminism
feminist
gag rule
genocide
hegemony
idealism
ideology
in vogue
interest
jingoism
just war
legalism
legality
Leninism
Leninist
majority
minority
moderate
momentum
monarchy
monopoly
moralism
nepotism
New Deal
New Left
Nihilism
nobility
pacifism
pan-Arab
partisan
passport
politics
populism
preamble
prestige
pro life
protocol
quisling
reprieve
republic
rhetoric
sabotage
scarcity
security
sedition
stimulus
strategy
strawman
subpoena
suffrage
taxation
tribunal
vanguard
vendetta
zero-sum

7

amnesty
anarchy
atavism
boycott
by-laws
cabinet
canvass
capital
charter
citizen
civitas
closure
commune
de jure
default
defunct
détente
diehard
dumping
dynasty
ecology
economy
elitism
embargo
embassy
enclave
entente
faction
fascism
hostage
infidel
keynote
leftist
liaison
liberal
liberty
mandate
Marxism
Marxist
militia
panacea
privacy
probate
radical
realism
refugee
royalty
secular
society
statute
subsidy
torture
treason
tyranny
utility
warhead

welfare
Zionism

6
accord
agenda
ballot
barter
budget
caucus
census
cohort
colony
comity
consul
curfew
deport

despot
empire
equity
ethics
ethnic
export
import
layman
market
masses
mayhem
monism
nation
nomads
parity
quorum
racism
reform
regime

status
strike
tariff
treaty
utopia
zealot

5
aegis
alien
cadre
caste
class
dogma
elite
envoy
ethos

exile
graft
guild
jihad
junta
lease
lobby
media
party
plank
probe
proxy
purge
Start
taboo
truce
usury

4
bias
bloc
clan
code
fiat
hack
lien
pact
peer
riot
sect
veto
visa
whip

Religion

19
Systematic theology
Unwritten doctrines

18
Intermediate state
Vincible ignorance

17
Consubstantiation
Pastoral Theology

16
Physico-theology

15
Total depravity

14
Infralapsarian
Moral theology

transformation
Unipersonalist
Visible church

13
Astrotheology
Justification
Oxford School
Pantheologist
Scholasticism
Strange woman

12
Atheological
Theologaster
Traducianism
Uncovenanted
Universalism
Universalist

11
Apologetics
Bartholomeo
Bonaventure
Incarnation

Inspiration
Pantheology
Theological

10
Bonhoeffer
Homiletics
Imputation
Isagogical
Licentiate
Patristics
Scholastic
Skepticism
Theologian
Theologics
Theologize
Yom Kippur

9
Atheology
Atonement
Berkouwer
Credendum
Ignorance
Isagogics
Neologist
Sacrament

Sceptical
Symbolics
Symbolism
Terminist
Testament
Tradition
Unitarian
Via media

8
Beaucamp
Covenant
Legalist
The Word
Tractate
Typology
Ubiquity
Vocation
Wesleyan

7
Bavinck
Berkhof
Erudite
Faculty
Hopkins
Irenics

Justify
Polemic
Trinity

6
Briggs
Impute
School
Shiloh
Throne

5
Karma
Selah
Softa
Study

4
Heim

Rivers

12
Murrumbidgee

11
Brahmaputra
Mississippi
Shattalarab

10
Shenandoah
Stlawrence

9
Euphrates
Irrawaddy
Mackenzie
Riogrande
Tennessee

Whitenile

8
Amudarya
Bluenile
Colorado
Klondike
Missouri

7
Darling
Dnieper
Huangho
Krishna
Limpopo
Moselle
Niagara
Orinoco
Potomac
Senegal
Shannon

Vistula
Waikato
Yangtse
Yangtze
Yenisey
Zambezi

6
Amazon
Danube
Ganges
Hudson
Irtysh
Jordan
Liffey
Mekong
Mersey
MurrayY
Orange
Parana
Thames
Tigris
Vltava

Yamuna
Yellow

5
Clyde
Congo
Forth
Indus
Jumna
Marne
Niger
PearlL
Plate
Rhine
Rhone
Seine
Tagus
Tiber
Volga
VoltaA
Yukon

4
Amur
East
Elbe
Lena
Main
Nile
Oder
Ouse
Ruhr
Ural

3
Don
Tay

2
Ob
Po

Russian Composers

14
Rimskykorsakov

13
Shosrakovitch

12
Dargomizhsky

11
Grechaninov
Rachmaninov
Tchaikovsky

10
Kabalevsky
Miaskovsky
Mussorgsky
Stravinsky

9
Balakirev
Prokofiev
Slominsky
Zimbalist

8
Glazunov
Scriabin

7
Borodin
Tiomkin

6
Gliere
Glinka

5
Elman

3
Cui

Russian Writers

12

Solzhenitsyn

10

Dostoevsky
Mayakovsky

9

Akhmatova
Goncharov
Lermontov
Pasternak
Shchedrin
Sholokhov
Tsvetaeva

8

Bulgakov
Nekrasov
Turgenev
Vysotsky

7

Brodsky
Chekov
Eessenin
Gumilev
Nabokov
Pushkin
Tolstoy

5

Bunin
Gogol
Gorky

4

Blok

Science Fiction

14

laurelindornan
neekerbreakers
slartybartfast
whitemountains

13

fattylumpkins
flourdumpling
latheofheaven
micheldelving
mistymountain
northfarthing
southfarthing
teethofmordor
threefarthing

12

blackcaptain
firemountain
graywanderer
mtlookatthat
mtlookitthat
pakprotector

11

barrowblade
bracegirdle
captainkirk
crackofdoom
deadmarshes
dunlendings

dwimmerlaik
easterlings
elvensmiths
fordprefect
greypilgrim
heathertoes
imladmorgul
isengarders
lampwrights
middleearth
minastirith
minusmorgul
misterspock
necromancer
neuromancer
numemoreans
oakenshield
pheriannath
smallburrow
thistlewool
thuganlitha
vernorvinge
westmarches
wizardsvale

10

arthurdent
beeblebrox
blackrider
blackstone
brandybuck
brandywine
brockhouse
bullroarer
cassiopeia
celebrimor

chimolitha
cloudyhead
crossroads
dentarthur
durinsbane
entmaidens
erkenbrand
fairbairns
fantastica
fimbrethil
gilthoniel
glorfindel
goldenhall
goldenwood
goodbodies
greymalkin
halloffire
hariseldon
hornblower
horselords
isenmouthe
ithilstone
larryniven
longbottom
lookatthat
lookitthat
lordofevil
middlearth
minasithil
mirrowmere
mitheithel
mithrandir
morgullord
morgulpass
morgulvale
overheaven
riddermark
ringwaiths

sandheaver
shadowhost
silverlode
simbelmyne
strawheads
thrandruil
timesaving
towerhills
whitedowns
whiterider
whiteskins
whitetower
wilderland
wolfriders
wormtongue
zirakzigil

9

admonfaye
ancalagon
angrenost
appledore
bandobras
barabduin
beechbone
beornings
beruthiel
blackgate
blackones
blackroot
bregaland
butterbur
buttercup
caradhras
carlcorey
celebrant

celebrian
darktower
dervoerin
dunharrow
durinsaxe
eastlands
ecthelion
elffriend
elvenhome
eorlingas
esmeralda
fallohide
fanuidhol
finduilas
firstborn
freelords
galadriel
gilgamesh
glamdring
goldberry
gorhendad
greatgate
greenhill
greenwood
grimbeorn
grishnakh
guardians
harkonnen
helmingas
helmsdike
helmsgate
heruggrim
highcourt
inglorion
khazaddum
landroval
lathspell
lockholes

longholes
loudwater
melnibone
methedras
minasanor
moonrider
mountdoom
mountfang
oldforest
oldnoakes
oliphaunt
osgiliath
peregrine
pickthorn
protector
proudfoot
puddifoot
quickbeam
ringworld
rivendell
rohanwold
rushlight
sackville
shadowfax
shirriffs
shriekers
snowbourn
southrons
stonecity
stonefolk
stormcrow
strongbow
supernova
swertings
telcontar
thaintook
thorondor
tnuctipun
treebeard
truenames
underhill
ungoliant
watchwood
whitehand
winnowill
witchlord
wolfrider
zarniwoop

8

argonath
asfaloth
atreides
baraddur
bbaggins
benedict

beregond
blackpit
bombadil
bounders
bradbury
breehill
brueinen
carmella
celebdil
celeborn
corsairs
darkcity
darkdoor
darklord
deadcity
denethor
deorwine
dernhelm
docsmith
earendil
eastroad
elbereth
elfhaven
elfstone
entwives
evenstar
fairfolk
firefoot
freawine
freefolk
gilgalad
gleowine
goatleaf
golasgil
goldwine
gorbadoc
grayhame
greyhost
greywood
guthwine
halbarad
halfling
haradrim
harfoots
heinlein
holbytla
holdwine
imladris
isengard
isengrim
leaflock
limlight
longlake
lumpkins
marigold
meduseld
meneldil
meneldor

meriadoc
mirkwood
morannon
muad dib
muad-dib
nameless
nimrodel
orodruin
outlands
palantir
pelennor
pipeweed
poohbear
radagast
raederle
robinton
rohangap
rohirrim
sandyman
skinbark
snowmane
startrek
stewards
sunlands
terminus
thechief
theedain
theodred
theshire
thetombs
thevalar
tindrock
tookland
trillian
valandil
vorondil
wanderer
wandlimb
waybread
wemadeit
westfold
westroad
whitfoot
wildwood
windfola
wingfoot
woodland

7

adelard
amonhem
amonsul
anarion
anduril
aragorn
arathon

argeleb
arrakis
arvedui
baggins
bagshot
baradur
barahir
baranor
bastian
benadar
benbova
bigfolk
boromir
brunner
burarum
burrows
bywater
caladan
citadel
crebain
crombie
delving
derufin
dimholt
dimrill
domingo
dorlyth
duinhir
dunadan
dunhere
dwarves
dworkin
eesmith
elendil
elessar
elladan
elrohir
entings
entwade
entwash
entwood
erestor
evendim
fangorn
faramir
felanor
felarof
finglas
fladrif
flaumel
forgoil
forlong
fornost
frealaf
frumple
galadon
galdrim
galmond

gamling
gandalf
ggildor
gothmog
guthlaf
gwaihir
halfast
hamfast
hasufel
haunted
haygate
hayward
henneth
hgwells
hirluin
hobbits
iarwain
imrahil
incanus
isildur
jinxian
lamedon
lazarus
legolas
lensman
lobelia
louiswu
lugdush
lumpkin
luthien
mablung
malbeth
melange
melilot
menolly
mithril
mrspock
muaddib
mugwort
mumakil
muzgash
numenor
oldbuck
onodrim
orcrist
orophin
orthanc
paladin
primula
rangers
redbook
renewer
roheryn
samwise
sandman
saradoc
saruman
selidor

shadows
shagrat
sharkey
skywise
slinker
smeagol
sorcery
stilgar
stinker
strider
telchar
tharkun
thecity
thedead
themule
thengel
thenine
theoden
theseer
thewise
thingol
trantor
tristan
tweener
tweeney
twofoot
urukhai
variags
watcher
westley
wldfara
wildman
wildmen
wizards
woodmen
wraiths

6

aiglos
amroth
anborn
anduin
angbor
angmar
asimov
atreyu
bagend
baldor
balrog
benden
bergil
bipohl
boffin
bolger
bombur
bowman

cirdan
cirion
cirith
clarke
corwin
cutter
damrod
deagol
duilin
duncan
dwalin
eagles
earnur
eeyore
elanor
elrond
elwing
eomund
eothan
feanor
fengel
fezzlk
finrod
fremen
fundin
gaffer
galdor
gamgee
garkin
garulf
gerard
gollum
gondor
gorbag
gorgor
gorgun
grubbs
gurney
haldir
hardin
harper
healer
heinox
hirgon
hobbit
holman
humfey
huorns
ingold
ioreth
iorlas
julian
kolvir
kossil
lagduf
leetah
lembas

lindir
maggot
mardil
marvin
mauhur
mearas
mentat
mordor
morgon
morgul
narsil
nazgul
nessus
newrow
noakes
noldor
oldodo
olorin
pelman
penthe
perian
piemur
piglet
pimple
radbug
random
ruatha
sancho
sauron
scatha
seldon
sharku
shelob
skeeve
slarty
stoors
stybba
targon
thorni
thrain
tigger
tirith
tobold
torech
trolls
tweeny
ufthak
vernor
warden
wights
winged
winnie
wizard
wraith
zaphod
zardoz

5

admon
aldor
amber
arden
arnor
arren
arwen
atuan
balin
baron
beorn
beppo
beren
bifur
bilbo
bofor
brand
brego
cabra
caine
ceorl
chani
chaos
chubb
clark
corey
drogo
durin
dyson
edain
eldar
elgin
elves
eomer
eored
eowyn
erech
ferny
folca
frodo
gimli
gleep
gloin
grima
guido
hador
hurin
inigo
ithil
jaxom
kanga
lotho
mogul
moria
motie

mumak
narvi
niven
ohtar
oisen
orald
orome
prill
rohan
rosha
rumil
runes
shire
smaug
snaga
spook
sting
tanda
tarks
thror
toran
trent
troll
turin
ugluk
umbar
ungol
uruks
valar
varda
verne
vicia
vinge
vogon
walda
wargs
wells
witch
woses
xanth
zirak

4

aahz
alia
anor
arha
arod
bink
bova
bree
dain
dent
deor
deth
dior

dora	frar	leto	otho	wolf
dori	frea	lune	pern	yrch
duny	gram	milo	pezi	yrth
elve	hama	momo	pohl	
ende	hari	mule	pooh	**3**
ents	hora	nali	rein	
eorl	isen	nibs	rory	ged
fang	jinx	nori	suth	nob
floi	kirk	nova	took	oin
forn	leof	orcs	weyr	pak

Seas

14
Bellingshausen

13
Mediterranean

10
Southchina
Tyrrhenian

9
Carribean
Eastchina

Greenland
Norwegian

8
Adriatic
Beaufort
Bismarck
Ligurian
Sargasso

7
Arabian
Arafura
Barents
Caspian
Celebes

Chukchi
Galilee
Marmara
Okhotsk
Weddell

6
Aegean
Baltic
Bering
Celtic
Inland
Ionian
Laptev
Tasman
Yellow

5
Banda
Black
Ceram
Coral
Irish
Japan
North
Timor
White

4
Aral
Azov
Dead
Java

Kara
Ross
Savu
Sulu

3
Red

Shakespeare's Words

20
allswellthatendswell
midsummernights-
dream
twogentle-
menofverona

16
merchantofvenice
tamingoftheshrew

15
titusandronicus

14
northumberland

13
julius caesar
three witches

12
falconbridge
fitz-patrick
guildenstern
juliuscaesar
marc anthony
mark anthony
threewitches
westmoreland

11
abergavenny
bolingbroke

fitzpatrick
henrythe8th
johnofgaunt
ladymacbeth
lancastrian
mackanthony
marc antony
marcanthony
mark antony
mustardseed
northampton
philostrate
plantaganet
rosencrantz
shakespeare
southampton

westminster
williampage

10
aguecheeck
alcibiades
andromache
andronicus
antipholus
archidamus
atemidorus
azerbaijan
barnardine
buckingham

calphurnia
canterbury
coriolanus
euphronius
fitz-peter
florentine
fortinbras
gloucester
graymalkin
greymalkin
holofernes
hortensius
jaquenetta
kissmekate
longaville
lysastrata
lysimachus
lysistrata
marcantony
margarelon
markantony
menecrates
messengers
montgomery
peasbottom
proculeius
richard3rd
richardiii
saturninus
sempronius
shakespear
shakespere
shakspeare
somerville
starveling
thetempest
titchfield
touchstone
willoughby
wriothesly

9

agamemnon
antiochus
apemantus
archibald
arviragus
autolycus
balthasar
balthazar
bassianus
biondello
brabantio
bridewell
caithness
calpurnia

cassandra
chatillon
cleomenes
cleopatra
coleville
constance
cornelius
cymbeline
dardanius
deiphobos
demetrius
desdemona
dolabella
donalbain
eastcheap
enobarbus
erpingham
ferdinand
fitzpeter
fitzwater
flaminius
francisca
francisco
glendower
grandpree
guiderius
guildford
helicanus
hippolyta
hortensio
hughevans
katahrine
katharina
kimbolton
kingjames
lancaster
longsword
lychorida
macmorris
mamillius
marcellus
mareshall
moonshine
nathaniel
oldcastle
patrician
patroclus
petruchio
poictiers
polixenes
pompeiius
posthumus
richardii
rousillon
salisbury
saturnius
sebastian

servilius
shakspear
shakspere
simonides
tearsheet
thersites
trebonius
valentine
ventidius
vincentio
voltimand
volumnius
westcheap
woodstock

8

abhorson
achilles
aemilius
anigonus
antiates
antigone
antonius
athenian
aufidius
baptista
bardolph
bassanio
beatrice
belarius
benedick
benvolio
bernardo
bohemian
borachio
bullcalf
burgundy
campeius
canidius
carlisle
charmian
chertsey
citizens
claudius
cominius
cordelia
cornwall
cressida
cytherea
cytheria
diomedes
dogberry
domitius
dramatis
eglamour
elsinore

falstaff
florence
florizel
fluellen
gadshill
gardiner
gertrude
glouster
gratiano
harcourt
hatfield
henry4th
henry8th
hereford
hermione
humphrey
isabella
kingjohn
kinglear
leonardo
leonatus
ligarius
lodovico
lucellus
lucentio
lucillus
lysander
malvolio
mamillus
margaret
marullus
mecaenus
menelaus
menenius
menteith
mercurio
mercutio
metellus
monmouth
montague
mortimer
mountjoy
octavius
overdone
pandarus
pandulph
panthino
parolles
pericles
personae
philario
philemon
phillipi
philotus
phyrynia
pindarus
poitiers

polonius
popilius
prospero
rambures
reynaldo
richard3
roderigo
rosalind
rosaline
salarino
seleucus
shrewish
sicilian
sicinius
soldiers
stephano
syracuse
tantalue
thaliard
timandra
titinius
touralne
triumvir
valerian
violenta
virgilia
volscian
volumnia

7

adriana
adriano
aediles
agrippa
alarbus
antenor
antonio
armando
arragon
aumerle
bedford
berkley
bertram
blanche
bohemia
bourbon
calchas
caliban
camillo
capulet
cassius
cecelia
cerimon
claudio
conrade
costard

cranmer
dauphin
deburgh
dionyza
ephesus
escalus
escanes
ethiope
eunuchs
flavius
fleance
florins
geffrey
gloster
goneril
gonzalo
helenus
henryiv
horatio
hotspur
iachimo
illyria
jessica
laertes
langley
lartius
lavinia
lecetta
lectors
leonato
leonine
leontes
lepidus
lictors
lorenzo
luciana
lucrece
macbeth
macduff
macedon
malcolm
marcius
mardian
mariana
marshal
martius
mecenus
mercade
messala
miranda
montano
montjoy
morimer
mowbray
navarre
nerissa
norfolk
octavia

ophelia
orlando
orleans
othello
paulina
perdita
pisanio
pompeii
proteus
provost
publius
pyramus
quickly
quintus
richard
rowland
rutland
salerio
sampson
shallow
shylock
sicilia
silvius
sirjohn
slender
solanio
solinus
suffolk
tempest
theseus
threnos
thyreus
titania
travers
triculo
troilus
tuscany
ulysses
valeria
varrius
velutus
vintner
warwick
windsor

6

adonis
adrian
aegeon
aemila
alexas
alonso
amiens
angelo
antony
athens

audrey
banquo
bianca
blanch
bottom
brutus
caesar
caphis
cassio
certes
chiron
cicero
cimber
clitus
cloten
clytus
cnidos
cobweb
curtis
decius
denier
denney
dorcas
dorset
dromio
dumain
duncan
edmund
egmund
elilia
elinor
emilia
ethiop
fabian
fenton
florin
fulvia
gallus
gaoler
gremio
grumio
gurney
guynes
hamlet
hector
helena
henry4
henry8
hermia
imogen
jaques
juliet
julius
junius
launce
lebeau
lector
lennox

lictor
lucius
mantua
marcus
marina
morton
mouldy
mutius
nestor
oberon
olivia
orsino
oswald
pedant
pistol
plaint
pompey
portia
quince
sardis
scarus
scroop
sexton
sextus
seyton
sicily
silius
silvia
simple
siward
sonnet
strabo
strato
surrey
tamora
taurus
thaisa
thisbe
thurio
tranio
tullus
tybalt
ursula
verges
vernon
verona
wolsey
yclept
yorick

5

aemil
aenas
aeson
ambas
angus

anjou
arden
ariel
audry
bagot
bates
bawdy
belch
bigot
biron
blunt
boult
boyet
bushy
butts
caius
casca
celia
ceres
cinna
cleon
clepe
clown
corin
curan
curio
egeus
elbow
emila
exton
firar
flute
froth
gaunt
gobbo
gower
henry
holla
hymen
julia
lafeu
lucio
maine
maria
melun
menas
milan
mopsa
osric
pedro
percy
phebe
philo
pinch
poins
priam
regan
robin

romeo	**4**	ford	luce	**3**
shrew		gaol	moth	
snout	ague	hugh	owen	ely
speed	ajax	iago	peto	nym
timon	arde	iras	puck	wye
titus	bawd	iris	ross	
tubal	cato	jamy	snug	
varro	davy	john	tyre	
viola	dido	juno	vaux	
yorik	dion	lear	wall	
	eros	lion	york	

Space

19

Collisional Process
Diffraction Grating
Galaxy Supercluster
Galilean satellites
Gravitational waves
Invisible Radiation
Observable Universe
Proton-Proton Chain
Schwarzschild Radius
Terrestrial Planets

18

Angular Resolution
Binary Star System
Chemical Evolution
Colliding Galaxies
Gravitational Lens
Infrared Telescope
Interstellar Space
Inverse Square Law
Molecular Velocity
Short-Period Comet
Stellar Black Hole
Terrestrial planet

17

Centrifugal force
Chemical Compound
Cosmic Abundances
Elliptical Galaxy
Extrasolar planet
Greenhouse Effect
Group of Galaxies
Image Intensifier

Interstellar Dust
Jovian Atmosphere
Long-Period Comet
Magellanic Clouds
Nautical Twilight
Neutrino Detector
Optical Telescope
Radiative Process
Stellar Evolution
Supernova Remnant
Termination shock
Thermal Radiation

16

Angular Momentum
Celestial Object
Celestial Sphere
Cepheid Variable
Critical Density
Electromagnetism
Extraterrestrial
Galactic Nucleus
Galaxy Evolution
Globular Cluster
Irregular Galaxy
Keck Observatory
Milky Way Galaxy
Planetary Nebula
Potential Energy
Secondary mirror
Starburst Galaxy
Stellar Parallax
White Dwarf Star

15

Absorption Line
Closed Universe

Collecting Area
Convection Zone
Dark Dust Cloud
Descending node
Differentiation
Electromagnetic
Escape Velocity
Galactic Center
Inferior planet
Io Plasma Torus
Lagrange points
Mean solar time
Molecular Cloud
Right Ascension
Semi-major axis
Standard Candle
Superior planet
Zenith Opposite

14

Accretion Disk
Ascending node
Atomic Nucleus
Civil Twilight
Doppler Effect
Galactic Plane
Galaxy Cluster
Gaseous Nebula
Geosynchronous
Gravity Assist
Great Red Spot
Habitable Zone
Interferometer
Jovian Planets
Kinetic Energy
Magnetic Field
Micrometeoroid
Nebular Theory
Periodic Comet

Pickoff Mirror
Primary Mirror
Reaction Wheel
Red Giant Star
Seyfert Galaxy
Shepherd moons
Solar Constant
Telemetry data
Van Allen Belt
Vela Satellite

13

Absolute Zero
Active Galaxy
Alpha Process
Asteroid Belt
Constellation
Degree of Arc
Digital Image
Emission Line
Event Horizon
Excited State
Filter Wheels
Flat Universe
Galactic Disk
Galactic Halo
Geostationary
Gravity waves
Kepler's Laws
Lunar Eclipse
Magnetopshere
Near-Infrared
Open Universe
Proper Motion
Radial Motion
Radio science
Radioactivity
Sidereal time
Solar Eclipse

Solar Maximum
Solar Minimum
Space Shuttle
Spectral Line
Spiral Galaxy
Sunspot Cycle
Tracking data
Variable Star
Visible Light
Walking orbit

12

Acceleration
Angular Size
Chromosphere
Command data
Coronal Hole
Dwarf Galaxy
Eccentricity
Fluorescence
Great circle
Ground State
Heliocentric
Hubble's Law
Impact Event
Jovian Winds
Kelvin Scale
Monitor data
Multiplexing
Neutron Star
Non-coherent
Open Cluster
Photovoltaic
Planck Curve
Planetesimal
Seismic Wave
Solar Arrays
Solar System
Spectroscopy

Star Cluster
Strong Force
True anomaly
T-Tauri Star

11

Brown Dwarf
Conjunction
Cosmic Rays
Dark Matter
Declination
Gravitation
Heliosphere
Host Galaxy
Inclination
Kuiper Belt
Leap Second
Light Curve
Light speed
Lithosphere
Local Group
Lyman Limit
Ozone Layer
Photosphere
Prime Focus
Protogalaxy
Protoplanet
Radio Waves
Roche Limit
Singularity
Solar Cycle
Spiral Arms
Temperature
Terrestrial
Transponder

10

Absorption
Antimatter
Arc Minute
Arc Second
Astronomer
Atmosphere
Barycenter
Black Hole
Cassegrain
Centimeter
Convection
Femtometer
Gamma Rays
Geocentric
Giant Star
Guide Star
Heliopause

Hour Angle
Ionization
Ionosphere
Light time
Light year
Light-Year
Local time
Luminosity
Major axis
Micrometer
Millimeter
Modulation
Oort Cloud
Opposition
Pathfinder
Perihelion
Periselene
Photometer
Photometry
Prominence
Reflection
Refraction
Relativity
Retrograde
Revolution
Shock Wave
Solar Wind
Subcarrier
Transducer
Turbulence
Wavelength
Weak Force

9

Afterglow
Amplitude
Asteroids
Attometer
Blue Star
Blueshift
Cosmology
Deuterium
Frequency
Gyroscope
Inflation
Intensity
Isotropic
Kilometer
Leap Year
Longitude
Meridians
Meteorite
Meteoroid
Milky Way
Parallels
Periapsis

Picometer
Protostar
Radiation
Red dwarf
Reflector
Refractor
Satellite
Spacetime
Supernova
Telescope
Three-way
VLBI data

8

Aphelion
Apoapsis
Apselene
Argument
Asteroid
Baseline
Big Bang
Bi-phase
Coherent
Downlink
Ecliptic
Electron
Ganymede
Infrared
Klystron
Latitude
MC-cubed
Molecule
Moonrise
Neutrino
Nutation
Parallax
Perijove
Perilune
Prograde
Redshift
Regolith
Rotation
Spectrum
Twilight
Universe
Velocity

7

Apojove
Apolune
Billion
Caltech
Carrier
Channel

Decibel
Density
Element
Ellipse
Equator
Equinox
Erosion
Fission
Horizon
Isotope
Jupiter
Keyhole
Mercury
Moonset
Neptune
Neutron
Nucleus
One-way
Opacity
Perigee
Sprites
Sunrise
Sunspot
Transit
Two-way
Volcano

6

Apogee
Apollo
Aurora
Beacon
Bolide
C-band
Comets
Corona
Crater
Filter
Fusion
Galaxy
Impact
Jovian
K-band
L-band
Mantle
Meteor
Micron
Packet
Photon
Planet
Plasma
Plunge
Proton
Pulsar
Quasar
Radian

Saturn
S-band
Sunset
Triton
Uplink
Uranus
X-band
X-Rays
Zenith

5

AMMOS
Bulge
CCSDS
CDSCC
Color
Comet
Earth
Fault
Flare
GDSCC
HDF-N
HDF-S
Laser
Light
Maria
Maser
MDSCC
MESUR
Nadir
NiCad
Nodes
OPNAV
Phase
Pixel
Pluto
Quark
SIRTF
Venus
X-ray

4

AAAS
AACS
Amor
Aten
Atom
C&DH
CNES
Coma
Core
CRAF
DSCC
DSMS

DSOT	**3**	GLL	**2**
Dyne		GMT	
Flux	AAS	GTL	µm
GSSR	ALT	GTO	AC
HEMT	AOS	HEF	AM
IPAC	BOT	HGA	AO
IRAS	BPS	ICE	AU
ISOE	BSF	IND	AZ
Jets	BVR	Ion	dB
LECP	BWG	IPC	DC
Mars	CCD	ISM	EL
Mass	CCS	ISO	EM
MCCC	CDR	IUS	ET
Moon	CDS	JGR	eV
MOSO	CDU	JPL	FE
NASA	CIT	kHz	FM
NIMS	CMC	KSC	HA
NIST	CRS	LAN	Hz
NOCC	CRT	LCP	Io
Nova	DEC	LEO	IR
OSSA	DKF	LGA	km
OWLT	DSN	LMC	MO
PN10	DSS	LNA	MR
PN11	EDL	LOS	NE
Rise	EDR	LOX	PE
RPIF	EHz	MCD	PI
RTLT	ELV	MCT	prn
SCET	EMF	MGA	RA
SCLK	EMR	MGN	RF
SEDR	EOT	MHz	SA
SEGS	ERC	MIT	SC
SFOF	ERT	NMC	SI
SFOS	ESA	OSI	UT
Star	ESP	OSR	UV
TMOD	FDS	OSS	
TWNC	Gal	OTM	
TWTA	GCF	PAM	
VGR1	GDS	PDS	
VGR2	GEO	PDT	
Wave	GHz	PHz	

			PIO	
			PLL	
			PST	
			PSU	
			RAM	
			RCP	
			RFI	
			RNS	
			ROM	
			RTG	
			SAF	
			SAR	
			Sec	
			SEF	
			Set	
			SMC	
			SNR	
			SOF	
			SPC	
			SSA	
			SSI	
			STD	
			STS	
			Sun	
			SWG	
			TAU	
			TCM	
			TDM	
			THz	
			TOS	
			TRK	
			TRM	
			TWT	
			TXR	
			UHF	
			ULS	
			USO	
			UTC	

Sports

13

Out of bounds
weightlifting

12

breaststroke
crosscountry
francoharris

11

closehauled
fieldhockey
goaltending
quarterback
rocklyblier
supersonics
tonylasorda

10

backstroke
basketball
benchpress
blackhawks
crosscheck
extrapoint
fullnelson
halfgainer

halfnelson
highdiving
linebacker
mapleleafs
northstars
racketball
rightfield
sidestroke
substitute

9

bellyflop
bigeightt
bigorange
bigviolet
bigyellow
bodycheck
canadiens
Cancelier

cardinals
cavaliers
defensive
favourite
fieldgoal
freestyle
freethrow
grandprix
grandslam
hat trick
home base
jackknife
leftfield
linedrive
mavericks
melblount
polevault
relayrace
starboard
strikeout
touchdown
waterpolo
wrestling

8

baseball
bigblack
biggreen
bigwhite
bluejays
bodyblow
bodylock
chargers
clippers
crabbing
defender
dibbling
dolphins
downhill
fastball
football
foulball
greenbay
halftime
hattrick
headblow
headlock
highbeam
highdive
highjump
Home run
hookshot

jumpshot
kayaking
knockout
lacrosse
longjump
marathon
mariners
offsides
overtime
patriots
penalize
penguins
peterose
phillies
seahawks
shooting
slamdunk
slapshot
steelers
swandive
swimming
takedown
ultimate
whitesox
xcountry

7

Allonge
bigblue
bowling
brewers
celtics
chicane
cougars
cowboys
creance
defence
dismiss
dodgers
dribble
endzone
faceoff
falcons
fensing
floorex
frisbee
hatrick
homerun
indians
infield
lasorda
leghold

lifting
luffing
orioles
packers
penalty
pirates
pistons
raiders
rangers
ribbies
riposte
rockets
running
sailing
toehold
vikings
weights
wrestle
yankees

6

49-ers
angels
astros
balked
b-ball
bigred
bigten
blount
boxing
braves
browns
bruins
buckos
career
centre
chiefs
crease
defend
dodger
endrun
flyers
franco
gainer
gaolie
giants
gloves
goalie
hiking
hockey
knicks
lakers

mallet
nstars
nymets
paddle
padres
pinned
popfly
racing
racket
redsox
royals
runner
Safety
saints
sixers
skiing
Soccer
sonics
spikes
squash
strike
tackle
teamen
teedee
tennis
thrust
tigers
triple
turkey

5

76ers
Balks
bball
bears
blier
block
bucks
bulls
colts
expos
glove
hawks
hiker
icing
kayak
kings
leash
lunge
parry
pbars
rings

rocky
rover
rugby
score
Slice
stern
touch
track
twins

4

6ers
ball
bars
bucs
Bunt
cope
cubs
goal
hook
mets
ncaa
open
pick
pins
polo
port
rams
rbis
reds
tack
walk
wood

3

aft
A's
bat
hit
mit
nfl
rbi

2

as
td

265

Tree Names

8
Beechnut
Magnolia
Mahogany
Mangrove

7
Dogwood
Hickory

6
Linden

Poplar
Walnut
Willow

5
Alder
Aspen

Birch
Cedar
Kauri
Maple

4
Palm

Pine
Teak

3
Ash
Fir
Oak

Trees

8
Beechnut
Chestnut
Hawthorn
Magnolia
Mahogany
Mangrove

7
Dogwood
Hickory

6
Acacia
Linden

Poplar
Spruce
Walnut
Willow

5
Alder
Aspen

Birch
Cedar
Kauri
Maple
Rowan

4
Palm

Pine
Teak

3
Ash
Elm
Fir
Oak

US Automobiles

10
Oldsmobile
Studebaker

9
Chevrolet

8
Cadillac
Chrysler
Delorean
Plymouth

7
Mercury

Packard
Pontiac

6
Desoto
Fraser
Hudson
Kaiser
Tucker

5
Buick
Dodge

4
Ford
Jeep

3
GMC

US Civil War

19
Harrietbeecherstowe

17
Alexanderstephens
Frederickdouglass

Generlbeauregard
Lifeamongthelowly
Outamericancousin

16
Chancellorsville
Margaretmitchell

Pittsburglanding
Sevendaysbattles

266

15

Ambroseburnside
Georgemcclellan
Gonewiththewind
Johnwilkesbooth
Lookoutmountain
Thomashigginson

14

Allanpinkerton
Fredericksburg
Hannibalhamlin
Jeffersondavis
Josephjohnston
Mechanicsville
Newyorktribune
Robertanderson
Savagesstation
Stephendouglas
Stephenmallory
Thomasjonathan
Uncletomscabin
Williamsherman
Williamwallace

13

Andrewjohnson
Georgepickett
Horacegreely
Irvinmcdowell
Judahbenjamin
Juliawardhowe
Southcarolina
Ulyssessgrant
Williamseward
Winfieldscott

12

Braxtonbragg
Edmundruffin
Edwinstanton
Emancipation
Fordstheatre
Fortdonelson
Fraysersfarm
Georgecuster
Gideonwelles
Hamptonroads
Harpersferry
Henryhalleck
Hiramulysses

Johnericsson
Marychestnut
Rapphannock
Theliberator
Varinahowell
Westvirginia

11

Edwardbaker
Gainessmill
Malvernhill
Marysurratt

10

Appomattox
Charleston
Coldharbor
Fortsumpter
Gatlinggun
Gettysburg
Jubalearly
Montgomery
Republican
Robertelee
Roberttodd
Samhouston

Sharpsburg
Shenandoah
Winchester

9

Fiveforks
Forthenry
Johnbrown
Merrimack
Natturner
Northstar
Peninsula
Sideburns
Stonewall
Tjjackson
Warishell

8

Anderson
Antietam
Douglass
Manassas
Marytodd
Monocact
Oakgrove
Richmond

Tecumseh
Uncletom
Virginia

7

Brinton
Bullrun
Liberia
Monitor
Simpson

6

Edward
Eleven
Shiloh

5

Bragg
Grant

3

Tad

US Presidents

18

Franklindroosevelt

17

Dwightdeisenhower
Theodoreroosevelt
Williamhowardtaft

16

Benjaminharrison
Georgewashington

Rutherfordbhayes
Williamhharrison

15

Grovercleveland
Johnquincyadams
Millardfillmore
Thomasjefferson
Williammckinley

14

Abrahamlincoln

Calvincoolidge
Chesteraarthur
Franklinpearce
Herbertchoover
Jamesagarfield
Lyndonbjohnson
Martinvanburen
warrengharding

13

Andrewjackson
Andrewjohnson
Jamesbuchanan
Richardmnixon

Ulyssessgrant
Woodrowwilson
Zacharytaylor

12

Harrystruman
Jamesmadison
Johnfkennedy
Ronaldreagan

11

Billclinton

Georgrwbush
Geraldford
Jamescarter
Jamesmonroe

10

Georgebush
Jameskpolk

9

Johnadams
Johntyler

US State Capitols

13	10	Frankfort Nashville	7	6
Jeffersoncity	Batonrouge		Atlanta	Albany
	Carsoncity	8	Augusta	Austin
12	Charleston		Concord	Boston
	Harrisburg	Bismarck	Jackson	Denver
Indianopolis	Littlerock	Cheyenne	Lansing	Helena
Oklahomacity	Montgomery	Columbia	Lincoln	Juneau
Saltlakecity	Montpelier	Columbus	Madison	Pierre
	Providence	Hartford	Olympia	Stpaul
11	Sacramento	Honolulu	Phoenix	Topeka
	Talahassee	Richmond	Raleigh	
Springfield			Santafe	5
	9		Trenton	
				Boise
	Annapolos			Dover
	Desmoines			Salem

US States

13	Northdakota Rhodeisland Southdakota	Wisconsin	7	Kansas Nevada Oregon
Massachusetts		8	Alabama	
Northcarolina	10		Arizona	5
Southcarolina		Arkansas	Florida	
	California	Colorado	Georgia	Idaho
12	Washington	Delaware	Indiana	Maine
		Illinois	Montana	Texas
Newhampshire	9	Kentucky	Newyork	
Pennsylvania		Maryland	Vermont	4
Westvirginia	Louisiana	Michigan	Wyoming	
	Minnesota	Missouri		Iowa
11	Newjersey	Nebraska	6	Ohio
	Newmexico	Oklahoma		Utah
Connecticut	Tennessee	Virginia	Alaska	
Mississippi			Hawaii	

Vegetable Names

11	8	7	Potato	4
Cauliflower	Broccoli	Cabbage	Radish	Corn
	Collards	Lettuce	Squash	Kale
10	Cucumber	Pumpkin	Tomato	Okra
	Eggplant	Spinach	Turnip	Peas
Watercress	Rutabaga			Rice
	Zuchinni	6	5	
9				3
		Carrot	Beans	
Asparagus		Pepper	Chili	Yam

Volcanoes

10	Soufriere	7	5	4
Galunggung	8	Tambora	Agung	Etna
Komagatake			Asama	Laki
Papandayan	Cotopaxi	6	Kelut	Ruiz
	Krakatau		Mayon	Taal
9	Pinatubo	Oshima	Unzen	
	Sthelens			
Lamington	Vesuvius			

Waterfalls

14	10	8	7	Tugela
Tyssestrengene	Sutherland	Cuquenan	Fachoda	Utiord
		Gavarnie	Niagara	Vettis
11	9	Mutarazi		
		Takkakaw	6	5
Basaseachic	Espelands	Victoria		
	Montezuma	Wallaman	Hunlen	Angel
		Yosemite	Ribbon	Kjell
				Monge

Words Used By Monty Python

26
executiveofficer-
fortheweek

25
dukhovskoknabileb-
skohatsk

24
trottetytrottetytrottety

23
leninaddressingthe-
crowd

22
fintimlinbinwhinbim-
lim

19
gotterdammer-
strasse

18
anarchosyndicalist

17
ekkyekkyekkyekkyz
josephthesomewhat
professionalement
psychoanalysister

16
anarchosyndicism
conspiratorially
magnaliumflanged
responsibilities
selfperpetuating
shakespearestyle

15
antiimperialist
authenticsender
barrowinfurness
britishrailways
divineonthehill
gastroenteritis
legbeforevicket
orchestraleader
philosophically
quintuplesmooth
stratfordonavon

14
absentmindedly
brontosauruses
confidentially
disappointedly
disappointment
existentialist
jewelencrusted
knowwhatahmean
manifestations
matteroffactly
musicannouncer
noninvolvement
qualifications
recordbreaking
responsibility
revolutionaire
uncontaminated

13
antichristian
anticlimactic
automatically
biscuitbarrel
bloodcurdling
boncentration
buuuuuurrrrnn
circumstances
colloquialism
comparatively
concilliatory
confectionary
consideration
consternation
contradicting
contradiction
determination
dingdingadong

entertainment
exaggeratedly
experimenting
goosecreature
gynaecologist
impersonation
incontinentia
ineffectually
international
manufacturers
mittelschmerz
outmanoeuvred
plasticcoated
possibilities
preservatives
psychological
regurgitation
semiexistence
sergeantmajor
stoutpamphlet
strattonsmith
strengthening
threecornered
transvestites
uncontrolable
understanding
unfortunately
ventriloquist
whittgenstein
whoopingcough
windowdresser
wolverhampton

12
accidentally
accomplished
alliteration
amphitheatre
bananashaped
blackballing
bloodstained
breathlessly
bridgekeeper
byacrocodile
cantilevered
cheesemakers
commentators
compromising
concentrated
consequently
considerable
considerably
constituency
construction

contradicted
conventional
decisiveness
deliberately
dictatorship
disappointed
disheartened
distributing
dramatically
easytohandle
elderberries
etceteragrad
exclamations
expectations
extraweekend
feeweeweewee
flyinganimal
frankincense
greengrocers
historically
hohohohohoho
increasingly
indcredulous
individually
inflammables
instructions
intelligence
intersection
kneetrembler
laboratories
lincolnshire
millionpound
motorcyclist
neighborhood
nightclothes
nonmigratory
obsequiously
occasionally
oldandyellow
oldfashioned
organization
outrrageous
particularly
peterborough
philosophers
preparations
psychologist
receptionist
redecorating
rhythmically
schopenhauer
semicarnally
soundproofed
specialities
staggeringly

stoatgobbler
superimposed
surroundings
suspiciously
unappetizing
unencumbered
unexpectedly
uninterested
unrestricted
unsuccessful
unsuspecting
verschnitzen
wisecracking

11
accompanied
allamerican
appelachian
approacheth
approaching
association
astrologers
bellydancer
blanketrope
bloodstains
brightening
brilliantly
byeelection
celebration
cognoscenti
comestibles
comfortable
comfortably
complaining
conclusions
confidently
confronting
corrections
correctment
deadlooking
decomposing
delightedly
derivatives
desperately
destination
deuteronomy
devastating
devastation
differences
dismembered
disparaging
earthquakes
effectively
elaborately

270

embarrassed
emotionally
emptyheaded
engineering
everybodies
exasperated
expansively
fascinating
fortunately
frivilously
functioning
grailshaped
hairraising
halfbrother
hammerstein
harmonizing
homosexuals
hospitality
hounourable
humiliation
hunchedover
immediately
imperialist
imploringly
incommoding
infiltrated
insincerely
insinuating
instruments
intellested
intercourse
interesting
interfering
interrupted
introducing
irritatedly
knickerless
lughtborrow
lumberjacks
meaningless
moneysaving
necessarily
neogeorgian
nightshirst
ninetyeight
ninetyseven
noncreative
pawaetonian
permanently
perpetuates
perplexedly
personality
photographs
plaintively
polevaulter
potentially
predictable

prestressed
proceedings
promotional
realization
reappearing
recognizing
regulations
remembering
reminiscing
replacement
respectable
restaurants
salmonmonia
sbeingeaten
selfcontrol
selfdefence
selfsealing
shrubberies
silhouetted
sixteenyear
snottyfaced
specialists
splintering
stickybates
stringettes
stronglyest
stuffynosed
sufferingly
suprisingly
surrounding
taissezvous
tchaikowsky
tellyvision
tentatively
thirtyseven
thouroughly
threeheaded
transcribed
transcriber
trenchcoats
twentyeight
twentyseven
unconscious
underground
utilization
voluntarily
walrustitty
wapscallion
welldressed
wensleydale
whitegarbed
worldfamous
youknowwhat

10

aborigones
absolutely
absorbatex
accusingly
acquainted
admissions
advantages
adventures
advertised
afterwards
apartments
apparently
applauding
approaches
architects
assistants
assortment
attachment
attatching
attempting
attracting
attributed
aubergines
australian
barbershop
barnstaple
beluntanks
bertenshaw
bewildered
blackheads
blasphemer
boatkeeper
bolsheviks
bossfellow
britischer
bromsgrove
bumcreland
caerphilly
capitalist
carshalton
cartmaster
celebrites
centurions
chassilier
cheerfully
chickening
chocolates
cigarettes
clausewitz
collection
collective
complainin
complaints
completely

considered
constantly
continuing
coperfield
coronworld
cottonwool
cricketers
crocodiles
crocodilic
cryingouts
cwackingup
davidovich
definately
definitely
depressing
destroying
determined
developing
diabolical
dibbingley
difference
dimensions
directions
disappears
discarding
discovered
disgusting
dishdrying
divergence
doctorthat
dostoievye
efficiency
especially
eurovision
eventually
excitement
excusezmoi
exploiting
expurgated
faithfully
fascinated
favourably
foodtrough
footlights
fortythree
foursecond
frightened
gainsaying
gangrenous
garnishing
generation
gillingham
glittering
gorgonzola
government
gramophone
haaaaaahhh

halfasleep
handlebars
handshakes
handtohand
haranguing
hysterical
ilfracombe
illchester
immigrants
imprisoned
incredibly
indicating
influences
interested
interviews
introduces
invisibile
jackinabox
knowlingly
laryngitis
laughingly
lesliegrad
lightyears
longswords
looseliver
lumberjack
malmesbury
malodorous
manusquire
marinating
mattresses
mechanised
membership
middleaged
monosodium
mussorgsky
newscaster
ninebladed
ninetynine
nuthatches
obediently
oesophagus
officially
okehampton
oppressing
oppressors
orangutans
originally
outconsume
paddington
personally
pestilence
plummeting
pommeyland
positivism
postulated
practising

preserving
preventers
principles
production
protesting
provencale
providence
psalmsthey
punishment
purveyance
quizmaster
rapesheake
reasonable
recommends
reconsider
recurrence
references
registered
rehearsing
relatively
remarkable
remembered
repeatedly
repressing
retirement
retreating
ribbentrop
sandwiches
scratching
shattering
shimmering
showjumper
signifying
soundtrack
spoonerism
sportscast
stalingrad
struggling
succsussor
suggesting
surprising
surrounded
suspenders
suspendies
suspicions
susscussor
tarmacadam
techniques
terrifying
thamesside
timetables
treblemilk
tupperware
twentyfour
twentynine
underbrush
undergoing

underlying
underneath
understand
undertaker
underwater
undressing
unextended
ungryloike
university
unofficial
unpleasant
unsingable
upstomivia
venezuelan
vibbentrop
wednesdays
wellheeled
whatahmean
whileuwait

9

accidents
according
achieving
activites
additives
addresses
afterburn
agnostics
agreement
amazement
amazingly
ambulance
animation
announcer
answering
antiroman
apartment
apologize
appalling
appearing
arguments
armaments
armchairs
armorclad
athletics
audessous
authority
available
awkwardly
backwards
bakewells
ballistic
bedsheets
behaviour
believing

bernofsky
bickering
blackpool
blinkered
bocialist
bolinaise
bouffants
braincell
britannia
brunettes
buddhists
buggering
buttockth
camenbert
cardinals
carefully
catholics
centurios
centurion
centuwion
certainly
chaaaarge
champions
chanteuse
checkered
chickened
classical
clicketty
collapsed
collapses
combining
comfidown
compasses
composers
composing
concealed
conchface
concludes
condemned
confirmed
confusing
connected
constable
consulted
container
continues
convinced
coronwold
coronworl
creatures
crowcombe
crunching
currently
curtailed
decisions
delerious
delighted

departing
depicting
deposited
detective
developed
dewpicked
dewwingdo
dinosaurs
diocisian
direction
disabling
disappear
disbelief
discovers
disliking
dismember
divisions
droitwich
droppings
dullsells
embracing
enchanter
enforcing
equipment
etessence
examining
excalibur
excepting
excitedly
excrement
exhausted
existence
expanding
expecting
explained
exploding
extremely
fanatical
fashioned
favourite
fermented
festering
fiveounce
flavoured
flustered
following
footsteps
forweight
fourpence
freemason
freetrial
gabriello
gallantly
galloping
gardening
garfunkel
garnished

generally
gesturing
goldblatt
goucester
gravesend
greaaaaat
guardedly
haegelian
hairstyle
halfprice
hammering
happening
happiness
harpenden
headaches
hedgerows
heideggar
heidegger
hopefully
horrified
hospitals
hurriedly
ignorance
impecable
impressed
including
increases
indicates
inflicted
inherited
innocence
insolence
intercity
interests
intermeal
involving
irishborn
irritated
itselfish
jarlsburg
jenkenson
johnstone
khristmas
knickleby
knighting
launcelot
leeringly
leicester
limburger
lingering
listening
literally
logically
loothesom
majorette
maritimes
mcgoering

megaphone
messianic
mightiest
miniskirt
minstrels
miserable
mohmedans
moistened
mountains
movements
mozarella
muttering
nearfatal
nervously
netlemeng
nevermind
nieizsche
niesewand
nightspot
ninepence
norweigan
nuremburg
obviously
onlookers
oooaaahhh
operating
outskirts
ownership
partially
particles
passersby
patiently
pedorasto
pendragon
perceived
perfectly
performed
perturbed
petrograd
political
posession
possessed
powerbase
predicted
presliced
processes
profusely
programme
prolonged
proposing
prospects
providing
purchased
questions
racialist
raindrops
realising
realizing

reappears
recommend
reduction
reference
reflected
registers
regularly
reiterate
rejoicing
remaining
remolarde
repeating
repressed
reputedly
returning
revealing
reverence
reverting
rewashing
roquefort
rubbethed
salterton
samarkind
satisfact
satisfied
saynomore
screaming
scribbles
searching
sensation
senseless
sepricely
sharpeyed
sheathing
shithouse
shoulders
shuffling
sidesteps
situation
sixfooter
sixtynine
socialism
sometimes
spaaaaaam
sparkling
specially
splashing
splitting
squeaking
squeezing
stainless
stalinist
statement
stationed
stickwick
stogumber
stoically
straining

strangely
strangers
stretched
strongest
struggles
stupidity
subjected
succeeded
succulent
suffering
suffrican
supposing
surprised
surprises
surveying
suspected
sustained
sweetmeat
tavistock
terrified
thermidor
tholdiewy
thousands
torturing
trampling
travelers
traveller
treatment
tunbridge
twentysix
twentytwo
twothirds
underwear
ungallant
unhealthy
uniformed
unloading
unplugged
villagers
walamaloo
walpoling
wapcaplet
watterlow
wellknown
wentworth
whaddayou
whispered
whistling
widiculed
wimbledon
wondering
zoomboing

8

aardvark
abattoir

abruptly
actually
adapting
admiring
againily
allowing
allright
anagrams
andahalf
anglaise
animated
animator
aqualung
atheists
attacked
attaturk
attempts
attended
austrian
avenging
averting
aviation
avoiding
bagpipes
balanced
bandaged
bandages
barnhart
bastards
battling
bayonets
beasties
becoming
bedevere
believes
belonged
bernaise
bideford
billions
biscuits
bisected
bitching
biweekly
bladders
bleating
bleeding
blessing
boggling
bookshop
borodins
bosworth
boulders
brackets
breaking
brightly
bringing
bristols
brothers

brrroooo
brushing
budleigh
bulganin
bursting
buttered
buttocks
cackling
cakehole
capitals
caressed
carnally
carrying
chamrent
chanteur
charging
charlton
chattily
cheapest
cheering
cherries
chickens
choruses
christof
churches
claiming
clambake
cleaners
cleansed
clearing
clenches
clicking
climbing
clothing
coconuts
coloring
commands
compared
comrades
concerts
conchito
concorde
confused
connolly
consists
contains
contents
contloll
controle
controll
controls
counting
cowering
crevette
crossing
crumples
crunchie
culdesac

cultured	fighting	jeanpaul	operated	reckoned
curtains	finished	kerensky	orbiting	reenters
cushions	flippers	kneecaps	organist	reformed
customer	flipping	kneeling	ospitals	regardez
darkness	floating	knitting	ottograd	register
deceased	followed	knocking	outdated	relative
defeated	foothigh	lancelot	outdoors	relieved
defeater	foottall	landlady	outraged	remained
deferens	forehead	lapschig	overcome	reolving
delights	forwards	latterly	parmesan	required
departed	founders	laughing	passable	requires
deported	frampton	learning	pastries	restored
deserted	freezing	liberals	pathorpe	returned
detached	friendly	lighting	patients	reunited
detected	froggies	lightish	peasants	revealed
disbands	fruitbat	llapgoch	penguins	rotating
discover	gardener	lockholm	physical	rounding
dishrack	gawwison	lovingly	planning	routines
dismount	generals	lumberjk	pointing	ruffians
displays	giacommo	macarios	politely	russians
distance	giggling	majority	politics	sampling
distress	goebells	matthias	poofters	sardines
dividing	grabbing	maudling	poohpooh	sargeant
divorced	greatest	mccluney	possibly	scarcely
divulged	gridenwa	mcnorton	praising	schlegel
doctored	gritting	measured	pramalot	sequence
dravenka	grunting	medieval	prepared	serpents
dressing	gulliver	meiabier	presents	serrated
drinking	hainault	mergerer	prixunis	servants
dropping	happened	minehead	probably	severely
edgeways	happenin	minister	problems	shallots
educated	havethat	misappre	proceeds	shooting
election	heathens	mohammed	produced	shopping
elements	heathrow	moonless	produces	shouting
ementhal	heavenly	moralize	products	shredded
engleska	hedgerow	morolowe	proffers	shrubber
enjoying	helpless	mortally	promised	shuffled
entering	herehere	moulting	promoted	sixpence
entirely	honestly	mounties	properly	skimming
entitled	honoured	mousebat	prophets	sleeping
entrance	hopeless	movement	proposed	slightly
escaping	horribly	narrator	provided	slipping
espresso	housinge	national	prowling	slithers
esuriant	hundreds	nestquoi	pursuers	slowotny
evolving	iddesley	newbruce	pursuing	smashing
examines	immanuel	nnothing	raggedly	smolensk
exciting	includes	noisiest	railings	snapping
exkorean	injuries	nononono	ramparts	sneaking
exparrot	insulted	nonsense	ratified	snorkels
explodes	intended	normally	reaching	socalled
explorer	involved	nostrils	reacting	soldiers
extended	ipswitch	noticing	reaction	soliders
eyebrows	ironical	observes	realised	sorrento
fashions	isolated	occupied	realized	spamalot
favorite	italians	offering	realizes	spanking
feathers	jaccuzzi	officers	recently	sparsely
fiercest	jeanette	onepound	recessed	spatters

speakers	unharmed	arguing	bullies	cutting
speaking	uniforms	armored	bundles	cycling
speeding	unjugged	arrived	burying	daisies
spitting	unlikely	arrives	buuuurn	damaged
spurised	unsteady	assured	bwavado	darkies
squashed	upstairs	attacks	byfleet	dashing
stammers	urgently	awaaaay	cackles	dawlish
standing	uttering	awfully	calling	decided
stardust	vacation	azalias	careers	defence
starting	valuable	bananas	carried	demibee
startled	viliborg	banging	carrier	demised
stepping	villager	barging	carries	derives
sticking	violence	barnaby	catarrh	designs
stinking	watching	baskets	causing	details
storming	weekends	bathing	cereals	dickuth
stronger	wellsish	bazouki	chabrol	dikkens
strongly	welshman	bearded	chances	dingkom
stuffing	whackett	beastly	changed	ditched
stunning	whaddaya	beating	changes	divined
subtitle	whatbarb	beckles	charged	doctors
succeeds	whispers	beckons	charges	donkeys
suddenly	whistles	becomes	chattin	dragged
suffered	whopping	beeches	cheaper	drawing
suffuses	williton	behinds	checked	dreaded
supposed	wondered	belongs	cheddar	dressed
suprised	wounding	beloved	chewing	dretsky
svetsana	wretched	benches	chockie	drinkee
swallows	yatlerot	bernerd	chunder	driving
switches	youngest	besides	circles	droning
taciturn		bewegen	claimed	dropped
tarpolin	7	biggest	classes	drummer
tastiest		biggles	cleaner	dustmen
tattooed		bigguth	cleared	eagerly
taunting	aaaaagh	bignose	clearly	earlier
teaching	aarthur	bimmler	clicket	ecrivez
teenager	abitoir	binding	clients	effects
tempting	abweise	bleedin	clodagh	ejected
terribly	accused	blessed	closely	emptied
thatthat	actions	blighty	closest	enemies
theories	adapted	blitish	closing	engaged
thilence	aerials	blondes	clothes	enjoyed
thilenth	affairs	bluveny	clubbed	entered
thinking	african	bobbing	coating	escaped
throwing	ahahaha	boldest	compere	escapes
tiverton	akawati	bombers	coughin	escorts
tovarich	alarmed	bottled	counter	estates
tracking	allonsy	bottles	covered	evening
training	allowed	bottoms	cracked	evicted
traveled	alright	bowling	creeper	exactly
triumphs	altered	bratbys	croaked	excited
tropical	amazing	bravely	crooked	expects
trousers	angrily	bravest	crossed	experts
tuppence	animals	bridges	crosses	expired
twolevel	annoyed	bringin	crowded	failing
ulcerous	answers	brisbon	crreoct	fainter
unbugged	anthrax	britons	crunchy	faintly
underway	anymore	budgies	crushed	falling
	appears			

fastest	helmets	loonies	parcels	recover
fathers	helpers	lustily	parrots	redhill
feeding	herring	maarten	parties	reigate
feeling	hitting	maggots	passing	removed
felling	holding	maidens	patabua	removes
fetchez	hopping	malliwi	peckish	renewed
fifties	horsham	manager	peering	replace
figures	housing	mangled	perches	requiem
finally	huddled	marched	perchin	resists
finding	huffing	marryin	periods	resting
fingers	hurling	masters	persons	results
firstly	hurries	matches	pickens	retired
fishing	hurting	maximus	picking	retreat
flanked	ignores	meaning	picnics	returns
flights	impaled	medical	pierced	reveals
flowers	injured	meeting	plgdogs	ribbons
flushed	insides	mellish	pigeons	rightly
follows	insists	mincing	pissant	ringing
fooling	islands	mingled	pissing	rioting
forgets	jacklin	minutes	pistols	risking
forming	jarring	missing	playing	rotting
founded	jumping	mistake	pleased	roughly
frankly	karnaby	mitzvah	plummer	rubbing
friends	keepers	moments	poached	ruffled
fromage	keeping	monkeys	pointed	rumours
frosted	kennels	morally	poisons	runnier
fucking	kichard	mormons	polling	running
fwendth	kicking	morning	poofski	rushing
galahad	killing	motions	poofter	russian
gallops	knights	muffled	pouring	sacking
gannets	knocked	mumbled	praised	sallied
germans	knotted	naaoooo	praline	salutes
gessiah	laborin	nabarro	praying	scalded
gestate	ladders	nastily	prefers	scarfed
getting	laertes	neewomm	propped	screams
gilliam	landing	nesting	proudly	seconds
goggles	largely	neville	prudish	secrets
goodies	largest	nibbled	puffing	selling
goooood	laurels	nightie	pursued	sercicf
grabbed	lavatry	nodding	pushing	serried
granada	leading	nortius	putting	setting
grating	leaning	noticed	pygmies	settled
gristle	leaping	notices	pyjamas	severed
grooves	leaving	nowdead	quickly	shagged
gruyere	legally	nudging	quietly	shaking
hacking	lengths	nursing	quipped	sharply
handles	lesbitt	nuzzled	raising	shekels
hapenin	letters	obediah	rallies	shephrd
happens	letting	officer	ranneth	shiftin
happier	lewgrad	oneeyed	rapidly	shining
happily	licence	ooooooh	rarnaby	shintus
harrest	lightly	oooover	reached	shocked
hastily	limping	opening	reaches	shoebox
hearing	lobbest	orating	reading	shoppin
heavens	logical	orrible	realise	shorter
heavily	longest	outside	reality	shouldn
heinous	looking	packing	realize	shouted

276

shrieks
silence
sillius
singing
sinners
sitting
situpon
slammed
sleekit
slicing
slogans
sloshed
sluices
smashed
smiling
smoking
snicker
soaring
sobbing
sonnets
sorting
spanked
speakee
spilled
spinman
spotted
squeals
stacked
stamped
standin
stapers
started
station
staying
steamed
stiffly
stifled
stilton
stoning
stopped
stories
strains
streams
streets
strides
strikes
stroked
stuckup
stuffed
stunned
subdued
suprise
surgoen
surveys
swindon
systems
tactics

talking
tangled
tapping
tarquin
tartlet
tatooed
taunton
teaches
teatime
tellers
telling
tenants
testing
theatre
thicker
thinker
thpiwit
throngs
thurmon
timidly
timrous
tiniest
titties
toadies
tongues
tooting
topples
torment
totally
tougher
touring
tourist
towards
trailer
trained
trapped
treated
treddle
trotsky
truffle
turning
typical
unaware
unboned
ungodly
unladen
unwraps
usually
utterly
valleys
vantyat
vending
viewers
viewing
vikings
virtues
visited

waiting
walking
wardens
warning
washing
wasting
watches
watford
weapons
wearily
wedding
weevils
wheeled
whining
whipped
whiskey
whizzes
whohoho
wickens
windows
winning
witches
workers
working
worried
worries
woughly
wounded
wrapped
wrapper
writhes
writing
wroking
ximinez
yalevmx
yelling
younger

6

aaaaah
aaaugh
acting
action
addock
afters
agrees
albans
alibut
allows
amazed
amazes
anoint
apples
arguer
arises
arrrgg

artist
asking
attila
babies
backed
badger
bakely
bangin
banner
barely
batter
beachy
beaked
beards
beeeen
begged
begins
beserk
better
bigger
biggus
bilbao
biolek
blazer
blimey
bodily
boring
bother
boxing
braces
breaks
brings
britan
bruces
bruson
budgie
bugged
bugger
bulges
burned
bursts
busily
butter
buying
byebye
cabbie
cadeau
called
camels
caring
caused
ceased
centre
chante
chants
cheeks
cheers

chewed
chords
chromo
chucks
chumps
chunks
chutes
claims
clears
cleese
climes
closed
closer
closes
closin
clouds
clough
colour
combed
coming
cooked
copper
corned
corner
coughs
couldn
counts
cowers
creaks
crimes
crisps
cristo
crowds
crufts
crying
cuiver
curses
cuttle
cweeps
cycles
daring
darkie
darles
dashes
deadly
deeply
dicing
dickie
dickus
dining
ditton
dodges
domine
dorsal
downmy
driver
drones

drying	goatee	kicked	months	polled
dumped	gotcha	killed	mooing	pommey
dundee	gouged	killer	mornay	poring
eartha	gracie	kindom	moscva	poster
easily	grasps	kipper	mounts	pounds
cating	groans	kissed	mouths	poured
ejects	groups	kneels	moving	pppass
elbows	guards	knocks	murals	prizes
elders	guests	ladder	nailed	proved
eliott	hacked	ladies	nearer	purely
eludes	halves	landed	nearly	purest
embeds	hammer	lapsed	needed	pushed
emetic	hamrag	lasted	neopok	pushes
endeth	hanged	latest	nestin	putrid
engicf	harder	laughs	newest	quests
enroll	hardly	laying	nigged	quieta
ension	hasset	leader	nights	racing
ensues	hauled	leaves	nnnnot	raggod
enters	having	letter	noises	raised
erbert	headed	licked	norisk	raises
evenin	heated	lifted	nothin	rarely
events	hehheh	likcly	notlob	ratbag
exeunt	heinri	lipped	nought	ratios
facing	helper	lively	number	reacts
fairly	hendon	living	nuthin	readln
farles	herron	loaded	odinga	really
farmer	herrys	lobbed	offers	reared
feebly	higher	lonely	oldham	recite
fiends	highly	longer	olives	record
fights	hiking	looked	opened	refers
filing	hllter	looney	orders	refuse
finest	hindus	louder	osledi	relics
firing	hooray	loudly	others	remain
fjords	hoping	lovely	ottery	remind
flames	hordes	lunged	ounces	remove
flavor	horned	lupins	ousted	restin
flends	horses	mainly	pagans	rhymes
flicks	houses	making	pagedn	riding
floats	housey	manger	panzer	rifles
floods	hovers	manier	partly	rising
floors	howait	manner	passed	rivers
flower	hunger	marked	passes	robins
flying	hunker	marles	paulin	rolled
fondue	immace	mashed	pauses	romans
forced	inglis	masses	paying	rubber
forces	inweek	master	pedals	rugged
freely	istory	mating	penses	rushes
frocks	jethro	matter	peters	sackly
fruits	jewith	medway	pianos	samite
fuhrer	joined	mercia	piglet	sanity
gained	joinin	merely	pining	sartre
garret	joking	millbo	pissed	sauced
gawain	jugged	missed	pither	saxons
gently	kaboom	missle	places	saying
gettin	keeeng	mister	played	scared
giving	keeper	mmmwah	player	scenes
glides	keepin	mnemot	points	scones

278

scowls
scruff
sealed
seated
seemed
senses
served
sewers
shakes
sharks
sheeps
sheets
shekel
shoots
shoppe
shorts
shouts
shrugs
signed
simian
singer
sirens
sittin
sleeps
slinks
slinky
slower
slowly
slurps
smacks
smiled
smiles
smoked
smokey
snacks
snarls
soddus
sooner
sorbet
sounds
speaks
spells
spiced
spikes
splosh
spurts
spying
stains
stairs
stalks
stamps
stands
starts
steals
sticks
stiffs
stiffy

stings
stoats
stoned
stonee
stones
straps
stwike
subway
sugary
summer
supper
surely
swells
swings
swords
tadger
taking
taller
tarred
tender
thames
thamle
thanks
theirs
theize
thighs
things
thinks
throws
thumps
tiiiny
tilsit
tiring
titles
titter
tracey
tracts
trades
trevor
trillo
troops
trusty
trying
turbot
turned
uhhhhh
unable
united
unless
unrest
unseen
untold
urgghh
uuuuuh
veined
verges
verily

verses
vested
vicars
vindow
visits
voices
voters
waddya
waking
walker
wanted
warmer
warned
wascal
wasted
watney
waving
weighs
wheels
whilst
whisks
whisky
whizzo
wicked
widely
wiggin
wildly
winces
winner
wishes
wistle
womens
worked
wotten
woulda
wouldn
writes
wymiss
yalevm
yappin
yessir
ygiene
younge

5

aaaaw
aargh
aaugh
abbos
abdul
acome
after
ahhhh
alpes
alves
angin

angor
aptly
areas
armed
armor
ashes
asked
aulds
avior
backs
badly
badon
baith
baked
baker
balls
bamps
bangs
based
bbbbe
beams
beans
beats
beaut
beery
bells
bidet
bimbo
bingo
birds
blows
blues
boils
boing
boite
bolts
bones
books
boozy
bored
botty
bovey
bowls
bruns
bwian
caked
cakes
calls
cards
chefs
ching
chips
chops
claps
clips
clubs
colin

color
combs
comes
comfy
coron
cower
crapp
creme
cries
crocs
cuffs
cwowd
darby
dates
deals
denis
dimly
doesn
doing
doors
draws
drops
drums
ducks
dumps
duped
early
earns
ector
edges
elgar
ended
enjoy
estce
exits
faces
fades
fakes
falls
favor
files
finds
finns
fiona
fires
fixed
fixes
flats
flies
fries
frogs
fwend
games
gasps
gents
girls
gives

glows	leige	nosir	rules	thrid
goats	letze	notes	rumor	thtop
goest	liege	oddly	runny	thwow
going	lieth	ohhhh	sadly	times
gonna	lifts	older	safer	tired
gotta	liked	ooooh	sales	tizer
grabs	likes	opens	salut	toads
grips	limbs	outer	saved	tools
gumby	lines	ovine	scots	trees
gweat	lions	owner	scuse	trent
hails	lipta	paese	seeds	tries
hairs	lived	palin	seems	tritt
hallo	liver	pants	selle	trots
hands	lives	parts	semen	tuned
hangs	livin	paune	shalt	turns
hated	lizst	peeks	shins	tuune
hates	loike	perdu	shoes	typed
heads	looks	pests	shots	typos
hears	loony	peter	shows	uhhhh
heels	lorry	picks	shroe	unsye
hegel	loved	pikes	sides	using
hhhow	lover	pinin	signs	uther
hmmmm	loves	plait	sings	vache
holds	lungs	plans	sizes	veins
holes	lupin	plays	skips	velly
homes	luton	poets	slams	vewwy
horns	mahal	polly	slaps	voles
hours	maker	ponds	slows	volts
howls	makes	posed	snaps	vorld
hullo	maman	pours	snips	votes
hurts	mandy	prang	snows	votre
idear	matey	prawn	soles	wabid
ilton	means	pucky	solly	waits
imply	meets	puked	soooo	wakes
innes	merci	pulls	sores	wakin
intro	mhmhm	pumps	sorts	wales
jjust	mihai	races	spake	walks
joins	mikes	raked	spank	wanna
joker	minds	ranks	speke	wants
judea	mixed	rasta	spelt	warms
jumps	moans	rated	spies	watai
keeps	monks	reads	spong	waves
kemel	moult	recap	spots	wavin
kicks	moved	recog	sshhh	wears
kings	moves	relax	stars	webel
knees	muska	rests	steps	weren
knows	naahs	rides	stops	wersh
kralk	nador	rings	surly	whene
krimt	named	rises	sward	whips
kursk	names	roars	swhat	whoah
lambs	needs	rober	takes	wight
lands	negus	rocks	talks	wilde
lanny	nests	rolls	tears	willy
laver	nicht	roofs	teens	wines
leads	nicky	rrrip	tells	wings
leans	noooo	rudge	temps	wiper
leaps	noses	ruled	terms	wogga

woken
words
works
worll
wowdy
wymer
yards
years
yours

4

aaah
aagh
aire
akil
allo
alot
apon
aren
argh
arms
arrr
asks
avec
aven
awed
ayes
baaa
bars
beds
bein
bink
bits
blah
bleu
bobs
bors
bows
boys
brat
bres
brie
brun
bude
buds
bugs
bunn
cait
cars
croc
cuss
cuts
daft
dans
days
dept

didn
dies
dips
does
dogs
doin
dona
dong
dwon
eads
ears
eats
ecce
edam
eggs
elks
ello
ends
ergo
ever
eyes
fans
fart
feta
fins
fuck
gaga
gath
gets
gran
guns
hadn
haff
hasn
hats
heil
hers
hits
hmph
holy
hooh
hsai
hume
hums
husk
hyah
iced
idly
ills
ints
isky
jesu
jews
kerb
kids
kilt
kitt

kung
lads
lahk
laws
legs
lets
lies
lips
lite
lots
mais
mein
ment
misc
moos
musn
nein
nets
news
niet
nihi
ning
nods
nono
nooo
nope
nuit
omsk
onan
ones
oohh
oooh
oops
ours
ovna
owns
pans
pays
peni
pets
phew
pisa
puts
quel
quoi
rapp
raps
rely
revy
ribs
runs
saki
saws
says
sees
sets
shhh

shit
sieg
sits
spam
sshh
stah
stig
stom
taht
taps
tath
ties
tins
tish
tisn
toga
tyre
uhhh
uhmm
unto
urgh
used
uses
vere
voom
vorn
vous
vows
waid
wasn
wath
ways
whow
wome
yeee
yeth
zoot

3

aah
aaw
ach
aha
ahh
ain
alf
arr
asn
aux
aww
bbc
bec
bot
bra
bro
bsl

cla
coq
das
der
dib
dos
dum
ead
eis
elp
erm
ext
feh
gen
git
hah
has
hee
hic
hmm
hoo
idn
iif
iit
ind
int
isn
ist
its
jrp
keo
kgb
kon
lbs
loo
lud
mam
mme
mon
naw
nev
nno
nom
noo
nuh
oho
ole
ooh
ooo
oui
owt
oww
pas
peu
phx
pox
que

reg	vas	**2**	hq	qu
roo	veq		im	sh
sey	ver	ay	ja	si
shh	vin	ce	lb	tg
shi	vor	cl	le	th
ssh	vos	da	ll	tu
taj	vot	di	mm	uh
tho	wha	ee	mp	um
tis	wor	el	ni	ve
tut	yeh	er	od	wm
uhh	yer	es	oi	ya
umm	yes	fu	oo	
und	yoo	fx	op	
urx	yup	gc	ot	
uth	yus	hm	pf	
uuh			ps	

World Cities

17
Bandarseribegawan

14
Andorralavella

13
Guatemalacity
Singaporecity

12
Antananarivo
Portauprince
Santodomingo
Yamoussoukro

11
Brazzaville
Buenosaires
Kualalumpur
Ouagadougou
Portmoresby
Portofspain
Sansalvador
Tegucigalpa

10
Addisababa
Basseterre
Bratislava
Bridgetown
Copenhagen
Georgetown
Kuwaitcity
Libreville
Mexicocity
Montevideo
Nouakchott
Panamacity
Paramaribo
Washington
Wellington

9
Amsterdam
Ashkhabad
Bucharest
Bujumbura
Islamabad
Jerusalem
Ljubljana
Mogadishu
Nukualofa
Phnompenh
Portlouis
Portonovo
Pyongyang
Reykjavik

Sanmarino
Stgeorges
Stockholm
Ulanbator
Vientiane

8
Abudhabi
Asuncion
Belgrade
Belmopan
Brasilia
Brussels
Budapest
Calcutta
Canberra
Castries
Chisinau
Damascus
Djibouti
Dushanbe
Freetown
Funafuti
Gaborone
Helsinki
Katmandu
Khartoum
Kingston
Kinshasha
Lilongwe
Monrovia
Ndlamena
Newdelhi
Pretoria

Santiago
Sarajevo
Tashkent
Valletta
Victoria

7
Algiers
Baghdad
Bangkok
Beijing
Bishkek
Caracas
Colombo
Conakry
Honiara
Jakarta
Kampala
Managua
Mbabane
Nairobi
Nicosia
Rangoon
Sanjose
Stjohns
Tallinn
Tbilis
Thimphu
Tripoli
Vilnus
Yaounde
Yerevan

6
Akmola
Ankara
Asmara
Athens
Bamako
Banjul
Beirut
Berlin
Bogota
Dodoma
Dublin
Geneva
Harare
Havana
Kigali
Lisbon
London
Luanda
Lusaka
Madrid
Malabo
Manama
Manila
Maputo
Maseru
Moroni
Moscow
Muscat
Nassau
Niamey
Ottawa
Prague
Riyadh

Roseau	Zagreb	Dhaka	Seoul	Doha
Skopje		Hanoi	Sofia	Kiev
Sydney	**5**	Kabul	Tokyo	Lima
Taipei		Lapaz	Tunis	Lome
Talinn	Abuja	Minsk	Vaduz	Male
Tarawa	Accra	Paris		Oslo
Tehran	Amman	Praia	**4**	Riga
Tirana	Berne	Quito		Rome
Vienna	Cairo	Rabat	Apia	Suva
Warsaw	Dakar	Sanaa	Baku	Vila

Writers

11

Shakespeare

10

Wordsworth

9

Stevenson
Thackeray

8

Lawrence

7

Carroll
Dickens
Durrell
Kipling
Spenser
Tolkien
Trollop

6

Austen
Bronte
Conrad
Orwell
Stoker

5

Blake
Burns
Byron
Doyle
Eliot
Hardy
Keats
Wilde
Woolf

Zoology

19

Aristotle's lantern
Asclepias butterfly
Grasshopper lobster
Grasshopper warbler
Lobster caterpillar
Paradise flycatcher
Pectorial sandpiper
Pileated woodpecker
Porcupine ant-eater
Prairie rattlesnake
Pride of the desert
Protective coloring
Reticulose rhizopod
Saint James's shell
Salt-marsh terrapin
Sculptured tortoise
Seasonal dimor-
phism
Snub-nosed
cachalot

Soft-shelled turtle
Stump-tailed lizard
Swallow-tailed duck
Swallow-tailed gull
Swallow-tailed moth
Wandering albatross
White-fronted goose
Woodpecker hornbill

18

Complemental males
Harnessed antelope
Hypermetamorpho-
sis
Lackey caterpillar
Lubber grasshopper
Magic humming bird
Marline-spike bird
Processionary moth
Pseudoneuropterous
Purple of mollusca

Rat-tailed serpent
Saint Peter's fish
Scotch nightingale
Slipper animalcule
Solitary sandpiper
Spine-tailed swift
Spur-winged plover
Testaceous animals
Thunderbolt beetle
Trachelobranchiate
Trumpet animalcule
Vulpine phalangist

17

Acanthopterygious
Cabbage butterfly
Hard-shelled clam
Humming-bird moth
Ischial callosity
Lamellibranchiata
Lamellibranchiate

Mountain antelope
Naked-eyed medusa
Ophthalmic region
Opisthobranchiata
Opisthobranchiate
Painted partridge
Peacock butterfly
Pectinibranchiata
Pectinibranchiate
Perennibranchiata
Perennibranchiate
Peristeromorphous
Perspective shell
Pharaoh's chicken
Phylactolaematous
Pied-billed grebe
Pigeon woodpecker
Plantain squirrel
Powder-down patch
Pulmonibranchiata
Pulmonibranchiate
Rhinoceros beetle

Ring-tailed eagle
Rough-legged hawk
Salt-water tailor
Secondary coverts
Seminal receptacl
Siphonobranchiata
Siphonobranchiate
Skiff caterpillar
Soft-shelled crab
Spangled coquette
Spur-winged goose
Squirrel petaurus
Steganophthalmata
Strawberry sawfly
Stylommatophorous
Summer yellowbird
Thistle butterfly
Thorn-headed worm
Tobacco-pipe fish
Tyrant flycatcher
Widow-in-mourning

16

Acanthocephalous
Acanthopterygian
Adjutant general
Agricultural ant
Alligator turtle
Ampullaceous sac
Asparagus beetle
Caducibranchiate
Cobra de capello
Coccygeal glands
Cock of the rock
Corneocalcareous
Cryptobranchiata
Cryptobranchiate
Cucumber beetle.
Curlew sandpiper
Geometric spider
Giant salamander
Goldsmith beetle
Green woodpecker
Ground parrakeet
Gynandromorphism
Gynandromorphous
Harlequin beetle
Hercules' beetle
Hystricomorphous
Inferobranchiata
Inferobranchiate
Labyrinthibranch
Laughing jackass
Madreporic plate
Magnolia warbler
Malacopterygious
Microlepidoptera
Migratory locust
Migratory thrush
Mock nightingale
Molly cottontail
Mountain sparrow
Mourning warbler
Neurosensiferous
Newfoundland dog
Nucleobranchiata
Obstetrical toad
Ocellated turkey
Opisthopulmonate
Organ-pipe coral
Palliobranchiata
Palliobranchiate
Paradise grackle
Passenger falcon
Passenger pigeon
Peach-tree borer
Peacock pheasant

Peregrine falcon
Pharyngobranchii
Plectospondylous
Plumed partridge
Prairie squirrel
Proboscis monkey
Procephalic lobe
Pseudoneuroptera
Pseudoscorpiones
Pulmogasteropoda
Radio-flagellata
Rat-tailed larva
Rat-tailed shrew
Respiratory tree
Scavenger beetle
Scissors grinder
Scorpion spiders
Sedentary spider
Segmental organs
Shepherd spider
Siphonal stomach
Siphonostomatous
Sloth animalcule
Spanish mackerel
Spectacled eider
Spectacled goose
Spectacled snake
Spermaceti whale
Spirit butterfly
Spruce partridge
Squawking thrush
Stalked barnacle
Strawberry borer
Striped squirrel
Summer sheldrake
Swordfish sucker
Tent caterpillar
Tracheobronchial
Tubulibranchiata
Ventricose shell
Viviparous shell
Wandering spider
Water chevrotain
Weavers' shuttle
Wheel animalcule
Whistling plover
Whistling thrush
White rhinoceros
Willow ptarmigan
Winter sheldrake
Woodland caribou

15

Acanthopterygii
Coachwhip snake
Colorado beetle

Comma butterfly
Cowper's glands
Crossopterygian
Gooseberry worm
Gossamer spider
Ground squirrel
Gymnophthalmata
Harlequin snake
Hepato-pancreas
Heterodactylous
Hog caterpillar
Horned screamer
Hunting leopard
Hydrobranchiata
Ichthyodorulite
Inferobranchian
Interambulacral
Interambulacrum
Intestinal worm
Jackass penguin
Jerboa kangaroo
Lantern carrier
Laughing falcon
Lophobranchiate
Malacopterygian
Man-of-war bird
Man-of-war hawk
Manx shearwater
Marmot squirrel
Marsipobranchia
Mermaid's glove
Mother-of-pearl
Mountain beaver
Mountain linnet
Mountain magpie
Myelencephalous
Native pheasant
Nutritive polyp
Odontostomatous
Ornithorhynchus
Osteopterygious
Pallial chamber
Pamprodactylous
Parasitic jager
Partridge shell
Pellibranchiata
Peristeropodous
Pharyngopneusta
Pheasant coucal
Pheasant parrot
Phylactolaemata
Pied flycatcher
Pinnated grouse
Plagiostomatous
Plec-tognathous
Porcelain shell
Prairie chicken

Prairie warbler
Prominent' moth
Prosobranchiata
Pseudonavicella
Pseudotetramera
Pulmobranchiate
Quince curculio
Red-tailed hawk
Restless thrush
Rhinoceros bird
Ringed dotterel
Ring-tailed cat
Robin redbreast
Sand-hill crane
Savanna sparrow
Scaly ant-eater
Scansorial tail
Scarlet admiral
Scarlet tanager
Scissors-tailed
Scutelliplantar
Scutibranchiata
Scutibranchiate
Serpent-tongued
Silver moonfish
Silver pheasant
Skeleton shrimp
Skunk blackbird
Snapping beetle
Snapping turtle
Sociable weaver
Soft-shell clam
Solitary thrush
Sooty albatross
South southerly
Southdown sheep
Spectacled bear
Spectacled duck
Spiculispongiae
Spini-spirulate
Squirrel monkey
Stag-horn coral
Staircase shell
Stalked crinoid
Stilt sandpiper
Stinking badger
Strawberry bass
Strawberry crab
Strawberry fish
Strawberry moth
Strawberry worm
Stylommatophora
Suchospondylous
Sucking stomach
Supra-auricular
Swallow warbler
Swamp blackbird

Swamp partridge
Tasmanian devil
Tectibranchiata
Tectibranchiate
Telescope shell
Tentacle sheath
Tentaculiferous
Terebratuliform
Tetrabranchiata
Tetrabranchiate
Tetractinellida
Tetrapnuemonian
Tooth coralline
Tortoise beetle
Tracheobranchia
Trapdoor spider
Triangle spider
Triangular crab
Turpentine moth
Upholsterer bee
Upland moccasin
Vespertilionine
Vine-leaf roper
Vitreous sponge
Viviparous fish
Wandering mouse
Watchman beetle
Water blackbird
Water partridge
Waxen chatterer
Wheat jointworm
Whistling eagle
Whistling snipe
White merganser
White partridge
Whiting pollack
Winter flounder
Zeugobranchiata

14

Acanthocephala
Acanthopterous
Alligator fish
Anarthropodous
Anisodactylous
Anthropomorpha
Appendicularia
Artiodactylous
Aspidobranchia
Cabbage beetle
Coarctate pupa
Cotton stainer
Crocodile bird
Crossopterygii
Crow blackbird
Curculionidous

Gastrovascular
Gentile-falcon
Golden warbler
Goliath beetle
Gonoblastidium
Grape curculio
Haematophilina
Harlequin duck
Harlequin moth
Harnessed moth
Harvest spider
Harvesting ant
Heath throstle
Hectocotylized
Hedgehog shell
Hermit warbler
Heterodactylae
Hexactinelline
Hill partridge
Holothurioidea
Honeycomb moth
Horned rattler
Horsehair worm
Howling monkey
Hunting spider
Hurricane bird
Ichthyophthira
Imaginal disks
Imperial eagle
Inequivalvular
Infrabranchial
Integropallial
Interbranchial
Interscapulars
Invisible bird
Jumping mullet
Jumping spider
Kangaroo mouse
Keyhole limpet
Keyhole urchin
King parrakeet
Lake whitefish
Lamellirostral
Lamellirostres
Laughing goose
Laughing hyena
Leaf butterfly
Leaping spider
Leather jacket
Leather turtle
Light-horseman
Lingual ribbon
Loeven's larva
Mackerel guide
Mackerel midge
Mackerel shark
Macrodactylous

Malacopterygii
Malacostracous
Marsupial frog
Measuring worm
Melolonthidian
Mermaid's head
Miller's thumb
Mocking thrush
Mountain ousel
Mountain quail
Mountain witch
Mule armadillo
Mushroom coral
Myrtle warbler
Nematelminthes
Northern diver
Notobranchiata
Notobranchiate
Nudibranchiata
Nudibranchiate
Numidian crane
Operculiferous
Operculigenous
Opossum shrimp
Ornithoscelida
Oyster catcher
Pachydactylous
Pachydermatous
Painted beauty
Painted turtle
Paleochinoidea
Paleocrinoidea
Paper nautilus
Parotic region
Partridge dove
Pavement teeth
Pectinate claw
Pectorial rail
Pelecaniformes
Pelican's foot
Perissodactyla
Phanerocodonic
Phanerodactyla
Phaneroglossal
Pharyngognathi
Pheasant shell
Phoenicopterus
Phylactolemata
Phyllobranchia
Picked dogfish
Pied blackbird
Plantain eater
Plathelminthes
Platyelminthes
Plectospondyli
Pleurobranchia
Pneumoskeleton

Podophthalmite
Podophthalmous
Polyplacophora
Polyprotodonta
Pomarine jager
Pomeranian dog
Porcelain crab
Porcupine crab
Porcupine fish
Porphyry shell
Potamospongiae
Prairie falcon
Prairie marmot
Prairie pigeon
Primary quills
Proboscidifera
Prosopocephala
Prosopulmonata
Prototracheata
Pseudonavicula
Pseudorhabdite
Purple grackle
Pygmy antelope
Queen's pigeon
Quinary system
Rainbow wrasse
Reciprocornous
Recurvirostral
Renidification
Rhinoceros auk
Rhomboganoidei
Rhynchobdellea
Rhynchocephala
Ring blackbird
River tortoise
Robin accentor
Rock parrakeet
Rock ptarmigan
Sable antelope
Sailor's choic
Salamandroidea
Salt-marsh hen
Sand partridge
Satellite moth
Saurobatrachia
Scaphognathite
Scapular tract
Scavenger crab
Schizognathism
Schizognathous
Schizonemertea
Scorpion shell
Screech thrush
Scutibranchian
Scyphobranchii
Sea pincushion
Sea wood louse

Secretary bird
Sergeant major
Serratirostral
Shrimp catcher
Silicispongiae
Silver whiting
Siphonostomata
Skunk porpoise
Snow partridge
Soldier beetle
Solitary snipe
Spanish curiew
Speckled trout
Speckled-belly
Specter candle
Specter shrimp
Spectral lemur
Spinning gland
Spittle insect
Spurious quill
Squirrel shrew
Stone crawfish
Strepsipterous
Striped mullet
Subturriculate
Sugar squirrel
Sulphur-bottom
Summer tanager
Sun animalcute
Suprabranchial
Swallow plover
Swallow shrike
Taenioglossate
Tasmanian wolf
Telescope carp
Telescope fish
Tenthredinides
Testudinarious
Tetractinellid
Tetradactylous
Thrasher whale
Thread herring
Thunder pumper
Trachelipodous
Tree porcupine
Trichite sheaf
Trichobranchia
Trichoscolices
Turkey buzzard
Turkey vulture
Turnicimorphae
Umbrella shell
Ursine dasyure
Venomous snake
Venus's basket
Venus's girdle
Vespertiliones

Viperine snake
Virginia quail
Water breather
Water elephant
Water laverock
Water measurer
Water moccasin
Water pheasant
Water scorpion
Whale's tongue
Whip-poor-will
Whip-tom-kelly
Whistling coot
Whistling Dick
Whistling duck
Whistling swan
Whistling teal
White elephant
White sturgeon
Whooping crane
Willow warbler
Window swallow
Winking monkey
Winter wagtail
Wood sheldrake
Zygobranchiate

13

Acetabulifera
Admiral shell
Alligator gar
Ambulacriform
Amphisbaenoid
Anallantoidea
Anencephalous
Animal flower
Antambulacral
Antenniferous
Anthobranchia
Aphanipterous
Aphidophagous
Appendiculata
Archencephala
Archiannelida
Aurichalceous
Aurocephalous
Bustard quail
Cabbage aphis
Calcispongiae
Campanularian
Catanadromous
Cephalocercal
Cephalopodous
Cephalothorax
Cephalotrocha
Cliff swallow

Clover weevil
Comprehensive
Compsognathus
Conchological
Corticiferous
Crebricostate
Crebrisulcate
Crow pheasant
Cucking stool
Cuckoo falcon
Currant borer
Cycloganoidei
Cycloid scale
Gadfly petrel
Galeopithecus
Garden spider
Gasteropodous
Gnathostegite
Golden oriole
Golden plover
Gorget hummer
Ground beetle
Ground cuckoo
Ground pigeon
Ground thrush
Gynandromorph
Haematotherma
Halichondriae
Hare kangaroo
Harlequin bat
Harvest mouse
Hedge sparrow
Hedgehog fish
Helianthoidea
Helmet beetle
Helmet shrike
Hemimetabolic
Hermit thrush
Hexactinellid
Hexadactylous
Hollow-horned
Holometabolic
Holophanerous
Holostomatous
Homogangliate
Honey buzzard
Honey creeper
Hop froth fly
Horned lizard
Horse mackerel
Horsehoe nose
House cricket
House sparrow
Hubble-bubble
Hydrocorallia
Hydrophyllium
Ichneumonidan

Ichneumonides
Ichthyomorpha
Implacentalia
Inequilateral
Interbrachial
Interepimeral
Interscapular
Isospondylous
Jumping louse
Jumping mouse
Jumping shrew
Kangaroo hare
Labrador duck
Ladder beetle
Lady's finger
Laemodipodous
Lake sturgeon
Lamellibranch
Lamellicornia
Laminiplantar
Lantern shell
Laughing gull
Leaf crumpler
Lepidopterist
Lepidopterous
Lightning bug
Lissencephala
Lobster louse
Locust beetle
Locust hunter
Looping snail
Lophobranchii
Lyencephalous
Mackerel bird
Mackerel cock
Mackerel gull
Madreporiform
Malacostomous
Malacostracan
Mandarin duck
Mandibuliform
Maneless lion
Mantis shrimp
Marsh harrier
Marsipobranch
Meadow mussel
Medusa's head
Mesobranchial
Metabranchial
Missel thrush
Money spinner
Monodactylous
Monothalamous
Monotrematous
Mosquito hawk
Mountain cock
Mountain goat

Mourning dove
Multicarinate
Multivalvular
Musk lorikeet
Musk parakeet
Mussel digger
Myelencephala
Myoepithelial
Myriacanthous
Naked mollusk
Native rabbit
Native thrush
Native turkey
Neptune's cup
Nettling cell
Night swallow
Night warbler
Nudibrachiate
Nutmeg pigeon
Odontophorous
Opisthoglypha
Opossum mouse
Orthoceratite
Ourang-outang
Oyster plover
Palisade worm
Pallial sinus
Palmidactyles
Panther cowry
Paradise bird
Paradise fish
Pectinibranch
Perissodactyl
Phalangistine
Phanerocarpae
Pharaoh's rat
Pheasant duck
Phragmosiphon
Phyllophagous
Pied antelope
Pigeon tremex
Pine grosbeak
Piping roller
Placoganoidei
Plagiostomous
Plagiotremata
Pleurobrachia
Pleuronectoid
Pneumatophore
Pneumonophora
Pocket gopher
Podophthalmia
Pole flounder
Polymeniscous
Polymorphosis
Polypomedusae
Polypteroidei

Polythalamous
Pompano shell
Porcellaneous
Postscutellum
Potato weevil
Pouched mouse
Prairie snake
Preacher bird
Pressirostral
Proliferation
Proteroglypha
Prussian carp
Pseudofilaria
Ptenoglossate
Pterobranchia
Pterylography
Puffing adder
Pulmoniferous
Quadricornous
Quadripennate
Quadrisulcate
Racket-tailed
Rainbow trout
Razor grinder
Red underwing
Rhipidoglossa
Rice troupial
River herring
Roan antelope
Rock barnacle
Rock kangaroo
Root barnacle
Ruffed grouse
Rusine antler
Sacred baboon
Sacred beetle
Sacred monkey
Sage thrasher
Saint Bernard
Salmon killer
Satin sparrow
Saurognathous
Saw sharpener
Scabbard fish
Scepterellate
Schizocoelous
Schizognathae
Schizopelmous
Sclerodermata
Sclerodermite
Sclerodermous
Scolecomorpha
Scombriformes
Scutibranchia
Scyphomedusae
Sea butterfly
Sea sandpiper

Sedge warbler
Semaeostomata
Serpent eater
Sexton beetle
Sheath-winged
Shepherd bird
Shield-bearer
Shuttle shell
Silver plover
Silver salmon
Siphoniferous
Siphonoglyphe
Siphonophoran
Siphunculated
Sipunculoidea
Skip mackerel
Slipper shell
Snow pheasant
Snowy lemming
Soft tortoise
Solidungulous
Spanish sheep
Sparrow spear
Speckled-bill
Spermatophore
Sphinx baboon
Spiculigenous
Spider hunter
Spider monkey
Spindle shell
Spinning mite
Spiny lobster
Split-tongued
Spring beauty
Spring beetle
Spruce grouse
Spurious wing
Squash beetle
Squirrel fish
Squirrel hake
Squirrel hawk
Standard-wing
Steganopodous
Stinging cell
Stomatopodous
Strand plover
Strepsipteran
Striped snake
Stubble goose
Subbrachiales
Subesophageal
Sulphur whale
Sundial shell
Superb warber
Supply system
Swamp sparrow
Sweet William

Swimming bell
Swimming crab
Synentognathi
Tangle picker
Tapestry moth
Telescope fly
Tentaculifera
Tentaculiform
Tentaculocyst
Testicardines
Tetradecapoda
Tetrapneumona
Thistle finch
Thoracostraca
Thunder snake
Thysanopteran
Tiger bittern
Timber beetle
Timber doodle
Timber grouse
Tippet grouse
Toad snatcher
Tomato sphinx
Toothed whale
Tracheophonae
Trachymedusae
Trachystomata
Tree kangaroo
Triarticulate
Trichiuriform
Trichopterous
Trichromatism
Trigonocerous
Trionychoidea
Trumpet conch
Trumpet shell
Tubulidentate
Turkey sponge
Turtle cowrie
Tyrant shrike
Umbrella bird
Unibranchiate
Unicorn shell
Unicorn whale
Upland plover
Ursine baboon
Ursine howler
Vaginopennous
Velvet runner
Velvet scoter
Velvet sponge
Venus's purse
Venus's shell
Vermiculation
Vine forester
Vine inchworm
Vitelligenous

Walking stick
Water boatman
Water buffalo
Water chicken
Water monitor
Water opossum
Water rattler
Water spinner
Wattle turkey
Wheatsel bird
Whip scorpion
White cricket
White flesher
White wagtail
White widgeon
Whooping swan
Willow grouse
Willow thrush
Window martin
Window oyster
Wingless bird
Wood engraver
Wood titmouse
Wood tortoise
Woolly macaco
Woolly monkey
Wormwood hare
Zygodactylous

12

Acanthopteri
Acephalocyst
Acrodactylum
Actinotrocha
Adambulacral
Adelocodonic
Ammonitoidea
Amphibiotica
Amphicoelous
Amphistomous
Anarthropoda
Angiostomous
Anisodactyls
Anseriformes
Anthophagous
Anthropoglot
Anthropoidea
Aphidivorous
Architeuthis
Arrenotokous
Arthrogastra
Arthropleura
Arthropomata
Arthrostraca
Artiodactyla
Artiodactyle

Ascidiozooid
Button quail
Cabbage worm
Cataphracted
Cephalophora
Cephaloptera
Clothes moth
Clypeastroid
Cobbler fish
Codling moth
Coelenterata
Coelenterate
Coleopterous
Conchologist
Copper finch
Coprophagous
Coral animal
Coryphaenoid
Cotton scale
Cotyligerous
Crepusculous
Crown antler
Ctenophorous
Ctenostomata
Cultirostral
Cultirostres
Currant worm
Curvicaudate
Curvirostral
Curvirostres
Cushion star
Cutlass fish
Cyclostomous
Gallinaceous
Ganoid scale
Garter snake
Gastropodous
Gastrotricha
Gastrotrocha
Geodephagous
Gila monster
Gizzard shad
Glass-sponge
Globe slater
Glove sponge
Glutton bird
Gnat catcher
Gnat snapper
Golden eagle
Golden robin
Gordian knot
Goroon shell
Grain weevil
Grape hopper
Grass spider
Grass sponge
Gray snapper

Green linnet
Green looper
Green monkey
Green turtle
Grizzly bear
Ground pearl
Ground robin
Ground snake
Gymnoblastea
Gymnoblastic
Gymnolaemata
Gym'norhinal
Gynaecophore
Gyrencephala
Hammer shell
Harrier hawk
Harvest fish
Harvest mite
Hazel grouse
Heart urchin
Hectocotylus
Hedgehog rat
Helmet shell
Hematotherma
Hemimetabola
Herring gull
Heterodactyl
Heterogynous
Heteromerous
Heteromyaria
Heteronereis
Heteropodous
Heterosomati
Heterotricha
Hickory shad
Hippocrepian
hippopotamus
Hognosesnake
Holometabola
Homomorphism
Honey badger
Honey weasel
Hopping Dick
Horned grebe
Horned horse
Horned snake
Horned viper
Horse mussel
Horse sponge
House martin
House spider
Humming bird
Hyalospongia
Hydractinian
Hypodactylum
Ichthyopsida
Indigo snake

Inoperculate
Intersternal
Intromittent
Invertebrata
Invertebrate
Ischiocerite
Ischiopodite
Jackass deer
Java sparrow
Jumping deer
Juniper worm
Kangaroo rat
King penguin
King vulture
Klipspringer
Labyrinthici
Ladder shell
Laemmergeyer
Lake herring
Lake whiting
Lark bunting
Lark sparrow
Latirostrous
Laughing owl
Leaf notcher
Leather carp
Lentil shell
Lepidoganoid
Lepidosauria
Leptocardian
Ligniperdous
Linguatulida
Linguatulina
Lithophagous
Little chief
Lizard snake
Longipennate
Longipennine
Longirostral
Longirostres
Loup-cervier
Lucky proach
Lumbriciform
Macropterous
Mademoiselle
Madreporaria
Malacobdella
Malacostraca
Malapterurus
Malashaganay
Mandibulated
Mange insect
Manna insect
Margate fish
Meadow mouse
Meadow pipit
Meadow snipe

Melon beetle
Menobranchus
Mermaid fish
Mesothoracic
Metagnathous
Metanauplius
Metathoracic
Microsthenic
Mimic beetle
Mineralogist
Mocking bird
Mocking wren
Mole cricket
Molluscoidal
Molluscoidea
Money cowrie
Monodelphian
Monodelphous
Monogoneutic
Monopneumona
Monothalaman
Moor buzzard
Moor titling
Mountain cat
Mouse galago
Mouth-footed
Mud tortoise
Musical fish
Myrmotherine
Myxocystodea
Nankeen bird
Native devil
Native sloth
Necrophagous
Needle shell
Negro monkey
Nematognathi
Neurochordal
Neuropterous
Night monkey
Night parrot
Nucleobranch
Nymphiparous
Ophiophagous
Orange cowry
Orange scale
Orang-outang
Ornithopappi
Orthopterous
Ostracodermi
Oyster shell
Pachydermata
Pachydermoid
Pachyglossal
Paedogenesis
Paedogenetic
Painted lady

Paleichthyes
Pantastomata
Paper sailor
Papilionides
Paradactylum
Paragnathous
Pardine lynx
Paridigitata
Peabody bird
Peacock fish
Pearl oyster
Pedicellaria
Pelican fish
Pelican ibis
Pentacrinite
Pentacrinoid
Pentastomida
Perichaetous
Periostracum
Peritracheal
Petalosticha
Peter's fish
Phalangoidea
Phryganeides
Phylactocarp
Phyllophagan
Phyllopodous
Physostomous
Phytophagous
Pigmy falcon
Pirate perch
Plant cutter
Plate-gilled
Plathelminth
Plectognathi
Pleurobranch
Plumed adder
Plumulaceous
Pluto monkey
Pneumatocyst
Pocket mouse
Podobranchia
Podophyllous
Podura scale
Polybranchia
Polycystidea
Polycyttaria
Polygastrian
Polygastrica
Polygoneutic
Polypiferous
Polypiparous
Polythalamia
Pomacentroid
Poor soldier
Post-abdomen
Pouched frog

Prairie hare
Prairie mole
Prairie wolf
Pressiroster
Proboscidate
Proboscidean
Proboscidial
Proboscidian
Procellarian
Protozoonite
Protracheata
Pseudohalter
Pseudo-heart
Pteroglossal
Pug-nose eel
Pumpkin seed
Pycnaspidean
Pycnodontini
Pygmy parrot
Pygobranchia
Quadrumanous
Queen pigeon
Razor-backed
Rectirostral
Red squirrel
Reed bunting
Reed sparrow
Reed warbler
Reef builder
Retinophoral
Retromingent
Rhabdocúlous
Rhabdopleura
Rhachiglossa
Rhamphotheca
Rhinocerical
Rhinolophine
Rhizocephala
Rhizostomata
Rhomboganoid
Rhynchonella
Rhynchophora
Rhynchophore
Ribbon snake
Ribborn worm
Rice bunting
Right-handed
Ringed snake
River limpet
River pirate
Rock builder
Rock lobster
Rock sparrow
Rock warbler
Rosary shell
Rough-footed
Rough-legged

Royston crow
Ruddy plover
Ruffed lemur
Saddle shell
Sage sparrow
Salamandrina
Salamandroid
Salmon trout
Sand cricket
Sand monitor
Sand skipper
Sand swallow
Sanguivorous
Saprophagous
Sarcophagous
Sarcorhamphi
Scale beetle
Scale insect
Scale-winged
Scaly-winged
Scaphocerite
Scarlet fish
Scarlet ibis
Scarlet mite
Schizorhinal
Scissorsbill
Scissorstail
Sciuromorpha
Scorpion fly
Scorpionidea
Screech hawk
Scutellation
Scytodermata
Sea crayfish
Sea cucumber
Sea dotterel
Sea elephant
Sea hedgehog
Sea partridg
Sea pheasant
Sea porcupin
Sea scorpion
Sea woodcock
Selachostomi
Semipalmated
Serpent eage
Serpent fish
Serpent star
Serrirostres
Sessile-eyed
Sheep's-wool
Shepherd dog
Shore plover
Shore teetan
Shovel-nosed
Siberian dog
Silver grebe

Silver lunge
Silver perch
Silver shell
Silver trout
Silver witch
Singing bird
Singing fish
Sinupalliate
Siphonophora
Siphonophore
Siphonostome
Siphorhinian
Sipunculacea
Skeletonizer
Sloth monkey
Snake killer
Snout beetle
Snow bunting
Snowy plover
Social whale
Soldier crab
Soldier fish
Soldier moth
Solenoconcha
Solenogastra
Solenoglypha
Solidungular
Solitary ant
Solitary bee
Song sparrow
Spanish flag
Sparrow hawk
Spatangoidea
Spider shell
Spider's web
Spine-finned
Spine-tailed
Spiralozooid
Spoon-billed
Squamigerous
Stake-driver
Steamer duck
Steganopodes
Stelleridean
Stelmatopoda
Stenodermine
Stick insect
Stiff-tailed
Stilt plover
Sting winkle
Stock pigeon
Stomach worm
Stone curlew
Stone falcon
Stone lugger
Stone marten
Stone plover

Stone roller
Stonesmickle
Storm petrel
Strepsiptera
Strepsorhina
Strepsorhine
Streptoneura
Stridulation
Striped bass
Strobilation
Struthioidea
Struthionine
Subcultrated
Subulicornes
Sucking fish
Sultana bird
Summer snipe
Sunset shell
Superciliary
Surf whiting
Surface grub
Surinam toad
Sweet marten
Sword shrimp
Syndactylous
Tadpole fish
Taenioglossa
Tail coverts
Tang sparrow
Tauricornous
Teleocephial
Telotrochous
Tentaculated
Tenuirostral
Tenuirostres
Terebratulid
Tetradactyle
Tetrapterous
Textile cone
Thalamophora
Thalassinian
Thistle bird
Thistle cock
Thorn hopper
Thysanoptera
Tiger beetle
Tippet grebe
Toad spittle
Tobacco worm
Trachelipoda
Tree creeper
Tree cricket
Tree lobster
Tree serpent
Tree sparrow
Tree swallow
Tree warbler

Triangulares
Trichopteran
Trichromatic
Trigger fish
Trochal disk
Trochosphere
Trough-shell
Truffle worm
Trumpet fish
Trunk turtle
Tube spinner
Turban-shell
Turbellarian
Turnip-shell
Turritelloid
Tussock moth
Twig girdler
Umbellularia
Umbrella ant
Under covert
Unicorn moth
Upper covert
Vaporer moth
Vare widgeon
Varying hare
Velvetbreast
Vent feather
Ventral fins
Venus's comb
Vermilinguia
Vicissy duck
Vine fretter
Violet shell
Visiting ant
Walking fish
Walking leaf
Wall creeper
Washing bear
Water beetle
Water junket
Water lizard
Water rabbit
Water spider
Water thrush
Water turkey
Watering pot
Wedge-tailed
Wheat beetle
Wheat maggot
Wheat thrips
Wheat weevil
Wheel urchin
Whin Sparrow
Whistle duck
White grouse
White hoolet
White miller

White rabbit
White salmon
White sucker
Whiting pout
Widow monkey
Willow biter
Window shell
Winter sleep
Winter snipe
Wood cricket
Wood fretter
Wood leopard
Wood puceron
Wood swallow
Wood warbler
Woolly louse
Woopher swan
Wreath-shell
Writing lark
Xenopterygii
Xylophagides
Yellowhammer
Yellowthroat
Zalambdodont
Zoochlorella
Zoerythrine
Zygobranchia
Zygodactylae

11

Abdominales
Abdominalia
Abranchiata
Abranchiate
Acadian owl
Accipitrine
Achlamydate
Acinetiform
Acorn-shell
Acrotarsium
Actinostome
Adipose fin
Aestivation
Alectorides
Allantoidea
Ametabolian
Ametabolous
Amorphozoic
Amphipneust
Amphipodous
Amphisbaena
Amphitrocha
Anatiferous
Ancon sheep
Angora goat
Anisopleura

Anthropical
Anthropidae
Antler moth
Aphaniptera
Aplacentata
Aplacophora
Apple borer
Apple midge
Apple snail
Arachnidial
Arachnidium
Arachnoidea
Archaeozoic
Archer fish
Argus shell
Ascidiarium
Ascidioidea
Aspergillum
Astrophyton
Auricularia
Cabbage fly
Cactus wren
Caddice fly
Cake urchin
Calamistrum
Calico bass
Candle coal
Carcinology
Caterpillar
Centriscoid
Cephalomere
Cephalopoda
Cephalopode
Cephalosome
Clover worm
Cochin fowl
Coenenchyma
Coleopteran
Colleterial
Colleterium
Communistic
Conchometer
Conchometry
Concolorous
Congo snake
Conirostral
Conirostres
Constrictor
Coprophagan
Coral snake
Coralligena
Corn weevil
Crab spider
Crocodilian
Crow shrike
Crown shell
Crustaceous

Cuckoo dove
Cuckoo fish
Cuckoo maid
Curlew Jack
Cycloganoid
Cyphonautes
Cyprinodont
Cypseliform
Cysticercus
Fastigiated
Gall insect
Galley-bird
Galley-worm
Gallinaceae
Gallinacean
Garter fish
Gasteropoda
Gastrostege
Gecarcinian
Generalized
German carp
Giant heron
Giant squid
Gier-falcon
Glass-snail
Glass-snake
Globiferous
Globigerina
Gnathostoma
Gnathotheca
Gold beetle
Golden wasp
Gonoblastid
Gorgoniacea
Grape borer
Grass snake
Grass snipe
Grasshopper
Gravedigger
Gray falcon
Gray mullet
Gray parrot
Grease moth
Green gland
Green snake
Grisly bear
Ground dove
Ground fish
Ground lark
Ground wren
Grugru worm
Grunting ox
Guinea worm
Gull teaser
Gymnoglossa
Gymnopaedic
Gymnophiona

Gymnosomata
Haematocrya
Hand-winged
Harbor seal
Hard oyster
Harvest fly
Haustellata
Haustellate
Heart shell
Helianthoid
Hellgramite
Hemathermal
Hemibranchi
Hemipterous
Hen harrier
Herbivorous
Hermit crab
Herring hog
Hesperidium
Hessian fly
Heteracanth
Heterophagi
High holder
High-palmed
Holaspidean
Holm thrush
Holocephali
Holostomata
Holostomate
Holothurian
Homotypical
Honey eater
Honey guide
Honeysucker
Hook-billed
Horned dace
Horned frog
Horned lark
Horned pout
Horned toad
Horse conch
Horse emmet
Horse finch
Horse-leech
House finch
House mouse
House snake
Hunting cat
Hunting dog
Hydrocaulus
Hydromedusa
Hylophagous
Hyoganoidei
Hyperoartia
Hyperotreta
Hypognatous
Hypopharynx

Hyporhachis
Ichthyoidal
Imber-goose
Imperforata
Implacental
Incrassated
Indigo bird
Infralabial
Infraocular
Insectivore
Intermediae
Invertebral
Isopodiform
Isopogonous
Isospondyli
Itch insect
Ivory shell
Jack curlew
Jack rabbit
Jack salmon
Jemlah goat
Jungle bear
Jungle cock
Kelp salmon
Keratophyte
King monkey
King mullet
King salmon
Kite falcon
Lace lizard
Lacertiloid
Lace-winged
Lackey moth
Laemodipoda
Lambda moth
Lamellicorn
Lammergeier
Lance snake
Lancet fish
Land turtle
Lappet moth
Larviparous
Latirostres
Latisternal
Leaf beetle
Leaf cutter
Leaf hopper
Leaf insect
Leaf roller
Leaf-footed
Leatherback
Leatherhead
Leatherneck
Leopard cat
Lepidoptera
Lepidosiren
Leptocardia

Leptodactyl
Leptostraca
Levirostres
Libelluloid
Lion lizard
Lipocephala
Lithodomous
Lithophytic
Liver shark
Lizard fish
Lobe-footed
Locust bird
Longicornia
Longipennes
Long-tongue
Lophobranch
Lucernarian
Lucernarida
Lyencephala
Lyre turtle
Maara shell
Macrochires
Macrodactyl
Macropodous
Macropteres
Madreporite
Magpie lark
Magpie moth
Maize eater
Maltese cat
Maltese dog
Mammillated
Mandibulate
Maned sheep
Marsebanker
Marsh quail
Marsupialia
Masked crab
Mason shell
Mastiff bat
Mastigopoda
Meadow lark
Meal beetle
Megasthenic
Merostomata
Mesogastric
Mesomyodian
Mesomyodous
Mesosternum
Mesotrochal
Metagastric
Metasternum
Microsthene
Mirror carp
Miter shell
Mollipilose
Monocardian

Monocondyla
Monodelphia
Monothalama
Monotremata
Moor monkey
Moss animal
Moth blight
Moth hunter
Moth miller
Mound maker
Mouse lemur
Multispiral
Muscallonge
Muscicapine
Museum pest
Music shell
Musk beaver
Musk beetle
Musk cattle
Musk turtle
Muskellunge
Mutton bird
Mutton fish
Myzostomata
Nasicornous
Natatorious
Native bear
Necrophagan
Nematocalyx
Nematognath
Nematoidean
Nematophora
Neomenoidea
Neuropodium
Neuropodous
Neuropteral
Neuropteran
Night churr
Night flyer
Night heron
Night raven
Nightingale
Nine-killer
Noctilionid
Noctilucine
Noctivagant
Nomopelmous
Notodontian
Nototherium
Nurse shark
Nutmeg bird
Oared shrew
Odontoblast
Odontophora
Odontophore
Oil sardine
Oligochaeta

Oligotokous
Onychophora
Operculated
Ophiomorpha
Ophiophagus
Ophiuroidea
Ophthalmite
Orange bird
Orbitolites
Orthopteran
Ostracoidea
Ostreaceous
Otter shell
Oyster crab
Oyster fish
Pachydactyl
Pachydermal
Paired fins
Palaeocarida
Palm weevil
Palmed deer
Palpigerous
Paludicolae
Pampas deer
Panther cat
Papillulate
Paragnathus
Paraphragma
Pariah kite
Parrot fish
Parson bird
Passeriform
Patelliform
Paucispiral
Pear blight
Pectostraca
Pedicellina
Pedipalpous
Pedunculata
Pennigerous
Pentacrinus
Pentamerous
Pentremites
Pepper moth
Perciformes
Percomorphi
Perigastric
Peripterous
Peristomial
Pernyi moth
Persian cat
Petromyzont
Phainopepla
Phalangious
Phenicopter
Phocodontia
Phragmocone

Phyllorhine
Phyllostome
Physoclisti
Physophorae
Phytophagic
Phytozoaria
Pigeon hawk
Pill beetle
Pill-willet
Pilot snake
Pilot whale
Pine lizard
Pine marten
Pine weevil
Piping frog
Pipistrelle
Piscivorous
Placentalia
Placoganoid
Plagiostome
Plagiostomi
Planipennia
Plant louse
Plantigrada
Plantigrade
Plastidozoa
Platyhelmia
Plectognath
Pleuroderes
Pleuroptera
Plum budder
Plum gouger
Plum weevil
Plumularian
Pneumootoka
Pneumophora
Podostomata
Poecilopoda
Poison fang
Polar whale
Polyactinia
Polycystina
Polycystine
Polygastric
Polygordius
Polymyodous
Polystomata
Polyzoarium
Pond turtle
Poor-willie
Potato worm
Potter wasp
Pouched dog
Pouched rat
Pouch-shell
Powder down
Prairie dog

Prairie hen
Priapulacea
Prick-eared
Pricklefish
Prickly rat
Prinpriddle
Proboscidea
Procephalic
Proliferate
Proliferous
Proostracum
Propithecus
Prosobranch
Prothoracic
Protocercal
Protomerite
Protoplasta
Protopodite
Protopterus
Protosomite
Prototheria
Pseudembryo
Pseudhaemal
Pseudo-cone
Pseudotinea
Psilopaedes
Psilopaedic
Ptenoglossa
Pterocletes
Pteropodous
Pterostigma
Ptilocerque
Ptilopaedes
Ptilopaedic
Puffing pig
Puff-legged
Pulmonarian
Pulmonifera
Purple bird
Pycnogonida
Pygmy goose
Quadrupedal
Quail snipe
Queen conch
Querquedule
Rabbit fish
Raccoon dog
Raccoon fox
Racing crab
Racket-tail
Radiolarian
Rapier fish
Rattlesnake
Rattlewings
Razor shell
Red admiral
Red empress

Red snapper
Regent bird
Reticularia
Retinophora
Rhabdophora
Rhachiodont
Rhinolophid
Rhipipteran
Rhizopodous
Rhopalocera
Rhynchocúla
Ribbon fish
Ribbon seal
Rice weevil
Right whale
Rimau dahan
Ring parrot
Ring plover
Ring thrush
Ringed seal
Ringed worm
Ringlestone
Ring-necked
Ring-tailed
River horse
River snail
Road runner
Robber crab
Robber gull
Robin snipe
Rock hopper
Rock pigeon
Rock plover
Rock rabbit
Rock thrush
Rose beetle
Rose chafer
Round robin
Rove beetle
Royal eagle
Royal tiger
Rudder fish
Rustic moth
Rypophagous
Sable mouse
Saccoglossa
Sack-winged
Sacred fish
Sage grouse
Sage rabbit
Sagittocyst
Saltatorial
Saltigradae
Sand badger
Sand collar
Sand darter
Sand dollar

Sand grouse
Sand hopper
Sand hornet
Sand launce
Sand lizard
Sand martin
Sand runner
Sand saucer
Saprophagan
Sarcophagan
Sarcoseptum
Saw whetter
Scalariform
Scaled dove
Schizognath
Scincoidian
Scolopacine
Scolopendra
Scopiferous
Scorpaenoid
Scotch duck
Scrag whale
Screech owl
Screw shell
Scrobicular
Scrub robin
Scutellated
Scutibranch
Scyphistoma
Scyphophori
Sea feather
Sea gudgeon
Sea lamprey
Sea leopard
Sea monster
Sea pudding
Sea saurian
Sea serpent
Sea surgeon
Sea swallow
Sea titling
Sea trumpet
Sea unicorn
Sea widgeon
Sea-blubber
Seed weevil
Selachoidei
Sepidaceous
Seraph moth
Sericterium
Sertularian
Shad-waiter
Shell gland
Shielddrake
Shore birds
Shufflewing
Silicioidea

Silk spider
Silk vessel
Silver chub
Silver hake
Silver moth
Silversides
Siphonopoda
Siphorhinal
Siphuncular
Sipunculoid
Skittle-dog
Sleepmarken
Sleepy duck
Sleuthhound
Smooth sole
Smother fly
Snail borer
Snail shell
Snake eater
Snow insect
Snow pigeon
Snowy heron
Soar falcon
Soft dorsal
Soft-finned
Soldier bug
Soldier fly
Solenaceous
Solenoglyph
Solenostomi
Solidungula
Song thrush
Sore falcon
Spanish fly
Sparrow owl
Spawn eater
Specter bat
Sperm whale
Spermatheca
Spermophile
Spermophore
Sphaeridium
Sphinx moth
Sphyraenoid
Spiculiform
Spider crab
Spider mite
Spike shell
Spindletail
Spindleworm
Spirit duck
Spongoblast
Sprat borer
Spur-winged
Squab-chick
Squat snipe
Squawk duck

Squid hound
Stag beetle
Stag-horned
Stalk borer
Staphylinid
Star lizard
Stickleback
Stomatopoda
Stone biter
Stone borer
Stone canal
Stone coral
Stone eater
Stone snipe
Stone toter
Stonerunner
Stony coral
Strand wolf
Streptures
Strongyloid
Struthiones
Subaduncate
Subbrachian
Subumbrella
Succoteague
Sucker tube
Suleah fish
Summer bird
Summer coot
Summer duck
Sun bittern
Supercilium
Superfamily
Supraocular
Swaddlebill
Swallowfish
Swamp robin
Swell shark
Swingletail
Sylvicoline
Symbranchii
Synallaxine
Synapticula
Syndactylic
Synthetical
Syrphus fly
Tachyglossa
Tailor bird
Tanystomata
Tapir tiger
Taxaspidean
Tectibranch
Teeter-tail
Ten-pounder
Tentaculata
Tenuiroster
Terebrantia

Terebrating
Terebratula
Termatarium
Terrienniak
Testudinata
Tetramerous
Tetrapteran
Tettigonian
Thamnophile
Thecodactyl
Thecosomata
Thelphusian
Thelytokous
Thorn devil
Thread cell
Thunderbird
Thunderfish
Thunderworm
Thysanopter
Thysanurous
Tibial spur
Tiger shark
Tiger shell
Timber worm
Tit babbler
Toad lizard
Tobacco box
Tobias fish
Tolypeutine
Tomato gall
Tomato worm
Totipalmate
Trachelidan
Trachelipod
Tree beetle
Tree hopper
Tree jobber
Tree lizard
Tree oyster
Tree pigeon
Tree shrike
Trichiuroid
Trichophore
Trichoptera
Trident bat
Triple-tail
Trochantine
Troglodytes
Tropic bird
Trout perch
Trumpet fly
Truttaceous
Tufted duck
Tulip-eared
Turbellaria
Turdiformes
Turkey bird

Turkey cock
Turkey pout
Turnip flea
Unguiculata
Unguiculate
Unguligrade
Unicolorous
Unimuscular
Urchin fish
Urosternite
Ursine seal
Valve-shell
Vampire bat
Vaza parrot
Velvet duck
Veneer moth
Ventriculus
Venus's fan
Vermiformia
Vermivorous
Verriculate
Vertebrated
Vesicularia
Vespertilio
Vine beetle
Vine hopper
Vine sawfly
Vine sphinx
Vine weevil
Vinegar eel
Virgularian
Vitellogene
Wading bird
Wall lizard
Warrior ant
Washerwoman
Water crake
Water devil
Water eagle
Water mouse
Water ouzel
Water shrew
Water snake
Water tiger
Water viper
Water witch
Weaver bird
Wedge-shell
Whale louse
Whale shark
Wheat aphis
Wheat louse
Wheat midge
Whidah bird
Whin Thrush
Whisky Jack
Whistlefish

Whistlewing
White brand
White coral
White mouse
White perch
White scale
White shark
White stork
White trout
White whale
Whitethroat
Whiting-mop
Whole snipe
Wild pigeon
Wild turkey
Willow gall
Willow lark
Wind-sucker
Wing covert
Wing-footed
Wing-handed
Winter duck
Winter gull
Winter moth
Winter shad
Winter teal
Winter wren
Wire-tailed
Wishtonwish
Wolf spider
Wood baboon
Wood culver
Wood grouse
Wood hoopoe
Wood pigeon
Wood rabbit
Wood shrike
Wood sucker
Wood tapper
Wood thrush
Woodcracker
Woodknacker
Woolly bear
Woolly maki
Xylophagous
Xylophilous
Yellowammer
Zeuglodonta
Zoantharian
Zoanthodeme
Zo^dendrium
Zo^phytical
Zygodactyle
Zygodactyli

10

Aberdevine
Abranchial
Acalephoid
Accipitres
Acephalous
Acropodium
Actinomere
Actinosome
Actinozoal
Actinozoan
Adactylous
Aftershaft
Ailuroidea
Alcyonacea
Alcyonaria
Amazon ant
Amber fish
Ambulacral
Ambulacrum
Amorphozoa
Amphineura
Amphipodan
Amphirhina
Anadromous
Anarthrous
Androphore
Anenterous
Angel fish
Angora cat
Angwantibo
Animalcule
Annelidous
Anomaliped
Ant thrush
Ant-cattle
Aphis lion
Apple worm
Arachnidan
Araneiform
Araneoidea
Arboricole
Arthroderm
Arthromere
Arthropoda
Arthrozoic
Articulata
Articulate
Ascidiform
Asiphonate
Asiphonida
Asteridian
Auriculars
Avicularia
Aviculture
Calicoback
Camelopard
Cankerworm

Canvasback
Caper bush
Capistrate
Catallacta
Cataphract
Catarrhine
Cavicornia
Cecidomyia
Cnidoblast
Coccinella
Cockchafer
Coddymoddy
Coelacanth
Coenoecium
Coffee bug
Coleoptera
Collembola
Collophore
Columbella
Complicant
Conchifera
Conchology
Condylopod
Conger sea
Coniroster
Copperhead
Copperworm
Copulatory
Coral fish
Corniplume
Corticifer
Cottontail
Cotyliform
Coulterneb
Crab louse
Craspedota
Craspedote
Crinoidean
Crocodilia
Croton bug
Crustacean
Ctenoidean
Ctenophora
Ctenophore
Cuckoo ray
Cucullated
Culiciform
Cushewbird
Cuttlefish
Cycloidian
Cyclostoma
Cyclostomi
Fenestrate
Foliaceous
Gall midge
Gasteropod
Gastrolith

Gastropoda
Gastrurous
Gemmipares
Germ stock
Ghost moth
Giant clam
Gier-eagle
Ginglymodi
Glass-crab
Glass-rope
Glochidium
Gnathidium
Goatsucker
Goggle-eye
Gold shell
Golden-eye
Gorgonacea
Gorse bird
Gorse chat
Gougeshell
Grain moth
Grain worm
Grallatory
Grape moth
Grape worm
Grass bass
Grass moth
Gravelling
Gravigrade
Gray snipe
Gray whale
Green crab
Green-leek
Greenshank
Gregarinae
Ground hog
Ground pig
Ground rat
Ground tit
Groundling
Guinea hen
Guinea pig
Gum animal
Gymnochroa
Haematitic
Halcyonoid
Hammerhead
Harp shell
Harvestman
Haustellum
Hawk eagle
Heath game
Heliconian
Hellbender
Hell-diver
Helminthes
Hematocrya

Hemelytrum
Hemerobian
Hemidactyl
Hemipteran
Herodiones
Heterocera
Heterodont
Heteromera
Heteropoda
Hexactinia
Hexapodous
Hippobosca
Holostraca
Holotricha
Homocercal
Homoeozoic
Honey bear
Honey kite
Hoonoomaun
Hoop snake
Horn shell
Horned bee
Horned owl
Horned ray
Hornet fly
Horse crab
Horse tick
House wren
Hover-hawk
Hydrachnid
Hydriodate
Hydrophora
Hydrorhiza
Hydrotheca
Hymenopter
Hyopastron
Hypoptilum
Hyporadius
Hypotricha
Hyracoidea
Hystricine
Ice petrel
Infuscated
Infusorial
Infusorian
Insessores
Involucrum
Ivory gull
Ivory-bill
Jack snipe
Jaguarondi
Jay thrush
Jonah crab
Jungle cat
Keratoidea
King conch
King eagle

King snake
Kingfisher
Koolokamba
Labipalpus
Lacertilia
Laemodipod
Lagomorpha
Lake trout
Lamnunguia
Lamp shell
Lamper eel
Lance fish
Land leech
Land snail
Lasso cell
Leaf louse
Leaf miner
Leaf sewer
Leaf-nosed
Lemon sole
Lemuroidea
Lepidopter
Lernaeacea
Libellulid
Limicoline
Limuloidea
Line conch
Lithodomus
Lithophyte
Locustella
Loggerhead
Lomatinous
Longshanks
Lophophore
Louse mite
Lucernaria
Lumbricoid
Lumpsucker
Lyriferous
Madreporic
Mail-shell
Malacoderm
Malacopoda
Malacozoic
Maned seal
Mango bird
Mango fish
Marginella
Marionette
Marsh hawk
Marsh wren
Marsupiate
Mask shell
Masked pig
Mason moth
Mason wasp
Massasauga

Mastigopod
Mattowacca
Maxilliped
Meadow hen
Meconidium
Medusa bud
Medusiform
Megasthene
Meleagrine
Meliphagan
Mercenaria
Meropodite
Mesopodium
Mesoscutum
Mesothorax
Metabolian
Metapodium
Metathorax
Midshipman
Milk snake
Mixogamous
Mole shrew
Molluscoid
Molluscous
Molly-mawk
Monkey-pot
Monocystic
Monogamous
Monomerous
Monomyaria
Monotocous
Moose bird
Moose yard
Mossbunker
Mound bird
Mouse bird
Mouse deer
Mouse hawk
Mud dauber
Mud minnow
Mullingong
Multivalve
Musk sheep
Musk shrew
Myeloneura
Nape-crest
Native hen
Natterjack
Necrophore
Nectocalyx
Needlefish
Nematelmia
Nematocera
Nematocyst
Nematogene
Nematoidea
Neossology

Nettlebird
Neuroptera
Nidamental
Night bird
Night hawk
Night moth
Nile goose
Noah's ark
Noctilucin
Nodosarine
Notidanian
Notopodium
Nudibranch
Nursehound
Nut weevil
Nutbreaker
Nutcracker
Nyctophile
Oak beauty
Oak pruner
Obliterate
Octocerata
Oculinacea
Odontocete
Oil beetle
Oligochete
Ommatidium
Omostegite
Onion fish
Ophiurioid
Orcheslian
Organ bird
Organ fish
Ortalidian
Orthoptera
Orycterope
Osmaterium
Osphradium
Ostraciont
Ovicapsule
Ovipositor
Ovotesttis
Owl monkey
Owl parrot
Owlet moth
Oxyrhyncha
Oysterling
Paddlecock
Paddlefish
Paddy bird
Palamedeae
Paleogaean
Palm swift
Palmerworm
Palmigrade
Palmipedes
Palpebrate

Paludicole
Paludinous
Pampas cat
Pantheress
Paper wasp
Papillones
Paradoxure
Paraglossa
Parapleura
Parapodium
Parapterum
Pariah dog
Parnassian
Pea maggot
Pea weevil
Pear shell
Pearl moth
Pectorials
Pediculate
Pediculati
Pediculina
Pedigerous
Pedimanous
Pedipalpus
Pelecypoda
Penguinery
Pennaceous
Pentameran
Pentremite
Percesoces
Perfoliate
Peritricha
Periwinkle
Pettichaps
Pettychaps
Phacochere
Phalangist
Phascolome
Phlox worm
Phryganeid
Phyllocyst
Phyllopoda
Phyllosoma
Phylloxera
Physemaria
Physoclist
Physograde
Physostomi
Phytophaga
Pichiciago
Piciformes
Pied finch
Pike perch
Pike whale
Pilot bird
Pilot fish
Pine borer

Pine finch
Pine mouse
Pine snake
Pinnatiped
Pinnigrada
Pinnigrade
Pinnipedes
Pinnipedia
Pinnothere
Pinnulated
Pin-tailed
Pit martin
Pithy gall
Placoidian
Placophora
Planarioid
Planoblast
Plasmodium
Platyptera
Platyrhine
Platyrhini
Pleurodont
Pleurotoma
Plume bird
Plume moth
Plumularia
Podobranch
Poecilopod
Poison sac
Polar bear
Polar hare
Polatouche
Polychaeta
Polycystid
Polyeidism
Polygamous
Polymyodae
Polynemoid
Polyp stem
Polyphemus
Polypifera
Polypterus
Polytocous
Pond snail
Pool snipe
Postocular
Potato bug
Potato fly
Praecocial
Pratincole
Proclivous
Procoelian
Proglottid
Proglottis
Prophragma
Prosternum
Prostomium

Protandric
Proteiform
Protoconch
Pseudopupa
Pseudovary
Psorosperm
Pteroceras
Pteropappi
Pterophore
Pterylosis
Ptilopteri
Puff adder
Pulmograde
Pulvinated
Pulvinulus
Pupigerous
Pupiparous
Pupivorous
Purse crab
Pycnogonid
Pygopodous
Quadricorn
Quadrumana
Quadrumane
Quail dove
Quail hawk
Quickhatch
Race horse
Rachiodont
Radiolaria
Radish fly
Ragamuffin
Rain goose
Rain quail
Raptorious
Rat-tailed
Razor fish
Rear-horse
Red grouse
Red maggot
Red mullet
Red spider
Red-riband
Reef heron
Republican
Reticulosa
Retinulate
Rhabdocúla
Rhabdomere
Rhinoceros
Rhinophore
Rhinotheca
Rhizophaga
Rhizostome
Rhombogene
Rice mouse
Rice-shell

Ring canal
Ring ousel
Ring snake
River chub
River crab
River duck
River jack
Robber fly
Rock pipil
Rock shell
Rock snake
Rock snipe
Rock trout
Rocksucker
Root louse
Rostrifera
Round clam
Royal tern
Rubythroat
Ruddy duck
Ruminantia
Rupicoline
Sabre fish
Saddleback
Sail fluke
Salamander
Saltatoria
Saltigrade
Sand birds
Sand canal
Sand mouse
Sand pride
Sand screw
Sand shark
Sand skink
Sand smelt
Sand snipe
Sand viper
Sanderling
Sandnecker
Sanguisuge
Sap sucker
Sarcoblast
Sarcophaga
Sarcophile
Sassorolla
Satin bird
Sauropsida
Saxicavous
Saxicoline
Scald crow
Scale carp
Scansorial
Scaphopoda
Scarabaeus
Scaup duck
Schizopoda

Scincoidea
Sclerobase
Scleroderm
Sclerotium
Sclerotome
Scomberoid
Scopuliped
Scorpiodea
Scorpiones
Screechers
Screw worm
Scrobicula
Scrub bird
Scyllarian
Scythewhet
Sea anemon
Sea barrow
Sea canary
Sea dragon
Sea flower
Sea ginger
Sea girkin
Sea lawyer
Sea mantis
Sea parrot
Sea salmon
Sea slater
Sea spider
Sea squirt
Sea urchin
Sea willow
Securifera
Securipalp
Seed eater
Sepiostare
Serpulidan
Sertularia
Setiparous
Sexradiate
Shagreened
Shawl goat
Shearwater
Sheathbill
Sheathfish
Sheep tick
Sheepshead
Sheerwater
Shell ibis
Shellapple
Shieldtail
Shore crab
Shore lark
Shovelbill
Shovelhead
Shovelnose
Shovelspur
Shrewmouse

Shriek owl
Sicklebill
Sidewinder
Silicoidea
Silk gland
Siluroidei
Silver eel
Silver fox
Silver gar
Silver owl
Silverback
Silverbill
Silverfish
Silverspot
Simple eye
Siphonarid
Siphoniata
Siphonifer
Siphuncled
Skeelgoose
Skieldrake
Sleepyhead
Sleevefish
Slit-shell
Sloth bear
Slothhound
Slow loris
Sminthurid
Snout moth
Snow goose
Snow mouse
Solpugidea
Somatocyst
Soothsayer
Sooty tern
Spatangoid
Spectacled
Spheniscan
Spheromere
Spherosome
Spider ant
Spider fly
Spinnerule
Split-tail
Spongiozoa
Spoutshell
Sprat loon
Spring fly
Springbuck
Springtail
Spur-shell
Squalodont
Squash bug
Squaterole
Squeteague
Stable fly
Stalk-eyed

Star coral
Starry ray
Starthroat
Statoblast
Steel duck
Steganopod
Stellerida
Stenostome
Sting moth
Stink shad
Stock duck
Stomatopod
Stomodaeum
Stone bass
Stone crab
Stone grig
Stone hawk
Stonehatch
Storm-beat
Stormfinch
Stridulate
Strongylid
Struthious
Sturionian
Subtypical
Subulipalp
Subumbonal
Sugar bird
Sugar mite
Sun beetle
Superorder
Supraloral
Suprapedal
Surf smelt
Swamp deer
Swan goose
Swarmspore
Swingdevil
Syndactyle
Synpelmous
Tabby moth
Taenioidea
Taeniosomi
Tamis bird
Tanglefish
Tapoa tafa
Tardigrada
Tardigrade
Tchawytcha
Teleophore
Teleostean
Teleostomi
Telotrocha
Tenderling
Tentacular
Tentaculum
Tercellene

Terricolae
Tessellata
Testudinal
Thalassian
Thecophora
Thick-knee
Thimbleeye
Thong seal
Threadfish
Threadworm
Thricecock
Thysanuran
Ticpolonga
Tiger moth
Tiger wolf
Timber sow
Tit thrush
Tittimouse
Toddy bird
Tomopteris
Tonguefish
Tongueworm
Toothshell
Top minnow
Tough-head
Toxoglossa
Trachearia
Trachinoid
Tree goose
Tree louse
Tree mouse
Tree pipit
Tree snake
Tree swift
Tree tiger
Trematodea
Trichiurus
Trichocyst
Trichopter
Tricurvate
Trillachan
Trimyarian
Tritozooid
Triungulus
Trochanter
Trochoidal
Troglodyte
Trophosome
Tschakmeck
Tube coral
Tube-nosed
Tuberculum
Tube-shell
Tubicolous
Tubularian
Tubularida
Tubulicole

Tubulipore
Tumbledung
Turbinated
Turbinella
Turkey hen
Turnip fly
Turritella
Turtledove
Tusk-shell
Twig borer
Typhlosole
Ularburong
Ungka-puti
Unicornous
Unossified
Urochordal
Urogastric
Vaginicola
Veretillum
Vermeology
Vertebrata
Vertebrate
Vesiculata
Vibraculum
Vida finch
Vine borer
Vine louse
Violet-tip
Viper fish
Viperoides
Vorticella
Waldheimia
Wall gecko
Ware goose
Warega fly
Warriangle
Wart snake
Water bear
Water bird
Water buck
Water cavy
Water cock
Water crow
Water deer
Water flea
Water hare
Water mite
Water newt
Water piet
Water pore
Water rail
Water tube
Water vole
Wattlebird
Wawaskeesh
Wax insect
Weaverfish

Whale bird	Acalephan	Calycozoa	Crossfish	Grayhound
Wheat duck	Accipiter	Campagnol	Crotaline	Green con
Wheat moth	Acephalan	Campanero	Crustacea	Green fly
Whip snake	Acipenser	Cantharis	Ctenocyst	Greenbone
White bass	Acraspeda	Carangoid	Ctenoidei	Greenfish
White bear	Actinaria	Carinaria	Cuirassed	Greengill
White game	Actinozoa	Carnivora	Cursorial	Greenhead
White grub	Aestivate	Carnivore	Cycloidei	Gregarine
White hake	Aggregate	Carrancha	Cyprinoid	Grenadier
White ibis	Albatross	Caruncula	Cystidean	Grossbeak
White lark	Alcyonium	Cassowary	Fasciated	Guardfish
White wolf	Alcyonoid	Catamount	Feathered	Guillemot
White wren	Alepidote	Cellepore	Flagellum	Gymnocopa
Whitebelly	Alligator	Cephalata	Funiculus	Gymnodont
Widow bird	Ambulator	Cephalate	Gall wasp	Gymnonoti
Wild drake	Ametabola	Cephalous	Gallature	Gymnotoka
Wild goose	Amphibian	Ceratodus	Galliform	Gynophore
Wildebeest	Amphidisc	Cetaceous	Gallinule	Gyrfalcon
Willow fly	Amphioxus	Clearwing	Galliwasp	Hair moth
Windowpane	Amphipoda	Clitellus	Game fowl	Hair seal
Wing shell	Anacanths	Coalgoose	Ganoidian	Hair worm
Wing-shell	Angleworm	Coalmouse	Garibaldi	Half-deck
Winter bud	Anior Ano	Coarctate	Garrulous	Half-fish
Winter egg	Anisopoda	Coast rat	Gaspereau	Haliotoid
Winter mew	Annelidan	Cockateel	Gastropod	Hamadryas
Wistonwish	Annellata	Cockroach	Geckotian	Hammerkop
Wood borer	Annulated	Coelodont	Gemitores	Harp seal
Wood guest	Annuloida	Coenosarc	Geometrid	Harpy bat
Wood louse	Annulosan	Coldfinch	Gephyrean	Harpy fly
Wood nymph	Ant-eater	Coleopter	Gerfalcon	Hartbeest
Wood pewee	Antennule	Coleperch	Germarium	Harvester
Wood quail	Anthobian	Colubrine	Ghostfish	Hawk moth
Wood shock	Anthozoan	Columella	Gibbartas	Heath hen
Wood snipe	Anthrenus	Comatulid	Glabellum	Heliconia
Woodhacker	Aphrodite	Commensal	Globefish	Heliopora
Woodpecker	Apneumona	Conchifer	Gnat hawk	Hematherm
Worm snake	Apple fly	Coralline	Gnathopod	Hemerobid
Worm-shell	Aproctous	Corallite	Goat moth	Hemiptera
Wound gall	Apteryges	Cormorant	Goldcrest	Herbivora
Xylophagan	Arachnida	Corncrake	Goldfinch	Herbivore
Xylophilan	Arachnoid	Coronamen	Goldfinny	Heronshaw
Yaffingale	Araneidan	Coronated	Goldsinny	Hesperian
Yaguarundi	Arctogeal	Coryphene	Gonangium	Heteropod
Yellowbill	Arctoidea	Coscoroba	Gonocalyx	Hill myna
Yellowbird	Argentine	Crabeater	Gonophore	Hirudinea
Yellowfish	Argonauta	Crampfish	Gonotheca	Hirundine
Yellowlegs	Ark shell	Crane fly	Gonozooid	Hoary bat
Yellowtail	Armadillo	Crankbird	Goosander	Hoemother
Yllanraton	Army worm	Creekfish	Goosefish	Hogchoker
Zeuglodont	Arrowworm	Cremaster	Gordiacea	Holostean
Zoanthacea	Arthropod	Cribellum	Gorgonian	Holostome
Zoantharia	Articulus	Crinoidal	Gourdworm	Holothure
Zoophytoid	Assapanic	Crinoidea	Gradatory	Homacanth
	Asteridea	Crocodile	Graduated	Homocercy
	Auchenium	Crookbill	Gray buck	Honey ant
	Autophagi	Crossbeak	Gray duck	Honey-bag
	Butterfly	Crossbill	Gray pike	Honeybird

9

Abdominal

Hook bill
Hornotine
Hornsnake
Hornwrack
Hornyhead
Horse ant
Horse bot
Horsefish
Horsefoot
Horsehead
horseshoe
Horsewood
Houndfish
House fly
Huia bird
Humblebee
Hyalonema
Hydriform
Hydroidea
Hydrophid
Hydrosoma
Hydrozoal
Hyena dog
Hypostoma
Ichneumon
Impennate
Impennous
Inca dove
Incumbent
Incurrent
Indian ox
Infumated
Infusoria
Ingluvial
Inquiline
Insistent
Irish elk
Ironsmith
Isogonism
Isopleura
Itch mite
Jaal goat
Jaculator
Jellyfish
Jenny ass
Jerfalcon
Jermoonal
John Dory
Jointworm
Kelp crab
Killifish
Killigrew
King duck
King hake
King rail
King tody
Kingstone

Kittiwake
Kleeneboc
Klipdachs
Kusimanse
Lacertian
Lacertine
Lady crab
Ladyclock
Lafayette
Lagomorph
Lampyrine
Land crab
Land pike
Larviform
Leaf flea
Leaf frog
Leaf tier
Leaf wasp
Lemniscus
Lepismoid
Leptiform
Leucosoid
Lich fowl
Limaceous
Limicolae
Lindiform
Lineolate
Ling-bird
Lintwhite
Lithocyst
Lithodome
Lithosian
Littorina
Log perch
Long clam
Longicorn
Longipalp
Lophiomys
Lophopoda
Loup-loup
Louse fly
Love bird
Lumbricus
Luna moth
Lyopomata
Lyre bird
Macartney
Macrodont
Macrotous
Macroural
Macruroid
Macrurous
Madrepora
Madrepore
Malacozoa
Malbrouck
Maldanian

Mallemoke
Man-eater
Manitrunk
Mantispid
Manubrium
Marimonda
Marsh hen
Marsupial
Marsupian
Martineta
Mason bee
Mastigure
Matagasse
Maxillary
Meal moth
Meal worm
Mealy bug
Meandrina
Medialuna
Megachile
Megastome
Meleagris
Mendregal
Merganser
Meroistic
Meropidan
Merulidan
Mesentery
Mesogloea
Mesonotum
Mesotheca
Metabolia
Metanotum
Metastome
Millepora
Millepore
Mino bird
Mire crow
Mistonusk
Mollemoke
Molluscan
Molossine
Monadaria
Monk seal
Monoecian
Monogenic
Monomyary
Monorhina
Monotreme
Moor cock
Moor coot
Moor fowl
Moor game
Moor hawk
Moth gnat
Mouldwarp
Mousefish

Mud devil
Mud puppy
Mudsucker
Mule deer
Multisect
Mummichog
Mummychog
Muscadine
Muscardin
Musciform
Musk deer
Musk duck
Musteline
Mute swan
Myomorpha
Myriapoda
Myrmicine
Mysticete
Natatores
Nautiloid
Nectosack
Nectostem
Negro bug
Negro fly
Nemertean
Nemertian
Nemertida
Nemertina
Neocarida
Nereidian
Neurocord
Neuropter
New light
Nile bird
Nine-eyes
Noctiluca
Nonagrian
Nose leaf
Nototrema
Nutjobber
Nutpecker
Nyctibune
Nymphales
Obomegoid
Obumbrant
Octopodia
Ocypodian
Oil gland
Oil shark
Old squaw
Onion fly
Oological
Oostegite
Ophidioid
Ophiurida
Opisthomi
Orbitelae

Organista
Organling
Orthopoda
Ossiculum
Ossifrage
Ostracean
Ostracion
Ostracoda
Ostracoid
Otter dog
Ouanderoo
Pachyderm
Pack moth
Pademelon
Palm crab
Palmarium
Palpicorn
Palpiform
Panoistic
Panorpian
Pantopoda
Parachute
Paragnath
Paraquito
Partridge
Passerine
Paste eel
Patellula
Pauhaugen
Pauropoda
Pear slug
Pearlfish
Pediculus
Pedipalpi
Penduline
Pennatula
Penny dog
Pentamera
Peraeopod
Perameles
Perciform
Percoidea
Perdicine
Perforata
Peripatus
Periproct
Peristome
Peritreme
Perradial
Perroquet
Petaurist
Petrogale
Phacellus
Phalaenid
Phalanger
Phalangid
Phalarope

Philander
Philomela
Phocacean
Phocodont
Pholadean
Phyllopod
Physaliae
Physopoda
Phytozoon
Pickering
Pig-jawed
Pine moth
Pinefinch
Pinionist
Pipemouth
Piririgua
Pit viper
Pithecoid
Placental
Placoides
Planarian
Planarida
Planorbis
Plant bug
Platanist
Platypoda
Plegepoda
Plenicorn
Plumicorn
Podotheca
Pollicate
Pollinate
Pollinose
Polyeidic
Polymyoid
Polypidom
Polystome
Polyzoary
Poor-john
Poor-will
Poppy bee
Porbeagle
Porcupine
Poriferan
Postfurca
Praecoces
Praetores
Predacean
Predatory
Preocular
Prescutum
Probeagle
Proboscis
Procerite
Procoelia
Proctucha
Prognathi

Promerops
Promethea
Promuscis
Prongbuck
Pronghorn
Propodite
Propodium
Proscolex
Prosimiae
Prosiphon
Proteidea
Prothorax
Protiston
Protozoan
Protozoic
Protozoon
Pseudopod
Pseudovum
Psittacid
Ptarmigan
Pteropoda
Puff bird
Pulmonata
Pulmonate
Pulvillus
Purse rat
Puss moth
Pygmy owl
Pygopodes
Quadruped
Quaketail
Queen bee
Queenfish
Quillback
Radicated
Raft duck
Rain bird
Rain fowl
Raptorial
Rat snake
Razorback
Razorbill
Red beard
Red coral
Red horse
Red perch
Red scale
Redbreast
Redthroat
Reermouse
Regularia
Reptantia
Reptation
Reptatory
Reptilian
Reremouse
Retriever

Rhinaster
Rhinopome
Rhipipter
Rhizodont
Rhizopoda
Rhopalium
Rhynchota
Ridgeling
Riflebird
River hog
Rock bass
Rock cavy
Rock cook
Rock crab
Rock dove
Rock duck
Rock goat
Rock seal
Rock wren
Rose gall
Rose slug
Rosefinch
Rotatoria
Roughhead
Roughtail
Roundfish
Roundworm
Roussette
Rucervine
Rush toad
Rust mite
Sabelloid
Sabrebill
Sage cock
Salmonoid
Salve bug
Sand cock
Sand crab
Sand cusk
Sand flea
Sand fluk
Sand lark
Sand mole
Sand snak
Sand star
Sand tube
Sand wasp
Sandpiper
Sarcoptes
Sarcoptid
Saturnian
Sauba ant
Savanilla
Saxicavid
Scaldfish
Scaleback
Scansores

Scaraboid
Scarecrow
Scarn bee
Schizopod
Schooling
Sciaenoid
Scombroid
Scopeline
Scopeloid
Scops owl
Scutellum
Sea acorn
Sea adder
Sea arrow
Sea beast
Sea bream
Sea devil
Sea drake
Sea goose
Sea grape
Sea horse
Sea jelly
Sea lemon
Sea loach
Sea louse
Sea mouse
Sea orang
Sea otter
Sea peach
Sea perch
Sea poker
Sea purse
Sea quail
Sea raven
Sea scurf
Sea snail
Sea snake
Sea snipe
Sea trout
Sea turtl
Seat worm
Secondary
Secretary
Sedentary
Sedge hen
Seed gall
Seed tick
Selachian
Semi pupa
Seminymph
Semiplume
Sericeous
Serranoid
Serricorn
Serrifera
Servaline

Sharpling
Sharptail
Shearbill
Sheartail
Sheatfish
Sheep bot
Sheep dog
Sheeprack
Sheldaple
Sheldfowl
Sheldrake
Shellfish
Shoemaker
Shortwing
Shovelard
Shredcook
Sigmodont
Silk fowl
Silk moth
Siluridan
Silverfin
Sing-sing
Sinistral
Siphonata
Siphonate
Siphuncle
Skin moth
Skirlcock
Skunkball
Skunkhead
Slave ant
Slime eel
Sloughing
Sly goose
Snailfish
Snake fly
Snakebird
Snakefish
Snakeneck
Snipefish
Snow cock
Snow flea
Snow gnat
Snowflake
Snowfleck
Snowy owl
Soft clam
Soft crab
Solenette
Solenodon
Solifugae
Solitaire
Song bird
Spadefish
Spadefoot
Spatangus
Spearfish

Sphenodon
Sphex fly
Spikebill
Spikefish
Spiketail
Spineback
Spinebill
Spinetail
Spinneret
Spirulate
Spitz dog
Splitfeet
Spongilla
Spoonbill
Spoonworm
Sporocyst
Sporogony
Spot rump
Spoutfish
Sprat mew
Sprigtail
Spur fowl
Squamduck
Squamipen
Squarrose
Stag tick
Staghound
Stank hen
Star worm
Stargaser
Steelhead
Steinbock
Stellerid
Stenoderm
Stiltbird
Sting ray
Stingaree
Stingbull
Stingfish
Stingtail
Stink rat
Stockdove
Stockfish
Stomapoda
Stomatoda
Stomatode
Stone cat
Stone fly
Stonebuck
Stonechat
Stonegall
Stragulum
Straw cat
Strisores
Stromboid
Struthian
Sturiones

Stylaster
Subcostal
Submedian
Submentum
Suctorial
Suctorian
Suffusion
Sun angel
Sun grebe
Sun trout
Surf bird
Surf clam
Surf duck
Surf fish
Surmullet
Swamp hen
Swartback
Sweetmeat
Swellfish
Swelltoad
Swiftfoot
Swimmeret
Swinefish
Swinepipe
Swordbill
Swordfish
Swordtail
Syllidian
Syncytium
Syngnathi
Taenidium
Tagnicate
Taguicati
Taintworm
Talegalla
Tanagrine
Tanagroid
Tangalung
Tangwhaup
Tank worm
Tapayaxin
Tarantula
Tectrices
Teleostei
Teleozoic
Teleozoon
Tentacled
Terebrant
Termatary
Testacean
Testicond
Tethyodea
Tetradont
Tetramera
Tetraonid
Tetraxile
Tetrodont

Thaliacea
Thoracica
Thornback
Thornbill
Thornbird
Thorntail
Threadfin
Throttler
Thylacine
Thysanura
Tiger cat
Tinamides
Tittlebat
Toddy cat
Toe biter
Tonnihood
Toothback
Toothbill
Top-shell
Tortricid
Totipalmi
Toupettit
Tracheary
Tracheata
Tracheate
Tree bear
Tree crab
Tree crow
Tree dove
Tree duck
Tree fish
Tree frog
Tree lark
Tree toad
Trematode
Trematoid
Tres-tyne
Trochilos
Trochilus
Trogonoid
Troopbird
Troopfowl
Troutbird
Trumpeter
Truncated
Trunkback
Trunkfish
Tube foot
Tubicolae
Tubicolar
Tubinares
Tubivalve
Tubularia
Tuko-tuko
Tunicated
Turbinoid
Turn-sick

Turnstone
Umbilicus
Undershot
Underwing
Undulated
Uniparous
Univalvia
Upokororo
Uran-utan
Urbicolae
Urocerata
Urochorda
Urodelian
Uropoetic
Vanessian
Veneracea
Vertebral
Vine grub
Vine slug
Viverrine
Viz-cacha
Vlissmaki
Wall newt
Wall wasp
Wall-plat
Wariangle
Warty egg
Water bug
Water dog
Water fox
Water hen
Water hog
Water pig
Water rat
Wave moth
Wedgebill
Weet-bird
Weet-weet
Wharf rat
Whealworm
Wheat fly
Wheatbird
Wheatworm
Wheel bug
Wheelbird
Whipparee
Whirligig
Whiskered
White ant
White nun
White owl
Whiteback
Whitebait
Whitebill
White-ear
White-eye
Whitefish

Whitehead
Whiteness
Whiterump
Whiteside
Whitetail
Whitewall
Whitewing
Wierangle
Wild boar
Wild fowl
Wind rush
Windhover
Wing case
Winninish
Wire grub
Wolf fish
Wolverine
Wood dove
Wood duck
Wood frog
Wood ibis
Wood lark
Wood mite
Wood sore
Wood star
Wood tick
Wood worm
Wood wren
Woodchuck
Woodhewer
Wreckfish
Wurbagool
Wynkernel
Xylophaga
Yellowfin
Yoke-toed
Zeuzerian
Zoanthoid
Zoocytium
Zoophagan
Zosterops

8

Acaridan
Accentor
Acephala
Achatina
Acinetae
Acontias
Acrodont
Actinula
Aculeate
Adelopod
Aglossal
Aigrette
Albacore

Albicore
Alcyones
Alcyonic
Alitrunk
Allmouth
Alouatte
Altrical
Altrices
Alveolus
Amadavat
Amioidei
Ammodyte
Amoebian
Amphibia
Amphipod
Amphiuma
Ampliate
Anaconda
Anatifer
Annellda
Anneloid
Annotine
Annulata
Annulate
Annuloid
Annulosa
Annulose
Anomoura
Anomuran
Anoplura
Anserine
Ant bird
Ant-bear
Antelope
Antennal
Ant-hill
Anthozoa
Ant-lion
Aphidian
Apterous
Aptychus
Araguato
Araneina
Arapaima
Archonts
Arctisca
Argonaut
Aristate
Arvicole
Ascidian
Ascidium
Asterias
Astraean
Athecata
Atherine
Auricula
Avifauna

Axillars
Azureous
Basilisk
Cabassou
Cabrilla
Cachalot
Cackerel
Caducous
Calamary
Calliope
Calymene
Cancroid
Capuchin
Capybara
Caraboid
Caracara
Carapace
Carapato
Carcaiou
Cargoose
Caseworm
Cassican
Cavicorn
Cavitary
Centiped
Cephalad
Cephalon
Cerastes
Cerberus
Cercopod
Cetacean
Clepsine
Clupeoid
Clypeate
Cnidaria
Cnidocil
Coachdog
Coachman
Coalfish
Cockatoo
Cocktail
Coenurus
Colocolo
Columbae
Comatula
Conepatl
Conodont
Cootfoot
Copelata
Copepoda
Coquette
Corallum
Corkwing
Corn fly
Corneule
Corselet
Craniota

Crayfish
Crevalle
Crotalus
Crypturi
Cuculoid
Curculio
Cursores
Cutwater
Cynoidea
Cystidea
Falconet
Forester
Frontlet
Gairfowl
Gallinae
Galloway
Gamecock
Ganoidal
Ganoidei
Gapeworm
Garefowl
Garganey
Gastrura
Gaverick
Geometer
Geophila
Gephyrea
Gerbille
Gilthead
Glasseye
Glossata
Glowworm
Gnathite
Gnatling
Gnatworm
Goatfish
Goldfish
Gonidial
Gonosome
Gonydial
Gorebill
Gorgelet
Gowdnook
Graduate
Graining
Gralline
Grapsoid
Gray hen
Gray owl
Grayback
Grayling
Greenlet
Grosbeak
Grubworm
Gryphaea
Guacharo
Gueparde

Guidguid
Guitguit
Gymnotus
Gyration
Hackbolt
Haemapod
Hag moth
Hairbird
Hairtail
Half ape
Halfbeak
Haliotis
Halteres
Haminura
Handfish
Hangbird
Hardhead
Hardtail
Harefoot
Hatterla
Hawfinch
Hawk fly
Hawk owl
Hawkbill
Headfish
Heckimal
Hedgehog
Heelspur
Helicoid
Heliozoa
Helminth
Hemionus
Hemipode
Hemipter
Hen clam
Hen hawk
Hesperid
Hexapoda
High-hoe
Hill ant
Hill tit
Hirudine
Hive bee
Hog deer
Holostei
Homopter
Honeybee
Hoot owl
Hop flea
Hop moth
Hornbill
Hornfish
Hornpout
Horntail
Horsefly
Horseman
Humpback

Hydranth
Hydrozoa
Hylobate
Hyracoid
Ianthina
Ichthyic
Iguanian
Iguanoid
Imaginal
Impennes
Inchworm
Indented
Indument
Infusory
Inghalla
Insessor
instinct
Involved
Irrorate
Isogonic
Janthina
Jararaca
Java cat
Jelerang
Jentling
June bug
Kabassou
Kangaroo
Karagane
Kelpfish
Keratosa
Keratose
Killdeer
King auk
Kingfish
Kinkajou
Kiwikiwi
Knobbler
Knoppern
Korrigum
Labellum
Lacewing
Ladybird
Ladyfish
Lagenian
Lake fly
Lamantin
Lampyris
Lancelet
Langarey
Lanneret
Larvalia
Lemurine
Lemuroid
Lepadite
Lepadoid
Leporine

Leucoryx	Menhaden	Neogaean	Panorpid	Pincpinc
Lim naea	Menopome	Nerfling	Papabote	Pinnated
Limacina	Mephitis	Neritina	Parakeet	Pinniped
Lineated	Merosome	Neuropod	Paramere	Pinpatch
Lion ant	Metapode	Notornis	Parasita	Pipefish
Lion dog	Metasome	Numbfish	Parasite	Pirarucu
Liparian	Metazoan	Nut crab	Parauque	Planaria
Liturate	Metazoic	Nuthatch	Parietal	Platypod
Lobefoot	Metazoon	Nutshell	Parkeria	Platypus
Long tom	Microzoa	Oat fowl	Paroquet	Pleurite
Longbeak	Milleped	Obtected	Parraqua	Plumiped
Longhorn	Milliped	Octodont	Passeres	Poachard
Longlegs	Mimicker	Octopede	Patagium	Podiceps
Longnose	Moccasin	Octopoda	Pavonine	Poephaga
Longspur	Mockbird	Oestrian	Paw clam	Policate
Lookdown	Mole rat	Old lady	Paxillus	Polliwog
Loricata	Molewarp	Old wife	Pea crab	Pollywog
Loricate	Mollusca	Ommateal	Pea dove	Polygamy
Lorikeet	Monk bat	Ommateum	Peachick	Polyneme
Lumpfish	Monkfish	Omnivora	Peasweep	Polypary
Lung sac	Monocule	Ootocoid	Pectoral	Polypean
Lungfish	Monogamy	Openbill	Pedimana	Polypide
Lungworm	Moon-eye	Ophidian	Pedimane	Polypite
Lyre bat	Moonfish	Ophidion	Pedipalp	Polypode
Macavahu	Moor hen	Ophiuran	Pedireme	Polypoid
Mackerel	Morepork	Ophiurid	Pegasoid	Polyzoan
Macropod	Mosquito	Orabassu	Pelasgic	Polyzoon
Macropus	Mucivore	Orbicula	Penelope	Pomarine
Macrural	Muckworm	Orbulina	Pengolin	Pond hen
Macruran	Mud bass	Oreosoma	Periderm	Pondfish
Mahoohoo	Mud crab	Oryctere	Perigone	Popinjay
Mallotus	Mud frog	Oscinian	Perisarc	Porifera
Mammalia	Mud wasp	Oscinine	Perisoma	Porpoise
Mammifer	Mugiloid	Osculant	Perisome	Potamian
Mandible	Multiped	Osteozoa	Pervious	Precoces
Mandrill	Murenoid	Ostracea	Phaethon	Primates
Mangabey	Muricoid	Ouistiti	Phalaena	Proceres
Manucode	Murrelet	Oulachan	Phatagin	Pronotum
Manx cat	Musquash	Ovariole	Pheasant	Proteles
Marbling	Musquito	Ovenbird	Phoronis	Protista
Margined	Mustache	Owl moth	Physalia	Protozoa
Marikina	Mutilate	Oxpecker	Physeter	Protract
Markhoor	Myogalid	Pachyote	Physopod	Psittaci
Marmoset	Myriapod	Pagurian	Picapare	Psychian
Martinet	Mystacal	Paliform	Picariae	Pteropod
Marysole	Mytiloid	Palm cat	Picarian	Ptilosis
Matamata	Myxinoid	Palmated	Piciform	Puff-leg
Mattages	Myzontes	Palmiped	Pickerel	Pupation
Meat fly	Nacreous	Palmworm	Pickmire	Pupipara
Medregal	Naticoid	Palpator	Piketail	Pupivora
Medusian	Nauplius	Palpebra	Pilchard	Pygargus
Medusoid	Nautilus	Palpifer	Pileated	Pygidium
Megaderm	Neelghau	Palpiger	Pileworm	Pyrenoid
Megalops	Nematode	Palpless	Pilidium	Pyrosome
Megapode	Nematoid	Palpocil	Pilifera	Qua-bird
Melanian	Nemertes	Paludina	Pill bug	Quirpele
Melanure	Nemertid	Pangolin	Pillworm	Racoonda

Radiated
Raindeer
Raptores
Rasorial
Rat mole
Ratitate
Rat-tail
Red bass
Red deer
Red duck
Red mite
Redbelly
Redfinch
Redmouth
Redshank
Redstart
Reedbird
Reedbuck
Reedling
Reptilia
Retepore
Retineum
Retinula
Retitelê
Rhabdite
Rhizopod
Rice hen
Ricebird
Ringbill
Ringbird
Ringdove
Ringneck
Ringtail
Rock cod
Rock eel
Rockfish
Rockling
Rodentia
Roncador
Roodebok
Rorulent
Rose bug
Rose fly
Rosefish
Roseworm
Rotatory
Roughleg
Rubytail
Ruminant
Rupicola
Rutilian
Sacalait
Sage hen
Saibling
Sailfish
Salagane
Sallyman

Salmonet
Sand bug
Sand dab
Sand eel
Sand fly
Sand pik
Sand rat
Sandfish
Sandworm
Sarcelle
Sassabye
Saurioid
Sawtooth
Saw-whet
Saxicava
Scalaria
Scapular
Scapulet
Scarabee
Scincoid
Sciurine
Sclerite
Scolytid
Scopiped
Scorpene
Scorpion
Screamer
Scuppaug
Scutella
Scutiger
Scutiped
Scyllaea
Sea bass
Sea bear
Sea bird
Sea calf
Sea clam
Sea cock
Sea coot
Sea corn
Sea crow
Sea dace
Sea dove
Sea duck
Sea eagl
Sea fern
Sea fowl
Sea gull
Sea hare
Sea hawk
Sea lark
Sea lily
Sea lion
Sea monk
Sea moss
Sea pear
Sea piet

Sea pork
Sea slug
Sea star
Sea toad
Sea whip
Sea wing
Sea wolf
Sea-mail
Sea-mell
Seashell
Seerfish
Seirfish
Selachii
Sembling
Sentinel
Serotine
Serrator
Setireme
Sewellel
Shadbird
Shanghai
Sharpsaw
Shelduck
Shipworm
Shockdog
Shoebill
Shoveler
Shuffler
Silkworm
Siluroid
Sinciput
Sinsring
Siphonet
Sirenian
Siscowet
Siskiwit
Skimback
Skipjack
Skirling
Skullcap
Skunktop
Slep obs
Slowworm
Slugworm
Snap bug
Snippack
Snowbird
Soapfish
Soft ray
Solarium
Solempne
Solpugid
Songster
Soricine
Spanworm
Sparhawk
Sparkler

Sparling
Speculum
Sperling
Sphingid
Spiculum
Spiracle
Spongiae
Sporosac
Sporozoa
Spurling
Squaloid
Squamata
Squatter
Squeaker
Squealer
Squirrel
Stag hog
Stagyard
Stagworm
Starfish
Starling
Starnose
Stayship
Steenbok
Stellion
Sternite
Stinkard
Stinkpot
Stomapod
Stopship
Strigate
Strigine
Strobila
Strobile
Strombus
Struthio
Studfish
Sturgeon
Sturnoid
Subbasal
Subbreed
Suberite
Subimago
Suckfish
Suctoria
Suffrago
Suilline
Sun bear
Sun star
Surmulot
Surroyal
Surucucu
Swiftlet
Swordick
Symphyla
Tabulata
Taeniada

Taeniata
Taenioid
Taeniola
Talapoin
Tamanoir
Tambreet
Tangfish
Tantalus
Tapeworm
Tapiroid
Tatouhou
Tatusiid
Taxicorn
Tea clam
Teguexln
Tentacle
Tercelet
Teredine
Terrapin
Tertiary
Terutero
Testacea
Tethydan
Tetradon
Tetrapod
Tetrodon
Thoracic
Thornbut
Throstle
Thrustle
Tilefish
Timaline
Tinkling
Tinmouth
Tipulary
Titmouse
Toadfish
Toadhead
Tocororo
Tomb bat
Tomnoddy
Tornaria
Torquate
Tortoise
Toucanet
Tow-head
Toxifera
Tragopan
Tree bug
Tree pie
Tree rat
Trichina
Tridacna
Triddler
Trigonia
Trimeran
Tringoid

Tristoma	Wanderoo	Abalone	Attagen	Diurnal
Tritovum	Warmouth	Abdomen	Aurelia	Fiddler
Trochili	Warragal	Acantha	Auricle	Fission
Troching	Wart hog	Acarina	Aurited	Flasher
Trochoid	Washdish	Acaroid	Aurochs	Flexure
Trombone	Waterbok	Acephal	Avicula	Footman
Troopial	Wax moth	Acerous	Axolotl	Fulcrum
Troupial	Weakfish	Acontia	Aye-aye	Gadwall
Tubeworm	Welshman	Acouchy	Azurine	Gallfly
Tubicole	Wheatear	Acrania	Bivalve	Gallnut
Tubicorn	Whinchat	Acritan	Buffalo	Ganoine
Tubipora	Whip ray	Actinal	Bulldog	Garfish
Tubipore	Whipworm	Actinia	Cabezon	Garpike
Tullibee	Whirlwig	Aculeus	Cacajo	Garrupa
Tunicary	Whistler	Admiral	Calamus	Gauffre
Tunicata	Whitecap	Adunque	Calicle	Gazelle
Tunicate	Whitling	Aeneous	Caparro	Gemsbok
Turf ant	Whittret	Agouara	Capelin	Genette
Turnspit	Whitwall	Alewife	Carabid	Geoduck
Twitlark	Wild bee	Alfione	Carabus	Gerlind
Tylopoda	Wild cat	Algazel	Caracal	Gherkin
Tympanum	Wine fly	Amebean	Catbird	Giraffe
Umbrella	Wingfish	Amniota	Catfish	Girdler
Umbrette	Wireworm	Amoebea	Cavally	Girrock
Uncinata	Witchuck	Anadrom	Cetacea	Gizzard
Ungulata	Wolf dog	Anatifa	Climber	Gladeye
Ungulate	Wolf eel	Anatine	Clumber	Gladius
Ungulous	Wood ant	Anchovy	Clypeus	Glaucus
Univalve	Wood hen	Anemone	Codfish	Glutton
Unpalped	Wood pie	Anhinga	Codling	Gobioid
Uplander	Wood rat	Annulet	Coendoo	Goéland
Urochord	Woodchat	Annulus	Coluber	Goggler
Uropodal	Woodcock	Anseres	Coolung	Goldney
Urostege	Woodpeck	Antenna	Copepod	Goldtit
Vadantes	Woodwall	Anurous	Corinne	Gorcock
Vagantes	Woodworm	Aphides	Coronal	Gorcrow
Vaginati	Woolhead	Aplysia	Cotinga	Gordian
Velarium	Wrymouth	Apodeme	Cottoid	Gordius
Veltfare	Wurraluh	Apodous	Courlan	Gorilla
Velutina	Xenurine	Aporosa	Courser	Goshawk
Venantes	Xiphioid	Aporose	Cowbird	Gourami
Venomous	Xylocopa	Aprocta	Cowfish	Gournet
Vermetid	Xylotrya	Apteral	Crappie	Grackle
Vermetus	Yakamilk	Apteran	Creeper	Grallae
Vestales	Yeorling	Apteria	Crested	Grallic
Vibrissa	Zandmole	Apteryx	Cricket	Grampus
Viperina	Ziphioid	AraÁari	Crinoid	Grayfly
Vitrella	Zoanthus	Areolet	Crissal	Graylag
Vivipara	Zooecium	Argulus	Crissum	Greylag
Vizcacha	Zoophaga	Armilla	Croaker	Gribble
Volution	Zoophyta	Artemia	Ctenoid	Griffon
Vondsira	Zoophyte	Ascarid	Cumacea	Grinder
Vorticel	Zoospore	Astacus	Cutworm	Grindle
Wainscot	Zopilote	Astarte	Cycloid	Grizzly
Wallaroo		Atlanta	Cymbium	Grooper
Wallbird	7	Atokous	Cypraea	Grouper
Wallhick		Atrocha	Cyprine	Growler

Grunter
Gryllus
Gryphon
Grysbok
Guanaco
Gudgeon
Guereza
Gurniad
Gustard
Gwiniad
Habitus
haddock
Halcyon
Halibut
Hamster
Hamulus
Haplomi
Harfang
Harrier
Haybird
Helamys
Henfish
Heritor
Herring
Hewhole
Hexapod
Hirling
Hirundo
Hoatzin
Hogfish
Holibut
Homarus
Hoolock
Hop fly
Hornbug
Hornowl
Huanaco
Hydatid
Hydrina
Hydroid
Hylodes
Hystrix
Icebird
Ignoble
Iguanid
Impalla
Impoofo
Inclusa
Ink bag
Ink sac
Insecta
Ischium
Isopoda
Iulidan
Ivy owl
Ixodian
Jacamar

Jacchus
Jackdaw
Jacksaw
Jacobin
Jar-owl
Jashawk
Jawfoot
Jet ant
Juddock
Jugular
Jugulum
Kalasie
Kaleege
Kamichi
Kanchil
Katydid
Keeling
Keitloa
Kestrel
Kholsun
Kinglet
Kirumbo
Kit fox
Knobber
Koklass
Kookoom
Kutauss
Labroid
Lacerta
Lacinia
Ladybug
Lampern
Lamprel
Lamprey
Lampron
Langaha
Langdak
Lanioid
Lapwing
Lavaret
Leaflet
Lemming
Lemurid
Leopard
Lepisma
Lernaea
Lernean
Leveret
Leviner
Limpkin
Limulus
Lingula
Linsang
Lioness
Lobiped
Lobster
Lobworm

Loculus
Lucifer
Lugworm
Lumbric
Lungoor
Lunulet
Lyerman
Lyncean
Macacus
Macaque
Macauco
Macrura
Madoqua
Maguari
Maharif
Maikong
Mallard
Malleus
Mammoth
Man ape
Manakin
Manatee
Marabou
Maracan
Marbled
Mariput
Marmose
Martern
Martlet
Mastiff
Maucaco
Mawworm
Maxilla
May bug
May fly
Maybird
Mayfish
Measles
Medrick
Meerkat
Meminna
Mendole
Merling
Merluce
Mesozoa
Metazoa
Miliary
Miliola
Milvine
Minivet
Mishcup
Molebut
Mollusc
Mollusk
Monarch
Moneran
Moneron

Mongoos
Mongrel
Monitor
Monozoa
Morinel
Morpion
Motacil
Mouflon
Mud dab
Mud eel
Mud hen
Mudfish
Mudwall
Mulloid
Mungoos
Muntjac
Muraena
Musimon
Musk ox
Muskrat
Musquaw
Mustang
Mycetes
Myophan
Mytilus
Myxopod
Nandine
Narwhal
Nebalia
Nefasch
Negrita
Nervure
Netfish
Neurula
Nicagua
Noctuid
Noctule
Notaeum
Nyentek
Oarfish
Oarfoot
Occiput
Ocellus
Oceloid
Octopod
Octopus
Oculina
Odonata
Oestrus
Oil bag
Oilbird
Ooecium
Ootheca
Opercle
Ophidia
Ophiura
Opossum

Oquassa
Oreades
Ortolan
Ortygan
Oscines
Osculum
Osselet
Osseter
Ossicle
Ostrich
Ouakari
Ouarine
Ovicell
Ovicyst
Ovipara
Oxbiter
Paddock
Painter
Paisano
Pallial
Palulus
Pampano
Pandora
Panther
Papagay
Papboat
Papilio
Pardale
Pardine
Paroket
Patella
Pea bug
Peabird
Peacock
Peafowl
Peccary
Pedicel
Pegador
Pegasus
Pelecan
Pelican
Pellack
Pellile
Penfish
Penguin
Pentail
Percoid
Peterel
Petiole
Phaeton
Phasmid
Phocine
Pictura
Piculet
Piddock
Piercer
Piewipe

Pigfish
Pigfoot
Pilcher
Pimlico
Pinchem
Pinfish
Pinnock
Pinnule
Pintado
Pintail
Pinworm
Piprine
Piscine
Pismire
Pitheci
Placoid
Plagate
Planula
Pleopod
Pleuron
Plumage
Plumula
Plumule
Pluteal
Pluteus
Pluvian
Poacher
Pochard
Podical
Podurid
Poebird
Pohagen
Pointer
Pokebag
Polecat
Polewig
Pollack
Pollard
Pollock
Polypus
Polyzoa
Pomfret
Pompano
Porcate
Porites
Porpita
Potoroo
Pouched
Pricket
Primary
Primate
Procris
Procyon
Prophet
Propleg
Procoma
Proteus

Protist
Pteryla
Puceron
Purpura
Puttock
Pygopod
Pyralid
Quahaug
Quinnat
Raccoon
Raddock
Radiale
Radiary
Radiata
Radiate
Radioli
Ralline
Ramulus
Rapaces
Rasores
Ratfish
Rectrix
Red ant
Red bug
Red fox
Redback
Redbird
Redfish
Redhead
Redhoop
Redhorn
Redlegs
Redpole
Redpoll
Redtail
Reduvid
Redwing
Remiges
Remiped
Reptant
Reptile
Retiary
Retiped
Rhabdom
Rhachis
Rheeboc
Rhytina
Rietboc
Rissoid
Robinet
Roebuck
Roedeer
Ronchil
Rorqual
Rosella
Rosette
Rostrum

Rotchet
Rotella
Rotifer
Ruddock
Ruminal
Rurales
Sabella
Saccate
Saddled
Saddler
Sagitta
Sakeret
Sapajou
Sardine
Sarigue
Saurian
Sauroid
Sautrie
Sawfish
Scallop
Scammel
Scapula
Scaroid
Schelly
Sciurus
Scolder
Scomber
Scooper
Scopate
Scopula
Scorpio
Scraber
Sculpin
Scurrit
Scutate
Sea ape
Sea bat
Sea bug
Sea cat
Sea cob
Sea cow
Sea dog
Sea eel
Sea egg
Sea fan
Sea fir
Sea fox
Sea hen
Sea hog
Sea mat
Sea maw
Sea mew
Sea owl
Sea pad
Sea pie
Sea pig
Sea pye

Sea rat
Sea-bar
Seaboat
Sea-ear
Sea-orb
Sea-pen
Seawife
Seriema
Serpent
Serpula
Serrula
Servage
Sessile
Setiger
Shallow
Sharded
Shedder
Shelled
Shirley
Shright
Sifilet
Signate
Silenus
Silicea
Sillock
Silurus
Simious
Siredon
Sirenia
Sirkeer
Sittine
Skaddon
Skegger
Skiddaw
Skimmer
Skipper
Skowitz
Skulpin
Skylark
Sleeper
Slobber
Smeared
Smerlin
Snapper
Snorter
Snowcap
Snuffer
Soldier
Soliped
Sondeli
Sorehon
Soulili
Sounder
Souslik
Spaniel
Sparada
Sparoid

Sparrow
Spawner
Spayade
Spectre
Speight
Spicule
Spinner
Spiodea
Spirula
Spitter
Squacco
Squilla
Squitee
Staniel
Stannel
Stanyel
Staynil
Steamer
Stentor
Sterlet
Stinker
Stipula
Striges
Stylops
Suckler
Sun gem
Sunbird
Sunfish
Surgeon
Suricat
Swallow
Sycones
Synapta
Synocil
Tabanus
Tachina
Tadpole
Tahaleb
Tajassu
Tamandu
Tamarin
Tanager
Tarente
Tarrier
Tarrock
Tarsius
Tataupa
Tatouay
Tattler
Taurine
Tea bug
Teleost
Tellina
Tendrac
Teneral
Terapin
Terebra

Tergite
Termite
Terrier
Tertial
Testudo
Thecata
Thwaite
Tigress
Tigrine
Tilt-up
Tinamou
Tinnock
Titlark
Tilling
Topknot
Torilto
Torpedo
Torques
Torrock
Tortrix
Touraco
Towllly
Toxotes
Trachea
Trepang
Trimera
Trionyx
Tripang
Trochal
Trochil
Trochus
Troilus
Trumpie
Truncus
Tschego
Tuatera
Tubfish
Tumbler
Tupaiid
Turacou
Tussock
Tylarus
Ulonata
Umbrine
Uncinus
Upeygan
Urocord
Urodela
Urodele
Uromere
Urosome
Vaagmer
Valvata
Valvule
Vampire
Vanessa
Vansire

Varanus
Velella
Veliger
Vendace
Vertigo
Vesicle
Vestlet
Viceroy
Vicugna
Vitrina
Viverra
Volador
Volator
Vultern
Vulture
Wagtail
Wallaby
Wapacut
Warbler
Waterie
Waxbill
Waxwing
Waybung
Webfoot
Webworm
Weroole
Wetbird
Whetile
Whitile
Whiting
Widegap
Widgeon
Wiggler
Willock
Wimbrel
Winglet
Witfish
Witwall
Woofell
Woolert
Wou-wou
Wow-wow
Wrybill
Wryneck
Xiphias
Xiphius
Xiphura
Yarwhip
Yellows
Zaerthe
Zamouse
Zebrine
Zinsang
Zonaria
Zoonite
Zoonule
Zorilla

Zygenid

6

Aboral
Acarus
Acrita
Acrite
Adnate
Agouta
Agouty
Alburn
Alcedo
Aliped
Alpaca
Alular
Amazon
Amioid
Amoeba
Amotus
Anabas
Angler
Anodon
Anolis
Anomia
Anopla
Antiae
Antler
Antlia
Aoudad
Aperea
Apodal
Apodan
Apodes
Aptera
Aquila
Argala
Argali
Asilus
Aswail
Ateles
Atrium
Avoset
Beaver
Becker
Cabiai
CabrÈe
Caddis
Caddow
Callow
Cancer
Caprid
Caranx
Carina
Carter
Castor
Caudad

Cayman
Cercal
Cerite
Ceroma
Clutch
Coaita
Cobweb
Coccus
Cocker
Cockle
Cockup
Cocoon
Collar
Collet
Collie
Colugo
Comber
Condor
Conger
Conner
Conure
Cooter
Corbie
Corona
Corsac
Corsak
Coucal
Cougar
Covert
Cowrie
Coyote
Craber
Crania
Crevis
Cuckoo
Cucujo
Cudden
Culmen
Cunner
Cupule
Curlew
Cururo
Cushat
Cygnet
Cypris
Cystid
Facies
Fascia
Fauces
Feeler
Frenum
Gadbee
Gadfly
Gadoid
Gaggle
Galago
Gambet

Gannet
Ganoid
Gardon
Garran
Garrot
Garvie
Gaviae
Gavial
Gelada
Gentle
Gerboa
Gibbon
Glires
Glossa
Gnawer
Godwit
Goldie
Goramy
Gorfly
Gorgon
Gorhen
Goslet
Gossat
Gouger
Gowdie
Grakle
Grilse
Grimme
Grison
Grivet
Grouse
Grubby
Guenon
Guffer
Gunnel
Gunner
Gurnet
Hackee
Haddie
Hagdon
Hapuku
Harder
Hareld
Harier
Hausen
Heifer
Hemuse
Hepper
Hirudo
Hoazin
Hooded
Hooper
Hoopoo
Hornel
Horner
Hornet
Houlet

306

Howler	Launce	Median	Nylgau	Phoebe
Howlet	Lé rot	Medusa	Nympha	Pholad
Huchen	Lecama	Megrim	Ocelot	Pholas
Hummer	Leipoa	Mental	Onager	Phylum
Hyaena	Leptus	Mentum	Onagga	Pianet
Hyalea	Ligula	Merino	Onappo	Piapec
Iguana	Limule	Merlin	Oorial	Pichey
Impoon	Linchi	Metope	Ootype	Picine
Ingena	Lindia	Midget	Opelet	Picked
Insect	Lingua	Miller	Orfray	Picoid
Island	Linnet	Milter	Orgeis	Pierid
Isopod	Lionel	Milvus	Oriole	Pigeon
Ixodes	Lionet	Minaul	Orthid	Pileus
Izzard	Lizard	Minnow	Orthis	Pilose
Jabiru	Lobosa	Mirror	Oscine	Pinion
Jacana	Locule	Mocker	Oscule	Piraya
Jacare	Locust	Moholi	Osprey	Pisces
Jackal	Loligo	Moloch	Ossean	Plaice
Jaguar	Lorica	Monera	Ostrea	Plaise
Jairou	Loriot	Moonie	Ourang	Pleura
Jerboa	Lotong	Mooruk	Ourebi	Plover
Jerker	Loutou	Moppet	Ox ray	Podium
Jerkin	Lugger	Morgay	Oxbird	Podley
Jharal	Lumper	Mormon	Oyster	Poiser
Jigger	Lungie	Morpho	Paddle	Pollan
Johnny	Lunule	Morris	Paguma	Polwig
Jowler	Lusern	Morrot	Palama	Polype
Jubate	Luwack	Motmot	Palmar	Polypi
Jugger	Maalin	Muflon	Palmer	Poodle
Jumper	Macaco	Mullet	Palola	Pookoo
Kadder	Mactra	Murine	Palped	Porite
Kaguan	Macula	Musang	Palpus	Possum
Kakapo	Maggot	Musket	Palule	Potter
Kalong	Magpie	Musmon	Papion	Poulpe
Keeled	Maholi	Mussel	Papula	Pouter
Kermes	Maiger	Mustac	Paries	Powter
Kholah	Maikel	Myaria	Parrot	Progne
Kickup	Mailed	Mydaus	Partan	Proleg
Kiddow	Maioid	Mygale	Paseng	Proped
Killer	Malmag	Myxine	Pastor	Pruner
Kipper	Mammal	Nanpie	Pavone	Psylla
Kitish	Mangue	Narica	Peahen	Pucras
Kittle	Mantis	Narwal	Pecary	Puffer
Koaita	Mantle	Natica	Pecora	Puffin
Kokama	Margay	Nayaur	Pecten	Pullus
Kokoon	Marlin	Nedder	Pectus	Punese
Komtok	Marmot	Nereid	Pedata	Punice
Koodoo	Marrot	Nereis	Peechi	Pupate
Koulan	Marten	Nerita	Peewit	Pyrula
Kukang	Martin	Nerite	Pelage	Python
Labial	Masked	Nestor	Pelick	Quacha
Labium	Mastax	Nickle	Peludo	Quagga
Labrum	Mataco	Nilgau	Pelvis	Quaily
Labrus	Maukin	Nipper	Perdix	Quaker
Lamina	Mazame	Nitter	Perlid	Quandy
Larine	Meagre	Nodose	Petrel	Quasje
Laroid	Measle	Nonett	Philip	Queest
Larval	Measly	Nucula	Phocal	Quesal

Rabbit	Sheath	Tamias	Tomcod	Warine
Radula	Sheely	Tampan	Tomium	Warrin
Ranine	Shilfa	Tanate	Tomtit	Warsaw
Rasher	Shough	Tangue	Toucan	Washed
Ratitê	Shrimp	Tangun	Towhee	Washer
Ratite	Sifter	Tanrec	Tremex	Wattle
Redeye	Silure	Tapeti	Tringa	Weasel
Redfin	Simial	Tapper	Trogon	Weaser
Reebok	Simian	Taring	Trophi	Weaver
Reeler	Simpai	Tarpan	Trygon	Webbed
Remora	Siphon	Tarpon	Tsetse	Weeper
Repent	Siskin	Tarpum	Turatt	Weesel
Repkie	Skater	Tarsal	Turban	Weever
Requin	Skitty	Tarsus	Turbit	Weevil
Rhesus	Skrike	Taster	Turbot	Weezel
Rictal	Skrite	Taurus	Turdus	Wekeen
Ridgel	Slater	Tautog	Turkey	Wellat
Roarer	Slider	Teaser	Turner	Wenona
Rochet	Smeath	Teeong	Turnix	Whewer
Rodent	Snacot	Teetan	Turnus	Wigeon
Rotoho	Social	Teetee	Turpin	Willet
Rother	Soland	Teewit	Turtle	Windle
Ruffle	Soosoo	Tegmen	Tusker	Winkle
Rusine	Sorghe	Tegula	Twaite	Wistit
Rytina	Sowbug	Teledu	Tystie	Wittol
Sagoin	Spadix	Tellen	Tzetze	Wivern
Saimir	Sparve	Telson	Uakari	Wombat
Saithe	Sphinx	Tenrec	Umhofo	Woohoo
Salmon	Spider	Teredo	Unguis	Wooyen
Salpid	Sponge	Tergal	Uraeum	Worble
Saltie	Sprite	Tergum	Urania	Worker
Samboo	Squali	Termes	Urchin	Wormal
Sambur	Squame	Tetard	Urchon	Wormil
Sandre	Squash	Tetaug	Urochs	Wormul
Sapajo	Squawk	Tethys	Uropod	Wornil
Sappho	Squill	Tettix	Ursula	Worrel
Sardel	Stemma	Teufit	Vagina	Wranny
Sarlyk	Sterre	Tewhit	Vanjas	Wrasse
Saurel	Stipes	Thamyn	Venada	Wurmal
Sauria	Stolon	Tharos	Venter	Xenomi
Sawfly	Strand	Thooid	Verdin	Yacare
Sawyer	Strany	Thrips	Vermes	Yaffle
Scaled	Strich	Thrush	Vervet	Yakare
Scarus	Stromb	Thunny	Victus	Yapock
Scolex	Stylet	Thysbe	Virgin	Yelper
Scorie	Summit	Tibrie	Voluta	Ynambu
Scoter	Surfer	Tidley	Volute	Yockel
Scutum	Surrow	Tinean	Volyer	Yowley
Semita	Suslik	Tineid	Vortex	Yuckel
Sennet	Sycock	Tingid	Vulpes	Zander
Sephen	Syrinx	Tingis	Wagati	Zarthe
Septum	Syzygy	Tinker	Walker	Zeekoe
Setter	Tabula	Tintie	Wallah	Zenick
Shahin	Tacaud	Tipula	Waller	Zibeth
Shammy	Taenia	Tip-up	Walrus	Zingel
Shanny	Taguan	Tirwit	Wapiti	Zonure
Shapoo	Tailor	Tockay	Wapper	Zoozoo

Zuisin

5

Aboma
Acorn
Addax
Adder
Agama
Agami
Aloof
Alose
Alula
Amzel
Anura
Apara
Aphid
Aphis
Apoda
Apode
Arara
Argus
Ariel
Arnee
Asker
Bleak
Brant
Cagit
Camel
Canis
Cardo
Caret
Clock
Cnida
Coati
Cobia
Colin
Conch
Coney
Conus
Coral
Costa
Coypu
Crake
Crane
Cuddy
Culex
Cutch
Drill
Facet
Fluke
Friar
Galei
Gaper
Gayal
Gazel
Gecko

Gemul
Genys
Gibel
Gilse
Gledd
Glide
Gnome
Golet
Gonys
Goody
Goral
Gorma
Goura
Grebe
Gripe
Grunt
Grype
Guana
Guara
Guevi
Gular
Gyall
Harle
Harpa
Heron
Hippe
Hobby
Hocco
Hoddy
Homer
Hoody
Horse
Hound
Houss
Huzza
Hyena
Hymar
Hymen
Hyrax
Igloo
Imago
Incus
Indri
Iulus
Izard
Jager
Jakie
Jenny
Junco
Jurel
Kaama
Kahau
Kalan
Kayko
Kevin
IGang
Konze
Korin

Krait
Kulan
Larva
Lates
Lemur
Lepas
Limax
Liver
Llama
Loach
Loche
Lodde
Longe
Loral
Loris
Louri
Lunge
Lurid
Lyrie
Lythe
Macao
Macaw
Macho
Madge
Magot
Maian
Maleo
Malma
Manid
Manis
Manta
Manul
Matie
M,tin
Mavis
Meloe
Melon
Menow
Merle
Merou
Mhorr
Midas
Midge
Miner
Minge
Minim
Minny
Molly
Momot
Monad
Monal
Monas
Moner
Moose
Moray
Morse
Mouse
Mugil

Munga
Murex
Murre
Murry
Musca
Mysis
Nacre
Nagor
Naiad
Naker
Nakoo
Nandu
Nasal
Nassa
Nates
Natka
Neddy
Nigua
Ninut
Noddy
Norie
Notum
Nucha
Nurse
Nymph
Nyula
Oared
Oliva
Olive
Ombre
Oozoa
Orang
Orbit
Ormer
Orvet
Otary
Otter
Ounce
Ousel
Ouzel
Owlet
Oxeye
Oxfly
Pacos
Padge
Padow
Palea
Palus
Panda
Pasan
Patas
Paugy
Pauxi
Pearl
Peele
Pekan
Pelma
Penna

Perca
Perch
Petal
Pewee
Pewet
Pewit
Phebe
Phoca
Phono
Physa
Pinna
Piper
Pipit
Pipra
Pique
Pirai
Pishu
Pitta
Plaga
Plica
Pluma
Plume
Poggy
Poker
Polyp
Pongo
Porgy
Potoo
Potto
Pouch
Powen
Power
Poyou
Prawn
Press
Pride
Prill
Prong
Pulex
Pupal
Puppy
Purre
Quail
Quarl
Quata
Quica
Quice
Quill
Quoll
Raash
Racer
Rache
Raker
Ranny
Rasse
Ratch
Ratel
Raven

Razor
Redia
Reeve
Roach
Robin
Rodge
Ronco
Royal
Ruffe
Sable
Sahui
Saiga
Sajou
Saker
Salpa
Sangu
Sargo
Sarpo
Sasin
Satyr
Saury
Scape
Scaup
Scink
Scole
Scray
Scull
Scute
Segge
Selch
Sepia
Serin
Sewen
Sewer
Sewin
Shama
Shank
Shard
Shark
Sheep
Shock
Shooi
Shote
Shrew
Siaga
Sifac
Simia
Siren
Sisel
Siwin
Skart
Skate
Skein
Skink
Skirr
Skout
Skunk
Sloth

Smelt
Smolt
Snail
Snake
Snigg
Snipe
Snook
Snout
Snowl
Soree
Sorex
Sound
Spade
Spece
Speck
Spent
Sphex
Spine
Spink
Spook
Sprat
Sprod
Squab
Squat
Squid
Stare
Starn
Stere
Stern
Stilt
Sting
Stint
Stoat
Stoma
Stork
Stote
Sunny
Swift
Swine
Sylph
Taira
Talon
Talpa
Tapir
Tardo
Tarin
Tatou
Taxel
Tayra
Tench
Tennu
Terin
Testa
Tetel
Theca
Thoth
Tibia
Tikus

Timal
Tinea
Togue
Topau
Topaz
Topet
Toque
Torsk
Torus
Toter
Trabu
Track
Trout
Trubu
Trunk
Tsebe
Tucan
Tugan
Tunny
Tupai
Turbo
Twink
Twite
Tyger
Ullet
Ulula
Umber
Umbra
Umbre
Uncus
Ungka
Upupa
Urite
Ursal
Urson
Ursuk
Ursus
Urubu
Varan
Vasum
Veery
Venus
Vespa
Viper
Vireo
Vison
Vitoe
Vitta
Vulva
Wader
Wavey
Wekau
Whaap
Whale
Whame
Whaup
Whelk
Whiff

Whilk
Whisp
Whoop
Whorl
Witch
Yakin
Yamma
Yarke
Youze
Yucca
zebra
Zebub
Zemni
Zenik
Zerda
Zizel
Zokor
Zooid
Zoril

4

Amia
Anas
Anoa
Apis
Apus
Asse
Aves
Axis
Cavy
Cero
Cete
Clee
Cleg
Cone
Cony
Cook
Coon
Coot
Coxa
Crab
Craw
Crew
Crow
Cusk
Cyst
Fish
Flag
Foot
Gade
Gall
Gape
Gaur
Gems
Gilt
Girl

Gnat
Goat
Goby
Gour
Grig
Grip
Grub
Guan
Guib
Gula
Gull
Haak
Haje
Hake
Hare
Hart
Hawk
Hebe
Herl
Hern
Hind
home
Honk
Horn
Houp
Huso
Ibex
Ibis
Inia
Isis
Isle
Jako
Joso
Juba
Kaka
Kate
Kite
Knee
Koba
Koel
Kuda
Kudu
Kyaw
Lama
Lamb
Lant
Lark
Leet
Ling
Lion
Liza
Lobe
Loir
Loma
Loom
Loon
Lore
Lori

Lory	Parr	Sile	Vark	Kid
Lote	Pavo	Skua	Vein	Kra
Lour	Pawk	Slab	Vent	Lag
Luce	Peal	Slug	Vole	Lar
Lurg	Peba	Smee	Waag	Lob
Luth	Peep	Smew	Waeg	Lug
Lynx	Pela	Snag	Wamp	Maa
Made	Pern	Soal	Wasp	Mad
Maha	Pica	Soko	weep	Maw
Maia	Pici	Sole	Weka	Mew
Maki	Piet	Sora	Welk	Moa
Mara	Pika	Sore	Wels	Mow
Melt	Pile	Spay	Whim	Mus
Mico	Pily	Spot	Wilk	Mya
Mida	Pink	Spur	Wipe	Nib
Milk	Pint	Stag	Wolf	Nit
Mill	Piot	Steg	Worm	Nun
Milt	Pipa	Sula	Wren	Olf
Mina	Pith	Swan	Wyla	Orc
Mink	Pogy	Syle	Xeme	Ork
Minx	Poor	Tahr	Yard	Owl
Mite	Pope	Tail	Yaup	Pad
Mitu	Pout	Tait	Yite	Par
Moco	Puck	Tana	Yoit	Pen
Moho	Pudu	Tant	Yolk	Pie
Mohr	Puet	Tatu	Yowe	Pig
Mola	Puma	Teal	Yuen	Pod
Mole	Pume	Team	Yunx	Pop
Mona	Pupa	Tern	Zati	Pup
Monk	Pupe	Teuk	Zebu	Rat
Mono	Purl	Thar	Zimb	Ray
Mort	Pyot	Tick	Zobo	Roe
Moth	Quet	Tidy	Zoea	Rud
Mule	Quin	Tike	Zoic	Sai
Musk	Quit	Titi	Zoon	Sao
Myna	Raia	Toad	Zope	Sod
Myxa	Raiê	Toco	Zubr	Sow
Naid	Rail	Tody		Tat
Nais	Rana	Tope	**3**	Tau
Napu	Reem	Tota		Tek
Neat	Rhea	Tuet	Ahu	Tit
Nems	Rheê	Tuna	Ant	Toe
Nepa	Rock	Turk	Ape	Ton
Newt	Roed	Tusk	Ara	Tue
Nope	Rook	Tuza	Ask	Tup
Nowd	Rudd	Tydy	Asp	Tur
Nowt	Rukh	Tyne	Ass	Ure
Once	Runt	Umbo	Auk	Wah
Opah	Saki	Unau	Cob	Yak
Orfe	Salp	Unio	Cod	Yet
Oryx	Scad	Unke	Gar	
Otis	Scar	Urox	Gnu	**2**
Owre	Scud	Urus	Goa	
Paca	Scup	Urva	Hen	Ai
Pacu	Seal	Utia	Hog	Id
Page	Seta	Vane	Ide	Oo
Palp	Shad	Vare	Jay	Ox
Pard	Shag	Vari		

Useful Notes:

Useful Notes: